Major Problems
in American Constitutional History

MAJOR PROBLEMS IN AMERICAN HISTORY SERIES

GENERAL EDITOR
THOMAS G. PATERSON

Major Problems
in American Constitutional
History
Volume II: From 1870
to the Present

DOCUMENTS AND ESSAYS

EDITED BY
KERMIT L. HALL
UNIVERSITY OF FLORIDA

D. C. HEATH AND COMPANY
Lexington, Massachusetts   Toronto

Address editorial correspondence to:

D. C. Heath
125 Spring Street
Lexington, MA 02173

Acquisitions Editor: James Miller
Developmental Editor: Sylvia Mallory
Production Editor: Sarah Doyle
Designer: Sally Thompson Steele
Production Coordinator: Charles Dutton
Text Permissions Editor: Margaret Roll

Cover: "Praying Ministers, 1962" by Jacob Lawrence. Spelman College.

Published simultaneously in Canada.

Printed in the United States of America.

International Standard Book Number: 0-669-21210-5

Library of Congress Catalog Number: 90-86143

10 9 8 7 6 5 4 3

Preface

Almost every major problem in American history has had, in one form or another, its constitutional reflection, and those reflections have been the stuff of constitutional history. As Alexis de Tocqueville, the famous French visitor to America in the 1830s, noted, "Scarcely any political question arises in the United States that is not revolved, sooner or later, into a judicial question." The fate of slavery in the pre–Civil War era, for example, generated an almost continuous debate over constitutional principles between North and South that culminated in the Supreme Court's decision in *Scott v. Sandford* (1857). More recently, conflicts in Vietnam and the Persian Gulf have raised questions about what powers the framers in Philadelphia intended for Congress and the president in "making" and "declaring" war. In our precedent-based common law system, in order for present law to be legitimate it must have some historical connection. In other words, we achieve stability in our constitutional system by linking the past to the present. For this reason, constitutional history has figured prominently in our public life and has emerged as a source of scholarly and political controversy. Time and again public officials, whether in Congress, the White House, or the Supreme Court, have turned to the history of the federal Constitution to support their positions. Just as often, given the past's ambiguity, historians have clashed with one another about what lessons previous constitutional struggles actually teach us.

The Constitution has been both a source of authority for government and a restraint on government. A constitution is an embodiment of principles, institutions, laws, and customs that form a framework of government. What makes such a document function is the concept of constitutionalism, which holds that political authority ought to be constrained through rules and procedures. In simple terms, the law should be above persons. At important landmarks in our history—World Wars I and II, the Great Depression, the civil-rights movement of the 1960s, for example—this most basic principle of government has come under attack, with government officials invoking community needs to set aside individual rights.

The history of rights in America reminds us that we have been deeply ambivalent about them. Survey after survey has disclosed as much. For example, when asked if an individual has a right to see or show a pornographic movie or to send or receive lewd materials through the mails, a majority of Americans respond negatively. Offered a choice between liberty and community control, they often select the latter. Yet these same respondents routinely insist—and insist in overwhelming numbers—that of the Constitution's provisions, the Bill of Rights is sacred. It would seem that we love to hate those provisions of our fundamental law that we most cherish.

As the documents that follow reveal, liberty is not an absolute. Granting total freedom to any individual could theoretically result in the restriction of freedom for everyone else. Social control is essential if rights are to have meaning. The challenge for the constitutional historian, therefore, is to understand how liberty has been distributed within the social order, and in what institutions—Congress, the Supreme Court, the presidency—this task has been lodged. This tension over the distribution of rights and powers within government (who is to enjoy them, and what institution is to allocate them) lies at the core of our constitutional history.

Today public officials and constitutional historians are locked in a sustained debate about how best to balance liberty and authority amid massive social change. Conservative scholars and public officials, among them Judge Robert Bork, proffer the doctrine of original intention as the best means of striking this balance. They insist that during the Chief Justiceship of Earl Warren (1954–1969) the Supreme Court became a continuing constitutional convention, in which the justices rewrote the nation's fundamental law to suit their own prejudices and redistributed rights in ways that favored minorities. The Court, they charge, became an "imperial judiciary" awash in its own personal excesses and gripped in a rapturous fit of liberalism and welfare statism. Under these circumstances, the rights of minorities took precedence over the rights of the majority, and reverse discrimination replaced plain old discrimination. If, the conservative argument runs, the justices only heeded the wishes—the intentions—of the framers, the present mess in which we supposedly find the Supreme Court subverting community control and unfairly redistributing rights would clear up.

Liberals have taken a different tack in responding to the challenge of balancing liberty and community control. They insist that the strength of the constitutional system depends on its ability to respond to social demands for justice through law. Old law, in short, must yield to new constitutional doctrines in order for fundamental law to retain legitimacy. Former Supreme Court Justice William J. Brennan and Justice Thurgood Marshall (the only African-American ever to sit on the Court) have taken exception to the arguments of Bork and other conservatives. Justice Brennan has observed that "an awareness of history and an appreciation of the aims of the Founding Fathers seldom resolve concrete problems." Justice Marshall has argued that the miracle of the Constitution was not its birth but its life—a life nurtured through two turbulent centuries marked by a pattern in which "suffering, struggle and sacrifice . . . has triumphed over much of what was wrong with the original Constitution." Marshall reminds us that the framers in 1787 respected neither African-Americans nor women as equals to white men before the law. Liberals further insist that, considering the heavy emphasis in American government on majority will, the federal judiciary in general and Supreme Court justices in particular offer the best means of making those less equal in life more equal in law.

The documents and essays in Volume I cover the period from the United States' founding through Reconstruction. Volume II begins with the 1870s and brings the story to the present. Both volumes reveal constitutional historians of different political and scholarly persuasions challenging one another's viewpoints and, in the process, contributing to the general debate over public policy. A better and more complete understanding of America's past is sure to emerge from this lively exchange.

Each chapter opens with a brief introduction that sets the historical scene. There follow a selection of documents and two or three essays examining the chapter topic. The essays show how differing interpretations can be drawn from the same historical evidence presented in the documents. Headnotes that place the readings in historical and interpretive perspective introduce the documents and essays. Readers wishing to explore the topics in greater depth should consult the books and articles listed under the end-of-chapter Further Reading.

Numerous people contributed wise counsel and professional expertise in the development of the two volumes. Detailed and extremely helpful written reviews of draft tables of contents were provided by Herman Belz, University of Maryland, College Park; Winfred Bernhard, University of Massachusetts, Amherst; Frederick Harrod, United States Naval Academy; Mary Beth Norton, Cornell University; Michael Parrish, University of California, San Diego; David Robson, John Carroll University; Ronald Seavoy, Bowling Green State University; John Semonche, University of North Carolina, Chapel Hill; David Sterling, University of Cincinnati; and Robert P. Sutton, Western Illinois University. Additional advice was generously extended by Richard Ellis, State University of New York, Buffalo; Robert Haws, University of Mississippi; R. Kent Newmyer, University of Connecticut; John Pratt, State University of New York, Stony Brook; Rebecca Shoemaker, Indiana State University; and George Suggs, Southeast Missouri State University. Finally, Stephen Prescott and Eric Rise helped to locate and photocopy the documents and essays. I extend my thanks to them, as well as to Sylvia Mallory, James Miller, Margaret Roll, Tina Beazer, Sarah Doyle, and Karen Wise of D. C. Heath, who were encouraging, professional, and patient beyond the call of duty.

K.L.H.

Contents

CHAPTER 1
Constitutional History and Constitutionalism
Page 1

ESSAYS

Hendrik Hartog • A History of Rights Consciousness 2

Herman Belz • In Defense of Liberal Pluralism and Constitutionalism 15

CHAPTER 2
Laissez-Faire Constitutionalism and Liberty in the Late Nineteenth Century
Page 23

DOCUMENTS 24

Jurist Thomas M. Cooley on Constitutional Limitations, 1869 25

The Slaughter-House Cases, 16 Wallace 36 (1873) 27

Munn v. *Illinois,* 94 U.S. 113 (1877) 31

United States v. *E. C. Knight,* 156 U.S. 1 (1895) 34

Pollock v. *Farmers' Loan and Trust Co.,* 158 U.S. 601 (1895) 41

In Re Debs, 158 U.S. 564 (1895) 44

The People's Party Platform, 1896 50

ESSAYS 53

Arnold M. Paul • Traditional Legal Conservatism 54

Michael Les Benedict • The Libertarian Foundations of Laissez-Faire Constitutionalism 62

CHAPTER 3
Paternalistic Sexism and Liberty to Contract, 1873–1923
Page 80

DOCUMENTS 81

Legal Scholar Christopher G. Tiedeman on the Limitations of Police Power, 1886 82

Ritchie v. *The People,* 155 Ill. 106 (1895) 85

Allgeyer v. *Louisiana,* 165 U.S. 578 (1897) 90

Holden v. *Hardy,* 169 U.S. 366 (1898) 92

Lochner v. *New York,* 198 U.S. 4 (1905) 94

AFL Leader Samuel Gompers on Why Married Women Should Not Work, 1906   **100**

Louis D. Brandeis and Josephine Goldmark on Women in Industry, 1908   **101**

Muller v. *Oregon,* 208 U.S. 412 (1908)   **103**

Roscoe Pound on Liberty of Contract, 1909   **106**

Adkins v. *Children's Hospital,* 261 U.S. 525 (1923)   **110**

E S S A Y S   **117**

Judith A. Baer • Women Workers and Liberty to Contract   **118**

Melvin I. Urofsky • The Courts and the Limits of Liberty to Contract   **129**

CHAPTER 4
The Emergence of Modern Civil Liberties
Page 142

D O C U M E N T S   **143**

The Espionage Act, 1917/1918   **143**

Schenck v. *United States,* 249 U.S. 47 (1919)   **144**

"Workers Wake Up," Version One, 1918   **146**

"Workers Wake Up," Version Two, 1918   **147**

Abrams v. *United States,* 250 U.S. 616 (1919)   **148**

Legal Scholar Zechariah Chafee, Jr., Considers Freedom of Speech in Wartime, 1918   **153**

Gitlow v. *New York,* 268 U.S. 652 (1925)   **157**

Near v. *Minnesota,* 283 U.S. 697 (1931)   **163**

E S S A Y S   **166**

Walter F. Berns • The Limits of Liberty   **166**

Richard Polenberg • Oliver Wendell Holmes, Jr., and Clear and Present Danger   **174**

Paul L. Murphy • Freedom of the Press and the Fourteenth Amendment   **182**

CHAPTER 5
Presidential Leadership and Court Packing
Page 188

D O C U M E N T S   **189**

Schechter v. *United States,* 295 U.S. 495 (1935)   **189**

Liberal Washington Journalists Drew Pearson and Robert S. Allen on the "Nine Old Men," 1936   **194**

The Judiciary Reform Act of 1937   **197**

President Franklin D. Roosevelt Advocates Judicial Reform, 1937   **198**

Chief Justice Charles Evans Hughes Defends the Supreme Court's Performance, 1937   **204**

The Senate Judiciary Committee's Report Rejects FDR's Plan, 1937   **206**

West Coast Hotel v. *Parrish,* 300 U.S. 397 (1937)   **213**

E S S A Y S   **216**

William E. Leuchtenburg • The Logic of FDR's Court-Packing Scheme   **216**

Michael Nelson • Court Packing as a Failure of Presidential Leadership   **226**

C H A P T E R   6
The Cold War and Civil Liberties
Page 242

D O C U M E N T S   **243**

John Dewey on Liberalism and Civil Liberties, 1936   **243**

The Alien Registration Act (Smith Act), 1940   **246**

Senate Judiciary Committee Hearings on the Smith Act, 1940   **247**

Dennis et al. v. *United States,* 341 U.S. 494 (1951)   **251**

Political Scientist John P. Roche Argues That We've Never Had More Freedom, 1956   **260**

Yates v. *United States,* 354 U.S. 298 (1957)   **265**

Brandenburg v. *Ohio,* 395 U.S. 444 (1969)   **269**

E S S A Y S   **270**

Michael Belknap • Anticommunist Hysteria and Political Persecution   **271**

Walter Berns • Free Speech Belongs to the Virtuous   **283**

C H A P T E R   7
The Modern Presidency
Page 293

D O C U M E N T S   **294**

Senator Robert A. Taft on President Harry S Truman's Power to Make War, 1950   **295**

Youngstown Sheet & Tube Co. et al. v. *Sawyer,* 343 U.S. 579 (1952)   **299**

The Gulf of Tonkin Resolution, 1964   **310**

President Richard M. Nixon Views the Problems Before Him, 1969   **311**

The War Powers Resolution, 1973   **313**

United States v. *Nixon,* 418 U.S. 683 (1974)   **317**

Senator Sam Ervin on Watergate and the Presidency, 1974   **324**

E S S A Y S   **331**

Arthur M. Schlesinger, Jr. • The Influence of Presidential Personality   **331**

Alexander M. Bickel • The Vietnam War as a Failure of Congress to Act   **344**

Philip B. Kurland • Watergate and Reform of the Presidency   **352**

C H A P T E R   8
Affirmative Action
Page 356

D O C U M E N T S   **357**

Plessy v. *Ferguson,* 163 U.S. 537 (1896)   **358**

Brown v. *Board of Education of Topeka, Kansas,* 347 U.S. 483 (1954)   **363**

Brown v. *Board of Education of Topeka, Kansas,* 349 U.S. 294 (1955)   **366**

The Southern Manifesto, 1956   **367**

The Civil Rights Act of 1964   **369**

Regents of the University of California v. *Bakke,* 438 U.S. 265 (1978)   **374**

Fullilove v. *Klutznick,* 448 U.S. 448 (1980)   **380**

Black Economist Thomas Sowell Asks, "Are Quotas Good for Blacks?" 1978   **383**

E S S A Y S   **391**

J. Harvie Wilkinson III • The Luminous but Flawed Goal of Racial Justice   **392**

J. Skelly Wright • The Morality of Affirmative Action   **398**

C H A P T E R   9
Women and Equal Rights
Page 407

D O C U M E N T S   **408**

Griswold v. *Connecticut,* 381 U.S. 419 (1965)   **409**

Frontiero v. *Richardson,* 411 U.S. 677 (1973)   **410**

The Equal Rights Amendment, 1972   **412**

Phyllis Schlafly Opposes the ERA, 1973   **412**

Marlow W. Cook Supports the ERA, 1973   **417**

The Reverend Jerry Falwell on the ERA, 1980   **422**

Roe v. *Wade,* 410 U.S. 113 (1973)   **423**

Webster v. *Reproductive Health Services* et al., 57 L.W. 5023 (1989)   **435**

E S S A Y S   **438**

John Hart Ely • Why *Roe* v. *Wade* Was a Mistake   **439**

Sylvia Law • The Reality of Biological Differences for Gender Equality   **447**

Deborah L. Rhode • Gender as Disadvantage Rather than Difference   **454**

C H A P T E R   10
Freedom of and Freedom from Religion
Page 462

D O C U M E N T S   **463**

James Madison Warns Against Religious Establishment, 1785   **464**

Everson v. *Board of Education of the Township of Ewing,* 330 U.S. 1 (1947)   **468**

Engel v. *Vitale,* 370 U.S. 421 (1962)   **474**

President John F. Kennedy Discusses the Supreme Court and Public-School Prayer, 1962   **480**

Ishmael Jaffree Opposes Public-School Prayer, 1985   **480**

Jaffree v. *The Board of School Commissioners of Mobile County,* 554 Fed. Supp. 1104 (1983)   **486**

Wallace v. *Jaffree,* 472 U.S. 38 (1985)   **489**

Senator Jesse Helms on Prayer in the Public Schools, 1985   **491**

E S S A Y S   **493**

James McClellan • The Supreme Court's Usurpation of Freedom of Religion   **493**

Leonard W. Levy • The Supreme Court's Defense of Freedom of Religion   **500**

C H A P T E R 11
The Constitutionality of the Death Penalty
Page 506

D O C U M E N T S   **507**

Louisiana ex rel. Francis v. *Resweber,* 329 U.S. 459 (1947)   **508**

Furman v. *Georgia,* 408 U.S. 238 (1972)   **510**

Gregg v. *Georgia,* 428 U.S. 153 (1976)   **516**

A Sample of Georgia Murder Cases, 1960–1978   **520**

McCleskey v. *Kemp,* 481 U.S. 279 (1987)   **522**

E S S A Y S   **532**

Walter Berns • The Morality of the Death Penalty   **533**

Charles L. Black • The Whim and Caprice of the Death Penalty   **539**

David Baldus et al. • Race and the Death Penalty   **543**

C H A P T E R 12
Original Intent and Constitutional Interpretation
Page 549

D O C U M E N T S   **550**

Former Attorney General Edwin Meese III on the Wisdom of Relying on the Framers' Original Intentions, 1985   **551**

Former Supreme Court Justice William J. Brennan, Jr., on the Failure of the Doctrine of Original Intent, 1985   **557**

Justice Thurgood Marshall on the Constitution's Bicentennial: Commemorating the Wrong Document? 1987   **566**

E S S A Y S   **567**

Raoul Berger • Original Intent as a Curb on Judicial Power   **568**

Leonard W. Levy • The Failure of Original Intent   **571**

A P P E N D I X

Page i

The Articles of Confederation and Perpetual Union   **i**

Constitution of the United States of America   **ix**

Amendments to the Constitution   **xviii**

The Constitution of the Confederate States of America   **xxvii**

Supreme Court Nominations, 1789–1990   **xl**

Constitutional History
and Constitutionalism

Radical, liberal, and conservative scholars of U.S. constitutional history have yet to produce a creative synthesis. The two leading textbooks, The American Constitution, *by Herman Belz, and* A March of Liberty, *by Melvin I. Urofsky, reflect the polarization in the field. The former presents the history of constitutionalism from an essentially conservative political perspective; the latter explores it from a liberal vantage point. Never have constitutional historians disagreed so vehemently over so many issues. For example, does public law embrace certain core values of justice, equality, and fairness that elevate it above political manipulation? Are the original intentions of the framers of the Constitution and the various amendments the best guide to constitutional understanding today? Can these intentions be known to us today, in any case? Should we examine constitutional history from the perspective of judges and courts? Or should we seek the ''aspirations'' of the people over constitutional rights? Does the legitimacy of constitutional values endure because succeeding generations maintain fidelity to the assumptions of those who have come before them? Or does the maintenance of an effective constitutional order depend on each generation's creatively adapting federal and state constitutions to ever-changing social and economic circumstances? For the time being, constitutional historians seem to agree only that they should disagree when answering these questions.*

 E S S A Y S

The two essays reprinted here reflect the current debate about the scope of and approaches to constitutional history. In the first selection, Hendrik Hartog, a professor of law at the University of Wisconsin, argues that constitutional historians should take seriously the development of "rights consciousness" in U.S. history by exploring how different groups interpret the Constitution. Hartog's approach, which draws from the critical legal studies perspective, underscores the ongoing conflict in the American experience about the meaning of the Constitution and the frequency with which lawmakers and ordinary citizens differ over rights. In short, Hartog emphasizes that the history of the Constitution is the history of many voices, not one, and especially not that of the Supreme Court.

Herman Belz approaches the issue of constitutionalism from a much different and politically more conservative perspective. Belz (far more than Hartog) stresses the nature of constitutionalism, but, like Hartog, he sees many connections between political life and constitutional developments. He reads the meanings differently, arguing that the interest-group pluralism that Hartog and others deplore is a vital part of the U.S. constitutional tradition. Belz dismisses charges that constitutionalism plays into the hands of those with power and influence; it merely aids those with social privilege; and it cannot deliver a meaningful solution to contemporary problems of race, gender, and economic equality. These questions of who benefits from the constitutional system, whether or not the system has been and is fair, and the extent to which it can adapt to ongoing change without losing its moorings in its historical foundations form the central issues of contemporary constitutional history.

A History of Rights Consciousness

HENDRIK HARTOG

This essay . . . suggest[s] a framework for writing a history of American constitutional rights consciousness. The first section describes characteristic practices of American constitutional rights consciousness, locating them in aspirations to freedom from bondage and from control by others. The second section poses some of the difficulties historians necessarily face in weighing the political and moral significance of those practices. The third criticizes the ordinary perspective of American constitutional history and suggests the difference that attention to constitutional rights consciousness might make.

The study of constitutional rights consciousness offers the possibility of integrating the subjects of American social history and American constitutional history. The study of constitutional rights consciousness also challenges tacit assumptions of both social and constitutional historians. Some social historians look for rights consciousness in the relative autonomy of particular social visions. They emphasize the features that, for example, differentiated black constitutional aspirations from those legitimated by a white Supreme Court, or married women's notions of their domestic rights from those of their husbands. Eventually, however, their subdiscipline ought to deal with the question of how distinctive and diverse groups learned to frame their claims in ways identified as "constitutional." They will have to deal with what binds us together as one people, as well as with what divides us. Legal scholars skeptical of the strategic value of devoting resources to claims to legal rights will have to confront groups' and individuals' convictions that constitutional struggles were meaningful. Historians certain of the transformative capacities inherent in rights discourses will have to deal with the demonstrated power of those discourses to deflect, contain, and delude those who place their hopes in rights.

Hendrik Hartog, "The Constitution of Aspiration and 'The Rights That Belong to Us All,' " *The Journal of American History*, 74 (December 1987): 1013–1034. Reprinted by permission.

It is helpful to think of rights talk as a relatively stable and permanent social convention . . . . But it is important to remember the distinctiveness of *this* constitutional convention. Constitutional rights (and their denial) have constituted Americans' political identities and engaged their imaginations. Rights are almost never gained painlessly. Their apparent durability may have made them seem valuable and worth the pain. But their apparent vulnerability and fragility—their capacity to be reimagined, repossessed, redistributed—have been another part of their value to the groups struggling for constitutional rights throughout American history.

Constitutional Aspirations and Constitutional Discontent

A history of constitutional rights consciousness needs to begin by confronting the immense symbolic power of an emancipatory vision of natural rights. It is this vision that one planter identified as the freed slaves' "wild notions of rights and freedom," and that Elizabeth Cady Stanton called "the inalienable right of all to be happy." This vision has justified continued struggle by groups in the face of (presumably temporary) judicial and political defeats.

The textual expression of that vision, the constitution of aspiration and struggle—the constitution relevant to constitutional rights consciousness—emerges from only a few phrases of the federal Constitution: portions of the Bill of Rights and the Civil War Amendments, and from the Declaration of Independence, which is not officially a constitutional text at all. And even those phrases may have had to carry moral weight and meaning that would have surprised their authors. An American emancipatory tradition of constitutional meaning must be rooted in the subversive and disruptive and utopian messages that people read into constitutional texts and drew from diverse and contradictory sources, including English common law, liberalism, Enlightenment philosophy, post-Reformation theology, and the medieval peasant's vision of self-ownership and freedom.

For the past two centuries, American understandings of constitutional rights have changed as understandings of the interrelated meanings of slavery and of political freedom have changed. The identification of the Constitution with a "Great Tradition" of emancipatory aspirations apparently resulted from the happenstance that a moral critique of slavery and a celebration of the virtues of free labor developed contemporaneously with American constitutionalism. The long contest over slavery did more than any other cause to stimulate the development of an alternate, rights conscious interpretation of the federal constitution. Still, a modern American understanding of constitutional rights could only become embedded in the Constitution after the Civil War and emancipation. All the varying meanings that have been derived from the phrase "equal protection of the laws" are rooted in contending visions of what it was that was overthrown by the end of slavery.

Which groups (sharecroppers? married women? children? welfare mothers? employees?) could lay claim metaphorically to the sense of outrage that since the Civil War has attached to legalized categories of dependence and servitude? What must government do to avoid legitimating enslaving relations? Those have been crucial questions for groups claiming constitutional rights. Underneath almost any claimed constitutional right, one can find an implicit claim that not to recognize the right would be a legitimation of the "badges and incidents" of a form of slavery.

Constitutional rights consciousness—at least in its typical American forms—has started from positive notions of self-ownership and of citizenship, from the ideal of an autonomous individual capable of imagining and realizing a personal future, from the Declaration of Independence's invocation of a universal right to the pursuit of happiness. The exaltation of freedom required the antithesis of enslavement. As Stanton wrote in 1857, "When we talk of woman's rights, is not the right to her person, to her happiness, to her life, the first on the list? If you go to a southern plantation and speak to a slave of his right to property, to the elective franchise, to a thorough education, his response will be a vacant stare. . . . The great idea of his right to himself, to his personal dignity, must first take possession of his soul." Such a statement, as description and as political program, suggests an aspiration to solitude and isolation. Individual autonomy—the freedom to be left alone and to lead a "private" life—was an overarching value.

American constitutional rights consciousness began with the dream of an autonomous identity, but critiques of law and other forms of official power and violence productive of hierarchy and social division have defined its political vision. Recognition of constitutional rights required the undoing of structures of illegitimate authority. The wrongs that constitutional rights would redress have usually been tied to a structure of status and dependency (slavery, peonage, coverture, childhood) reinforced and reproduced by public power. And the constitution that claimants looked to embodied a structure of rights that rose above and countered the "real" social order of oppressive relations.

The vision of autonomy incorporated an ideal of community. Autonomous, rights-bearing individuals would live in groups and collectivities and participate in public life. Their "happiness," as Thomas Jefferson knew, required community. They would know themselves, as individuals and as citizens, through their capacity to construct intentional and voluntary forms of solidarity. And many, particularly the many in the nineteenth century raised within a powerful Christian culture, interpreted the development of individual capacities as an overarching right, because it enabled one to fulfill a variety of duties to others. One was obliged then to become an autonomous citizen, so that one could participate usefully in communities.

Who was entitled to the status of citizen and of rights bearer? At the heart of the constitutional aspiration one finds a critique of all restrictive definitions of citizenship, as reproductions of illegitimate hierarchy. Government cannot know in advance who will be capable of exercising rights. And rights holders are those who do what rights holders do. Those who act as autonomous individuals—choosing, constructing, protecting—whether through collective or solitary activities, grow entitled to rights identified with the choices they have made. More, government ought to treat as adult citizens those who take on citizenship's burdens and responsibilities, perhaps especially when they (women, minorities, children, the handicapped) fit received and legitimated categories of the naturally dependent.

The problem of dependency, what might be called the parental problem of how to prepare dependents for autonomous adulthood, strikes me as a key to a history of struggles over constitutional rights consciousness. Those who drew on visions of constitutional rights often recognized themselves as still dependent and vulnerable, even as they aspired to autonomy. They knew they needed help, and they sought to draw on (and, in the process, to construct) a continuing pragmatic tradition of care and responsibility, which many have aspired to impose on public authority. Within this tradition, government (after the Civil War, in particular the federal government) would have a particular responsibility to give dependent groups the means and the capacity for citizenship, to protect as well as to recognize.

Yet, the appropriate quantity of protection that the federal government, as well as other structures of authority, ought to provide, has also been a continuing source of division and conflict. The aspiration to undo dependency has led some to attack all governmental care as paternalistic. The desire to destroy the bonds of past legal servitudes drew Stanton and Samuel Gompers to an acceptance of a formalistic voluntarism or privatism that denied continuing dependencies. A commitment to negative liberty may justify leaving the newly enfranchised unprotected to their fates. The emancipatory project identified with constitutional rights consciousness sometimes became nothing more than the removal of formal legal constraints.

If American constitutional rights consciousness has been rooted in utopian aspirations to an autonomous life, freed of hierarchies and status, how have those aspirations been expressed in constitutional struggles? What is it that groups hoped would be the result of their recourse to rights? The papers in the symposium reveal three forms of constitutional claims made by groups seeking to realize their constitutional aspirations. By forms of constitutional claims, I do not mean the conventional lawyers' categories—free exercise, free speech, due process, equal protection—used in constitutional law, but three distinct, yet interrelated, ways of characterizing the rights required to secure constitutional aspirations. The first characterization, and the most familiar, is that of the right as a "trump," a claim that, once established, triumphs over competing values and claims. The second, and the most important for a historical understanding of American constitutional rights consciousness, is that of a right as a duty on public authority to undo—to destroy—the structures that maintain hierarchy and oppression. The third is that of a right as a duty on public authority to reconstruct itself or its relations to its citizens, or lose legitimacy. They offer three ways of describing the demand that lies behind the assertion of a claimed right. The first says, "Mine!" The second says, "Not theirs!" The third says, "Do what is necessary, or I will never again trust you!"

The first of these characterizations, the trump, is what most of us ordinarily mean when we say that we have a right. The goal of the claim is to assert the autonomy and capacity of the rights holder and the complementary disempowerment of all others, in particular of the state. That understanding of a right is implicit in the statement of the United States Supreme Court in *Pierce* v. *Society of Sisters* that Oregon had no capacity "to standardize its children by forcing them to accept instruction from public [school] teachers only." It also is what freedmen who in 1867 refused to leave a Richmond, Virginia, streetcar meant when they shouted, "Let's have our rights."

That form of asserting a right borrows from property law an almost spatial sense of the bounded self—of what in the eighteenth century were called the "fences" that constituted the liberties of free men. As with property law, the form of the constitutional claim often masks the dependence of the rights holder on a world of others. Black freedmen learned that they had a right to walk the sidewalks of southern towns as free men, but they also knew or quickly learned that that right depended, as all rights depend, on the willingness of public authority to enforce it. They knew then that their freedom rested on the temporary presence of the Union army. Likewise, the assertion of a right to a distinctive religious practice has given various devotional communities a sense of their possession of a distinctive identity. Yet, the use of secular courts to enforce rights of communities whose frames of reference place them in opposition to secular authority suggests the compromising posture of an identity founded on rights.

As with property law, the claim to a constitutional right as a trump has often been countered by assertions of a "larger" public interest, or expedience, that balanced or constrained individual freedoms and autonomy. So Mormon claims that polygamy represented the free exercise of religious beliefs and was therefore immune to challenge were countered by federal insistence that conventional Christian "monogamy was necessary for democratic and republican forms of government." Parents' insistence on a right to raise children as they see fit has regularly run up against public authority's interest in "the best interests of the child." And Stanton's belief that Radical Republicans owed her and other abolitionist women the right to vote was countered by the male apologia that securing rights for the freedman was so important that no political capital could be expended on ancillary concerns. Few rights really do trump the prudential assertions of organized public power.

Likening a constitutional claim to a property right also implies the rights holder's separation from a governing authority that can only legitimate itself by recognizing the autonomy and independence of the rights holder. Such a republican separation is assuredly what some religious minorities have hoped to realize through invocation of free exercise rights. It may also be what W. E. B. Du Bois was after when he argued that the equality guaranteed by the Fourteenth Amendment did not preclude a separate black identity. But the metaphor of property appears inconsistent with postrevolutionary notions of the sovereignty of the people. If the goal of constitutional struggle is membership in "We, the People," then it hardly seems appropriate to found one's constitutional identity on a metaphorical image of rights as possessions that isolate the holder from the larger political community.

Except for religious minorities, [no other] groups . . . devoted as much energy to gaining constitutional recognition for their rights, conceived of as private possessions, as to the destruction of the settled rights of those who oppressed them. Divesting vested rights—obtaining constitutional recognition of the "no right" of others—is thus a second way of characterizing the goals of constitutional struggles. When groups have insisted on their constitutional rights, they have usually insisted on the end to some illegitimate yet legal form of power, a form itself almost always bearing the imprimatur of a right. They have read into the Constitution an implied destabilization of those vested—and often constitutionally recognized—rights of others that constrained their capacities and their autonomy.

Establishment of a new constitutional right has often been little else than the disestablishment of an older constitutional right or structure of rights. Rights seekers, say the National Association for the Advancement of Colored People in the mid-twentieth century, have justified invoking public power by their opponents' possession of previously unquestioned rights. They knew that without a reappraisal of previously constitutional practices there could be no positive right worth having. School integration is a meaningful right only in the context of the destruction of locally imposed racial segregation. For 140 years, feminists have made male possession of their sexuality and of their wealth and of their children the hallmarks of a constitutionally corrupt society. Women's rights may have meant nothing more (or less) than the end of male patriarchal rights. When ex-slaves went out on their own, when they moved about and sought to control their work and personal lives, they were not simply asserting their possession of individual rights. Such behavior consciously challenged their ex-masters, confronting them with the destruction of previously settled rights over what was once theirs. When scholars explore labor's long struggle to establish a constitutional right to organize collectively, they may better understand that right, not as a search for a personal possession, but as a struggle to overturn a history of judicial confirmation of managerial rights over the employment relation. Even "the idea of a community right to industrial property" that Youngstown's steelworkers have recently learned to make their own is first of all about divesting steel companies of their traditional rights to do whatever they choose (including abandoning profitable factories). To reformulate such constitutional rights claims in positive and possessory terms robs them of the meanings they held for those who mobilized them.

When presented as claims to negate rights, rights readily become a focus for group organization and identity. As possessive individualists, rights holders may lack collective political identities, but to uproot common opponents they must join together. Black struggles for civil rights coalesced into a movement when leaders organized to uproot the vested rights of southern (and northern) white communities to enforce segregation by law. . . . [A]ttempts to organize a feminist antipornography movement have relied on a confrontation with the expectations of men who believe that they have a constitutional right to take erotic pleasure from whatever they choose.

. . . By focusing on the wrongs to be undone, rights claimants have transformed an inherited libertarian rhetoric, so that it could at times be made an instrument of collective organization and collective identities.

The aspiration to forms of constitutional divestment has often carried an unsettling and radical edge. When freed slaves and married women asserted their common citizenship with whites and married men, they knew (as did their opponents) that their citizenship—their potential status as members of a transformed political community—depended on taking vested and settled rights away. Likewise, both employers and employees always understood that the latters' gains derived from the formers' losses. One cannot imagine being freed from vested structures of servitude without imagining the correlative of those who have been served losing their perquisites. Masking rhetorics has sometimes allowed Americans to feel as if everyone benefited from changes in constitutional rights, but such rhetorics have been less convincing than the "instrumentalist" arguments for legal changes said to promote economic growth.

More importantly, this second form of constitutional claim suggests an apparently contradictory conception of the Constitution as a permanent structure of authority. At the same time that newly freed blacks, early feminists, and others mobilized a strategy to destabilize others' rights, they also invested the constitutional rights they sought with immanent and unchanging meaning. Many of the rights attacked by them were rights that, as in the case of the right to segregate affirmed in *Plessy* v. *Ferguson,* had been explicitly recognized by constitutional authority. If they could be changed, why not the newer rights as well?

Both the yearning for permanent statements of rights and the insistence on the contingency of present structures of authority are central features of American constitutional rights consciousness. Groups have been able to draw from constitutional language ways of demonstrating that those who exercised power over them did so illegitimately, immorally, and wrongly, and therefore had nothing worthy of recognition as vested rights. At the same time, groups have made aspirations to a life free from legally recognized hierarchies—to a life without the badges and incidents of slavery—into a super-constitution that has taken permanent precedence over any merely transitory determination of constitutional meaning. Some rights should never have been recognized. And some constitutional changes (involving the denial of previously vested rights) could only be imagined as returns to forms of permanent truth and moral meaning forgotten by earlier constitutional interpreters.

While many rights claimants have rested visions of constitutional legitimacy on the need to redistribute rights from oppressor to oppressed, few have stated their public claims so starkly. As a people, Americans may be "constitutionally" incapable of characterizing rights claims as moves in a zero-sum game. Lawyers know that a new, increased, or transformed public good must always be alleged as the necessary consequence of any recognition of previously unrecognized rights; there must be some net benefit to the public welfare. Americans have never simply righted wrongs; they have always been making things better.

Occasionally, however, particular rights claimants have gone beyond the easy and lawyerlike assertion of an increase in the public good. Instead, they have insisted on characterizing particular claims as preconditions to any future public legitimacy. This is a third way of characterizing constitutional rights. In some cases such claims have taken the form of demands for structures of effective legal remedies. For minorities and women, affirmative action today makes the formal rights secured in the constitutional order something other than empty and fraudulent assurances. Without it, they would come to see themselves as fooled by rights, as having misdirected their aspirations.

Alternatively, groups have at times declared one particular constitutional right as primary and superior to all others. Nineteenth-century feminists, for example, eventually designated the franchise as the first of all rights. Their characterization rested on the common equation of citizenship with the vote and their complementary understanding that the continuation of patriarchy was inconsistent with female citizenship. Without the ballot, women remained vulnerable and dependent, less than autonomous individuals. With it, feminists could imagine the reconstruction of a legitimate public order. Likewise, for religious minorities with deviant religious practices, the free exercise clause of the First Amendment has been seen as "the axis on which the wheel of history turns," the only foundation for life within a crushingly secular American society.

To historians, the notion that the constitutional order must legitimate itself by recognizing a particular right may suggest a strikingly tentative and contingent commitment to the American constitutional arena. Such demands imply a threat: If you (the state, the courts, the Department of Labor) don't do this one thing, then we (women, minorities, religious deviationists) will have learned the foolishness of identifying personal aspirations with constitutional rights. They imply the threat of withdrawal and of a loss of constitutional faith.

Dilemmas of a Convention

. . . [H]istorians ought not fool themselves that a return to the middle— somewhere between essential truth and no truth, somewhere between permanent moral values and aesthetics and power—will resolve their own feelings about rights. Like other Americans, they cherish deep ambivalences about the virtues of rights and rights discourses. Seeing constitutional rights consciousness as conventional in nature and structure may permit them to avoid apocalyptic excesses; it will discourage the ruminations that take some on a conceptual banister ride from rights aspirants' visions of autonomy and self-ownership to totalitarianism and despair. Yet I am sure the conflict between immanence and plasticity . . . will be recreated in the middle ground of convention. We cannot escape the conflict, because it is inherent in our inherited language of rights.

Let me briefly sketch two sources of the conflict. First, the claims of outsiders, no less than those of insiders, resonate with conceptions drawn from long-standing constitutional traditions. Those conceptions have been rooted in particular social and historical contexts and reflect the values of a variety of constitutional winners. The result is that the recourse to rights will, at times, produce distortions of outsiders' aspirations. Second, persistent struggle about conceptions of rights may call into question the value of the rights themselves, as relatively permanent measures of political stability and legitimacy.

The recourse to rights rhetoric has constrained the claims of some of those who struggled for constitutional rights, precluding some positions and cabining some aspirations. Consider the power of notions of possessive individualism, for example. The Lockean tradition has lived in the constitutional claims Americans have made, for all of the valor and imagination of the legal and historical scholarship that has tried to recover alternative intellectual foundations. The inherited meanings drawn from that tradition shaped the claims of a labor movement, which from the early twentieth century on conceded many of the prerogatives of management, as the representative of company-owning shareholders. The influence of possessive individualism also helps explain the relative unavailability of constitutional language for litigants asserting the collective rights of families. Either family rights became the individualistic, libertarian rights of individuals within a family, or they were equated with the property rights of a patriarchal head of household.

To use our individualistic Bill of Rights and Fourteenth Amendment as sources of language to constitute, recognize, and legitimate group identities and to represent group aspirations is, at minimum, an odd way to articulate a collective faith. For the past century and more, lawyers have devoted much ingenuity to formulating group claims in ways that have made them appear to conform to the categories of a distinctly individualistic constitutional rights discourse. Their work has often been heroic and sometimes successful. Yet, it has also failed frequently enough that historians may wonder whether clients might not have sought better weapons in struggles for respect and legitimacy.

Using the inherited categories of rights talk as a way of articulating grievances, wants, and hopes disciplines the speaker. Not all wants can be posed as rights. Rights talk has shaped what groups demand as their rights, so that what is demanded has often ended close to what those with power wanted to give. For example, black parents in Boston (and elsewhere) who struggled for decades to compel school boards to shift resources to their impoverished and segregated schools ended up watching their children being bused to equally impoverished, but hostile, white schools. They were taught through constitutional rights litigation, as interpreted by their lawyers, that integration had to take precedence over any redistribution of resources to the education of their children. What they got was what their lawyers asked for.

Another difficulty must be faced by those who would write a "conventional" history of rights incorporating the struggles and achievements of constitutional outsiders. . . . Americans have often thought of the word *right* in terms of constraints and barriers against change. They have known rights as the distinctive attributes of legitimate constitutional government, because rights reveal that government's intention not to invade the private identities of its citizens. Thus, gaining a constitutional right—gaining public recognition that you have a right, and not just a want—should mean that you have gained some protection against fickle and transitory political judgments.

But such an interpretation of constitutional rights as conservative, as barriers to change, flies in the face of the histories explored in this symposium, many of which describe the articulation through rights of visions of change and transformation. Indeed, groups claiming rights have often aimed to end a preexisting regime of substantive rights. How else can we understand black freedmen's claimed right to much of the lands of their former masters? Groups wish "their" rights, once established, to be permanent and stable. They insist that only other, opposing, rights must be temporary and changeable. To make the obvious interpretive point, the attractiveness of permanence is always from a particular perspective.

To the extent then that constitutional historians integrate the perspectives of those outside the constitutional mainstream with mainstream understandings, they will, almost necessarily, weaken commitments to a traditional rights convention. At minimum, historians will have to rethink their inherited understandings of rights. At maximum, they may find themselves forced to abandon notions of a distinctively legal or constitutional history, abandoning a perspective founded on the American Constitution's separation from the indeterminacies of American social and political history.

Constitutional History from the Bottom Up

Constitutional historians have disagreed sharply over many issues: political, moral, methodological. Virtually all, however, have taken it as a given that the goal of historical inquiry should be an examination and evaluation of a body of authoritative interpretations—constitutional law—typically identified with the pronouncements of the United States Supreme Court. Largely banished from the domain of constitutional history have been the activities and beliefs of all who were not official interpreters. Thus, we have had a surfeit of studies of the racial beliefs of the drafters and official interpreters of the Fourteenth Amendment. But, until recently, we knew little of the distinctive constitutional beliefs that informed black activism in the post–Civil War period. And still, today, no constitutional historian has made Afro-American constitutional vision a prominent feature of post–Civil War constitutionalism.

The prevailing conception of constitutional history's proper subject matter has not required constitutional historians to deny the significance of social and cultural change. Today, work in constitutional history often rests on an assumption that various nonconstitutional inputs—social, cultural, ideological, economic, political—produce outputs, or constitutional texts, that are, or express, constitutional law. Insofar as conventional constitutional history has concerned itself with the constitutional faiths and values of blacks and others of the constitutionally disinherited, it has done so by considering them as inputs, helping to produce the outputs of doctrine embodied in constitutional law. The historical inquiry assesss the contribution of inputs to outputs and analyzes changes in both over time. But such historical analyses, no less than older methodologies, assume that only certain authoritative texts and certain authoritative textual interpretations can have the status of constitutional output. Recovering their meaning and their place within a continuing sequence of authoritative texts and interpretations is the proper business of constitutional history.

Scholars have often pointed to various long traditions of constitutionalism—traditions that distinguish fundamental law from (presumably democratic or, at minimum, unruly) politics—as shaping American deference to a text and to a privileged group of interpreters. The emphasis on authoritative texts tends to imply the near inevitability of the American pattern of discovering constitutional meaning and of establishing constitutional legitimacy. . . . [T]he typical forms of American constitutional history may themselves be the consequence of the machinations of two generations of jurisprudes who worked to make the federal Constitution appear an objective, external, and completed document, interpretable only by legal mandarins. One reason, then, why historians have seen the Constitution as they have is because two generations of "Framers" intended them to see it that way.

The result, in any event, is a constitutional history that provides no account of perhaps the most salient and interesting feature of American public culture: its rights consciousness. . . . Americans have been especially inclined to phrase their demands and "needs" in arguments about constitutional rights, to expect remedies for their wrongs to be provided through processes provided by formal legal institutions, and to view their activities as touching on issues of constitutional interpretation. Such consciousness has thrived among those who did not benefit from mainstream interpretations of the Constitution.

The persistent presence of constitutional rights consciousness, articulated by and embodied in a changing array of groups, ought to call into question American constitutional history's received perspective. If constitutional law were really nothing but a body of texts authoritatively interpreted by a specialized and distant elite, why would so many Americans have ceaselessly organized to validate in legal arenas distinctive constitutional claims and perceived entitlements? If American constitutionalism were really about the evolution of a univocal meaning, about getting the right historical answer to the constitutional question of the moment, could historians ever account for the contingency and the variety of wildly different right answers that have been derived from the texts over the past two centuries? If particular opinions and holdings were conclusive of struggles for legal rights, then those who lost in court should have either accepted the loss as legal and slunk into passivity or insisted on power through nonlegal means. Yet, neither alternative has attracted many groups throughout American history. . . .

Constitutional historians are so used to thinking of the business of constitutional history as explaining the origins of various statements of constitutional law doctrine that it is difficult to even imagine alternatives. To learn to see the constitutional rights consciousness as constitutional output, no less than constitutional input, would require historians to deal with the American Constitution as contested interpretive terrain, as an arena of struggle between contending and changing normative orders. They would have to recognize that constitutional history incorporates many voices, that there has rarely been a monolithic understanding of constitutional meaning, that the position of the United States Supreme Court as our preeminent constitutional interpreter is a problematic feature of our history.

Such a vision of constitutional history requires a perspective wide enough to incorporate the relations between official producers of constitutional law, and those who at particular times and in particular circumstances resisted or reinterpreted constitutional law. It would recognize the significance of a variety of groups who worked to reconstruct constitutional law for their own purposes—including the purpose of reconstructing a legitimate constitutional order. Lawyers' categories, formal legalistic language, would remain important subjects of study, but as translations and as mediations of aspirations and claims, not as the ends of inquiry.

Supreme Court cases should be only one portion of the descriptive detail of American constitutional history. As important would be the small, everyday contests, arguments, negotiations, and understandings in which legal rights and constitutional assumptions have been constructed and exercised. Labor contracts, divorce decrees, zoning variances, municipal ordinances, children's claimed right to keep their parents out of their closets, parents' exercise of their asserted right to discipline their children—all are the stuff of our constitutional history as well.

Formal constitutional rights talk translates and reconstructs conflict. It does not initiate it. Constitutional history's distinctiveness as a domain of inquiry should result from the historical experiences of groups and individuals throughout American history who have invested that arena of struggle with meaning and significance. It is not important for itself. . . . I do not believe we will ever discover a relatively stable truth about ourselves from the nature of American rights talk. We can only use American constitutional struggles as ways of learning about "the history of a people contending about power, identity, and justice."

Conclusion

. . . Our uncertainties, our discomforts, our ambivalence about the salience and significance of rights in American history should not be repressed as exploratory work proceeds. They are themselves sources of historical insight into rights' moral place. Historians cannot hope to write a social history of

American constitutional experience without confronting the peculiar eva-
nescence of rights. Constitutional rights have been valuable because they
appear as solid and permanent commitments by the society, as guarantees
of an unchanging vision of free human subjectivity. Yet we know that their
meanings have changed dramatically and frequently over time. The very
successes of particular groups in insisting on the perquisites of membership
within a common American citizenry suggest the changeability of constitutional claims.

Constitutional history has traditionally assumed responsibility for con-
serving an inherited American constitutionalism. Its practitioners have assumed the task laid out by Lincoln in his Springfield Lyceum address. What
is constitutionalism? While there are many definitions, all orient themselves
around the notion of the rule of law—around the notion that legitimate
government is, to use the famous phrase of John Adams and James Har-
rington, "a government of laws, not of men."

In most versions, the idea of a government of laws has been said to
lead to a vision of limited government. Government is legitimate only so
long as it recognizes that there are things that it cannot do, particularly to
the "private" identities and possessions of its citizens. At the same time,
the notion of a government of laws also has suggested a government that
must justify itself by its congruence with external standards and norms. There
is within our inherited Anglo-American notions of constitutionalism no inherent right to rule. Government, ruling, must be justified. And the right
to govern, therefore, rests on government's obligation to do particular
things—to prevent forms of bondage, to protect property rights, to guarantee
people security from the cruelty and the chaos of a life without structures
of political authority.

Can inherited notions of American constitutionalism—of the primacy
of a government of laws—coexist with a reconstructed constitutional history
founded on the study of constitutional rights consciousness? I can imagine
a constitutionalism of rights consciousness, a populist reinterpretation of the
government of laws, locating those laws in the changing aspirations of diverse
groups within the society. Yet I do not know whether such an understanding
would satisfy yearnings for stable external standards against which to hold
governmental processes.

Historians will conserve a constitutional heritage. What they conserve—
what future writings in American constitutional history will include and
exclude, what will be regarded as salient, what will be recognized as pe-
ripheral—is for them to decide. Their decisions ought to leave readers with
an understanding of the moral complexity of American constitutional experience, and the passion invested in constitutional rights, as well as the
costs of commitment to American constitutional values. The task is to interpret the constitutional history of a society that has been and remains
structured by divisions of wealth, gender, and race, yet, at the same time,
has been and remains committed to values of democracy, fairness, and
respect.

In Defense of Liberal Pluralism and Constitutionalism

HERMAN BELZ

Every state has a constitution—a body of principles, institutions, laws, and customs that forms the framework of government—but not every state is a constitutional state. The latter is distinguished by a commitment to constitutionalism, which in essence is the idea that political life ought to be carried on according to procedures and rules that paradoxically are in some degree placed beyond politics: procedures in other words that are fundamental. Nothing so positive as a written constitution, but rather the belief that the law as the embodiment of a society's most important values is powerful, characterizes government under the rule of law.

Apprehension about the future of constitutional government in the United States . . . increased in [the sixties and seventies.] Political assassination, urban riots, the resort to civil disobedience by groups as disparate as striking postal workers and university students, the idea that politics is important enough to be the object of secret intelligence operations—all of this is evidence of a crisis in which the very legitimacy of public authority is called into question. In the long run, however, perhaps even more unsettling than these turbulent events is the intellectual and ideological challenge to constitutionalism that they have produced.

This challenge appears most significantly, I believe, not in the revelations of former White House aides, alarming as these are, but rather in the crisis literature of political science [and history] which has attempted to explain the upheaval of the past several years and offer a new theory of politics. The most obvious feature of this literature is its critique of pluralism. Interest-group liberalism, the antipluralists emphatically conclude, is the dead end, not the vital center, of American democracy. Dissatisfaction with liberal pluralism is not new, however, and in the . . . literature it does not provide the special animus of the attack on the liberal state. Rather impatience with constitutionalism, which runs pretty deep amid the consciousness raising and political involvement of our time, forms the essential theme of the attack on pluralism.

The fundamental charge against pluralism is that it is not real democracy, but rather a system of special privilege by which the rich and powerful protect their interests at the expense of the people. American politics, the antipluralists insist, simply does not work the way it is supposed to in theory. It is fatuous, they say, to think that a vast number of competing and roughly equal groups interact freely in the political decision-making structure. On the contrary, a few corporate giants control the political system. An even more damning indictment of pluralism is that it excludes many groups from the political process entirely. Blacks, the poor, students, women, and sundry

Herman Belz, "New Left Reverberations in the Academy: The Antipluralist Critique of Constitutionalism," *Review of Politics*, 36 (1974): 265–283. Reprinted by permission.

minorities are all seen as relegated to a condition of noncitizenship outside the political arena.

If it is suggested that American politics is actually responsive to demands from nonelite groups, the antipluralist answer is that the system may work after a fashion, but the workings are all trivial and irrelevant. The root of the trouble is said to be the biased context in which interest-group politics operates. The political process may be open, the media relatively accessible, freedom of speech and of the press secure. All this is beside the point, however, for what is really important, say the critics, is "the other face of power," that is, the class bias of pluralist politics which prevents issues of real concern to the community from being brought into the political arena. The groups which control the system ignore problems such as urban blight, public transportation, worker alienation, and environmental destruction. What officials do not do, the argument runs—the nondecisions they make— are more important than the decisions they make about insignificant matters.

From here it is but a short distance to the doctrine of repressive tolerance. Because the political system is managed in the interests of dominant economic groups, . . . there is an objective contradiction between the political structure and the theory of pluralist toleration. In practice equality of tolerance becomes abstract and spurious, an instrument of coordination and control rather than a means of effecting change. . . . [W]hen toleration is examined in the context of liberalism, with its assumption of a utilitarian and individualistic ethic, it is revealed as negligence of the public interest. The attitude which this kind of criticism encourages will be recognized by anyone who has been on a college campus [in the late sixties and early seventies]. Student radicals take part in an election, work hard for a candidate, and then if the candidate loses decry the system for failing once again. . . . The procedures of democratic pluralism become in this view mere legitimizing rituals and the right of dissent an instrument of oppression. . . .

. . . [T]he critique of pluralism goes beyond an accounting of the specific failures of the liberal state in America. What is being challenged is the very idea of constitutionalism itself. This is most apparent in the antipluralists' preoccupation with political action.

Constitutionalism, they contend, even in its original eighteenth-century formulation, was flawed by its failure to contain a concept of political action. Beguiled by the idea of applying science to politics, the founders of constitutionalism sought to control human behavior by devising rules and procedures for the conduct of government that would eliminate the need for political leadership and citizen participation. Placing their faith in institutions rather than men, they provided no space for political action and designed a mechanistic system which depersonalized, trivialized, and fragmentized political life. Antipluralists charge further that constitutionalism comprehends and protects mere private economic interests. It thus denies the vision of politics as an educational and salvational activity, and the possibility of defining and achieving a true public purpose. In liberal society a "nondirective constitutionalism" aimed at containing competing interests is substituted for authentic political community.

Those who think of politics as the art of achieving the possible and see in the constitutional system broad scope for political action may wonder about the criteria used to reach these negative conclusions. And indeed skepticism is warranted, for the antipluralists' critique of constitutionalism depends heavily upon a conception of political action drawn more from philosophy than from ordinary language and experience.

. . . [C]ritics of pluralism hold that political action refers to acts which are novel, consequential, purposive, irreversible, and indeterminate. All else, including the routine and often predictable responses which characterize a stable constitutional regime, are defined—and dismissed—as behavior. Perhaps not every antipluralist critic would subscribe to precisely this formulation of the issue, but the demands for relevant action and meaningful change heard so often these days come pretty close to capturing the more technical definition. A corollary notion . . . is the idea of public space. As used by the antipluralists, public space refers to opportunities in which men can appear to others and disclose themselves in speech and action. This seems familiar enough, and we readily think of the range of legally protected liberties under the first and fourteenth amendments. But if speech and action and petitioning of the government avail nothing in the way of boundless, novel, unanticipated and indeterminate results—nothing that meets the criteria of political action—then there is evidently no true public space or genuine political freedom.

If constitutionalism is seen as defective in its original conception, it is criticized all the more in its present-day reality for suppressing authentic politics. This emerges most clearly in the attack on the "process theory" of democracy. Classical democratic thought, the critics argue, posited broad popular participation in politics in pursuit of the common good. In the Cold War era, however, pluralists revised the classical theory by concluding that democracy consisted in procedures and practices which assured a stable political system characterized by low popular participation. Liberal democracy became in essence a process distinguished by voter apathy and elite manipulation.

Although the antipluralists do not quite say that procedure is unimportant, they believe it has too often been honored at the expense of higher values. . . . Wilson Carey McWilliams has suggested that any solution to the contemporary political crisis must involve an abandonment of our fascination for a government of mechanical contrivances designed to avoid conflict, if not to eliminate politics altogether.

Impatient, if not scornful of procedure, antipluralists regard politics as a matter of commitment and values and substantive results. Pluralism in contrast is seen as excessively concerned with stability and efficiency and, therefore, as essentially antipolitical. Christian Bay epitomizes the antipluralist animus in condemning what he calls the liberal myth that American society is democratic and that only by working within the constitutional system can a more just society be created. The most urgent contemporary need, says Bay, is to destroy this myth.

Certainly the critics of liberal pluralism have done their demythologizing best. It remains to ask, however, what they would have in its place and how their reform ideas stand in relation to constitutionalism.

In the . . . crisis literature three tendencies can be discerned on the question, what is to be done? One looks to civil disobedience as a source of political renewal, a second contemplates the democratization of economic organizations, and a third urges a new theory of politics based upon a revival of citizenship.

Although practitioners of civil disobedience may see it as a way of bringing down the system, scholarly interpreters contend on the contrary that it can make the political system work better. Civil disobedience, they reason, can become a new form of representation with the potential to revitalize democratic citizenship. Those who engage in civil disobedience are seen as a legitimate opposition whose political actions may enlighten the government and, by informing it of its misuse of power, actually enhance the rule of law. Tyranny being the exclusion of the public from the political, reasons Wilson Carey McWilliams, we are perilously near that condition now. Yet a way out is provided by civil disobedience, which by enabling citizens to gain access to the public can be a means of constitutional reform. Hannah Arendt views civil disobedients as organized minorities expressing their disagreement with the majority. Placing recent protesters in the tradition of voluntary associations, Arendt's novel argument envisions formal recognition of a lobbyist, group representation role for civil-disobedient minorities.

The hostility that people feel toward a nameless bureaucracy may lead in the future to further spasms of civil disobedience. It is hard to take seriously, however, the suggestion that "disciplined civil disobedience is possibly a creative way to ask citizens of the state if they are satisfied with other aspects of the delegational model that has served well but which may not have produced the most equitable and efficient allocation of power and resources to deal with emergent disaffection and unmet needs in the national polity." If civil-disobedient groups do somehow become "constitutionalized" they will be part of the pluralist political structure, a curious and disappointing conclusion, it would seem, from the radical point of view. Should civil disobedience increase, however, and produce a body of concerned participating magistrates as McWilliams urges, the result will more likely be an expedient people's justice than constitutional government as we have known it historically.

A second reformist theme of the antipluralists concerns the enforcing of accountability and responsibility in the economic power structure. It has become a commonplace to observe that corporations wield political power and make policies no different in substance and effect from those of public officials. What is needed is to broaden the definition of the political to include these nominally private but actually public institutions.

One way of constitutionalizing corporations is through judicial and administrative regulation. Because this would mean more of the same sort of centralized national regulation that has seemed so ineffectual in the past, however, antipluralists take a dim view of it. They argue instead for "participatory democracy." This is surely one of the more imprecise terms of contemporary political discourse, but in the present context it means control of corporations by those who work in and are affected by them. The system of self-management that exists in Yugoslavia is taken as model. Workers would form the board of directors or governing council of a business or industry, or in larger enterprises elect delegates to a council. The point is not to redistribute property, but rather to encourage democratic participation at the place of work in order to reduce people's sense of powerlessness and contribute to their self-development. Industrial democracy would make workers citizens of the enterprise rather than corporate subjects. And by enabling them to see the relationship between public and private spheres it would in turn make them better citizens of the state.

A politically engaged citizenry, the ultimate objective of both civil disobedience strategy and participatory economic democracy, lies at the very center of the third tendency in antipluralist reformism, the quest for a new theory of politics. The immediate purpose of this quest is a regeneration of citizenship and the creation of opportunities for genuine political action. . . .

It may be, as anthropologist Stanley Diamond argues, that the rule of law is a symptom of the disorder of customary institutions and the decline of a civilization. Believing that the second coming of true democracy, community, and participation would obviate the whole rule structure of the modern liberal state, the antipluralists seem to share this view. Until our political salvation is assured, however, we are justified in asking what the implications of the new politics and the new political theory are for constitutionalism.

Although the question usually is of interest to liberals and conservatives, some radical antipluralists, despite intense criticism of the liberal state, profess concern for constitutionalism. Theorists of civil disobedience and economic democracy seek ways of legitimizing new forms of dissent and constitutionalizing the great aggregates of economic power. A few theorists of the new politics say their purpose is to revise constitutionalism to provide greater scope for political action, diminishing the height of government but not removing the restraints upon it. In fighting for their causes, moreover, radicals will rely on constitutional rules for protection. Some caution further against rejecting bourgeois liberal constitutional ideals simply because they have often been a cloak for oppression, and express concern for constitutional processes within the radical movement, lest violence and brutality obliterate peaceful procedures. This is evidence that the attack on the pluralist system does not necessarily mean repudiation of the idea of constitutionalism.

Nevertheless, the new political theory of the antipluralists contradicts the fundamental ideas of constitutionalism. Those critics who profess to revise the theory of constitutionalism are mistaken, I believe, in their understanding of its essential meaning. To them—and inferentially to the antipluralists in general—constitutionalism means, or ought to mean, the people as constituent power, the source of authority and ground of law. It means further the people creating political power by forming a social compact and exercising that power in governing themselves. The ancient notion of popular sovereignty, dating from the founding of the republic, epitomizes this conception of constitutionalism.

Its root idea is politicism, the belief, that is, that political will and the force of personality, knowledge of the good and the will to realize it in acts of wisdom, are more important for good government—and more decisive in determining the course of events—than any institutional framework or procedural arrangements. Governments are like clocks, runs the old aphorism, and go from the motion men give them, not from anything in themselves. This politicist argument has always had considerable appeal. When it is applied to the people as a whole, and they are invested with the power of political action—especially as the antipluralists would define political action—it acquires even greater force, if indeed it does not become irresistible.

But while flexibility, discretion, personal character and freedom of political action—the elements of politicism—have had a place in the constitutional tradition, they have not formed the essence of it. In essence constitutionalism has meant adherence to certain formal procedures embodying and promoting the fundamental values of liberty, equality, and justice; to ways of conducting politics and managing public affairs which preserve a space immune to or beyond politics. In order words, while the people have been the constituent power, their power to govern—popular sovereignty— has been limited by their own constitutional creation. At its inception in the eighteenth century American constitutionalism was marked by an extraordinarily democratic basis, and the people as constituent power was the most startling of the revolutionary ideas. Yet the idea that a constitution was superior to and controlling of the political power of government, even when the people themselves exercised that power either through established institutions or outside them, was also part of revolutionary constitutionalism.

In the history of Western political thought this idea of fundamental law was as remarkable an innovation as the notion of the people as constituent power. In the long run it became the truly distinctive feature of American constitutionalism. The constitution was conceived of as a means of conducting politics, but it did not consist in a mere declaration of purposes or a set of exhortations, as the French constitution of 1791 did. It was on the contrary explicitly declared to be law, the supreme law of the land along with treaties of the United States and acts of Congress made in pursuance of it. Ordinary law, as between private persons, was to be used to regulate the acts of government and the energies and passions of politics. And this political law maintaining the structure of the body politic and protecting individual liberty against encroachment by the government, a paradoxical and contradictory thing according to the best learning of the day, was to be enforced by ordinary courts of justice. It was altogether a curious amalgam which, in conjunction with the division of power between national and state governments known as federalism, effectively destroyed sovereignty as it was then known. And it meant too that popular sovereignty must be stillborn, must be placed under constitutional restraints as well.

It is the age-old politicist drive to be free of procedural restraints which informs the antipluralist appeal for a new politics. Expressing this appeal in modern terms of commitment, transcendence, and self-fulfillment, the critics resurrect the classic democratic ideal of an engaged citizenry exercising political and legal sovereignty and standing above institutions. But no better than anyone else are the antipluralists able to explain how fundamental fairness can obtain in a system of government in which all is politicized.

The essence of the political is discretion, discrimination, expediency, adjustment of conflicting claims on a pragmatic basis. The essence of the legal is general and prospective rules that result in regular and predictable procedure. A constitution must of course generate power as well as channel it. It must comprehend both the political and legal dimension. And in a strict sense we cannot say that one is more important than the other; both are essential. Yet while we can be pretty sure that political energies and passions and conflicts will continue to manifest themselves, with the insistence and power seemingly of natural forces, the experience of the twentieth century tells us that the existence of a stable and fair system for restraining these forces cannot be taken for granted. The opposite of constitutionalism—arbitrary and coercive government which denies political liberty and free public criticism—must be guarded against. And this means keeping in mind, to use the language of social science, a contrast-model.

From the 1930s to the 1950s totalitarian regimes in Europe provided a vivid contrast-model which led intellectuals in the United States to reconsider their own constitutional tradition. Instead of dismissing the rule of law as a conservative fiction and a device for maintaining the status quo, as many had done, they came to see it as a valid distinction between systems of government. A revival of interest in constitutionalism occurred which made it a principal theme in modern liberalism.

The antipluralists have reacted against liberal constitutionalism as though it were entirely ideological—a reflection of the false consciousness of its adherents—and lacking any basis in historical reality. They deny the validity of the totalitarian contrast-model on the ground that it fosters complacency and, by failing to emphasize problems, forecloses the possibility of change. Yet it is difficult to ignore recent history—right down to the latest interdiction of free speech and academic inquiry by student radicals—and hard not to be apprehensive about a political theory that exalts popular participation and political action to the extent that the new politics does. It may seem entirely clear to the heralds of the new citizenship that the mass participation of modern technological society is completely different from the true democratic participation they envision, but a skeptical view of this distinction seems warranted. How realistic is it to think that men and women will engage in politics for the sheer love of it, apart from practical purposes? Benjamin R. Barber states that "a new era of *philopoly* might help to make life for man in the post-historical epoch livable." It would be more accurate to say that only after history ends—in the world to come—will people play at politics for the love of the thing itself, as some antipluralists believe.

If the present crisis is rooted in an erosion of community which has released proliferating forces of conflict, calling into question the authority of government and politicizing all manner of social processes and relationships, the solution lies not in further encouragement of politicist tendencies but in their being brought into a more stable equilibrium with the essential ideas and procedures of constitutionalism. This will not be accomplished by stern admonitions from high officials to respect law and order, especially now in the light of the Watergate revelations. Whether the crisis can be surmounted according to prescriptions offered meanwhile by political scientists in the liberal constitutional tradition may also be doubted. These solutions range from Lowi's juridical democracy, to Friedrich's call for inspirational democratic leadership, to Tugwell's new model constitution. Appealing as these suggestions are, they seem to assume against the evidence that someone somewhere has the knowledge and power to set things right.

The crux of the matter is the tendency and habit of ordinary citizens to regard political institutions and procedures as legitimate. In the United States legitimate authority derives in large part from the direct link with the eighteenth-century framers' act of foundation and the consensual basis on which it rested. This basis has been seriously challenged, but how far the disintegration of community has gone is not clear. Probably it has not gone as far as the dramatic events [in the late sixties and early seventies] seemed to indicate. The structure of assumptions, beliefs, and practices in which constitutionalism consists may be more solidly based than it appears in the crisis literature. Nevertheless, the antipluralists' insistence on ever greater political participation and action reflects and represents a challenge to constitutionalism that is not merely academic. If the liberal constitutional order collapses, the critics of pluralism might consider, it is not at all likely that a left-wing movement dedicated to participatory democracy will take its place.

⊞ *F U R T H E R   R E A D I N G*

Paul Finkelman, "The Constitution and the Intentions of the Framers: The Limits of Historical Analysis," *University of Pittsburgh Law Review* 50 (1989): 349–398

Lawrence M. Friedman, *A History of American Law*, 2nd ed. (1985)

Kermit L. Hall, *The Magic Mirror: Law in American History* (1989)

———, ed. *Main Themes in United States Constitutional and Legal History* (1987)

Michael Kammen, *A Machine That Would Go of Itself: The Constitution in American Culture* (1986)

Alfred H. Kelly, Winfred A. Harbison, and Herman J. Belz, *The American Constitution: Its Origins and Development*, 6th ed. (1983)

Melvin I. Urofsky, *A March of Liberty: A Constitutional History of the United States* (1988)

William M. Wiecek, "Clio as Hostage: The United States Supreme Court and the Uses of History," *California Western Law Review* 24 (1988): 227–276

CHAPTER
2

Laissez-Faire Constitutionalism and Liberty in the Late Nineteenth Century

Jolting social and economic transformations unsettled late nineteenth-century America. Massive immigration, which altered the nation's cultural and ethnic mix, figured prominently in these changes. The newcomers merged with a steady flow of Americans leaving the farm to form a mighty river of urbanization. The nation's changed character appeared even more dramatically in its explosive economic growth. Every significant measure of economic activity soared. Railroad-track mileage, for example, increased from about 30,000 miles in 1860 to more than 240,000 miles in 1910. Nowhere in the world was economic growth so spectacular as in the United States, already among the richest nations.

The Industrial Revolution in America fostered increasing competition between capital and labor that in turn bred unprecedented social unrest. The infamous Haymarket Riot in Chicago in 1886 touched off a public panic that radical immigrant laborers threatened the internal security of the nation. Widespread outbursts of labor militancy only added to popular fears, as did the Populist party's crusades for free silver, taxes on the incomes of the rich, and new laws to bust the trusts.

Contemporaries widely viewed measures such as the income tax as radical, or even socialist or communist in origin. Nineteenth-century Americans, after all, had given great weight to laissez-faire individualism. This doctrine held that the greatest and cheapest productivity would occur only if employer and employee were left free to set their own terms of employment and if the markets for capital and labor were allowed to work unobstructed by governmental action. Perhaps President Grover Cleveland captured the essence of this view when he vetoed an 1887 appropriation for drought-stricken Texas farmers with the remark that *"though the people support the Government, the Government should not support the people."*

This chapter concentrates on the relationship of the Constitution to free-market ideology; the next chapter examines the concepts of substantive due process and freedom to contract. In both instances, the ideas of a free market and of freedom to contract complemented the then dominant theory of Social Darwinism. In articulating the latter, the Yale sociologist William Graham Sumner borrowed from the evolutionary biology of Charles Darwin to proclaim that the advancement of the economy depended on competition among human beings, with the fittest (including corporations) surviving. Any governmental interference in this process merely directed the flow of wealth away from the talented and able toward the undeserving.

The constitutional developments of the era, of course, turned on more than laissez-faire ideology. There was a broad consensus about the virtues of economic growth; disagreements arose mainly over how best to distribute the costs and benefits of that growth. Legislators and judges worried about the distribution and protection of rights to property, the control of which, in turn, dictated the distribution of wealth generally.

✠ D O C U M E N T S

Thomas M. Cooley was chief judge of the Michigan Supreme Court from 1864 to 1885 and one of the nineteenth century's most prolific legal treatise writers. His most important work, *Treatise on the Constitutional Limitations Which Rest upon the Legislative Power of the States of the American Nation* (referred to commonly as *Constitutional Limitation*), a portion of which is excerpted as the first document, dealt with the relationship between state legislative authority (the so-called police powers of the states to provide for health, safety, morals, and welfare) and the judiciary. State and federal courts seized on Cooley's arguments to overturn a host of regulatory measures that had been designed ostensibly to promote the public welfare.

The U.S. Supreme Court initially embraced legislative efforts to reign in the consequences of industrialization, but the justices disagreed sharply about whether a measure was genuinely designed to promote the public welfare, which the Court approved of, or whether it was intended instead to redistribute wealth, something that the justices rejected. In the *Slaughterhouse Cases* (1873), for example, the justices upheld by a 5–4 margin a Louisiana law that granted to a single company the franchise for one slaughterhouse built away from the residential areas of New Orleans. The dissenters in the *Slaughterhouse Cases* eventually became the majority of the Court, and when they did, they struck down measures such as the federal income tax in *Pollock* v. *Farmers' Loan and Trust Co.* (1895), which is reprinted as document 3. In *Munn* v. *Illinois* (1877), the fourth document, the justices sustained a measure designed to regulate the grain-elevator business in Chicago. Not quite twenty years later, with popular anxiety about the intrusion of government into business at fever pitch, the Court in *United States* v. *E. C. Knight* (1895), document 5, found that a company controlling more than 90 percent of the nation's sugar-refining capacity did not violate the Sherman Antitrust Act. In *In Re Debs* (1895), excerpted as the sixth document, the justices overwhelmingly endorsed the broad powers of the federal government to regulate unions.

The decisions in *Pollock*, *Debs*, and *E. C. Knight* confirmed the view of many labor and farm groups that not only was the Supreme Court hostile to them, but the entire constitutional system required a massive overhaul. The Populist party's 1896 platform, which is the last document, offered at the time what seemed a radical constitutional vision, although after almost 100 years it appears strikingly benign.

Jurist Thomas M. Cooley on Constitutional Limitations, 1869

It must be evident to any one that the power to declare a legislative enactment void is one which the judge, conscious of the fallibility of the human judgment, will shrink from exercising in any case where he can conscientiously and with due regard to duty and official oath decline the responsibility. The legislative and judicial are co-ordinate departments of the government, of equal dignity; each is alike supreme in the exercise of its proper functions, and cannot directly or indirectly, while acting within the limits of its authority, be subjected to the control or supervision of the other, without an unwarrantable assumption by that other of power which, by the constitution, is not conferred upon it. The constitution apportions the powers of government, but it does not make any one of the three departments subordinate to another, when exercising the trust committed to it. The courts may declare legislative enactments unconstitutional and void in some cases, but not because the judicial power is superior in degree or dignity to the legislative. Being required to declare what the law is in the cases which come before them, they must enforce the constitution as the paramount law, whenever a legislative enactment comes in conflict with it. But the courts sit, not to review or revise the legislative action, but to enforce the legislative will; and it is only where they find that the legislature has failed to keep within its constitutional limits, that they are at liberty to disregard its action; and in doing so, they only do what every private citizen may do in respect to the mandates of the courts when the judges assume to act and to render judgments or decrees without jurisdiction. "In exercising this high authority, the judges claim no judicial supremacy; they are only the administrators of the public will. If an act of the legislature is held void, it is not because the judges have any control over the legislative power, but because the act is forbidden by the constitution, and because the will of the people, which is therein declared, is paramount to that of their representatives expressed in any law."

Nevertheless, in declaring a law unconstitutional, a court must necessarily cover the same ground which has already been covered by the legislative department in deciding upon the propriety of enacting the law, and they must indirectly overrule the decision of that co-ordinate department. The task is therefore a delicate one, and only to be entered upon with reluctance and hesitation. It is a solemn act in any case to declare that that body of men to whom the people have committed the sovereign function of making the laws for the commonwealth, have deliberately disregarded the limitations imposed upon this delegated authority, and usurped power which the people have been careful to withhold; and it is almost equally so when the act which is adjudged to be unconstitutional appears to be chargeable rather to careless and improvident action, or error in judgment, than to intentional disregard of obligation. But the duty to do this in a proper case, though at one time doubted, and by some persons persistently denied, it is now generally agreed that the courts cannot properly decline, and in its performance they seldom fail of proper support if they proceed with due caution and circumspection, and under a proper sense as well of their own responsibility, as of the respect due to the action and judgment of the law-makers. . . .

In the American constitutional system, the power to establish the ordinary regulations of police has been left with the individual States, and cannot be assumed by the national government. Neither can the national government through any of its departments or officers assume any supervision of the police regulations of the States, so long as they do not invade the sphere of national sovereignty, and obstruct or impede the exercise of any authority which the Constitution has confided to the nation. But on the other hand it is easy to see that the power in the States might be so employed as to interfere with the jurisdiction of the general government; and some of the most serious questions regarding the police of the States concerns the cases in which authority has been conferred upon Congress. In those cases it has sometimes been claimed that the ordinary police jurisdiction is by necessary implication excluded, and that, if it were not so, the State would be found operating within the sphere of the national powers, and establishing regulations which would either abridge the rights which the national Constitution undertakes to render absolute, or burden the privileges which, being conferred by law of Congress, cannot properly be subject to control by any other authority. But any accurate statement of the theory upon which the police power rests, will render it apparent that a proper exercise of it by the State cannot come in conflict with the provisions of the Constitution of the United States. If the power only extends to a just regulation of rights with a view to the due protection and enjoyment of all, and does not deprive any one of that which is justly and properly his own, it is obvious that its possession by the State, and its exercise for the regulation of the property and actions of its citizens, cannot well constitute an invasion of national jurisdiction, or afford a basis for an appeal to the protection of the national authorities.

This subject has often been considered in its bearings upon the clause of the Constitution of the United States which forbids the States passing any laws violating the obligation of contracts; and invariably it has been held that this clause does not so far remove from State control the rights and properties which depend for their existence or enforcement upon contracts, as to relieve them from the operation of such general regulations for the good government of the State and the protection of the rights of individuals as may be deemed important. All contracts and all rights, it is held, are subject to this power; and regulations which affect them may not only be established by the State, but must also be subject to change from time to time, with reference to the general well-being of the community, as circumstances change, or as experience demonstrates the necessity.

The Slaughter-House Cases,
16 Wallace 36 (1873)

[5–4: Miller, Clifford, Davis, Hunt, Strong;
Bradley, Chase, Field, Swayne]

Mr. Justice Miller delivered the opinion of the Court.

The regulation of the place and manner of conducting the slaughtering of animals is among the most necessary and frequent exercises of the police power. The 1869 law is aptly framed to remove from the more densely populated part of the city, the noxious slaughter-houses, and large and offensive collections of animals necessarily incident to them, and to locate them where the convenience, health, and comfort of the people require they shall be located. And it must be conceded that the means adopted by the act for this purpose are appropriate, are stringent, and effectual. But it is said that in creating a corporation for this purpose, and conferring upon it exclusive privileges—privileges which it is said constitute a monopoly—the legislature has exceeded its power. . . .

The most cursory glance at [the Civil War Amendments] discloses a unity of purpose, when taken in connection with the history of the times, which cannot fail to have an important bearing on any question of doubt concerning their true meaning. . . . Fortunately that history is fresh within the memory of us all, and its leading features, as they bear upon the matter before us, free from doubt.

. . . The overshadowing and efficient cause [of the Civil War] was African slavery. In that struggle slavery, as a legalized social relation, perished. It perished as a necessity of the bitterness and force of the conflict. . . . But the war being over, those who had succeeded in re-establishing the authority of the Federal government were not content to permit this great act of emancipation to rest on the actual results of the contest or the proclamation of the Executive, both of which might have been questioned in after times, and they determined to place this main and most valuable result in the Constitution of the restored Union as one of its fundamental articles. Hence the [13th Amendment].

To withdraw the mind from the contemplation of this grand yet simple declaration of the personal freedom of all the human race within the jurisdiction of this government—a declaration designed to establish the freedom of four millions of slaves—and with a microscopic search endeavor to find in it a reference to servitudes, which may have been attached to property in certain localities, requires an effort, to say the least of it. That a personal servitude was meant is proved by the use of the word "involuntary," which can only apply to human beings. [The] word servitude is of larger meaning than slavery, as the latter is popularly understood in this country, and the obvious purpose was to forbid all shades and conditions of African slavery. . . .

. . . Notwithstanding the formal recognition by those [Southern] States of the abolition of slavery, the condition of the slave race would, without further protection of the Federal government, be almost as bad as it was before. Among the first acts of legislation adopted by several of the States were laws which imposed upon the colored race onerous disabilities and burdens, and curtailed their rights in the pursuit of life, liberty, and property to such an extent that their freedom was of little value, while they had lost the protection which they had received from their former owners from motives both of interest and humanity. They were in some States forbidden to appear in the towns in any other character than menial servants. They were required to reside on and cultivate the soil without the right to purchase or own it. They were excluded from many occupations of gain, and were not permitted to give testimony in the courts in any case where a white man was a party. It was said that their lives were at the mercy of bad men, either because the laws for their protection were insufficient or were not enforced.

These circumstances, whatever of falsehood or misconception may have been mingled with their presentation, forced upon the statesmen who had conducted the Federal government in safety through the crisis of the rebellion, and who supposed that by the thirteenth article of amendment they had secured the result of their labors, the conviction that something more was necessary in the way of constitutional protection to the unfortunate race who had suffered so much. They accordingly [proposed the 14th Amendment].

A few years' experience satisfied the thoughtful men who had been the authors of the other two amendments that, notwithstanding the restraints of those articles on the States, and the laws passed under the additional powers granted to Congress, these were inadequate for the protection of life, liberty, and property, without which freedom to the slave was no boon. They were in all those States denied the right of suffrage. The laws were administered by the white man alone. It was urged that a race of men distinctively marked as was the negro, living in the midst of another and dominant race, could never be fully secured in their person and the property without the right of suffrage. Hence [the 15th Amendment].

We repeat, then, in the light of this recapitulation of events, almost too recent to be called history, but which are familiar to us all; and on the most casual examination of the language of these amendments, no one can fail to be impressed with the one pervading purpose found in them all, lying at the foundation of each, and without which none of them would have been even suggested; we mean the freedom of the slave race, the security and firm establishment of that freedom, and the protection of the newly-made freeman and citizen from the oppressions of those who had formerly exercised unlimited dominion over him. . . .

We do not say that no one else but the negro can share in this protection. Both the language and spirit of these articles are to have their fair and just weight in any question of construction. Undoubtedly while negro slavery alone was in the mind of the Congress which proposed the thirteenth article, it forbids any other kind of slavery, now or hereafter. . . .

Up to the adoption of the recent amendments, no claim or pretence was set up that those rights depended on the Federal government for their existence or protection, beyond the very few express limitations which the Federal Constitution imposed upon the States—such, for instance, as the prohibition against ex post facto laws, bills of attainder, and laws impairing the obligation of contracts. But with the exception of these and a few other restrictions, the entire domain of the privileges and immunities of citizens of the States, as above defined, lay within the constitutional and legislative power of the States, and without that of the Federal government. Was it the purpose of the fourteenth amendment, by the simple declaration that no State should make or enforce any law which shall abridge the privileges and immunities of *citizens of the United States,* to transfer the security and protection of all the civil rights which we have mentioned, from the States to the Federal government? And where it is declared that Congress shall have the power to enforce that article, was it intended to bring within the power of Congress the entire domain of civil rights heretofore belonging exclusively to the States?

All this and more must follow, if the proposition of the plaintiffs in error be sound. For not only are these rights subject to the control of Congress whenever in its discretion any of them are supposed to be abridged by State legislation, but that body may also pass laws in advance, limiting and re-stricting the exercise of legislative power by the States, in their most ordinary and usual functions, as in its judgment it may think proper on all such subjects. And still further, such a construction followed by a reversal of the judgments of the Supreme Court of Louisiana in these cases, would constitute this court a perpetual censor upon all legislation of the States, on the civil rights of their own citizens, with authority to nullify such as it did not approve as consistent with those rights, as they existed at the time of the adoption of this amendment. The argument we admit is not always the most conclusive which is drawn from the consequences urged against the adoption of a particular construction of an instrument. But when, as in the case before us, these consequences are so serious, so far-reaching and pervading, so great a departure from the structure and spirit of our institutions; when the effect is to fetter and degrade the State governments by subjecting them to the control of Congress, in the exercise of powers heretofore universally conceded to them of the most ordinary and fundamental character; when in fact it radically changes the whole theory of the relations of the State and Federal governments to each other and of both these governments to the people; the argument has a force that is irresistible, in the absence of language which expresses such a purpose too clearly to admit of doubt. We are convinced that no such results were intended by the Congress which proposed these amendments, nor by the legislatures of the States which ratified them. . . .

[The war] added largely to the number of those who believe in the necessity of a strong National government. But, however pervading this sentiment, and however it may have contributed to the adoption of the amendments we have been considering, we do not see in those amendments any purpose to destroy the main features of the general system. Under the pressure of all the excited feeling growing out of the war, our statesmen have still believed that the existence of the States with powers for domestic and local government, including the regulation of civil rights—the rights of person and of property—was essential to the perfect working of our complex form of government, though they have thought proper to impose additional limitations on the States, and to confer additional power on that of the Nation.

But whatever fluctuations may be seen in the history of public opinion on this subject during the period of our national existence, we think it will be found that this court, so far as its functions required, has always held with a steady and an even hand the balance between State and Federal power, and we trust that such may continue to be the history of its relation to that subject. Affirmed.

Mr. Justice Field, joined by Chief Justice Chase and Justices Swayne and Bradley, dissenting.

Upon the theory on which the exclusive privileges granted by the act in question are sustained, there is no monopoly, in the most odious form, which may not be upheld. The question presented is, therefore, one of the gravest importance, not merely to the parties here, but to the whole country. It is nothing less than the question whether the recent amendments to the Federal Constitution protect the citizens of the United States against the deprivation of their common rights by State legislation. In my judgment the fourteenth amendment does afford such protection. . . .

The amendment does not attempt to confer any new privileges or immunities upon citizens, or to enumerate or define those already existing. It assumes that there are such privileges and immunities which belong of right to citizens as such, and ordains that they shall not be abridged by State legislation. If this inhibition has no reference to privileges and immunities of this character, but only refers, as held by [the majority], to such privileges and immunities as were before its adoption specifically designated in the Constitution or necessarily implied as belonging to citizens of the United States, it was a vain and idle enactment, which accomplished nothing, and most unnecessarily excited Congress and the people on its passage. With privileges and immunities thus designated or implied no State could ever have interfered by its laws, and no new constitutional provision was required to inhibit such interference. The supremacy of the Constitution and the laws of the United States always controlled any State legislation of that character. But if the amendment refers to the natural and inalienable rights which belong to all citizens, the inhibition has a profound significance. . . .

The terms, privileges and immunities, are not new in the amendment; they were in the Constitution before the amendment was adopted. . . . The privileges and immunities designated are those *which of right belong to the citizens of all free governments*. Clearly among these must be placed the right to pursue a lawful employment in a lawful manner, without other restraint than such as equally affects all persons. . . .

What [Art. IV, § 2] did for the protection of the citizens of one State against hostile and discriminating legislation of other States, the fourteenth amendment does for the protection of every citizen of the United States against hostile and discriminating legislation against him in favor of others, whether they reside in the same or in different States. If under the fourth article of the Constitution equality of privileges and immunities is secured between citizens of different States, under the fourteenth amendment the same equality is secured between citizens of the United States. . . .

This equality of right, with exemption from all disparaging and partial enactments, in the lawful pursuits of life, throughout the whole country, is the distinguishing privilege of citizens of the United States. To them, everywhere, all pursuits, all professions, all avocations are open without other restrictions than such as are imposed equally upon all others of the same age, sex, and condition. The State may prescribe such regulations for every pursuit and calling of life as will promote the public health, secure the good order and advance the general prosperity of society, but when once prescribed, the pursuit or calling must be free to be followed by every citizen who is within the conditions designated, and will conform to the regulations. This is the fundamental idea upon which our institutions rest, and unless adhered to in the legislation of the country our government will be a republic only in name. The fourteenth amendment, in my judgment, makes it essential to the validity of the legislation of every State that this equality of right should be respected. It is to me a matter of profound regret that the validity [of the Louisiana law] is recognized by a majority of this court, for by it the right of free labor, one of the most sacred and imprescriptible rights of man, is violated. Grants of exclusive privileges are opposed to the whole theory of free government, and it requires no aid from any bill of rights to render them void. That only is a free government, in the American sense of the term, under which the inalienable right of every citizen to pursue his happiness is unrestrained, except by just, equal, and impartial laws.

Munn v. Illinois, 94 U.S. 113 (1877)

[7–2: Waite, Bradley, Clifford, Davis, Hunt,
Miller, Swayne; Field, Strong]

Chief Justice Waite delivered the opinion of the Court.

The question to be determined in this case is whether the general assembly of Illinois can, under the limitations upon the legislative power of the States imposed by the Constitution of the United States, fix by law the maximum of charges for the storage of grain in warehouses at Chicago and other places in the State having not less than one hundred thousand inhabitants, "in which grain is stored in bulk, and in which the grain of different owners is mixed together, or in which grain is stored in such a manner that the identity of different lots or parcels cannot be accurately preserved."

1. To that part of sect. 8, art. 1, of the Constitution of the United States which confers upon Congress the power "to regulate commerce with foreign nations and among the several States";

2. To that part of sect. 9 of the same article which provides that "no preference shall be given by any regulation of commerce or revenue to the ports of one State over those of another"; and

3. To that part of amendment 14 which ordains that no State shall "deprive any person of life, liberty, or property, without due process of law, nor deny to any person within its jurisdiction the equal protection of the laws."

We will consider the last of these objections first. . . .

The Constitution contains no definition of the word "deprive," as used in the Fourteenth Amendment. To determine its signification, therefore, it is necessary to ascertain the effect which usage has given it, when employed in the same or a like connection.

While this provision of the amendment is new in the Constitution of the United States, as a limitation upon the powers of the States, it is old as a principle of civilized government. It is found in Magna Charta, and, in substance if not in form, in nearly or quite all the constitutions that have been from time to time adopted by the several States of the Union. By the Fifth Amendment, it was introduced into the Constitution of the United States as a limitation upon the powers of the national government, and by the Fourteenth, as a guaranty against any encroachment upon an acknowledged right of citizenship by the legislature of the States. . . .

When one becomes a member of society, he necessarily parts with some rights or privileges which, as an individual not affected by his relations to others, he might retain. "A body politic," as aptly defined in the preamble of the Constitution of Massachusetts, "is a social compact by which the whole people covenants with each citizen, and each citizen with the whole people, that all shall be governed by certain laws for the common good." This . . . authorize[s] the establishment of laws requiring each citizen to so conduct himself, and to use his own property, as not unnecessarily to injure another. . . . From this source come the police powers. . . . Under these powers the government regulates the conduct of its citizens one towards another, and the manner in which each shall use his own property, when such regulation becomes necessary for the public good. In their exercise it has been customary in England from time immemorial, and in this country from its first colonization, to regulate ferries, common carriers, hackmen, bakers, millers, wharfingers, innkeepers, &c., and in so doing to fix a maximum of charge to be made for services rendered, accommodations furnished, and articles sold. To this day, statutes are to be found in many of the States upon some or all these subjects; and we think it has never yet been successfully contended that such legislation came within any of the constitutional prohibitions against interference with private property. . . .

From this it is apparent that, down to the time of the adoption of the Fourteenth Amendment, it was not supposed that statutes regulating the use, or even the price of the use, of private property necessarily deprived an owner of his property without due process of law. Under some circumstances they may, but not under all. The amendment does not change the law in this particular: it simply prevents the States from doing that which will operate as such a deprivation.

This brings us to inquire as to the principles upon which this power of regulation rests, in order that we may determine what is within and what without its operative effect. Looking, then, to the common law, from whence came the right which the Constitution protects, we find that when private property is "affected with a public interest, it ceases to be *juris privati* only." This was said by Lord Chief Justice Hale more than two hundred years ago. . . . Property does become clothed with a public interest when used in a manner to make it of public consequence, and affect the community at large. When, therefore, one devotes his property to a use in which the public has an interest, he, in effect, grants to the public an interest in that use, and must submit to be controlled by the public for the common good, to the extent of the interest he has thus created. He may withdraw his grant by discontinuing the use; but, so long as he maintains the use, he must submit to the control. . . .

But we need not go further. Enough has already been said to show that, when private property is devoted to a public use, it is subject to public regulation. It remains only to ascertain whether the warehouses of these plaintiffs in error, and the business which is carried on there, come within the operation of this principle. . . .

In this connection it must also be borne in mind that, although in 1874 there were in Chicago fourteen warehouses adapted to this particular business, and owned by about thirty persons, nine business firms controlled them. . . . Thus it is apparent that all the elevating facilities through which these vast productions "of seven or eight great States of the West" must pass on the way "to four or five of the States on the seashore" may be a "virtual" monopoly.

Under such circumstances it is difficult to see why, if the common carrier, or the miller, or the ferryman, or the innkeeper, or the wharfinger, or the baker, or the cartman, or the hackney-coachman, pursues a public employment and exercises "a sort of public office," these plaintiffs in error do not. They stand, to use again the language of their counsel, in the very "gateway of commerce," and take toll from all who pass. Their business most certainly "tends to a common charge, and is become a thing of public interest and use." . . .

For our purposes we must assume that, if a state of facts could exist that would justify such legislation, it actually did exist when the statute now under consideration was passed. For us the question is one of power, not of expediency. If no state of circumstances could exist to justify such a statute, then we may declare this one void, because . . . in excess of the legislative power of the State. But if it could, we must presume it did. Of the propriety of legislative interference within the scope of legislative power, the legislature is the exclusive judge. . . .

It matters not in this case that these plaintiffs in error had built their warehouses and established their business before the regulations complained of were adopted. What they did was from the beginning subject to the power of the body politic to require them to conform to such regulations as might be established by the proper authorities for the common good. They entered upon their business and provided themselves with the means to carry it on subject to this condition. If they did not wish to submit themselves to such interference, they should not have clothed the public with an interest in their concerns. The same principle applies to them that does to the proprietor of a hackney-carriage, and as to him it has never been supposed that he was exempt from regulating statutes or ordinances because he had purchased his horses and carriage and established his business before the statute or the ordinance was adopted.

It is insisted, however, that the owner of property is entitled to a reasonable compensation for its use, even though it be clothed with a public interest, and that what is reasonable is a judicial and not a legislative question.

As has already been shown, the practice has been otherwise. In countries where the common law prevails, it has been customary from time immemorial for the legislature to declare what shall be a reasonable compensation under such circumstances, or, perhaps more properly speaking, to fix a maximum beyond which any charge made would be unreasonable. Undoubtedly, in mere private contracts, relating to matters in which the public has no interest, what is reasonable must be ascertained judicially. But this is because the legislature has no control over such a contract. So, too, in matters which do affect the public interest, and as to which legislative control may be exercised, . . . the courts must determine what is reasonable. The controlling fact is the power to regulate at all. If that exists, the right to establish the maximum of charge, as one of the means of regulation, is implied. . . .

We know that this is a power which may be abused; but that is no argument against its existence. For protection against abuses by legislatures the people must resort to the polls, not to the courts. . . .

United States v. *E. C. Knight,* 156 U.S. 1 (1895)

[8–1: Fuller, Blatchford, Brewer, Brown, Gray,
Jackson, Shiras, White; Harlan]

Mr. Chief Justice Fuller . . . delivered the opinion of the court.

By the purchase of the stock of the four Philadelphia refineries, with shares of its own stock, the American Sugar Refining Company acquired nearly complete control of the manufacture of refined sugar within the United States. The bill charged that the contracts under which these purchases were made constituted combinations in restraint of trade, and that in entering into them the defendants combined and conspired to restrain the trade and commerce in refined sugar among the several States and with foreign nations, contrary to the act of Congress of July 2, 1890. . . .

The fundamental question is, whether conceding that the existence of a monopoly in manufacture is established by the evidence, that monopoly can be directly suppressed under the act of Congress in the mode attempted by this bill.

It cannot be denied that the power of a State to protect the lives, health, and property of its citizens, and to preserve good order and the public morals, "the power to govern men and things within the limits of its dominion," is a power originally and always belonging to the States, not surrendered by them to the general government, nor directly restrained by the Constitution of the United States, and essentially exclusive. The relief of the citizens of each State from the burden of monopoly and the evils resulting from the restraint of trade among such citizens was left with the States to deal with, and this court has recognized their possession of that power even to the extent of holding that an employment or business carried on by private individuals, when it becomes a matter of such public interest and importance as to create a common charge or burden upon the citizen; in other words, when it becomes a practical monopoly, to which the citizen is compelled to resort and by means of which a tribute can be exacted from the community, is subject to regulation by state legislative power. On the other hand, the power of Congress to regulate commerce among the several States is also exclusive. The Constitution does not provide that interstate commerce shall be free, but, by the grant of this exclusive power to regulate it, it was left free except as Congress might impose restraints. Therefore it has been determined that the failure of Congress to exercise this exclusive power in any case is an expression of its will that the subject shall be free from restrictions or impositions upon it by the several States, and if a law passed by a State in the exercise of its acknowledged powers comes into conflict with that will, the Congress and the State cannot occupy the position of equal opposing sovereignties, because the Constitution declares its supremacy and that of the laws passed in pursuance thereof; and that which is not supreme must yield to that which is supreme. "Commerce, undoubtedly, is traffic," said Chief Justice Marshall, "but it is something more; it is intercourse. It describes the commercial intercourse between nations and parts of nations in all its branches, and is regulated by prescribing rules for carrying on that intercourse." That which belongs to commerce is within the jurisdiction of the United States, but that which does not belong to commerce is within the jurisdiction of the police power of the State. . . .

The argument is that the power to control the manufacture of refined sugar is a monopoly over a necessary of life, to the enjoyment of which by a large part of the population of the United States interstate commerce is indispensable, and that, therefore, the general government in the exercise of the power to regulate commerce may repress such monopoly directly and set aside the instruments which have created it. But this argument cannot be confined to necessaries of life merely, and must include all articles of general consumption. Doubtless the power to control the manufacture of a given thing involves in a certain sense the control of its disposition, but this is a secondary and not the primary sense; and although the exercise of that power may result in bringing the operation of commerce into play, it does not control it, and affects it only incidentally and indirectly. Commerce succeeds to manufacture, and is not a part of it. The power to regulate commerce is the power to prescribe the rule by which commerce shall be governed, and is a power independent of the power to suppress monopoly. But it may operate in repression of monopoly whenever that comes within the rules by which commerce is governed or whenever the transaction is itself a monopoly of commerce.

It is vital that the independence of the commercial power and of the police power, and the delimitation between them, however sometimes perplexing, should always be recognized and observed, for while the one furnishes the strongest bond of union, the other is essential to the preservation of the autonomy of the States as required by our dual form of government; and acknowledged evils, however grave and urgent they may appear to be, had better be borne, than the risk be run, in the effort to suppress them, of more serious consequences by resort to expedients of even doubtful constitutionality.

It will be perceived how far-reaching the proposition is that the power of dealing with a monopoly directly may be exercised by the general government whenever interstate or international commerce may be ultimately affected. The regulation of commerce applies to the subjects of commerce and not to matters of internal police. Contracts to buy, sell, or exchange goods to be transported among the several States, the transportation and its instrumentalities, and articles bought, sold, or exchanged for the purposes of such transit among the States, or put in the way of transit, may be regulated, but this is because they form part of interstate trade or commerce. The fact that an article is manufactured for export to another State does not of itself make it an article of interstate commerce, and the intent of the manufacturer does not determine the time when the article or product passes from the control of the State and belongs to commerce. . . .

[I]n *Kidd* v. *Pearson*, . . . where the question was discussed whether the right of a State to enact a statute prohibiting within its limits the manufacture of intoxicating liquors, except for certain purposes, could be overthrown by the fact that the manufacturer intended to export the liquors when made, it was held that the intent of the manufacturer did not determine the time when the article or product passed from the control of the State and belonged to commerce, and that, therefore, the statute, in omitting to except from its operation the manufacture of intoxicating liquors within the limits of the State for export, did not constitute an unauthorized interference with the right of Congress to regulate commerce. . . .

In *Kidd* v. *Pearson* the refusal of a State to allow articles to be manufactured within her borders even for export was held not to directly affect external commerce, and state legislation which, in a great variety of ways, affected interstate commerce and persons engaged in it, has been frequently sustained because the interference was not direct.

Contracts, combinations, or conspiracies to control domestic enterprise in manufacture, agriculture, mining, production in all its forms, or to raise or lower prices or wages, might unquestionably tend to restrain external as well as domestic trade, but the restraint would be an indirect result, however inevitable and whatever its extent, and such result would not necessarily determine the object of the contract, combination, or conspiracy.

Again, all the authorities agree that in order to vitiate a contract or combination it is not essential that its result should be a complete monopoly; it is sufficient if it really tends to that end and to deprive the public of the advantages which flow from free competition. Slight reflection will show that if the national power extends to all contracts and combinations in manufacture, agriculture, mining, and other productive industries, whose ultimate result may affect external commerce, comparatively little of business operations and affairs would be left for state control.

It was in the light of well-settled principles that the act of July 2, 1890, was framed. Congress did not attempt thereby to assert the power to deal with monopoly directly as such; or to limit and restrict the rights of corporations created by the States or the citizens of the States in the acquisition, control, or disposition of property; or to regulate or prescribe the price or prices at which such property or the products thereof should be sold; or to make criminal the acts of persons in the acquisition and control of property which the States of their residence or creation sanctioned or permitted. Aside from the provisions applicable where Congress might exercise municipal power, what the law struck at was combinations, contracts, and conspiracies to monopolize trade and commerce among the several States or with foreign nations; but the contracts and acts of the defendants related exclusively to the acquisition of the Philadelphia refineries and the business of sugar refining in Pennsylvania, and bore no direct relation to commerce between the States or with foreign nations. The object was manifestly private gain in the manufacture of the commodity, but not through the control of interstate or foreign commerce. It is true that the bill alleged that the products of these refineries were sold and distributed among the several States, and that all the companies were engaged in trade or commerce with the several States and with foreign nations; but this was no more than to say that trade and commerce served manufacture to fulfil its function. Sugar was refined for sale, and sales were probably made at Philadelphia for consumption, and undoubtedly for resale by the first purchasers throughout Pennsylvania and other States, and refined sugar was also forwarded by the companies to other States for sale. Nevertheless it does not follow that an attempt to monopolize, or the actual monopoly of, the manufacture was an attempt, whether executory or consummated, to monopolize commerce, even though, in order to dispose of the product, the instrumentality of commerce was necessarily invoked. There was nothing in the proofs to indicate any intention to put a restraint upon trade or commerce, and the fact, as we have seen, that trade or commerce might be indirectly affected was not enough to entitle conplainants to a decree. The subject-matter of the sale was shares of manufacturing stock, and the relief sought was the surrender of property which

had already passed and the suppression of the alleged monopoly in manufacture by the restoration of the *status quo* before the transfers; yet the act
of Congress only authorized the Circuit Courts to proceed by way of preventing and restraining violations of the act in respect of contracts, combinations, or conspiracies in restraint of interstate or international trade or
commerce.

The Circuit Court declined, upon the pleadings and proofs, to grant the
relief prayed, and dismissed the bill, and we are of opinion that the Circuit
Court of Appeals did not err in affirming that decree. *Decree affirmed.*

Mr. Justice Harlan, dissenting.

Prior to the 4th day of March, 1892, the American Sugar Refining
Company, a corporation organized under a general statute of New Jersey
for the purpose of buying, manufacturing, refining, and *selling sugar in
different parts of the country,* had obtained the control of *all* the sugar
refineries in the United States except five, of which four were owned and
operated by Pennsylvania corporations—the E. C. Knight Company, the
Franklin Sugar Refining Company, Spreckels' Sugar Refining Company, and
the Delaware Sugar House—and the other, by the Revere Sugar Refinery
of Boston. These five corporations were all in active competition with the
American Sugar Refining Company and with each other. The product of
the Pennsylvania companies was about thirty-three per cent, and that of the
Boston company about two per cent, of the entire quantity of sugar refined
in the United States.

In March, 1892, by means of contracts or arrangements with stockholders
of the four Pennsylvania companies, the New Jersey corporation—using for
that purpose its own stock—purchased the stock of those companies, and
thus obtained absolute control of the entire business of sugar refining in the
United States except that done by the Boston company, which is too small
in amount to be regarded in this discussion.

"The object," the court below said, "in purchasing the Philadelphia
refineries was to obtain a greater influence or *more perfect control* over *the
business* of refining *and selling* sugar *in this country.*" This characterization
of the object for which this stupendous combination was formed is properly
accepted in the opinion of the court as justified by the proof. I need not
therefore analyze the evidence upon this point.

In *Kidd* v. *Pearson* we recognized, as had been done in previous cases,
the distinction between the mere transportation of articles of interstate commerce and the *purchasing* and *selling* that *precede transportation.* It is said
that manufacture precedes commerce and is not a part of it. But it is equally
true that when manufacture ends, that which has been manufactured becomes
a subject of commerce; that buying and selling succeed manufacture, come
into existence after the process of manufacture is completed, precede transportation, and are as much commercial intercourse, where articles are bought
to be carried from one State to another, as is the manual transportation of
such articles after they have been so purchased. The distinction was recognized by this court in *Gibbons* v. *Ogden,* where the principal question

was whether commerce included navigation. Both the court and counsel recognized buying and selling or barter *as included in commerce.* Chief Justice Marshall said that the mind can scarcely conceive a system for regulating commerce, which was "*confined* to prescribing rules for the conduct of individuals in the actual employment of buying and selling, or of barter." . . .

The power of Congress covers and protects the absolute freedom of such intercourse and trade among the States as may or must succeed manufacture and precede transportation from the place of purchase. This would seem to be conceded; for, the court in the present case expressly declare that "*contracts to buy,* sell, or exchange goods *to be transported among the several States,* the transportation and its instrumentalities, and articles bought, sold, or exchanged for the purpose of such transit among the States, or put in the way of transit, *may be regulated,* but this is *because they form part of interstate trade or commerce.*" Here is a direct admission—one which the settled doctrines of this court justify—that contracts to buy and the purchasing of goods *to be transported from one State to another,* and transportation, with its instrumentalities, are all *parts* of interstate trade or commerce. Each part of such trade is then under the protection of Congress. And yet, by the opinion and judgment in this case, if I do not misapprehend them, Congress is without power to protect the commercial intercourse that such purchasing necessarily involves against the restraints and burdens arising from the existence of *combinations* that meet purchasers, from whatever State they come, with the threat—for it is nothing more nor less than a threat—that they *shall not* purchase what they desire to purchase, *except at the prices fixed by such combinations.* A citizen of Missouri has the right to go in person, or send orders, to Pennsylvania and New Jersey for the purpose of purchasing refined sugar. But of what value is that right if he is confronted in those States by a vast *combination* which absolutely controls the price of that article by reason of its having acquired all the sugar refineries in the United States in order that they may fix prices in their own interest exclusively?

In my judgment, the citizens of the several States composing the Union are entitled, of right, to buy goods in the State where they are manufactured, or in any other State, without being confronted by an illegal combination whose business extends throughout the whole country, which by the law everywhere is an enemy to the public interests, and which prevents such buying, except at prices arbitrarily fixed by it. I insist that the free course of trade among the States cannot coexist with such combinations. When I speak of trade I mean the buying and selling of articles of every kind that are recognized articles of interstate commerce. Whatever improperly obstructs the free course of interstate intercourse and trade, as involved in the buying and selling of articles to be carried from one State to another, may be reached by Congress, under its authority to regulate commerce among the States. The exercise of that authority so as to make trade among the States, in all recognized articles of commerce, absolutely free from unreasonable or illegal restrictions imposed by combinations, is justified by an express grant of power to Congress and would redound to the welfare of the whole country. I am unable to perceive that any such result would imperil the autonomy of the States, especially as that result cannot be attained through the action of any one State.

Undue restrictions or burdens upon the purchasing of goods, in the market for sale, to be transported to other States, cannot be imposed even by a State without violating the freedom of commercial intercourse guaranteed by the Constitution. But if a *State* within whose limits the business of refining sugar is exclusively carried on may not constitutionally impose burdens upon purchases of sugar *to be transported to other States*, how comes it that combinations of corporations or individuals, within the same State, may not be prevented by the national government from putting unlawful restraints upon the purchasing of that article *to be carried from the State in which such purchases are made?* If the national power is competent to repress *State* action in restraint of interstate trade as it may be involved in purchases of refined sugar to be transported from one State to another State, surely it ought to be deemed sufficient to prevent unlawful restraints attempted to be imposed by combinations of corporations or individuals upon those identical purchases; otherwise, illegal combinations of corporations or individuals may—so far as national power and interstate commerce are concerned—do, with impunity, what no State can do. . . .

A decree recognizing the freedom of commercial intercourse as embracing the right to buy goods to be transported from one State to another, without buyers being burdened by unlawful restraints imposed by combinations of corporations or individuals, so far from disturbing or endangering, would tend to preserve the autonomy of the States, and protect the people of all the States against dangers so portentous as to excite apprehension for the safety of our liberties. If this be not a sound interpretation of the Constitution, it is easy to perceive that interstate traffic, so far as it involves the price to be paid for articles necessary to the comfort and well-being of the people in all the States, may pass under the absolute control of overshadowing combinations having financial resources without limit and an audacity in the accomplishment of their objects that recognizes none of the restraints of moral obligations controlling the action of individuals; combinations governed entirely by the law of greed and selfishness—so powerful that no single State is able to overthrow them and give the required protection to the whole country, and so all-pervading that they threaten the integrity of our institutions.

We have before us the case of a combination which absolutely controls, or may, at its discretion, control the price of all refined sugar in this country. Suppose another *combination*, organized for private gain and to control prices, should obtain possession of all the large flour mills in the United States; another, of all the grain elevators; another, of all the oil territory; another, of all the salt-producing regions; another, of all the cotton mills; and another, of all the great establishments for slaughtering animals, and the preparation of meats. What power is competent to protect the people of the United States against such dangers except a national power—one that is capable of exerting its sovereign authority throughout every part of the territory and over all the people of the nation?

To the general government has been committed the control of commercial intercourse among the States, to the end that it may be free at all times from any restraints except such as Congress may impose or permit for the benefit of the whole country. The common government of all the people is the only one that can adequately deal with a matter which directly and injuriously affects the entire commerce of the country, which concerns equally all the people of the Union, and which, it must be confessed, cannot be adequately controlled by any one State. Its authority should not be so weakened by construction that it cannot reach and eradicate evils that, beyond all question, tend to defeat an object which that government is entitled, by the Constitution, to accomplish. "Powerful and ingenious minds," this court has said, "taking, as postulates, that the powers expressly granted to the government of the Union, are to be contracted by construction into the narrowest possible compass, and that the original powers of the States are retained if any possible construction will retain them, may, by a course of well digested, but refined and metaphysical reasoning, founded on these premises, explain away the Constitution of our country, and leave it, a magnificent structure, indeed, to look at, but totally unfit for use. They may so entangle and perplex the understanding as to obscure principles which were before thought quite plain, and induce doubts where, if the mind were to pursue its own course, none would be perceived." *Gibbons* v. *Ogden* . . . .

While a decree annulling the contracts under which the combination in question was formed, may not, in view of the facts disclosed, be effectual to accomplish the object of the act of 1890, I perceive no difficulty in the way of the court passing a decree declaring that that combination imposes an unlawful restraint upon trade and commerce among the States, and perpetually enjoining it from further prosecuting any business pursuant to the unlawful agreements under which it was formed or by which it was created. Such a decree would be within the scope of the bill, and is appropriate to the end which Congress intended to accomplish, namely, to protect the freedom of commercial intercourse among the States against combinations and conspiracies which impose unlawful restraints upon such intercourse.

For the reasons stated I dissent from the opinion and judgment of the court.

Pollock v. *Farmers' Loan and Trust Co.,* 158 U.S. 601 (1895)

[5–4: Fuller, Blatchford, Brewer, Grey, Shiras; Harlan, Jackson, Brown, White]

Mr. Chief Justice Fuller delivered the opinion of the Court.

The Constitution divided Federal taxation into two great classes, the class of direct taxes, and the class of duties, imports, and excises; and prescribed two rules which qualified the grant of power as to each class.

The power to lay direct taxes apportioned among the several States in proportion to their representation in the popular branch of Congress, a representation based on population as ascertained by the census, was plenary and absolute; but to lay direct taxes without apportionment was forbidden. The power to lay duties, imposts, and excises was subject to the qualification that the imposition must be uniform throughout the United States.

Our previous decision was confined to the consideration of the validity of the tax on the income from real estate, and on the income from municipal bonds. . . .

We are now permitted to broaden the field of inquiry, and to determine to which of the two great classes a tax upon a person's entire income, whether derived from rents, or products, or otherwise, of real estate, or from bonds, stocks, or other forms of personal property, belongs; and we are unable to conclude that the enforced subtraction from the yield of all the owner's real or personal property, in the manner prescribed, is so different from a tax upon the property itself, that it is not a direct, but an indirect tax, in the meaning of the Constitution. . . .

Whatever the speculative views of political economists or revenue reformers may be, can it be properly held that the Constitution, taken in its plain and obvious sense, and with due regard to the circumstances attending the formation of the government, authorizes a general unapportioned tax on the products of the farm and the rents of real estate, although imposed merely because of ownership and with no possible means of escape from payment, as belonging to a totally different class from that which includes the property from whence the income proceeds?

There can be but one answer, unless the constitutional restriction is to be treated as utterly illusory and futile, and the object of its framers defeated. We find it impossible to hold that a fundamental requisition, deemed so important as to be enforced by two provisions, one affirmative and one negative, can be refined away by forced distinctions between that which gives value to property, and the property itself.

Nor can we perceive any ground why the same reasoning does not apply to capital in personalty held for the purpose of income or ordinarily yielding income, and to the income therefrom. All the real estate of the country, and all its invested personal property, are open to the direct operation of the taxing power if an apportionment be made according to the Constitution. The Constitution does not say that no direct tax shall be laid by apportionment on any other property than land; on the contrary, it forbids all unapportioned direct taxes; and we know of no warrant for excepting personal property from the exercise of the power, or any reason why an apportioned direct tax cannot be laid and assessed. . . .

. . . Cannot Congress, if the necessity exist of raising thirty, forty, or any other number of million dollars for the support of the government, in addition to the revenue from duties, imposts, and excises, apportion the quota of each State upon the basis of the census, and thus advise it of the payment which must be made, and proceed to assess that amount on all the real and personal property and the income of all persons in the State, and collect the same if the State does not in the meantime assume and pay its quota and collect the amount according to its own system and in its own way? Cannot Congress do this, as respects either or all these subjects of taxation, and deal with each in such manner as might be deemed expedient . . . ? Inconveniences might possibly attend the levy of an income tax, notwithstanding the listing of receipts, when adjusted, furnishes its own valuation; but that it is apportionable is hardly denied, although it is asserted that it would operate so unequally as to be undesirable. . . .

We are not here concerned with the question whether an income tax be or be not desirable, nor whether such a tax would enable the government to diminish taxes on consumption and duties on imports, and to enter upon what may be believed to be a reform of its fiscal and commercial system. Questions of that character belong to the controversies of political parties, and cannot be settled by judicial decision. In these cases our province is to determine whether this income tax on the revenue from property does or does not belong to the class of direct taxes. If it does, it is, being unapportioned, in violation of the Constitution, and we must so declare.

Differences have often occurred in this court—differences exist now—but there has never been a time in its history when there has been a difference of opinion as to its duty to announce its deliberate conclusions unaffected by considerations not pertaining to the case in hand. . . .

Our conclusions may, therefore, be summed up as follows:

First. We adhere to the opinion already announced, that, taxes on real estate being indisputably direct taxes, taxes on the rents or income of real estate are equally direct taxes.

Second. We are of opinion that taxes on personal property, or on the income of personal property, are likewise direct taxes.

Third. The tax imposed by sections twenty-seven to thirty-seven, inclusive, of the act of 1894, so far as it falls on the income of real estate and of personal property, being a direct tax within the meaning of the Constitution, and, therefore, unconstitutional and void because not apportioned according to representation, all those sections, constituting one entire scheme of taxation, are necessarily invalid. . . .

Mr. Justice Harlan dissenting.

[T]his decision may well excite the gravest apprehensions. It strikes at the very foundations of national authority, in that it denies to the general government a power which is, or may become, vital to the very existence and preservation of the Union in a national emergency, such as that of war with a great commercial nation, during which the collection of all duties upon imports will cease or be materially diminished. It tends to reestablish that condition of helplessness in which Congress found itself during the period of the Articles of Confederation, when it was without authority by laws operating directly upon individuals, to lay and collect, through its own agents, taxes sufficient to pay the debts and defray the expenses of government, but was dependent, in all such matters, upon the good will of the States, and their promptness in meeting requisitions made upon them by Congress. . . .

I cannot assent to an interpretation of the Constitution that impairs and cripples the just powers of the National Government in the essential matter of taxation, and at the same time discriminates against the greater part of the people of our country.

The practical effect of the decision to-day is to give to certain kinds of property a position of favoritism and advantage inconsistent with the fundamental principles of our social organization, and to invest them with power and influence that may be perilous to that portion of the American people upon whom rests the larger part of the burdens of the government, and who ought not to be subjected to the dominion of aggregated wealth any more than the property of the country should be at the mercy of the lawless.

In Re Debs, 158 U.S. 564 (1895)

(Unanimous)

Mr. Justice Brewer . . . delivered the opinion of the court.

The case presented by the bill is this: The United States, finding that the interstate transportation of persons and property, as well as the carriage of the mails, is forcibly obstructed, and that a combination and conspiracy exists to subject the control of such transportation to the will of the conspirators, applied to one of their courts, sitting as a court of equity, for an injunction to restrain such obstruction and prevent carrying into effect such conspiracy. Two questions of importance are presented: First. Are the relations of the general government to interstate commerce and the transportation of the mails such as authorize a direct interference to prevent a forcible obstruction thereof? Second. If authority exists, as authority in governmental affairs implies both power and duty, has a court of equity jurisdiction to issue an injunction in aid of the performance of such duty[?]

First. What are the relations of the general government to interstate commerce and the transportation of the mails? They are those of direct supervision, control, and management. While under the dual system which prevails with us the powers of government are distributed between the State and the Nation, and while the latter is properly styled a government of enumerated powers, yet within the limits of such enumeration it has all the attributes of sovereignty, and, in the exercise of those enumerated powers, acts directly upon the citizen, and not through the intermediate agency of the State. . . .

Among the powers expressly given to the national government are the control of interstate commerce and the creation and management of a post office system for the nation. Article I, section 8, of the Constitution provides that "the Congress shall have power. . . . Third, to regulate commerce with foreign nations and among the several States, and with the Indian tribes. . . . Seventh, to establish post offices and post roads."

Congress has exercised the power granted in respect to interstate commerce in a variety of legislative acts. . . .

Under the power vested in Congress to establish post offices and post roads, Congress has, by a mass of legislation, established the great post office system of the country, with all its detail of organization, its machinery for the transaction of business, defining what shall be carried and what not, and the prices of carriage, and also prescribing penalties for all offences against it.

Obviously these powers given to the national government over interstate commerce and in respect to the transportation of the mails were not dormant and unused. Congress had taken hold of these two matters, and by various and specific acts had assumed and exercised the powers given to it, and was in the full discharge of its duty to regulate interstate commerce and carry the mails. The validity of such exercise and the exclusiveness of its control had been again and again presented to this court for consideration. It is curious to note the fact that in a large proportion of the cases in respect to interstate commerce brought to this court the question presented was of the validity of state legislation in its bearings upon interstate commerce, and the uniform course of decision has been to declare that it is not within the competency of a State to legislate in such a manner as to obstruct interstate commerce. If a State with its recognized powers of sovereignty is impotent to obstruct interstate commerce, can it be that any mere voluntary association of individuals within the limits of that State has a power which the State itself does not possess? . . .

But there is no such impotency in the national government. The entire strength of the nation may be used to enforce in any part of the land the full and free exercise of all national powers and the security of all rights entrusted by the Constitution to its care. The strong arm of the national government may be put forth to brush away all obstructions to the freedom of interstate commerce or the transportation of the mails. If the emergency arises, the army of the Nation, and all its militia, are at the service of the Nation to compel obedience to its laws.

But passing to the second question, is there no other alternative than the use of force on the part of the executive authorities whenever obstructions arise to the freedom of interstate commerce or the transportation of the mails? Is the army the only instrument by which rights of the public can be enforced and the peace of the nation preserved? Grant that any public nuisance may be forcibly abated either at the instance of the authorities, or by any individual suffering private damage therefrom, the existence of this right of forcible abatement is not inconsistent with nor does it destroy the right of appeal in an orderly way to the courts for a judicial determination, and an exercise of their powers by writ of injunction and otherwise to accomplish the same result. . . . ". . . As a rule, injunctions are denied to those who have adequate remedy at law. Where the choice is between the ordinary and the extraordinary processes of law, and the former are sufficient, the rule will not permit the use of the latter. In some cases of nuisance and in some cases of trespass the law permits an individual to abate the one and prevent the other by force, because such permission is necessary to the complete protection of property and person. When the choice is between redress or prevention of injury by force and by peaceful process, the law is well pleased if the individual will consent to waive his right to the use of force and await its action. Therefore, as between force and the extraordinary writ of injunction, the rule will permit the latter."

So, in the case before us, the right to use force does not exclude the right of appeal to the courts for a judicial determination and for the exercise of all their powers of prevention. Indeed, it is more to the praise than to the blame of the government, that, instead of determining for itself questions of right and wrong on the part of these petitioners and their associates and enforcing that determination by the club of the policeman and the bayonet of the soldier, it submitted all those questions to the peaceful determination of judicial tribunals, and invoked their consideration and judgment as to the measure of its rights and powers and the correlative obligations of those against whom it made complaint. And it is equally to the credit of the latter that the judgment of those tribunals was by the great body of them respected, and the troubles which threatened so much disaster terminated.

Neither can it be doubted that the government has such an interest in the subject-matter as enables it to appear as party plaintiff in this suit. It is said that equity only interferes for the protection of property, and that the government has no property interest. A sufficient reply is that the United States have a property in the mails, the protection of which was one of the purposes of this bill. . . .

We do not care to place our decision upon this ground alone. Every government, entrusted, by the very terms of its being, with powers and duties to be exercised and discharged for the general welfare, has a right to apply to its own courts for any proper assistance in the exercise of the one and the discharge of the other, and it is no sufficient answer to its appeal to one of those courts that it has no pecuniary interest in the matter. The obligations which it is under to promote the interest of all, and to prevent the wrongdoing of one resulting in injury to the general welfare, is often of itself sufficient to give it a standing in court. This proposition in some of its relations has heretofore received the sanction of this court. . . .

It is obvious . . . that while it is not the province of the government to interfere in any mere matter of private controversy between individuals, or to use its great powers to enforce the rights of one against another, yet, whenever the wrongs complained of are such as affect the public at large, and are in respect of matters which by the Constitution are entrusted to the care of the Nation, and concerning which the Nation owes the duty to all the citizens of securing to them their common rights, then the mere fact that the government has no pecuniary interest in the controversy is not sufficient to exclude it from the courts, or prevent it from taking measures therein to fully discharge those constitutional duties.

The national government, given by the Constitution power to regulate interstate commerce, has by express statute assumed jurisdiction over such commerce when carried upon railroads. It is charged, therefore, with the duty of keeping those highways of interstate commerce free from obstruction, for it has always been recognized as one of the powers and duties of a government to remove obstructions from the highways under its control. . . .

Up to a recent date commerce, both interstate and international, was mainly by water, and it is not strange that both the legislation of Congress and the cases in the courts have been principally concerned therewith. The fact that in recent years interstate commerce has come mainly to be carried on by railroads and over artificial highways has in no manner narrowed the scope of the constitutional provision, or abridged the power of Congress over such commerce. On the contrary, the same fulness of control exists in the one case as in the other, and the same power to remove obstructions from the one as from the other.

Constitutional provisions do not change, but their operation extends to new matters as the modes of business and the habits of life of the people vary with each succeeding generation. The law of the common carrier is the same to-day as when transportation on land was by coach and wagon, and on water by canal boat and sailing vessel, yet in its actual operation it touches and regulates transportation by modes then unknown, the railroad train and the steamship. Just so is it with the grant to the national government of power over interstate commerce. The Constitution has not changed. The power is the same. But it operates to-day upon modes of interstate commerce unknown to the fathers, and it will operate with equal force upon any new modes of such commerce which the future may develop.

It is said that seldom have the courts assumed jurisdiction to restrain by injunction in suits brought by the government, either state or national, obstructions to highways, either artificial or natural. This is undoubtedly true, but the reason is that the necessity for such interference has only been occasional. Ordinarily the local authorities have taken full control over the matter, and by indictment for misdemeanor, or in some kindred way, have secured the removal of the obstruction and the cessation of the nuisance. . . . .

That the bill filed in this case alleged special facts calling for the exercise of all the powers of the court is not open to question. The picture drawn in it of the vast interests involved, not merely of the city of Chicago and the State of Illinois, but of all the States, and the general confusion into which the interstate commerce of the country was thrown; the forcible interference with that commerce; the attempted exercise by individuals of powers belonging only to government, and the threatened continuance of such invasions of public right, presented a condition of affairs which called for the fullest exercise of all the powers of the courts. If ever there was a special exigency, one which demanded that the court should do all that courts can do, it was disclosed by this bill, and we need not turn to the public history of the day, which only reaffirms with clearest emphasis all its allegations.

The difference between a public nuisance and a private nuisance is that the one affects the people at large and the other simply the individual. The quality of the wrong is the same, and the jurisdiction of the courts over them rests upon the same principles and goes to the same extent. Of course, circumstances may exist in one case, which do not in another, to induce the court to interfere or to refuse to interfere by injunction, but the jurisdiction, the power to interfere, exists in all cases of nuisance. True, many more suits are brought by individuals than by the public to enjoin nuisances, but there are two reasons for this. First, the instances are more numerous of private than of public nuisances; and, second, often that which is in fact a public nuisance is restrained at the suit of a private individual, whose right to relief arises because of a special injury resulting therefrom. . . .

. . . It surely cannot be seriously contended that the court has jurisdiction to enjoin the obstruction of a highway by one person, but that its jurisdiction ceases when the obstruction is by a hundred persons. It may be true, as suggested, that in the excitement of passion a mob will pay little heed to processes issued from the courts, and it may be, as said by counsel in argument, that it would savor somewhat of the puerile and ridiculous to have read a writ of injunction to Lee's army during the late civil war. It is doubtless true that *inter arma leges silent,* and in the throes of rebellion or revolution the processes of civil courts are of little avail, for the power of the courts rests on the general support of the people and their recognition of the fact that peaceful remedies are the true resort for the correction of wrongs. But does not counsel's argument imply too much? Is it to be assumed that these defendants were conducting a rebellion or inaugurating a revolution, and that they and their associates were thus placing themselves beyond the reach of the civil process of the courts? We find in the opinion of the Circuit Court a quotation from the testimony given by one of the defendants before the United States Strike Commission, which is sufficient answer to this suggestion:

"As soon as the employés found that we were arrested, and taken from the scene of action, they became demoralized, and that ended the strike. It was not the soldiers that ended the strike. It was not the old brotherhoods that ended the strike. It was simply the United States courts that ended the strike. Our men were in a position that never would have been shaken, under any circumstances, if we had been permitted to remain upon the field among them. Once we were taken from the scene of action, and restrained from sending telegrams or issuing orders or answering questions, then the minions of the corporations would be put to work. . . . Our headquarters were temporarily demoralized and abandoned, and we could not answer any messages. The men went back to work, and the ranks were broken, and the strike was broken up, . . . not by the army, and not by any other power, but simply and solely by the action of the United States courts in restraining us from discharging our duties as officers and representatives of our employés."

Whatever any single individual may have thought or planned, the great body of those who were engaged in these transactions contemplated neither rebellion nor revolution, and when in the due order of legal proceedings the question of right and wrong was submitted to the courts, and by them decided, they unhesitatingly yielded to their decisions. The outcome, by the very testimony of the defendants, attests the wisdom of the course pursued by the government, and that it was well not to oppose force simply by force, but to invoke the jurisdiction and judgment of those tribunals to whom by the Constitution and in accordance with the settled conviction of all citizens is committed the determination of questions of right and wrong between individuals, masses, and States.

It must be borne in mind that this bill was not simply to enjoin a mob and mob violence. It was not a bill to command a keeping of the peace; much less was its purport to restrain the defendants from abandoning whatever employment they were engaged in. The right of any laborer, or any number of laborers, to quit work was not challenged. The scope and purpose of the bill was only to restrain forcible obstructions of the highways along which interstate commerce travels and the mails are carried. And the facts set forth at length are only those facts which tended to show that the defendants were engaged in such obstructions.

A most earnest and eloquent appeal was made to us in eulogy of the heroic spirit of those who threw up their employment, and gave up their means of earning a livelihood, not in defence of their own rights, but in sympathy for and to assist others whom they believed to be wronged. We yield to none in our admiration of any act of heroism or self-sacrifice, but we may be permitted to add that it is a lesson which cannot be learned too soon or too thoroughly that under this government of and by the people the means of redress of all wrongs are through the courts and at the ballot-box, and that no wrong, real or fancied, carries with it legal warrant to invite as a means of redress the coöperation of a mob, with its accompanying acts of violence.

We have given to this case the most careful and anxious attention, for we realize that it touches closely questions of supreme importance to the people of this country. Summing up our conclusions, we hold that the government of the United States is one having jurisdiction over every foot of soil within its territory, and acting directly upon each citizen; that while it is a government of enumerated powers, it has within the limits of those powers all the attributes of sovereignty; that to it is committed power over interstate commerce and the transmission of the mail; that the powers thus conferred upon the national government are not dormant, but have been assumed and put into practical exercise by the legislation of Congress; that in the exercise of those powers it is competent for the nation to remove all obstructions upon highways, natural or artificial, to the passage of interstate commerce or the carrying of the mail; that while it may be competent for the government (through the executive branch and in the use of the entire executive power of the nation) to forcibly remove all such obstructions, it is equally within its competency to appeal to the civil courts for an inquiry and determination as to the existence and character of any alleged obstructions, and if such are found to exist, or threaten to occur, to invoke the powers of those courts to remove or restrain such obstructions; that the jurisdiction of courts to interfere in such matters by injunction is one recognized from ancient times and by indubitable authority; that such jurisdiction is not ousted by the fact that the obstructions are accompanied by or consist of acts in themselves violations of the criminal law; that the proceeding by injunction is of a civil character, and may be enforced by proceedings in contempt; that such proceedings are not in execution of the

criminal laws of the land; that the penalty for a violation of injunction is
no substitute for and no defence to a prosecution for any criminal offences
committed in the course of such violation; that the complaint filed in this
case clearly showed an existing obstruction of artificial highways for the
passage of interstate commerce and the transmission of the mail—an obstruction not only temporarily existing, but threatening to continue; that
under such complaint the Circuit Court had power to issue its process of
injunction; that it having been issued and served on these defendants, the
Circuit Court had authority to inquire whether its orders had been disobeyed,
and when it found that they had been, then to proceed under section 725,
Revised Statutes, which grants power "to punish, by fine or imprisonment,
. . . disobedience, . . . by any party . . . or other person, to any lawful writ,
process, order, rule, decree or command," and enter the order of punishment
complained of; and, finally, that, the Circuit Court, having full jurisdiction
in the premises, its finding of the fact of disobedience is not open to review
on *habeas corpus* in this or any other court; . . .

The petition for a writ of *habeas corpus* is *denied.*

The People's Party Platform, 1896

The People's Party, assembled in National Convention, reaffirms its allegiance to the principles declared by the founders of the Republic, and also
to the fundamental principles of just government as enunciated in the platform of the party in 1892.

We recognize that through the connivance of the present and preceding
Administrations the country has reached a crisis in its National life, as
predicted in our declaration four years ago, and that prompt and patriotic
action is the supreme duty of the hour.

We realize that, while we have political independence, our financial and
industrial independence is yet to be attained by restoring to our country the
Constitutional control and exercise of the functions necessary to a people's
government, which functions have been basely surrendered by our public
servants to corporate monopolies. The influence of European moneychangers
has been more potent in shaping legislation than the voice of the American
people. Executive power and patronage have been used to corrupt our
legislatures and defeat the will of the people, and plutocracy has thereby
been enthroned upon the ruins of democracy. To restore the Government
intended by the fathers, and for the welfare and prosperity of this and future
generations, we demand the establishment of an economic and financial
system which shall make us masters of our own affairs and independent of
European control, by the adoption of the following declaration of principles:

The Finances

1. We demand a National money, safe and sound, issued by the General
Government only, without the intervention of banks of issue, to be a full
legal tender for all debts, public and private; a just, equitable, and efficient

means of distribution, direct to the people, and through the lawful disbursements of the Government.

2. We demand the free and unrestricted coinage of silver and gold at the present legal ratio of 16 to 1, without waiting for the consent of foreign nations.

3. We demand that the volume of circulating medium be speedily increased to an amount sufficient to meet the demand of the business and population, and to restore the just level of prices of labor and production.

4. We denounce the sale of bonds and the increase of the public interest-bearing debt made by the present Administration as unnecessary and without authority of law, and demand that no more bonds be issued, except by specific act of Congress.

5. We demand such legislation as will prevent the demonetization of the lawful money of the United States by private contract.

6. We demand that the Government, in payment of its obligation, shall use its option as to the kind of lawful money in which they are to be paid, and we denounce the present and preceding Administrations for surrendering this option to the holders of Government obligations.

7. We demand a graduated income tax, to the end that aggregated wealth shall bear its just proportion of taxation, and we regard the recent decision of the Supreme Court relative to the income-tax law as a misinterpretation of the Constitution and an invasion of the rightful powers of Congress over the subject of taxation.

8. We demand that postal savings-banks be established by the Government for the safe deposit of the savings of the people and to facilitate exchange.

Railroads and Telegraphs

1. Transportation being a means of exchange and a public necessity, the Government should own and operate the railroads in the interest of the people and on a non-partisan basis, to the end that all may be accorded the same treatment in transportation, and that the tyranny and political power now exercised by the great railroad corporations, which result in the impairment, if not the destruction of the political rights and personal liberties of the citizens, may be destroyed. Such ownership is to be accomplished gradually, in a manner consistent with sound public policy.

2. The interest of the United States in the public highways built with public moneys, and the proceeds of grants of land to the Pacific railroads, should never be alienated, mortgaged, or sold, but guarded and protected for the general welfare, as provided by the laws organizing such railroads. The foreclosure of existing liens of the United States on these roads should at once follow default in the payment thereof by the debtor companies; and at the foreclosure sales of said roads the Government shall purchase the same, if it becomes necessary to project its interests therein, or if they can be purchased at a reasonable price and the Government shall operate said railroads as public highways for the benefit of the whole people, and not in

the interest of the few, under suitable provisions for protection of life and property, giving to all transportation interests equal privileges and equal rates for fares and freight.

3. We denounce the present infamous schemes for refunding these debts, and demand that the laws now applicable thereto be executed and administered according to their intent and spirit.

4. The telegraph, like the Post Office system, being a necessity for the transmission of news, should be owned and operated by the Government in the interest of the people.

The Public Lands

1. True policy demands that the National and State legislation shall be such as will ultimately enable every prudent and industrious citizen to secure a home, and therefore the land should not be monopolized for speculative purposes. All lands now held by railroads and other corporations in excess of their actual needs should by lawful means be reclaimed by the Government and held for actual settlers only, and private land monopoly, as well as alien ownership, should be prohibited.

2. We condemn the land grant frauds by which the Pacific railroad companies have, through the connivance of the Interior Department, robbed multitudes of *bona-fide* settlers of their homes and miners of their claims, and we demand legislation by Congress which will enforce the exemption of mineral land from such grants after as well as before the patent.

3. We demand that *bona-fide* settlers on all public lands be granted free homes, as provided in the National Homestead Law, and that no exception be made in the case of Indian reservations when opened for settlement, and that all lands not now patented come under this demand.

The Referendum

We favor a system of direct legislation through the initiative and referendum, under proper Constitutional safeguards.

Direct Election of President and Senators by the People

We demand the election of President, Vice-President, and United States Senators by a direct vote of the people. . . .

The Territories

We favor home rule in the Territories and the District of Columbia, and the early admission of the Territories as States.

Public Salaries

All public salaries should be made to correspond to the price of labor and its products.

Employment to Be Furnished by Government

In times of great industrial depression, idle labor should be employed on public works as far as practicable.

Arbitrary Judicial Action

The arbitrary course of the courts in assuming to imprison citizens for indirect contempt and ruling by injunction should be prevented by proper legislation.

Pensions

We favor just pensions for our disabled Union soldiers.

A Fair Ballot

Believing that the elective franchise and an untrammeled ballot are essential to a government of, for, and by the people, the People's party condemns the wholesale system of disfranchisement adopted in some States as unrepublican and undemocratic, and we declare it to be the duty of the several State legislatures to take such action as will secure a full, free and fair ballot and an honest count.

The Financial Question: "The Pressing Issue"

While the foregoing propositions constitute the platform upon which our party stands, and for the vindication of which its organization will be maintained, we recognize that the great and pressing issue of the pending campaign, upon which the present election will turn, is the financial question, and upon this great and specific issue between the parties we cordially invite the aid and co-operation of all organizations and citizens agreeing with us upon this vital question.

✥ *E S S A Y S*

The traditional explanation of constitutional developments during the late nineteenth century stressed the Supreme Court's conservative nature. Laissez-faire ideology, so the argument went, permeated the Court, giving its justices an intellectual hook on which to hang their conservative economic views. As the retired political scientist Arnold Paul argues in the first essay, the justices specifically, and the judges of state and federal courts generally, turned a hostile face to regulatory measures. The judiciary arrogated power to itself as it went about restricting popularly based legislative measures unpalatable to capitalists. More recently, however, historian Michael Les Benedict of Ohio State University has offered a different vision of laissez-faire constitutionalism. In the second essay, Benedict argues that the Supreme Court was far more concerned with protecting liberty than with simply defending monopolistic business practices and greedy captains of industry. In this sense, therefore, the courts were most concerned with protecting rights, as they have been historically according to Benedict. When we understand the intellectual climate in which judges operated in the late nineteenth century, then their behavior seems far less economically expedient and much more constitutionally principled.

Traditional Legal Conservatism

ARNOLD M. PAUL

. . . The social protests of the post–Civil War era stemmed from the great pace of industrialization, and, more particularly, from the swift concentration of economic power in the large corporation. Midwestern and Southern farmers, unable to control their marketing through organization and suffering from a long-term international price decline, complained bitterly of monopolistic rates by railroads, grain elevators, and banks. Factory workers and miners, crowded in slums with insecure status in a rapidly changing economy, periodically rebelled at low wages, long hours, and bad working conditions. Small businessmen, faced with the more efficient, and frequently more ruthless, competition of the large corporation, charged that the continued consolidation of capital was destroying individual opportunity. And many professional and white-collar people, uneasy over the accumulation of great wealth and the growing disparity of rich and poor, feared that the traditional fluidity of American society was fast disappearing. The near-unanimous passage of the Sherman Anti-Trust Act in 1890 revealed the pervasiveness of popular dissatisfaction with many aspects of the new industrialism.

As popular discontents grew more menacing in the 1890s, and conservative alarm for the security of property increased accordingly, the role of the courts assumed a new importance. Gradually at first, and then with rapid strides, the judiciary emerged in the mid-1890s as the principal bulwark of conservative defense. The transformation of the due process clause into a substantive check upon legislative regulation, the development of the labor injunction as an antistrike weapon, the near-emasculation of the Sherman Anti-Trust Act in the *E. C. Knight* case, and the overthrow of the federal income tax in the *Pollock* case were related aspects of a massive judicial entry into the socioeconomic scene. American constitutionalism underwent a revolution in the 1890s, a conservative-oriented revolution which vastly expanded the scope of judicial supremacy, with important consequences for American economic and political history. . . .

Reprinted from Arnold M. Paul, *Conservative Crisis and the Rule of Law: Attitudes of Bar and Bench, 1887–1895* (Ithaca, N.Y.: Cornell University Press, 1960), pp. 1–14, 229–237. Copyright © 1960 by the American Historical Association. Used by permission of the publisher, Cornell University Press.

As tensions mounted after the Haymarket riot, and the leading cases establishing the new judicialism passed in review, lawyers and judges appeared before the bar associations, contributed articles to the law journals, made speeches at commencement exercises, and otherwise made known their views on the great problems of the day. What issues loomed largest in the minds of these articulate members of the legal profession? How far did they think it wise for courts to go in interposing judicial blocks between the demands of reform and the interests of conservatism? How did they regard the growing conflict between capital and labor, and what role did they think proper for the judiciary in that conflict? And most important perhaps, how did they evaluate the implications for the democratic process in the expanded concept of judicial review then being developed. . . .

Of major significance were important differences within the general framework of what may be called the conservative point of view. Two main streams of legal conservative thought could be distinguished: a laissez-faire conservatism, drawing heavily on the antipaternalism doctrines of Herbert Spencer and dedicated to the utmost freedom for economic initiative and the utmost restriction upon legislative interference; and a more traditional conservatism, which, while assigning the protection of private property to a high status in the hierarchy of values, was especially concerned with the problems of maintaining an ordered society in a world where the forces of popular democracy might become unmanageable. From the professional standpoint, legal conservatism as a whole, and particularly traditional legal conservatism, set great store by precedent and the proprieties of judicial procedure.

Within all these categories of opinion there were wide variations from moderate to extreme—or, as may be said, from center to left (for the progressives) and from center to right (for the conservatives). And in tracing the changing attitudes of lawyers and judges from 1887 to 1895, when court intervention reached its climax, we shall find that it was a significant movement to the right within traditional legal conservatism that finally determined the triumph of the new judicialism.

. . . Under the pressure of social discontent, legislators had begun to act in the 1870s and 1880s in regard to railroad and grain elevator rates, labor relations, and other matters affecting large business concerns. In turn, corporation lawyers had been pressing the courts to protect more vigilantly the rights of property against legislative regulation. The newly adopted Fourteenth Amendment, with its general phraseology prohibiting the states from abridging the "privileges and immunities" of citizens of the United States, or from depriving "any person of life, liberty, or property, without due process of law," or from denying to any person "the equal protection of the laws," was repeatedly offered as a suitable constitutional vehicle for judicial interposition. The due process clause especially, corporation lawyers maintained, should be understood as embodying guarantees of fundamental private rights against legislative infringement—especially in regard to such matters as the labor contract and the rate schedules of railroads and other public service corporations. The claim made was threefold: that the legislature had no power to intervene in these matters; that if the legislature did have the power, it had to exercise it "reasonably"; and that the final arbiter of reasonableness was the judiciary. And the interpretation of reasonableness urged upon the judges by corporate counsel often meant at the very least a substantial diminution of the legislative power, and in some types of cases—the freedom-of-contract cases for example—the impressment upon the Constitution of a laissez-faire ideology.

But "due process of law" historically had connoted procedural and not substantive restrictions upon the powers of government, and to adopt the interpretations of the corporation lawyers would mean a drastic extension of judicial review beyond its traditional limitations. The courts were cautious; the United States Supreme Court in particular, which must ultimately set the pattern for constitutional trends throughout all American courts, was yielding very little, formally at least, to the arguments of corporation lawyers. To be sure, the Court had acceded in January, 1886, to the claim of Roscoe Conkling that the word "person" in the Fourteenth Amendment was intended to apply to corporations as well as to natural persons. But as a leading authority has pointed out, this alone was only of potential value to corporations seeking relief from state regulatory laws; for on the critical issue of whether the Fourteenth Amendment should be regarded as imposing substantive restraints upon state social and economic legislation, the Court was firmly upholding the legislative power.

The basis of the Court's position had been established in 1877 in the great case of *Munn* v. *Illinois*, one of the famous "Granger" cases resulting from the reform movements of the 1870s. Rendered by a 7–2 majority of the Court, Justices Field and Strong dissenting, *Munn* v. *Illinois* seemed for many years an impregnable barrier to the new constitutionalism. Long the bête noire of laissez-faire conservatism, the case merits restatement here.

At issue was an Illinois law of 1871 requiring a license for the operation of public warehouses in cities of not less than 100,000 population (Chicago was the only city affected) and prescribing a maximum schedule of rates for the storage and handling of grain. Chief Justice Morrison R. Waite for the Court, rejecting the contention of the plaintiff that he was being deprived of property without due process of law, sustained the law as a legitimate exercise of the police power. Under this power, continued the Chief Justice,

> the government regulates the conduct of its citizens one towards another, and the manner in which each shall use his own property, when such regulation becomes necessary for the public good. In their exercise it has been customary in England from time immemorial, and in this country from its first colonization, to regulate ferries, common carriers, hackmen, bakers, millers, wharfingers, innkeepers, etc., and in so doing to fix a maximum of charge to be made for services rendered, accommodations furnished, and articles sold.

Thus, regulation of private property was not per se a deprivation of property without due process of law. But what were the circumstances which governed the determination of whether such regulation was or was not a deprivation? Here Waite had recourse to the 200-year-old common-law treatise *De Portibus Maris* by Lord Chief Justice Hale, wherein it was stated that when private property is "affected with a public interest, it ceases to be *juris privati* only." Said Waite, in what was to be the most oft-quoted passage of his opinion:

> Property does become clothed with a public interest when used in a manner to make it of public consequence, and affect the community at large. When, therefore, one devotes his property to a use in which the public has an interest, he, in effect, grants to the public an interest in that use, and must submit to be controlled by the public for the common good, to the extent of the interest he has thus created.

The grain storage business in Chicago, lying squarely astride the great stream of interstate commerce in grain, was thus affected with the public interest. And the elevator facilities in Chicago, having always charged agreed-upon rates and able to "take toll from all who pass," constituted therefore a "virtual monopoly."

Possibly the critical hinge of the whole opinion was in regard to the claim of appellant that in any event the owner of the property was entitled to a reasonable compensation for its use, and "reasonable" was a matter for judicial and not legislative decision. To this Waite answered:

> The controlling fact is the power to regulate at all. If that exists, the right to establish the maximum of charge, as one of the means of regulation, is implied. . . .
>
> We know that this is a power which may be abused; but that is no argument against its existence. For protection against abuses by legislatures the people must resort to the polls, not to the courts.

The Chief Justice was adhering firmly to judicial restraint: the reasonableness of public regulation would remain a political question, and not become a legal one.

In subsequent cases the Court upheld and expanded further its broad acknowledgment of legislative power, reaching close to its high point in this line of decisions with the 1886 case of *Stone* v *Farmers' Loan and Trust Co.* In that case a railroad's charter granted in 1884 specifically empowered the company to fix its own rates and charges. Nevertheless, Chief Justice Waite, again speaking for the Court, sustained the application to the company of a newly established railroad commission's findings as to what rates the company should charge. Since the company had conceded that its power to set rates was limited by the common-law rule that all charges must be reasonable, it could not complain, said Waite, if the legislature determined for itself in the first instance what was reasonable, for this was simply another example of statutory implementation of the common law, always a recognized practice.

Having thus refined away the charter rights in respect to rates almost to the vanishing point—and weakened further the protections of the *Dartmouth College* case—the Chief Justice felt obliged to insert this concession:

From what has thus been said, it is not to be inferred that this power of limitation or regulation is itself without limit. This power to regulate is not a power to destroy, and limitation is not the equivalent of confiscation. Under pretence of regulating fares and freights, the State cannot require a railroad corporation to carry persons or property without reward; neither can it do that which in law amounts to a taking of private property for public use without just compensation, or without due process of law.

In extreme cases then, the Court agreed, it might set aside an act as contrary to due process. In ensuing years this passage was much quoted by railroad counsel, and it has since been regarded by many scholars as an important springboard for substantive due process. At the time, however, no such favorable prognosis was foreseen by corporation lawyers or by laissez-faire conservatives generally, who saw only continued judicial obeisance to the legislative will. Nor did the two dissenting opinions of Justices Harlan and Field, the former on narrow, the latter on broad grounds, seem sufficient to promise an early reversal of the Court's position.

In contrast to this continued insistence by the United States Supreme Court upon the flexibility of legislative discretion, matters affecting the state courts had already produced a basis for possible restrictions on the legislative will. For by 1887 the doctrine of freedom of contract had been developed, and its initial applications established. The first great step toward this end after the Civil War was the publication by Thomas M. Cooley in 1868 of his famous *Constitutional Limitations,* wherein he gathered together the scattered constitutional law of the different states into a convenient, organized whole which could serve as a principal source for citation in the state courts. In his preface Cooley said he had written "in full sympathy with the restraints" that the Fathers had imposed upon government in America. Although Cooley was conscientious enough to mark out areas of state power as well as restrictions upon states, the over-all emphasis of the book was on "Limitations."

But Cooley did not merely collect for exposition; in the process he also enlarged upon and created afresh. His discussion of "law of the land" and "due process of law" was a contribution of considerable importance to laissez-faire constitutionalism; so also was his impugnment as "class legislation" of laws which unwarrantably infringed the "capacity to make contracts." These and other passages of his writings were to be frequently quoted by counsel, and by judges, as authority for judicial invalidation of state regulatory acts.

Cooley's path-breaking work on the state level was soon supplemented from an entirely different source, the individualist opinions of Justice Stephen J. Field of the United States Supreme Court. Not the least fascinating of the many unusual elements of the rise of the new constitutionalism was the acceptance of Field's ideas on the state level before they finally attained sanction from the majority of his colleagues on the supreme federal bench.

In the famous *Slaughter-House Cases,* Field's dissenting opinion extolled as inalienable the right of the citizen "to pursue his own calling" and arrogated to the judiciary operating through the Fourteenth Amendment the obligation to protect that and all the other "inalienable rights" against hostile state action. . . .

. . . [B]y the 1890s it was a root principle of American conservatism that in a time of social crisis, when rampant populism might threaten the established order, the Supreme Court must act as counterweight to the election returns, as defender of minority rights against majority rule. From the conservative point of view, this meant primarily the protection of property rights. In America the signpost of status was not place but property, and the denominator of the ordered society not respect for hierarchies of station but regard for differences in possessions. The great danger to be guarded against in America, so the conservative tradition ran, was a thrust from below, an upsurge of *the democracy* resentful at the growth of concentrated wealth and determined to use its majority power to effect redistribution. If an age of tension should create a drawing of class lines, with property the divisive factor, and if universal suffrage should become the vehicle for legislative leveling, then only the judiciary could redress the balance, "the final breakwater . . . against the tumultuous ocean of democracy."

Although the Constitutional Convention of 1787 had probably assumed some judicial review, the majority at Philadelphia had placed their main reliance for restraining the excesses of democracy upon the check-and-balance system in the broader sense, the "competing factions" of James Madison. The main body of conservatives in 1787, though seeking to dilute and channelize the Revolutionary enthusiasm for direct democracy, had not intended, for the most part, more than procedural limitations on the representative process. True, in some future time of crisis, it was agreed, the work of 1787 might require a major readjustment; but so long as economic opportunity remained abundant and class tensions were readily reducible, no all-pervading judicial guardianship seemed essential.

The right-wing Federalists, however, led by Hamilton and later by Marshall, had early regarded the judiciary as potentially the key bulwark of conservative defense. Certainly, in the Jeffersonian and Jacksonian periods the federal judiciary became the principal exponent of the conservative interest, the development of the contract clause and the vested-rights doctrine representing to conservatives just the kind of additional counterbalances deemed imperative to protect property rights and creditor claims in an era of advancing democracy and aggressive equalitarianism. By the 1840s, although conservatism in America was temporarily losing its vitality (because its postulate of an aristocracy-democracy antagonism was inapplicable to the American scene), the tradition of judicial guardianship had already attained a pre-eminent place in the conservative firmament.

Some forty years later, in the 1880s, with legislative regulation on the increase, with the rise of a new social tension perceptible, the constitutional and legal doctrines developed in earlier decades had lost their efficacy. The *Dartmouth College* case, that great anchor of the contract clause, had been weakened by construction and bypassed by legislation; while the old vested-rights doctrine had withered away from disuse. Nor was the new Fourteenth Amendment, the almost desperate appeals of corporation lawyers notwithstanding, proving an adequate substitute: the *Slaughter-House Cases* and *Munn* v. *Illinois* seemed to have rendered it largely unserviceable. Even the teachings of Herbert Spencer and the economists, unvarying though they were in disparaging legislative interference with economic liberty, had thus far made only a small impression on the law reports. Though Justice Field's persistence—and Roscoe Conkling's ingenuity—had extracted some concessions from the Court in the mid-1880s, though Cooley and Tiedeman had prescribed the patterns for restricting legislative police power and a number of the state courts were beginning to show responsiveness, though equity jurisprudence was revealing new expansiveness in protection of property rights against labor unrest, in the late 1880s all these tendencies, still unexplored and often ambiguous, were receiving only limited application.

The pleas of corporate counsel and laissez-faire doctrinaires for vigorous judicial interventionism, only partially answered in the 1880s by the cautious moderates in control of the courts, received a new hearing with the turn of the decade. To the conservative mind the crisis of the 1890s was not merely a matter of discrete political and economic conflicts over legislative policy and labor relations; the entire equilibrium of American society was being called into question. The long-assumed fluidity of the American class structure was seen as disappearing before the increasing concentration of wealth, the interests of capital and labor appeared more deeply antagonistic, and class struggle between the have's and the seeking-to-have's seemed a real possibility. America was creating a Rhine in its midst, lamented United States District Judge Peter S. Grosscup in a Memorial Day address of 1894, "and conflicts like those of the Teuton and the Gaul must be expected."

The line of conservative thought thus emerging may well be termed a form of neo-Federalism, a recrudescence of a traditional conservatism fearful of restless majorities upsetting the social order and the rights of property. The forebodings of the Federalists of 1787, that some future time of tension would severely strain the American experiment, seemed on the verge of fulfillment. What could stay the expected depredations of the propertyless? If the present tendencies continued, declaimed United States Circuit Judge William Howard Taft in June, 1894, "our boasted constitutional guaranties of property rights will not be worth the parchment upon which they were originally written." The secure constitutionalism of 1787 was collapsing. The Presidency was becoming a popular office, unbalancing John Adams' mixed government; classes and parties seemed increasingly nationalized, weakening Madison's structure of competing factions. At the same time the state police power was rapidly expanding; the national commerce power was invading immensely important economic relationships; and the federal taxing power, innocuous since the early post-bellum period, was being revived boldly as an incipient leveling device. What the times demanded of a neo-Federalist conservatism was a new period of creative constitutionalism, a refurbished Constitution brought up to date as a conservative instrument.

As the tensions of the time steadily mounted, and the demands of laissez-faire right-wing conservatives grew more insistent upon judicial intervention, the attitudes of the moderate center of the legal profession, and particularly traditional legal conservatism, became decisive. This group had often held the balance between the progressives and the right-wing conservatives in the profession. Moderate in their views on government regulation and the rights of property, and concerned professionally with preserving the traditional principles and procedures of legal and constitutional construction, most traditional conservatives had long opposed any fundamental change in the nature or extent of judicial power. The pressures of the 1890s, however, weakened the position of the moderates; the course of judicial decision moved relentlessly toward increasing interposition; and as the crisis reached its height in 1894 and 1895 and conservative fears approached near panic, a major sector of the moderates finally broke from the center position, as in the *Pollock* decision, coalesced with the right wing in the burgeoning neo-Federalism, and sealed the triumph of the new judicialism.

The resultant constitutional and legal revolution was, from the conservative point of view, indeed creative, in its way as significant for the laissez-faire conservatism of the 1890s as the constitutionalism of 1787 for the conservatism of that era. Due process of law, once primarily procedural, was now solidly substantive as well; the police power, once freely malleable as adjuster of social imbalance, was now encased by freedom of contract; the ancient process of equity, once applicable only to named individuals and as safeguard for physical property, was now an instrument of public, i.e., judicial, policy and applicable to "all persons whomsoever"; the commerce power, once "plenary" under Marshall, was now divided under Fuller; and a hundred years of tax law precedent, thought inviolable by the rule of *stare decisis*, was now shattered by the *Pollock* case. Traditional legal conservatism, forced to choose between *traditionalism* and *conservatism*—ironic choice—had chosen the latter. The conservative attachment to the ordered society, demanding as it seemed the firmest judicial interposition in protection of property from social upheaval, had outranked in value the more formalistic virtues of legal tradition.

In strengthening the right-wing position on the issue of the role of the judiciary and thus promoting the advance of judicial supremacy, the traditional legal conservatism of the 1890s had also prepared the way, unintentionally, I believe, for the enshrinement of laissez-faire philosophy in constitutional law. With the various precedents and legal principles developed in the 1890s available as stepping stones, laissez-faire doctrinaires could far more easily have their way with the courts. Pre-1890 traditionalism, driven by the mid-nineties into alliance with laissez-faire doctrinairism, was largely absorbed by it; laissez-faire philosophy became, in the minds of many, *the* tradition of the courts. And progressives defending social legislation, rather than argue that the courts were exceeding their traditional functions, for the most part accepted the new conditions and tried to accomplish their aims by sustaining, in effect, the burden of proof in the matter of "reasonableness."

Whether the sweep of laissez-faire ideology would have encompassed the judiciary in the course of time without the special impetus of the 1890s is highly doubtful. A number of scholars have noted, without satisfactory explanation, the paradox that laissez-faire doctrines so thoroughly invaded the law considerably after their full effects in philosophy, politics, and economics were felt and passed and when *laissez faire* and Social Darwinism were already in full retreat in the body politic. Certainly the crisis of the 1890s and the concomitant movement to right-wing conservatism forced decisively a dramatic quickening of the pace for laissez-faire constitutionalism, a sudden overmounting of hurdles at a time when constitutional doctrine was still not assured in its direction. Had the legal and constitutional traditions overturned in the 1890s been maintained by the courts but another few years, the changed social atmosphere of the 1900s would have made unlikely, I suggest, the advanced judicial supremacy developed by the 1920s and 1930s.

As it turned out, however, the neo-Federalism of the 1890s opened the door to what was to prove in succeeding decades a full proliferation of judicial obstructionism. The Supreme Court of the United States became, instead of an instrument of constitutional democracy, an impediment to constitutional democracy. Exaggerating its powers beyond proportion in the period 1890–1937, confusing its proper role in the American scheme of government, the Court for a long while seriously weakened its real value. In the unfolding of these unfortunate developments, the bar and the bench of the 1890s, and not least the usually tradition-minded legal conservatives, had no little part.

The Libertarian Foundations of Laissez-Fairre Constitutionalism

MICHAEL LES BENEDICT

I. Legal Scholarship and Laissez-Faire Constitutionalism

Until recently, historians of American constitutionalism agreed that, except for the infamous Dred Scott decision, the most unfortunate decisions of the Supreme Court were those that incorporated the notion of laissez-faire into the Constitution in the late nineteenth century. These decisions permitted the Court to frustrate efforts to secure a more just economic order in the United States until the 1930s. The intellectual foundations of laissez-faire constitutionalism have been so alien to most legal scholars since the 1930s (and equally unintelligible to many even earlier) that they have found it difficult to believe these decisions were the result of efforts to enforce "neutral" principles of constitutional law, to utilize the terms of Herbert Wechsler's famous analysis. They could not conceive of the Court's rhetoric about liberty and due process as anything but cant, a subterfuge designed to camouflage other purposes.

"Laissez-Faire and Liberty: A Reevaluation of the Meaning and Origins of the Laissez-Faire Constitutionalism," by Michael Les Benedict, *Law and History Review* (Fall 1985), pp. 293–314, 327–331. Reprinted by permission of Cornell University Press.

The orthodox view became that, beneath the rhetoric, "the major value of the Court . . . was the protection of the business community against government." During the era of laissez-faire constitutionalism, the "Supreme Court . . . in fact was an arm of the capital-owning class," legal scholars and historians charged. "Capitalist enterprise in America generated . . . forces in government and in the underlying classes hostile to capitalist expansion; . . . it became the function of the Court to check those forces and to lay down the lines of economic orthodoxy." Thus when John P. Frank summarized the instances in which the Supreme Court had invalidated national acts and laws up to 1954, he found that the overwhelming majority "had no direct bearing on basic liberties." Rather they involved, among other things, "economic matters."

It was to protect the privileges of the wealthy and of corporations, legal scholars concluded, that American judges engrafted upon the Constitution the economic principle of laissez-faire, the admonition that government ought not to interfere with the natural laws that govern economic relations. They did this primarily by reinterpreting the phrase "due process of law" found in the fifth and fourteenth Amendments to give judges the power to rule laws unconstitutional when their substance, not merely the mode of enforcing them, infringed property rights. This, constitutional scholars insisted, was a perversion of the original meaning of the due process clauses. Although the standard studies of the origins of "substantive" due process of law found ante-bellum antecedents in the doctrine of "vested rights," they concluded that the concept of "substantive" due process had made slight, if any, headway. The Supreme Court had rejected the idea firmly in key cases after the Civil War and adopted it only in the 1880s and 1890s when those opposed to business interests threatened to gain control of the other branches of the national government.

Although challenged, this view is still widely accepted. It plays a key role in the ongoing debate over the proper mode of judicial review. Legal scholars have cited the incorporation of the doctrine of laissez-faire into the Constitution as one of the worst examples of judicial abuse of power. When Justice Rehnquist denounced the judicial-activist notion of "a living Constitution" in 1976, he cited the apogee of laissez-faire constitutionalism, *Lochner* v. *New York*, and *Dred Scott* together in this *argumentum ad horrendum*. Nothing can so damn a decision as to compare it to *Lochner* and its ilk. As John Hart Ely has written, these laissez-faire cases "are now universally acknowledged to have been constitutionally improper."

However, this traditional interpretation reflects the depth of the chasm separating the world view of the twentieth century from that of the nineteenth more than it reflects the real origins and meaning of laissez-faire constitutionalism. Law does not develop in isolation from the perceptions and ideas of the general community. Changing understandings of how society operates, changing standards of fundamental right and wrong help to shape legal doctrine. When those general perceptions and standards change, whole areas of the law based on them may become unintelligible to those who imbibe the new.

The world view of most Americans—and the mainstream of the American intellectual community—gradually underwent such a change between the 1880s and the 1930s. Common to most western societies, this shift constituted "one of the greatest intellectual and moral upheavals in western history," according to a legal scholar who has described its impact on American law. It left the era of laissez-faire constitutionalism a "dark age," in the sense described by the great philosopher of history, R. G. Collingwood: "[S]ometimes whole generations of historians . . . find in certain periods of history nothing intelligible, and call them dark ages; . . . such phrases tell us nothing about those ages themselves, though they tell us . . . the persons who use them . . . are unable to re-think the thoughts that were fundamental to their life."

As the intellectual commitments forged in the Progressive and New Deal eras have faded, and as older notions we now call "conservative" have revived, it has become possible once more to make sense of laissez-faire constitutionalism. As a consequence, the traditional interpretation has slowly been eroding. Scholars have pointed out that government regulation was widespread throughout the nineteenth century. Courts entertained challenges to relatively few of these regulations and overturned even fewer; they can hardly be denominated rigidly laissez-faire in outlook, these analysts have suggested. A series of reassessments sympathetic to such pillars of laissez-faire constitutionalism as Thomas McIntyre Cooley, Stephen J. Field, and even David J. Brewer, have appeared. In the case of each jurisprudent, scholars have found that their ideas transcended mere devotion to business interests. Rather, their concern after all was the relation of individual liberty to government, and they were willing to take positions counter to those of powerful economic interests when their principles called upon them to do so. The most recent edition of the leading American constitutional history textbook reflects some of this revisionism, recognizing the Jacksonian origins of some of the doctrines that made up laissez-faire constitutionalism and stating merely that they were "*used* for a generation to organize and protect the new system of industrial and finance capitalism" (italics mine), rather than charging that the justices intended them for that purpose.

But despite nascent revisionism, there is as yet no full description of the ethical, libertarian foundation of laissez-faire constitutionalism. It is the purpose of this essay to provide that description and to show how traditional American constitutional and legal beliefs suggested constitutional sanctions for laissez-faire.

In doing so, I do not mean to suggest that economic interests played no role in establishing laissez-faire constitutionalism. People rarely will pursue a grievance unless they have some stake in rectifying it. The parties who believed that economic regulations violated their rights had something to gain from pursuing the matter; so have defendants who have challenged criminal procedures and so have black Americans who have pressed for racial equality. On the other hand we all acquiesce every day to rules that run against our self-interest; we concede their legitimacy and we feel no grievance. The thing to be understood is, why did those who challenged

various economic regulations in the later nineteenth century feel that grievance, and why did judges, lawyers, the overwhelming majority of intellectuals, and millions of ordinary Americans agree with them? Once we understand that, we will be able to accept laissez-faire constitutionalism for
what it was—not an embarrassment but part of a long heritage of protection
for liberty, as it has been understood by Americans at different times in our
history.

To arrive at that understanding one must recognize that there were two
related but distinct justifications for the laissez-faire principle in the later
nineteenth century. The first was based directly upon classical economists'
conception of the "laws" of economics. It suggested that almost any government effort to overcome or channel those laws was doomed to failure.
The second was based on a concept of human liberty implicit in the principles
of classical economics. It militated only against certain kinds of government
interferences in the economy, not against all interference. That concept was
that the power of government could not legitimately be exercised to benefit
one person or group at the expense of others. It was this conviction—not
the notion that all government economic activity violated "immutable" economic laws—that lay at the heart of laissez-faire constitutionalism. It was
a principle in which Americans had long believed, that drew upon a libertarian heritage broader than classical economics, and that judges had enforced against legislative transgressions long before capitalists used it to
defend what they believed to be their rights. Laissez-faire constitutionalism
received wide support in late nineteenth-century America not because it was
based on widely adhered-to economic principles, and certainly not because
it protected entrenched economic privilege, but rather because it was con-
gruent with a well-established and accepted principle of American liberty.

II. Classical Economics and Laissez-Faire

At the foundation of classical economics lay the conviction that it was man's
nature to seek to gratify his desires with the least possible pain and effort.
From this basic fact "scientific" analysis could adduce a whole series of laws
that governed men's economic relationships. (By "scientific" nineteenth-
century economists meant the careful classification and definition of terms;
they did not mean the process of hypothesis-formation and testing that we
would today say defines the scientific method.) Since they were based on
unalterable human nature, the laws discovered by this process were natural
laws, as much so as those that governed the physical elements of the universe.
Furthermore, insofar as God had created human nature (and in America
many leading economists were also clergymen), those laws could be said to
reflect divine will.

Among the laws classical economists posited was that the value of any
good or service was determined by the intensity of the demand for it compared to its scarcity. Another was that men would always seek to produce
goods or provide services that brought the greatest return for the least
expense and effort. These they would trade for goods they could provide

for themselves only at greater expense and with more effort. Their trading partners, of course, were doing the same thing and thus both sides benefited by getting the most goods possible with least possible expense and effort. Therefore the most complete freedom of exchange promised the greatest prosperity for all.

Labor was a form of service. As any service, its value was determined in a bargain based on supply and demand. The supply of labor depended, of course, on the number of workers available but also upon their character. The individual members of an educated working class that valued its leisure time would refuse to sell their labor too cheaply, thus raising wages in general. Moreover, educated, responsible, sober workers would be in greater demand than shiftless ignorant ones. On the other hand, most laissez-faire economists believed there was a limit to the possible demand for workers, as expressed in wages. Workers could not be paid more than the amount of accumulated capital in the country less other costs of production. This amount was what laissez-faire economists called a "wage fund." A few classical economists also believed the notion developed by Malthus that the needs and numbers of human beings inevitably outstripped production, and that therefore the prices of most goods would always be out of the reach of most men and women. But by no means did all American classical economists share such pessimism; on the contrary, many were joyfully optimistic that the ability of men and women to control population growth and their desire to produce goods in order to acquire other goods promised ever-increasing production and prosperity.

Once men progressed beyond the stage of mere barter, classical economists believed, the value of goods, services, and labor was expressed according to a standard of value, that is, money. In the opinions of some of them, God had ordained that precious metals, especially gold, serve that purpose. In the opinion of others, precious metals, and especially gold, had simply proved to be the best possible measure of value over the centuries, because of the universal desire for it, its easy transportability, and the general stability of its supply.

All classical economists agreed that these natural laws provided the most efficient mechanism possible for the promotion of prosperity and the maintenance of economic stability. When particular goods became too scarce and the demand for them drove prices up, men would rush to increase production in order to take advantage of the high prices, thus increasing supply and bringing prices down. Likewise, when a particular good became too plentiful in relation to demand and therefore prices dropped, men would shift their productive capacities to other goods, thus lowering supplies and raising prices. No producer could keep the prices of goods artificially high, because consumers would turn to his competitors, who would take advantage of the opportunity to sell more goods at fair prices. Goods would always be available to each person at the lowest possible cost because he would purchase them with money earned from that activity which offered him the highest return for the least effort. If there were a real demand for a good or service, men would provide it, and at a cost commensurate with the demand. If men were unwilling to pay a price that made the production of a service worthwhile, then they could not have been so anxious for it after all, and productive energies would be better spent on something else.

However, the forces of supply and demand could maintain this ideal balance only if men were free to enter and leave the market in response to the push and pull of higher returns in the production of one good or another, or the provision of one service or another. Thus classical economists demanded a system of "unfettered competition." Government had the responsibility of assuring that no one used force or fraud to restrain such competition, whether labor unions or business conspirators cooperating to rig prices or markets. But human laws could not improve on the system itself; they could only interfere with it, thus the adage "laissez-faire," the "let-alone principle."

At its extreme the doctrine of laissez-faire ran almost to anarchism. Herbert Spencer, the Social Darwinist philosopher who was better known here than in his native England (though hardly as influential as some historians have believed), urged the elimination of public education, sanitation laws, and the public postal system, among other government institutions. But no Anmerican devotee of laissez-faire went this far. Instead they demanded that government cease its interference with freedom of trade through protective tariffs; stop its subsidization of industrial and transportation development through tax policies, tariffs, postal subsidies, and land grants; permit nothing but gold to be legal tender; resist the temptation to cure economic abuses with regulation; and desist from efforts to improve wages and many shortcomings in working conditions through legislation.

Merely cataloging these positions on the issues of the late nineteenth century indicates that most Americans found unpersuasive the argument that government could not improve upon the "natural" laws of economy. Over laissez-faire objections the national government maintained protective tariffs throughout the last half of the nineteenth century; until the mid-1870s it subsidized railroad development; throughout the era it provided postal subsidies to steamship and other transportation companies. In the 1860s and 1870s the national government augmented the nation's supply of currency with "legal tenders" that were not backed by specie. It regulated the money supply by speeding and slowing and sometimes reversing the rate that these notes were withdrawn from circulation. In 1878 the national government began coining limited amounts of silver. In 1887 it created the first great regulatory agency, the Interstate Commerce Commission, to regulate railroads and their customers; in 1890 it passed the Sherman Anti-Trust Act. As early as the 1870s Congress passed a law limiting the working day to eight hours for government employees and after a good deal of debate decreed that there would be no proportional reduction in pay, even if that led to wages higher than those that would have been dictated by the laws of supply and demand. All this was enough to persuade the authors of the leading textbook in American constitutional history to dub the late nineteenth century "The First Era of National Economic Regulation."

On the state level government was more active, and in more active violation of laissez-faire economic tenets. Local authorities in many areas continued to promote transportation development with tax abatements, debt guarantees, and public subscriptions to stock issues. At the same time, many states passed stiff new regulations to govern the conduct of their transportation enterprises. In yearly addresses on the state of American law, the presidents of the American Bar Association reported law after law promoting and subsidizing economic development, regulating business practices, employment conditions, and labor relations. As one scholar, reviewing the literature on the relation between government and private enterprise in the nineteenth century has concluded, "From Missouri to Maine, from the beginning to the end of the nineteenth century, governments were deeply involved in lending, borrowing, building, and regulating."

Those who urged the government to adhere to the "let-alone principle" certainly did not perceive their ideas to be in the saddle. They perceived themselves to be reformers, not defenders of the status quo. They continually deplored the American tendency to over-legislation. Early in the 1870s a contributor to the *North American Review* lamented: "The average man . . . is singularly subject to all kinds of political deception; he loves above all things, to be doctored; and, if a political organization desire, it will take no great cunning or skill to compound some soothing syrup . . . to meet the present demand; an additional, 'lie upon the statute-book' is a matter of no great consequence." Fifteen years later, in what is generally thought of as the heart of the laissez-faire era, the dean of American laissez-faire propagandists, William Graham Sumner, complained that exponents of the laissez-faire principle still were received "with . . . irritation and impatience."

If the principle of laissez-faire was less than compelling to the public at large in the years that the Supreme Court developed the doctrine of substantive due process, neither was it widely held among the businessmen whom it was supposed to protect. Of course it was businessmen who pressed Congress for the protective tariff and who sought public support for economic development. But businessmen, especially merchants, were also active promoters of state regulation of railroads and later of federal regulation. Businessmen were hardly united behind the laissez-fairist's beloved gold standard, many of them urging inflation as a tool to promote economic prosperity. Of course they were willing to marshal laissez-faire economic arguments against legislation that they perceived to be contrary to their interests, and they shared a vague notion that economic problems were not amenable to government-imposed solutions. But they conceded that government activity was useful in too many cases to be called laissez-fairist. As a leading business historian has concluded, businessmen developed "an unformulated pragmatic social philosophy that accorded with their economic interests but not with any existing system of thought."

The justices of the Supreme Court were no more dogmatic than businessmen when it came to evaluating laws that attempted to "interfere" with the "natural" laws of economics. For example, they conceded government power to regulate practices, rates, and prices in a broad category of economic enterprise: those businesses "affected with a public interest." They regularly sustained government regulations of property, business practices, contracts, and working conditions when they were designed to promote the safety, morals, or health of the community. They sustained national power to determine what constituted legal tender.

Of course the limits the justices put upon these powers were crucial. The "public interest" in a business that government had subjected to economic regulation had to be demonstrable; the regulations had to be "reasonable" and not "confiscatory." Regulations of businesses not affected with a public interest had to be designed to protect health, morals, or safety, not to secure economic benefits to any particular group.

But it is in these limitations that the libertarian rather than economic basis of the Court's position becomes apparent. The *economic* argument for laissez-faire was based on the conviction that all government regulation of economic relations were inefficient, if not unenforceable. But the limitations that the justices put upon the power of government to regulate economic enterprises were quite irrelevant to this objection, which would have imposed barriers to almost any regulation, if the justices had accepted it.

Neither the justices in their opinions, nor counsel in their briefs and arguments, objected to economic regulations because of their interference with immutable economic laws. Rather, they insisted that certain kinds of legislation violated rights. Those rights were closely enough related to principles of classical economics to impart apparent justification to Justice Holmes's famous complaint that decisions protecting them were "decided upon an economic theory which a large part of the country does not entertain." But it was a concept of rights implicit in classical economics and not a total inhibition on government action that the court was enforcing. This is apparent in Holmes's indictment itself. It was Herbert Spencer's *Social Statics*, not Adam Smith's *Wealth of Nations*, that Holmes complained was being written into the Constitution, and Spencer's opus was not an economic study at all. It was rather an effort to define "a strictly scientific morality" as deduced from a fundamental moral, not economic, principle, what Spencer called the "law of equal freedom," the principle that "every man has freedom to do all that he wills, provided he infringes not on the equal freedom of any other man."

III. "Class Legislation"

Classical economics implied both a broad definition of property rights and a definition of liberty that made government regulation an object of suspicion. As already noted, according to classical economists no object or service had any intrinsic value; value was always determined by the bargain between buyer and seller, which in turn was dependent on supply and demand. Therefore any government attempt to interfere with that bargaining process affected property in the only way that had any meaning: by changing its value. To differentiate diminution of the value of property from deprivation of property itself made no logical sense. Moreover, it was natural for classical economists to look upon the value set upon goods or services by the laws of supply and demand as their *real* value. Insofar as government action either raised or lowered prices by interfering with the operation of a free marketplace, it was taking the property of one party to the bargain and giving it to another. This was "class," or "special" legislation—using the power of government for the benefit of a particular group at the expense of the rest of society. It made government the means of theft, the direct antithesis of the legitimate purpose of government, which all knew was to offer protection against such wrongs. It was this conviction, a fundamental idea about right and wrong, not a doctrinaire belief in the inefficiency of government economic intervention, that lay at the heart of American laissez-faire constitutionalism.

Despite their commitment to a value-free, "scientific" approach to economics, many of the laissez-faire economists explicitly challenged the justice of such legislation. But this was not the primary thrust of their "scientific" works, and it is unlikely that economic texts were very widely read, even by the American elite or by that portion of it that practiced law. Rather, the laissez-faire doctrine of liberty was drummed into the conscience of American intellectual (and legal) leaders in the course of public debate on specific issues. Laissez-faire propagandists—such as professor and former special revenue commissioner of the Treasury Department David A. Wells, Boston textile manufacturer Edward Atkinson, Yale sociologist William Graham Sumner, journalists Edwin L. Godkin and Horace White, and professional economists Lyman Atwater, Arthur L. Perry, and Simon Newcomb (who was also a respected astronomer)—wrote hundreds of articles and tracts and delivered just as many lectures and poltical addresses denouncing specific instances of "special" and "class" legislation and the tendency towards such injustice in general.

In the opinion of the laissez-faire propagandists, the great danger to liberty had always emanated from the temptation to misuse the powers of government for the benefit of those who controlled it. In darker ages it had been princes and aristocrats who had possessed such power. But in modern, democratic times, the danger seemed to lie in the opposite direction. As Sumner worried, "Now that the governmental machine is brought within everyone's reach the seduction of power is just as masterful over a democratic faction as ever it was over king or barons."

To the laissez-fairist this willingness to enact "class legislation"—to use government power to improve the condition of one group in society at the expense of another, or to alter through state action the relative bargaining positions of laborers and employers or consumers and producers—defined socialism and communism. No matter how limited the interference, the principle was the same. "There are no socialistic schemes . . . which do not upon analysis, turn out to mak[e] those who have share with those who have not," Sumner explained. "If . . . the question is raised, what ought the State to do . . . for a class or an interest, it really is the question . . . . What ought Some-of-us to do for Others-of-us. Or as the great, and by no means reactionary, economist, Francis A. Walker, put it: "I should apply the term 'socialistic' to all efforts, under popular impulse, to enlarge the functions of government, to the diminution of individual initiative and enterprise, for a supposed public good."

As advocates of laissez-faire looked about them, they grew ever gloomier about the prospects for liberty in the United States. "[T]he activity of the State, under the new democractic system, shows itself every year more at the mercy of clamorous factions," Sumner mourned, "and legislators find themselves constantly under greater pressure to act . . . in such a way as to quell clamor." The omens were particularly grim in the teeming and growing cities. "Here the dangerous classes are most numerous and strong, and the effects of flinging the suffrage to the mob are most disastrous," the historian Francis Parkman wrote. In cities democracy "hands over great municipal corporations, the property of those who hold stock in them, to the keeping of greedy and irresponsible crowds controlled by adventurers as reckless as themselves, whose object is nothing but plunder."

Parkman's comments were especially trenchant, but his concern was widely shared. For example, future President James A. Garfield confided to a friend, "It has long been my opinion that universal suffrage is a failure as applied to municipal corporations . . . . The root of the difficulty is this: one naturalized foreigner can by his vote neutralize the vote of A. T. Stewart [the millionarie New York merchant]. Thus two men without a dollar can dispose of the pecuniary interests of a man worth many millions." "Our money is spent and our taxes are laid by insignificant ephemeral creatures," laissez-fairists grieved. Because of the influence of Tammany-style corruptionists upon the ignorant and propertyless mass of urban voters, "the educated and wealthy [man] . . . felt himself as much disfranchised as if he had been excluded from the polls by law." Under such circumstances the taxes levied upon urban property holders took on the character of confiscation, "organized communism and destruction of property under the guise of taxation," Simon Stern called it.

Given such convictions and fears, it was natural that the laissez-fairists should have supported efforts to weaken the power of the political "machines" through reform of the civil service and that they should have sympathized when southern Conservatives used similar arguments to justify the elimination of Negro influence from southern politics.

Even more obvious examples of class legislation, of "socialism" and "communism," were efforts to improve the conditions of labor, either by direct government regulation of the terms of labor contracts or by removing legal obstacles to the right of unions to strike for higher wages or better working conditions. In the former case, for example, restricting the work day to eight hours or banning payment of wages in company scrip, the state plainly was interfering on the behalf of one of the parties to a bargain, insofar as unfettered bargaining based on the supply of and demand for labor would have led to a different outcome. Moreover it was not only, perhaps not primarily, the employer who was being deprived of his rights through the state's intervention. The real loser, according to the laissez-faire theorists, was the worker who would have been willing to work longer hours or accept company scrip in exchange for the job in question. The "lazier" worker had used the power of government to protect himself from the competition of the more diligent.

Modifying conspiracy laws so as to permit effective strikes raised the same objection. A worker or group of workers might have the right to refuse to work for a certain wage or under objectionable conditions, but they could not deprive other workers of the right to accept the terms they had rejected. Nor could they seek to limit access to crafts by requiring apprenticeship before entry. To do either was as much to engage in a combination in restraint of trade as was a conspiracy among producers to raise prices by preventing goods from reaching the market. Government tolerance of such behavior would sanction the grossest kind of private wrong, depriving men of protection for the fundamental right to exchange labor for sustenance. Finally, since most laissez-fairists believed that only a fixed amount of capital was available to employ labor—a wage fund—any artificial rise in the remuneration of one worker had to come at the expense of others.

To seek these goals through political pressure was to promote the most obvious sort of class legislation. To labor reformers' complaints that workers were merely seeking to defend themselves against the political power of monopolistic corporations, laissez-faire analysts responded, "If capital has gained an advantage by special legislation, this is to be counter-balanced, not by special legislation to favor the other side . . . but by earnest united protests against all special legislation." By doing otherwise workers "play into the very hands of monopoly, by following its example. . . . The era of social justice will not be ushered in by those who have nothing better to urge than the old strife of classes for supremacy."

Another piece of plainly class legislation was the "discriminating" income tax, one that exempted incomes below a certain level. Such an act "has no claim to be considered a tax, but is simply confiscation," the laissez-faire tax expert, David A. Wells, expostulated. "[I]f the State may take five per cent from the man with $5,000 income, and ten per cent from the man with more than $5,000, why stop at these limits? . . . Why not take all that such individuals receive in excess of the average income of the masses? . . . The individual proposing such a tax [is], then, in theoretical intent, a communist of the most radical type. . . ." It could be defended, said a congressional opponent, "only . . . on the same ground that the highwayman defends his acts." It was "[c]lass legislation on a tremendous scale."

Laissez-faire libertarians hardly looked more kindly upon what they believed to be farmer efforts to set aside the normal bargaining process that set railroad rates. No matter what the farmers' grievances, "[w]hen the Grangers had once proclaimed that their object was to 'fix rates', or, in other words, to declare by law what proportion of the market value of services they themselves should pay . . . it was perfectly clear that the Granger movement was rank communism," Godkin thundered.

But more crucial than any of these issues were the two that dominated political discourse throughout the late nineteenth century, regulation of the currency and reduction of the protective tariff. It may seem strange today that expounders of laissez-faire liberty identified protectionism with socialism, but one must remember that most of its advocates justified the protective tariff on the grounds that it protected American workers from competition with products made by cheap foreign labor. To Sumner the issue was simple: the protective tariff raised the price everyone had to pay in order to protect those engaged in a particular industry; it was a "question whether the government shall make A give a part of his product to B, to support B in an unproductive industry." The counter-argument that society was obligated to guarantee a worker's "right" to labor for a high wage did not persuade the free traders. "The argument is pretty much that of the communists to this day," they responded. "Would a tariff bill be tolerated for a moment, if its object was declared in the title as 'An act to maintain high wages for a small portion of the people . . . by means of a heavy tax on the remainder' . . . ?" they asked. Do protectionists "believe in communism?" Are they "prepared to say it is within the proper function of government to attempt to fix the rate of wages and to provide specific work for all?"

Laissez-fairists recognized that the primary beneficiaries of the protective tariff were industrialists rather than workers. But that did not vitiate the equivalence between protectionism and socialism. No matter who received its benefits, the protective tariff was "an adoption by the National legislature of the *principle of special legislation*." "Protection differs from communism only in this," Atkinson insisted, "that it attempts to enforce inequitable distribution of our annual product . . . , while communism, or socialism, invokes the force of law under the mistaken idea that a more equitable division may be had . . . ."

The currency question involved the same issues. It was bad enough that the government had turned to the expedient of issuing "greenbacks," legal tender not redeemable in gold, in order to finance the Civil War. Insofar as a debtor paid a creditor in that depreciated currency instead of the gold-backed currency the creditor had expected when he agreed to the contract, the creditor had been forced to loan the government his gold, without any interest. He was left with notes that the government promised to repay in gold at some unspecified date. "It was a direct violation of the law of ownership," one economist complained. "The government took the property of the owner without consent either granted or even asked." When the Treasury Department released another tide of greenbacks in the wake of the Panic of 1873, Atkinson made the same objection. It was "a precedent for a Secretary of the Treasury to collect a forced loan . . . at any time."

Even worse was pressure to issue greenbacks, or later to coin silver, for the direct purpose of stimulating the economy by making debts easier to pay. This was class legislation pure and simple, taking from the creditor and giving to the debtor. "Men ought to be made to pay what they agreed and expected to have to pay," Godkin wrote in the *Nation*. "Their escape from this obligation, through the laxity of the laws, is a great misfortune; but their escape through the connivance . . . of government is a still greater misfortune." Artificial inflation of the currency amounted to a "sanction given by the law to the wholesale cheating by fraudulent debtors." It was "a license . . . to defraud . . . creditors." Laissez-faire opponents of inflation consistently inveighed against the morality, perhaps even more than against the policy, of the proposal. In a typical expression of disgust, Charles Francis Adams, Jr., wrote a friend, "We are now educating ourselves into a nation of swindlers; who, whenever their debts press upon them, ease themselves off by invalidating all existing contracts." For laissez-fairists, only gold was "honest money."

Modern scholars of American legal and intellectual history have not been kind to late nineteenth century laissez-faire spokesmen. Their laissez-faire principles may have been part of a liberal heritage, but the laissez-fairists had forgotten its essence, Sidney Fine concluded. "Those . . . who continued to advocate the laissez-faire brand of liberalism tended to establish economic freedom as an end in itself rather than a means to an end." Louis Hartz, the great historian of American liberalism, charged that the "wealthier, conservative strand" of American liberalism had turned the tenets of the more egalitarian, libertarian strand against its advocates, Whigs masquerading as Democrats, he described them.

But the purpose of the laissez-faire propagandists was not to protect the property of the rich from the ravages of the poor. Their purpose was to preserve liberty. They were convinced of one truth beyond doubt: liberty could not survive in a polity where control of government enabled those in power to secure their interests at the expense of those without. It made control of government too important. It invited strife. It invited corruption. Adams, himself Massachusett's first Commissioner of Railroads, expressed their common conviction when he warned of the dangers inherent in government regulation of the railways: "He who owns the thing knows that he must also own the legislature which regulates the thing. . . . The man who owns will possess himself of the man who regulates." As usual, Sumner expressed it best: "[T]he advocate of interference takes it for granted that he and his associates will have the administration of their legislative device in their own hands. . . . They never appear to remember that the device, when once set up, will itself be the prize of a struggle; that it will serve one set of purposes as well as another, so that after all the only serious question is: who will get it?" To press for legislation to benefit the majority at the expense of those who accumulated capital was suicidal to democracy, Sumner insisted. Unable to resist the will of the majority in a democratic system, capitalists inevitably would try to protect their interests by subverting it. "Modern plutocrats buy their way through elections and legislatures, in the confidence of being able to get powers which will recoup them for all the outlay and yield and ample surplus besides." Plutocracy, the "political form in which the real controlling force is wealth," "the most sordid and debasing form of political energy known to us," not an ideal, egalitarian society, was the inevitable consequent to class legislation. This was what was "new and threatening" and "the issue which menaces modern society."

Throughout his life Sumner feared that the great threat to liberty emanated from below, from the subversion of democratic liberty that would follow the demand for class legislation on behalf of the have-nots. But most laissez-fairists perceived the danger as running the other way. It was the unfair advantages sought by the rich and powerful that taught workers and farmers to turn to government to promote their interests. Commenting on the railroads, even the rigidly laissez-faire economist Julian Sturtevant observed, "Surely while these great companies set so stupendous an example of combination to resist competition, no one should be surprised that their employees combine for higher wages, and that everywhere strikes are of frequent occurrence. Such examples in high places are very likely to be followed." When Massachusetts bankers persuaded their state legislature to stay debt collections during a liquidity crisis in 1878, Henry Adams called it "infamous"—"as flagrant a breach of faith as was ever sanctioned by a legislature." It overshadows the western granger legislation," he exploded. Sumner inveighed against efforts to subsidize the restoration of the American shipbuilding and shipping industry. It was the demand of the rich and powerful for special legislation that inspired similar demands by others. Since "the mass of the people . . . perceive that some are made richer by means of one statute, they infer that others may gain either high wages or leisure, or some other desirable end, by the enactment of another statute," Edward Atkinson explained.

Nowhere was this more apparent than in capitalists' pressure to maintain protective tariffs. Of all the special legislation sought and acquired by business interests, the protective tariff was the most colossal fraud. Repudiating the fiction that the tariff was designed to protect the wages of American workers, its laissez-faire opponents characterized it as "the aggrandizement of capital by law," an abuse of the taxing power by special legislation. Laissez-faire reformers warned capitalists that protectionism was the parent of socialism. "It is a significant fact that the agitation of the labor question in this country comes most urgently from persons employed in those branches of occupation which are most affected by a protective tariff." Atkinson observed. "It cannot but be obvious to . . . workers that many of their employers have thus gained wealth by force of law." "Both grow in the same soil," another free trade advocate insisted. "[T]he common conditions for the existence of both . . . are to be found in the doctrine of State aid and governmental interference." Exasperated by the failure of such logic to shake capitalists' commitment to the protective system, Sumner fumed, "The English land-owners [who fought repeal of the Corn Laws] were no whit worse than American manufacturers."

To what we might call laissez-faire libertarians, all these instances of special legislation, whether to promote the interests of businessmen, or farmers, or laborers, were of a piece. "Whether they are paper-money schemes, tariff schemes, subsidy schemes, internal improvement schemes, or usury laws, they all have this in common with the most vulgar of the communist projects," Sumner wrote, "and the errors of this sort in the past which have been committed in the interest of the capitalist class now furnish precedents, illustration and encouragement for the new category of demands."

The laissez-faire concept of liberty became the common currency among the elite in the United States. It formed the basis upon which discussions of liberty proceeded. Inevitably it made a tremendous impact upon lawyers and judges, and their arguments and decisions are redolent of its concepts. But the widespread acceptance of laissez-faire notions of liberty must be attributed, at least in part, to the fact that its major thrust, hostility to "special" and "class" legislation, was already ingrained in American law and political theory. . . .

V. Symbiosis: Laissez-Faire Constitutionalism

In the 1850s the focus of American legislation slowly began to shift from promotion of economic development towards greater regulation of that development. As a consequence, lawyers launched an ever-increasing number of attacks upon laws that they claimed exceeded legislative power. Some of these challenged regulations involved morals; but more and more involved some degree of redistribution of resources. Lawyers challenged prohibition statutes, early zoning-type regulations, special assessments, disaster relief, public payment of Civil War draftees' commutation fees, tax exemptions and subsidies for businesses, and railroad regulations.

The judicial response is instructive. In those cases where counsel complained merely that legislation was a "retrospective" violation of "vested rights," that is, that it made it illegal to hold property that was legal when acquired, judges nearly always sustained the legislative power. Thus only the courts of Indiana and New York ruled prohibition unconstitutional. Other judges sustained it as a health and moral measure well within the police power. Likewise, courts sustained ordinances restricting the operation of dangerous, unsanitary, or entertainment-oriented businesses to certain locations. But in these cases there was no suggestion of "class legislation," no clear transfer of property or its benefits from one portion of the community to another. Judges were far less sympathetic to legislation where such a transfer could be demonstrated.

The famous *Slaughterhouse Cases* had elements of both. The challenged law was designed to protect public health by establishing a single slaughterhouse for the use of New Orleans' butchers, away from residential areas. But it authorized a single company of seventeen incorporators to build it and its appurtenances. The butchers would be forced to rent facilities from them. The butchers "claim an interest, a privilege, a property, in their labor, and the faculty of applying their labor in useful occupations; of which they cannot be deprived for the profit or gain of other persons or corporations," their counsel, former Supreme Court Justice John Archibald Campbell, insisted. Their business "by this Act . . . has been converted into a *Monopoly* for the benefit of *Seventeen selected* persons." As is well known, the Supreme Court sustained the law by the narrowest possible majority, with the dissenters deeming it unconstitutional both as a violation of the privileges and immunities of citizens of the United States and as a deprivation of liberty and property without due process of law.

In other cases the transfer of property from one group to another was even plainer, and in those cases judges by the 1860s were establishing the clear foundations of laissez-faire constitutionalism and, more slowly, substantive due process of law. For example, several states permitted local communities to levy taxes to pay commutation fees that would enable their young men to escape the draft. But in the opinion of many judges, such a tax was too clearly an imposition on the taxpayers of the community for the benefit of a smaller class. The commutation fee was really a penalty for refusing to serve, a Maine judge explained as he concurred in ruling such laws unconstitutional. "A tax for such purpose is not only a tax on A. for the benefit of B., but it is also a tax on A. to reimburse B. the amount of the penalty."

Special assessments for local improvements raised similar problems. Did not the whole community get the benefit at the expense of those assessed? That concern led the New Jersey courts to impose a strict requirement that local government compensate the difference between an assessment and the actual value of the improvement to those assessed. Finally in 1874 they ruled unconstitutional all frontage assessments for street improvements. The New York courts, on the other hand, regularly sustained special assessments, holding that "there is nothing in the Constitution of this State, which requires taxation to be general . . . or that it shall be equal. . . ." But by 1872 the weight of anti-class legislation legal opinion forced a *caveat*. When residents of Brockport challenged a law requiring them alone to pay for a normal school open to all state residents, the Court of Appeals sustained the law, citing earlier recognition of expansive state taxing power. However, the judges added, "It would be going too far to deny that the provisions of the Constitution, which declare that no person shall be deprived of property without due process of law, and that property shall be taken for public use upon just compensation, would afford no protection to the citizen against impositions made nominally in the form of taxes, but which were in fact forced levies upon individuals or confiscations of private property . . . to pay for benefits conferred upon others who bore no proportion of the burden."

But it was subsidies for private businesses that were most likely to offend judges' constitutional sensibilities, and they were among the first to be overturned in a large number of jurisdictions. Such subsidies of millers, manufacturers, and railroad companies blurred the line "between what is for public and governmental, and what is for private purposes, between general legislation for the whole people and special for the individual," Maine's Supreme Court warned. "If it were proposed to pass an act enabling the inhabitants of the several towns by vote to transfer the farms or the horses or oxen . . . from the rightful owner or owners to some manufacturer whom the majority might select, the monstrousness of such proposed legislation would be transparent. But the mode by which the property would be taken from one or many and given to another or others can make no difference in the principle." Maine's constitution forbade the deprivation of one's property except by "judgment of his peers or the law of the land," the court pointed out. "Property taken by taxation is not taken by the judgment of our peers. A statute in direct violation of the primary principles of justice is not 'the law of the land' within the meaning of the constitution." "[T]hough the money demand of the citizen is called a tax, it is not such," wrote Iowa's Judge John F. Dillon in ruling Iowa's railroad subsidy law unconstitutional. It "is, in fact, a coercive contribution in favor of private railway corporations, and violative, not only of the general spirit of the [Iowa] Constitution . . . , but of that specific provision which declares *that no man shall be deprived of his property without due process of law.*"

In 1863, as lawyers and judges ever more clearly linked the concept of "class" or "special legislation" to that of "due process of law," Thomas McIntyre Cooley, the locofoco Democrat-turned-Republican, published his immensely influential *Treatise on Constitutional Limitations.* That treatise made him "the principal contributor to the cause of constitutional laissez-faire in the era following the Civil War," scholars have agreed.

Cooley gathered together and organized the disparate cases in which judges had applied different specific constitutional prohibitions in order to protect vested rights from retrospective and class legislation. Despite his own stress upon enforcing such prohibitions with restraint, he provided judges with a catalogue of justifications for restriction of state power. His treatise was by no means designed to protect special interests from government regulation. Far from it. Two years after its appearance, Cooley suggested his real animus when as a justice of the Michigan Supreme Court he used its principles not to sustain but to reject the power of states to subsidize private corporations. "[W]hen the State once enters upon the business of subsidies, the strong and powerful are most likely to control legislation, and . . . the weaker will be taxed to enhance the profits of the stronger," he wrote.

Nonetheless, Cooley's *Treatise on Constitutional Limitations* merits Benjamin R. Twiss's description as "almost . . . a direct counter" in the world of law "to the appearance of Karl Marx's *Das Kapital.*" After all, the heart of *Das Kapital,* and of socialism, is the conviction that class warfare is inevitable and that control of the institutions of the state is its object until the final victory of the proletariat and establishment of socialism makes it irrelevant to the social order; the heart of Cooley's *Treatise,* and of laissez-faire constitutionalism, was opposition to class and special legislation. State subsidies were illicit no matter who they were intended to benefit, weak or powerful, Cooley insisted from the Michigan court's bench. "[T]he discrimination . . . is an invasion of the equality of right and privilege which is a maxim in State government. . . . [I]t is not the business of the State to make discriminations in favor of one class against another."

Cooley's views are emblematic of the symbiotic relationship between the concept of rights articulated by laissez-faire propagandists in the Gilded Age and the legal and political heritage of hostility towards "class legislation" which seemed to sanction their views. The attacks that laissez-fairists levied upon "class legislation" in post–Civil War America resonated with principles already deeply embedded in American legal thought. Inevitably, the two merged. When John F. Dillon, now federal judge and American Bar Association president, described the income tax as "a forced contribution from the rich to the poor" and "class legislation of the most pronounced and vicious type" he was not only engaging in a laissez-faire polemic; he was calling for judicial intervention against any proposal so manifestly "violative of the constitutional rights of the property owner."

Ultimately, the courts responded to this sort of appeal, made in speech after speech, legal and popular article after article, legal brief after brief. It would require a new essay to discuss how courts, both state and national, slowly came to do so. That is a study that wants doing, and which requires far more than the traditional account of the progression from *Slaughterhouse* and *Munn* to *Lochner*, by way of the Mississippi and Minnesota rate cases, *Smyth* v. *Ames*, and *Allgeyer* v. *Louisiana*.

However, it should be clear from the foregoing that when the courts did respond, they did not simply spin the doctrine of "substantive due process of law" and the other underpinnings of laissez-faire constitutionalism out of thin air, in order to protect the position of the privileged. They responded because they perceived "class legislation" where a new generation would see laws designed to benefit everyone. An American heritage of liberty dictated revulsion against such enactments, and a concept of "due process of law" that had been developing for almost a century seemed to provide a sanction against them.

⊹ *F U R T H E R   R E A D I N G*

Loren Beth, *The Development of the American Constitution, 1877–1917* (1971)
———, "The Slaughterhouse Cases," *Louisiana Law Review* 23 (1963): 487–505
Gerald Eggert, "Richard Olney and the Income Tax Cases," *Mississippi Valley Historical Review* 48 (1961): 24–41
Sidney Fine, *Laissez-Faire and the General-Welfare State* (1956)
Richard Hofstadter, *The Age of Reform* (1955)
William Letwin, *Law and Economic Policy in America: The Evolution of the Sherman Antitrust Act* (1965)
Charles McCurdy, "The *Knight* Sugar Decision of 1895 and the Modernization of American Corporate Law, 1869–1903," *Business History Review* 53 (1979): 304–342
William E. Nelson, *The Fourteenth Amendment: From Political Principle to Judicial Doctrine* (1988)
Mary Cornelia Porter, "That Commerce Shall Be Free: A New Look at the Old Laissez-Faire Court," *Supreme Court Review* (1979): 135–159
Harry N. Scheiber, "The Road to *Munn:* Eminent Domain and the Concept of Public Purpose in the State Courts," *Perspectives in American History* 5 (1971): 329–404
John Semonche, *Charting the Future: The Supreme Court Responds to a Changing Society, 1890–1920* (1978)
William F. Swindler, *Court and Constitution in the Twentieth Century: The Old Legality, 1889–1932* (1968)
Christopher L. Tomlins, *The State and the Unions: Labor Relations, Law, and the Organized Labor Movement, 1880–1960* (1985)

Paternalistic Sexism and Liberty to Contract, 1873–1923

Conservative legal commentators joined with business leaders in the late nineteenth century to oppose any use of the police power that interfered with their economic interests. This opposition took constitutional expression in the doctrines of substantive due process of law and liberty to contract.

Through most of the nineteenth century, due process had essentially one meaning: procedural. The due-process provisions in state constitutions and the Fifth and Fourteenth amendments to the federal Constitution provided that every person was entitled to an orderly proceeding that afforded an opportunity to be heard and to be protected in his or her rights. Due process also acquired a substantive meaning, however, one that derived from the old doctrine of vested rights. Substantive due process meant that there existed an irreducible sum of rights that was vested in the individual and with which government could not arbitrarily interfere. In short, there were substantive, not just procedural, limitations on the legislature's exercise of the police powers.

By the mid-1890s the doctrine emerged full-blown. It was, first of all, antiredistributive. State and federal courts held that certain kinds of regulatory legislation could so affect property as to amount to a violation of individual (or corporate) rights. When courts acted to overturn such legislation, they invariably favored the wealthy over the poor, and capital over labor. Substantive due process had another dimension, which was not exclusively, or even predominantly, aimed at protecting the rich. The courts invoked this dimension to void special, or class, legislation—measures that clearly favored one group over another. Many of the pertinent decisions involved businesses competing with one another rather than poor individuals fighting to resist the rich and powerful.

Substantive due process also reinforced the concept of liberty to contract, which had its roots in the free-labor ideology of the pre–Civil War era. The doctrine of free labor flourished among northern Republicans, who widely claimed that democracy depended on men and women who were free to work

*where and for whom they wanted, free to seek the best wages and working con-
ditions they could attain, and free to move wherever they wished. Substantive
due process of law turned one's "free" labor into a property right to make
whatever arrangements one wanted with an employer. Such a "right" presumed a degree of equality in bargaining over the terms and conditions of employment that did not exist, however, in an industrial marketplace dominated by
capital rather than labor.*

*Liberty to contract created tension with another nineteenth-century cultural
assumption—that women were physically inferior to men and that as the mothers of future generations they required special legislative protection. Antebellum
free-labor ideology excluded women, of course, but their entry into the work
force after the Civil War stirred debate about their legal status. If the state protected them but not men, then the assumptions behind liberty to contract were
suspect. If lawmakers treated women as men's equals, however, they threatened
the structure on which gender relations rested.*

⊕ D O C U M E N T S

Christopher J. Tiedeman, a professor of law at the University of Missouri, was a
doctrinaire critic of the police power. In his most renowned work, *A Treatise on
the Limitations of Police Power in the United States*, parts of which are excerpted
as the first document, Tiedeman urged judges to construe that power narrowly.
State and federal judges translated Tiedeman's notions into decisions, of which
Ritchie v. *The People* (1895), the second document, was among the most famous.
Judge Benjamin D. Magruder of the Illinois Supreme Court struck down a law
that prohibited the employment of women in workshops or factories for more
than eight hours a day or forty-eight hours a week. Substantive due process
triumphed in the Supreme Court in *Allgeyer* v. *Louisiana* (1897), the third
document.

A year later, however, the Court signaled a willingness to take the new industrial conditions into account when weighing state protective legislation. In *Holden* v. *Hardy*, the fourth document, the justices upheld by a 7–2 vote a Utah law
that provided for the health and safety of workers in dangerous industries, such as
mining smelters. This new standard did not prevent the justices from invoking
substantive due process and freedom to contract to strike down state legislation
where the danger to workers, while real, was less palpable. *Lochner* v. *New York*
(1905), the fifth document, involved Joseph Lochner, a baker who objected to a
New York State statute prohibiting the employment of workers in bakeries for
more than ten hours a day and sixty hours a week. A sharply divided Court
struck the measure down, provoking Justice Oliver Wendell Holmes, Jr., to issue
one of the Court's most famous dissents.

The year following *Lochner*, Samuel Gompers, the founder of the American
Federation of Labor, asserted that married women should not work; see the sixth
selection. Such paternalism blended with arguments by Progressive reformers in
support of protective legislation for women. Josephine Goldmark, of the National
Consumers' League, a Progressive reform group, joined with Louis Brandeis to
prepare a new kind of legal brief, one that stressed the social, psychological, and
economic necessity of legislation rather than its particular legal qualities. Brandeis's almost one-hundred-page brief, reprinted as the seventh document, defended an Oregon statute that established a ten-hour workday for women. In

Muller v. *Oregon* (1908), the eighth document, Justice David J. Brewer's opinion, part of which is excerpted as the ninth document, added a thick layer of paternalism to Brandeis's brief in sustaining the statute. Roscoe Pound, the Dean of Harvard Law School, argued in a 1909 article in the *Yale Law Journal*, document 10, that individual rights, when threatened by uneven bargaining power, could be protected only through state intervention.

The notion of freedom to contract persisted, however, surfacing once again in *Adkins* v. *Children's Hospital* (1923), the last document. Justice George Sutherland's opinion not only rested on the due-process clause of the Fourteenth Amendment but drew strength from the recent passage of the Nineteenth Amendment, granting women the vote. Protective legislation like that in the District of Columbia, Sutherland observed, undermined the freedom of women. Justice Sutherland proclaimed that freedom to contract in the economic arena was a corollary of genuine political equality. Was he right?

Legal Scholar Christopher G. Tiedeman on the Limitations of Police Power, 1886

. . . The private rights of the individual, apart from a few statutory rights, which when compared with the whole body of private rights are insignificant in number, do not rest upon the mandate of municipal law as a source. They belong to man in a state of nature; they are natural rights, rights recognized and existing in the law of reason. But the individual, in a state of nature, finds in the enjoyment of his own rights that he transgresses the rights of others. Nature wars upon nature, when subjected to no spiritual or moral restraint. The object of government is to impose that degree of restraint upon human actions, which is necessary to the uniform and reasonable conservation and enjoyment of private rights. Government and municipal law protect and develop, rather than create, private rights. The conservation of private rights is attained by the imposition of a wholesome restraint upon their exercise, such a restraint as will prevent the infliction of injury upon others in the enjoyment of them; it involves a provision of means for enforcing the legal maxim, which enunciates the fundamental rule of both the human and the natural law, *sic utere tuo, ut alienum non lædas* [use your own property in such a way as not to injure another's]. The power of the government to impose this restraint is called POLICE POWER. By this "general police power of the State, persons and property are subjected to all kinds of restraints and burdens, in order to secure the general comfort, health and prosperity of the State; of the perfect right in the legislature to do which no question ever was or upon acknowledged general principles ever can be made, so far as natural persons are concerned." Blackstone defines the police power to be "the due regulation and domestic order of the kingdom, whereby the inhabitants of a State, like members of a well-governed family, are bound to conform their general behavior to the rules of propriety, good neighborhood and good manners, and to be decent, industrious and inoffensive in their respective stations." . . . The continental jurists include, under the term *Police Power*, not only those restraints upon private rights which are imposed for the general welfare of all, but also all the governmental institutions, which are established with public funds for the better promotion of the public good, and the alleviation of private want and suffering. Thus they would include the power of the government to expend the public moneys in the construction and repair of roads, the establishment of hospitals and asylums and colleges, in short, the power to supplement the results of individual activity with what individual activity can not accomplish. "The governmental provision for the public security and welfare in its daily necessities, that provision which establishes the needful and necessary, and therefore appears as a bidding and forbidding power of the State, is the scope and character of the police." But in the present connection, as may be gathered from the American definitions heretofore given, the term must be confined to the imposition of restraints and burdens upon persons and property. The power of the government to embark in enterprises of public charity and benefit can only be limited by the restrictions upon the power of taxation, and to that extent alone can these subjects in American law be said to fall within the police power of the State.

It is to be observed, therefore, that the police power of the government, as understood in the constitutional law of the United States, is simply the power of the government to establish provisions for the enforcement of the common as well as civil-law maxim, *sic utere tuo, ut alienum non lædas.* . . . Any law which goes beyond that principle, which undertakes to abolish rights, the exercise of which does not involve an infringement of the rights of others, or to limit the exercise of rights beyond what is necessary to provide for the public welfare and the general security, cannot be included in the police power of the government. It is a governmental usurpation, and violates the principles of abstract justice, as they have been developed under our republican institutions. . . .

30. Personal Liberty—How Guaranteed

It is altogether needless in this connection to indulge in a panegyric upon the blessings of guaranteed personal liberty. The love of liberty, of freedom from irksome and unlawful restraints, is implanted in every human breast. In the American Declaration of Independence, and in the bills of rights of almost every State constitution, we find that personal liberty is expressly guaranteed to all men equally. But notwithstanding the existence of these fundamental and constitutional guaranties of personal liberty, the astounding anomaly of the slavery of an entire race in more than one-third of the States of the American Union, during three-fourths of a century of national existence, gave the lie to their own constitutional declarations, that "*all* men are endowed by their Creator, with certain inalienable rights, among which are the right to life, liberty, and the pursuit of happiness." But, happily, this contradiction is now a thing of the past, and in accordance with the provisions of the thirteenth amendment to the constitution of the United States, it is now the fundamental and practically unchangeable law of the land, that "neither slavery nor involuntary servitude, except as a punishment for crime whereof the party shall have been duly convicted, shall exist within the United States, or any place subject to their jurisdiction.

But to a practical understanding of the effect of these constitutional guaranties, a clear idea of what personal liberty consists is necessary. It is not to be confounded with a license to do what one pleases. Liberty, according to Montesquieu, consists "only in the power of doing what we ought to will, and in not being constrained to do what we ought not to will." No man has a right to make such a use of his liberty as to commit an injury to the rights of others. His liberty is controlled by the oft quoted maxim, *sic utere tuu, ut alienum non lædas.* Indeed liberty is that amount of personal freedom, which is consistent with a strict obedience to this rule. . . . While liberty does not consist in a paucity of laws, still it is only consistent with a limitation of the restrictive laws to those which exercise a wholesome restraint. "That man is free who is protected from injury," and his protection involves necessarily the restraint of other individuals from the commission of the injury. In the proper balancing of the contending interests of individuals, personal liberty is secured and developed; any further restraint is unwholesome and subversive of liberty. As Herbert Spencer has expressed it, "every man may claim the fullest liberty to exercise his faculties compatible with the possession of like liberty by every other man."

The constitutional guaranties are generally unqualified, and a strict construction of them would prohibit all limitations upon liberty, if any other meaning but the limited one here presented were given to the word. But these guaranties are to be liberally construed, so that the object of them may be fully attained. They do not prohibit the exercise of police power in restraint of licentious trespass upon the rights of others, but the restrictive measures must be kept within these limits. "Powers, which can be justified only on this specific ground (that they are police regulations), and which would otherwise be clearly prohibited by the constitution, can be such only as are so clearly necessary to the safety, comfort and well-being of society, or so imperatively required by the public necessity, as to lead to the rational and satisfactory conclusion that the framers of the constitution could not, as men of ordinary prudence and foresight, have intended to prohibit their exercise in the particular case, notwithstanding the language of the prohibition would otherwise include it."

The restrictions upon personal liberty, permissible under these constitutional limitations, are either of a public or private nature. In consequence of the mental and physical disabilities of certain classes, in the law of domestic relations, their liberty is more or less subjected to restraint, the motive being their own benefit. These restraints are of a private nature, imposed under the law by private persons who stand in domestic relation to those whose liberty is restrained. . . . In this connection we are only concerned with those restraints which are of a public nature, *i.e.,* those which are imposed by government. They may be subdivided under the following headings: 1. The police control of the criminal classes. 2. The police control of dangerous classes, other than by criminal prosecutions. 3. The regulation of domicile and citizenship. 4. Police control of morality and religion. 5. Police regulation of the freedom of speech and of the press. 6. Police regulation of trades and professions.

Ritchie v. *The People,* 155 Ill. 106 (1895)

. . . Mr. Justice Magruder delivered the opinion of the court.

Upon complaint of the factory inspector appointed under the law hereinafter named, a warrant was issued by a justice of the peace of Cook County against plaintiff in error, and, upon his appearance and waiver in writing of jury trial, a trial was had resulting in a finding of guilty, and the imposition of a fine of $5.00, and costs. The complaint charged that, on a certain day in February, 1894, plaintiff in error employed a certain adult female of the age of more than eighteen years to work in a factory for more than eight hours during said day. The plaintiff in error took an appeal to the Criminal Court of Cook County, and waived a jury, and upon trial in that court before the judge without a jury, he was convicted and fined. The case is brought to this Court by writ of error for the purpose of reviewing such judgment of the Criminal Court. . . .

The present prosecution, as is conceded by counsel on both sides, is for an alleged violation of section 5 of said Act [to regulate the manufacture of clothing]. That section is as follows: "No female shall be employed in any factory or workshop more than eight hours in any one day or forty-eight hours in any one week.". . .

The main objection urged against the Act, and that to which the discussion of counsel on both sides is chiefly directed, relates to the validity of section 5. It is contended by counsel for plaintiff in error, that that section is unconstitutional as imposing unwarranted restrictions upon the right to contract. On the other hand, it is claimed by counsel for the People, that the act is a sanitary provision, and justifiable as an exercise of the police power of the State.

Does the provision in question restrict the right to contract? The words, "no female shall be employed," import action on the part of two persons. There must be a person who does the act of employing, and a person who consents to the act of being employed. Webster defines employment as not only "the act of employing," but "also the state of being employed." The prohibition of the statute is, therefore, twofold, first, that no manufacturer, or proprietor of a factory or workshop, shall employ any female therein more than eight hours in one day, and, second, that no female shall consent to be so employed. It thus prohibits employer and employee from uniting their minds, or agreeing, upon any longer service during one day than eight hours. In other words, they are prohibited, the one from contracting to employ, and the other from contracting to be employed, otherwise than as directed. "To be 'employed' in anything means not only the act of doing it, but also to be engaged to do it; to be under contract or orders to do it."
. . . Hence, a direction, that a person shall not be employed more than a specified number of hours in one day, is at the same time a direction, that such person shall not be under contract to work for more than a specified

number of hours in one day. It follows, that section 5 does limit and restrict the right of the manufacturer and his employee to contract with each other in reference to the hours of labor.

Is the restriction thus imposed an infringement upon the constitutional rights of the manufacturer and the employee? Section 2 of article 2 of the constitution of Illinois provides, that "no person shall be deprived of life, liberty or property, without due process of law." A number of cases have arisen within recent years in which the courts have had occasion to consider this provision, or one similar to it, and its meaning has been quite clearly defined. The privilege of contracting is both a liberty and property right. . . . Liberty includes the right to acquire property, and that means and includes the right to make and enforce contracts. . . . The right to use, buy and sell property and contract in respect thereto is protected by the constitution. Labor is property, and the laborer has the same right to sell his labor, and to contract with reference thereto, as has any other property owner. In this country the legislature has no power to prevent persons who are *sui juris* from making their own contracts, nor can it interfere with the freedom of contract between the workman and the employer. The right to labor or employ labor, and make contracts in respect thereto upon such terms as may be agreed upon between the parties, is included in the constitutional guaranty above quoted. . . . The protection of property is one of the objects for which free governments are instituted among men. . . . The right to acquire, possess and protect property includes the right to make reasonable contracts. . . . And when an owner is deprived of one of the attributes of property, like the right to make contracts, he is deprived of his property within the meaning of the constitution. . . . The fundamental rights of Englishmen, brought to this country by its original settlers and wrested from time to time in the progress of history from the sovereigns of the English nation, have been reduced by Blackstone to three principal or primary articles: "the right of personal security, the right of personal liberty, and the right of private property." . . . The right to contract is the only way by which a person can rightfully acquire property by his own labor. "Of all the 'rights of persons' it is the most essential to human happiness." . . .

This right to contract, which is thus included in the fundamental rights of liberty and property, cannot be taken away "without due process of law." The words: "due process of law:" have been held to be synonymous with the words: "law of the land." . . . Blackstone says: "The third absolute right, inherent in every Englishman, is that of property, which consists in the free use, enjoyment and disposal of all his acquisitions, without any control or diminution, save only by the laws of the land." . . . The "law of the land" is "general public law binding upon all the members of the community, under all circumstances, and not partial or private laws, affecting the rights of private individuals or classes of individuals." . . . The "law of the land" is the opposite of "arbitrary, unequal and partial legislation." . . . The legislature has no right to deprive one class of persons of privileges allowed to other persons under like conditions. The man, who is forbidden to acquire and enjoy property in the same manner in which the rest of the community is permitted to acquire and enjoy it, is deprived of liberty in particulars of primary importance to his pursuit of happiness. If one man is denied the right to contract as he has hitherto done under the law, and as others are still allowed to do by the law, he is deprived of both liberty and property to the extent to which he is thus deprived of such right. In line with these principles, it has been held that it is not competent, under the constitution, for the legislature to single out owners and employers of a particular class, and provide that they shall bear burdens not imposed on other owners of property or employers of labor, and prohibit them from making contracts which other owners or employers are permitted to make. . . .

We are not unmindful, that the right to contract may be subject to limitations growing out of the duties which the individual owes to society, to the public or to the government. These limitations are sometimes imposed by the obligation to so use one's own as not to injure another, by the character of property as affected with a public interest or devoted to a public use, by the demands of public policy or the necessity of protecting the public from fraud or injury, by the want of capacity, by the needs of the necessitous borrower as against the demands of the extortionate lender. But the power of the legislature to thus limit the right to contract must rest upon some reasonable basis, and cannot be arbitrarily exercised. It has been said, that such power is based in every case on some condition, and not on the absolute right to control. Where legislative enactments, which operate upon classes of individuals only, have been held to be valid, it has been where the classification was reasonable, and not arbitrary. . . .

Applying these principles to the consideration of section 5, we are led irresistibly to the conclusion, that it is an unconstitutional and void enactment. While some of the language of the Act is broad enough to embrace within its terms the manufacture of all kinds of goods or products, other provisions are limited to the manufacture of "coats, vests, trousers, knee-pants, overalls, cloaks, shirts, ladies' waists, purses, feathers, artificial flowers or cigars, or any wearing apparel of any kind whatsoever." The Act is entitled "An Act to regulate the manufacture of clothing, wearing apparel and other articles," etc. Under the rule of construction heretofore laid down by this Court, that general and specific words, which are capable of an analogous meaning, being associated together, take color from each other, so that the general words are restricted to a sense analogous to the less general, it would seem that the general words: "and other articles:" should be restricted to a meaning analogous to the meaning of the words: "clothing, wearing apparel:" and, consequently, that they would only embrace articles of the same kind as those expressly enumerated. . . . But whether this is so, or not, we are inclined to regard the Act as one which is partial and discriminating in its character. If it be construed as applying only to manufacturers of clothing, wearing apparel and articles of a similar nature, we can see no reasonable ground for prohibiting such manufacturers and their employees from contracting for more than eight hours of work in one day, while other manufacturers and their employees are not forbidden to so contract. If the Act be construed as applying to manufacturers of all kinds of products, there is no good reason why the prohibition should be directed against manufacturers and their employees, and not against merchants, or builders, or contractors, or carriers, or farmers, or persons engaged in other branches of industry, and their employees therein. Women, employed by manufacturers, are forbidden by section 5 to make contracts to labor longer than eight hours in a day, while women employed as saleswomen in stores, or as domestic servants, or as book-keepers, or stenographers, or type-writers, or in laundries, or other occupations not embraced under the head of manufacturing, are at liberty to contract for as many hours of labor in a day as they choose. The manner, in which the section thus discriminates against one class of employers and employees and in favor of all others, places it in opposition to the constitutional guaranties hereinbefore discussed, and so renders it invalid.

But aside from its partial and discriminating character, this enactment is a purely arbitrary restriction upon the fundamental right of the citizen to control his or her own time and faculties. It substitutes the judgment of the legislature for the judgment of the employer and employee in a matter about which they are competent to agree with each other. It assumes to dictate to what extent the capacity to labor may be exercised by the employee, and takes away the right of private judgment as to the amount and duration of the labor to be put forth in a specified period. When the legislature thus undertakes to impose an unreasonable and unnecessary burden upon any one citizen or class of citizens, it transcends the authority entrusted to it by the constitution, even though it imposes the same burden upon all other citizens or classes of citizens. General laws may be as tyrannical as partial laws. A distinguished writer upon constitutional limitations has said, that general rules may sometimes be as obnoxious as special, if they operate to deprive individual citizens of vested rights, and that, while every man has a right to require that his own controversies shall be judged by the same rules which are applied in the controversies of his neighbors, the whole community is also entitled, at all times, to demand the protection of the ancient principles which shield private rights against arbitrary interference, even though such interference may be under a rule impartial in its operation. (Cooley on Cons. Lim.—5 ed.—top page 434, marg. page 355. . . .) Section 1 of article 2 of the constitution of Illinois provides as follows: "All men are by nature free and independent, and have certain inherent and inalienable rights; among these are life, liberty and the pursuit of happiness. To secure these rights and the protection of property, governments are instituted among men, deriving their just powers from the consent of the governed." Liberty, as has already been stated, includes the right to make contracts, as well with reference to the amount and duration of labor to be performed, as concerning any other lawful matter. Hence, the right to make contracts is an inherent and inalienable one, and any attempt to unreasonably abridge it is opposed to the constitution. . . .

But it is claimed on behalf of defendant in error, that this section can be sustained as an exercise of the police power of the State. The police power of the State is that power which enables it to promote the health, comfort, safety and welfare of society. It is very broad and far reaching, but is not without its limitations. Legislative acts passed in pursuance of it must not be in conflict with the constitution, and must have some relation to the ends sought to be accomplished; that is to say, to the comfort, welfare or safety of society. Where the ostensible object of an enactment is to secure the public comfort, welfare or safety, it must appear to be adapted to that end; it cannot invade the rights of person and property under the guise of a mere police regulation, when it is not such in fact; and where such an act takes away the property of a citizen or interferes with his personal liberty, it is the province of the Courts to determine whether it is really an appropriate measure for the promotion of the comfort, safety and welfare of society. . . .

There is nothing in the title of the Act of 1893 to indicate that it is a sanitary measure. . . .

It is not the nature of the things done, but the sex of the persons doing them, which is made the basis of the claim that the Act is a measure for the promotion of the public health. It is sought to sustain the Act as an exercise of the police power upon the alleged ground, that it is designed to protect woman on account of her sex and physique. It will not be denied, that woman is entitled to the same rights, under the constitution, to make contracts with reference to her labor as are secured thereby to men. The first section of the fourteenth amendment to the constitution of the United States provides: "No State shall make or enforce any law which shall abridge the privileges or immunities of citizens of the United States, nor shall any State deprive *any person* of life, liberty or property without due process of law, nor deny to any person within its jurisdiction the equal protection of the law." It has been held that a woman is both a "citizen" and a "person" within the meaning of this section. . . . The privileges and immunities here referred to are, in general, "protection by the government, with the right to acquire and possess property of every kind, and to pursue and obtain happiness and safety, subject, nevertheless, to such restraints as the government may prescribe for the general good of the whole." (*Slaughter House cases.* . . .) As a citizen, woman has the right to acquire and possess property of every kind. As a "person," she has the right to claim the benefit of the constitutional provision that she shall not be deprived of life, liberty or property without due process of law. Involved in these rights thus guaranteed to her is the right to make and enforce contracts. The law accords to her, as to every other citizen, the natural right to gain a livelihood by intelligence, honesty and industry in the arts, the sciences, the professions or other vocations. Before the law, her right to a choice of vocations cannot be said to be denied or abridged on account of sex. . . .

The tendency of legislation in this State has been to recognize the rights of woman in the particulars here specified. The Act of 1867, as above quoted, by the use of the words, "he or she," plainly declares that no woman shall be prevented by anything therein contained from working as many hours overtime or extra hours as she may agree; and thereby recognizes her right to contract for more than eight hours of work in one day. An Act approved

March 22, 1872, entitled "An Act to secure freedom in the selection of an occupation," etc., provides that "no person shall be precluded or debarred from any occupation, profession or employment (except military) on account of sex." . . . The Married Woman's Act of 1874 authorizes a married woman to sue and be sued without joining her husband, and provides that contracts may be made and liabilities incurred by her and enforced against her to the same extent and in the same manner as if she were unmarried, and that she may receive, use and possess her own earnings, and sue for the same in her own name, free from the interference of her husband, or his creditors. . . .

Section 5 of the Act of 1893 is broad enough to include married women and adult single women, as well as minors. As a general thing, it is the province of the legislature to determine what regulations are necessary to protect the public health and secure the public safety and welfare. But inasmuch as sex is no bar, under the constitution and the law, to the endowment of woman with the fundamental and inalienable rights of liberty and property which include the right to make her own contracts, the mere fact of sex will not justify the legislature in putting forth the police power of the State for the purpose of limiting her exercise of those rights, unless the courts are able to see, that there is some fair, just and reasonable connection between such limitation and the public health, safety or welfare proposed to be secured by it. . . .

Our conclusion is, that section 5 of the Act of 1893, and the first clause of section 10 thereof, are void and unconstitutional for the reasons here stated. These are the only portions of the Act, which have been attacked in the argument of counsel. No reason has been pointed out why they are not distinct and separable from the balance of the Act. The rule is that, where a part of a statute is unconstitutional, the remainder will not be declared to be unconstitutional also, if the two are distinct and separable so that the latter may stand, though the former becomes of no effect. . . . We do not wish to be understood by anything herein said as holding that section five (5) would be invalid if it was limited in its terms to females who are minors.

The judgment of the Criminal Court of Cook County is reversed, and the cause is remanded to that Court with directions to dismiss the prosecution. *Reversed and remanded.*

Allgeyer v. *Louisiana,* 165 U.S. 578 (1897)

(Unanimous)

Mr. Justice Peckham delivered the opinion of the Court.

In this case the only act which it is claimed was a violation of the statute in question consisted in sending the letter through the mail notifying the company of the property to be covered by the policy already delivered. We have then a contract which it is conceded was made outside and beyond the limits of the jurisdiction of the State of Louisiana, being made and to be performed within the State of New York, where the premiums were to be paid and losses, if any, adjusted. . . .

It is natural that the state court should have remarked that there is in this "statute an apparent interference with the liberty of defendants in restricting their rights to place insurance on property of their own whenever and in what company they desired." Such interference is not only apparent, but it is real, and we do not think that it is justified for the purpose of upholding what the State says is its policy with regard to foreign insurance companies which had not complied with the laws of the State for doing business within its limits. . . .

The Supreme Court of Louisiana says that the act of writing within that State, the letter of notification, was an act therein done to effect an insurance on property then in the State, in a marine insurance company which had not complied with its laws, and such act was, therefore, prohibited by the statute. As so construed we think the statute is a violation of the Fourteenth Amendment of the Federal Constitution, in that it deprives the defendants of their liberty without due process of law. The statute which forbids such act does not become due process of law, because it is inconsistent with the provisions of the Constitution of the Union. The liberty mentioned in that amendment means not only the right of the citizen to be free from the mere physical restraint of his person, as by incarceration, but the term is deemed to embrace the right of the citizen to be free in the enjoyment of all his faculties; to be free to use them in all lawful ways; to live and work where he will; to earn his livelihood by any lawful calling; to pursue any livelihood or avocation, and for that purpose to enter into all contracts which may be proper, necessary and essential to his carrying out to a successful conclusion the purposes above mentioned. . . .

Has not a citizen of a State, under the provisions of the Federal Constitution above mentioned, a right to contract outside of the State for insurance on his property—a right of which state legislation cannot deprive him? . . . When we speak of the liberty to contract for insurance or to do an act to effectuate such a contract already existing, we refer to and have in mind the facts of this case, where the contract was made outside the State, and as such was a valid and proper contract. The act done within the limits of the State under the circumstances of this case for the purpose therein mentioned, we hold a proper act, one which the defendants were at liberty to perform and which the state legislature had no right to prevent, at least with reference to the Federal Constitution. To deprive the citizen of such a right as herein described without due process of law is illegal. Such a statute as this in question is not due process of law, because it prohibits an act which under the Federal Constitution the defendants had a right to perform. This does not interfere in any way with the acknowledged right of the State to enact such legislation in the legitimate exercise of its police or other powers as to it may seem proper. In the exercise of such right, however, care must be taken not to infringe upon those other rights of the citizen which are protected by the Federal Constitution.

Holden v. *Hardy*, 169 U.S. 366 (1898)

[7–2: Brown, Fuller, Gray, Harlan, Shiras,
McKenna, White; Brewer, Peckham]

Mr. Justice Brown delivered the opinion of the Court.

This case involves the constitutionality of an act of the legislature of Utah, of March 30, 1896, c. 72, entitled "An act regulating the hours of employment in underground mines and in smelters and ore reduction works." . . .

The validity of the statute in question is, however, challenged upon the ground of an alleged violation of the Fourteenth Amendment to the Constitution of the United States, in that it abridges the privileges or immunities of citizens of the United States; deprives both the employer and the laborer of his property without due process of law, and denies to them the equal protection of the laws. As the three questions of abridging their immunities, depriving them of their property, and denying them the protection of the laws, are so connected that the authorities upon each are, to a greater or less extent, pertinent to the others, they may properly be considered together.

Prior to the adoption of the Fourteenth Amendment there was a similar provision against deprivation of life, liberty or property without due process of law incorporated in the Fifth Amendment; but as the first eight amendments to the Constitution were obligatory only upon Congress, the decisions of this court under this amendment have but a partial application to the Fourteenth Amendment, which operates only upon the action of the several States. The Fourteenth Amendment, which was finally adopted July 28, 1868, largely expanded the power of the Federal courts and Congress, and for the first time authorized the former to declare invalid all laws and judicial decisions of the States abridging the rights of citizens or denying them the benefit of due process of law. . . .

An examination of . . . cases under the Fourteenth Amendment will demonstrate that, in passing upon the validity of state legislation under that amendment, this court has not failed to recognize the fact that the law is, to a certain extent, a progressive science; that in some of the States methods of procedure, which at the time the Constitution was adopted were deemed essential to the protection and safety of the people, or to the liberty of the citizen, have been found to be no longer necessary; that restrictions which had formerly been laid upon the conduct of individuals, or of classes of individuals, had proved detrimental to their interests; while, upon the other hand, certain other classes of persons, particularly those engaged in dangerous or unhealthful employments, have been found to be in need of additional protection. . . .

Of course, it is impossible to forecast the character or extent of these changes, but in view of the fact that from the day Magna Charta was signed to the present moment, amendments to the structure of the law have been made with increasing frequency, it is impossible to suppose that they will not continue, and the law be forced to adapt itself to new conditions of society, and, particularly, to the new relations between employers and employés, as they arise. . . .

This court has never attempted to define with precision the words "due process of law," nor is it necessary to do so in this case. It is sufficient to say that there are certain immutable principles of justice which inhere in the very idea of free government which no member of the Union may disregard, as that no man shall be condemned in his person or property without due notice and an opportunity of being heard in his defence. . . .

As the possession of property, of which a person cannot be deprived, doubtless implies that such property may be acquired, it is safe to say that a state law which undertakes to deprive any class of persons of the general power to acquire property would also be obnoxious to the same provision. Indeed, we may go a step further, and say that, as property can only be legally acquired as between living persons by contract, a general prohibition against entering into contracts with respect to property, or having as their object the acquisition of property, would be equally invalid. . . .

This right of contract, however, is itself subject to certain limitations which the State may lawfully impose in the exercise of its police powers. While this power is inherent in all governments, it has doubtless been greatly expanded in its application during the past century, owing to an enormous increase in the number of occupations which are dangerous, or so far detrimental to the health of employés as to demand special precautions for their well-being and protection, or the safety of adjacent property. While this court has held . . . that the police power cannot be put forward as an excuse for oppressive and unjust legislation, it may be lawfully resorted to for the purpose of preserving the public health, safety or morals, or the abatement of public nuisances, and a large discretion "is necessarily vested in the legislature to determine not only what the interests of the public require, but what measures are necessary for the protection of such interests." . . .

While the business of mining coal and manufacturing iron began in Pennsylvania as early as 1716, and in Virginia, North Carolina and Massachusetts even earlier than this, both mining and manufacturing were carried on in such a limited way and by such primitive methods that no special laws were considered necessary, prior to the adoption of the Constitution, for the protection of the operatives; but, in the vast proportions which these industries have since assumed, it has been found that they can no longer be carried on with due regard to the safety and health of those engaged in them, without special protection against the dangers necessarily incident to these employments. In consequence of this, laws have been enacted in most of the States designed to meet these exigencies and to secure the safety of persons peculiarly exposed to these dangers. Within this general category are ordinances providing for fire escapes for hotels, theatres, factories and other large buildings, a municipal inspection of boilers, and appliances designed to secure passengers upon railways and steamboats against the dangers necessarily incident to these methods of transportation. In States where manufacturing is carried on to a large extent, provision is made for the protection of dangerous machinery against accidental contact, for the cleanliness and ventilation of working rooms, for the guarding of well holes, stairways, elevator shafts and for the employment of sanitary appliances. In others, where mining is the principal industry, special provision is made for the shoring up of dangerous walls, for ventilation shafts, bore holes, escapement shafts, means of signalling the surface, for the supply of fresh air and the elimination, as far as possible, of dangerous gases, for safe means of hoisting and lowering cages, for a limitation upon the number of persons permitted to enter a cage, that cages shall be covered, and that there shall be fences and gates around the top of shafts, besides other similar precautions. . . .

But if it be within the power of a legislature to adopt such means for the protection of the lives of its citizens, it is difficult to see why precautions may not also be adopted for the protection of their health and morals. It is as much for the interest of the State that the public health should be preserved as that life should be made secure. . . .

Upon the principles above stated, we think the act in question may be sustained as a valid exercise of the police power of the State. The enactment does not profess to limit the hours of all workmen, but merely those who are employed in underground mines, or in the smelting, reduction or refining of ores or metals. These employments, when too long pursued, the legislature has judged to be detrimental to the health of the employés, and, so long as there are reasonable grounds for believing that this is so, its decision upon this subject cannot be reviewed by the Federal courts. . . .

We are of opinion that the act in question was a valid exercise of the police power of the State, and the judgments of the Supreme Court of Utah are, therefore, *Affirmed.*

Lochner v. New York, 198 U.S. 4 (1905)

[5–4: Peckham, Brown, Brewer, Fuller, McKenna;
Day, Harlan, Holmes, White]

Mr. Justice Peckham . . . delivered the opinion of the court.

The indictment, it will be seen, charges that the plaintiff in error violated the one hundred and tenth section of article 8, chapter 415, of the Laws of 1897, known as the labor law of the State of New York, in that he wrongfully and unlawfully required and permitted an employé working for him to work more than sixty hours in one week. There is nothing in any of the opinions delivered in this case, either in the Supreme Court or the Court of Appeals of the State, which construes the section, in using the word "required," as referring to any physical force being used to obtain the labor of an employé. It is assumed that the word means nothing more than the requirement arising from voluntary contract for such labor in excess of the number of hours specified in the statute. There is no pretense in any of the opinions that the statute was intended to meet a case of involuntary labor in any form. All the opinions assume that there is no real distinction, so far as this question is concerned, between the words "required" and "permitted." The mandate of the statute that "no employé shall be required or permitted to work," is the substantial equivalent of an enactment that "no employé shall contract or agree to work," more than ten hours per day, and as there is no provision for special emergencies the statute is mandatory in all cases. It is not an act merely fixing the number of hours which shall constitute a legal day's work, but an absolute prohibition upon the employer, permitting, under any circumstances, more than ten hours work to be done in his establishment. The employé may desire to earn the extra money, which would arise from his working more than the prescribed time, but this statute forbids the employer from permitting the employé to earn it.

The statute necessarily interferes with the right of contract between the employer and employés, concerning the number of hours in which the latter may labor in the bakery of the employer. The general right to make a contract in relation to his business is part of the liberty of the individual protected by the Fourteenth Amendment of the Federal Constitution. *Allgeyer* v. *Louisiana.* . . . Under that provision no State can deprive any person of life, liberty or property without due process of law. The right to purchase or to sell labor is part of the liberty protected by this amendment, unless there are circumstances which exclude the right. There are, however, certain powers, existing in the sovereignty of each State in the Union, somewhat vaguely termed police powers, the exact description and limitation of which have not been attempted by the courts. Those powers, broadly stated and without, at present, any attempt at a more specific limitation, relate to the safety, health, morals and general welfare of the public. Both property and liberty are held on such reasonable conditions as may be imposed by the governing power of the State in the exercise of those powers, and with such conditions the Fourteenth Amendment was not designed to interfere. . . .

The State, therefore, has power to prevent the individual from making certain kinds of contracts, and in regard to them the Federal Constitution offers no protection. If the contract be one which the State, in the legitimate exercise of its police power, has the right to prohibit, it is not prevented from prohibiting it by the Fourteenth Amendment. Contracts in violation of a statute, either of the Federal or state government, or a contract to let one's property for immoral purposes, or to do any other unlawful act, could obtain no protection from the Federal Constitution, as coming under the liberty of person or of free contract. Therefore, when the State, by its legislature, in the assumed exercise of its police powers, has passed an act which seriously limits the right to labor or the right of contract in regard to their means of livelihood between persons who are *sui juris* (both employer and employé), it becomes of great importance to determine which shall prevail—the right of the individual to labor for such time as he may choose, or the right of the State to prevent the individual from laboring or from entering into any contract to labor, beyond a certain time prescribed by the State.

This court has recognized the existence and upheld the exercise of the police powers of the States in many cases which might fairly be considered as border ones, and it has, in the course of its determination of questions regarding the asserted invalidity of such statutes, on the ground of their violation of the rights secured by the Federal Constitution, been guided by rules of a very liberal nature, the application of which has resulted, in numerous instances, in upholding the validity of state statutes thus assailed. Among the later cases where the state law has been upheld by this court is that of *Holden* v. *Hardy*. . . .

It must, of course, be conceded that there is a limit to the valid exercise of the police power by the State. There is no dispute concerning this general proposition. Otherwise the Fourteenth Amendment would have no efficacy and the legislatures of the States would have unbounded power, and it would be enough to say that any piece of legislation was enacted to conserve the morals, the health or the safety of the people; such legislation would be valid, no matter how absolutely without foundation the claim might be. The claim of the police power would be a mere pretext—become another and delusive name for the supreme sovereignty of the State to be exercised free from constitutional restraint. This is not contended for. In every case that comes before this court, therefore, where legislation of this character is concerned and where the protection of the Federal Constitution is sought, the question necessarily arises: Is this a fair, reasonable and appropriate exercise of the police power of the State, or is it an unreasonable, unnecessary and arbitrary interference with the right of the individual to his personal liberty or to enter into those contracts in relation to labor which may seem to him appropriate or necessary for the support of himself and his family? Of course the liberty of contract relating to labor includes both parties to it. The one has as much right to purchase as the other to sell labor.

This is not a question of substituting the judgment of the court for that of the legislature. If the act be within the power of the State it is valid, although the judgment of the court might be totally opposed to the enactment of such a law. But the question would still remain: Is it within the police power of the State? and that question must be answered by the court.

The question whether this act is valid as a labor law, pure and simple, may be dismissed in a few words. There is no reasonable ground for interfering with the liberty of person or the right of free contract, by determining the hours of labor, in the occupation of a baker. There is no contention that bakers as a class are not equal in intelligence and capacity to men in other trades or manual occupations, or that they are not able to assert their rights and care for themselves without the protecting arm of the State, interfering with their independence of judgment and of action. They are in no sense wards of the State. Viewed in the light of a purely labor law, with no reference whatever to the question of health, we think that a law like the one before us involves neither the safety, the morals nor the welfare of the public, and that the interest of the public is not in the slightest degree affected by such an act. The law must be upheld, if at all, as a law pertaining to the health of the individual engaged in the occupation of a baker. It does not affect any other portion of the public than those who are engaged in that occupation. Clean and wholesome bread does not depend upon whether the baker works but ten hours per day or only sixty hours a week. The limitation of the hours of labor does not come within the police power on that ground.

It is a question of which of two powers or rights shall prevail—the power of the State to legislate or the right of the individual to liberty of person and freedom of contract. The mere assertion that the subject relates though but in a remote degree to the public health does not necessarily render the enactment valid. The act must have a more direct relation, as a means to an end, and the end itself must be appropriate and legitimate, before an act can be held to be valid which interferes with the general right of an individual to be free in his person and in his power to contract in relation to his own labor. . . .

We think the limit of the police power has been reached and passed in this case. There is, in our judgment, no reasonable foundation for holding this to be necessary or appropriate as a health law to safeguard the public health or the health of the individuals who are following the trade of a baker. If this statute be valid, and if, therefore, a proper case is made out in which to deny the right of an individual, *sui juris,* as employer or employé, to make contracts for the labor of the latter under the protection of the provisions of the Federal Constitution, there would seem to be no length to which legislation of this nature might not go. The case differs widely, as we have already stated, from the expressions of this court in regard to laws of this nature, as stated in *Holden* v. *Hardy.* . . .

We think that there can be no fair doubt that the trade of a baker, in and of itself, is not an unhealthy one to that degree which would authorize the legislature to interfere with the right to labor, and with the right of free contract on the part of the individual, either as employer or employé. In looking through statistics regarding all trades and occupations, it may be true that the trade of a baker does not appear to be as healthy as some other trades, and is also vastly more healthy than still others. To the common understanding the trade of a baker has never been regarded as an unhealthy one. Very likely physicians would not recommend the exercise of that or of any other trade as a remedy for ill health. Some occupations are more healthy than others, but we think there are none which might not come under the power of the legislature to supervise and control the hours of working therein, if the mere fact that the occupation is not absolutely and perfectly healthy is to confer that right upon the legislative department of the Government. It might be safely affirmed that almost all occupations more or less affect the health. There must be more than the mere fact of the possible existence of some small amount of unhealthiness to warrant legislative interference with liberty. . . .

It is also urged, pursuing the same line of argument, that it is to the interest of the State that its population should be strong and robust, and therefore any legislation which may be said to tend to make people healthy must be valid as health laws, enacted under the police power. If this be a valid argument and a justification for this kind of legislation, it follows that the protection of the Federal Constitution from undue interference with liberty of person and freedom of contract is visionary, wherever the law is sought to be justified as a valid exercise of the police power. Scarcely any law but might find shelter under such assumptions, and conduct, properly so called, as well as contract, would come under the restrictive sway of the legislature. Not only the hours of employés, but the hours of employers, could be regulated, and doctors, lawyers, scientists, all professional men, as well as athletes and artisans, could be forbidden to fatigue their brains and bodies by prolonged hours of exercise, lest the fighting strength of the State be impaired. We mention these extreme cases because the contention is extreme. We do not believe in the soundness of the views which uphold this law. On the contrary, we think that such a law as this, although passed in the assumed exercise of the police power, and as relating to the public health, or the health of the employés named, is not within that power, and is invalid. The act is not, within any fair meaning of the term, a health law, but is an illegal interference with the rights of individuals, both employers and employés, to make contracts regarding labor upon such terms as they may think best, or which they may agree upon with the other parties to such contracts. Statutes of the nature of that under review, limiting the hours in which grown and intelligent men may labor to earn their living, are mere meddlesome interferences with the rights of the individual, and they are not saved from condemnation by the claim that they are passed in the exercise of the police power and upon the subject of the health of the individual whose rights are interfered with, unless there be some fair ground, reasonable in and of itself, to say that there is material danger to the public health or to the health of the employés, if the hours of labor are not curtailed. If this be not clearly the case the individuals, whose rights are thus made the subject of legislative interference, are under the protection of the Federal Constitution regarding their liberty of contract as well as of person; and the legislature of the State has no power to limit their right as proposed in this statute. . . .

It was further urged on the argument that restricting the hours of labor in the case of bakers was valid because it tended to cleanliness on the part of the workers, as a man was more apt to be cleanly when not overworked, and if cleanly then his "output" was also more likely to be so. What has already been said applies with equal force to this contention. We do not admit the reasoning to be sufficient to justify the claimed right of such interference. The State in that case would assume the position of a supervisor, or *pater familias*, over every act of the individual, and its right of governmental interference with his hours of labor, his hours of exercise, the character thereof, and the extent to which it shall be carried would be recognized and upheld. In our judgment it is not possible in fact to discover the connection between the number of hours a baker may work in the bakery and the healthful quality of the bread made by the workman. The connection, if any exists, is too shadowy and thin to build any argument for the interference of the legislature. If the man works ten hours a day it is all right, but if ten and a half or eleven his health is in danger and his bread may be unhealthful, and, therefore, he shall not be permitted to do it. This, we think, is unreasonable and entirely arbitrary. . . .

It is manifest to us that the limitation of the hours of labor as provided for in this section of the statute under which the indictment was found, and the plaintiff in error convicted, has no such direct relation to and no such substantial effect upon the health of the employé, as to justify us in regarding the section as really a health law. It seems to us that the real object and purpose were simply to regulate the hours of labor between the master and his employés (all being men, *sui juris*), in a private business, not dangerous in any degree to morals or in any real and substantial degree, to the health of the employés. Under such circumstances the freedom of master and employé to contract with each other in relation to their employment, and in defining the same, cannot be prohibited or interfered with, without violating the Federal Constitution.

The judgment of the Court of Appeals of New York as well as that of the Supreme Court and of the County Court of Oneida County must be reversed and the case remanded to the County Court for further proceedings not inconsistent with this opinion. *Reversed.*

Mr. Justice Holmes dissenting.

I regret sincerely that I am unable to agree with the judgment in this case, and that I think it my duty to express my dissent.

This case is decided upon an economic theory which a large part of the country does not entertain. If it were a question whether I agreed with that theory, I should desire to study it further and long before making up my mind. But I do not conceive that to be my duty, because I strongly believe that my agreement or disagreement has nothing to do with the right of a majority to embody their opinions in law. It is settled by various decisions of this court that state constitutions and state laws may regulate life in many ways which we as legislators might think as injudicious or if you like as tyrannical as this, and which equally with this interfere with the liberty to contract. Sunday laws and usury laws are ancient examples. A more modern one is the prohibition of lotteries. The liberty of the citizen to do as he likes so long as he does not interfere with the liberty of others to do the same, which has been a shibboleth for some well-known writers, is interfered with by school laws, by the Post Office, by every state or municipal institution which takes his money for purposes thought desirable, whether he likes it or not. The Fourteenth Amendment does not enact Mr. Herbert Spencer's Social Statics. The other day we sustained the Massachusetts vaccination law. *Jacobson* v. *Massachusetts.* . . . United States and state statutes and decisions cutting down the liberty to contract by way of combination are familiar to this court. *Northern Securities Co.* v. *United States.* . . . Two years ago we upheld the prohibition of sales of stock on margins or for future delivery in the constitution of California. *Otis* v. *Parker.* . . . The decision sustaining an eight hour law for miners is still recent. *Holden* v. *Hardy.* . . . Some of these laws embody convictions or prejudices which judges are likely to share. Some may not. But a constitution is not intended to embody a particular economic theory, whether of paternalism and the organic relation of the citizen to the State or of *laissez faire*. It is made for people of fundamentally differing views, and the accident of our finding certain opinions natural and familiar or novel and even shocking ought not to conclude our judgment upon the question whether statutes embodying them conflict with the Constitution of the United States.

General propositions do not decide concrete cases. The decision will depend on a judgment or intuition more subtle than any articulate major premise. But I think that the proposition just stated, if it is accepted, will carry us far toward the end. Every opinion tends to become a law. I think that the word liberty in the Fourteenth Amendment is perverted when it is held to prevent the natural outcome of a dominant opinion, unless it can be said that a rational and fair man necessarily would admit that the statute proposed would infringe fundamental principles as they have been understood by the traditions of our people and our law. It does not need research to show that no such sweeping condemnation can be passed upon the statute before us. A reasonable man might think it a proper measure on the score of health. Men whom I certainly could not pronounce unreasonable would uphold it as a first instalment of a general regulation of the hours of work. Whether in the latter aspect it would be open to the charge of inequality I think it unnecessary to discuss.

AFL Leader Samuel Gompers on Why Married Women Should Not Work, 1906

In undertaking to answer the question as to whether the wife should help to support the family, I take it that what is meant is the wife of a mechanic, a laborer, a workman, not the well-to-do or the fairly well-to do, for among the latter there is not even the false pretense of necessity. Taking, then, my conception of what is implied by the question, I have no hesitancy in answering, positively and absolutely, "No." . . .

Imagine the wife leaving her home and children unprotected and uncared for during the working hours, which among women generally, by reason of their comparative lack of organization, are much longer than the day's work of men. . . .

It is not for any real preference for their labor that the unscrupulous employer gives work to girls and boys and women, but because of his guilty knowledge that he can easily compel them to work longer hours and at a lower wage than men. It is the so-called competition of the unorganized, defenseless woman worker, the girl and the wife, that often tends to reduce the wages of the father and husband, so that frequently in after years, particularly in factory towns, the combined wages of the husband and wife, the father and daughter, have been reduced to the standard of the wages earned by the father or husband in the beginning.

I contend that the wife or mother, attending to the duties of the home, makes the greatest contribution to the support of the family. The honor, glory, and happiness that come from a beloved wife and the holiness of motherhood are a contribution to the support and future welfare of the family that our common humanity does not yet fully appreciate.

It is with keen gratification that observers have noticed in recent years that the wife of the wage-earner, where the husband has been a fair bread-winner for the family, has taken up beautiful needlework, embroidery, and the cultivation of her better, but heretofore latent, talents.

There is no reason why all the opportunities for the development of the best that women can do should be denied her, either in the home or else-where. I entertain no doubt but that from the constant better opportunity resultant from the larger earning power of the husband the wife will, apart from performing her natural household duties, perform that work which is most pleasurable for her, contributing to the beautifying of her home and surroundings. . . .

Louis D. Brandeis and Josephine Goldmark on Women in Industry, 1908

VII. Laundries

The specific prohibition in the Oregon Act of more than ten hours' work in laundries is not an arbitrary discrimination against that trade. Laundries would probably not be included under the general terms of "manufacturing" or "mechanical establishments"; and yet the special dangers of long hours in laundries, as the business is now conducted, present strong reasons for providing a legal limitation of the hours of work in that business. . . .

B. Bad Effect upon Health. *Report of British Chief Inspector of Factories and Workshops, 1900.*

The whole work of a laundry is done standing, and the practice of so apportioning the legal "sixty hours a week" that on three or four days in the week the women have to work from 8 A.M. to 10 or 11 at night—a practice which could be, and where there is proper organization often is, rendered needless—has its natural result in the form of disease to which laundry workers are extremely liable. It is well known that they suffer much from varicose veins, and terrible ulcers on the legs; but the extraordinary extent to which they are afflicted is, I think, not generally known. In many other trades standing is a necessary condition, and it is difficult to account for the far greater prevalence of this disease among laundry workers than among others of the same class engaged in ordinary factory occupations, except on the ground of the long and irregular hours. . . .

With a view to arriving, if possible, at some definite knowledge of the position of laundry workers as compared with other women of their class and situation, in regard to the question of health, I have this year devoted some time to inquiring into the subject in the districts under my charge and in neighboring localities. . . . By the kindness of the superintendents of the two first infirmaries (Islesworth, and Wandsworth and Clapham) I have been able to examine the carefully kept records of the number, ages, occupations, and diseases of the patients. . . .

D. Bad Effect upon Morals. *Report of British Chief Inspector of Factories and Workshops, 1900.*

One of the most unsatisfactory results of the present system or lack of system of working hours in laundries is the unfortunate moral effect on the women and girls of this irregularity. The difficulty of securing steady regular work from employees and of insuring punctual attendance is complained of on all sides, and the more intelligent employers are beginning to see that this is the natural result of the irregularity in working hours, which is still too readily fostered by many who do not realize its mischievous effect. Women who are employed at arduous work till far into the night are not likely to be early risers nor given to punctual attendance in the mornings, and workers who on one or two days in the week are dismissed to idleness or to other occupations, while on the remaining days they are expected to work for abnormally long hours, are not rendered methodical, industrious, or dependable workers by such an unsatisfactory training. The self-control and good habits engendered by a regular and definite period of moderate daily employment, which affords an excellent training for the young worker in all organized industries, is sadly lacking, and, instead, one finds periods of violent over-work alternating with hours of exhaustion. The result is the establishment of a kind of "vicious circle"; bad habits among workers make compliance by their employers with any regulation as to hours very difficult, while a lack of loyal adherence to reasonable hours of employment by many laundry occupiers increases the difficulty for those who make the attempt in real earnestness. . . .

Dangerous Trades. Thomas Oliver, M.D., *Medical Expert to Dangerous Trades Committee of the Home Office. 1902.* The ten minutes or quarter-hour "lunch" of "beer" is common, and the "beer-man" who goes his rounds at 10 A.M. and 6 or 7 P.M. to all the laundries, delivering his cans of beer from the nearest public house, is an institution which is, I believe, unknown in any other trade. Imagine the amazement of the master of a mill or weaving factory if his employees were to stop in a body for a quarter of an hour twice a day between meals to drink beer! Yet in many laundries the beer is kept on the premises for the purpose, and it is certain that as long as time thus wasted (to put it on the lowest grounds) can be made up by each separate woman "working it out" at the end of the day, irregular dawdling and intemperate habits will be encouraged. On the other hand, a woman who is expected on Thursdays or Fridays to be in the laundry from 8 or 8:30 in the morning till 9 or 10 or 11 at night may claim with some show of reason that only by some kind of spur can she keep her over-tired body from flagging. . . .

Conclusion

We submit that in view of the facts above set forth and of legislative action extending over a period of more than sixty years in the leading countries of Europe, and in twenty of our States, it cannot be said that the Legislature of Oregon had no reasonable ground for believing that the public health, safety, or welfare did not require a legal limitation on women's work in manufacturing and mechanical establishments and laundries to ten hours in one day. . . .

Muller v. *Oregon,* 208 U.S. 412 (1908)

(Unanimous)

Mr. Justice Brewer delivered the opinion of the Court.

. . . The single question is the constitutionality of the statute under which the defendant was convicted so far as it affects the work of a female in a laundry. That it does not conflict with any provisions of the State constitution is settled by the decision of the Supreme Court of the State. The contentions of the defendant, now plaintiff in error, are thus stated in his brief:

"(1) Because the statute attempts to prevent persons, *sui juris,* from making their own contracts, and thus violates the provisions of the Fourteenth Amendment, as follows:

" 'No State shall make or enforce any law which shall abridge the privileges or immunities of citizens of the United States; nor shall any State deprive any person of life, liberty, or property, without due process of law; nor deny to any person within its jurisdiction the equal protection of the laws.'

"(2) Because the statute does not apply equally to all persons similarly situated, and is class legislation.

"(3) The statute is not a valid exercise of the police power. The kinds of work prescribed are not unlawful, nor are they declared to be immoral or dangerous to the public health; nor can such a law be sustained on the ground that it is designed to protect women on account of their sex. There is no necessary or reasonable connection between the limitation prescribed by the act and the public health, safety, or welfare."

It is the law of Oregon that women, whether married or single, have equal contractual and personal rights with men. . . .

It thus appears that, putting to one side the elective franchise, in the matter of personal and contractual rights they stand on the same plane as the other sex. Their rights in these respects can no more be infringed than the equal rights of their brothers. We held in *Lochner* v. *New York* . . . that a law providing that no laborer shall be required or permitted to work in bakeries more than sixty hours in a week or ten hours in a day was not as to men a legitimate exercise of the police power of the State, but an unreasonable, unnecessary, and arbitrary interference with the right and liberty of the individual to contract in relation to his labor, and as such was in conflict with, and void under, the Federal Constitution. That decision is invoked by plaintiff in error as decisive of the question before us. But this assumes that the difference between the sexes does not justify a different rule respecting a restriction of the hours of labor.

In patent cases counsel are apt to open the argument with a discussion of the state of the art. It may not be amiss, in the present case, before examining the constitutional question, to notice the course of legislation as well as expressions of opinion from other than judicial sources. In the brief filed by Mr. Louis D. Brandeis, for the defendant in error, is a very copious collection of all these matters. . . .

The legislation and opinions referred to . . . may not be, technically speaking, authorities, and in them is little or no discussion of the constitutional question presented to us for determination, yet they are significant of a widespread belief that woman's physical structure, and the functions she performs in consequence thereof, justify special legislation restricting or qualifying the conditions under which she should be permitted to toil. Constitutional questions, it is true, are not settled by even a consensus of present public opinion, for it is the peculiar value of a written constitution that it places in unchanging form limitations upon legislative action, and thus gives a permanence and stability to popular government which otherwise would be lacking. At the same time, when a question of fact is debated and debatable, and the extent to which a special constitutional limitation goes is affected by the truth in respect to that fact, a widespread and long continued belief concerning it is worthy of consideration. We take judicial cognizance of all matters of general knowledge.

It is undoubtedly true, as more than once declared by this court, that the general right to contract in relation to one's business is part of the liberty of the individual, protected by the Fourteenth Amendment to the Federal Constitution; yet it is equally well settled that this liberty is not absolute and extending to all contracts, and that a State may, without conflicting with the provisions of the Fourteenth Amendment, restrict in many respects the individual's power of contract. Without stopping to discuss at length the extent to which a State may act in this respect, we refer to the following cases in which the question has been considered: *Allgeyer* v. *Louisiana* . . . , *Holden* v. *Hardy* . . . , *Lochner* v. *New York*. . . .

That woman's physical structure and the performance of maternal functions place her at a disadvantage in the struggle for subsistence is obvious. This is especially true when the burdens of motherhood are upon her. Even when they are not, by abundant testimony of the medical fraternity continuance for a long time on her feet at work, repeating this from day to day, tends to injurious effects upon the body, and as healthy mothers are essential to vigorous offspring, the physical well-being of woman becomes an object of public interest and care in order to preserve the strength and vigor of the race.

Still again, history discloses the fact that woman has always been dependent upon man. He established his control at the outset by superior physical strength, and this control in various forms, with diminishing intensity, has continued to the present. As minors, though not to the same extent, she has been looked upon in the courts as needing especial care that her rights may be preserved. Education was long denied her, and while now the doors of the school-room are opened and her opportunities for acquiring knowledge are great, yet even with that and the consequent increase of capacity for business affairs it is still true that in the struggle for subsistence she is not an equal competitor with her brother. Though limitations upon personal and contractual rights may be removed by legislation, there is that in her disposition and habits of life which will operate against a full assertion of those rights. She will still be where some legislation to protect her seems necessary to secure a real equality of right. Doubtless there are individual exceptions, and there are many respects in which she has an advantage over him; but looking at it from the viewpoint of the effort to maintain an independent position in life, she is not upon an equality. Differentiated by these matters from the other sex, she is properly placed in a class by herself, and legislation designed for her protection may be sustained, even when like legislation is not necessary for men and could not be sustained. It is impossible to close one's eyes to the fact that she still looks to her brother and depends upon him. Even though all restrictions on political, personal, and contractual rights were taken away, and she stood, so far as statutes are concerned, upon an absolutely equal plane with him, it would still be true that she is so constituted that she will rest upon and look to him for protection; that her physical structure and a proper discharge of her maternal functions—having in view not merely her own health, but the well-being of the race—justify legislation to protect her from the greed as well as the passion of man. The limitations which this statute places upon her contractual powers, upon her right to agree with her employer as to the time she shall labor, are not imposed solely for her benefit, but also largely for the benefit of all. Many words cannot make this plainer. The two sexes differ in structure of body, in the functions to be performed by each, in the amount of physical strength, in the capacity for long-continued labor, particularly when done standing, the influence of vigorous health upon the future well-being of the race, the self-reliance which enables one to assert full rights, and in the capacity to maintain the struggle for subsistence. This difference justifies a difference in legislation and upholds that which is designed to compensate for some of the burdens which rest upon her.

We have not referred in this discussion to the denial of the elective franchise in the State of Oregon, for while that may disclose a lack of political equality in all things with her brother, that is not of itself decisive. The reason runs deeper, and rests in the inherent difference between the two sexes, and in the different functions in life which they perform.

For these reasons, and without questioning in any respect the decision in *Lochner* v. *New York,* we are of the opinion that it cannot be adjudged that the act in question is in conflict with the Federal Constitution, so far as it respects the work of a female in a laundry, and the judgment of the Supreme Court of Oregon is *Affirmed.*

Roscoe Pound on Liberty of Contract, 1909

"The right of a person to sell his labor," says Mr. Justice Harlan, "upon such terms as he deems proper, is in its essence, the same as the right of the purchaser of labor to prescribe the conditions upon which he will accept such labor from the person offering to sell it. So the right of the employee to quit the service of the employer, for whatever reason, is the same as the right of the employer, for whatever reason, to dispense with the services of such employee. . . . In all such particulars the employer and the employee have equality of right, and any legislation that disturbs that equality is an arbitrary interference with the liberty of contract, which no government can legally justify in a free land." With this positive declaration of a lawyer, the culmination of a line of decisions now nearly twenty-five years old, a statement which a recent writer on the science of jurisprudence has deemed so fundamental as to deserve quotation and exposition at an unusual length, as compared with his treatment of other points, let us compare the equally positive statement of a sociologist:

"Much of the discussion about 'equal rights' is utterly hollow. All the ado made over the system of contract is surcharged with fallacy."

To everyone acquainted at first hand with actual industrial conditions the latter statement goes without saying. Why, then do courts persist in the fallacy? Why do so many of them force upon legislation an academic theory of equality in the face of practical conditions of inequality? Why do we find a great and learned court in 1908 taking the long step into the past of dealing with the relation between employer and employee in railway transportation, as if the parties were individuals—as if they were farmers haggling over the sale of a horse? Why is the legal conception of the relation of employer and employee so at variance with the common knowledge of mankind? The late President has told us that it is because individual judges project their personal, social and economic views into the law. A great German publicist holds that it is because the party bent of judges has dictated decisions. But when a doctrine is announced with equal vigor and held with equal tenacity by courts of Pennsylvania and of Arkansas, of New York and of California, of Illinois and of West Virginia, of Massachusetts and of Missouri, we may not dispose of it so readily. Surely the sources of such a doctrine must lie deeper. Let us inquire then, what further and more potent causes may be discovered, how these causes have operated to bring about the present state of the law as to freedom of contract, what the present doctrine of the courts is upon that subject, and how far we may expect amelioration thereof in the near future. . . .

. . . [O]ur ideal of justice has been to let every force play freely and exert itself completely, limited only by the necessity of avoiding friction. As a result, and as a result of our legal history, we exaggerate the importance of property and of contract, as an incident thereof. A leader of the bar, opposing the income tax, argues that a fundamental object of our polity is "preservation of the rights of private property." Text writers tell us of the divine origin of property. The Supreme Court of Wisconsin tells us that the right to take property by will is an absolute and inherent right, not depending upon legislation. The absolute certainty which is one of our legal ideals, an ideal responsible for much that is irritatingly mechanical in our legal system, is demanded chiefly to protect property. And our courts regard the right to contract, not as a phase of liberty—a sort of freedom of mental motion and locomotion—but as a phase of property, to be protected as such. A further result is to exaggerate private right at the expense of public interest. Blackstone's proposition that "the public good is in nothing more essentially interested than in the protection of every individual's private rights," has been quoted in more than one American decision; and one of these is a case often cited in support of extreme doctrines of liberty of contract. It is but a corollary that liberty of contract cannot be restricted merely in the interest of a contracting party. His right to contract freely is to yield only to the safety, health, or moral welfare of the public. Still another result is that bench and bar distrust and object to legislation. . . . Suffice it to say here that the doctrine as to liberty of contract is bound up in the decisions of our courts with a narrow view of what constitutes special or class legislation that greatly limits effective law-making. If we can only have laws of wide generality of application, we can have only a few laws; for the wider their application the more likelihood there is of injustice in concrete cases. But from the individualist standpoint a minimum of law is desirable. The common law antipathy to legislation sympathizes with this, and in consequence we find courts saying that it is not necessary to consider the reasons that led up to the type of legislation they condemn and that the maxim that the government governs best which governs least is proper for courts to bear in mind in expounding the Constitution.

The second cause [is] mechanical jurisprudence. . . . The effect of all system is apt to be petrifaction of the subject systematized. Legal science is not exempt from this tendency. Legal systems have their periods in which system decays into technicality, in which a scientific jurisprudence becomes a mechanical jurisprudence. In a period of growth through juristic speculation and judicial decision, there is little danger of this. But whenever such a period has come to an end, when its work has been done and its legal theories have come to maturity, jurisprudence tends to decay. Conceptions are fixed. The premises are no longer to be examined. Everything is reduced to simple deduction from them. Principles cease to have importance. The law becomes a body of rules. This is the condition Professor Henderson refers to when he speaks of the way of social progress as barred by barricades of dead precedents. Manifestations of mechanical jurisprudence are conspicuous in the decisions as to liberty of contract. A characteristic one is the rigorous logical deduction from predetermined conceptions in disregard of and often in the teeth of the actual facts, which was noted at the outset. Two courts in passing on statutes abridging the power of free contract have noted the frequency of such legislation in recent times but have said that it was not necessary to consider the reasons for it. Another court has asked what right the legislature has to "*assume* that one class has the need of protection against another." Another has said that the remedy for the company store evil "is in the hands of the employee," since he is not compelled to buy from the employer, forgetting that there may be a compulsion in fact where there is none in law. Another says, that "theoretically there is among our citizens no inferior class," and of course no facts can avail against that theory. Another tells us that man and woman have the same rights, and hence a woman must be allowed to contract to work as many hours a day as a man may. We have already noted how Mr. Justice Harlan insists on a legal theory of equality of rights in the latest pronouncement of the Federal Supreme Court. Legislation designed to give laborers some measure of practical independence, which, if allowed to operate, would put them in a position of reasonable equality with their masters, is said by courts, because it infringes on a theoretical equality, to be insulting to their manhood and degrading, to put them under guardianship, to create a class of statutory laborers, and to stamp them as imbeciles. I know of nothing akin to this artificial reasoning in jurisprudence unless it be the explanation given by Pomponius for the transfer of legislative power from the Roman people during the Empire: "The *plebs* found, in course of time, that it was difficult for them to meet together, and the general body of the citizens no doubt found it more difficult still." No doubt they did. Caesar or the praetorian prefect would have seen to that.

Survival of a purely juristic notion of the state and of economics and politics, in contrast with the social conception of the present, the third cause suggested, can be looked at but briefly. Formerly the juristic attitude obtained in religion, in morals, and in politics as well as in law. This fundamentally juristic conception of the world, due possibly to Roman law being the first subject of study in the universities, which gave a form of legality even to theology, has passed away elsewhere. But it lingers in the courts. Jurisprudence is the last in the march of the sciences away from the method of deduction from predetermined conceptions. The sociological movement in jurisprudence, the movement for pragmatism as a philosophy of law, the movement for the adjustment of principles and doctrines to the human conditions they are to govern rather than to assumed first principles, the movement for putting the human factor in the central place and relegating logic to its true position as an instrument, has scarcely shown itself as yet in America. Perhaps the dissenting opinion of Mr. Justice Holmes in *Lochner v. New York,* is the best exposition of it we have.

Another factor of no mean importance in producing the line of decisions we are considering is the training of lawyers and judges in eighteenth century theories of natural law. . . . Until a comparatively recent date, all legal education, whether in school or in office, began with the study of Blackstone. Probably all serious office study begins with Blackstone or some American imitator to-day. Many schools make Blackstone the first subject of instruction to-day, and in others Blackstone is a subject of examination for admission or of prescribed reading after admission, or there are courses on elementary law in which texts reproducing the theories of the introduction to and the first book of the *Commentaries* are the basis of instruction. A student who is college-trained may have had a course or courses that brought him in contact with modern thought. It is quite as likely he has not, or if he has, the natural law theories which are a matter of course in all our law books are not unlikely to persuade him that what he learned in college is immaterial in the domain of law. Constitutional law is full of natural law notions. For one thing, there is the doctrine that apart from constitutional restrictions there are individual rights resting on a natural basis, to which courts must give effect "beyond the control of the state." In the judicial discussions of liberty of contract this idea has been very prominent. . . . These natural law ideas are carried to an extreme by the Supreme Court of Illinois in *Ritchie* v. *People,* in which case it is announced that women have a natural equality with men and that no distinction may be drawn between them with respect to power of engaging to labor.

Closely related to the ideas just considered, and, indeed, a product of the same training, is a deep-seated conviction of the American lawyer that the doctrines of the common law are part of the universal jural order. Just as in nine cases out of ten, natural law meant for the seventeenth century and eighteenth century jurist the Roman law which he knew and had studied, for the common law lawyer it means the common law. For one thing, this feeling leads to a narrow attitude toward legislation; a tendency to hold down all statutory innovations upon the common law as far as possible. In like spirit, on this subject of liberty of contract, most of the courts which have overthrown legislation as being in derogation of liberty of contract, most of the courts which have overthrown legislation as being in derogation of liberty, have insisted that only common law incapacities can be given legal recognition; that new incapacities in fact, growing out of new conditions in business and industry, cannot be taken advantage of in legislation; that the ordinary farm-hand and the laborer in the beet fields, for example, must be treated alike. But, even more important for our purpose, this feeling operates in constitutional law to lead judges to try statutes by the measure of common law doctrines rather than by the Constitution.

Not only, however, is natural law the fundamental assumption of our elementary books and of professional philosophy, but we must not forget that it is the theory of our bills of rights. Not unnaturally, therefore, courts have clung to it as being the orthodox theory of our constitutions. But the fact that the framers held that theory by no means demonstrates that they intended to impose the theory upon us for all time. It is contrary to their principles to assume that they intended to dictate philosophical or juristic beliefs and opinions to those who were to come after them. What they did intend was the *practical* securing of each individual against arbitrary and capricious governmental acts. They intended to protect the people against their rulers, not against themselves. They laid down principles, not rules, and rules can only be illustrations of those principles so long as facts and opinions remain what they were when the rules were announced. . . .

Last of the causes suggested, but by no means the least efficient in bringing about the line of decisions under consideration, is the sharp line between law and fact in our legal system, due originally to the exigencies of trial by jury. The line between what is for the court to pass upon and what is for the jury, has come to be called a line between law and fact. For purposes of jury trial the line itself has to be drawn often very artificially. But, beyond that, when it is drawn the tendency is to assume that questions which analytically are pure questions of fact, when they become questions for the court to decide, must be looked at in a different way from ordinary questions of fact and must be dealt with in an academic and artificial manner because they have become questions of law. The tendency to insist upon such a line and to draw it arbitrarily, has spread from the law of trials to every part of the law. . . .

The attitude of many of our courts on the subject of liberty of contract is so certain to be misapprehended, is so out of the range of ordinary understanding, the decisions themselves are so academic and so artificial in their reasoning, that they cannot fail to engender such feelings. Thus, those decisions do an injury beyond the failure of a few acts. These acts can be replaced as legislatures learn how to comply with the letter of the decisions and to evade the spirit of them. But the lost respect for courts and law cannot be replaced. The evil of those cases will live after them in impaired authority of the courts long after the decisions themselves are forgotten.

Adkins v. *Children's Hospital,* 261 U.S. 525 (1923)

[5–3: Sutherland, Butler, McKenna, McReynolds,
VanDevanter; Holmes, Taft, Sandford]

Mr. Justice Sutherland delivered the opinion of the Court.

. . . The judicial duty of passing upon the constitutionality of an act of Congress is one of great gravity and delicacy. The statute here in question has successfully borne the scrutiny of the legislative branch of the government, which, by enacting it, has affirmed its validity; and that determination must be given great weight. This Court, by an unbroken line of decisions from Chief Justice Marshall to the present day, has steadily adhered to the rule that every possible presumption is in favor of the validity of an act of Congress until overcome beyond rational doubt. But if by clear and indubitable demonstration a statute be opposed to the Constitution we have no choice but to say so. The Constitution, by its own terms, is the supreme law of the land, emanating from the people, the repository of ultimate sovereignty under our form of government. A congressional statute, on the other hand, is the act of an agency of this sovereign authority and if it conflict with the Constitution must fall; for that which is not supreme must yield to that which is. To hold it invalid (if it be invalid) is a plain exercise of the judicial power—that power vested in courts to enable them to administer justice according to law. From the authority to ascertain and determine the law in a given case, there necessarily results, in case of conflict, the duty to declare and enforce the rule of the supreme law and reject that of an inferior act of legislation which, transcending the Constitution, is of no effect and binding on no one. This is not the exercise of a substantive power to review and nullify acts of Congress, for no such substantive power exists. It is simply a necessary concomitant of the power to hear and dispose of a case or controversy properly before the court, to the determination of which must be brought the test and measure of the law. . . .

The statute now under consideration is attacked upon the ground that it authorizes an unconstitutional interference with the freedom of contract included within the guaranties of the due process clause of the Fifth Amendment. That the right to contract about one's affairs is a part of the liberty of the individual protected by this clause, is settled by the decisions of this Court and is no longer open to question. . . .

Within this liberty are contracts of employment of labor. In making such contracts, generally speaking, the parties have an equal right to obtain from each other the best terms they can as the result of private bargaining. . . .

There is, of course, no such thing as absolute freedom of contract. It is subject to a great variety of restraints. But freedom of contract is, nevertheless, the general rule and restraint the exception; and the exercise of legislative authority to abridge it can be justified only by the existence of exceptional circumstances. Whether these circumstances exist in the present case constitutes the question to be answered. It will be helpful to this end to review some of the decisions where the interference has been upheld and consider the grounds upon which they rest.

(1) *Those dealing with statutes fixing rates and charges to be exacted by businesses impressed with a public interest.* . . .

(2) *Statutes relating to contracts for the performance of public work.* . . .

(3) *Statutes prescribing the character, methods and time for payment of wages.* . . .

(4) *Statutes fixing hours of labor.* It is upon this class that the greatest emphasis is laid in argument and therefore, and because such cases approach most nearly the line of principle applicable to the statute here involved, we shall consider them more at length. In some instances the statute limited the hours of labor for men in certain occupations and in others it was confined in its application to women. No statute has thus far been brought to the attention of this Court which by its terms, applied to all occupations. In *Holden* v. *Hardy* . . . , the Court considered an act of the Utah legislature, restricting the hours of labor in mines and smelters. This statute was sustained as a legitimate exercise of the police power, on the ground that the legislature had determined that these particular employments, when too long pursued, were injurious to the health of the employees, and that, as there were reasonable grounds for supporting this determination on the part of the legislature, its decision in that respect was beyond the reviewing power of the federal courts.

That this constituted the basis of the decision is emphasized by the subsequent decision in *Lochner* v. *New York* . . . , reviewing a state statute which restricted the employment of all persons in bakeries to ten hours in any one day. The Court referred to *Holden* v. *Hardy, supra,* and, declaring it to be inapplicable, held the statute unconstitutional as an unreasonable, unnecessary and arbitrary interference with the liberty of contract and therefore void under the Constitution. . . .

Subsequent cases in this Court have been distinguished from that decision [*Lochner*], but the principles therein stated have never been disapproved. . . .

The essential characteristics of the statute now under consideration, which differentiate it from the laws fixing hours of labor, will be made to appear as we proceed. It is sufficient now to point out that the latter . . . deal[s] with incidents of the employment having no necessary effect upon the heart of the contract, that is, the amount of wages to be paid and received. A law forbidding work to continue beyond a given number of hours leaves the parties free to contract about wages and thereby equalize whatever additional burdens may be imposed upon the employer as a result of the restrictions as to hours, by an adjustment in respect of the amount of wages. Enough has been said to show that the authority to fix hours of labor cannot be exercised except in respect of those occupations where work of long continued duration is detrimental to health. This Court has been careful in every case where the question has been raised, to place its decision upon this limited authority of the legislature to regulate hours of labor and to disclaim any purpose to uphold the legislation as fixing wages, thus recognizing an essential difference between the two. It seems plain that these decisions afford no real support for any form of law establishing minimum wages.

If now, in the light furnished by the foregoing exceptions to the general rule forbidding legislative interference with freedom of contract, we examine and analyze the statute in question, we shall see that it differs from them in every material respect. It is not a law dealing with any business charged with a public interest or with public work, or to meet and tide over a temporary emergency. It has nothing to do with the character, methods or periods of wage payments. It does not prescribe hours of labor or conditions under which labor is to be done. It is not for the protection of persons under legal disability or for the prevention of fraud. It is simply and exclusively a price-fixing law, confined to adult women (for we are not now considering the provisions relating to minors), who are legally as capable of contracting for themselves as men. It forbids two parties having lawful capacity—under penalties as to the employer—to freely contract with one another in respect of the price for which one shall render service to the other in a purely private employment where both are willing, perhaps anxious, to agree, even though the consequence may be to oblige one to surrender a desirable engagement and the other to dispense with the services of a desirable employee. The price fixed by the board need have no relation to the capacity or earning power of the employee, the number of hours which may happen to constitute the day's work, the character of the place where the work is to be done, or the circumstances or surroundings of the employment; and, while it has no other basis to support its validity than the assumed necessities of the employee, it takes no account of any independent resources she may have. It is based wholly on the opinions of the members of the board and their advisers—perhaps an average of their opinions, if they do not precisely agree—as to what will be necessary to provide a living for a woman, keep her in health and preserve her morals. It applies to any and every occupation in the District, without regard to its nature or the character of the work. . . .

The feature of this statute which, perhaps more than any other, puts upon it the stamp of invalidity is that it exacts from the employer an arbitrary payment for a purpose and upon a basis having no causal connection with his business, or the contract or the work the employee engages to do. The declared basis, as already pointed out, is not the value of the service rendered, but the extraneous circumstance that the employee needs to get a prescribed sum of money to insure her subsistence, health and morals. The ethical right of every worker, man or woman, to a living wage may be conceded. One of the declared and important purposes of trade organizations is to secure it. And with that principle and with every legitimate effort to realize it in fact, no one can quarrel; but the fallacy of the proposed method of attaining it is that it assumes that every employer is bound at all events to furnish it. The moral requirement implicit in every contract of employment, viz., that the amount to be paid and the service to be rendered shall bear to each other some relation of just equivalence, is completely ignored. The necessities of the employee are alone considered and these arise outside of the employment, are the same when there is no employment, and as great in one occupation as in another. Certainly the employer by paying a fair equivalent for the service rendered, though not sufficient to support the employee, has neither caused nor contributed to her poverty. On the contrary, to the extent of what he pays he has relieved it. In principle, there can be no difference between the case of selling labor and the case of selling goods. If one goes to the butcher, the baker or grocer to buy food, he is morally entitled to obtain the worth of his money but he is not entitled to more. If what he gets is worth what he pays he is not justified in demanding more simply because he needs more; and the shopkeeper, having dealt fairly and honestly in that transaction, is not concerned in any peculiar sense with the question of his customer's necessities. Should a statute undertake to vest in a commission power to determine the quantity of food necessary for individual support and require the shopkeeper, if he sell to the individual at all, to furnish that quantity at not more than a fixed maximum, it would undoubtedly fall before the constitutional test. The fallacy of any argument in support of the validity of such a statute would be quickly exposed. The argument in support of that now being considered is equally fallacious, though the weakness of it may not be so plain. A statute requiring an employer to pay in money, to pay at prescribed and regular intervals, to pay the value of the services rendered, even to pay with fair relation to the extent of the benefit obtained from the service, would be understandable. But a statute which prescribes payment without regard to any of these things and solely with relation to circumstances apart from the contract of employment, the business affected by it and the work done under it, is so clearly the product of a naked, arbitrary exercise of power that it cannot be allowed to stand under the Constitution of the United States.

We are asked, upon the one hand, to consider the fact that several States have adopted similar statutes, and we are invited, upon the other hand, to give weight to the fact that three times as many States, presumably as well informed and as anxious to promote the health and morals of their people, have refrained from enacting such legislation. We have also been furnished with a large number of printed opinions approving the policy of the minimum wage, and our own reading has disclosed a large number to the contrary. These are all proper enough for the consideration of the lawmaking bodies, since their tendency is to establish the desirability or undesirability of the legislation; but they reflect no legitimate light upon the question of its validity, and that is what we are called upon to decide. The elucidation of that question cannot be aided by counting heads.

It is said that great benefits have resulted from the operation of such statutes, not alone in the District of Columbia but in the several States, where they have been in force. A mass of reports, opinions of special observers and students of the subject, and the like, has been brought before us in support of this statement, all of which we have found interesting but only mildly persuasive. That the earnings of women now are greater than they were formerly and that conditions affecting women have become better in other respects may be conceded, but convincing indications of the logical relation of these desirable changes to the law in question are significantly lacking. They may be, and quite probably are, due to other causes. We cannot close our eyes to the notorious fact that earnings everywhere in all occupations have greatly increased—not alone in States where the minimum wage law obtains but in the country generally—quite as much or more among men as among women and in occupations outside the reach of the law as in those governed by it. No real test of the economic value of the law can be had during periods of maximum employment, when general causes keep wages up to or above the minimum; that will come in periods of depression and struggle for employment when the efficient will be employed at the minimum rate while the less capable may not be employed at all.

Finally, it may be said that if, in the interest of the public welfare, the police power may be invoked to justify the fixing of a minimum wage, it may, when the public welfare is thought to require it, be invoked to justify a maximum wage. The power to fix high wages connotes, by like course of reasoning, the power to fix low wages. If, in the face of the guaranties of the Fifth Amendment, this form of legislation shall be legally justified, the field for the operation of the police power will have been widened to a great and dangerous degree. If, for example, in the opinion of future lawmakers, wages in the building trades shall become so high as to preclude people of ordinary means from building and owning homes, an authority which sustains the minimum wage will be invoked to support a maximum wage for building laborers and artisans, and the same argument which has been here urged to strip the employer of his constitutional liberty of contract in one direction will be utilized to strip the employee of his constitutional liberty of contract in the opposite direction. A wrong decision does not end with itself: it is a precedent, and, with the swing of sentiment, its bad influence may run from one extremity of the arc to the other.

It has been said that legislation of the kind now under review is required in the interest of social justice, for whose ends freedom of contract may lawfully be subjected to restraint. The liberty of the individual to do as he pleases, even in innocent matters, is not absolute. It must frequently yield to the common good, and the line beyond which the power of interference may not be pressed is neither definite nor unalterable but may be made to move, within limits not well defined, with changing need and circumstance. Any attempt to fix a rigid boundary would be unwise as well as futile. But, nevertheless, there are limits to the power, and when these have been passed, it becomes the plain duty of the courts in the proper exercise of their authority to so declare. To sustain the individual freedom of action contemplated by the Constitution, is not to strike down the common good but to exalt it; for surely the good of society as a whole cannot be better served than by the preservation against arbitrary restraint of the liberties of its constituent members. . . .

Chief Justice Taft, dissenting.

I regret much to differ from the Court in these cases.

The boundary of the police power beyond which its exercise becomes an invasion of the guaranty of liberty under the Fifth and Fourteenth Amendments to the Constitution is not easy to mark. Our Court has been laboriously engaged in pricking out a line in successive cases. We must be careful, it seems to me, to follow that line as well as we can and not to depart from it by suggesting a distinction that is formal rather than real.

Legislatures in limiting freedom of contract between employee and employer by a minimum wage proceed on the assumption that employees, in the class receiving least pay, are not upon a full level of equality of choice with their employer and in their necessitous circumstances are prone to accept pretty much anything that is offered. They are peculiarly subject to the overreaching of the harsh and greedy employer. The evils of the sweating system and of the long hours and low wages which are characteristic of it are well known. Now, I agree that it is a disputable question in the field of political economy how far a statutory requirement of maximum hours or minimum wages may be a useful remedy for these evils, and whether it may not make the case of the oppressed employee worse than it was before. But it is not the function of this Court to hold congressional acts invalid simply because they are passed to carry out economic views which the Court believes to be unwise or unsound.

Legislatures which adopt a requirement of maximum hours or minimum wages may be presumed to believe that when sweating employers are prevented from paying unduly low wages by positive law they will continue their business, abating that part of their profits, which were wrung from the necessities of their employees, and will concede the better terms required by the law; and that while in individual cases hardship may result, the restriction will enure to the benefit of the general class of employees in whose interest the law is passed and so to that of the community at large.

The right of the legislature under the Fifth and Fourteenth Amendments to limit the hours of employment on the score of the health of the employee, it seems to me, has been firmly established. As to that, one would think, the line had been pricked out so that it has become a well formulated rule. In *Holden* v. *Hardy* . . . , it was applied to miners and rested on the unfavorable environment of employment in mining and smelting. In *Lochner* v. *New York* . . . , it was held that restricting those employed in bakeries to ten hours a day was an arbitrary and invalid interference with the liberty of contract secured by the Fourteenth Amendment. Then followed a number of cases beginning with *Muller* v. *Oregon* . . . sustaining the validity of a limit on maximum hours of labor for women . . . , and following these cases came *Bunting* v. *Oregon* . . . In that case, this Court sustained a law limiting the hours of labor of any person, whether man or woman, working in any mill, factory or manufacturing establishment to ten hours a day with a proviso as to further hours to which I shall hereafter advert. The law covered the whole field of industrial employment and certainly covered the case of persons employed in bakeries. Yet the opinion in the *Bunting Case* does not mention the *Lochner Case*. No one can suggest any constitutional distinction between employment in a bakery and one in any other kind of a manufacturing establishment which should make a limit of hours in the one invalid, and the same limit in the other permissible. It is impossible for me to reconcile the *Bunting Case* and the *Lochner Case* and I have always supposed that the *Lochner Case* was thus overruled *sub silentio*. Yet the opinion of the Court herein in support of its conclusion quotes from the opinion in the *Lochner Case* as one which has been sometimes distinguished but never overruled. Certainly there was no attempt to distinguish it in the *Bunting Case*.

However, the opinion herein does not overrule the *Bunting Case* in express terms, and therefore I assume that the conclusion in this case rests on the distinction between a minimum of wages and a maximum of hours in the limiting of liberty to contract. I regret to be at variance with the Court as to the substance of this distinction. In absolute freedom of contract the one term is as important as the other, for both enter equally into the consideration given and received, a restriction as to one is not any greater in essence than the other, and is of the same kind. One is the multiplier and the other the multiplicand.

If it be said that long hours of labor have a more direct effect upon the health of the employee than the low wage, there is very respectable authority from close observers, disclosed in the record and in the literature on the subject quoted at length in the briefs, that they are equally harmful in this regard. Congress took this view and we can not say it was not warranted in so doing.

With deference to the very able opinion of the Court and my brethren who concur in it, it appears to me to exaggerate the importance of the wage term of the contract of employment as more inviolate than its other terms. Its conclusion seems influenced by the fear that the concession of the power to impose a minimum wage must carry with it a concession of the power to fix a maximum wage. This, I submit, is a *non sequitur*. A line of distinction like the one under discussion in this case is, as the opinion elsewhere admits, a matter of degree and practical experience and not of pure logic. Certainly the wide difference between prescribing a minimum wage and a maximum wage could as a matter of degree and experience be easily affirmed. . . .

Without, however, expressing an opinion that a minimum wage limitation can be enacted for adult men, it is enough to say that the case before us involves only the application of the minimum wage to women. If I am right in thinking that the legislature can find as much support in experience for the view that a sweating wage has as great and as direct a tendency to bring about an injury to the health and morals of workers, as for the view that long hours injure their health, then I respectfully submit that *Muller* v. *Oregon* . . . controls this case. The law which was there sustained forbade the employment of any female in any mechanical establishment or factory or laundry for more than ten hours. This covered a pretty wide field in women's work and it would not seem that any sound distinction between that case and this can be built up on the fact that the law before us applies to all occupations of women with power in the board to make certain exceptions. Mr. Justice Brewer, who spoke for the Court in *Muller* v. *Oregon*, based its conclusion on the natural limit to women's physical strength and the likelihood that long hours would therefore injure her health, and we have had since a series of cases which may be said to have established a rule of decision. . . .

I am not sure from a reading of the opinion whether the Court thinks the authority of *Muller* v. *Oregon* is shaken by the adoption of the Nineteenth Amendment. The Nineteenth Amendment did not change the physical strength or limitations of women upon which the decision in *Muller* v. *Oregon* rests. The Amendment did give women political power and makes more certain that legislative provisions for their protection will be in accord with their interests as they see them. But I don't think we are warranted in varying constitutional construction based on physical differences between men and women, because of the Amendment. . . .

⊞ *E S S A Y S*

Historians once argued that the judiciary during the Progressive era was an enemy of both reform and women, at least where protective legislation was concerned. This conclusion rested not only on scholars' definition of liberty but on the importance they attached to the states' police powers. The traditional view, espoused by political scientist Judith Baer of the University of Massachusetts and argued in the first essay, is that judges relied on freedom to contract to strike down vast bodies of protective legislation. A revisionist interpretation insists, however, that Baer and other scholars overstated the legal impact of freedom to contract and exaggerated the role played by substantive due process in framing the judiciary's response to industrialization. In the second essay, Melvin Urofsky, a leading scholar of American constitutional history and a professor at Virginia Commonwealth University, reexamines the role played by the state judiciary. He argues that courts were not total enemies of reform; that state judges were sensitive to the legislatures' role in protecting health, safety, morals, and welfare; and that, after initially disapproving of protective legislation, most state courts—even the most conservative, as in New York and Illinois—acquiesced to these measures.

Women Workers and Liberty to Contract

JUDITH A. BAER

. . . Before 1908, special regulations for women usually took one of two forms. The more common was hours regulation, either establishing a maximum number of hours women could work or prohibiting them from working during certain hours, typically at night. Twenty-one states had passed maximum hours laws by 1908; one—New York—had such a law applying only to women under twenty-one; and four had night work laws. The latter type of regulation was proposed not only as a means of protecting safety and preserving family life, but in the hope that it would act as an aid to the enforcement of maximum-hours laws. . . .

The first women's hours laws were the product of agitation by labor organizations, including the few women's unions. The men's unions which fought for such laws were not very vulnerable to the charge that their primary concern was to eliminate competition. This motive was present. . . . But as we shall see, the legislation was not primarily intended to have, nor, apparently, did it have, the effect of removing female competition. Some skilled unions found better ways to keep women out of the trades: one was to demand strict observance of apprenticeship rules, and another, paradoxically, was to demand equal pay for the women who did get jobs, so they could not drive the men out by accepting lower wages. But not all skilled unions were hostile to women workers. The International Typographical Union, for example, not only had a long-standing equal pay regulation, but amended its constitution in 1869 to prohibit sex-based discrimination in subordinate unions.

Up to 1890, the unions were the chief proponents of legislation. After that time, this role was assumed by middle-class reformist organizations, the most influential of which was the National Consumers' League, under the leadership of women like [Florence] Kelley and the Goldmark sisters, Josephine and Pauline. The League and similar organizations led the fight for labor legislation from then until the New Deal, lobbying for bill after bill and instigating lawsuit after lawsuit. The leading labor organizations, first

Reprinted by permission of Greenwood Publishing Group, Inc., Westport, CT. Judith A. Baer, *The Chains of Protection: The Judicial Response to Women's Labor Legislation* (Westport, CT: Greenwood Press, 1978), pp. 16–18, 21, 23, 29–34, 38, 51–54, 56–57, 59–67, 93–97.

the Knights of Labor and then the American Federation of Labor, supported this legislation, but with neither the commitment nor the effect of the reformist groups. (Women's suffrage groups neither supported nor opposed these laws actively, although the reformist groups supported women's suffrage.)

One must be careful to separate consideration of the *motives* which produced the drive for this legislation from consideration of its *effects*. The fact that few of the supporters of protective legislation were motivated by male fear of female competition does not necessarily mean that the laws did not have the effect of removing this threat. It is difficult to determine what the effects of the legislation were, since in making a judgment like that one is trying to decide what *would* have happened *if* certain conditions had not prevailed. As late as 1928, the U.S. Women's Bureau's concluded that legislation had almost never restricted women's employment opportunities, because occupations were so rigidly segregated by sex that women's opportunities were effectively limited without legislation. The laws, they concluded, took no opportunities from women that they would have had in their absence. These investigators found only two instances of protective legislation being used to limit opportunities, and in one instance the women affected won an eight-year battle for an exemption.

This evidence is corroborated by other sources. The conclusion are, however, open to question. They amount to an assertion that without legislation, no one would have hired women for work usually performed by men, anyway. But there are instances of the displacement of one sex by another in an occupation—clerical work and cigar-making, for example—and, since women usually could be paid less than men, it is equally plausible that employers might have tried to replace men with women in the absence of legislation. Furthermore, the Women's Bureau conclusions have to be called into question because of the way the advisory committee which wrote its report was set up. Violent disagreement among its original members forced the representative of the Woman's Party—a group of feminists which had already begun to question the legitimacy of protective legislation—to resign, leaving on the committee representatives of the AFL, the National Women's Trade Union League, and the League of Women Voters, groups which had consistently supported protective legislation. Thus, the people predisposed toward finding evidence of discrimination against women in employment, caused by legislation, were not represented while those predisposed toward viewing the effects of legislation favorably remained.

The motives of the labor organizations and the reformist groups were quite similar. [M]ost of the evidence indicates that unions were motivated by a sincere desire to improve the lot of women workers as well as their own. However, in the minds of labor leaders these motives frequently were fused, or confused. . . .

Trade unionists, usually male, and middle-class social workers, frequently female, argued for restrictions according to their views of the women workers' interests. Manufacturing and business interests, opposed to these laws, insisted that they violated these workers' rights to freedom of contract.

On neither side of the controversy did women workers regularly speak for themselves; on both sides, others spoke for them. The women were given little chance to determine what it was that they themselves might want. . . .

The adjudication of hours laws provided . . . significant—and erratic—precedents. . . .

We must recognize the fact that these judges were reasoning within a box they had gotten themselves into. With the exception of the Oregon Supreme Court in 1906, the year after *Lochner*, they were not forced to accept the principle of freedom of contract or to apply it to hours legislation. As I have suggested, not all judges shared the prevailing ideas, and they were not always accepted by a majority within every court. In New York, Minnesota, and West Virginia, laws regulating labor conditions were upheld against the charge that they violated freedom of contract. There is no reason why other courts could not have done the same. Until *Lochner*, state courts were never forced either by precedent or by unanimity of professional opinion to invalidate labor laws. Those courts which did so were exercising considerable freedom of choice.

[By 1895,] twelve states had such laws. The Illinois Supreme Court overturned an eight-hour law for women in factories or workshops under both the Due Process and Equal Protection Clauses. *Ritchie* v. *People* was decided the year after the Pullman strike; it probably would have been a bad year for any labor law in Illinois. The court insisted that women were entitled to the same liberty of contract as men, regardless of differences of "sex and physique." The legislature, it declared, "has sought to impose an unreasonable and unnecessary burden upon . . . one citizen or class of citizens." The arguments and the result would have been satisfying only, perhaps, to a feminist who was also a judicial conservative. The *Ritchie* decision probably discouraged enactment of women's hours laws in other states. Between 1896 and 1908, nevertheless, nine states passed such laws. . . .

By January 1908, with oral argument in *Muller* scheduled for that month, seven cases involving women's hours laws had been decided by state supreme courts over a period of thirty-two years. Four laws had been upheld, and three overturned. . . . The decisions formed no discernible pattern, chronological, geographic, or theoretical. The weight of precedent fell on neither side. The states had provided the Supreme Court with little guidance. *Lochner* indicated strong disapproval of hours legislation, but in 1898 in *Holden* v. *Hardy* the Court had indicated willingness to sustain limitations in special circumstances. The *Muller* case could go either way, and the result would be crucial.

The law's supporters were determined to win, not only to sustain protective legislation for women but also to mount a successful attack on "the highest bastion of legal conservatism." The fact that the law at issue pertained only to women was to some extent an accident. The major goal was to establish "a factual connection between the law and the conditions of life which had provoked it." Reformers developed a startlingly innovative strategy. Instead of emphasizing legal precedents, they marshalled empirical evidence to convince the Court of the law's wisdom.

It was not the State of Oregon, but the National Consumers' League, which originally assumed this task. The League approached Louis Brandeis, the brother-in-law of its publications secretary Josephine Goldmark. Brandeis had distinguished himself from his colleagues at the bar by his sympathy to reform. The League asked him to represent it as *amicus curiae.* Brandeis refused to take the case unless he was hired as special counsel for the State of Oregon. This was agreed to, and the lawyer, the League, and the state joined forces. Josephine Goldmark supervised the collection of data, and she and Brandeis organized it into a brief which was filed before the Supreme Court.

This was the first Brandeis brief, and it made the term "brief" seem a misnomer. It may have been the longest the Court had ever seen, but it would not hold that record for long. In the opinion, Justice Brewer referred to Brandeis' "very copious collection of all these matters." In comparison with later Brandeis briefs, which could run over a thousand pages, "copious" seems a gross exaggeration. The *Muller* brief was 113 pages long. Two pages were devoted to precedent and legal argument, thirteen to a list of all the hours laws enacted so far anywhere in the world, one to a conclusion, and the remaining eighty-seven to empirical evidence.

It is usually a risky business to persuade any group out of a position it took as recently as three years previous, especially a court. Here, that might have been possible. The *Lochner* vote had been five to four, and one of the justices in the majority had since retired. But it is much safer to try to persuade people that the circumstances of a present case are distinguishable from those of an earlier one, and therefore not controlled by it. That was the tack Brandeis took, both in the brief and in oral argument. The obvious difference between the New York law and the Oregon one was that the former applied to all adults in a certain occupation and the latter only to women. So Brandeis was naturally encouraged to emphasize sexual differences, which he did. . . .

One feature of the brief (also characteristic of later Brandeis briefs) is the amount of space devoted to proving that this law does not subvert the interests of employers: almost one-fourth of the brief. This indicates the extent to which Brandeis and Goldmark had assumed the task of furnishing the Court with the relevant facts.

What kinds of data does the brief contain? One kind it does *not* contain is arguments about women's "primary role" or "inherent nature." Views like these are sometimes implied, but they are not stated. The brief sticks to observable conditions. Most of the data are anecdotal rather than statistical, consisting of selections from reports of factory or health inspectors both in the United States and in foreign countries; testimony before legislative investigating committees of witnesses such as physicians or social workers; quotes from medical texts and journal articles; and similar sources. There are a few examples of questionable data such as Havelock Ellis' statement that women's muscles and blood had more water in them than men's, but for the most part the brief contains presumably accurate reports of witnesses about conditions they observed.

The methodological sophistication of the reports, however, is not very great. The experts did not seem to realize that a report of injury and illness among workers does not suggest, let alone prove, a causal relationship between working conditions and health unless it is accompanied by statistics which show that the incidence of pathology is significantly greater among workers than in the general population. Even if such controls are available, no causal connection would be proved. Intervening variables might still be controlling, as in the matter of maternal employment and infant mortality. (The data available to Brandeis, Goldmark, Felix Frankfurter, and Mary Dewson for later briefs is better in this respect).

In these pages, we find report after report of a high incidence of tuberculosis, lead-poisoning, menstrual problems, miscarriages, deformed joints, and general ill health among women workers, with occasional pointed references to ill health among men workers. But there are few attempts at finding a control group. There are three exceptions to this generalization— the testimony of a British physician on sterility among working women but not among nonworkers in the same family, the report of two other doctors that in one town, women operatives had far more digestive problems than women in general, and a statement that infant mortality was highest in industrial areas—but even these are very small, contain no statistics, and are not duplicated elsewhere.

The data provide convincing evidence that women factory and laundry workers are subject to disease and injury, and that fatigue tends to increase accidents, but does not prove that women are more vulnerable than men are. Most of the reports were of shops, factories, or laundries where all or most of the employees were women. There was little evidence that men would have withstood the same conditions better. There are exceptions here, too, such as a report from Massachusetts compositors that women, unlike men, could not stand at the "case" and therefore suffered from muscle pain, menstrual difficulties, and general weakness. But most of the evidence does not prove that women suffered because of their physical characteristics any more than the Triangle Fire [Triangle Shirtwaist Co., New York City, 1910] did.

The part of the brief which discusses the effect of shorter hours is more persuasive as evidence of causal relationships; we find testimony that when hours were reduced, health improved. Whether or not long hours caused injury, disease, alcoholism, or infant mortality, amelioration of these conditions frequently followed reduction of hours. The evidence here is as anecdotal as that in the rest of the brief, but here there is, at least, a control group, with conditions before hours were reduced compared with conditions after reduction.

The portions of the brief which deal with the health of infants and children contain many references to the "puny, sickly, partly developed children" of factory workers, but they do not indicate a causal relationship between the employment of the mother and such pathology. We have already discussed the problem of infant mortality, prominent in the brief. And many of the children described as puny and sickly were themselves factory workers, and would probably have been weak no matter what their mothers did. Presumably, malnutrition was also a factor, but it is not suggested that, after weaning, this is caused by maternal employment.

One set of conditions which is ignored in the brief are the political ones. Brandeis makes no effort to argue that women need the protection of the state because they lack the political power to protect themselves. Throughout the brief we find not only a failure to prove causal connections between long hours and ill health (probably not Brandeis' and Goldmark's fault, considering the data available to them), but failure to distinguish physical causes from economic ones. The brief permits either of two conclusions: that working women suffer because of their physical structure, or that they suffer because the only jobs open to them are particularly dangerous and unpleasant.

The Supreme Court records of the *Muller* case contain no brief for the plaintiff, although the headnote to the opinion states that one was filed. Its argument is summarized here. The attorneys not only insisted that freedom of contract was protected by the Fourteenth Amendment, but that "women . . . as persons and citizens are entitled to all the privileges and immunities provided, and are as competent to contract with reference to their labor as are men." It cited the usual long string of precedents on the former point, and *Richie, Williams,* and, mystifyingly, *Wenham* on the latter.

The Decision: Woman in a Class by Herself

The case decided by the Supreme Court on February 24, 1908, became a landmark case not for its relevance to women's rights, but for its implications for economic regulation. It put a crack in the *Lochner* doctrine, and paved the way for "shift[ing] the emphasis from the fact that they are *women* to the fact that it is *industry* and relation of industry to the community that is regulated." The decision is not usually analyzed as I shall analyze it here, with an emphasis on the discussion of women. Even contemporary feminist scholars do not spend much time on it. They may, like Kate Millett, deplore its "patronizing air of concessions made to the physically inferior" or, like Leo Kanowitz, criticize its "male supremacist notions"—and these are valid and necessary criticisms—but no writer that I know of has yet examined in detail precisely what the opinion has to say about women.

The opinion for a unanimous Court was written by Justice David Brewer, a leading judicial conservative who had concurred in *Lochner* and dissented in *Holden* v. *Hardy*. . . .

Brewer has weighed most of the distinguishing features of the situation of working women, and has chosen to emphasize those which are physical and, in his view, unalterable in impact. He does not mention the economic conditions which might place women "at a disadvantage in the struggle for existence." He does discuss women's social and political disadvantages, but suggests that in the present case they are rather beside the point. He insists that even if these disabilities were removed, and the need for some kinds of special regulations perhaps eliminated thereby, women's physical and, perhaps, psychological nature ("disposition and habits of life") would still necessitate some special protection. Labor legislation based on women's physical characteristics is ruled permissible and advisable not only now, but for all time.

The assignment of this opinion to a judge who held to the principle of freedom of contract even more rigidly than most of his colleagues did probably had significant influence on the reasoning employed, and thus on the development of American constitutional law in the area of sex equality. (It is fascinating to speculate what the decision would have said if Justice Holmes, say, had written it instead). Considering Brewer's constitutional views, his choice of emphasis is understandable. If he had stressed the social and economic disabilities, he would have left the door open for later conclusion that any workers who suffered such disabilities could claim governmental protection—a conclusion contrary to his entire philosophy. He was on safer ground arguing as he did. "Grown and intelligent men" might someday be at a disadvantage in the struggle for subsistence, but they would surely never bear children.

Brewer makes the assumption, unsupported here by evidence, that the sexes differ psychologically as well as physically. This assumption bolsters his argument, but is not essential to it and is not, therefore, a very important part of it. Positing psychological differences makes it easier to identify the interests of women, as he *explicitly* does, with those of "the race." Surely, if women were psychologically constructed as men are, they would not yield willingly to limitations on their contractual rights. But Brewer does not need to, and indeed does not, dwell on this point. He emphasizes known physical facts rather than engaging in theorizing about female psychology.

That kind of theorizing would not have been unprecedented for Supreme Court opinions. Thirty-six years earlier, Justice Bradley, concurring in the affirmance of Illinois' denial of bar admission to a woman, had waxed eloquent in a manner very similar to the National Trades Union's 1836 report. Bradley had written of the "natural and proper timidity and delicacy which belongs to the female sex," unfitting it for many coarse occupations in favor of its "paramount design and mission . . . to fulfill the noble and benign offices of wife and mother." He had even gone so far as to refer to "the law of the Creator." Neither Brewer nor the justices who reviewed later employment laws produced anything like this. Given their evident views, they did not have to.

If one believes that freedom of contract is a constitutional right, which workers actually enjoy, the limitation of this freedom for women can be defended only if one agrees that women should have less freedom under the Constitution than men. The opinion does not flinch from this necessity. It declares that women may be denied rights which men enjoy, both for what the state views as their own benefit and in the interests of the larger society. Of course, any law which limits the working hours of a particular group of workers—miners, for example—curtails their freedom of contract relative to other workers. Viewed in this light, *Muller* would not seem startling—until we remember that it is possible to choose to be, or cease to be a miner; but one does not choose to be, or cease to be a woman.

Brewer has made the problem fairly easy to solve with his assumption that the interests of women coincide nicely with societal interests. Fusion of these two sets of interests obscures the possibility of conflict between them, conflict which, I have suggested, is a crucial problem in determining the legitimacy of a restriction. In this case, the assumption the Court has made appears reasonable. When one must stand all day in a hot, crowded factory, interest in one's own health demands shorter hours, which would also further society's interest in the production of healthy children.

But it is easy to envision situations in which these interests would conflict, as anyone informed on the abortion controversy knows. All steps which could be taken in the interests of women would not necessarily also protect actual or potential children. Indeed, one good way to help safeguard the health of women would be to discourage them from having children at all. This argument is, admittedly, extreme, but it is not therefore groundless. Despite medical advances, pregnancy and childbirth can be hazardous to health. The risk of death from pregnancy is statistically higher than the risk of death from any form of contraception, and even without death, pregnancy carries an appreciable risk of attendant dangerous, disabling complications. But anyone who suggests, as Shulamith Firestone does, that "Childbirth HURTS. And it isn't good for you," and draws the obvious conclusion from this statement, is ignored.

When we turn from specific considerations of physical health to more general considerations of interests, it is even easier to see the possibility of conflict, unless we accept the Court's tentatively articulated, and empirically unsupported belief about the nature of women. Women who are free to select occupations which involve considerable physical exertion might be willing to jeopardize their childbearing capacities. Women who enjoy working for long periods of time, or at unorthodox times of the day, might want to minimize domestic tasks. To make things even more complicated, some women might want one kind of life, and some another. The *Muller* ruling implicitly places the balance overwhelmingly on the side of "societal" interests, identified with family interests.

The opinion is fascinating not only as constitutional law, but as an interpretation of history. In three pages, Brewer has advanced two conflicting interpretations of the origin of the inequality of women, without resolving the apparent contradiction. First, he informs us that man "established his control at the outset by superior physical strength." The stronger dominated the weaker. There was apparently initial reluctance, if superior physical strength was needed. But a few lines later, Brewer discusses how woman "looks to her brother and depends upon him" for protection. This suggests that women voluntarily submitted to male dominance because of their own recognized need for protection.

We do not expect judges to be either historians or anthropologists. Indeed, considering some of their efforts in the former area, many of us might prefer that they stay out of the latter. But when they do venture into these disciplines, they invite, and usually deserve criticism. Brewer presents no evidence whatsoever for either of his contradictory conclusions. His historio-anthropological excursion is not crucial to his conclusion, but it is significant for its implications and applications. Men establish control over women, but women seek the protection of men. Somehow protection is inextricably intertwined with domination—a point which will become increasingly important as the need for protection decreases and men struggle to maintain their dominant position.

In *Muller*, the Court was presented with much evidence that people who worked in the kind of occupations in which women were usually employed needed shorter hours. But the conclusion that the Court drew from this evidence was that women could not work as many hours per day as men could. As I have suggested, this choice of emphasis was probably dictated in large part by the justices' need to reconcile the principle of freedom of contract with the need for some kind of regulation, a need powerfully argued by the Brandeis brief. The easiest way to make that reconciliation was to stress the most obvious and most persistent differences between women and "grown and intelligent men": not the economic and social differences, but the physical ones.

As precedent, *Muller* was able to become even more controlling in the area of sex equality than in the area of economic regulation. For more than sixty years, courts upheld nearly all cases of sex discrimination, citing this case as binding precedent, following its lead in emphasizing permanent rather than temporary, physical rather than economic or social, aspects of women's condition. Indeed, the one important deviant case seemed to be the product of judicial inability to believe that any factors other than permanent physical differences could justify special legislation. The slavish following of the *Muller* precedent was to persist long after technological advances had ameliorated the conditions which had made restrictions necessary.

The emphasis on sex differences in *Muller* and the decisions leading up to it were necessitated in part by a highly artificial set of circumstances, such as the creation of the exaggerated doctrine of freedom of contract and the traducing of the principle of reasonable classification. In the next thirty years the courts would abandon these doctrines, thus legitimizing governmental regulation over economic activity, and completely overturning the principle that "like legislation for men . . . could not be sustained." But the courts did not rethink their position on sex discrimination, finding it as valid in the modern constitutional era as it had been before.

[A]fter World War I, the movement for minimum wage met with discouragement. Although these laws had originally found a ready public acceptance, postwar advocates of minimum wage laws found employers vigorously opposed and the public apathetic. . . .

. . . The manufacturers had realized what had hit them, and were arming themselves against it. The fact that wages had risen in the years since the war helped buttress their argument. Unfortunately, despite these increases, many women's earnings still were not sufficient for their needs. Investigations of the Women's Bureau and various state agencies in the postwar years showed that throughout the country thousands of women workers in factories, laundries, and other mercantile establishments did not earn a living wage, and that despite postwar increases, real wages had frequently dropped in relation to the cost of living, determined by standards similar to those employed earlier.

But only one new minimum-wage law was passed between the war and the Depression. In 1918, Congress, by an overwhelming majority, enacted a law authorizing the fixing of minimum wages for adult women in the District of Columbia. A year later, Women's Bureau investigators found that the average rate of pay for women hotel, restaurant, and hospital workers was $15.40 per week; the Bureau of Labor Statistics estimated that the minimum cost of living that year was $18.43 per week. In March 1920, the wage board established by the law issued an order setting a minimum wage of $16.50 per week for women working in hotels, lodging houses, apartment houses, or hospitals. . . . The Children's Hospital of the District of Columbia, and a woman elevator operator in a hotel, sued to enjoin enforcement. Because the illness of a judge on the Supreme Court of the District of Columbia necessitated reargument (which got to be a thorny issue itself), the case took over three years to get to the U.S. Supreme Court, accompanied by the one Brandeis brief which failed to convince a court.

The opinion, issued on April 9, 1923, ranks with *Lochner* as an exhibit in the Chamber of Horrors of Substantive Due Process. The law was invalidated on the grounds that it unduly restricted freedom of contract, and that it bore no reasonable relation to health and morals. The case was decided by a vote of five to three (Brandeis not participating because his daughter was a member of the Minimum Wage Commission), and the dissents were as emphatic as those in *Lochner* had been. The public reaction was overwhelmingly critical, indicating that this decision was out of step with opinion on all sides, even in the legal profession. Law reviews had nothing good to say about it. The New York *World* typified the reaction of the press in a cartoon showing Justice Sutherland, the author of the majority opinion, holding out the decision to a figure labelled, "Woman wage earner." The caption read: "This decision, madam, affirms your constitutional right to starve." So much for the freedom that the law curtailed.

[T]he important parts of the opinion are those in which Sutherland rejects the argument that the government may provide special legislation for wage protection for women. His first task was to distinguish this from the hours cases . . . .

. . . Although Brewer had explicitly denied that the disfranchisement of women was a factor in that decision, the *Adkins* court appears to see the vote as a matter of primary importance. The majority apparently assumes that, since the Nineteenth Amendment, the only differences between the sexes which can justify special legislation are the physical ones—which, admittedly, do not seem to be directly related to living expenses. Except for the reliance on suffrage, however, the reasoning in *Adkins* is entirely

compatible with that in *Muller*. Brewer had implied that changes in the social
position of women might eventually make some special legislation for women
obsolete, but that the physical differences between the sexes would always
necessitate some special protection for women. Sutherland has accepted both
portions of this argument. He insists that the changes anticipated by Brewer
have now occurred: that women no longer suffer contractual, political, and
civil disadvantages which formerly might have justified regulations like that
at issue here. But he agrees with Brewer that physical differences may still
provide a basis for regulations reasonably connected with them . . . . Since
Sutherland can see no connection between women's physical characteristics
and wages, he concludes that minimum wage laws for women are
unconstitutional.

As Brewer had done, Sutherland ignores economic differences between
the sexes, in their incomes and working opportunities and in the conditions
they had to endure—differences whose existence was demonstrated, in both
cases, by the evidence in the briefs. In *Muller*, that inattention did not make
much difference, since physical distinction provided plausible justification
for hour limitation. But no such clear connection obtains between physical
distinctions and wage regulation. In the latter area, economic factors are
crucial. However great the political and social changes since 1908—and
surely the *Adkins* Court exaggerates them—the economic differences between the sexes were nowhere near the vanishing point, Nineteenth Amendment or no Nineteenth Amendment. . . .

The dissents, too, betray confusion as to what *Muller* had decided and
what was being decided now. Chief Justice Taft was uncertain as to what
the status of *Muller* now was . . . . On its face, that passage seems to me
to say quite plainly that hours limitations are justified by physical differences
even if the political ones have diminished (which is, of course, exactly what
Brewer said), but Taft was apprehensive. He argued that the present case
was controlled by *Muller*, declaring, "I don't think we are warranted in
varying constitutional construction based on physical differences between
men and women, because of the Nineteenth Amendment." But Taft does
not explain how the wage regulations are "based on physical differences
between men and women." Do women need a certain minimum income
because they may bear children, or because they are usually weaker than
most men? If so, precisely what is the connection between either or both
of these characteristics and living expenses? Taft does not give us any useful
hint. . . .

The significant division on the Court seems to be between those who
think that now that women have gained political, contractual, and civil rights,
only physical differences can justify special legislation, and do not justify
this type of it (the majority), and those who believe that the physical differences do justify this, and probably, from their language, any kind of
differential treatment (the dissenters). . . . These two decisions indicate the
extent to which judges' attention was increasingly focused on the physical
and permanent differences. They also indicate great confusion on the part
of these judges about what the real issue was. For the question is not whether

there is a rational relationship between sexual characteristics and a given regulation. The question should be, rather, whether there is a rational relationship between an evil which is substantive and a law which purports to mitigate that evil. For example, certainly there is a rational connection between physical strength and working hours. But the important point is whether there is a causal connection between ill health, accidents and so forth, and the number of hours one works. In night work, the question is whether prohibition of this work can reasonably be said to prevent the evils identified. In minimum wage regulation, the point is whether the dangers of an inadequate income can be mitigated by a fixed wage. But the courts obscure this question. Ironically, the result is that women's freedom of contract is sustained in a situation where in fact it did not exist, and curtailed in a situation where it did exist. This comment is not a defense of minimum-wage laws which apply only to women—I find them vulnerable to the same criticisms I made of women's hours laws—but I include it to emphasize the fact that the result of . . . *Adkins* was not to help, but to harm, women workers. . . .

The Courts and the Limits of Liberty to Contract

MELVIN I. UROFSKY

For a number of years, courts during the Progressive Era have been characterized as enemies of reform. Judges, according to that view, read their own conservative biases into law in order to nullify child labor legislation, efforts to establish maximum hours, minimum wages, and workmen's compensation, and revisions of traditional rules governing employer liability in job-related accidents. Theodore Roosevelt, Gilbert Roe, Roscoe Pound, and others were only a few voices in the chorus that condemned courts for their allegedly reactionary attitudes toward social legislation. Louis D. Brandeis, for example, on the eve of his nomination to the United States Supreme Court, charged judges with being blind to the great social and economic changes of the past half-century and with erecting their own prejudices into legal barriers to reform.

Recent studies of the United States Supreme Court have led to a revision of that institution's image as a thoroughgoing enemy of reform. Despite its decisions in such cases as *Lochner* v. *New York, Adair* v. *United States,* and *Coppage* v. *Kansas,* which have often been portrayed as epitomizing its opposition to protective legislation, the Court in fact upheld the vast majority of protective statutes it reviewed. A similar analysis needs to be done for state courts, which, if anything, enjoyed an even more reactionary reputation. Decisions such as those in *In re Jacobs, Godcharles & Company* v. *Wigeman, Ritchie* v. *People,* and *Ives* v. *South Buffalo Railway Company* gave contemporary critics the fuel they needed to declare, as did William

"State Courts and Protective Legislation during the Progressive Era: A Reevaluation" by Melvin I. Urofsky, *Journal of American History* 72 (June 1985), pp. 63–68, 71–74, 77–79, 88–91. Reprinted by permission.

F. Dodd, that "the greater number of our state courts are illiberal and, under our present constitutional and judicial organization, are able to block needed social and industrial legislation."

Yet if one looks at the larger spread of state court decisions, that view must be revised. In surveying state court decisions prior to World War I involving the basic elements of the Progressive program to protect workers— laws involving child labor, maximum hours, minimum wages, employer liability, and workmen's compensation—one finds that, with only a few exceptions, state courts moved consistently toward approval of a wide range of reform legislation. In attempting to enact their program, Progressives, although occasionally delayed in the courts, were not blocked there.

The general legislative outline of that protective program emerged fairly early in the Progressive Era: minimal standards to reduce the incidence of child labor; maximum working hours for women and children, as well as for men employed in dangerous occupations; payment of wages in cash, to eliminate the abuses of the scrip system and company stores; safety and sanitary standards for factories and mines; the establishment of a minimum wage, first for women and children, then for men; elimination of employers' common law defenses against liability for injury to their workers; the creation of workmen's compensation plans to insure against the hazards of death and disability in the factory; and, finally, laws to protect workers' rights to organize into unions. As Richard Hofstadter concluded, "it was expected that the [neutral] state, dealing out evenhanded justice, would meet the gravest complaints. Industrial society was to be humanized through the law."

The reformers, operating mainly in the state legislatures, succeeded in securing much, but not all, of their program and, in the first two decades of the twentieth century, significantly transformed the environment of industrial workers. How Progressives secured their victories, however, concerns us less than do the opposition they faced within the legal community and the question of how state courts responded to protective legislation. Common wisdom had long held the judiciary as a barrier to reform, and in many states sufficient evidence can be found to support that view. As one Nebraska judge noted disapprovingly in 1894, "There has in modern times arisen a sentiment favorable to paternalism in matters of legislation," and he, for one, intended to oppose the trend. Many other state judges shared that attitude.

For those opposed to what they considered unwarranted legislative interference in the natural workings of the economy, Thomas M. Cooley and Christopher G. Tiedeman provided an intellectual scaffolding upon which to erect the barriers. Cooley, whose *Treatise on Constitutional Limitations* may have been the most cited legal treatise in American law, made it plain that he relied on the courts to protect the nation against kindhearted but ill-advised attempts to meddle with the social and economic order. Tiedeman saw the limits on legislative power as even more restricted than did Cooley. In Tiedeman's view the proper role of government consisted of no more "than to provide for the public order and personal security by the prevention and punishment of crimes and trespasses." Writing during the growth of demands for greater legislative involvement in the marketplace, Tiedeman explicitly set out to prove that the police power, on which reformers relied to legitimate their proposals, could not go beyond the ancient legal maxim *sic utere tuo, ut alienum non laedas*—"use your own property in such a way as to not injure another's property."

In the new industrial age, however, property extended far beyond its traditional physical manifestations. In 1902 Judge Peter Grosscup declared that property "is not, in its modern sense, confined to that which may be touched by the hand, or seen by the eye. What is called tangible property has come to be, in most great enterprises, but the embodiment, physically, of an underlying life, a life that, in its contribution to success, is immeasurably more effective than the mere physical embodiment." The "underlying life" included the policies adopted by entrepreneurs to carry out their business goals and encompassed the terms on which they hired their laborers.

The laissez-faire rationalism of the nineteenth century found its judicial expression through the creation and sanctification of freedom of contract. As first articulated by Justice Rufus Peckham in 1897, the due process clause of the Fourteenth Amendment covered substantive as well as procedural guaranties. Those rights included the freedom to "pursue any livelihood or avocation, and for that purpose to enter into all contracts which may be proper, necessary and essential to . . . carrying out to a successful conclusion the purposes above mentioned." Proponents of freedom to contract hailed it as the cornerstone of a free society and argued that legislatures retained practically no power to interfere with private arrangements between employer and employee setting the terms and conditions of labor. Labor, too, was a property right, which free men could exercise and contract for as they desired, and as a Georgia judge noted, "I know of no right more precious, and one which laboring men ought to guard with more vigilance, than the right to fix by contract the terms upon which their labor shall be engaged."

Despite the assertions of contemporary critics or of later writers such as Benjamin R. Twiss, Clyde E. Jacobs, and Judith A. Baer, freedom of contract never achieved the dominant position in American law claimed by its adherents or denounced by its foes. First of all, the common law itself never viewed the right to contract as absolute. Fraud, duress, considerations of public policy, and other exceptions had long been accepted by courts as legitimate reasons to restrict or to nullify contracts. Although many judges persisted in the legal fiction that employer and employee stood as equals in the bargaining process, as early as 1762 Lord Northington had argued that "necessitous men are not, truly speaking, free men, but, to answer a present exigency, will submit to any terms that the crafty may impose upon them." When courts recognized that significant inequalities existed, or were persuaded of the fact, they were prepared to negate the agreement or to permit the state to impose limitations on the contractual process.

To justify those restrictions, reformers relied on the police power of the state. All commentators recognized that as part of its sovereign powers, a state could override both individual and property rights in order to preserve the health, safety, and welfare of the populace. Conservatives, even while conceding the existence of that authority, argued for severe limits on its use. Cooley, for example, had seen the power as necessary for any well-ordered society but insisted that such regulations have direct and immediate "reference to the comfort, safety, or welfare of society . . . and they must not, under pretense of regulation, take from the corporation any of the essential rights and privileges which the charter confers." Progressives, on the other hand, saw the power as far more extensive, by which the authority of the state could be exercised on behalf of the oppressed. "The police power," said Oliver Wendell Holmes in 1911, "may be put forth in aid of what is sanctioned by usage, or held by the prevailing morality, or strong and preponderant opinion to be greatly and immediately necessary to the public welfare." By that reading, the police power, instead of being limited, could reach almost anything the legislature wished to regulate.

In the police power lay the key to constitutional approval or denial of protective legislation. In those courts that adopted a narrow view of the power, protective legislation had tough sledding; where judges took a more expansive view of how the state could further public welfare, reformers found a sympathetic hearing. In the years following the Civil War, both the United States Supreme Court and states courts had numerous occasions to pass on the limits of the police power, and in so doing they created the precedents by which to judge legislative efforts to control the labor contract. Because that power derived from the ancient residual powers of the state, it could not be formally spelled out by legislatures or by constitutional conventions; the police power at any time was essentially what the courts declared it to be. Looking at state cases of the period, one can find numerous examples of expansive as well as restrictive interpretations of state power. . . .

Merely declaring that certain policies promoted the public good did not by itself bring measures within the sanction of the police power. The laws had to relate specifically to a clearly recognized health or safety objective and to be "clearly necessary for the safety, comfort or well-being of society [and which] the framers of the constitution . . . as men of ordinary prudence, cannot be supposed to have intended to prohibit." Some courts went further and demanded that the regulations meet the test of "reasonableness" as well. Not only did there have to be a substantive threat to the public welfare, but also the response chosen by the legislature had to be reasonable in the eyes of the court. Although some courts saw the police power as superior to private property rights, others saw property as the limit beyond which the state could not go. The legislature, said a Nebraska court in 1896, "cannot, under the guise of a police regulation, arbitrarily invade private property or personal rights." In one of the most famous cases negating a police regulation, Judge Robert Earl, speaking in 1885 for a unanimous New York court, struck down a statute prohibiting cigar making in tenements. The law bore no relation to health or safety, he declared, no matter what the legislature had factually determined, but "interferes with the profitable and free use of his property by the owner or lessee of a tenement-house who is a cigarmaker, and trammels him in the application of his industry and the disposition of his labor, and thus, in a strictly legitimate sense, it arbitrarily deprives him of his property and some portion of his personal liberty."

Two facts, however, remained clear to the proponents of protective legislation. First, courts had long put restrictions not only on contract but on other liberties as well. Even the phrase *sic utere* . . . itself implied limits on the absolute use of property. Not even the most ardent advocates of laissez-faire denied that the state had, in the police power, the tool and the obligation to prevent individuals from so exercising their own liberty in a way to abuse the rights of others or to harm the health, safety, and welfare of society. Second, in looking at the conditions spawned by industrialization, reformers found just those dangers that they believed justified police regulation to mitigate social evils.

The debate over the limits of the police power had not been resolved when cases testing protective legislation began to come before state courts. Tiedeman's assertion that "the unwritten law of this country is in the main against the exercise of police power" was, by the time he wrote, more wish than reality. In fact, in the introduction to his later revised two-volume treatise on the subject, he declared that his purpose was to halt the growing latitude given to that power. On the other hand, Charles M. Hough's claim at the end of the Progressive Era, that states had learned to get around due process and property restrictions by calling on the police power, is too strong an assertion in the other direction. Lawrence M. Friedman's statement that one cannot find a consistent economic theory governing court cases of the period seems the most considered judgment, and he well notes that "some of the most ringing affirmations of laissez-faire appeared in dissent." The same may be said of labor cases; no clear pattern is discernible. State courts had ample precedents on which to judge the plethora of labor regulations reformers pushed through state legislatures. They could, and at times did, find in favor of property rights as against those measures; but more often than not they validated protective legislation under the police power. . . .

Child labor legislation [for example] found easy acceptance in the state courts. The fact that children had always been a protected class made it easy for even conservative judges to approve extensive police regulations. Defendants rarely argued that such laws violated contract but, rather, pleaded that shifting liability placed an unfair burden on them, thus denying due process. That argument never commanded any more support in the state courts than it received from Justice Hughes.

The special leeway given to children opened the door in another area of protective legislation, the regulation of hours, since the initial efforts of reformers focused on another legally disadvantaged group, women. By emphasizing the special restraints on women, as well as their unique status as "mothers of the race," Progressives were able to establish a bridgehead, as it were, before striking out in pursuit of their larger goal, an eight-hour day for all workers.

The struggle to reduce the number of working hours constituted one of the major reforms of the period and was part of a larger campaign for shorter hours dating back to the early nineteenth century. In 1874 Massachusetts had enacted legislation for minors and women (the two were often grouped together, since both labored under substantial limitations on their rights), restricting their work week to no more than sixty hours. Although the call for an eight-hour day for all workers became a standard demand of organized labor by the end of the century, American workers in 1899 averaged over fifty-seven hours per week on the job, and a decade later the figure had declined by only two and one-half hours. In the face of such conditions, it is little wonder that by 1918 forty-three states, Puerto Rico, and the District of Columbia had enacted statutes regulating hours.

For purposes of analysis, hours legislation, aside from the child labor regulation discussed above, can be grouped into three major categories: hours of women; hours of laborers on public works; and hours of men in special occupations. Although there is considerable chronological overlap in those categories, such grouping will help highlight the particular arguments employed by both sides with the proponents relying on the police power and with employers appealing to liberty of contract.

The earliest case dealing with restrictions on hours for women arose in Massachusetts, when in 1876 *Commonwealth* v. *Hamilton Manufacturing Company* tested the 1874 statute prohibiting employment of women for more than sixty hours per week. In a short opinion the court brushed aside employers' arguments that the law violated freedom of contract and impinged on the rights granted the corporation in its charter. The court found that the statute violated no rights and represented a valid exercise of the police power. "This principle has been so frequently recognized in the Commonwealth," the court concluded, "that reference to the decisions is unnecessary." Although *Hamilton Manufacturing* would be cited in nearly every case involving women's hours, one wishes that the learned judges had spelled out their reasoning in more detail or at least had cited the "unnecessary" precedents. A suspicion lingers that the court decided the case more on an intuitive, rather than on an analytical, basis, a situation not unknown to the common law.

Ritchie v. *People*, the next case dealing with women's hours, did not evade the issue, and in one of the most condemned state court decisions of the period, the Illinois Supreme Court in 1895 struck down an 1893 statute limiting women's hours in factories or workshops to no more than eight hours in any one day and forty-eight in a week. While conceding that the police power of the state is extensive, the court declared that it must be directly related to the comfort, welfare, or safety of society. The law in question did not meet that test. "It is not the nature of the things done, but the sex of the persons doing them, which is made the basis of the claim that the act is a measure for the promotion of the public health." Women, intended to be the beneficiaries of the law, became, in the eyes of the court, its victims, since they were deprived of an essential constitutional right, the freedom to contract. Although Judge Benjamin D. Magruder conceded that the right to contract was subject to some limitations under the police power, he noted that those limitations had to "rest upon some reasonable basis, and cannot be arbitrarily exercised." A distinction based merely on sex could not be held reasonable and, therefore, could not stand.

Ritchie v. *People* became a paradigm of how those courts opposed to protective legislation would act. Even while conceding the long reach of the police power, they subjected that power to tests of directness and reasonableness and then found the laws lacking in those areas. They set up in opposition to the police power a constitutional right, sometimes due process but more often liberty of contract, which they would then, while also conceding some limits, hold as controlling in the particular instance. Although courts granted the legislature power to make policy distinctions, judges would then attack those distinctions as arbitrary, unreasonable, and interfering with the worker's right to dispose freely of his or her labor. Moreover, by insisting that all persons be treated *sui juris,* the courts could charge legislatures with attempting to put free people, entitled to constitutional protection, under a demeaning tutelage.

For all the condemnation *Ritchie* v. *People* received, however, few courts in fact adopted it as precedent. Between 1895 and 1908, when in *Muller* v. *Oregon* the United States Supreme Court validated an Oregon law restricting women's hours, only two states, one being Colorado, struck down similar statutes, and the Colorado Supreme Court based its ruling on technical deficiencies in the statute, not on substantive grounds. Only in New York, in *People* v. *Williams,* did the state's highest court adopt Judge Magruder's reasoning in *Ritchie* v. *People.* There Judge John C. Gray, with whom all six of his fellow judges concurred, also made note of the police power but immediately declared that the statute, prohibiting employment of women in factories between 9:00 P.M. and 6:00 A.M., "overstepped the limits set by the constitution of the state to the exercise of the power to interfere with the rights of citizens."

Judge Gray's opinion, with its effort to deny any reasonable basis for that law, can be seen as the New York tribunal's effort to discount the fact that by 1907 several state courts had upheld laws regulating women's hours. Pennsylvania, Nebraska, Washington, and Oregon statutes had all passed judicial muster, whereas other state laws had never faced challenge in the courts. In Pennsylvania an 1897 act limited minors and females to a workday of no more than twelve hours and a maximum of sixty hours per week. In its reasoning the Pennsylvania court found the justification that Judge Gray deemed absent in New York's law, namely, the physical inferiority of women and their unique status as potential mothers: "Surely an act which prevents the mothers of our race from being tempted to endanger their life and health by exhaustive employment can be condemned by none save those who expect to profit by it." The court noted that the legislature had certainly acted reasonably in its exercise of the police power by differentiating between men, on the one hand, and women and children, on the other. "If such legislation savors of paternalism," the court declared, "it is in its least objectionable form in that it cares for those who from their own necessities . . . may be prompted or required to jeopardize their health . . . hence the interests of the state itself."

Two other states, Nebraska and Washington, upheld hours laws in 1902 and adopted the reasoning of the Pennsylvania court. Four years later, in *State* v. *Muller,* an Oregon law limiting the hours of women working in factories and laundries to no more than ten per day received approval from that state's high court. Chief Justice Robert S. Bean noted that any labor contract is "subject to such reasonable limitations as are essential to the peace, health, welfare and good order of the community." The question to be determined, therefore, was whether that particular law constituted a reasonable exercise of the police power. The legislature had deemed it a matter of public policy to protect the physical well-being of women working in environments potentially dangerous to their health. He found nothing exceptional in that belief, and the court held that the law did not violate any constitutional rights of either employer or employee.

Unlike employers in the earlier cases, however, Curt Muller, the defendant laundry owner, appealed that decision to the United States Supreme Court, believing that the Court's 1905 opinion in *Lochner* would lead it to overturn the Oregon decision. In *Lochner* a New York law limiting the hours of bakery workers had been struck down as exceeding the police power because it bore no reasonable relation to health or safety. The National Consumers' League arranged for Brandeis, the "people's attorney," to represent Oregon, and he based his defense of the state law on the reasoning used in the earlier state cases. He saw that the Court had not held that *any* hours regulation was impermissible; in fact, the Court had previously upheld both state hours laws that had come before it. In *Lochner* the Court had asserted that it could not find the relation of the law to accepted areas of police regulation. In his now famous brief, Brandeis set out to show that relation, with more than one hundred pages devoted to economic and social data detailing the effect of long hours on women's health and the experience of other nations in that field. Without mentioning *Lochner*, the Court unanimously, in *Muller* v. *Oregon,* upheld the Oregon law, thus putting the constitutional imprimatur on women's hours legislation. . . .

Women, therefore, as a protected class, fell within the ambit of the police power, and the state could set terms for its own labor contracts; but reformers sought to cut down excessive hours for all workers, men as well as women, in private as well as public work. Early efforts in that direction immediately ran into difficulty. In Nebraska the legislature set eight hours as a day's labor, except for those in farm or domestic work. In 1894 the state's high court struck the statute down because it discriminated against farm and domestic laborers, thus violating Cooley's stricture against special legislation. But more than that, the court declared, the statute denied persons "the right to make and enforce the most ordinary, every-day contracts—a right accorded to all other persons. This denial of the right to contract is based upon a classification which is purely arbitrary, because the ground of the classification has no relation whatever to the natural capacity of persons to contract."

So-called special, or class, legislation could be justified under the police power only if it could be shown to have a direct bearing on the limited concerns of that power, namely, health, safety, or public comfort. New York tried that approach in an 1892 statute providing that ten hours of labor performed within twelve consecutive hours would constitute a day's labor for railroad workers, on the grounds that tired employees were a menace to the safety of the public. The New York court upheld the statute, but in such a way as to emasculate it. The ten-hour provision (which applied only in the absence of an express contract for other arrangements), was held to be no more than a statutory definition, thus unenforceable. While the court acknowledged the state's power to place some restrictions on working hours, it seemed to say that only minor limitations would be valid.

In Utah, however, the state constitution required the legislature to "pass laws to provide for the health and safety of the employees in factories, smelters and mines." Two cases tested these laws. In *State* v. *Holden* the Utah court in 1896 found that working conditions in smelters, where workers would be exposed to noxious gases for long periods, constituted a health danger, and the legislative judgment that men ought not to be exposed to such conditions for more than eight hours per day was, in the court's view, a reasonable decision. Of interest is the court's comment that it did not base its opinion merely on the state constitution; the court noted that even absent a specific constitutional clause, the state undoubtedly had the authority to pass the law under its police power. In the case of mine workers, the court took an even broader view and rejected Cooley's claim that class legislation was per se invalid. Under the police power the state could find that certain classes of workers needed special protection because certain types of business activity introduced particular problems: "In this way, laws are designed and adapted to the peculiarities attending each class of business. By such laws, different classes of people are protected by various acts and provisions. In this way, various classes of business are regulated, and the people protected, by appropriate laws, from dangers and evils that beset them." By such reasoning, legislatures could fine tune their police regulations almost on a business-by-business basis. Freedom of contract, in the court's view, had little claim against the larger interests of health and safety.

In *Holden* v. *Hardy* in 1898, the United States Supreme Court, by a seven-to-two vote, affirmed the Utah decisions. Speaking through Justice Henry B. Brown, the court set forth a liberal interpretation of how states might use their police powers that closely followed the state court's reasoning. But the Court went further. It dismissed the right to contract argument because employer and employee did not stand in a position of bargaining equality. When such disparity existed the state could intervene if necessary to protect the welfare of the party with a significantly lesser bargaining power. That discretion resided in the legislature, and although the police power was not limitless, within its rather broad parameters the courts would not second-guess the wisdom of elected representatives.

Holden v. *Hardy* became the paradigmatic case for approving protective legislation, with its holding that special and dangerous conditions justified the intervention of the state. In the next few years, several state courts used that reasoning to uphold hours laws for men. A Rhode Island ten-hour law for street railway workers, a Missouri statute limiting miners to eight hours, and Nevada acts to the same effect all received judicial blessing in opinions that cited and followed *Holden* v. *Hardy.* Only the Colorado court refused to go along and struck down the state's eight-hour law for miners as class legislation that violated freedom to contract. The court deemed *Holden* v. *Hardy* inapplicable because Colorado lacked the constitutional provision for such legislation found in Utah, although both the Utah and the United States supreme courts had emphasized that the authority for such legislation lay in the police power. As for the legislative judgment to which Justice Brown had said the courts ought to defer, the Colorado court pointedly declared that it was up to the judiciary "to determine what are the subjects upon which the [police] power is to be exercised, and the reasonableness of that exercise."

The Colorado position, however, appeared to be a minority view until, like a bombshell, the United States Supreme Court in 1905 invalidated a New York law establishing a ten-hour day and sixty-hour week for bakery workers. Justice Peckham, who had dissented in both *Holden* v. *Hardy* and *Atkin* v. *Kansas,* now spoke for a bare five-man majority in condemning the statute as being, not a true police measure, but an effort "simply to regulate the hours of labor between the master and his employees (all being men, *sui juris*), in a private business, not dangerous in any degree to morals or in any real and substantive degree, to the health of the employees." In the odium surrounding *Lochner,* the fact is often lost that in the three state courts that had earlier heard the case, the law had thrice been upheld. The case first arose in the Oneida County court, where the sitting judge ruled in its favor. In the Appellate Division, the court split three to two to uphold the law, and the Court of Appeals, by four to three, also voted to sustain it. Of the twenty-two judges who participated in the four decisions, twelve thought it constitutional, but because five of the ten who disagreed sat on the United States Supreme Court, the law went down.

Lochner, given the range of hours legislation that the United States Supreme Court approved, ought to be seen as an aberration, rather than as an epitome of the Court's attitude toward protective legislation. More important, it had only a limited impact on state courts. The Missouri court, relying on *Lochner,* struck down a six-day work week for bakers, and a Louisiana law establishing eight hours for certain jobs also fell in an opinion heavily laden with references to freedom of contract. As late as 1915, in a rather unusual opinion, the normally liberal Massachusetts court struck down a nine-hour day for certain railroad employees as an infringement of contract, with *Lochner* held to be governing. Most state courts, however, either ignored *Lochner* or distinguished it from the cases before them. Montana's eight-hour law for miners was held a valid exercise of the police power, which presumably limited contract, as was a similar California statute. In New York a limitation on railroad employees of no more than eight hours' work in a twenty-four-hour period received court approval as a valid police regulation, since its goal was to prevent accidents caused by fatigue. By that time legislatures were proving bolder, and some passed hours laws affecting all workers, not just women, minors, and those in public works or in dangerous occupations. . . .

Why then, if state courts were as receptive to protective legislation as this survey would indicate, did both contemporary as well as later writers label them so conservative and opposed to reform? There are several reasons, none of which by itself might have created the misperception but which together painted a bleak portrait of judges adamantly invalidating humane and progressive legislation.

First, uniformity did not prevail across all forty-eight state-court systems. Some courts, such as those in New York and Illinois, appear to have been far more conservative than others, while Massachusetts and Oregon, among others, enjoyed courts sympathetic to reform. As we have seen, nearly identical laws dealing with hours, wage regulation, employer liability, and workmen's compensation met with completely different judicial responses even in neighboring states; only laws controlling child labor received universal approbation.

A second reason is that although only a few decisions, in cases such as *Godcharles, Ritchie* v. *People,* and *Ives,* came down to invalidate protective laws, they invariably generated the majority of press commentary about the courts. In perusing the contemporary popular journals, one would never guess that state courts normally approved that type of legislation; one would see only attacks on the courts for usurping power and thwarting the popular will. In a similar fashion contemporary criticism of the courts often found its way into later scholarly articles and monographs, which also distorted the actual records of the courts. Attacks by Roosevelt, Brandeis, Robert M. La Follette, and others appeared in numerous works, especially those written during the constitutional crisis of the 1930s. Charles Warren's defense of the United States Supreme Court, on the other hand, was apparently forgotten by all save a handful of legal scholars.

A fourth factor to take into account is the sharp shift in the United States Supreme Court toward the end of the Progressive Era, after which the conservatism of that bench appeared to undo many of the reformers' earlier gains. Thus federal child labor laws were twice declared invalid, once for exceeding the commerce power and the other time for going beyond the limits of proper taxation. In *Adkins* v. *Children's Hospital,* the Court struck down a minimum-wage statute and resurrected *Lochner,* which nearly everyone, including Chief Justice William Howard Taft (certainly no liberal), had thought dead. The Court's decisions often constrained state courts, which felt bound to follow the constitutional rulings of the nation's highest tribunal. The long era of conservative domination, which chilled numerous reform programs, did not end until 1937, and it has continued to color our perceptions of the earlier period.

Another consideration is that even when reformers pushed protective measures through legislatures and then secured court approval, the laws often lacked decent enforcement mechanisms or failed to ameliorate the problem. As labor leader John B. Lennon argued, workers ought not to rely on laws alone: "If one half of these [current] laws were enforced, the condition of the wage-earners would be fairly good; but this, unfortunately, is not the case." One ought not to blame the courts for absence of effective laws or for the failure to provide sufficient funds and personnel for enforcement.

One cannot impose any consistent pattern on judicial decisions in that period. If in some cases courts struck down protective legislation and invoked the sanctity of contract, in far more cases they upheld reform efforts and either differentiated the circumstances so as to avoid the contract issue or, in many instances, merely dismissed it, relegating it to an inferior position vis-à-vis the police power. That is less true, however, in an area where courts did evince a decided bias against labor unions. Although an 1842 Massachusetts decision showed that courts could, if they wished, find ground to support unions, many did not. In 1900 Judge Magruder, who had delivered the opinion in *Ritchie* v. *People,* also spoke for the Illinois court in striking down a law requiring contractors on public works to hire only laborers belonging to unions. The act, he declared, discriminated between classes and therefore violated the state constitution. A later Massachusetts statute, which the American Federation of Labor hailed as a "model labor law," provided that a person's labor shall be construed as a personal, not a property, right and that no injunction should issue in labor matters. The state court, noting that the United States Supreme Court had already ruled that labor was property, invalidated the statute as denying workers equal protection. "The right to make contracts to earn money by labor," declare the court in *Bogni* v. *Perotti,* "is at least as essential to the laborer as is any property right to other members of society."

In *Bogni* the Massachusetts judges relied on two of the more notorious anti-union decisions of the United States Supreme Court. In *Adair* the Court struck down a federal law against "yellow dog" contracts on railroads, which required workers to sign pledges not to join or to remain members of a union while employed. The second case, *Coppage,* invalidated a similar state law, and Justice Pitney specifically attacked the statute for attempting to adjust inequities in the bargaining process. "[W]herever the right of private property" exists, he declared, "there must and will be inequalities of fortune. . . . [I]t is from the nature of things impossible to uphold freedom of contract and the right of private property without at the same time recognizing as legitimate those inequalities." Often overlooked is the fact that in *Coppage* the Court reversed the state court, which had upheld the law on grounds that it protected the worker in the bargaining process, by allowing the worker, through the union, to compensate somewhat for an unequal position in facing the employer.

The majority of state court decisions, however, did go against laws that attempted to support unions. If one wishes to consider such statutes as "protective legislation," then they must be conceded as exceptions to the pattern that prevailed in other areas. But it may be better to view laws dealing with labor unions as different in type. The protective legislation described herein aimed at preventing abuses of labor by employers through setting certain minima below which the employers could not force workers to go. Pro-union measures, on the other hand, aimed at increasing the bargaining power of one side in order to ensure a fairer bargaining process, thus a more equitable contract. To many judges the old common-law prohibitions against conspiracy appeared too strong to permit the state's intervention in a nonprotective manner, one that up until then had been clearly beyond the recognized limits of the police power. It would be many years before that attitude would change.

If I have read the cases correctly, however, then it appears that the doctrine of contract, while exalted by conservatives and set in opposition to the police power, was far from triumphant at the state level, just as it also failed to carry the day in the United States Supreme Court. Despite an occasional decision such as [that] in *Ritchie* v. *People* . . . , which naturally upset reformers, in most cases the courts reflected the mildly reformist views of the country at large. Rather than as bastions of reaction, most state courts could be fairly characterized as upholders of the best common-law tradition, attempting to meet the new social and economic conditions of the country. In doing so they did not embrace one doctrine to the exclusion of others but, in most instances, balanced legal doctrines, contract and police power, and, again in most instances, deferred to legislative judgment in policy matters. The Progressives, for all their complaints, could really have asked for no more.

✤ *F U R T H E R   R E A D I N G*

William F. Dodd, "Social Legislation and the Courts," *Political Science Quarterly* 28 (March 1913): 1–17

Clyde E. Jacobs, *Law Writers and the Courts: The Influence of Thomas M. Cooley, Christopher Tiedeman, and John F. Dillon upon American Constitutional Law* (1954)

Paul Kens, *Judicial Power and Reform Politics: The Anatomy of Lochner* v. *New York* (1990)

Charles W. McCurdy, "The Roots of Liberty of Contract Reconsidered," *Yearbook of the Supreme Court Historical Society* 20 (1984): 20–33

Alpheus T. Mason, "The Case of the Overworked Laundress," in John Garraty, ed., *Quarrels That Have Shaped the Constitution* (1975), pp. 176–190

Joseph F. Paschal, *Mr. Justice Sutherland: A Man Against the State* (1951)

John Semonche, *Charting the Future: The Supreme Court Responds to a Changing Society, 1890–1920* (1978)

D. Grier Stephenson, Jr., "The Supreme Court and Constitutional Change: *Lochner* v. *New York* Revisited," *Villanova Law Review* 21 (1975): 217–243

Benjamin R. Twiss, *Lawyers and the Constitution: How Laissez Faire Came to the Supreme Court* (1942)

Melvin Urofsky, *A Mind of One Piece: Brandeis and American Reform* (1971)

CHAPTER
4

The Emergence of Modern
Civil Liberties

Rampant nativism, combined with fever-pitch patriotism, resulted in serious violations of civil liberties during World War I. The Austrian-born violinist Fritz Kreisler, for example, and the famous Swiss-born conductor of the Boston Symphony, Dr. Karl Muck, were barred from U.S. music halls during the war. In a more deadly vein, 500 citizens of Collinsville, Illinois, who had decided that a fellow townsman, Roger Prager, was a German spy, dragged him into the street, wrapped him in the American flag, and murdered him.

Tough government policies during and following the war echoed these popular sentiments. The administration of Woodrow Wilson pushed through a willing Congress the draconian Espionage Act of 1918, a measure premised on the idea that restrictions on civil liberties would hasten the end of the conflict. Immediately following the peace settlement, Wilson's attorney general, A. Mitchell Palmer, established an antiradicalism division in the Department of Justice and assigned a young attorney, J. Edgar Hoover, to oversee its operation. Based on intelligence gathered by Hoover, Palmer in late 1919 and early 1920 carried out raids that resulted in the arrest of more than 6,000 alleged "radicals" and the deportations of hundreds of people. State governments followed suit, passing antiradical and antilabor laws to blunt the growing force of union organizing.

Traditionally, the states rather than the federal government had dealt with questions of civil liberty; throughout the nineteenth century, the Supreme Court had never invoked either the speech or the press clause of the First Amendment to decide a case. World War I and its aftermath permanently altered this pattern, however, as the justices reluctantly weighed national security against individual liberty. The Court also embraced the idea of incorporation; that is, that the due-process clause of the Fourteenth Amendment extended the rights of speech and press in the First Amendment against state action. This process of nationalizing—of extending the protection of the Bill of Rights against state action through the Fourteenth Amendment—occurred gradually, incrementally, but inexorably. These early years of First Amendment development laid the foundation for the subsequent dramatic expansion of civil liberty more than thirty years later during the chief justiceship of Earl Warren (1953–1969).

The Espionage Act of 1918, the first document, was the most far-reaching limitation on civil liberty in American history. The Supreme Court affirmed its constitutionality in two landmark cases, *Schenck* v. *U.S.* (1919) and *Abrams* v. *U.S.* (1919), the second and fourth documents, respectively. In the latter case, the government's prosecution rested on a leaflet entitled "Workers—Wake Up." The particular version used by the government to prosecute the defendants is reprinted as the third document. The work contains statements strongly critical of the government, probably because its translator apparently had only modest skills in the Yiddish language. A more faithful translation, document 5, features a more moderate tone. One of the most striking aspects of the *Schenck* and *Abrams* cases was the switch of Justice Oliver Wendell Holmes, Jr., from supporting the law in the former instance to eloquently dissenting against it in the latter case.

The change in Holmes's position is explained at least partially by his association with Zechariah Chafee, Jr., a professor at Harvard Law School and one of the most influential writers on First Amendment issues during this century. In "Freedom of Speech in War Time," the sixth document, Chafee argued for a balancing test that would account for both the public interest and individual rights. The Espionage Act was contrary to the open political discourse on which representative government depended.

Antiradical hysteria also surfaced in the states, which passed various criminal-anarchy statutes that curbed free speech. In *Gitlow* v. *New York* (1924), the seventh document, the justices voted 7–2 (Holmes and Brandeis dissenting) to sustain the conviction of Benjamin Gitlow, a member of the American Communist party and publisher of a "Left-Wing Manifesto." Justice Edward Terry Sanford's majority opinion accepted the idea, however, that the due-process clause of the Fourteenth Amendment incorporated fundamental rights such as freedom of speech and freedom of the press. The Court, therefore, put itself in the highly controversial role of holding state laws affecting speech and press up to federal First Amendment standards. The justices had already reached the conclusion, through the use of substantive due process, that property could be protected against state action. The implications of this new approach became clear in 1931, when the Court, in *Stromberg* v. *California* and *Near* v. *Minnesota*, struck down state laws curbing speech and press. The latter case, portions of which are excerpted in the last document, was not only the first great censorship case decided by the justices but a dramatic example of the constitutional consequences of nationalizing the Bill of Rights.

The Espionage Act, 1917/1918

Be it enacted, That section three of the Act . . . approved June 15, 1917, be . . . amended so as to read as follows:

"Sec. 3. Whoever, when the United States is at war, shall wilfully make or convey false reports or false statements with intent to interfere with the operation or success of the military or naval forces of the United States, or to promote the success of its enemies, or shall wilfully make or convey false reports, or false statements, or say or do anything except by way of bona fide and not disloyal advice to an investor . . . with intent to obstruct the sale by the United States of bonds . . . or the making of loans by or to the

United States, or whoever, when the United States is at war, shall wilfully cause . . . or incite . . . insubordination, disloyalty, mutiny, or refusal of duty, in the military or naval forces of the United States, or shall wilfully obstruct . . . the recruiting or enlistment service of the United States, and whoever, when the United States is at war, shall wilfully utter, print, write, or publish any disloyal, profane. scurrilous, or abusive language about the form of government of the United States, or the Constitution of the United States, or the military or naval forces of the United States, or the flag . . . or the uniform of the Army or Navy of the United States, or any language intended to bring the form of government . . . or the Constitution . . . or the military or naval forces . . . or the flag . . . of the United States into contempt, scorn, contumely, or disrepute . . . or shall wilfully display the flag of any foreign enemy, or shall wilfully . . . urge, incite, or advocate any curtailment of production in this country of any thing or things . . . necessary or essential to the prosecution of the war . . . and whoever shall wilfully advocate, teach, defend, or suggest the doing of any of the acts or things in this section enumerated and whoever shall by word or act support or favor the cause of any country with which the United States is at war or by word or act oppose the cause of the United States therein, shall be punished by a fine of not more than $10,000 or imprisonment for not more than twenty years, or both. . . .

Schenck v. *United States*, 249 U.S. 47 (1919)

(Unanimous)

Mr. Justice Holmes delivered the opinion of the court.

This is an indictment in three counts. The first charges a conspiracy to violate the Espionage Act of June 15, 1917, c. 30, § 3, 40 Stat. 217, 219, by causing and attempting to cause insubordination, &c., in the military and naval forces of the United States, and to obstruct the recruiting and enlistment service of the United States, when the United States was at war with the German Empire, to-wit, that the defendants wilfully conspired to have printed and circulated to men who had been called and accepted for military service under the Act of May 18, 1917, a document set forth and alleged to be calculated to cause such insubordination and obstruction. . . . The defendants were found guilty on all the counts. They set up the First Amendment to the Constitution forbidding Congress to make any law abridging the freedom of speech, or of the press, and bringing the case here on that ground have argued some other points also of which we must dispose. . . .

The document in question upon its first printed side recited the first section of the Thirteenth Amendment, said that the idea embodied in it was violated by the Conscription Act and that a conscript is little better than a convict. In impassioned language it intimated that conscription was despotism in its worst form and a monstrous wrong against humanity in the interest of Wall Street's chosen few. It said "Do not submit to intimidation," but in form at least confined itself to peaceful measures such as a petition for the repeal of the act. The other and later printed side of the sheet was headed "Assert Your Rights." It stated reasons for alleging that any one violated the Constitution when he refused to recognize "your right to assert your opposition to the draft," and went on "If you do not assert and support your rights, you are helping to deny or disparage rights which it is the solemn duty of all citizens and residents of the United States to retain." It described the arguments on the other side as coming from cunning politicians and a mercenary capitalist press, and even silent consent to the conscription law as helping to support an infamous conspiracy. It denied the power to send our citizens away to foreign shores to shoot up the people of other lands, and added that words could not express the condemnation such cold-blooded ruthlessness deserves, &c., &c., winding up "You must do your share to maintain, support and uphold the rights of the people of this country." Of course the document would not have been sent unless it had been intended to have some effect, and we do not see what effect it could be expected to have upon persons subject to the draft except to influence them to obstruct the carrying of it out. The defendants do not deny that the jury might find against them on this point.

But it is said, suppose that that was the tendency of this circular, it is protected by the First Amendment to the Constitution. Two of the strongest expressions are said to be quoted respectively from well-known public men. It well may be that the prohibition of laws abridging the freedom of speech is not confined to previous restraints, although to prevent them may have been the main purpose. . . . We admit that in many places and in ordinary times the defendants in saying all that was said in the circular would have been within their constitutional rights. But the character of every act depends upon the circumstances in which it is done. . . . The most stringent protection of free speech would not protect a man in falsely shouting fire in a theatre and causing a panic. It does not even protect a man from an injunction against uttering words that may have all the effect of force. . . . The question in every case is whether the words used are used in such circumstances and are of such a nature as to create a clear and present danger that they will bring about the substantive evils that Congress has a right to prevent. It is a question of proximity and degree. When a nation is at war many things that might be said in time of peace are such a hindrance to its effort that their utterance will not be endured so long as men fight and that no Court could regard them as protected by any constitutional right. It seems to be admitted that if an actual obstruction of the recruiting service were proved, liability for words that produced that effect might be enforced. The statute of 1917 in § 4 punishes conspiracies to obstruct as well as actual obstruction. If the act, (speaking, or circulating a paper,) its tendency and the intent with which it is done are the same, we perceive no ground for saying that success alone warrants making the act a crime. . . . Indeed that case might be said to dispose of the present contention if the precedent covers all *media concludendi*. But as the right to free speech was not referred to specially, we have thought fit to add a few words.

It was not argued that a conspiracy to obstruct the draft was not within the words of the Act of 1917. The words are "obstruct the recruiting or enlistment service," and it might be suggested that they refer only to making it hard to get volunteers. Recruiting heretofore usually having been accomplished by getting volunteers the word is apt to call up that method only in our minds. But recruiting is gaining fresh supplies for the forces, as well by draft as otherwise. It is put as an alternative to enlistment or voluntary enrollment in this act. The fact that the Act of 1917 was enlarged by the amending Act of May 16, 1918, c. 75, 40 Stat. 553, of course, does not affect the present indictment and would not, even if the former act had been repealed. . . . *Judgments affirmed.*

"Workers Wake Up," Version One, 1918

The preparatory work for Russia's emancipation is brought to an end by his Majesty, Mr. Wilson, and the rest of the gang; dogs of all colors!

America, together with the Allies, will march to Russia, not, "God Forbid," to interfere with the Russian affairs, but to help the Czecho-Slovaks in their struggle against the Bolsheviki.

Oh, ugly hypocrites; this time they shall not succeed in fooling the Russian emigrants and the friends of Russia in America. Too visible is their audacious move.

Workers, Russian emigrants, you who had the least belief in the honesty of our government, must now throw away all confidence, must spit in the face the false, hypocritic, military propaganda which has fooled you so relentlessly, calling forth your sympathy, your help, to the prosecution of the war. With the money which you have loaned, or are going to loan them, they will make bullets not only for the Germans but also for the Workers Soviets of Russia. Workers in the ammunition factories, you are producing bullets, bayonets, cannon, to murder not only the Germans, but also your dearest, best, who are in Russia and are fighting for freedom.

You who emigrated from Russia, you who are friends of Russia, will you carry on your conscience in cold blood the shame spot as a helper to choke the Workers Soviets? Will you give your consent to the inquisitionary expedition to Russia? Will you be calm spectators to the fleecing blood from the hearts of the best sons of Russia?

America and her Allies have betrayed (the workers). Their robberish aims are clear to all men. The destruction of the Russian Revolution, that is the politics of the march to Russia.

Workers, our reply to the barbaric intervention has to be a general strike! An open challenge only will let the government know that not only the Russian worker fights for freedom, but also here in America lives the spirit of revolution.

Do not let the government scare you with their wild punishment in prisons, hanging and shooting. We must not and will not betray the splendid fighters of Russia. Workers, up to fight.

Three hundred years had the Romanoff dynasty taught us how to fight.

Let all rulers remember this, from the smallest to the biggest despot, that the hand of the revolution will not shiver in a fight.

Woe unto those who will be in the way of progress. Let solidarity live!

The Rebels

"Workers Wake Up," Version Two, 1918

The preparatory work for Russia's "deliverance" is finished, and has been made clear by his Majesty, Mr. Wilson, and his comrades: dogs of all colors.

America together with the Allies will march after Russia, not, God forbid, to intervene in its internal affairs but only to help the Czecho-Slovaks in their fight against the Bolsheviks.

Oh, the ugly hypocrites! This time may it not work out for them to lie to the Russian emigrants and the friends of Russia in America. Too open is their audacious attitude.

Workers, wanderers from Russia, you who had the least faith in the earnestness of the government, must now throw away every trust, must spit in the face of the lying, hypocritical, military propaganda, which has lied to you in an ugly way in order to elicit your sympathy and your help in conducting the war. With your poor monies which you have loaned or will loan, they will make bullets not only for the Germans but also for the Workers' Soviets in Russia. While working in the ammunition factories you are creating bullets, swords, cannons to murder not only Germans but also your most beloved, your best ones, who are in Russia and who are fighting for freedom.

Wanderers and friends of Russia, will you carry on your consciences cold-bloodedly the stain of shame as accomplices in the strangulation of the Workers' Soviets? Will you add your vote to the inquisition-like expedition after Russia? Silent bywatchers of the blood flowing from the hearts of the best sons of Russia.

America and the Allies have lied. Their larcenous goals are clear to every person—the elimination of the Russian Revolution—this is the politics of the march after Russia.

Workers, our answer to the barbaric intervention has to be a general strike! A public resistance alone can let the government know that not only the Russian worker fights for freedom but that also here in America lives the spirit of revolution. Let the government not frighten you with its wild penalties of imprisonment, hanging and shooting.

We must not and shall not betray the brave fighters of Russia.

Workers, up to the battle!

Three hundred years the Romanovs have taught us how to fight. Let all rulers remember this, from the smallest to the biggest despot, that the hand of the revolutionary will not tremble in the fight.

Woe to those who stand in the way of progress!

Solidarity lives.

Rebels

Abrams v. United States, 250 U.S. 616 (1919)

[7–2: Clarke, Day, McKenna, McReynolds,
Pitney, Van Devanter, White; Holmes,
Brandeis]

Mr. Justice Clarke delivered the opinion of the court.

On a single indictment, containing four counts, the five plaintiffs in error, hereinafter designated the defendants, were convicted of conspiring to violate provisions of the Espionage Act of Congress (§ 3, Title I, of Act approved June 15, 1917, as amended May 16, 1918, 40 Stat. 553).

Each of the first three counts charged the defendants with conspiring, when the United States was at war with the Imperial Government of Germany, to unlawfully utter, print, write and publish: In the first count, "disloyal, scurrilous and abusive language about the form of Government of the United States"; in the second count, language "intended to bring the form of Government of the United States into contempt, scorn, contumely and disrepute"; and in the third count, language "intended to incite, provoke and encourage resistance to the United States in said war." The charge in the fourth count was that the defendants conspired "when the United States was at war with the Imperial German Government, . . . unlawfully and wilfully, by utterance, writing, printing and publication, to urge, incite and advocate curtailment of production of things and products, to wit, ordnance and ammunition, necessary and essential to the prosecution of the war." The offenses were charged in the language of the act of Congress.

It was charged in each count of the indictment that it was a part of the conspiracy that the defendants would attempt to accomplish their unlawful purpose by printing, writing and distributing in the City of New York many copies of a leaflet or circular, printed in the English language, and of another printed in the Yiddish language, copies of which, properly identified, were attached to the indictment.

All of the five defendants were born in Russia. They were intelligent, had considerable schooling, and at the time they were arrested they had lived in the United States terms varying from five to ten years, but none of them had applied for naturalization. Four of them testified as witnesses in their own behalf and of these, three frankly avowed that they were "rebels," "revolutionists," "anarchists," that they did not believe in government in any form, and they declared that they had no interest whatever in the Government of the United States. The fourth defendant testified that he was a "socialist" and believed in "a proper kind of government, not capitalistic," but in his classification the Government of the United States was "capitalistic."

It was admitted on the trial that the defendants had united to print and distribute the described circulars and that five thousand of them had been printed and distributed about the 22d day of August, 1918. The group had a meeting place in New York City, in rooms rented by defendant Abrams, under an assumed name, and there the subject of printing the circulars was discussed about two weeks before the defendants were arrested. The defendant Abrams, although not a printer, on July 27, 1918, purchased the printing outfit with which the circulars were printed and installed it in a basement room where the work was done at night. The circulars were distributed some by throwing them from a window of a building where one of the defendants was employed and others secretly, in New York City.

The defendants pleaded "not guilty," and the case of the Government consisted in showing the facts we have stated, and in introducing in evidence copies of the two printed circulars attached to the indictment, a sheet entitled "Revolutionists Unite for Action," written by the defendant Lipman, and found on him when he was arrested, and another paper, found at the headquarters of the group, and for which Abrams assumed responsibility.

Thus the conspiracy and the doing of the overt acts charged were largely admitted and were fully established.

On the record thus described it is argued, somewhat faintly, that the acts charged against the defendants were not unlawful because within the protection of that freedom of speech and of the press which is guaranteed by the First Amendment to the Constitution of the United States, and that the entire Espionage Act is unconstitutional because in conflict with that Amendment.

This contention is sufficiently discussed and is definitely negatived in *Schenck* v. *United States*. . . .

It will not do to say, as is now argued, that the only intent of these defendants was to prevent injury to the Russian cause. Men must be held to have intended, and to be accountable for, the effects which their acts were likely to produce. Even if their primary purpose and intent was to aid the cause of the Russian Revolution, the plan of action which they adopted necessarily involved, before it could be realized, defeat of the war program of the United States, for the obvious effect of this appeal, if it should become effective, as they hoped it might, would be to persuade persons of character such as those whom they regarded themselves as addressing, not to aid government loans and not to work in ammunition factories, where their work would produce "bullets, bayonets, cannon" and other munitions of war, the use of which would cause the "murder" of Germans and Russians. . . .

[E]xcerpts sufficiently show, that while the immediate occasion for this particular outbreak of lawlessness, on the part of the defendant alien anarchists, may have been resentment caused by our Government sending troops into Russia as a strategic operation against the Germans on the eastern battle front, yet the plain purpose of their propaganda was to excite, at the supreme crisis of the war, disaffection, sedition, riots, and, as they hoped, revolution, in this country for the purpose of embarrassing and if possible defeating the military plans of the Government in Europe. A technical distinction may perhaps be taken between disloyal and abusive language applied to the *form* of our government or language intended to bring the *form* of our government into contempt and disrepute, and language of like character and intended to produce like results directed against the President and Congress, the agencies through which that form of government must function in time of war. But it is not necessary to a decision of this case to consider whether such distinction is vital or merely formal, for the language of these circulars was obviously intended to provoke and to encourage resistance to the United States in the war, as the third count runs, and, the defendants, in terms, plainly urged and advocated a resort to a general strike of workers in ammunition factories for the purpose of curtailing the production of ordnance and munitions necessary and essential to the prosecution of the war as is charged in the fourth count. Thus it is clear not only that some evidence but that much persuasive evidence was before the jury tending to prove that the defendants were guilty as charged in both the third and fourth counts of the indictment and under the long established rule of law hereinbefore stated the judgment of the District Court must be *Affirmed.*

Mr. Justice Holmes dissenting.

. . . The first . . . says that the President's cowardly silence about the intervention in Russia reveals the hypocrisy of the plutocratic gang in Washington. . . .

The other leaflet, headed "Workers—Wake Up," with abusive language says that America together with the Allies will march for Russia to help the Czecko-Slovaks in their struggle against the Bolsheviki, and that this time the hypocrites shall not fool the Russian emigrants and friends of Russia in America. It tells the Russian emigrants that they now must spit in the face of the false military propaganda by which their sympathy and help to the prosecution of the war have been called forth and says that with the money they have lent or are going to lend "they will make bullets not only for the Germans but also for the Workers Soviets of Russia," and further, "Workers in the ammunition factories, you are producing bullets, bayonets, cannon, to murder not only the Germans, but also your dearest, best, who are in Russia and are fighting for freedom." It then appeals to the same Russian emigrants at some length not to consent to the "inquisitionary expedition to Russia," and says that the destruction of the Russian revolution is "the politics of the march to Russia." The leaflet winds up by saying "Workers, our reply to this barbaric intervention has to be a general strike!," and after a few words on the spirit of revolution, exhortations not to be afraid, and some usual tall talk ends "Woe unto those who will be in the way of progress. Let solidarity live! The Rebels."

No argument seems to me necessary to show that these pronunciamentos in no way attack the form of government of the United States, or that they do not support either of the first two counts. What little I have to say about the third count may be postponed until I have considered the fourth. With regard to that it seems too plain to be denied that the suggestion to workers in the ammunition factories that they are producing bullets to murder their dearest, and the further advocacy of a general strike, both in the second leaflet, do urge curtailment of production of things necessary to the prosecution of the war within the meaning of the Act of May 16, 1918 . . . . But to make the conduct criminal that statute requires that it should be "with intent by such curtailment to cripple or hinder the United States in the prosecution of the war." It seems to me that no such intent is proved.

I am aware of course that the word intent as vaguely used in ordinary legal discussion means no more than knowledge at the time of the act that the consequences said to be intended will ensue. Even less than that will satisfy the general principle of civil and criminal liability. A man may have to pay damages, may be sent to prison, at common law might be hanged, if at the time of his act he knew facts from which common experience showed that the consequences would follow, whether he individually could foresee them or not. But, when words are used exactly, a deed is not done with intent to produce a consequence unless that consequence is the aim of the deed. It may be obvious, and obvious to the actor, that the consequence will follow, and he may be liable for it even if he regrets it, but he does not do the act with intent to produce it unless the aim to produce it is the proximate motive of the specific act, although there may be some deeper motive behind.

It seems to me that this statute must be taken to use its words in a strict and accurate sense. They would be absurd in any other. A patriot might think that we were wasting money on aeroplanes, or making more cannon of a certain kind than we needed, and might advocate curtailment with success, yet even if it turned out that the curtailment hindered and was thought by other minds to have been obviously likely to hinder the United States in the prosecution of the war, no one would hold such conduct a crime. I admit that my illustration does not answer all that might be said but it is enough to show what I think and to let me pass to a more important aspect of the case. I refer to the First Amendment to the Constitution that Congress shall make no law abridging the freedom of speech.

I never have seen any reason to doubt that the questions of law that alone were before this Court in the cases of *Schenck, Frohwerk* and *Debs* . . . were rightly decided. I do not doubt for a moment that by the same reasoning that would justify punishing persuasion to murder, the United States constitutionally may punish speech that produces or is intended to produce a clear and imminent danger that it will bring about forthwith certain substantive evils that the United States constitutionally may seek to prevent. The power undoubtedly is greater in time of war than in time of peace because war opens dangers that do not exist at other times.

But as against dangers peculiar to war, as against others, the principle of the right to free speech is always the same. It is only the present danger of immediate evil or an intent to bring it about that warrants Congress in setting a limit to the expression of opinion where private rights are not concerned. Congress certainly cannot forbid all effort to change the mind of the country. Now nobody can suppose that the surreptitious publishing of a silly leaflet by an unknown man, without more, would present any immediate danger that its opinions would hinder the success of the government arms or have any appreciable tendency to do so. Publishing those opinions for the very purpose of obstructing however, might indicate a greater danger and at any rate would have the quality of an attempt. So I assume that the second leaflet if published for the purposes alleged in the fourth count might be punishable. But it seems pretty clear to me that nothing less than that would bring these papers within the scope of this law. An actual intent in the sense that I have explained is necessary to constitute an attempt, where a further act of the same individual is required to complete the substantive crime. . . . It is necessary where the success of the attempt depends upon others because if that intent is not present the actor's aim may be accomplished without bringing about the evils sought to be checked. An intent to prevent interference with the revolution in Russia might have been satisfied without any hindrance to carrying on the war in which we were engaged.

I do not see how anyone can find the intent required by the statute in any of the defendants' words. The second leaflet is the only one that affords even a foundation for the charge, and there, without invoking the hatred of German militarism expressed in the former one, it is evident from the beginning to the end that the only object of the paper is to help Russia and stop American intervention there against the popular government—not to impede the United States in the war that it was carrying on. To say that two phrases taken literally might import a suggestion of conduct that would have interference with the war as an indirect and probably undesired effect seems to me by no means enough to show an attempt to produce that effect. . . .

Persecution for the expression of opinions seems to me perfectly logical. If you have no doubt of your premises or your power and want a certain result with all your heart you naturally express your wishes in law and sweep away all opposition. To allow opposition by speech seems to indicate that you think the speech impotent, as when a man says that he has squared the circle, or that you do not care whole-heartedly for the result, or that you doubt either your power or your premises. But when men have realized that time has upset many fighting faiths, they may come to believe even more than they believe the very foundations of their own conduct that the ultimate good desired is better reached by free trade in ideas—that the best test of truth is the power of the thought to get itself accepted in the competition of the market, and that truth is the only ground upon which their wishes safely can be carried out. That at any rate is the theory of our Constitution. It is an experiment, as all life is an experiment. Every year if not every day we have to wager our salvation upon some prophecy based upon imperfect knowledge. While that experiment is part of our system I think that we should be eternally vigilant against attempts to check the expression of opinions that we loathe and believe to be fraught with death, unless they so imminently threaten immediate interference with the lawful and pressing purposes of the law that an immediate check is required to save the country. I wholly disagree with the argument of the Government that the First Amendment left the common law as to seditious libel in force. History seems to me against the notion. I had conceived that the United States through many years had shown its repentance for the Sedition Act of 1798, by repaying fines that it imposed. Only the emergency that makes it immediately dangerous to leave the correction of evil counsels to time warrants making any exception to the sweeping command, "Congress shall make no law . . . abridging the freedom of speech." Of course I am speaking only of expressions of opinion and exhortations, which were all that were uttered here, but I regret that I cannot put into more impressive words my belief that in their conviction upon this indictment the defendants were deprived of their rights under the Constitution of the United States.

Mr. Justice Brandeis concurs with the foregoing opinion.

Legal Scholar Zechariah Chafee, Jr., Considers Freedom of Speech in Wartime, 1918

Never in the history of our country, since the Alien and Sedition Laws of 1798, has the meaning of free speech been the subject of such sharp controversy as to-day. Over two hundred prosecutions and other judicial proceedings during the war, involving speeches, newspaper articles, pamphlets, and books, have been followed since the armistice by a widespread legislative consideration of bills punishing the advocacy of extreme radicalism. It is becoming increasingly important to determine the true limits of freedom of expression, so that speakers and writers may know how much they can properly say, and governments may be sure how much they can lawfully and wisely suppress. The United States Supreme Court has recently handed down several decisions upon the Espionage Act, which put us in a much better position than formerly to discuss the war-time aspects of the general problem of liberty of speech, and this article will approach the general problem from that side. At some later day it may be possible to discuss the proper limits of radical agitation in peace, and also to make a detailed historical examination of the events and documents leading up to the free speech clauses in our state and federal constitutions. For the present it is not feasible to do more than consider the application of those clauses to the treatment of opposition to war. . . .

Clearly, the problem of the limits of freedom of speech in war time is no academic question. On the one side, thoughtful men and journals are asking how scores of citizens can be imprisoned under this constitution only for their disapproval of the war as irreligious, unwise, or unjust. On the other, federal and state officials point to the great activities of German agents in our midst and to the unprecedented extension of the business of war over the whole nation, so that in the familiar remark of Ludendorff, wars are no longer won by armies in the field, but by the *morale* of the whole people. The widespread Liberty Bond campaigns, and the shipyards, munition factories, government offices, training camps, in all parts of the country, are felt to make the entire United States a theater of war, in which attacks upon our cause are as dangerous and unjustified as if made among the soldiers in the rear trenches. The government regards it as inconceivable that the Constitution should cripple its efforts to maintain public safety. Abstaining from countercharges of disloyalty and tyranny, let us recognize the issue as

"Freedom of Speech in Wartime" by Zechariah Chafee, Jr. *Harvard Law Review* 32 (June 1918), pp. 932–934, 936–938, 943–945, 958–960, 968–969. Reprinted by permission.

a conflict between two vital principles, and endeavor to find the basis of reconciliation between order and freedom.

At the outset, we can reject two extreme views in the controversy. First, there is the view that the Bill of Rights is a peacetime document and consequently freedom of speech may be ignored in war. This view has been officially repudiated. At the opposite pole is the belief of many agitators that the First Amendment renders unconstitutional any Act of Congress without exception "abridging the freedom of speech, or of the press," that all speech is free, and only action can be restrained and punished. This view is equally untenable. The provisions of the Bill of Rights cannot be applied with absolute literalness but are subject to exceptions. . . . The difficulty, of course, is to define the principle on which the implied exceptions are based, and an effort to that end will be made subsequently.

Since it is plain that the true solution lies between these two extreme views, and that even in war time freedom of speech exists subject to a problematical limit, it is necessary to determine where the line runs between utterance which is protected by the Constitution from governmental control and that which is not. . . .

We can, of course, be sure that certain forms of utterance, which have always been crimes or torts at common law, are not within the scope of the free speech clauses. The courts in construing such clauses have, for the most part, done little more than place obvious cases on this or that side of the line. They tell us, for instance, that libel and slander are actionable, or even punishable, that indecent books are criminal, that it is contempt to interfere with pending judicial proceedings, and that a permit can be required for street meetings; and on the other hand, that some criticism of the government must be allowed, that a temperate examination of a judge's opinion is not contempt, and that honest discussion of the merits of a painting causes no liability for damages. But when we ask where the line actually runs and how they know on which side of it a given utterance belongs, we find no answer in their opinions. Justice Holmes in his Espionage Act decisions had a magnificent opportunity to make articulate for us that major premise, under which judges ought to classify words as inside or outside the scope of the First Amendment. He, we hoped, would concentrate his great abilities on fixing the line. Instead, like the other judges, he has told us that certain plainly unlawful utterances are, to be sure, unlawful.

> The First Amendment . . . obviously was not intended to give immunity for every possible use of language. . . . We venture to believe that neither Hamilton nor Madison, nor any other competent person then or later, ever supposed that to make criminal the counselling of a murder . . . would be an unconstitutional interference with free speech.
>
> The most stringent protection of free speech would not protect a man in falsely shouting fire in a theatre and causing a panic.

How about the man who gets up in a theater between the acts and informs the audience honestly but perhaps mistakenly that the fire exits are too few or locked? He is a much closer parallel to Schenck or Debs. How about James Russell Lowell when he counseled, not murder, but the cessation of murder, his name for war? The question whether such perplexing cases are within the First Amendment or not cannot be solved by the multiplication of obvious examples, but only by the development of a rational principle to mark the limits of constitutional protection.

"The gradual process of judicial inclusion and exclusion," which has served so well to define other clauses in the federal Constitution by blocking out concrete situations on each side of the line until the line itself becomes increasingly plain, has as yet been of very little use for the First Amendment. The cases are too few, too varied in their character, and often too easily solved, to develop any definite boundary between lawful and unlawful speech. Even if some boundary between the precedents could be attained, we could have little confidence in it unless we knew better than now the fundamental principle on which the classification was based. Indeed, many of the decisions in which statutes have been held to violate free speech seem to ignore so seriously the economic and political facts of our time, that they are precedents of very dubious value for the inclusion and exclusion process. Nearly every free speech decision, outside such hotly litigated portions as privilege and fair comment in defamation, appears to have been decided largely by intuition. . . .

The true meaning of freedom of speech seems to be this. One of the most important purposes of society and government is the discovery and spread of truth on subjects of general concern. This is possible only through absolutely unlimited discussion, for, as Bagehot points out, once force is thrown into the argument, it becomes a matter of chance whether it is thrown on the false side or the true, and truth loses all its natural advantage in the contest. Nevertheless, there are other purposes of government, such as order, the training of the young, protection against external aggression. Unlimited discussion sometimes interferes with these purposes, which must then be balanced against freedom of speech, but freedom of speech ought to weigh very heavily in the scale. The First Amendment gives binding force to this principle of political wisdom.

Or to put the matter another way, it is useless to define free speech by talk about rights. The agitator asserts his constitutional right to speak, the government asserts its constitutional right to wage war. The result is a deadlock. Each side takes the position of the man who was arrested for swinging his arms and hitting another in the nose, and asked the judge if he did not have a right to swing his arms in a free country. "Your right to swing your arms ends just where the other man's nose begins." To find the boundary line of any right, we must get behind rules of law to human facts. In our problem, we must regard the desires and needs of the individual human being who wants to speak and those of the great group of human beings among whom he speaks. That is, in technical language, there are individual interests and social interests, which must be balanced against each other, if they conflict, in order to determine which interest shall be sacrificed under the circumstances and which shall be protected and become the foundation of a legal right. It must never be forgotten that the balancing cannot be properly done unless all the interests involved are adequately ascertained, and the great evil of all this talk about rights is that each side is so busy denying the other's claim to rights that it entirely overlooks the human desires and needs behind that claim. . . .

The First Amendment protects two kinds of interests in free speech. There is an individual interest, the need of many men to express their opinions on matters vital to them if life is to be worth living, and a social interest in the attainment of truth, so that the country may not only adopt the wisest course of action but carry it out in the wisest way. This social interest is especially important in war time. Even after war has been declared there is bound to be a confused mixture of good and bad arguments in its support, and a wide difference of opinion as to its objects. Truth can be sifted out from falsehood only if the government is vigorously and constantly cross-examined, so that the fundamental issues of the struggle may be clearly defined, and the war may not be diverted to improper ends, or conducted with an undue sacrifice of life and liberty, or prolonged after its just purposes are accomplished. Legal proceedings prove that an opponent makes the best cross-examiner. Consequently it is a disastrous mistake to limit criticism to those who favor the war. Men bitterly hostile to it may point out evils in its management like the secret treaties, which its supporters have been too busy to unearth. The history of the last five years shows how the objects of a war may change completely during its progress, and it is well that those objects should be steadily reformulated under the influence of open discussion not only by those who demand a military victory but by pacifists who take a different view of the national welfare. Further argument for the existence of this social interest becomes unnecessary if we recall the national value of the opposition in former wars.

The great trouble with most judicial construction of the Espionage Act is that this social interest has been ignored and free speech has been regarded as merely an individual interest, which must readily give way like other personal desires the moment it interferes with the social interest in national safety. The judge who has done most to bring social interests into legal thinking said years ago, "I think that the judges themselves have failed adequately to recognize their duty of weighing considerations of social advantage. The duty is inevitable, and the result of the often proclaimed judicial aversion to deal with such considerations is simply to leave the very ground and foundation of judgments inarticulate and often unconscious." The failure of the courts in the past to formulate any principle for drawing a boundary line around the right of free speech has not only thrown the judges into the difficult questions of the Espionage Act without any well-considered standard of criminality, but has allowed some of them to impose standards of their own and fix the line at a point which makes all opposition to this or any future war impossible. . . .

The true boundary line of the First Amendment can be fixed only when Congress and the courts realize that the principle on which speech is classified as lawful or unlawful involves the balancing against each other of two very important social interests, in public safety and in the search for truth. Every reasonable attempt should be made to maintain both interests unimpaired, and the great interest in free speech should be sacrificed only when the interest in public safety is really imperiled, and not, as most men believe, when it is barely conceivable that it may be slightly affected. In war time, therefore, speech should be unrestricted by the censorship or by punishment, unless it is clearly liable to cause direct and dangerous interference with the conduct of the war.

Thus our problem of locating the boundary line of free speech is solved. It is fixed close to the point where words will give rise to unlawful acts. . . . There is a similar balancing in the determination of what is "due process of law." And we can with certitude declare that the First Amendment forbids the punishment of words merely for their injurious tendencies. The history of the Amendment and the political function of free speech corroborate each other and make this conclusion plain.

The Espionage Act of 1917 seems on its face constitutional under this interpretation of the First Amendment, but it may have been construed so extremely as to violate the Amendment. Furthermore, freedom of speech is not only a limit on Congressional power, but a policy to be observed by the courts in applying constitutional statutes to utterance. . . .

Justice Holmes seems to discuss the constitutionality of the Espionage Act of 1917 rather than its construction. There can be little doubt that it is constitutional under any test if construed naturally, but it has been interpreted in such a way as to violate the free speech clause and the plain words of the statute, to say nothing of the principle that criminal statutes should be construed strictly. If the Supreme Court test had been laid down in the summer of 1917 and followed in charges by the District Courts, the most casual perusal of the utterances prosecuted makes it sure that there would have been many more acquittals. Instead, bad tendency has been the test of criminality, a test which this article has endeavored to prove wholly inconsistent with freedom of speech, or any genuine discussion of public affairs.

Furthermore, it is regrettable that Justice Holmes did nothing to emphasize the social interest behind free speech, and show the need of balancing even in war time. The last sentence of the passage quoted from the Schenck case seems to mean that the Supreme Court will sanction any restriction of speech that has military force behind it, and reminds us that the Justice used to say when he was young, "that truth was the majority vote of that nation that could lick all others." His liberalism seems held in abeyance by his belief in the relativity of values. It is not by giving way to force and the majority that truth has been won. Hard it may be for a court to protect those who oppose the cause for which men are dying in France, but others have died in the past for freedom of speech. . . .

Gitlow v. *New York,* 268 U.S. 652 (1925)

[7–2: Sanford, Butler, McKenna, McReynolds,
Sutherland, Taft, Van Devanter; Holmes,
Brandeis]

Mr. Justice Sanford delivered the opinion of the Court.

Benjamin Gitlow was indicted in the Supreme Court of New York, with three others, for the statutory crime of criminal anarchy. New York Penal

Laws, §§ 160, 161. He was separately tried, convicted, and sentenced to imprisonment. The judgment was affirmed by the Appellate Division and by the Court of Appeals. . . . The case is here on writ of error to the Supreme Court, to which the record was remitted.

The contention here is that the statute, by its terms and as applied in this case, is repugnant to the due process clause of the Fourteenth Amendment. . . .

The following facts were established on the trial by undisputed evidence and admissions: The defendant is a member of the Left Wing Section of the Socialist Party, a dissenting branch or faction of that party formed in opposition to its dominant policy of "moderate Socialism." Membership in both is open to aliens as well as citizens. The Left Wing Section was organized nationally at a conference in New York City in June, 1919, attended by ninety delegates from twenty different States. The conference elected a National Council, of which the defendant was a member, and left to it the adoption of a "Manifesto." This was published in The Revolutionary Age, the official organ of the Left Wing. The defendant was on the board of managers of the paper and was its business manager. He arranged for the printing of the paper and took to the printer the manuscript of the first issue which contained the Left Wing Manifesto, and also a Communist Program and a Program of the Left Wing that had been adopted by the conference. Sixteen thousand copies were printed, which were delivered at the premises in New York City used as the office of the Revolutionary Age and the headquarters of the Left Wing, and occupied by the defendant and other officials. These copies were paid for by the defendant, as business manager of the paper. Employees at this office wrapped and mailed out copies of the paper under the defendant's direction; and copies were sold from this office. It was admitted that the defendant signed a card subscribing to the Manifesto and Program of the Left Wing, which all applicants were required to sign before being admitted to membership; that he went to different parts of the State to speak to branches of the Socialist Party about the principles of the Left Wing and advocated their adoption; and that he was responsible for the Manifesto as it appeared, that "he knew of the publication, in a general way and he knew of its publication afterwards, and is responsible for its circulation."

There was no evidence of any effect resulting from the publication and circulation of the Manifesto. . . .

The specification of the errors relied on relates solely to the specific rulings of the trial court in the matters hereinbefore set out. The correctness of the verdict is not questioned, as the case was submitted to the jury. The sole contention here is, essentially, that as there was no evidence of any concrete result flowing from the publication of the Manifesto or of circumstances showing the likelihood of such result, the statute as construed and applied by the trial court penalizes the mere utterance, as such, of "doctrine" having no quality of incitement, without regard either to the circumstances of its utterance or to the likelihood of unlawful sequences; and that, as the exercise of the right of free expression with relation to government is only punishable "in circumstances involving likelihood of substantive evil," the statute contravenes the due process clause of the Fourteenth Amendment. The argument in support of this contention rests primarily upon the following propositions: 1st, That the "liberty" protected by the Fourteenth Amendment includes the liberty of speech and of the press; and 2nd, That while liberty of expression "is not absolute," it may be restrained "only in circumstances where its exercise bears a causal relation with some substantive evil, consummated, attempted or likely," and as the statute "takes no account of circumstances," it unduly restrains this liberty and is therefore unconstitutional.

The precise question presented, and the only question which we can consider under this writ of error, then is, whether the statute, as construed and applied in this case by the state courts, deprived the defendant of his liberty of expression in violation of the due process clause of the Fourteenth Amendment.

The statute does not penalize the utterance or publication of abstract "doctrine" or academic discussion having no quality of incitement to any concrete action. It is not aimed against mere historical or philosophical essays. It does not restrain the advocacy of changes in the form of government by constitutional and lawful means. What it prohibits is language advocating, advising or teaching the overthrow of organized government by unlawful means. These words imply urging to action. Advocacy is defined in the Century Dictionary as: "1. The act of pleading for, supporting, or recommending; active espousal." It is not the abstract "doctrine" of overthrowing organized government by unlawful means which is denounced by the statute, but the advocacy of action for the accomplishment of that purpose. It was so construed and applied by the trial judge, who specifically charged the jury that: "A mere grouping of historical events and a prophetic deduction from them would neither constitute advocacy, advice or teaching of a doctrine for the overthrow of government by force, violence or unlawful means. [And] if it were a mere essay on the subject, as suggested by counsel, based upon deductions from alleged historical events, with no teaching, advice or advocacy of action, it would not constitute a violation of the statute. . . . "

The Manifesto, plainly, is neither the statement of abstract doctrine nor, as suggested by counsel, mere prediction that industrial disturbances and revolutionary mass strikes will result spontaneously in an inevitable process of evolution in the economic system. It advocates and urges in fervent language mass action which shall progressively foment industrial disturbances and through political mass strikes and revolutionary mass action overthrow and destroy organized parliamentary government. It concludes with a call to action in these words: "The proletariat revolution and the Communist reconstruction of society—*the struggle for these*—is not indispensible. . . . The Communist International calls the proletariat of the world to the final struggle!" This is not the expression of philosophical abstraction, the mere prediction of future events; it is the language of direct incitement.

The means advocated for bringing about the destruction of organized parliamentary government, namely, mass industrial revolts usurping the functions of municipal government, political mass strikes directed against the parliamentary state, and revolutionary mass action for its final destruction, necessarily imply the use of force and violence, and in their essential nature are inherently unlawful in a constitutional government of law and order. That the jury were warranted in finding that the Manifesto advocated not merely the abstract doctrine of overthrowing organized government by force, violence and unlawful means, but action to that end, is clear.

For present purposes we may and do assume that freedom of speech and of the press—which are protected by the First Amendment from abridgment by Congress—are among the fundamental personal rights and "liberties" protected by the due process clause of the Fourteenth Amendment from impairment by the States. We do not regard the incidental statement in *Prudential Ins. Co.* v. *Cheek* . . . that the Fourteenth Amendment imposes no restrictions on the States concerning freedom of speech, as determinative of this question.

It is a fundamental principle, long established, that the freedom of speech and of the press which is secured by the Constitution, does not confer an absolute right to speak or publish, without responsibility, whatever one may choose, or an unrestricted and unbridled license that gives immunity for every possible use of language and prevents the punishment of those who abuse this freedom. . . . Reasonably limited, . . . this freedom is an inestimable privilege in a free government; without such limitation, it might become the scourge of the republic.

That a State in the exercise of its police power may punish those who abuse this freedom by utterances inimical to the public welfare, tending to corrupt public morals, incite to crime, or disturb the public peace, is not open to question. . . .

Thus it was held by this Court in the *Fox Case,* that a State may punish publications advocating and encouraging a breach of its criminal laws; and, in the *Gilbert Case,* that a State may punish utterances teaching or advocating that its citizens should not assist the United States in prosecuting or carrying on war with its public enemies.

And, for yet more imperative reasons, a State may punish utterances endangering the foundations of organized government and threatening its overthrow by unlawful means. These imperil its own existence as a constitutional State. Freedom of speech and press . . . does not protect disturbances to the public peace or the attempt to subvert the government. It does not protect publications or teachings which tend to subvert or imperil the government or to impede or hinder it in the performance of its governmental duties. . . . It does not protect publications prompting the overthrow of government by force; the punishment of those who publish articles which tend to destroy organized society being essential to the security of freedom and the stability of the State. . . . And a State may penalize utterances which openly advocate the overthrow of the representative and constitutional form of government of the United States and the several States, by violence or other unlawful means. . . . In short this freedom does not deprive a State of the primary and essential right of self preservation; which, so long as human governments endure, they cannot be denied. . . .

By enacting the present statute the State has determined, through its legislative body, that utterances advocating the overthrow of organized government by force, violence and unlawful means, are so inimical to the general welfare and involve such danger of substantive evil that they may be penalized in the exercise of its police power. That determination must be given great weight. Every presumption is to be indulged in favor of the validity of the statute. . . . And the case is to be considered "in the light of the principle that the State is primarily the judge of regulations required in the interest of public safety and welfare"; and that its police "statutes may only be declared unconstitutional where they are arbitrary or unreasonable attempts to exercise authority vested in the State in the public interest." . . . That utterances inciting to the overthrow of organized government by unlawful means, present a sufficient danger of substantive evil to bring their punishment within the range of legislative discretion, is clear. Such utterances, by their very nature, involve danger to the public peace and to the security of the State. They threaten breaches of the peace and ultimate revolution. And the immediate danger is none the less real and substantial, because the effect of a given utterance cannot be accurately foreseen. The State cannot reasonably be required to measure the danger from every such utterance in the nice balance of a jeweler's scale. A single revolutionary spark may kindle a fire that, smouldering for a time, may burst into a sweeping and destructive conflagration. It cannot be said that the State is acting arbitrarily or unreasonably when in the exercise of its judgment as to the measures necessary to protect the public peace and safety, it seeks to extinguish the spark without waiting until it has enkindled the flame or blazed into the conflagration. It cannot reasonably be required to defer the adoption of measures for its own peace and safety until the revolutionary utterances lead to actual disturbances of the public peace or imminent and immediate danger of its own destruction; but it may, in the exercise of its judgment, suppress the threatened danger in its incipiency. . . .

We cannot hold that the present statute is an arbitrary or unreasonable exercise of the police power of the State unwarrantably infringing the freedom of speech or press; and we must and do sustain its constitutionality.

This being so it may be applied to every utterance—not too trivial to be beneath the notice of the law—which is of such a character and used with such intent and purpose as to bring it within the prohibition of the statute. . . . In other words, when the legislative body has determined generally, in the constitutional exercise of its discretion, that utterances of a certain kind involve such danger of substantive evil that they may be punished, the question whether any specific utterance coming within the prohibited class is likely, in and of itself, to bring about the substantive evil, is not open to consideration. It is sufficient that the statute itself be constitutional and that the use of the language comes within its prohibition.

It is clear that the question in such cases is entirely different from that involved in those cases where the statute merely prohibits certain acts involving the danger of substantive evil, without any reference to language itself, and it is sought to apply its provisions to language used by the defendant for the purpose of bringing about the prohibited results. There, if it be contended that the statute cannot be applied to the language used by the defendant because of its protection by the freedom of speech or press, it must necessarily be found, as an original question, without any previous determination by the legislative body, whether the specific language used involved such likelihood of bringing about the substantive evil as to deprive it of the constitutional protection. In such cases it has been held that the general provisions of the statute may be constitutionally applied to the specific utterance of the defendant if its natural tendency and probable effect was to bring about the substantive evil which the legislative body might prevent. *Schenck* v. *United States.* . . . And the general statement in the *Schenck Case* . . . that the "question in every case is whether the words are used in such circumstances and are of such a nature as to create a clear and present danger that they will bring about the substantive evils,"—upon which great reliance is placed in the defendant's argument—was manifestly intended, as shown by the context, to apply only in cases of this class, and has no application to those like the present, where the legislative body itself has previously determined the danger of substantive evil arising from utterances of a specified character. . . .

And finding, for the reasons stated, that the statute is not in itself unconstitutional, and that it has not been applied in the present case in derogation of any constitutional right, the judgment of the Court of Appeals is *Affirmed.*

Mr. Justice Holmes, dissenting.

Mr. Justice Brandeis and I are of opinion that this judgment should be reversed. The general principle of free speech, it seems to me, must be taken to be included in the Fourteenth Amendment, in view of the scope that has been given to the word "liberty" as there used, although perhaps it may be accepted with a somewhat larger latitude of interpretation than is allowed to Congress by the sweeping language that governs or ought to govern the laws of the United States. If I am right, then I think that the criterion sanctioned by the full Court in *Schenck* v. *United States* . . . applies. "The question in every case is whether the words used are used in such circumstances and are of such a nature as to create a clear and present danger that they will bring about the substantive evils that [the State] has a right to prevent." It is true that in my opinion this criterion was departed from in *Abrams* v. *United States* . . . , but the convictions that I expressed in that case are too deep for it to be possible for me as yet to believe that it [has] settled the law. If what I think the correct test is applied, it is manifest that there was no present danger of an attempt to overthrow the government by force on the part of the admittedly small minority who shared the defendant's views. It is said that this manifesto was more than a theory, that it was an incitement. Every idea is an incitement. It offers itself for belief and if believed it is acted on unless some other belief outweighs it or some failure of energy stifles the movement at its birth. The only difference between the expression of an opinion and an incitement in the narrower sense is the speaker's enthusiasm for the result. Eloquence may set fire to reason. But whatever may be thought of the redundant discourse before us it had no chance of starting a present conflagration. If in the long run the beliefs expressed in proletarian dictatorship are destined to be accepted by the dominant forces of the community, the only meaning of free speech is that they should be given their chance and have their way.

If the publication of this document had been laid as an attempt to induce an uprising against government at once and not at some indefinite time in the future it would have presented a different question. The object would have been one with which the law might deal, subject to the doubt whether there was any danger that the publication could produce any result, or in other words, whether it was not futile and too remote from possible consequences. But the indictment alleges the publication and nothing more.

Near v. *Minnesota*, 283 U.S. 697 (1931)

[5–4: Hughes, Brandeis, Holmes, Roberts,
Stone; Butler, McReynolds, Sutherland,
Van Devanter]

Chief Justice Hughes delivered the opinion of the Court.

This statute, for the suppression as a public nuisance of a newspaper or periodical, is unusual, if not unique, and raises questions of grave importance transcending the local interests involved in the particular action. It is no longer open to doubt that the liberty of the press, and of speech, is within the liberty safeguarded by the due process clause of the Fourteenth Amendment from invasion by state action. . . .

In maintaining this guaranty, the authority of the State to enact laws to promote the health, safety, morals and general welfare of its people is necessarily admitted. The limits of this sovereign power must always be determined with appropriate regard to the particular subject of its exercise. . . . Liberty of speech, and of the press, is also not an absolute right, and the State may punish its abuse. . . . Liberty, in each of its phases, has its history and connotation and, in the present instance, the inquiry is as to the historic conception of the liberty of the press and whether the statute under review violates the essential attributes of that liberty. . . .

If we cut through more details of procedure, the operation and effect of the statute in substance is that public authorities may bring the owner or publisher of a newspaper or periodical before a judge upon a charge of conducting a business of publishing scandalous and defamatory matter—in particular that the matter consists of charges against public officers of official dereliction—and unless the owner or publisher is able and disposed to bring competent evidence to satisfy the judge that the charges are true and are published with good motives and for justifiable ends, his newspaper or periodical is suppressed and further publication is made punishable as a contempt. This is of the essence of censorship.

The question is whether a statute authorizing such proceedings in restraint of publication is consistent with the conception of the liberty of the press as historically conceived and guaranteed. In determining the extent of the constitutional protection, it has been generally, if not universally, considered that it is the chief purpose of the guaranty to prevent previous restraints upon publication. The struggle in England, direct against the legislative power of the licenser, resulted in renunciation of the censorship of the press. . . .

[P]unishment for the abuse of the liberty accorded to the press is essential to the protection of the public, and . . . the common law rules that subject the libeler to responsibility for the public offense, as well as for the private injury, are not abolished by the protection extended in our constitutions. . . . In the present case, we have no occasion to inquire as to the permissible scope of subsequent punishment. For whatever wrong the appellant has committed or may commit, by his publications, the State appropriately affords both public and private redress by its libel laws. As has been noted, the statue in question does not deal with punishments; it provided for no punishment, except in case of contempt for violation of the court's order, but for suppression and injunction, that is, for restraint upon publication.

The objection has also been made that the principle as to immunity from previous restraint is stated too broadly, if every such restraint is deemed to be prohibited. That is undoubtedly true; the protection even as to previous restraint is not absolutely unlimited. But the limitation has been recognized only in exceptional cases; "When a nation is at war many things that might be said in time of peace are such a hindrance to its effort that their utterance will not be endured so long as men fight and that no Court could regard them as protected by any unconstitutional right." *Schenck* v. *United States*. . . .

The exceptional nature of its limitations places in a strong light the general conception that liberty of the press, historically considered and taken up by the Federal Constitution, has meant, principally although not exclusively, immunity from previous restraints or censorship. The conception of the liberty of the press in this country had broadened with the exigencies of the colonial period and with the efforts to secure freedom from oppressive administration. That liberty was especially cherished for the immunity it afforded from previous restraint of the publication of censure of public officers and charges of official misconduct. . . .

The importance of this immunity has not lessened. While reckless assaults upon public men, and efforts to bring obloquy upon those who are endeavoring faithfully to discharge official duties, exert a baleful influence and deserve the severest condemnation in public opinion, it cannot be said that this abuse is greater, and it is believed to be less, than that which characterized the period in which our institutions took shape. Meanwhile, the administration of government has become more complex, the opportunities for malfeasance and corruption have multiplied, crime has grown to most serious proportions, and the danger of its protection by unfaithful officials and of the impairment of the fundamental security of life and property by criminal alliances and official neglect, emphasizes the primary need of a vigilant and courageous press, especially in great cities. The fact that the liberty of the press may be abused by miscreant purveyors of scandal does not make any the less necessary the immunity of the press from previous restraint in dealing with official misconduct. Subsequent punishment for such abuses as may exist is the appropriate remedy, consistent with constitutional privilege.

The statute in question cannot be justified by reason of the fact that the publisher is permitted to show, before injunction issues, that the matter published is true and is published with good motives and for justifiable ends. If such a statute, authorizing suppression and injunction on such a basis, is constitutionally valid, it would be equally permissible for the legislature to provide that at any time the publisher of any newspaper could be brought before a court, or even an administrative officer (as the constitutional protection may not be regarded as resting on mere procedural details) and required to produce proof of the truth of his publication, or of what he intended to publish, and of his motives, or stand enjoined. If this can be done, the legislature may provide machinery for determining in the complete exercise of its discretion what are justifiable ends and restrain publication accordingly. And it would be but a step to a complete system of censorship. The recognition of authority to impose previous restraint upon publication in order to protect the community against the circulation of charges of misconduct, and especially of official misconduct, necessarily would carry with it the admission of the authority of the censor against which the constitutional barrier was erected. The preliminary freedom, by virtue of the very reason for its existence, does not depend, as this Court has said, on proof of truth. . . .

Equally unavailing is the insistence that the statute is designed to prevent the circulation of scandal which tends to disturb the public peace and to provide assaults and the commission of crime. Charges of reprehensible conduct, and in particular of official malfeasance, unquestionably create a public scandal, but the theory of the constitutional guaranty is that even a more serious public evil would be caused by authority to prevent publication. . . . There is nothing new in the fact that charges of reprehensible conduct may create resentment and the disposition to resort to violent means of redress, but this well-understood tendency did not alter the determination to protect the press against censorship and restraint upon publication. . . . The danger of violent reactions becomes greater with effective organization of defiant groups resenting exposure, and if this consideration warranted legislative interference with the initial freedom of publication, the constitutional protection would be reduced to a mere form of words.

For these reasons we hold the statute . . . to be an infringement of the liberty of the press guaranteed by the Fourteenth Amendment. We should add that this decision rests upon the operation and effect of the statute, without regard to the question of the truth of the charges contained in the particular periodical. . . .

✥ *E S S A Y S*

Scholars of American liberty have disagreed over the path taken by the Supreme Court in the early civil-liberties cases. In the first selection, Walter F. Berns, a political scientist at the American Enterprise Institute, is sharply critical of Justice Oliver Wendell Holmes, Jr.; the growing intervention by the Supreme Court in matters associated with civil liberties; and the nationalization of the First Amendment. Richard Polenberg, a historian teaching at Cornell University, takes an opposite position in the second essay, finding in Holmes's dissent in *Abrams* the core values of modern civil-liberties theory. In the final essay, Paul L. Murphy, regents professor of history at the University of Minnesota, insists that the Court's decision in *Near* v. *Minnesota* demonstrated the wisdom of Holmes's approach and the need for judicial protection of civil liberties.

The Limits of Liberty

WALTER F. BERNS

. . . In *Schenck*, the Court, in an opinion written by Justice Holmes, took it for granted that Congress not only had the authority but the duty to protect the integrity of the military and naval services—insubordination and obstruction were "substantive evils that Congress has a right to prevent." The only question of interest here is whether the conviction of these two defendants under this statute [Espionage Act] violated the First Amendment. Holmes conceded that in other circumstances their anticonscription leaflets would have been protected, but the "character of every act depends upon the circumstances in which it is done," and Schenck . . . had acted during wartime. "The most stringent protection of free speech would not protect a man in falsely shouting fire in a theater, and causing a panic," Holmes said, though he did not explain whether this was so because the man shouted falsely or simply because his shout, whatever his intention, was instrumental in causing a panic. . . .

Schenck lacked the elements of a great case, the sort of case whose solution requires the Court to expound the fundamental principles of the constitution and thereby to provide the rule by which public life is to be measured. . . . Nevertheless, *Schenck* bequeathed us the clear-and-present-danger formula, which was soon to become the clear-and-present-danger test, and that test was to play a prominent role in the disposition of subsequent cases, and especially in the free speech literature built up around these cases. In *Schenck* it served to remind us . . . that while freedom of

From *The First Amendment and the Future of American Democracy* by Walter F. Berns. (New York: Basic Books, 1976), pp. 148–164, 166–168, 185–187. Reprinted by permission of Basic Books, Inc., Publishers, New York.

speech is the rule, there are exceptions to the rule—and war is a prolific generator of exceptions to rules. The exceptions are based on an appreciation of the importance and power of speech, as well as on the knowledge that the exercise of this power is not always compatible with ends the government is entitled and sometimes required to pursue, such as victory in a war which will determine the fate of republican government itself. This was clearly Lincoln's view, and had it been his fate to serve on the Court instead of in the Presidency, he surely would have fashioned a law of the First Amendment that takes this into account. Thus, despite the argument that Justice Black was later to make famous, not all speech is protected, even though the First Amendment specifically says Congress shall make *no* law abridging the freedom of speech.

Within a few months of its decision in *Schenck,* the Court was given the opportunity to decide a case involving an authentic sedition law, a law enacted in 1918 as an amendment to the 1917 Espionage Act, under which Schenck had been convicted. This amendment forbade, when the United States was at war with Germany, the uttering or publishing of "disloyal, scurrilous and abusive language about the form of government of the United States, or language intended to bring the form of government of the United States into contempt, scorn, contumely and disrepute, or intended to incite [etc.] resistance to the United States in said war. . . ." Five self-styled "rebels," "revolutionists," "anarchists," or "socialists" were convicted of having conspired to violate the provisions of this law by printing pamphlets attacking the sending of American forces to Russia and calling upon the "Workers of the World" to rise against the "capitalist" enemy, who was accused of fighting not only Imperial Germany but the "Workers Soviets of Russia." The Court, in a majority opinion written by Justice Clarke, devoted most of its attention to the question of whether there was sufficient evidence to support the jury's guilty verdicts, and dismissed the First Amendment defense in a one-sentence reference to *Schenck* (and a lesser-known case following *Schenck*). As to whether anyone could be punished for publishing abusive language about the "form of government," as opposed to language intended to provoke resistance to the war effort, the Court found it unnecessary to say. The distinction may be "vital or merely formal," but in either case it was irrelevant here, Clarke said, because the defendants had clearly intended to provoke a general strike and thereby to curtail production of war material. One could not know from this opinion that the case presented questions that concern fundamental principles of republican government. But such questions were present, and if they were to receive the careful consideration they deserve, it would have to be in the dissent that Holmes wrote for himself and Brandeis.

Holmes's dissenting opinion has been called "the most eloquent and moving defense of free speech since Milton's *Areopagitica*" and praised for putting the case against suppression of opinion in "perhaps its most perfect literary form for modern times." He doubted that the pamphlets involved, which he referred to as "silly" and as "puny anonymities [unable] to turn the color of legal litmus paper," came close to creating a clear and present danger of disrupting the war effort; and in the absence of such a danger, there could be no exception to the First Amendment's guarantee of freedom of speech. And he now addressed himself seriously to the question of the intent of the utterances, saying that, strictly speaking, "a deed is not done with intent to produce a consequence unless that consequence is the aim of the deed." . . .

With all respect for those who have praised this [*Abrams* dissent] it is not at all evident that it can provide a sound foundation for the law of the First Amendment. In the first place, it is by no means clear, especially in its implications. Does it mean that the "thought" that wins acceptance in the market will, whatever its substance, be labeled the truth? Or, on the contrary, that the truth has an advantage that enables it to win in any competition? If the latter, then of course persecution is illogical because it is unnecessary. But since Holmes has suggested that there can never be any basis for certainty and that all "fighting faiths" come and go in the seasons of history, he must mean that the thought that wins is a relative "truth," not a truth strictly so-called. If this is what he means, it does not follow that other doctrines may not logically be suppressed. By the only relevant criteria—those supplied by the marketplace—they are false and, to say the same thing, unpopular; and to the extent that they are unpopular, they can be "safely" suppressed. The more obnoxious they are held to be, the more unpopular they will be; and the more unpopular they are, the more safely those who hold them may be persecuted. It would seem, therefore, that the "truth" that wins in the market provides a very good ground indeed upon which those who subscribe to it can "safely" carry out their wishes, including a wish to extirpate the last vestiges of what the market has characterized as obnoxious "thought." Instead of issuing in a rule of "freedom for the thought that we hate"—or as Holmes puts it in *Abrams,* loathe—it seems to permit suppression of that thought. On what possible basis may one complain if one's own opinion is no longer tolerated by those who speak in the name of the truth and are entitled so to speak because they won the competition? Unlike Jefferson's argument for toleration of all religious opinions, Holmes's argument for toleration collapses under analysis. Jefferson was able to tolerate all religious opinions because, kept in their proper place, they were all politically irrelevant; and their proper place was defined by a political doctrine that he held to be self-evidently true.

Still, the *Abrams* dissent was Holmes's first attempt to elaborate a theory of the First Amendment—if we ignore his somewhat casual treatment of the issue as it appeared in *Schenck*—and it was not to be his last. Within six years the Court had the case that foreshadowed the most troubling cases of the modern era, and Holmes's dissent in it was destined to be accepted by the foremost libertarians of our day as the basis on which they would build the law.

Gitlow v. *New York* was significantly different from *Schenck*; here the offense was specified in terms of speech, political speech, and, much more clearly than in *Abrams,* political speech concerning the "form of government," or better, the very basis of the regime. Gitlow, an American disciple of Stalin, had been convicted under a New York statute that made it a criminal offense for anyone to advocate, advise, or teach, or to publish a paper that advocated, advised, or taught, that government should be overthrown by force or violence. Students of constitutional law will recognize it as the model for the Smith Act enacted by Congress in 1940. A divided Supreme Court affirmed Gitlow's conviction on the grounds that a state may punish "utterances endangering the foundation of organized government by unlawful means, and may regard utterances advocating the forceful overthrow of government as among those that endanger the foundation of organized government." Furthermore, by way of emphasizing the intrinsic illegality of some speech—that is, its illegality irrespective of the circumstances in which it is uttered—the Court went on to stress that the Constitution does not require the state to wait until the "revolutionary utterances lead to actual disturbances of the public peace or imminent and immediate danger of its own destruction." On the contrary, it may punish "every utterance—not too trivial to be below the notice of the law—which is of such a character and used with such intent and purpose as to bring it within the prohibition of the statute." The difference between the Espionage Act of 1917, under which Schenck had been convicted, and this New York Criminal Anarchy Act consisted in the difference between the substantive evils they sought to prevent; the former sought to prevent insubordination in the armed forces (to state it simply), while the latter sought to prevent the utterances themselves (and, thereby, to protect organized, constitutional government). There was, so far as the Court was concerned, no question present in *Gitlow* the answer to which required the use of the danger test. . . . What this means, among other things, is that Gitlow's political purpose was an illegal purpose, and that the law may take cognizance of the illegality of certain political purposes and may punish utterances made with the intent to effect these purposes. It may do this because, unlike the case of religious doctrines—which may be freely espoused—some political doctrines are incompatible with the principles upon which the country is built. It was with this last proposition especially that Holmes disagreed.

The organization to which Gitlow belonged (the precursor of the American Communist Party) was surely not a political party in the ordinary American sense. The argument of its "Left Wing Manifesto" was precisely that socialism could not be introduced by ordinary political action. It was "necessary to destroy the parliamentary state" by the use of such means as *"the political mass strike"* against the state itself, and to "overthrow . . . the political organization upon which capitalistic exploitation depends." "Revolutionary socialism does not propose to 'capture' the bourgeois parliamentary state, but to conquer and destroy it . . . by means of political action . . . in the revolutionary Marxian sense [which means] the *class action* of the proletariat *in any form* having as its objective the conquest of the power of the state" and its replacement by a new state "functioning as a dictatorship of the proletariat." Gitlow and his associates in the United States in 1919 were no more reticent in expressing their contempt for the institutions of constitutional government than are some of the spokesmen of radical movements, left and right, in our own day.

There is probably no question, even among the most devoted followers of Holmes, that the American government has the authority to punish anyone who acts along the lines advocated by Gitlow's manifesto. Indeed, not even Gitlow argued, or would argue, that the Constitution required the government to remain indifferent to his *attempts* to overthrow constitutional government. . . .

It is commonly held, and with good reason, that the opinion of the Court in [the Gitlow] case is not, to say the least, fully satisfactory. Whatever has been said by others, it seems clear that the Court failed fully to appreciate the extent to which the power it left in the hands of the state is a power that lends itself readily to abuse, and that the Court failed in making no effort to delineate constitutional restrictions designed to prevent that abuse. In this respect, Holmes's opinion was clearly better. Properly applied, the danger test reduces, even if it does not eliminate, the possibilities of such abuse; and to the extent that it accomplishes this end, it is an appropriate rule of the First Amendment, a rule that we might expect Marshall to have formulated, in substance if not in form, had he been given the opportunity. Yet Sanford's opinion for the Court has the merit of never losing sight of the connection between freedom of speech and republican government, and in this respect it is defensible. The same cannot be said of Holmes's. In one of his most frequently cited statements, he made explicit what he had implied in *Abrams*—namely, that freedom of speech has no necessary connection with republican government.

> If, in the long run, the beliefs expressed in proletarian dictatorship are destined to be accepted by the dominant forces of the community the only meaning of free speech is that they should be given their chance and have their way.

This well-known statement makes clear what his *Abrams* dissent had left in some doubt: the First Amendment, in his view, protects the expression of all political doctrines, and leaves to the marketplace of ideas alone the determination of the winner. In the long run, the advocates of proletarian dictatorship may win; in the short run, they must be allowed to compete freely and thereby be given the chance to become the dominant force of the community and "have their way." But the dominant forces in the New York community of 1925 may not have *their* way, because their way, embodied in the Criminal Anarchy Act under which Gitlow was convicted, is incompatible with "the only meaning of free speech."

Holmes took no cognizance of the obvious and awkward question this poses: on what basis can freedom of speech be granted to those who would deny freedom of speech to others? Or to state this in its traditional form, does it make sense to tolerate the intolerant? And the traditional answer was that it did not. Before religious toleration could be established, religion had to be reformed, subordinated . . . , and made politically irrelevant. Each sect had to be willing to live in peace with the others, and the basis of that agreement to live in peace was the common political doctrine to which they all subscribed and deferred. This is what the subordination of religion meant in practice, and it implied that each sect could trust the others to allow it to live in peace—so long as it obeyed the laws that applied to all. It is quite clear that the Republicans and Democrats and Socialists and Progressives and Populists and Whigs, and all the rest, cannot trust Gitlow's party to allow them to live in peace; they have Gitlow's word for that. He would "conquer and destroy" them. The only basis on which he and his friends can be tolerated is their weakness . . . .

The Strange Case of Oliver Wendell Holmes, Jr.

All this would be unimportant were it not for the esteem in which Holmes is held, and the fact that such esteem reflects the extent to which his opinions have been accepted by "the dominant forces" of the constitutional law community. . . .

The question is whether Holmes's was an appropriate "philosophy" to be expounded from the Supreme Court of the United States. In answering this question, one is required to pay tribute to his "wit, eloquence, and a certain grandeur of manner that captured for him the loyalty of many admirable men of the law" . . . . One must also acknowledge that much of Holmes's fame as a judge is richly deserved: he led the attack on the doctrinaire jurisprudence that had captured the Court of his day and had fashioned, largely from the due process clauses, a property right that sometimes threatened the very possibility of state or national government. . . .

Holmes [however] owes his fame partly to his good fortune in serving on the Court at a time when his views on the judicial power happened to be compatible with the political interests of the common man and happened to correspond to the views of the academic constitutional lawyers and the others who wrote the histories of the period. Holmes was no reformer—in fact, he was contemptuous of the efforts of the reformers, with their "tinkering with the institution of property," and said that "social regeneration" could be effected "only by taking in hand life and trying to build a race"— but his view of the Constitution and of the role of the Court allowed him to write those famous dissenting opinions upholding legislation establishing maximum hours of labor, for example, or outlawing "yellow-dog" contracts, opinions cited in preference to those of other justices. . . . Holmes wrote memorable opinions ("To quote from Mr. Justice Holmes' opinions," Frankfurter once said, "is to string pearls"), and when he said that "if there is any principle of the Constitution that more imperatively calls for attachment than any other it is the principle of free thought—not free thought for those who agree with us but freedom for the thought that we hate," it did not matter that he said it in a dissenting opinion, and it did not matter that he cited no authority and provided no argument: his words carried weight. . . . And it is his dissent in *Lochner* v. *New York*, rather than the carefully modulated dissent of Justice Harlan's, that is the one usually printed in the casebooks, picked up by the commentators, and thereby transmitted to succeeding generations. The Founders to the contrary notwithstanding, it became the accepted view that the Constitution, as Holmes put it in *Lochner,* was made "for people of fundamentally differing views." The Constitution is here, as in *Abrams* and *Gitlow,* understood to be essentially a set of rules for a game open not merely to all religious players but to all political players as well, and it has no interest in the outcome of the competition among them—even if the winner promises to abolish the rules of the game.

This view of the Constitution is not readily reconciled with Holmes's denial of the rights of man. If men do not possess rights, or if there is no foundation for the rights they claim to possess, it would seem to follow that justice is merely the right of the stronger, and Holmes in fact says this in one of his legal papers . . . . And if justice is the rule of the stronger, or the "dominant power," there is no basis for what might be called his un- limited pluralism, according to which all groups are entitled to play the political game—no basis, that is, except a First Amendment that constitutes nothing more than a trick played at the beginning by the numerically weaker, whereby the numerically stronger were induced to limit their power. There is, of course, an element of truth to this; the Constitution as a whole is, and was openly said to be, "a republican remedy for the diseases most incident to republican government," and these diseases were defined as abuses of the power that the majority would otherwise exercise by right. . . . Madison could justify the Bill of Rights, and all the other constitutional devices for limiting the power of the majority, potentially the stronger power, only insofar as it could be shown that these provisions were calculated to protect not only minority interests but also minority rights, rights for which there was some foundation other than the desires of the minor party. Without such a foundation, the constitutional restrictions on majority rule would indeed have been a trick played by the clever few on the sleeping or stupid many. By denying a foundation for rights, Holmes deprived civil liberty of its only firm foundation. Strangely, however, this did not prevent his inter- pretation of the First Amendment from being accepted as the "prevailing view," or his *Gitlow* formulation from being considered the "classic state- ment" of that view.

The fact that his *Gitlow* statement has come to be accepted as the correct formulation of the meaning of the First Amendment was undoubtedly as- sisted by the fact that *Gitlow* was, for another and unrelated reason, an unusually significant case. It was here that the Court took the radical step of nationalizing the law of freedom of speech and press by "incorporating" the First Amendment's provisions into the word "liberty" of the Fourteenth Amendment, thereby making them apply to the states as well as to the national government. This had the effect of bringing to the Supreme Court cases that earlier had been decided finally in the courts of the various states, and these now number in the hundreds. *Gitlow* was not a run-of-the-mill case, and what was done there proved to be of great consequence to the nation; and because Holmes was not a run-of-the-mill Supreme Court justice, what he said there proved to be more memorable than the opinion of the

Court, even though what he said there cannot provide a sound foundation for the law of the First Amendment. What he said there, as well as in *Abrams*, was, in effect, that freedom of speech is absolute but that it does not matter if freedom of speech is abolished (by a "proletarian dictatorship"). This is, of course, an untenable position.

Madison and Hamilton . . . cared deeply about freedom of speech because they cared deeply about republican government, and they applied their considerable powers to the task of defining the place free speech should properly occupy in a republican regime; but Holmes was indifferent to these larger constitutional questions. The Constitution occupied no special place in his thoughts; he never wrote a significant article or delivered a significant speech on the Constitution or on any of its provisions. Instead of attempting to guide the development of American political life informed by the principles of the Constitution, he turned to the study of private law, and found the law of its development in something resembling history. . . . He was indifferent, unconcerned with the substance or the consequences of the doctrines espoused. He could refer to *Gitlow* as a case involving the right "of an anarchist (so-called) to talk drool in favor of proletarian dictatorship." And when Eugene Debs was sentenced under the Espionage Act to ten years imprisonment for making what was mainly a socialist speech to a Socialist Party audience, Holmes, who wrote the opinion of the Court sustaining the conviction, could dismiss Debs's First Amendment defense as having been "disposed of in Schenck v. United States," and leave it at that; then, with reference to the case, he could say in a letter to Pollock that "there was a lot of jaw about free speech." It was in this same spirit that he wrote his *Abrams* and *Gitlow* dissents: the freedom of this kind of speech is absolute because this kind of speech is nothing but "drool" and "jaw." . . .

Conclusion

It is interesting—and it proved to be important—that Holmes, in his exposition of the First Amendment, should have used the term "fighting faiths." Men should realize, he said, that "time has upset many fighting faiths." But it was the specific purpose of the religious clauses of the First Amendment to cause the disappearance not of many but of *all* fighting faiths, the sort of religious faiths for which men in the past had demonstrated too great a willingness to fight. But since fighting faiths would not disappear of their own accord, they had to be superseded by a political truth. This truth, which was meant to endure, consigned all religious beliefs to a subordinate position where, having lost their militant proclivities, they could safely be ignored by the law. Religious beliefs and religious differences would then be politically irrelevant. By speaking of fighting faiths in the context of the speech and press provisions of the First Amendment, Holmes consigned political doctrines to the same category of irrelevancy. Whether a person is a liberal democrat or a Communist is, according to Holmes, of no more concern to the law than whether a person is a Methodist or a Baptist. This, he said, is the "only meaning of free speech."

But those who are ruled by tyrants have no need to speak politically because they are permitted no opportunity to act politically. It is sufficient that they "express" themselves by their presence at Nuremberg rallies or in Red Square, by a shout of *Sieg Heil* or the raising of a clenched fist. It is probably not by chance that it was only after Holmes's became the "prevailing view" of the First Amendment that the term "freedom of expression" made its appearance in the literature. . . . Freedom of expression is a commodious term, capable of encompassing not only speech but . . . all forms of communication, including those that have nothing whatever to do with self-government. The essential difference between the term "speech," the uniquely human capacity, and the term "expression" is that the former is connected to rationality, and it is man's rationality that makes him, unlike other animals, a being capable of governing himself. Speech makes possible the discussion and the reasoning requisite to the determination of how best to secure the rights with which men alone are endowed. Men may agree to be governed for self-interested reasons (to secure their rights), but it is the function of speech (of discussion, of reading, of thinking) to make known to men what is truly in their interests. It was only after a good deal of discussion that the Constitution was written and government instituted among Americans, and the form of government instituted requires discussion to continue—in Brandeis's words, "public discussion is a political duty"—precisely to enable Americans to govern themselves. Speech is a condition of *republican* government, which is why the Founders accorded it constitutional protection. In Madison's words, freedom of speech is an essential element of the process whereby the people choose the members of the government, and "the right of electing the members of the Government constitutes . . . the essence of a free and responsible government." The Founders' use of the phrase "freedom of *speech*" was not inadvertent, any more than Emerson's use of the word "expression" was inadvertent, although it probably was inadvertence that led him to remove the word speech from the First Amendment and put in its stead the word expression: "In construing specific legal doctrines which . . . will govern concrete issues, the main function of the courts is not to balance the interest in freedom of expression against other social interests but to define the key elements in the First Amendment: 'expression,' 'abridge,' and 'law.' " He can be excused for this because . . . the term "expression" comes closer to describing the kinds of utterances the Court has brought within the range of the First Amendment's protection. The Court has done this without considering the consequences for republican government.

Oliver Wendell Holmes, Jr., and Clear and Present Danger

RICHARD POLENBERG

. . . The Justice who listened most attentively to the contending presentations by Harry Weinberger and Assistant Attorney General Robert P. Stewart

From *Fighting Faiths* by Richard Polenberg, pp. 207–208, 211–212, 215–219, 222–224, 227–

may have been Oliver Wendell Holmes, Jr. Seven months earlier, in March 1919, when the Court had decided the first Espionage Act cases that came before it, Holmes had formulated the "clear and present danger" standard. That standard was consistent with everything that Holmes, in a legal career spanning fifty years, had written about the relationship between law and human nature, and about the proper balance between social order and individual rights. The clear and present danger test, in its original form, was not at all solicitous of the rights of dissenters. Between March and November . . . Holmes's thinking would undergo a significant change, and the Abrams case would play a central role in that change. . . .

Writing to friends in the years [before] the wartime Espionage Act cases, Holmes referred scornfully to softheaded social reformers who failed to realize that order would always come before liberty, the state before the individual. To many, Holmes may have appeared cynical, but surely he preferred to think that he possessed a realistic understanding of human nature. It was not his fault, as he put it, that "man's destiny is to fight." In November 1915 he asked an acquaintance, Dean John Wigmore of the Northwestern University Law School, "doesn't this squashy sentimentality of a big minority of our people about human life make you puke?" Holmes said he was thinking of several groups: those who condemn "the sensible doctor and parents who don't perform an operation to keep a deformed and nearly idiot baby alive—also of pacifists—of people who believe there is an upward and onward—who talk of uplift—who think that something particular has happened and that the universe is no longer predatory. Oh bring in a basin."

In the summer of 1918 Holmes explained his view of free speech, a view to which forty years of reflection had led him. A nation would protect itself against the expression of dangerous opinions, he said, as readily as it would against the spread of smallpox. "Free speech stands no differently than freedom from vaccination," he told Judge Learned Hand. "The occasions would be rarer when you cared enough to stop it but if for any reason you did care enough you wouldn't care a damn for the suggestion that you were acting on a provisional hypothesis and might be wrong." In a letter to Harold Laski, Holmes succintly restated the same argument: "My thesis would be (1) if you are cocksure, and (2) if you want it very much, and (3) if you have no doubt of your power—you will do what you believe efficient to bring about what you want—by legislation or otherwise. In most matters of belief we are not cocksure—we don't care very much—and we are not certain of our power. But in the opposite case we should deal with the act of speech as we deal with any other overt act that we don't like."

This was how Holmes saw things when, late in January 1919, the first three Espionage Act cases—*Schenck*, *Frohwerk*, and *Debs*—came before the Supreme Court. Arguing each case for the government were the Special Assistants to the Attorney General, John Lord O'Brian and Alfred Bettman. The Court unanimously upheld all three convictions, and Holmes wrote all three opinions. *Schenck* was decided on March 3, *Frohwerk* and *Debs* on March 10. Although the facts in the cases were substantially different, the clear and present danger standard which Holmes formulated to justify the ruling in *Schenck* also served as the basis for the two other decisions. . . .

Of course, one can be guilty of conspiring to violate a law even if the conspiracy fails. As Holmes pointed out, "we perceive no ground for saying that success alone warrants making the act a crime." But in the case of a conspiracy to violate the Espionage Act, as Holmes had stated, the elements of "proximity and degree" were crucial. The trial hardly demonstrated that the Socialist Party's circular created a "clear and present" danger of bringing about "the substantive evils that Congress has a right to prevent." Holmes would have rendered the facts in *Schenck* far more accurately—but far less memorably—had he written, "The most stringent protection of free speech would not protect a man in falsely advising theatregoers that a 'no smoking' ordinance deprived them of their rights, and causing the audience to turn him in as a troublemaker." . . .

While writing the opinion in *Schenck*, Holmes said that the case had "wrapped itself around me like a snake in a deadly struggle to present the obviously proper in the forms of logic—the real substance being: Damn your eyes—that's the way 'it's' going to be." He had recently reread John Stuart Mill's *On Liberty*, Holmes added, and perhaps he was influenced by Mill's argument that speech could properly be limited when—and only when—it caused "harm" to society. Opinions "lost their immunity," according to Mill, "when the circumstances in which they are expressed are such as to constitute in their expression a positive instigation to some mischievous act." The opinion that all corn dealers are starvers of the poor, Mill explained, could be printed in a newspaper but not "delivered orally to an excited mob assembled before the house of a corn dealer" or even "handed about among the same mob in the form of a placard."

Holmes may have thought that the clear and present danger standard made a similar distinction, but his formulation, as historian Fred D. Ragan has pointed out, served nevertheless "as a negative or restraining device rather than as a positive, libertarian or permissive rule." The Oliver Wendell Holmes who wrote the Court's decisions in *Schenck*, *Frohwerk*, and *Debs* was the Civil War veteran, the legal theorist, and the jurist who thought that individual rights must yield when society felt threatened, who sneered at the squashy sentimentality of those who denied that the universe was predatory, and who drew a comparison between laws prohibiting certain kinds of speech and laws requiring vaccination against smallpox. As yet, Holmes was "quite insensitive to any claim for special judicial protection of free speech."

Holmes and the Libertarians

Shortly after the Supreme Court handed down the Debs decision, Holmes received a letter from Judge Learned Hand. The two men had begun to correspond the previous June, after a chance meeting on a train as each was traveling to his summer home, Holmes to Beverly Farms, Massachusetts, and Hand to Cornish, New Hampshire. They had started to talk about "Tolerance" ("that rarest of the gods," as Hand once termed it) and continued their discussion in an exchange of letters. "Opinions are at best provisional hypotheses, incompletely tested," Hand had written at the time, ". . . they are never absolutes. So we must be tolerant of opposite opinions or varying opinions by the very fact of the incredulity of our own." Hand proposed a standard of "direct incitement" that was extraordinarily protective of free speech: only "direct advocacy" of unlawful acts could be punished; all other speech, no matter how critical of government policies, would be protected. He had earlier applied this "absolute and objective test" in deciding that *The Masses* could not be barred from the mails.

Now, in late March 1919, Learned Hand resumed his dialogue with Holmes. Writing about Debs's conviction under the Espionage Act, Hand claimed that "the thing against which the statute aims is positive impediments to raising an army. Speech may create such by its influence on others' conduct." But speech only violated the Act "when the words were directly an incitement." In effect, Hand was saying, whatever Debs's intent may have been, and whatever the effect of his speech, his conviction should have been upheld only if he had directly incited his listeners to violate the law. Holmes replied on April 3, saying, "I don't quite get your point," and adding that he could not see any difference between Hand's direct incitement test and his own clear and present danger standard. Inasmuch as Hand agreed that certain kinds of speech could violate the statute, Holmes wrote, "I don't know what the matter is, or how we differ so far as your letter goes." This uncharacteristically obtuse response, according to constitutional lawyer Gerald Gunther, indicates "the primitiveness of Holmes's first amendment thinking at that time." . . .

It was in this somewhat unsettled frame of mind that Holmes read Zechariah Chafee's article, "Freedom of Speech in War Time," in the June issue of the *Harvard Law Review*. Chafee, a professor of law at Harvard, conceded that the First Amendment did not protect all speech. The problem was to determine "where the line runs" between speech that is protected and speech that is not. In the Espionage Act cases, he said, Holmes had missed a "magnificent opportunity" to indicate where to draw that line. The clear and present danger standard, Chafee explained, only suggests that "certain plainly unlawful utterances are, to be sure, unlawful." Citing Holmes's sentence about falsely shouting fire in a theatre and causing a panic, Chafee offered a rejoinder. "How about the man who gets up in a theater between the acts and informs the audience honestly but perhaps mistakenly that the fire exits are too few or locked. He is a much closer parallel to Schenck or Debs." What was required, Chafee concluded, was not "the multiplication of obvious examples" but rather "the development of a rational principle."

Chafee suggested that Holmes, without fully realizing it, had already discovered such a rational principle; he merely had to construe his clear and present danger test to mean what Learned Hand had meant by direct incitement in *Masses.* Holmes had said, in *Schenck,* that the question was whether words create a clear and present danger "that they will bring about the substantive evils that Congress has a right to prevent"; and this, Chafee thought, "substantially agrees with the conclusion reached by Judge Hand." Speech should be unrestricted, Chafee argued, "unless it is clearly liable to cause direct and dangerous interference with the conduct of the war"; the line should be drawn "close to the point where words will give rise to unlawful acts." If by substantive evils were meant overt acts of interference, "then Justice Holmes draws the boundary line very close to the test of incitement at common law and clearly makes the punishment of words for their bad tendency impossible." Of course, Chafee admitted, this is not the way Holmes had construed the clear and present danger test in *Debs* (otherwise "it is hard to see how he could have been held guilty"), but what was to stop him from construing it that way in the future?

To help Holmes along, Chafee made the following argument: "The true meaning of freedom of speech seems to be this. One of the most important purposes of society and government is the discovery and spread of truth on subjects of general concern. This is possible only through absolutely unlimited discussion, for, as [Walter] Bagehot points out, once force is thrown into the argument, it becomes a matter of chance whether it is thrown on the false side or the true, and truth loses all its natural advantage in the contest." Conceding that government had other purposes, such as the preservation of order, and that "unlimited discussion sometimes interferes with these purposes," Chafee nevertheless insisted there was a "social interest in the attainment of truth" and that "truth can be sifted out from falsehood only if the government is vigorously and constantly cross-examined." As if directing his message to one reader, and one reader only, Chafee buttressed his argument by quoting "the judge who had done most to bring social interests into legal thinking." Oliver Wendell Holmes, he noted pointedly, had once criticized judges who "have failed adequately to recognize their duty of weighing considerations of social advantage."

Not only did Holmes read the article, but he met Chafee during the summer of 1919 when Harold Laski invited them for tea. Laski was himself much taken by the article—"we must fight on it," he told Chafee. "I've read it twice, and I'll go to the stake for every word"—and had already recommended it to Holmes. So we may assume that free speech was one of the topics of conversation that afternoon. By then, it seems clear, Holmes had begun to reconsider his original view of the subject, the view expressed in *Schenck, Frohwerk,* and *Debs.* While he still thought that a nation at war was going to restrict speech, he did not believe that it was necessary, or desirable, for Eugene Debs or other "poor devils" to go to jail. While the national interest might call for limitations on speech, those limitations had to be weighed against the social interest in obtaining the truth. Holmes had been led to this reconsideration by the criticisms he received from Learned Hand, Ernst Freund, and Zechariah Chafee, and also, perhaps, by other authors he was reading. . . .

By October 1919 Holmes had begun to view the issue of free speech differently than he had in March. He had not accepted Learned Hand's "incitement" test, or Ernst Freund's still more libertarian outlook, or even the theoretical arguments advanced by Zechariah Chafee and Harold Laski. But his reading of history, biography, and political philosophy had made Holmes more sensitive to the value of free speech as a means of getting at the truth, to the importance of experimentation, and to the need to treat dissenters mercifully, or, as Locke had said, "to mitigate the severity of the law." Holmes expressed his view in a letter to Harold Laski. "I fear we have less freedom of speech here than they have in England. Little as I believe in it as a theory I hope I would die for it and I go as far as anyone whom I regard as competent to form an opinion, in favor of it. Of course when I say I don't believe in it as a theory I don't mean that I do believe in the opposite as a theory. . . . When you are thoroughly convinced that you are right—wholeheartedly desire an end—and have no doubt of your power to accomplish it—I see nothing but municipal regulations to interfere with your using your power to accomplish it." Holmes wrote this letter on October 20, the day before the Supreme Court heard argument in the case of *Abrams et al.* v. *United States.*

The Dissent

[S]hortly after circulating a draft of his dissent in the Abrams case, Oliver Wendell Holmes was visited at his home by three of his brethren. The story of this pilgrimage to 1720 I Street was related to Dean Acheson, who was Louis Brandeis's clerk, by Stanley Morrison, who was Holmes's. Willis Van Devanter, Mahlon Pitney, and a third Justice whose identity Acheson could not recall, accompanied by Holmes's wife, Fanny, entered the Justice's study. "They laid before him their request that in this case, which they thought affected the safety of the country, he should, like the old soldier he had once been, close ranks and forego individual predilections. Mrs. Holmes agreed. The tone of the discussion was at all times friendly, even affectionate. The Justice regretted that he could not do as they wished. They did not press." It is likely that at some point in the discussion Pitney said, "I think there was a case for the jury," since that is the comment he jotted on the dissent Holmes circulated. Holmes, who had anticipated this pressure to go along with the majority, and had commented that he would "perhaps be persuaded to shut up, but I don't expect it," stood his ground. As he later told a friend, "I thought as I was given the Debs case and some others when the convictions were upheld, it was my duty and my right to state my opinion as to the limit."

Louis D. Brandeis told Holmes, "I join you heartily & gratefully. This is fine—very." The opinion to which Brandeis referred consists of twelve paragraphs; the first ten are unremarkable, but the eleventh and the twelfth are among the most eloquent in the annals of American law. The first paragraph summarizes the charges in the four counts of the indictment; the second summarizes the English leaflet, "The Hypocrisy of the United States and Her Allies" (reprinting in full the postscript beginning "It is absurd to call us pro-German"); and the third summarizes the Yiddish leaflet, "Workers—Wake Up!!" Holmes either quoted the leaflets directly or else paraphrased them. He also commented that the Yiddish leaflet used "abusive language" and engaged in "some usual tall talk."

In the fourth paragraph Holmes said that "no argument seems to me necessary" to show that the leaflets did not support either of the first two counts of the indictment, and continued, "What little I have to say about the third count" (conspiring to encourage resistance to the United States) "may be postponed until I have considered the fourth" (conspiring to incite curtailment of production of things necessary for the war). "It seems too plain to be denied," Holmes said, that the remarks directed at munitions workers and the advocacy of a general strike "do urge curtailment of production of things necessary to the prosecution of the war." For such advocacy to be criminal, however, the Sedition Act "requires that it should be 'with intent by such curtailment to cripple or hinder the United States in the prosecution of the war.' It seems to me that no such intent is proved."

Having raised the issue of intent, Holmes devoted the fifth and sixth paragraphs to defending his interpretation. He conceded that "the word intent as vaguely used in ordinary legal discussion means no more than knowledge at the time of the act that the consequences said to be intended will ensue" but that "when words are used exactly, a deed is not done with intent to produce a consequence unless that consequence is the aim of the deed." In other words, Holmes argued that the word "intent" in the statute required that just such an aim be present. An act is not done with the "intent" to produce a particular consequence, he went on, "unless the aim to produce it is the proximate motive of the specific act, although there may be some deeper motive behind." The Sedition Act should "be taken to use its words in a strict and accurate sense." Otherwise, Holmes pointed out, an "absurd" situation would result: "A patriot might think that we were wasting money on aeroplanes . . . and might advocate curtailment with success, yet even if it turned out that the curtailment hindered and was thought by other minds to have been obviously likely to hinder the United States in the prosecution of the war, no one would hold such conduct a crime." Then, almost apologetically, he remarked, "I admit that my illustration does not answer all that might be said but it is enough to show what I think and to let me pass to a more important aspect of the case."

That aspect was the First Amendment protection of freedom of speech, which Holmes addressed in the seventh and eighth paragraphs. He asserted that in the Schenck, Frohwerk, and Debs cases "the questions of law that alone were before this court . . . were rightly decided." He adverted to the example he had given in *Frohwerk:* just as Congress could punish speech persuading to murder, it "constitutionally may punish speech that produces or is intended to produce a clear and imminent danger that it will bring about forthwith certain substantive evils that the United States constitutionally may seek to prevent." In restating the clear and present danger standard, however, Holmes modified it significantly, by changing "present" to "imminent" and by adding the critical qualifying word "forthwith." The power to restrict speech would necessarily be greater in wartime because of the special dangers involved. But "Congress certainly cannot forbid all effort to change the mind of the country." Even during a war "the principle of the right to free speech is always the same," which is to say that only "the present danger of immediate evil," or an intent to bring it about, warrants restriction. No such danger was present in the Abrams case, Holmes said. "Now nobody can suppose that the surreptitious publishing of a silly leaflet by an unknown man, without more, would present any immediate danger that its opinions would hinder the success of the government arms or have any appreciable tendency to do so." Admitting that the law could properly punish speech made "for the very purpose of obstructing" the war, Holmes concluded: "So I assume that the second leaflet if published for the purposes alleged in the fourth count might be punishable."

By now Holmes had circled back to the question of intent, and resumed the discussion in the ninth and tenth paragraphs. "I do not see how anyone can find the intent required by the statute in any of the defendant's words." The crucial document was the Yiddish leaflet, and "it is evident from the beginning to the end that the only object of the paper is to help Russia and stop American intervention there against the popular government—not to impede the United States in the war that it was carrying on." To "attempt" to do something required an "actual intent." "To say that two phrases"— the lines addressed to munitions workers and the call for a general strike— "taken literally might import a suggestion of conduct that would have interference with the war as an indirect and probably undesired effect seems to me by no means enough to show an attempt to produce that effect." Returning to a consideration of the third count, which he had earlier postponed, Holmes wrote, "I think that resistance to the United States means some forcible act of opposition to some proceeding of the United States in pursuance of the war. . . . For the reasons that I have given I think that no such intent was proved or existed in fact." . . .

Unlike Justice Clarke's majority opinion, which conceded that the anarchists were intelligent and well-educated, Holmes, to demonstrate the absence of a clear and present danger, belittled the anarchists, their beliefs, and their leaflets (as he had earlier, when he referred to a "silly leaflet by an unknown man"). Moreover, Holmes virtually admitted that he dissented, at least in part, because he believed that the long prison sentences were indefensible. Although the appropriateness of the sentences was not before the Court, it was a very real issue to the Justice who had wanted, and expected, Eugene Debs to be pardoned, who had been reading about the years spent in Dorchester gaol by Richard Carlile, the friend of Francis Place, and who perhaps recalled John Locke's advice that "even the guilty are to be spared, where it can prove no prejudice to the innocent."

Holmes's final paragraph discussed the connection between freedom of speech, the search for truth, and the value of experimentation. Reading Laski, Chafee, and Hand, he had been mulling over that connection for many months. . . .

Holmes had again reformulated the clear and present danger test so as to permit speech unless "an immediate check is required to save the country." So defined, the standard surely would not support the conviction of Abrams, Steimer, Lipman, and Lachowsky, but neither would it uphold the convictions of Charles T. Schenck, Jacob Frohwerk, or Eugene Debs. That is why one scholar has claimed that Holmes's dissent transformed "the phrase 'clear and present danger' from an apology for repression into a commitment to oppose authority," and another has noted that it "did at last provide a real basis for regarding clear and present danger as a speech-protective doctrine."

Holmes soon had second thoughts about his view that the jury had no basis for finding the defendants guilty on the fourth count. "I think it possible that I was wrong in thinking that there was no evidence on the Fourth Count," he wrote on December 14. But Holmes never doubted that his interpretation of intent was correct. "I still am of opinion that I was right, if I am right in what I devoutly believe, that an actual intent to hinder the U.S. in its war with Germany must be proved." Insisting that "the only object of the leaflets was to hinder our interference with Russia," Holmes only regretted that he had not "developed this in the opinion. But that is ancient history now." To Harold Laski, Holmes explained that "I assumed, but I ought to have made it clearer," that it was "necessary that the overt act laid should be proved to be done with intent to forward a conspiracy to interfere with the war with Germany," not merely to block intervention in Russia. . . .

Freedom of the Press and the Fourteenth Amendment
PAUL L. MURPHY

. . . In their brief to the Minnesota Supreme Court attacking that body's earlier validation of the state's newspaper "Gag Law" and the use of an injunction to silence a publication, the attorneys for the *Chicago Daily Tribune* set forth an extensive historical exposition of freedom of the press. The brief contended that from the death of Socrates through the fall of the Roman Empire until after the Renaissance, authorities prohibited discussion and proscribed scientific works. During this period, the Inquisition flourished, and censorship was in the hands of church and state. The brief pointed out that the Tudor and Stuart dynasties censored the English press, and that during the Commonwealth, until the latter years of the 17th century, the government frequently used the hated licensing technique against the press. Western civilization, it contended, then came to see the error of suppressing ideas. If governments, particularly corrupt ones, could silence written opposition to their actions, they could speedily crush all attempts to reform existing evils. Characterizing the Minnesota law as "despotic," the brief argued that "such laws give birth to violence and revolution; when the people are forbidden to speak and write, they begin to act." "Surely," its authors argued, "it is better to permit the free publication of defamation with responsibility therefor afterwards. 'No abuse of a free press can be so great

Paul L. Murphy, "*Near* v. *Minnesota* in the Context of Historical Developments," *Minnesota Law Review* 66 (November 1981): 95–97, 147–157. Used by permission of the author and the *Minnesota Law Review.*

as the evils of its suppression.' " The brief ended with the plea, "[w]e therefore ask this Court to vindicate the freedom of the press and to protect a right for which so much blood has been shed down through the centuries."

The Minnesota Supreme Court, which considered the case two years earlier, remained unimpressed. It rejected both the pleas based on history and the strong arguments regarding the limits of state governmental authority and followed its earlier decision. In that opinion, Chief Justice Samuel B. Wilson noted the deference accorded to the legislature in promoting the public welfare. More specifically, the Chief Justice found that a court may enjoin a newspaper as a public nuisance when existing libel laws did not adequately protect the public.

The case of *Near* v. *Minnesota* resulted from the defendant's appeal to the United States Supreme Court from the Minnesota Supreme Court's decision. Contemporaries saw *Near* as a landmark, with one legal commentator on freedom of the press characterizing the case as "the most important decision rendered since the adoption of the first amendment." Subsequent authorities continue to view it in a similar light. The opinion represents an important development in American public law; it had important impacts upon a wide range of historical developments. These include the relationship between government and the broad dispersal of public information; the general history of public regulation in the United States; the use of law in America to criminalize certain forms of behavior, and the subsequent forms of social control which emerged from that process; the development of the fourteenth amendment as an instrument for the proper definition of state authority and state responsibility within the federal system; and the changed role of law vis-à-vis the media as the United States underwent the modernization process, including all of the implications which that process produced for the operation of democratic institutions within a mass, impersonal society. . . .

In addition to the [U.S. Supreme] Court, other elements in the 1920s were deeply concerned over free press issues and involved themselves actively to achieve their favorable resolution. For example, the American Newspaper Publishers Association (ANPA), founded in 1887 as a daily newspaper trade association, worked to free the press. By the 1920s, the ANPA represented the great majority of American newspapers, serving principally as an instrument for advancing the business interests of daily newspapers and as a negotiator of adjustments and conflicts with advertisers, labor, communications competitors, newsprint makers, and the government. In the immediate post World War I period, the organization expressed strong concern over continuing government interference with the media and took the position that the nation no longer needed the wartime rules, regulations, and frequent coercion, and that deregulation and decriminalization were required. . . .

The ANPA based part of its concern on a fear that if sizable portions of the American public came to regard the press as solely a business enterprise, it would be open to economic regulation under the authority of state police power. On the other hand, it feared the press would lose public sympathy for its freedom as an information source protected by the first amendment. Thus, the ANPA, sensitive to rising public criticism of the press's behavior and to the press's sins not only of commission, but also of omission, particularly in its highly partisan treatment of many political issues, found itself more on the defensive than usual.

One of the movers and shakers in the ANPA was Colonel Robert R. McCormick, the colorful, autocratic owner and publisher of the *Chicago Tribune*. McCormick, long concerned with keeping the politicians off the back of the media, in fact opened the decade defending a long and colorful libel action against the city of Chicago. The city sued the *Tribune* for the sum of ten million dollars for alleged libel, because the newspaper criticized the fiscal administration of the city and, thereby, injured its credit. The *Tribune* rested its defense on the argument that the state and federal constitutional guarantees of freedom of the press precluded a government's suit for libel. McCormick won. The Chief Justice of Illinois handed down a unanimous decision, vigorously asserting the right of the media to inform the public regarding the performance of its officials: "When the people became sovereign, as they did when our government was established under our constitution and the ministers became the servants of the people, the right to discuss government followed as a natural sequence." McCormick's efforts soon realized even greater rewards.

The *Near* Litigation Draws National Attention

In 1928, partly in response to the first prosecution under the Minnesota Gag Law earlier that year, McCormick accepted the chairmanship of a new ANPA Committee on Freedom of the Press. Not surprisingly, as the first Gag Law case under the Minnesota statute began to work its way through the Minnesota courts, the ANPA and McCormick quickly lent support to the defendant Minneapolis publishers, by furnishing financial assistance and legal counsel. McCormick saw the law as authority for a repeat performance, this time through an injunction proceeding, of the political assault he had overcome in Chicago five years earlier. At the 1929 ANPA meeting, he submitted a committee report decrying the statute as "tyrannical, despotic, un-American and oppressive," as resuscitating "obsolete libels on the government" and "permitting suppression of publications exposing corruption in government." The report asserted that courts of equity should not be permitted to censor the press and suppress writings in advance of publication, and that "this statute was the first attempt of a legislature since the foundation of the Union to gag the press in so drastic a manner." At its 1930 meeting, the ANPA adopted another resolution condemning the Minnesota act as "a violation of the First and Fourteenth Amendments of the Constitution of the United States, a peril to the right of property and a menace to republican institutions . . . and as a dangerous and vicious invasion of personal liberties."

ANPA members were particularly troubled by the Minnesota Supreme Court ruling in the initial Gag Law case sustaining the use of the Gag Law. The court reasoned that the current tendency in American law was to extend, rather than to restrict, the police power; accordingly, the legislature could legitimately place certain conditions on the way a person conducts a business. Since the newspaper business was no different than any other business, and the distribution of scandalous material disturbed the public peace, provoked assaults and the commission of crimes, and was therefore detrimental to public morals and to the general welfare, the law was valid. The case, the court noted, was not unlike a number of other recent precedents in which the states legitimately restrained the press. Moreover, the due process clause of the fourteenth amendment was never intended to limit the subjects on which the police power of the states might be lawfully exerted. If this position were to be sustained on appeal, the free press, which the body was pledged to defend, would clearly be endangered. Editorials and general expression of pained protest from the national press underlined this concern.

The Supreme Court heard arguments in the case of *Near* v. *Minnesota* on January 30, 1931, handing down its ruling on June 1 of that year. Between those two dates it heard a case challenging the use of a California Red Flag law to silence the leaders of a left-wing summer camp, and ruled large portions of that law a deprivation of liberty without due process, contrary to the fourteenth amendment. . . .

Chief Justice Hughes, joined by Holmes, Brandeis, Stone, and Roberts, clearly embraced the liberal position. He stated early on that "in the present case, we have no occasion to inquire as to the permissible scope of subsequent punishment." The subject was the "no prior restraint" doctrine and its protection of the publication of material which could well be the subject of subsequent punishment under criminal libel or other laws. Hughes's argument concerning prior restraint was far more historical than analytical. As Thomas Emerson pointed out, "the Court never undertook to explain the functional basis of the prior restraint doctrine." It preferred to find in the "general conception" of liberty of the press, as adopted by the Federal Constitution, the essential attribute of freedom from prior restraint, which the Court was convinced the statute violated. On the other hand, possibly reflecting the emerging legal realism of the day, Hughes did not care to be drawn into the abstract question of whether the Minnesota law authorized prior restraint. Rather, he believed the test was whether in operation the law worked that way—whether in its administration and techniques of enforcement, it served to preclude in advance the dispersal of certain ideas and information. Proceeding from these assumptions, Hughes ruled that the Minnesota law was an unconstitutional infringement of the freedom of the press safeguarded by the due process clause of the fourteenth amendment. In the process, he asserted finally, after 150 years, the principle that restraint before publication is, with few exceptions, unconstitutional. In finally reducing the broad prohibition against prior restraint to a working principle of constitutional law, he recognized that minor exceptions existed. Contemporary commentators, however, viewed the exceptions as insignificant and hypothetical. The broader implications of the majority, speaking through the Chief Justice, gave the decision its historical significance as a turning point in American law and public policy.

The ruling brought to a significant new stage Brandeis's long crusade for redefining the term "liberty" in human rights rather than in property rights terms. By actually using that concept to strike down a state law, the decision also logically extended the incorporation theory as it related to freedom of the press, a theory which Justice Sanford launched in his *Gitlow* opinion. Considered with the *O'Gorman* decision of the previous January 5, which downgraded the property rights objection to states' use of police power, *Near* seemed to shift presumptions regarding the constitutionality of state laws. Laws restricting personal liberties now demanded new and vigorous justification, while laws restricting property rights were to be given the judicial benefit of the doubt. Thus, the ruling culminated more than 60 years of struggle over the proper relationship among the federal government, the states, and the citizen regarding first amendment issues. The press now joined speech in being protected not only from formal federal government restraint, but from state restraint and more subtle forms of local restraint such as those authorized by the Minnesota law.

In the first amendment area, the ruling was a clear triumph for Learned Hand and Zechariah Chafee; Hughes even cited Chafee's influential book *Freedom of Speech* in his opinion. The ruling was clearly "market-place" in its orientation. It strongly stressed the importance in a democratic society of the press being free to carry out its proper function of informing the electorate, particularly about the behavior of the people's public officials. The behavior of the editors of the *Saturday Press* obviously troubled the Chief Justice—the form of exposé writing they engaged in clearly was styled to arouse passion rather than to disperse knowledge and information. The opinion, however, in some ways blurred this distinction, focusing instead upon the importance of editors to be able to criticize public officials, consequently downplaying any illicit motives, defamation, racial and religious bigotry, and general irresponsibility. Hughes focused upon what was defensible about Near's operation, rather than what was indefensible.

In this regard, the opinion came directly to terms with the changing and modernizing conditions that produced much of the new journalism. . . .

In a different context, the ruling represented an important development in the area of deregulation and decriminalization, an issue of considerable concern at this time. The World War I and immediate postwar federal and state legislation attaching criminal penalties to certain forms of expression, belief, and association was a form of public regulation. Not unlike the prohibition amendment, its critics increasingly viewed it as unwarranted interference with personal rights and personal choices, which many people believed did not deserve to be classified with criminal behavior. The *Near* decision, along with the *Stromberg* ruling two weeks earlier, was actually a form of decontrol striking at the use of state police power to curtail freedom of expression. Decontrol was not only popular at the time, but indicated the general public's distaste for the heavy handed enforcement of sedition, criminal syndicalism, and red flag laws, as well as for state and local censorship of various forms of publication. In this regard, the majority opinion was in sharp contrast to that of both Minnesota Supreme Court rulings and of the minority dissent, all of which supported and encouraged a greater use of state police power to deal with virtually every unseemly aspect of society and human behavior.

The majority opinion also questioned and rejected some of the assumptions and overtones of the earlier word crime laws. Suspicion emerged regarding whether they were really precautionary laws designed not as punishment for actual wrong conduct, but as a means to prevent future evils by a series of restrictions and qualifications which local officials could use to control conduct which the majority found somehow unacceptable. . . .

Finally, the *Near* case, along with *Stromberg* v. *California,* was an attempt to move away, and move the country away, from the use of informal local controls to limit freedom of expression. Just as the majority condemned the ongoing use of the police power to restrict civil liberties, so it condemned a situation which made it possible for local officials, often acting at the behest of private local power, to selectively use their discretion in the law enforcement process to curtail expression that was distasteful or threatening to the local power establishment. While the Civil Rights movement of the 1950s and 1960s quickly demonstrated that such controls could be swiftly revived and reinvigorated, the realistic recognition of their potential as devices to inhibit free expression by the *Near* court marked an important judicial acknowledgement of a process long overlooked by legal literalists. . . .

✛ *F U R T H E R   R E A D I N G*

Alexis J. Anderson, "The Formative Period of First Amendment Theory, 1870–1915," *American Journal of Legal History* 24 (1980): 56–75

Jerold S. Auerbach, "The Patrician as Libertarian: Zechariah Chafee, Jr., and Freedom of Speech," *New England Quarterly* 24 (December 1969): 511–531

David Bogen, "The Free Speech Metamorphosis of Mr. Justice Holmes," *Hofstra Law Review* 11 (1982): 97–189

Richard C. Cortner, *The Supreme Court and the Second Bill of Rights: The Fourteenth Amendment and the Nationalization of the Bill of Rights* (1981)

Paul L. Murphy, *The Meaning of Freedom of Speech: First Amendment Freedoms from Wilson to FDR* (1972)

———, *World War I and the Origin of Civil Liberties in the United States* (1979)

David M. Rabban, "The Emergence of Modern First Amendment Doctrine," *University of Chicago Law Review* 50 (1983): 1207–1355

———, "The First Amendment in Its Forgotten Years," *Yale Law Journal* 90 (1981): 516–595

Fred D. Ragan, "Justice Oliver Wendell Holmes, Jr., Zechariah Chafee, Jr., and the Clear and Present Danger Test for Free Speech: The First Year, 1919," *Journal of American History* 58 (June 1971): 24–45

Frank R. Strong, "Fifty Years of 'Clear and Present Danger': From Schenck to Brandenburg—And Beyond," *Supreme Court Review* (1969): 41–80

David B. Tyack, "The Perils of Pluralism: The Background of the Pierce Case," *American Historical Review* 74 (October 1968): 74–98

Stephen Vaugh, "First Amendment Liberties and the Committee on Public Information," *American Journal of Legal History* 23 (1979): 95–119

CHAPTER
5

Presidential Leadership and Court Packing

⁜

The Great Depression inspired a reevaluation by the American people of the relationship between law and society and between government and the governed. The economic collapse staggered the middle class, prompting millions of previously productive workers to question the highly individualistic assumptions of laissez-faire constitutionalism while demanding that government provide a collective social-welfare approach to economic hardship. Democratic president Franklin Roosevelt responded directly to these needs; the New Deal that he sponsored after entering the White House in 1933 offered a safety net (modest by today's standards) with which to catch the victims of an industrial order gone bust. Infusing the presidency with new energy, FDR created an alphabet soup of new administrative agencies and he took extraordinary actions, such as closing banks throughout the nation during 1933.

When in 1935 the Supreme Court began striking down some of the most important of the New Deal initiatives, among them the National Industrial Recovery Act (NIRA) and the Agricultural Adjustment Act (AAA), the president responded with a plan to alter the Court's composition. Following his landslide victory in the 1936 election, FDR submitted to Congress a blueprint for reorganizing the federal courts generally and the Supreme Court specifically. Throughout American history, other presidents had sought to mold the courts in their political image, but none had launched so bold a plan. Roosevelt's scheme centered on altering the historical rules by which vacancies became available. He called, first, for the appointment of additional judges to all the federal courts. With regard to the Supreme Court, he proposed that once a justice reached age seventy, he or she would have six months in which to retire. If he or she failed to do so, the president would be permitted to appoint an additional justice, up to a maximum of six new appointees. At the time FDR advanced the bill, six justices would have qualified.

The so-called court-packing scheme failed in the end, partly because Congress and the public viewed it with suspicion and partly because the Court itself sensed that its continued opposition to the New Deal might ultimately undermine its own legitimacy. In early 1937 the justices began to sustain several pieces of state and federal New Deal legislation designed to relieve the pressures of the Depression. On a broader plane, FDR's plan demonstrated the seeming pliability of the modern constitutional order. Roosevelt's action indicated that law was clearly related to the political and personal interests of the justices who sat on the Court. Constitutional law was not something that judges mechanically applied; instead, it was a shifting body of principles that had to be shaped to changing social and economic conditions.

✣ *D O C U M E N T S*

One of the most controversial aspects of the New Deal programs was the power that Congress delegated to administrative bodies to make policies, such as fixing prices and production quotas under the National Industrial Recovery Act. In *Schechter Poultry Corp.* v. *United States* (1935), reprinted as the first document, the Supreme Court struck down the NIRA on May 27, 1935, "Black Monday," so called because on that same day the Court declared several other pieces of New Deal legislation unconstitutional. Journalists Drew Pearson and Robert S. Allen in *Nine Old Men* (1936), excerpted in the second document, chronicled the popular hostility to this and other Court decisions. This book ridiculed the Court's insensitivity to the impact of the Depression.

Following his 1936 election, Roosevelt on March 9, 1937, presented one of his fireside chats to the nation (see the third document), in which he explained his reasons for sponsoring the Judicial Reform Act of 1937 in Congress. Chief Justice Charles Evans Hughes disagreed sharply with the president's plan, and his letter of March 22, 1937, to Senator Burton K. Wheeler, the fourth document, reveals that the supposedly apolitical Supreme Court was capable of exercising political punch on matters it deemed crucial. The Senate Judiciary Committee agreed with Hughes; its report to the full Senate, document 5, urged rejection of the bill. The proposal shocked even New Deal supporters, who feared that the measure would erode the independence of the judiciary and subvert the doctrine of separation of powers. The Court also shifted ground, as its decisions in *West Coast Hotel* v. *Parrish* (1937), document 6, demonstrate.

Shortly thereafter three of the most conservative members of the Court left the bench, permitting FDR to make his first appointments. While the president lost the battle for the judiciary act, he clearly won the larger war over the direction of the Supreme Court.

Schechter v. *United States,* ## 295 U.S. 495 (1935)

(Unanimous)

Mr. Chief Justice Hughes delivered the opinion of the Court.

Petitioners in No. 854 were convicted in the District Court of the United States for the Eastern District of New York on eighteen counts of an indictment charging violations of what is known as the "Live Poultry Code," and on an additional count for conspiracy to commit such violations. By demurrer to the indictment and appropriate motions on the trial, the defendants contended (1) that the Code had been adopted pursuant to an unconstitutional delegation by Congress of legislative power; (2) that it attempted to regulate intrastate transactions which lay outside the authority of Congress; and (3) that in certain provisions it was repugnant to the due process clause of the Fifth Amendment. . . .

First. Two preliminary points are stressed by the Government with respect to the appropriate approach to the important questions presented. We are told that the provision of the statute authorizing the adoption of codes must be viewed in the light of the grave national crisis with which Congress was confronted. Undoubtedly, the conditions to which power is addressed are always to be considered when the exercise of power is challenged. Extraordinary conditions may call for extraordinary remedies. But the argument necessarily stops short of an attempt to justify action which lies outside the sphere of constitutional authority. Extraordinary conditions do not create or enlarge constitutional power. The Constitution established a national government with powers deemed to be adequate, as they have proved to be both in war and peace, but these powers of the national government are limited by the constitutional grants. Those who act under these grants are not at liberty to transcend the imposed limits because they believe that more or different power is necessary. Such assertions of extra-constitutional authority were anticipated and precluded by the explicit terms of the Tenth Amendment—"The powers not delegated to the United States by the Constitution, nor prohibited by it to the States, are reserved to the States respectively, or to the people."

The further point is urged that the national crisis demanded a broad and intensive coöperative effort by those engaged in trade and industry, and that this necessary coöperation was sought to be fostered by permitting them to initiate the adoption of codes. But the statutory plan is not simply one for voluntary effort. It does not seek merely to endow voluntary trade or industrial associations or groups with privileges or immunities. It involves the coercive exercise of the law-making power. The codes of fair competition which the statute attempts to authorize are codes of laws. If valid, they place all persons within their reach under the obligation of positive law, binding equally those who assent and those who do not assent. Violations of the provisions of the codes are punishable as crimes.

Second. The question of the delegation of legislative power. We recently had occasion to review the pertinent decisions and the general principles which govern the determination of this question. *Panama Refining Co.* v. *Ryan.* . . . The Constitution provides that "All legislative powers herein granted shall be vested in a Congress of the United States, which shall consist of a Senate and House of Representatives." Art. I, § 1. And the Congress is authorized "To make all laws which shall be necessary and proper for carrying into execution" its general powers. Art. I, § 8, par. 18. The Congress is not permitted to abdicate or to transfer to others the essential legislative functions with which it is thus vested. We have repeatedly recognized the necessity of adapting legislation to complex conditions involving a host of details with which the national legislature cannot deal directly. We pointed out in the *Panama Company* case that the Constitution has never been regarded as denying to Congress the necessary resources of flexibility and practicality, which will enable it to perform its function in laying down policies and establishing standards, while leaving to selected instrumentalities the making of subordinate rules within prescribed limits and the determination of facts to which the policy as declared by the legislature is to apply. But we said that the constant recognition of the necessity and validity of such provisions, and the wide range of administrative authority which has been developed by means of them, cannot be allowed to obscure the limitations of the authority to delegate, if our constitutional system is to be maintained. . . .

Accordingly, we look to the statute to see whether Congress has overstepped these limitations—whether Congress in authorizing "codes of fair competition" has itself established the standards of legal obligation, thus performing its essential legislative function, or, by the failure to enact such standards, has attempted to transfer that function to others. . . .

In providing for codes, the National Industrial Recovery Act dispenses with this administrative procedure and with any administrative procedure of an analogous character. But the difference between the code plan of the Recovery Act and the scheme of the Federal Trade Commission Act lies not only in procedure but in subject matter. We cannot regard the "fair competition" of the codes as antithetical to the "unfair methods of competition" of the Federal Trade Commission Act. The "fair competition" of the codes has a much broader range and a new significance. The Recovery Act provides that it shall not be construed to impair the powers of the Federal Trade Commission, but, when a code is approved, its provisions are to be the "standards of fair competition" for the trade or industry concerned, and any violation of such standards in any transaction in or affecting interstate or foreign commerce is to be deemed "an unfair method of competition" within the meaning of the Federal Trade Commission Act. § 3 (b). . . .

The Government urges that the codes will "consist of rules of competition deemed fair for each industry by representative members of that industry—by the persons most vitally concerned and most familiar with its problems." Instances are cited in which Congress has availed itself of such assistance; as *e.g.,* in the exercise of its authority over the public domain, with respect to the recognition of local customs or rules of miners as to mining claims, or, in matters of a more or less technical nature, as in designating the standard height of drawbars. But would it be seriously contended that Congress could delegate its legislative authority to trade or industrial associations or groups so as to empower them to enact the laws they deem to be wise and beneficent for the rehabilitation and expansion of their trade or industries? Could trade or industrial associations or groups be constituted legislative bodies for that purpose because such associations or groups are familiar with the problems of their enterprises? And, could an effort of that sort be made valid by such a preface of generalities as to permissible aims as we find in section 1 of title I? The answer is obvious. Such a delegation of legislative power is unknown to our law and is utterly inconsistent with the constitutional prerogatives and duties of Congress.

The question, then, turns upon the authority which § 3 of the Recovery Act vests in the President to approve or prescribe. If the codes have standing as penal statutes, this must be due to the effect of the executive action. But Congress cannot delegate legislative power to the President to exercise an unfettered discretion to make whatever laws he thinks may be needed or advisable for the rehabilitation and expansion of trade or industry. . . .

Accordingly we turn to the Recovery Act to ascertain what limits have been set to the exercise of the President's discretion. *First,* the President, as a condition of approval, is required to find that the trade or industrial associations or groups which propose a code, "impose no inequitable restrictions on admission to membership" and are "truly representative." That condition, however, relates only to the status of the initiators of the new laws and not to the permissible scope of such laws. *Second,* the President is required to find that the code is not "designed to promote monopolies or to eliminate or oppress small enterprises, and will not operate to discriminate against them." And, to this is added a proviso that the code "shall not permit monopolies or monopolistic practices." But these restrictions leave virtually untouched the field of policy envisaged by section one, and, in that wide field of legislative possibilities, the proponents of a code, refraining from monopolistic designs, may roam at will and the President may approve or disapprove their proposals as he may see fit. . . .

Nor is the breadth of the President's discretion left to the necessary implications of this limited requirement as to his findings. As already noted, the President in approving a code may impose his own conditions, adding to or taking from what is proposed, as "in his discretion" he thinks necessary "to effectuate the policy" declared by the Act. Of course, he has no less liberty when he prescribes a code on his own motion or on complaint, and he is free to prescribe one if a code has not been approved. The Act provides for the creation by the President of administrative agencies to assist him, but the action or reports of such agencies, or of his other assistants—their recommendations and findings in relation to the making of codes—have no sanction beyond the will of the President, who may accept, modify or reject them as he pleases. Such recommendations or findings in no way limit the authority which § 3 undertakes to vest in the President with no other conditions than those there specified. And this authority relates to a host of different trades and industries, thus extending the President's discretion to all the varieties of laws which he may deem to be beneficial in dealing with the vast array of commercial and industrial activities throughout the country.

Such a sweeping delegation of legislative power finds no support in the decisions upon which the Government especially relies. . . .

To summarize and conclude upon this point: Section 3 of the Recovery Act is without precedent. It supplies no standards for any trade, industry or activity. It does not undertake to prescribe rules of conduct to be applied to particular states of fact determined by appropriate administrative procedure. Instead of prescribing rules of conduct, it authorizes the making of codes to prescribe them. For that legislative undertaking, § 3 sets up no standards, aside from the statement of the general aims of rehabilitation, correction and expansion described in section one. In view of the scope of that broad declaration, and of the nature of the few restrictions that are imposed, the discretion of the President in approving or prescribing codes, and thus enacting laws for the government of trade and industry throughout the country, is virtually unfettered. We think that the code-making authority thus conferred is an unconstitutional delegation of legislative power.

Third. The question of the application of the provisions of the Live Poultry Code to intrastate transactions. . . .

The undisputed facts thus afford no warrant for the argument that the poultry handled by defendants at their slaughterhouse markets was in a *"current"* or *"flow"* of interstate commerce and was thus subject to congressional regulation. The mere fact that there may be a constant flow of commodities into a State does not mean that the flow continues after the property has arrived and has become commingled with the mass of property within the State and is there held solely for local disposition and use. So far as the poultry here in question is concerned, the flow in interstate commerce had ceased. The poultry had come to a permanent rest within the State. It was not held, used, or sold by defendants in relation to any further transactions in interstate commerce and was not destined for transportation to other States. Hence, decisions which deal with a stream of interstate commerce— where goods come to rest within a State temporarily and are later to go forward in interstate commerce—and with the regulations of transactions involved in that practical continuity of movement, are not applicable here. . . .

(2) Did the defendants' transactions directly *"affect"* interstate commerce so as to be subject to federal regulation? The power of Congress extends not only to the regulation of transactions which are part of interstate commerce, but to the protection of that commerce from injury. It matters not that the injury may be due to the conduct of those engaged in intrastate operations. Thus, Congress may protect the safety of those employed in interstate transportation "no matter what may be the source of the dangers which threaten it." . . .

In determining how far the federal government may go in controlling intrastate transactions upon the ground that they "affect" interstate commerce, there is a necessary and well-established distinction between direct and indirect effects. The precise line can be drawn only as individual cases arise, but the distinction is clear in principle. Direct effects are illustrated by the railroad cases we have cited, as *e.g.,* the effect of failure to use prescribed safety appliances on railroads which are the highways of both interstate and intrastate commerce, injury to an employee engaged in interstate transportation by the negligence of an employee engaged in an intrastate movement, the fixing of rates for intrastate transportation which unjustly discriminate against interstate commerce. But where the effect of intrastate transactions upon interstate commerce is merely indirect, such transactions remain within the domain of state power. If the commerce clause were construed to reach all enterprises and transactions which could be said to have an indirect effect upon interstate commerce, the federal authority would embrace practically all the activities of the people and the authority of the State over its domestic concerns would exist only by sufferance of the federal government. . . .

It is not the province of the Court to consider the economic advantages or disadvantages of such a centralized system. It is sufficient to say that the Federal Constitution does not provide for it. Our growth and development have called for wide use of the commerce power of the federal government in its control over the expanded activities of interstate commerce, and in protecting that commerce from burdens, interferences, and conspiracies to restrain and monopolize it. But the authority of the federal government may not be pushed to such an extreme as to destroy the distinction, which the commerce clause itself establishes, between commerce "among the several States" and the internal concerns of a State. The same answer must be made to the contention that is based upon the serious economic situation which led to the passage of the Recovery Act—the fall in prices, the decline in wages and employment, and the curtailment of the market for commodities. Stress is laid upon the great importance of maintaining wage distributions which would provide the necessary stimulus in starting "the cumulative forces making for expanding commercial activity." Without in any way disparaging this motive, it is enough to say that the recuperative efforts of the federal government must be made in a manner consistent with the authority granted by the Constitution.

We are of the opinion that the attempt through the provisions of the Code to fix the hours and wages of employees of defendants in their intrastate business was not a valid exercise of federal power. . . .

Liberal Washington Journalists Drew Pearson and Robert S. Allen on the "Nine Old Men," 1936

When the Nine Old Men declared the National Industrial Recovery Act unconstitutional they passed judgment, not on the fact that four Jewish boys in Brooklyn sold a few crates of sick chickens in violation of the poultry code, but upon a chapter in the history of the United States as important and as bizarre as any since the Civil War. . . .

[The *Schechter*] case offered two important advantages. First, the Supreme Court only one year before had passed upon the conviction of Toots Herbert and Joe Weiner, and in doing so definitely found that racketeering in the chicken industry of Brooklyn was in restraint of interstate commerce. Second, the Schechter attorneys had stipulated regarding the points in the case, thus obviating any necessity on the government's part to prove what the code was. This, because of the slipshod manner in which codes were

Excerpt from "The Nine Old Men" by Drew Pearson and Robert S. Allen, copyright 1937 by Drew Pearson and Robert S. Allen. Used by permission of Doubleday, a division of Bantam Doubleday Dell Publishing Group, Inc.

filed at the White House and State Department—as discovered in the hot-oil case—might be embarrassing and difficult.

However, the Schechter case had one grave drawback. The Justice Department had brought a criminal action against Joseph and his brethren, and if their convictions were upheld by the Supreme Court, Joe would serve three months, Alex two, and Martin and Aaron one month each in jail. It was possible that some of the Nine Old Men might go along with the NRA if the Schechters were charged only with a civil breach of the law. But to send four insignificant Jewish poultry dealers to jail for violation of a system at which the big steel moguls were thumbing their noses was bound to grate upon the susceptibilities of the liberal judges, and New Deal legalists should have known it.

Nevertheless, faced with the rapid molting of the Blue Eagle's feathers, Donald Richberg took a one-hundred-to-one shot. He decided upon an immediate test of the NRA, and on April 8, 1935, the Department of Justice joined with the Schechter Live Poultry Corporation of Brooklyn in asking the Supreme Court for an immediate review of the latter's appeal.

The argument was heard in the old red-plush courtroom in the Capitol, and the Schechter brothers enjoyed it more than anyone else. Joe Schechter pushed his way through the crowd, only to be stopped by a guard.

"Who are you?" the guard demanded.

"Me?" Joe gasped. "You dun't know who I am?"

"No, who are you?"

"I am Joe Schechter!"

Joe regarded the black-robed justices a little nervously and slid into a seat. But Attorney Heller, soaring far beyond his wildest ambition, was not in the least awed. His East Side accent in fullest flower, he described the tribulations of his clients under the tyranny of the NRA; how customers walked into Joe's Brooklyn market and tried to take their pick of the chickens in the coops, but, alas, were compelled under the code to accept the first bird that came out of the coop; and told how the rabbis shrugged their shoulders at Joe and remarked, "Vell, if I kent have the chicken I vant from you, Joe, I go someplace else," which they did. . . .

Justice McReynolds, listening with grim interest, leaned forward and asked:

"And it was for that your client went to jail?"

In his inexperienced way, Heller drew an excellent picture of the interference in petty business which the NRA entailed. Probably he did more to win the case than the great Wood, who followed with a learned discussion of the interstate-commerce question. Stanley, Reed and Richberg divided the government's time, the latter painting an eloquent picture of the chaos sure to follow if the NRA were junked. He described the great social progress which the act had brought, and envisioned the collapse sure to follow an unfavorable decision.

Joe Schechter, overwhelmed by Richberg's speech, whispered to a near-by spectator:

"I hope they gives it a conviction, so NRA will stand."

Eventually the Nine Old Men filed out, to reappear on May 27, 1935—an eventful day in New Deal history.

The announcement of decisions began uneventfully, Justice Butler reading an opinion involving the New York Life Insurance Company. Justice Sutherland followed with a unanimous opinion that President Roosevelt had grossly exceeded his authority by removing William E. Humphrey from the Federal Trade Commission without cause. The New Deal had lost its first skirmish of the day.

Justice Brandeis then began a gentle and scholarly opinion branding unconstitutional the Frazier-Lemke Act. Although not a New Deal measure, this was signed by Roosevelt and permitted farmers to retain their land for five years despite mortgage foreclosure and with the privilege of paying the mortgage later at a new appraisal. This decision also was unanimous.

Then the Chief Justice began to read the opinion for which the courtroom waited. Using oratorical emphasis, and shifting about in his chair, Mr. Hughes spent some time outlining the background of the Schechter case and describing the methods of moving poultry in New York. Ultimately he dropped this significant sentence:

"The defendants do not sell poultry in interstate commerce."

Richberg and Reed seemed to slump deeper in their chairs. They knew their case was lost. Just one year before, the same Nine Old Men, passing upon the conspiracy of Joe Weiner and Toots Herbert to interfere with the New York poultry trade, unanimously held that "unquestionably it [poultry] is in interstate commerce."

But now they held, with equal unanimity, that the Schechter sick chickens had "come to rest."

At his next press conference President Roosevelt, for perhaps the first time, lost his smile.

"The gravest question," he said, "revolves around the Court's interpretation of the government's powers over interstate commerce. These powers constitute the only weapon we have to fight conditions not even dreamed of a hundred and fifty years ago.

"When the Constitution was written, this country was in the horse-and-buggy stage. Almost ninety per cent of our trade was intrastate. There was no problem of earning and buying power. There was no social question, such as health, to be reckoned with on a national basis. Ethics were different. If one fellow could get away with skinning another fellow—well, that was all right.

"But now things have changed. The country thought it was solving its problems gradually on a national basis, but now its attempted solutions are thrown back in the face of the American people, and the country is right back in the horse-and-buggy stage where it started.

"The issue," concluded the President, "is second in importance only to war."

Mrs. Roosevelt sat beside him, calmly knitting a blue sock.

But the rest of the country was not so calm. With the press and a good part of the public, the NRA was anything but popular. And the general exclamation escaping from a General-Johnson-wearied public was: "Whoopee! Good for the Supreme Court!"

The Nine Old Men are only human, and those hosannas rang in their ears for a long time. Probably if the Schechter hosannas had not been so loud, the story of the AAA and the New York minimum-wage and the Guffey acts might have been different.

One year later, Joseph and his brethren, back in Brooklyn, were wondering about the ultimate effect of what they had done to NRA.

On the streets of London on the day of the Schechter decision, the London *Express* blazed forth with these headlines: "AMERICA STUNNED! ROOSEVELT'S WORK KILLED IN TWENTY MINUTES." . . .

The Judiciary Reform Act of 1937

1. Proposed Bill

Be it enacted, That—

(a) When any judge of a court of the United States, appointed to hold his office during good behavior, has heretofore or hereafter attained the age of seventy years and has held a commission or commissions as judge of any such court or courts at least ten years, continuously or otherwise, and within six months thereafter has neither resigned nor retired, the President, for each such judge who has not so resigned or retired, shall nominate, and by and with the advice and consent of the Senate, shall appoint one additional judge to the court to which the former is commissioned: *Provided,* That no additional judge shall be appointed hereunder if the judge who is of retirement age dies, resigns, or retires prior to the nomination of such additional judge.

(b) The number of judges of any court shall be permanently increased by the number appointed thereto under the provisions of subsection (a) of this section. No more than fifty judges shall be appointed thereunder, nor shall any judge be so appointed if such appointment would result in (1) more than fifteen members of the Supreme Court of the United States, (2) more than two additional members so appointed to a circuit court of appeals, the Court of Claims, the United States Court of Customs and Patent Appeals, or the Customs Court, or (3) more than twice the number of judges now authorized to be appointed for any district or, in the case of judges appointed for more than one district, for any such group of districts. . . .

(d) An additional judge shall not be appointed under the provisions of this section when the judge who is of retirement age is commissioned to an office as to which Congress has provided that a vacancy shall not be filled.

Sec. 2. (a) Any circuit judge hereafter appointed may be designated and assigned from time to time by the Chief Justice of the United States for service in the circuit court of appeals for any circuit. Any district judge hereafter appointed may be designated and assigned from time to time by the Chief Justice of the United States for service in any district court, or, subject to the authority of the Chief Justice, by the senior circuit judge of his circuit for service in any district court within the circuit. A district judge designated and assigned to another district hereunder may hold court separately and at the same time as the district judge in such district. . . . The designation and assignment of any judge may be terminated at any time by order of the Chief Justice or the senior circuit judge, as the case may be. . . .

Sec. 3 (a) The Supreme Court shall have power to appoint a proctor. It shall be his duty (1) to obtain and, if deemed by the Court to be desirable, to publish information as to the volume, character, and status of litigation in the district courts and circuit courts of appeals, and such other information as the Supreme Court may from time to time require by order, and it shall be the duty of any judge, clerk, or marshal of any court of the United States promptly to furnish such information as may be required by the proctor; (2) to investigate the need of assigning district and circuit judges to other courts and to make recommendations thereon to the Chief Justice; (3) to recommend, with the approval of the Chief Justice, to any court of the United States methods for expediting cases pending on its dockets; and (4) to perform such other duties consistent with his office as the Court shall direct. . . .

Sec. 5. When used in this Act—

(a) The term "judge of retirement age" means a judge of a court of the United States, appointed to hold his office during good behavior, who has attained the age of seventy years and has held a commission or commissions as judge of any such court or courts at least ten years, continuously or otherwise, and within six months thereafter, whether or not he is eligible for retirement, has neither resigned nor retired. . . .

President Franklin D. Roosevelt Advocates Judicial Reform, 1937

. . . Tonight, sitting at my desk in the White House, I make my first radio report to the people in my second term of office. . . .

The American people have learned from the depression. For in the last three national elections an overwhelming majority of them voted a mandate that the Congress and the President begin the task of providing . . . protection—not after long years of debate, but now.

The courts, however, have cast doubts on the ability of the elected Congress to protect us against catastrophe by meeting squarely our modern social and economic conditions.

We are at a crisis in our ability to proceed with that protection. It is a quiet crisis. There are no lines of depositors outside closed banks. But to the far-sighted it is far-reaching in its possibilities of injury to America.

I want to talk with you very simply about the need for present action in this crisis—the need to meet the unanswered challenge of one-third of a nation ill-nourished, ill-clad, ill-housed.

Last Thursday I described the American form of government as a three-horse team provided by the Constitution to the American people so that their field might be plowed. The three horses are, of course, the three branches of government—the Congress, the executive, and the courts. Two of the horses are pulling in unison today; the third is not. Those who have intimated that the President of the United States is trying to drive that team overlook the simple fact that the President, as Chief Executive, is himself one of the three horses.

It is the American people themselves who are in the driver's seat.

It is the American people themselves who want the furrow plowed.

It is the American people themselves who expect the third horse to pull in unison with the other two.

I hope that you have reread the Constitution of the United States. Like the Bible, it ought to be read again and again.

It is an easy document to understand when you remember that it was called into being because the Articles of Confederation under which the Original Thirteen States tried to operate after the Revolution showed the need of a National Government with power enough to handle national problems. In its preamble the Constitution states that it was intended to form a more perfect Union and promote the general welfare; and the powers given to the Congress to carry out those purposes can be best described by saying that they were all the powers needed to meet each and every problem which then had a national character and which could not be met by merely local action.

But the framers went further. Having in mind that in succeeding generations many other problems then undreamed of would become national problems, they gave to the Congress the ample broad powers "to levy taxes . . . and provide for the common defense and general welfare of the United States."

That, my friends, is what I honestly believe to have been the clear and underlying purpose of the patriots who wrote a Federal Constitution to create a National Government with national power, intended as they said, "to form a more perfect union . . . for ourselves and our posterity."

For nearly 20 years there was no conflict between the Congress and the Court. Then, in 1803, . . . [t]he Court claimed the power to declare it [a statute] unconstitutional and did so declare it. But a little later the Court itself admitted that it was an extraordinary power to exercise and through Mr. Justice Washington laid down this limitation upon it: "It is but a decent respect due to the wisdom, the integrity, and the patriotism of the legislative body, by which any law is passed, to presume in favor of its validity until its violation of the Constitution is proved beyond all reasonable doubt."

But since the rise of the modern movement for social and economic progress through legislation, the Court has more and more often and more and more boldly asserted a power to veto laws passed by the Congress and State legislatures in complete disregard of this original limitation.

In the last 4 years the sound rule of giving statutes the benefit of all reasonable doubt has been cast aside. The Court has been acting not as a judicial body, but as a policy-making body.

When the Congress has sought to stabilize national agriculture, to improve the conditions of labor, to safeguard business against unfair competition, to protect our national resources, and in many other ways to serve our clearly national needs, the majority of the Court has been assuming the power to pass on the wisdom of these acts of the Congress—and to approve or disapprove the public policy written into these laws.

That is not only my accusation. It is the accusation of most distinguished Justices of the present Supreme Court. I have not the time to quote to you all the language used by dissenting Justices in many of these cases. But in the case holding the Railroad Retirement Act unconstitutional, for instance, Chief Justice Hughes said in a dissenting opinion that the majority opinion was "a departure from sound principles," and placed "an unwarranted limitation upon the commerce clause." And three other Justices agreed with him.

In the case holding the A.A.A. unconstitutional, Justice Stone said of the majority opinion that it was a "tortured construction of the Constitution." And two other Justices agreed with him.

In the case holding the New York Minimum Wage Law unconstitutional, Justice Stone said that the majority were actually reading into the Constitution their own "personal economic predilections," and that if the legislative power is not left free to choose the methods of solving the problems of poverty, subsistence, and health of large numbers in the community, then "government is to be rendered impotent." And two other Justices agreed with him.

In the face of these dissenting opinions, there is no basis for the claim made by some members of the Court that something in the Constitution has compelled them regretfully to thwart the will of the people.

In the face of such dissenting opinions, it is perfectly clear that as Chief Justice Hughes has said, "We are under a Constitution, but the Constitution is what the judges say it is."

The Court in addition to the proper use of its judicial functions has improperly set itself up as a third House of the Congress—a superlegislature, as one of the Justices has called it—reading into the Constitution words and implications which are not there, and which were never intended to be there.

We have, therefore, reached the point as a Nation where we must take action to save the Constitution from the Court and the Court from itself. We must find a way to take an appeal from the Supreme Court to the Constitution itself. We want a Supreme Court which will do justice under the Constitution—not over it. In our courts we want a government of laws and not of men.

I want—as all Americans want—an independent judiciary as proposed by the framers of the Constitution. That means a Supreme Court that will enforce the Constitution as written—that will refuse to amend the Constitution by the arbitrary exercise of judicial power—amendment by judicial say-so. It does not mean a judiciary so independent that it can deny the existence of facts universally recognized.

How, then, could we proceed to perform the mandate given us? It was said in last year's Democratic platform, "If these problems cannot be effectively solved within the Constitution, we shall seek such clarifying amendment as will assure the power to enact those laws, adequately to regulate commerce, protect public health and safety, and safeguard economic security." In other words, we said we would seek an amendment only if every other possible means by legislation were to fail.

When I commenced to review the situation with the problem squarely before me, I came by a process of elimination to the conclusion that short of amendments the only method which was clearly constitutional, and would at the same time carry out other much-needed reforms, was to infuse new blood into all our courts. We must have men worthy and equipped to carry out impartial justice. But at the same time we must have judges who will bring to the courts a present-day sense of the Constitution—judges who will retain in the courts the judicial functions of a court and reject the legislative powers which the courts have today assumed.

In 45 out of 48 States of the Union, judges are chosen not for life but for a period of years. In many States judges must retire at the age of 70. Congress has provided financial security by offering life pensions at full pay for Federal judges on all courts who are willing to retire at 70. In the case of Supreme Court Justices, that pension is $20,000 a year. But all Federal judges, once appointed, can, if they choose, hold office for life no matter how old they may get to be.

What is my proposal? It is simply this: Whenever a judge or justice of any Federal court has reached the age of 70 and does not avail himself of the opportunity to retire on a pension, a new member shall be appointed by the President then in office, with the approval, as required by the Constitution, of the Senate of the United States.

That plan has two chief purposes: By bringing into the judicial system a steady and continuing stream of new and younger blood, I hope, first, to make the administration of all Federal justice speedier and therefore less costly; secondly, to bring to the decision of social and economic problems younger men who have had personal experience and contact with modern facts and circumstances under which average men have to live and work. This plan will save our National Constitution from hardening of the judicial arteries.

The number of judges to be appointed would depend wholly on the decision of present judges now over 70 or those who would subsequently reach the age of 70.

If, for instance, any one of the six Justices of the Supreme Court now over the age of 70 should retire as provided under the plan, no additional place would be created. Consequently, although there never can be more than 15, there may be only 14, or 13, or 12, and there may be only 9.

There is nothing novel or radical about this idea. It seeks to maintain the Federal bench in full vigor. It has been discussed and approved by many persons of high authority ever since a similar proposal passed the House of Representatives in 1869.

Why was the age fixed at 70? Because the laws of many States, the practice of the civil service, the regulations of the Army and Navy, and the rules of many of our universities and of almost every great private business enterprise commonly fix the retirement age at 70 years or less.

The statute would apply to all the courts in the Federal system. There is general approval so far as the lower Federal courts are concerned. The plan has met opposition only so far as the Supreme Court of the United States itself is concerned. If such a plan is good for the lower courts, it certainly ought to be equally good for the highest court, from which there is no appeal.

Those opposing this plan have sought to arouse prejudice and fear by crying that I am seeking to "pack" the Supreme Court and that a baneful precedent will be established.

What do they mean by the words "packing the Court"?

Let me answer this question with a bluntness that will end all honest misunderstanding of my purposes.

If by that phrase "packing the Court" it is charged that I wish to place on the bench spineless puppets who would disregard the law and would decide specific cases as I wished them to be decided, I make this answer: That no President fit for his office would appoint, and no Senate of honorable men fit for their office would confirm, that kind of appointees to the Supreme Court.

But if by that phrase the charge is made that I would appoint and the Senate would confirm Justices worthy to sit beside present members of the Court who understand those modern conditions; that I will appoint Justices who will not undertake to override the judgment of the Congress on legislative policy; that I will appoint Justices who will act as Justices and not as legislators—if the appointment of such Justices can be called "packing the Courts"—then I say that I, and with me the vast majority of the American people, favor doing just that thing—now.

Is it a dangerous precedent for the Congress to change the number of the Justices? The Congress has always had, and will have, that power. The number of Justices has been changed several times before—in the administrations of John Adams and Thomas Jefferson, both signers of the Declaration of Independence, Andrew Jackson, Abraham Lincoln, and Ulysses S. Grant.

I suggest only the addition of Justices to the bench in accordance with a clearly defined principle relating to a clearly defined age limit. Fundamentally, if in the future America cannot trust the Congress it elects to refrain from abuse of our constitutional usages, democracy will have failed far beyond the importance to it of any kind of precedent concerning the judiciary.

We think it so much in the public interest to maintain a vigorous judiciary that we encourage the retirement of elderly judges by offering them a life pension at full salary. Why then should we leave the fulfillment of this public policy to chance or make it dependent upon the desire or prejudice of any individual Justice?

It is the clear intention of our public policy to provide for a constant flow of new and younger blood into the judiciary. Normally, every President appoints a large number of district and circuit judges and a few members of the Supreme Court. Until my first term practically every President of the United States had appointed at least one member of the Supreme Court. President Taft appointed five members and named a Chief Justice; President Wilson three; President Harding four, including a Chief Justice; President Coolidge one; President Hoover three, including a Chief Justice.

Such a succession of appointments should have provided a court well balanced as to age. But chance and the disinclination of individuals to leave the Supreme Bench have now given us a Court in which five Justices will be over 75 years of age before next June and one over 70. Thus a sound public policy has been defeated.

I now propose that we establish by law an assurance against any such ill-balanced Court in the future. I propose that hereafter, when a judge reaches the age of 70, a new and younger judge shall be added to the Court automatically. In this way I propose to enforce a sound public policy by law instead of leaving the composition of our Federal courts, including the highest, to be determined by chance or the personal decision of individuals.

If such a law as I propose is regarded as establishing a new precedent, is it not a most desirable precedent?

Like all lawyers, like all Americans, I regret the necessity of this controversy. But the welfare of the United States, and indeed of the Constitution itself, is what we all must think about first. Our difficulty with the Court today rises not from the Court as an institution but from human beings within it. But we cannot yield our constitutional destiny to the personal judgment of a few men who, being fearful of the future, would deny us the necessary means of dealing with the present.

This plan of mine is no attack on the Court; it seeks to restore the Court to its rightful and historic place in our system of constitutional government and to have it resume its high task of building anew on the Constitution "a system of living law."

I have thus explained to you the reasons that lie behind our efforts to secure results by legislation within the Constitution. I hope that thereby the difficult process of constitutional amendment may be rendered unnecessary. . . .

I am in favor of action through legislation—

First, because I believe that it can be passed at this session of the Congress.

Second, because it will provide a reinvigorated, liberal-minded judiciary necessary to furnish quicker and cheaper justice from bottom to top.

Third, because it will provide a series of Federal courts willing to enforce the Constitution as written, and unwilling to assert legislative powers by writing into it their own political and economic policies.

During the past half century the balance of power between the three great branches of the Federal Government has been tipped out of balance by the courts in direct contradiction of the high purposes of the framers of the Constitution. It is my purpose to restore that balance. You who know me will accept my solemn assurance that in a world in which democracy is under attack I seek to make American democracy succeed.

Chief Justice Charles Evans Hughes Defends the Supreme Court's Performance, 1937

My Dear Senator Wheeler:

In response to your inquiries, I have the honor to present the following statement with respect to the work of the Supreme Court:

1. The Supreme Court is fully abreast of its work. When we rose on March 15 (for the present recess) we had heard argument in cases in which certiorari had been granted only four weeks before, Feb. 1.

During the current term, which began last October and which we call October Term, 1936, we have heard argument on the merits in 150 cases (180 numbers) and we have 28 cases (30 numbers) awaiting argument. We shall be able to hear all these cases, and such others as may come up for argument, before our adjournment for the term. There is no congestion of cases upon our calendar.

This gratifying condition has obtained for several years. We have been able for several terms to adjourn after disposing of all cases which are ready to be heard. . . .

3. The statute relating to our Appellate jurisdiction is the act of Feb. 13, 1925; 43 stat. 936. That act limits to certain cases the appeals which come to the Supreme Court as a matter of right. Review in other cases is made to depend upon the allowance by the Supreme Court of a writ of certiorari.

Where the appeal purports to lie as a matter of right, the rules of the Supreme Court (Rule 12) require the appellant to submit a jurisdictional statement showing that the case falls within that class of appeals and that a substantial question is involved. We examine that statement and the supporting and opposing briefs, and decide whether the court has jurisdiction. As a result, many frivolous appeals are forthright dismissed and the way is open for appeals which disclose substantial questions.

4. The act of 1925 . . . was most carefully considered by Congress. . . . That legislation was deemed to be essential to enable the Supreme Court to perform its proper function. No single court of last resort, whatever the number of judges, could dispose of all the cases which arise in this vast country and which litigants would seek to bring up if the right of appeal were unrestricted.

Hosts of litigants will take appeals so long as there is a tribunal accessible. In protracted litigation, the advantage is with those who command a long purse. Unmeritorious appeals cause intolerable delays. Such appeals clog the calendar and get in the way of those that have merit. . . .

If further review [of cases] is to be had by the Supreme Court it must be because of the public interest in the questions involved. The review, for example, should be for the purpose of resolving conflicts in judicial decisions between different Circuit Courts of Appeal or between Circuit Courts of

Appeal and State courts where the question is one of State law; or for the purpose of determining constitutional questions or settling the interpretation of statutes; or because of the importance of the questions of law that are involved. Review by the Supreme Court is thus in the interest of the law, not in the mere interest of the litigants.

It is obvious that if appeal as a matter of right is restricted to certain described cases, the question whether the review should be allowed in other cases must necessarily be confined to some tribunal for determination, and of course, with respect to review by the Supreme Court, that court should decide.

5. Granting certiorari is not a matter of favor but of sound judicial discretion. It is not the importance of the parties or the amount of money involved that is in any sense controlling. . . .

Furthermore, petitions for certiorari are granted if four justices think they should be. A vote by a majority is not required in such cases. Even if two or three of the justices are strongly of the opinion that certiorari should be allowed, frequently the other justices will acquiesce in their view but the petition is always granted if four so vote.

6. The work of passing upon these applications for certiorari is laborious but the court is able to perform it adequately. Observations have been made as to the vast number of pages of records and briefs that are submitted in the course of a term. The total is imposing, but the suggested conclusion is hasty and rests on an illusory basis.

Records are replete with testimony and evidence of facts. But the questions on certiorari are questions of law. So many cases turn on the facts, principles of law not being in controversy. It is only when the facts are so interwoven with the questions of law which we should review that the evidence must be examined and then only to the extent that it is necessary to decide the questions of law.

This at once disposes of a vast number of factual controversies where the parties have been fully heard in the courts below and have no right to burden the Supreme Court with the dispute which interests no one but themselves. . . .

I think it safe to say that about 60 per cent of the applications for certiorari are wholly without merit and ought never to have been made. There are probably about 20 per cent or so in addition which have a fair degree of plausibility but which fail to survive critical examination. The remainder, falling short, I believe, of 20 per cent, show substantial grounds and are granted. I think that it is the view of the members of the court that if any error is made in dealing with these applications it is on the side of liberality.

An increase in the number of justices of the Supreme Court, apart from any question of policy, which I do not discuss, would not promote the efficiency of the court. It is believed that it would impair that efficiency so long as the court acts as a unit. There would be more judges to hear, more judges to confer, more judges to discuss, more judges to be convinced and to decide.

The present number of justices is thought to be large enough so far as the prompt, adequate and efficient conduct of the work of the court is concerned. . . .

I understand that it has been suggested that with more justices the court could hear cases in divisions. It is believed that such a plan would be impracticable. A large proportion of the cases we hear are important and a decision by a part of the court would be unsatisfactory.

I may also call attention to the provision of Article III, Section 1, of the Constitution that the judicial power of the United States shall be vested "in one Supreme Court" and in such inferior courts as the Congress may from time to time ordain and establish. The Constitution does not appear to authorize two or more Supreme Courts or two or more parts of a Supreme Court functioning in effect as separate courts.

On account of the shortness of time I have not been able to consult with the members of the court generally with respect to the foregoing statement, but I am confident that it is in accord with the views of the justices. I should say, however, that I have been able to consult with Mr. Justice Van Devanter and Mr. Justice Brandeis, and I am at liberty to say that the statement is approved by them.

The Senate Judiciary Committee's Report Rejects FDR's Plan, 1937

. . . The Committee on the Judiciary, to whom was referred the bill to reorganize the judicial branch of the Government, after full consideration, having unanimously amended the measure, hereby report the bill adversely with the recommendation that it do not pass. . . .

The Argument

The committee recommends that the measure by rejected for the following primary reasons:

I. The bill does not accomplish any one of the objectives for which it was originally offered.

II. It applies force to the judiciary and in its initial and ultimate effect would undermine the independence of the courts.

III. It violates all precedents in the history of our Government and would in itself be a dangerous precedent for the future.

IV. The theory of the bill is in direct violation of the spirit of the American Constitution and its employment would permit alteration of the Constitution without the people's consent or approval; it undermines the protection our constitutional system gives to minorities and is subversive of the rights of individuals.

V. It tends to centralize the Federal district judiciary by the power of assigning judges from one district to another at will.

VI. It tends to expand political control over the judicial department by adding to the powers of the legislative and executive departments respecting the judiciary. . . .

Objectives as Originally Stated

As offered to the Congress, this bill was designed to effectuate only three objectives, described as follows in the President's message:

1. To increase the personnel of the Federal courts "so that cases may be promptly decided in the first instance, and may be given adequate and prompt hearing on all appeals";

2. To "invigorate all the courts by the permanent infusion of new blood";

3. To "grant to the Supreme Court further power and responsibility in maintaining the efficiency of the entire Federal judiciary."

The third of these purposes was to be accomplished by the provisions creating the office of the Proctor and dealing with the assignment of judges to courts other than those to which commissioned.

The first two objectives were to be attained by the provisions authorizing the appointment of not to exceed 50 additional judges when sitting judges of retirement age, as defined in the bill, failed to retire or resign. How totally inadequate the measure is to achieve either of the named objectives, the most cursory examination of the facts reveals. . . .

Question of Age Not Solved

The next question is to determine to what extent "the persistent infusion of new blood" may be expected from this bill.

It will be observed that the bill before us does not and cannot compel the retirement of any judge, whether on the Supreme Court or any other court, when he becomes 70 years of age. It will be remembered that the mere attainment of three score and ten by a particular judge does not, under this bill, require the appointment of another. The man on the bench may be 80 years of age, but this bill will not authorize the President to appoint a new judge to sit beside him unless he has served as a judge for 10 years. In other words, age itself is not penalized; the penalty falls only when age is attended with experience.

No one should overlook the fact that under this bill the President, whoever he may be and whether or not he believes in the constant infusion of young blood in the courts, may nominate a man 69 years and 11 months of age to the Supreme Court, or to any court, and if confirmed, such nominee, if he never had served as a judge, would continue to sit upon the bench unmolested by this law until he had attained the ripe age of 79 years and 11 months.

We are told that "modern complexities call also for a constant infusion of new blood in the courts, just as it is needed in executive functions of the Government and in private business." Does this bill provide for such? The answer is obviously no. As has been just demonstrated, the introduction of old and inexperienced blood into the courts is not prevented by this bill.

More than that, the measure, by its own terms, makes impossible the "constant" or "persistent" infusion of new blood. It is to be observed that the word is "new," not "young."

The Supreme Court may not be expanded to more than 15 members. No more than two additional members may be appointed to any circuit court of appeals, to the Court of Claims, to the Court of Customs and Patent Appeals, or to the Customs Court, and the number of judges now serving in any district or group of districts may not be more than doubled. There is, therefore, a specific limitation of appointment regardless of age. That is to say, this bill, ostensibly designed to provide for the infusion of new blood, sets up insuperable obstacles to the "constant" or "persistent" operation of that principle. . . .

It thus appears that the bill before us does not with certainty provide for increasing the personnel of the Federal judiciary, does not remedy the law's delay, does not serve the interest of the "poorer litigant" and does not provide for the "constant" or "persistent infusion of new blood" into the judiciary. What, then, does it do?

The Bill Applies Force to the Judiciary

The answer is clear. It applies force to the judiciary. It is an attempt to impose upon the courts a course of action, a line of decision which, without that force, without that imposition, the judiciary might not adopt. . . .

Those of us who hold office in this Government, however humble or exalted it may be, are creatures of the Constitution. To it we owe all the power and authority we possess. Outside of it we have none. We are bound by it in every official act.

We know that this instrument, without which we would not be able to call ourselves presidents, judges, or legislators, was carefully planned and deliberately framed to establish three coordinate branches of government, every one of them to be independent of the others. For the protection of the people, for the preservation of the rights of the individual, for the maintenance of the liberties of minorities, for maintaining the checks and balances of our dual system, the three branches of the Government were so constituted that the independent expression of honest difference of opinion could never be restrained in the people's servants and no one branch could overawe or subjugate the others. That is the American system. It is immeasurably more important, immeasurably more sacred to the people of America, indeed, to the people of all the world than the immediate adoption of any legislation however beneficial.

That judges should hold office during good behavior is the prescription. It is founded upon historic experience of the utmost significance. Compensation at stated times, which compensation was not to be diminished during their tenure, was also ordained. Those comprehensible terms were the outgrowths of experience which was deep-seated. . . . This judicial system is the priceless heritage of every American.

By this bill another and wholly different cause is proposed for the intervention of executive influence, namely, age. Age and behavior have no connection; they are unrelated subjects. By this bill, judges who have reached 70 years of age may remain on the bench and have their judgment augmented if they agree with the new appointee, or vetoed if they disagree. This is far from the independence intended for the courts by the framers of the Constitution. This is an unwarranted influence accorded the appointing agency, contrary to the spirit of the Constitution. The bill sets up a plan which has as its stability the changing will or inclination of an agency not a part of the judicial system. Constitutionally, the bill can have no sanction. The effect of the bill, as stated by the Attorney General to the committee, and indeed by the President in both his message and speech, is in violation of the organic law.

Object of Plan Acknowledged

No amount of sophistry can cover up this fact. The effect of this bill is not to provide for an increase in the number of Justices composing the Supreme Court. The effect is to provide a forced retirement or, failing in this, to take from the Justices affected a free exercise of their independent judgment. . . .

Let us, for the purpose of the argument, grant that the Court has been wrong, wrong not only in that it has rendered mistaken opinions but wrong in the far more serious sense that it has substituted its will for the congressional will in the matter of legislation. May we nevertheless safely punish the Court?

Today it may be the Court which is charged with forgetting its constitutional duties. Tomorrow it may be the Congress. The next day it may be the Executive. If we yield to temptation now to lay the lash upon the Court, we are only teaching others how to apply it to ourselves and to the people when the occasion seems to warrant. Manifestly, if we may force the hand of the Court to secure our interpretation of the Constitution, then some succeeding Congress may repeat the process to secure another and a different interpretation and one which may not sound so pleasant in our ears as that for which we now contend.

There is a remedy for usurpation or other judicial wrongdoing. If this bill be supported by the toilers of this country upon the ground that they want a Court which will sustain legislation limiting hours and providing minimum wages, they must remember that the procedure employed in the bill could be used in another administration to lengthen hours and to decrease wages. If farmers want agricultural relief and favor this bill upon the ground that it gives them a Court which will sustain legislation in their favor, they must remember that the procedure employed might some day be used to deprive them of every vestige of a farm relief.

When members of the Court usurp legislative powers or attempt to exercise political power, they lay themselves open to the charge of having lapsed from that "good behavior" which determines the period of their official life. But, if you say, the process of impeachment is difficult and uncertain, the answer is, the people made it so when they framed the Constitution. It is not for us, the servants of the people, the instruments of the Constitution, to find a more easy way to do that which our masters made difficult.

But, if the fault of the judges is not so grievous as to warrant impeachment, if their offense is merely that they have grown old, and we feel, therefore, that there should be a "constant infusion of new blood," then obviously the way to achieve that result is by constitutional amendment fixing definite terms for the members of the judiciary or making mandatory their retirement at a given age. Such a provision would indeed provide for the constant infusion of new blood, not only now but at all times in the future. The plan before us is but a temporary expedient which operates once and then never again, leaving the Court as permanently expanded to become once more a court of old men, gradually year by year falling behind the times. . . .

A Measure Without Precedent

This bill is an invasion of judicial power such as has never before been attempted in this country. It is true that in the closing days of the administration of John Adams, a bill was passed creating 16 new circuit judges while reducing by one the number of places on the Supreme Court. It was charged that this was a bill to use the judiciary for a political purpose by providing official positions for members of a defeated party. The repeal of that law was the first task of the Jefferson administration.

Neither the original act nor the repealer was an attempt to change the course of judicial decision. And never in the history of the country has there been such an act. The present bill comes to us, therefore, wholly without precedent.

It is true that the size of the Supreme Court has been changed from time to time, but in every instance after the Adams administration, save one, the changes were made for purely administrative purposes in aid of the Court, not to control it. . . .

A Precedent of Loyalty to the Constitution

Shall we now, after 150 years of loyalty to the constitutional ideal of an untrammeled judiciary, duty bound to protect the constitutional rights of the humblest citizen even against the Government itself, create the vicious precedent which must necessarily undermine our system? The only argument for the increase which survives analysis is that Congress should enlarge the Court so as to make the policies of this administration effective.

We are told that a reactionary oligarchy defies the will of the majority, that this is a bill to "unpack" the Court and give effect to the desires of the majority; that is to say, a bill to increase the number of Justices for the express purpose of neutralizing the views of some of the present members. In justification we are told, but without authority, by those who would rationalize this program, that Congress was given the power to determine the size of the Court so that the legislative branch would be able to impose its will upon the judiciary. This amounts to nothing more than the declaration that when the Court stands in the way of a legislative enactment, the Congress may reverse the ruling by enlarging the Court. When such a principle is adopted, our constitutional system is overthrown!

This, then, is the dangerous precedent we are asked to establish. When proponents of the bill assert, as they have done, that Congress in the past has altered the number of Justices upon the Supreme Court and that this is reason enough for our doing it now, they show how important precedents are and prove that we should now refrain from any action that would seem to establish one which could be followed hereafter whenever a Congress and an executive should become dissatisfied with the decisions of the Supreme Court.

This is the first time in the history of our country that a proposal to alter the decisions of the court by enlarging its personnel has been so boldly made. Let us meet it. Let us now set a salutary precedent that will never be violated. Let us, of the Seventy-fifth Congress, in words that will never be disregarded by any succeeding Congress, declare that we would rather have an independent Court, a fearless Court, a Court that will dare to announce its honest opinions in what it believes to be the defense of the liberties of the people, than a Court that, out of fear or sense of obligation to the appointing power, or factional passion, approves any measure we may enact. We are not the judges of the judges. We are not above the Constitution.

Even if every charge brought against the so-called "reactionary" members of this Court be true, it is far better that we await orderly but inevitable change of personnel than that we impatiently overwhelm them with new members. Exhibiting this restraint, thus demonstrating our faith in the American system, we shall set an example that will protect the independent American judiciary from attack as long as this Government stands. . . .

True it is, that courts like Congresses, should take account of the advancing strides of civilization. True it is that the law, being a progressive science, must be pronounced progressively and liberally; but the milestones of liberal progress are made to be noted and counted with caution rather than merely to be encountered and passed. Progress is not a mad mob march; rather, it is a steady, invincible stride. . . .

If, under the "hydraulic pressure" of our present need for economic justice, we destroy the system under which our people have progressed to a higher degree of justice and prosperity than that ever enjoyed by any other people in all the history of the human race, then we shall destroy not only all opportunity for further advance but everything we have thus far achieved. . . .

Even if the case were far worse than it is alleged to be, it would still be no argument in favor of this bill to say that the courts and some judges have abused their power. The courts are not perfect, nor are the judges. The Congress is not perfect, nor are Senators and Representatives. The Executive is not perfect. These branches of government and the office[s] under them are filled by human beings who for the most part strive to live up to the dignity and idealism of a system that was designed to achieve the greatest possible measure of justice and freedom for all the people. We shall destroy the system when we reduce it to the imperfect standards of the men who operate it. We shall strengthen it and ourselves, we shall make justice and liberty for all men more certain when, by patience and self-restraint, we maintain it on the high plane on which it was conceived.

Inconvenience and even delay in the enactment of legislation is not a heavy price to pay for our system. Constitutional democracy moves forward with certainty rather than with speed. The safety and the permanence of the progressive march of our civilization are far more important to us and to those who are to come after us than the enactment now of any particular law. The Constitution of the United States provides ample opportunity for the expression of popular will to bring about such reforms and changes as the people may deem essential to their present and future welfare. It is the people's charter of the powers granted those who govern them. . . .

Summary

We recommend the rejection of this bill as a needless, futile, and utterly dangerous abandonment of constitutional principle.

It was presented to the Congress in a most intricate form and for reasons that obscured its real purpose.

It would not banish age from the bench nor abolish divided decisions.

It would not affect the power of any court to hold laws unconstitutional nor withdraw from any judge the authority to issue injunctions.

It would not reduce the expense of litigation nor speed the decision of cases.

It is a proposal without precedent and without justification.

It would subjugate the courts to the will of Congress and the President and thereby destroy the independence of the judiciary, the only certain shield of individual rights.

It contains the germ of a system of centralized administration of law that would enable an executive so minded to send his judges into every judicial district in the land to sit in judgment on controversies between the Government and the citizen.

It points the way to the evasion of the Constitution and establishes the method whereby the people may be deprived of their right to pass upon all amendments of the fundamental law.

It stands now before the country, acknowledged by its proponents as a plan to force judicial interpretation of the Constitution, a proposal that violates every sacred tradition of American democracy.

Under the form of the Constitution it seeks to do that which is unconstitutional.

Its ultimate operation would be to make this Government one of men rather than one of law, and its practical operation would be to make the Constitution what the executive or legislative branches of the Government choose to say it is—an interpretation to be changed with each change of administration.

It is a measure which should be so emphatically rejected that its parallel will never again be presented to the free representatives of the free people of America. . . .

West Coast Hotel v. *Parrish*, 300 U.S. 397 (1937)

[5–4: Hughes, Brandeis, Cardozo, Roberts,
Stone; Butler, McReynolds, Sutherland,
Van Devanter]

. . . Mr. Chief Justice Hughes delivered the opinion of the Court.

This case presents the question of the constitutional validity of the minimum wage law of the State of Washington. . . .

The principle which must control our decision is not in doubt. The constitutional provision invoked is the due process clause of the Fourteenth Amendment governing the States, as the due process clause invoked in the *Adkins* case governed Congress. In each case the violation alleged by those attacking minimum wage regulation for women is deprivation of freedom of contract. What is this freedom? The Constitution does not speak of freedom of contract. It speaks of liberty and prohibits the deprivation of liberty without due process of law. In prohibiting that deprivation the Constitution does not recognize an absolute and uncontrollable liberty. Liberty in each of its phases has its history and connotation. But the liberty safeguarded is liberty in a social organization which requires the protection of law against the evils which menace the health, safety, morals and welfare of the people. Liberty under the Constitution is thus necessarily subject to the restraints of due process, and regulation which is reasonable in relation to its subject and is adopted in the interests of the community is due process.

This essential limitation of liberty in general governs freedom of contract in particular. More than twenty-five years ago we set forth the applicable principle in these words, after referring to the cases where the liberty guaranteed by the Fourteenth Amendment had been broadly described . . . .

This power under the Constitution to restrict freedom of contract has had many illustrations. That it may be exercised in the public interest with respect to contracts between employer and employee is undeniable. . . .

The point that has been strongly stressed that adult employees should be deemed competent to make their own contracts was decisively met nearly forty years ago in *Holden* v. *Hardy* . . . , where we pointed out the inequality in the footing of the parties. . . .

It is manifest that this established principle is peculiarly applicable in relation to the employment of women in whose protection the State has a special interest. That phase of the subject received elaborate consideration in *Muller* v. *Oregon* (1908) . . . , where the constitutional authority of the State to limit the working hours of women was sustained. We emphasized the consideration that "woman's physical structure and the performance of maternal functions place her at a disadvantage in the struggle for subsistence" and that her physical well being "becomes an object of public interest and care in order to preserve the strength and vigor of the race." We emphasized the need of protecting women against oppression despite her possession of contractual rights. We said that "though limitations upon personal and contractual rights may be removed by legislation, there is that in her disposition and habits of life which will operate against a full assertion of those rights. She will still be where some legislation to protect her seems necessary to secure a real equality of right." Hence she was "properly placed in a class by herself, and legislation designed for her protection may be sustained even when like legislation is not necessary for men and could not be sustained." We concluded that the limitations which the statute there in question "placed upon her contractual powers, upon her right to agree with her employer as to the time she shall labor" were "not imposed solely for her benefit, but also largely for the benefit of all." . . .

This array of precedents and the principles they applied were thought by the dissenting Justices in the *Adkins* case to demand that the minimum wage statute be sustained. The validity of the distinction made by the Court between a minimum wage and a maximum of hours in limiting liberty of contract was especially challenged. . . . That challenge persists and is without any satisfactory answer. As Chief Justice Taft observed: "In absolute freedom of contract the one term is as important as the other, for both enter equally into the consideration given and received, a restriction as to the one is not greater in essence than the other and is of the same kind. One is the multiplier and the other the multiplicand." And Mr. Justice Holmes, while recognizing that "the distinctions of the law are distinctions of degree," could "perceive no difference in the kind or degree of interference with liberty, the only matter with which we have any concern, between the one case and the other. The bargain is equally affected whichever half you regulate." . . .

One of the points which was pressed by the Court in supporting its ruling in the *Adkins* case was that the standard set up by the District of Columbia Act did not take appropriate account of the value of the services rendered. In the *Morehead* case, the minority thought that the New York statute had met that point in its definition of a "fair wage" and that it accordingly presented a distinguishable feature which the Court could recognize within the limits which the *Morehead* petition for certiorari was deemed to present. The Court, however, did not take that view and the New York Act was held to be essentially the same as that for the District of Columbia. The statute now before us is like the latter, but we are unable to conclude that in its minimum wage requirement the State has passed beyond the boundary of its broad protective power.

The minimum wage to be paid under the Washington statute is fixed after full consideration by representatives of employers, employees and the public. It may be assumed that the minimum wage is fixed in consideration of the services that are performed in the particular occupations under normal conditions. Provision is made for special licenses at less wages in the case of women who are incapable of full service. The statement of Mr. Justice

Holmes in the *Adkins* case is pertinent: "This statute does not compel anybody to pay anything. It simply forbids employment at rates below those fixed as the minimum requirement of health and right living. It is safe to assume that women will not be employed at even the lowest wages allowed unless they earn them, or unless the employer's business can sustain the burden. In short the law in its character and operation is like hundreds of so-called police laws that have been upheld." . . . And Chief Justice Taft forcibly pointed out the consideration which is basic in a statute of this character: "Legislatures which adopt a requirement of maximum hours or minimum wages may be presumed to believe that when sweating employers are prevented from paying unduly low wages by positive law they will continue their business, abating that part of their profits, which were wrung from the necessities of their employees, and will concede the better terms required by the law; and that while in individual cases hardship may result, the restriction will enure to the benefit of the general class of employees in whose interest the law is passed and so to that of the community at large." . . .

We think that the views thus expressed are sound and that the decision in the *Adkins* case was a departure from the true application of the principles governing the regulation by the State of the relation of employer and employed. . . .

With full recognition of the earnestness and vigor which characterize the prevailing opinion in the *Adkins* case, we find it impossible to reconcile that ruling with these well-considered declarations. What can be closer to the public interest than the health of women and their protection from unscrupulous and overreaching employers? And if the protection of women is a legitimate end of the exercise of state power, how can it be said that the requirement of the payment of a minimum wage fairly fixed in order to meet the very necessities of existence is not an admissible means to that end? The legislature of the State was clearly entitled to consider the situation of women in employment, the fact that they are in the class receiving the least pay, that their bargaining power is relatively weak, and that they are the ready victims of those who would take advantage of their necessitous circumstances. The legislature was entitled to adopt measures to reduce the evils of the "sweating system," the exploiting of workers at wages so low as to be insufficient to meet the bare cost of living, thus making their very helplessness the occasion of a most injurious competition. The legislature had the right to consider that its minimum wage requirements would be an important aid in carrying out its policy of protection. The adoption of similar requirements by many States evidences a deepseated conviction both as to the presence of the evil and as to the means adopted to check it. Legislative response to that conviction cannot be regarded as arbitrary or capricious, and that is all we have to decide. Even if the wisdom of the policy be regarded as debatable and its effects uncertain, still the legislature is entitled to its judgment.

There is an additional and compelling consideration which recent economic experience has brought into a strong light. The exploitation of a class of workers who are in an unequal position with respect to bargaining power and are thus relatively defenceless against the denial of a living wage is not only detrimental to their health and well being but casts a direct burden for their support upon the community. What these workers lose in wages the taxpayers are called upon to pay. The bare cost of living must be met. We may take judicial notice of the unparalleled demands for relief which arose during the recent period of depression and still continue to an alarming extent despite the degree of economic recovery which has been achieved. It is unnecessary to cite official statistics to establish what is of common knowledge through the length and breadth of the land. While in the instant case no factual brief has been presented, there is no reason to doubt that the State of Washington has encountered the same social problem that is present elsewhere. The community is not bound to provide what is in effect a subsidy for unconscionable employers. The community may direct its law-making power to correct the abuse which springs from their selfish disregard of the public interest. The argument that the legislation in question consti-tutes an arbitrary discrimination, because it does not extend to men, is unavailing. This Court has frequently held that the legislative authority, acting within its proper field, is not bound to extend its regulation to all cases which it might possibly reach. . . .

Our conclusion is that the case of *Adkins* v. *Children's Hospital, supra,* should be, and it is, overruled. The judgment of the Supreme Court of the State of Washington is *Affirmed.*

⧾ E S S A Y S

Scholars usually treat President Franklin D. Roosevelt's court-packing plan as a dramatic episode of American constitutional history that most fully implicated the Supreme Court. That is the approach taken in the first essay by William Leuchten-burg, Kennan professor of history at the University of North Carolina, Chapel Hill. Leuchtenburg's interpretation, while examining the president's leadership role and the scheme's political origins, stresses the implications of the episode for the history of the Court. Michael Nelson, a professor of political science at Van-derbilt University, in the second selection views the entire affair in another way— as an important event in the emergence of the modern American presidency. Nel-son argues that in FDR's overreaching of power is a larger lesson about what happens in modern constitutional democracy when a president garners an over-whelming base of popular support. The court-packing plan was as much a test of the presidency as it was a test of the Court.

The Logic of FDR's Court-Packing Scheme

WILLIAM E. LEUCHTENBURG

. . . On "Black Monday," May 27, 1935, in three 9-to-0 decisions, the Court invalidated the National Industrial Recovery Act and the Frazier-Lemke Act and ruled, in the *Humphrey* case, that the President could not remove

William E. Leuchtenburg, "The Origins of Franklin D. Roosevelt's 'Court-Packing' Plan," *The Supreme Court Review* (1966): 356–365, 380–387, 390–395, 400. Reprinted by permission of the University of Chicago Press.

members of independent regulatory commissions save as Congress provided. Roosevelt was incensed by the overturning of the NRA, the keystone of his industrial recovery program. The Court's language in denouncing the delegation of powers and its narrow construction of the Commerce Clause appeared to place other New Deal laws in jeopardy and to bar the way to new legislation. He was even more outraged by the *Humphrey* decision, which, in view of the history of the *Myers* opinion, seemed a deliberate assault by the Court on his own prerogatives. The unanimity of the Court in all three cases was bewildering. "Well, where was Ben Cardozo?" he asked. "And what about old Isaiah?"

For four days, while the country speculated about what he would do, the President said nothing. On May 31, reporters were summoned to the White House. As they filed in, they saw on the President's desk a copy of the *Schechter* opinion and a sheaf of telegrams. Eleanor Roosevelt, seated next to her friend Mrs. Felix Frankfurter, busied herself knitting on a blue sock. For the next hour and a half, while reporters listened intently, Roosevelt, in an unusually somber mood, discoursed on the implications of the Court's opinion. Thumbing the copy of the *Schechter* decision as he spoke, the President argued that the Court's ruling had stripped the national government of its power to cope with critical national problems. "We are facing a very, very great national non-partisan issue," he said. "We have got to decide one way or the other . . . whether in some way we are going to . . . restore to the Federal Government the powers which exist in the national Governments of every other Nation in the world." Of all the words the President spoke at the extraordinary conference, newspapermen singled out one sentence which headline writers emblazoned on late afternoon newspapers: "We have been relegated to the horse-and-buggy definition of interstate commerce."

. . . Most commentators upbraided the President severely. The Washington *Post* typified much of the newspaper response with an editorial bluntly titled, "A President Leaves His Party." Henry Stimson wrote Roosevelt a long letter in which he protested that the "horse-and-buggy" observation "was a wrong statement, an unfair statement and, if it had not been so extreme as to be recognizable as hyperbole, a rather dangerous and inflammatory statement." Senator Arthur Vandenberg, Michigan Republican, declared: "I don't think the President has any thought of emulating Mussolini, Hitler or Stalin, but his utterance as I have heard it is exactly what these men would say." . . .

From both within and outside the Administration, Roosevelt was urged to act immediately. In the confusion after the horse-and-buggy conference, Raymond Moley, one of the original members of the Brain Trust, called Vice President John N. Garner and Senators [James] Byrnes and Robert M. La Follette, Jr., together and found that they, like he, favored a constitutional amendment. Encouraged by the meeting, Moley wrote an editorial for *Today* advocating this course, and Byrnes spoke in support of the idea in Charleston, South Carolina. In Congress, the demand for action produced a freshet of new proposals. Some wanted to make constitutional grants of power to Congress more explicit; others, like Senator [George] Norris, wished to require at least a 7-to-2 vote by the Supreme Court to invalidate legislation.

In the nation there was growing anti-Court sentiment, which those who wished to act right away might tap. To the forces arrayed against the Court by the rail pension opinion, the *Schechter* decision had added both those groups which had benefited from the NRA and people who resented any setback to Roosevelt and the New Deal. A Memphis man advised the President to balk the Court by declaring martial law, and a Kentucky attorney wrote: "I should think that you and Congress were as tired of the Supreme Court stunts as the people are."

But Roosevelt decided against immediate action. For a moment, Moley recalls, the President showed a "flicker of enthusiasm," but this soon dwindled. Roosevelt sensed that the time was not yet ripe. The NRA had its supporters, but its detractors were more numerous; he could not go to the country with that kind of an appeal. The clamor raised by the horse-and-buggy conference indicated that the Court would have to antagonize a much larger portion of the nation before it would be politically safe to challenge it. The difficulties in the way of winning approval for a constitutional amendment were inhibiting. Norris conceded: "It looks now as though it would be an absolute impossibility to pass it through the Senate or the House by the necessary two-thirds majority in order to submit it to the states." Nor had the explorations in the Department of Justice proceeded far enough so that Roosevelt was ready with a specific proposal.

For the next year Roosevelt bided his time. He made no public reference to the Supreme Court even when additional adverse decisions appeared to require some sort of response. He left the impression that he was accepting the Court's verdicts without complaint and that, after having had his knuckles rapped for his horse-and-buggy remarks, he proposed neither to say nor to do anything further. In fact, as Tugwell has written, "If open battle was not at once joined, a kind of twilight war did begin." . . .

If and when the time came to act, the amendment route seemed the most promising path, although not everyone agreed about this. Some thought that the problem lay not in the Constitution but the Court; hence, they reasoned either that the composition of the Court must be altered or that the Court must, and perhaps could, be persuaded to change its views. The Felix Frankfurter cadre, which had always disliked the NRA anyway, opposed the amendment approach. From a different standpoint, [Attorney General] Homer Cummings, angered by the *Schechter* decision, fumed: "I tell you, Mr. President, they mean to destroy us. . . . We will have to find a way to get rid of the present membership of the Supreme Court." Yet the unanimity of the Court made it seem unlikely that the New Deal could win a majority, and it argued against solving the problem by appointing a few additional judges. After the *Schechter* opinion was handed down, Raymond Clapper wrote: "Talk of blackjacking the court by enlarging its membership collapsed when all nine justices joined in the decision. That subterfuge of packing the court, a weak and uncertain one at best, becomes ridiculous to think of now." . . .

Finding a satisfactory plan was only one part of Roosevelt's strategy; another part was building popular support for such a move. The horse-and-buggy conference had been one move toward that end. In August the President took another step when he met at the White House with George Creel. In collaboration with Creel, a veteran of reform wars, Roosevelt sometimes used the pages of *Collier's* to launch trial balloons. For an article entitled "Looking Ahead with Roosevelt," the President now dictated to Creel:

> In the next few months, the Supreme Court will hand down fresh pronouncements with respect to New Deal laws, and it is possible the President will get another "licking." If so, much will depend on the language of the licking. In the event that unconstitutionality is found, perhaps the decisions will point the way to statutory amendments. If, however, the Constitution is construed technically; if it is held that one hundred and fifty years have no bearing on the case, and that the present generation is powerless to meet social and economic problems that were not within the knowledge of the founding fathers, and therefore not made the subject of their specific consideration, then the President will have no other alternative than to go to the country with a Constitutional amendment that will lift the Dead Hand, giving the people of today the right to deal with today's vital issues.

He told Creel grimly: "Fire that as an opening gun."

Contrary to Roosevelt's expectation, the trial balloon attracted almost no notice. Most of the nation in 1935 was still either indifferent to the Court question or outrightly opposed to tethering the Court. . . .

Despite this discouraging response, the President pushed ahead quietly with his plans. At a long lunch at the White House on November 12, 1935, [Interior Secretary Harold] Ickes and Roosevelt fell to talking about the Court. The President remarked that he did not think that any Justices would retire and permit him to make new appointments. "Then," Ickes noted, "he said that while the matter could not be talked about now, he believed that the way to mend the situation was to adopt a constitutional amendment which would give the Attorney General the right, if he has any doubt of the constitutionality of a legislative act, to apply to the Supreme Court for a ruling, that ruling to state specifically in which respects the act is unconstitutional. Then, if the next succeeding Congress, with this opinion of the Supreme Court before it, should re-enact that statute, it would, by that fact, be purged of its unconstitutionality and become the law of the land." . . .

In essence, the President's strategy was to leave the power of decision to the Supreme Court. If the Court upheld New Deal legislation, the issue would fade away. But if all the legislation were thrown out, Roosevelt warned, there would be "marching farmers and marching miners and marching workingmen throughout the land." For almost half a year, while the Court was recessed, the conflict between the President and the Court had simmered on a low flame. But during those months, as Roosevelt was keenly aware, such significant questions as the AAA processing tax had been making their way through the lower courts; the Supreme Court could be expected to render decisions on such matters early in 1936. "If the Court does send the AAA flying like the NRA," the President had told [Department of Labor solicitor Charles] Wyzanski, "there might even be a revolution." . . .

In November 1936, Franklin Roosevelt rolled up the greatest landslide victory in the history of two-party competition by capturing the electoral votes of all but two of the forty-eight states. His political opponents routed, his policies vindicated, he could now give full attention to the challenge posed by the Supreme Court. Time was short. In just two more months the Court would reconvene; awaiting it were tests of the validity of the Social Security Act, the Wagner Labor Relations Act, the Railway Labor Act, the Commodity Exchange Act, state minimum-wage and unemployment compensation laws, and of the powers of the PWA, the SEC, and the Federal Communications Commission. Even the gold clause resolution faced another contest.

In view of this prospect, what was Roosevelt to do? He might just wait for vacancies to develop. The laws of nature were on his side, for never in our history had a Court been composed of so elderly a group. Moreover, Justices Van Devanter and Sutherland had talked of retiring. Yet Roosevelt had seen nearly four years go by without one opportunity to make an appointment, an experience that had occurred in no other full presidential term save for the special instance of Andrew Johnson's tenure. Anyone familiar with the conversation of Justices knew enough to place a high discount on talk of retiring, and these particular Justices seemed determined to stay on the bench so long as Roosevelt was in the White House. At the first cabinet meeting after the election, the President, in a spirit of gallows humor, said that Justice McReynolds would still be on the tribunal when he was 105.

Still, Roosevelt might wait to see whether the Court would follow the election returns. The switch of even one Justice could be decisive. It might be anticipated that the emphatic outcome of the election would surprise some Justices who had believed that they were speaking for a nation outraged by the New Deal. (It is clear from Van Devanter's correspondence that he thought the election would be close.) Nor, it has been argued, was Justice Roberts as set aginst the New Deal as he appeared to be.

Yet there were risks in waiting. The Court had behaved so arrogantly in the spring of 1936 that the prospects for a change of views seemed slim. Not only did the Court's line of reasoning in its last term leave little reason to suppose that the Court would not strike down such landmarks as the Wagner Act and the Social Security law, but it barred the way to new legislation. Returned to office with a tremendous grant of power, Roosevelt might be denied by the Court the opportunity to use that power. If he waited to see what the Court did, he might find himself with his past achievements obliterated and the momentum for future change lost.

Roosevelt had a strong sense of his own place in history. He would not countenance being written off in the history books as a man who had been frustrated in his attempts to lead the country out of the depression and to create a more humane social order. . . .

Both Roosevelt and Cummings had a tacit understanding that at some point action would have to be taken, and they now agreed that the Court was unlikely to be changed in its ways by the election returns. Yet the President still did not indicate that the time to act had come. He treated the meeting as yet another occasion on which the Attorney General had been asked for a progress report, and told him to come back as soon as he had something new to recommend. Meanwhile he was to maintain the closest secrecy on his research. . . .

Roosevelt dismissed the amendment route as unacceptable for a number of reasons. In the first place, he thought an amendment would be difficult to frame. Two years of study in the Justice Department had not yet yielded a satisfactory draft, and liberals outside the government were far from a consensus. When the National Consumers' League, which had spearheaded the drive for minimum-wage legislation, polled national legal experts after the *Tipaldo* decision on whether a campaign for an amendment should be launched, the results were discouraging. Half of those polled—including Felix Frankfurter—opposed agitation for an amendment, and the other half were so far apart on what kind of an amendment should be sought that the League decided against any action at all.

Even if an amendment could be framed, and approved by two-thirds of each house of Congress, it would have to run the gantlet of ratification by three-fourths of the states. . . .

At best, ratification would take a long time, and time was invaluable. Conscious of the brief span allotted to reform movements, Roosevelt wanted to exploit his landslide victory to drive through legislation such as a wages and hours bill while Congress still felt the full force of his popular indorsement. To be sure, the Norris lame-duck amendment had been adopted quickly, but that, he thought, was because it had not been opposed by any strongly entrenched interest. A constitutional amendment affecting the courts would not only be rejected by business interests but would encounter state legislatures largely composed of lawyers, who would be likely to be more disapproving of tinkering with the courts than would other groups. . . .

Even if all these objections were overcome and an amendment went through, any legislation enacted under authorization of such an amendment would still be subject to review in the courts, unless such an amendment was purely procedural. "In view of what Mr. Justice Roberts did to a clause as broad and sweeping as 'the general welfare,' " wrote Charles A. Beard, "I can see other justices of his mental outlook macerating almost any clarifying amendment less generous in its terms. If there is any phrase wider than providing for the general welfare, I am unable to conjure it up in my mind." Besides, if the President should sponsor an amendment enlarging federal powers, it might seem tantamount to conceding that he had been wrong and the Supreme Court right in their dispute over the constitutionality of New Deal measures, and this Roosevelt, especially after his bracing election triumph, was less willing than ever to do.

After eliminating amendment proposals, Roosevelt and Cummings next looked into various suggestions that would require only an act of Congress. First, they considered a bill stipulating more than a majority of Justices to invalidate a law; they dismissed this, because they feared that the Court would void such a statute. As [Donald] Richberg later explained: "A mere statute to this effect would either be disregarded by the court, or have the result that Justices anxious to preserve the prestige of the court would join unwillingly with the majority so as to make a decision of the court effective." Moreover, such a law would limit the Court's role as a protector of civil liberties. They then examined a bill to withdraw appellate jurisdiction, but they were troubled by the recognition that the Court would still have original jurisdiction, especially in cases involving conflicts among states, and that the lower courts would retain their powers. By the end of the nine days, both men were leaning toward court-packing as the only feasible solution, but they were not yet committed to it, nor had they decided on the form it should take.

Just before departing for South America, Roosevelt met once more with Cummings in the President's office. This time the President told an elated Cummings that he had made his decision; he would present a Court bill to Congress as soon as one was ready. Cummings gave him two stout volumes of proposed amendments and bills to take aboard ship to study, and they agreed that if any new ideas were developed they would be dispatched to the President at his ports of call. Roosevelt also took with him two lengthy memorandums from Donald Richberg, which stated that he "should not simply *defend* reasonable exercises of legislative power, but should aggressively *attack* the unconstitutional exercise of judicial power." On November 18, the President set sail for southern waters, after charging Cummings to have a plan ready for him on his return. . . .

During the four weeks the President was touring South America, Cummings and his aides worked prodigiously at canvassing the possibilities for judicial reform. But when Roosevelt returned on December 15, they still had not found a solution. . . .

By now, it had become commonplace to refer to the Justices as the "nine old men." A. A. Berle had used the term in passing in 1933, and a column in a Kentucky newspaper reflected a popular notion when it referred to the Court as "nine old back-number owls (appointed by by-gone Presi-. dents) who sit on the leafless, fruitless limb of an old dead tree." But it was the publication on October 26, 1936 of *The Nine Old Men* by Drew Pearson and Robert S. Allen which made the phrase a household word. The book quickly climbed onto the best-seller lists, and it was serialized in newspapers across the country. Even critics of the Justices were disturbed by the book's tone and by its inaccuracies, but this exposé helped concentrate popular attention on both the age and the viewpoint of the Court as a more sober account might not have done. Representative Thomas Amlie of Wisconsin, while regretting the book's innuendos, thought "that Pearson and Allen have done a particularly good job on the Constitutional law angle," and Senator Joseph Guffey of Pennsylvania called for a Senate investigation of the allegations made in the book. Guffey called the volume "the most disturbing— I would say shocking book on public officials I have ever read. Its purported disclosures are sensational." . . .

At some point [between December 17 and 22], Cummings found his answer. While carrying on his other duties, the Attorney General had also been writing a history of his department, in collaboration with his aide, Carl McFarland. One passage in *Federal Justice,* which was about to be published, now stood out from the pages as it had not before, a recommendation that Justice McReynolds, when serving as Wilson's Attorney General, had made in 1913.

McReynolds' recommendation stated:

> Judges of the United States Courts, at the age of 70, after having served 10 years, may retire upon full pay. In the past, many judges have availed themselves of this privilege. Some, however, have remained upon the bench long beyond the time that they are able to adequately discharge their duties, and in consequence the administration of justice has suffered. . . . I suggest an act providing that when any judge of a Federal court below the Supreme Court fails to avail himself of the privilege of retiring now granted by law, that the President be required, with the advice and consent of the Senate, to appoint another judge, who would preside over the affairs of the court and have precedence over the older one. This will insure at all times the presence of a judge sufficiently active to discharge promptly and adequately the duties of the court.

Cummings now reasoned that [o]nce the principle of retirement was adopted, any age might be stipulated, but 70 seemed especially compelling. It had been the age that, on different occasions, McReynolds, Cummings, and [constitutional law expert Edward S.] Corwin had all hit upon, and it had the not inconsiderable advantage of having biblical sanction. That summer, an Oklahoma newspaper had proposed to retire Supreme Court Justices at seventy, "as set out in Holy Writ as the reasonable span of human life." With the retirement age fixed at 70, Roosevelt would be able to name six new Justices, thus practically assuring a bench that would approve New Deal legislation.

Before presenting the plan to Roosevelt, Cummings directed his assistants in the Justice Department to prepare a series of reports. He deliberately parceled out work so that the scheme would be kept a secret even from his own aides. Except for Cummings and [Stanley] Reed, no one in the department save for [Alexander] Holtzoff and [Carl] McFarland appears to have known the full scope of the proposal until it was announced. When his assistants reported back to Cummings, each gave a favorable reply. One report approved the plan's constitutionality. Another turned up historical precedent in an 1869 bill that had passed the House of Representatives. A third pulled together statistics to show that the formula would also supply enough new judges for the lower courts.

Cummings' search had ended. On December 22, he sent a penciled note to the President: "I am 'bursting' with ideas anent our constitutional problems; and have a plan (of substance & approach) I would like to talk over with you when you have the time." By this point, Roosevelt was already determined to "pack" the Court, but he did not yet know how, and he still thought of the idea as a birch rod to be taken out of the closet only if the Court did not mend its ways in the new term.

He now summoned George Creel to the White House once more to prepare an article, this one to be called "Roosevelt's Plans and Purposes." During the afternoon and evening they worked together, Creel was struck by the fact that the President, understandably, viewed the election as a purely personal victory. He told Creel that the social objectives he cherished would all have to run the gantlet of the Supreme Court. But his face brightened as he said: "I've thought of a better way than a constitutional amendment stripping the Court of its power to nullify acts of Congress. The time element makes that method useless. Granted that Congress could agree on such an amendment for submission to the several states, it would be two, three, or four years before the legislatures could or would act. What do you think of this?" From a drawer in his desk, he extracted a heavily marked copy of the Constitution and riffled the pages as he read off passages and commented on the powers of Congress to act for the general welfare.

After reading Article III, § 1, he asked: "Where is there anything in that which gives the Supreme Court the right to override the legislative branch?" As the President talked, Creel wrote afterward, "I was amazed by his reading on the subject and by the grip of his mind on what he conceived to be essential facts. For example, he quoted at length from Madison's *Journal* and Elliot's *Debates,* citing them as his authority for the statement that the framers of the Constitution had voted on four separate occasions against giving judges the power to pass upon the constitutionality of acts of Congress."

If Congress was to reclaim the powers that had been usurped from it, Roosevelt reasoned, it should add a rider to each bill at the next session charging the Supreme Court to remember that the Constitution vested all legislative power in Congress and authorized it to provide for the general welfare. Suppose this proved ineffective? Creel related: " 'Then,' said the President, his face like a fist,'Congress can *enlarge* the Supreme Court, increasing the number of justices so as to permit the appointment of men in tune with the spirit of the age.' " When *Collier's* published this article on December 26, with three columns discussing the Supreme Court, Creel expected an explosion in Congress and the press. Yet, once again, the President's explicit words were ignored.

On the same day that Creel's article appeared, Cummings went to the White House to report on Roosevelt. According to one account, not altogether probable, the Attorney General handed the President a packet of plans with the new scheme on the bottom. He then watched agitatedly while Roosevelt turned over each in turn until he came to Cummings' favorite; to the Attorney General's immense pleasure, Roosevelt was delighted. However it happened, it is clear that the President gave his approval that day. He was gratified that the proposal was unquestionably constitutional, and he took a mischievous pleasure in the fact that it could be attributed to McReynolds.

Buoyed by the President's approval, Cummings now turned his hand to sketching the remaining details of the plan. He wanted not only to liberalize the Court but to reform the entire judiciary. By presenting "court-packing" in the guise of judicial reform, he would make the plan more palatable. Yet Cummings' interest in reform was not just expedient. He had long cherished the aim of overhauling the structure of the courts, and Roosevelt shared some of his ardor. Once they launched what they knew would be a historic fight, they wanted it to be remembered for improving the judicial system as well as for overcoming the intransigence of the Supreme Court.

For two years, William Denman, Judge of the Ninth Circuit Court of Appeals, had been bombarding Roosevelt with pleas for more lower-court judges in order to relieve congestion in the courts and prevent miscarriages of justice. Denman also argued that the lower-court system was illogically organized, and, he proposed, among other suggestions, the appointment of a proctor of the Supreme Court to supervise lower courts and the creation of "roving judges" to clear up congestion. The Judicial Conference had also, more than once, pointed out the need for additional district judges. Cummings now decided to tie all these ideas together into a single package, but to relate the call for more lower-court judges to the principle of age.

By the end of the year, the Justice Department had prepared the first draft of the bill. In all, it went through twelve full drafts and numerous minor revisions. The measure embraced four proposals: (1) that when a judge of a federal court who had served ten years did not resign or retire within six months after his seventieth birthday, the President might name another judge as co-adjutor; (2) that the Supreme Court should not have more than six added Justices, nor any lower-court bench more than two, nor the total federal judiciary more than fifty; (3) that lower-court judges might be assigned to exceptionally busy courts; and (4) that the lower courts should be supervised by the Supreme Court through a proctor.

Roosevelt and Cummings decided it would be helpful to accompany the bill with both a message from the President and a letter from the Attorney General. Instead of concentrating on the desirability of a more liberal court, both documents would stress the incapacity of aged judges and the need for additional appointments to get the Court abreast to its work. By emphasizing the theme of greater efficiency, they hoped the whole plan would be accepted as a project for judicial reform rather than a stratagem to pack the Court. Once again, Cummings parceled out assignments within the department so that men were called on to supply statistics on denial of certiorari or the ages of judges without ever being told why this information was wanted or being given enough to do to be able to piece together what was happening. . . .

Of the plan itself, few have found much good to say. Much of this criticism is surely justified. Yet the presentation of the plan was not a capricious act but the result of a long period of gestation. During this time, other alternatives were carefully examined, favored for a while, and then discarded on not unreasonable grounds. Throughout this same period, Roosevelt was called on repeatedly to take action, and it appeared, in particular, that he would have a sizable following for a recommendation which would justify the appointment of additional Justices by stressing the infirmity of the Hughes Court. That Roosevelt misjudged the state of opinion seems probable in retrospect, but, at the time, the plan seemed to have an inherent logic and even inevitability. . . .

Court Packing as a Failure of Presidential Leadership

MICHAEL NELSON

The Court and the President

Franklin Roosevelt's problems with the Supreme Court are an oft-told tale. Four of the nine justices who served on the Court during his first term were ardent conservatives who appeared to regard the New Deal brand of governmental intervention in the economy as constitutionally unacceptable almost by definition. Dubbed the Four Horsemen, they were: Willis Van Devanter, James C. McReynolds, George Sutherland, and Pierce Butler. Another group of three justices seemed more disposed to allow the elected branches of government wide latitude in framing public policies: Louis D. Brandeis, Harland Fiske Stone, and Benjamin N. Cardozo. The remaining two justices, Chief Justice Charles Evans Hughes and Owen J. Roberts, were swing votes, not consistently aligned with either bloc. By the end of Roosevelt's first term, six of these justices, including all four conservatives, were in their seventies, the oldest collection of justices ever to sit on the Court. Roosevelt had appointed none of them; he was the first president since James Monroe to serve a full term with no opportunities to nominate one or more justices.

Sensing the Court's hostility almost from the start, the Roosevelt administration delayed cases that challenged the constitutionality of New Deal measures from coming before the Court for as long as possible, but the judicial hammer blows began falling in 1935. In May the justices invalidated the Railway Pension Act, the National Industrial Recovery Act, the Frazier-Lemke Act, and a presidential decision to fire a member of the Federal Trade Commission. (The last three decisions were handed down on 27 May, thenceforth known as Black Monday to New Dealers). In January 1936 the Court voided the tax provision of the Agricultural Adjustment Act, then in May (after approving the Tennessee Valley Authority Act in February) struck down the Guffey Coal Act and the Municipal Bankruptcy Act. Finally, in *Morehead* v. *Tipaldo,* its most controversial decision of all, the Court ruled in June that New York's minimum-wage law for women was unconstitutional, thus nearly precluding even a state government role in depression-fighting. In all these cases the Four Horsemen voted against the New Deal; sometimes they were joined by Roberts, sometimes by Roberts and Hughes, sometimes (as in the three Black Monday decisions) by all the other justices.

What, from the vantage point of mid-1936, was Roosevelt to do? Simply

Michael Nelson, "The President and the Court: Reinterpreting the Court-Packing Episode of 1937," *Political Science Quarterly* 103 (Summer 1988): 268–270, 273–278, 281–293. Reprinted with permission.

to wait for the justices to change their minds or leave the Court was to him intolerable. The logic of the majority opinions in the Court's recent decisions seemed to leave no room for other New Deal measures whose constitutionality had not yet been tested, such as the Social Security Act and the Wagner Labor Relations Act, much less for legislation concerning wages and hours and other subjects that Roosevelt was planning to introduce. And he was convinced that no vacancies on the Court would occur for him to fill: McReynolds would still be on the bench when he was 105, the President groused. Conflict with the Court seemed inevitable.

Yet Roosevelt knew from experience that to attack the Court would create serious problems of its own. In the aftermath of Black Monday, he had chastised the justices for "relegat[ing] us to the horse-and-buggy definition of interstate commerce." The outraged public reaction to this offhand remark, not just from conservatives, was evidence enough that any effort to change the situation by law or constitutional amendment would require Roosevelt to do nothing less than summon all the elements of political power that he had been able to bring together in the first term. . . .

The Court-Packing Episode

[I]n order to accomplish a dramatic legislative victory of the kind he felt he needed over the Supreme Court, Roosevelt would require intellectually and politically suitable policy ideas, an empowering election, and a fully deployed repertoire of political skills.

Ideas.   Roosevelt had no shortage of ideas to draw from about how to resolve his problems with the Supreme Court. The populist and progressive movements of the late nineteenth and early twentieth centuries had made courts a target of reform. As William Leuchtenburg notes, "Roosevelt began his political career at the time that his distant cousin Theodore was assaulting the sanctity of the courts and the air was loud with cries for the recall of judges and judicial decisions." In the 1920s, such proposals increasingly were aimed at the Supreme Court, which seemed under Chief Justice William Howard Taft to have gone to the extreme in its conservatism. More recently, the first round of anti–New Deal Court decisions in early 1935 (including the anticipation, false as it turned out, that the Court would rule against Roosevelt and Congress in the gold clause cases) had lent unprecedented urgency to some liberals' desire to rein in the Court. The years 1935–1937 saw more "Court-curbing" bills introduced in Congress than in any other three-year (or thirty-five year) period in history. A few of these, including some endorsed by Vice President Garner and Senators James M. Byrnes and Robert M. La Follette, Jr., proposed to amend the Constitution to define Congress's legislative powers more expansively. Most, however, were aimed at the Court itself, some in the form of constitutional amendments, others as simple legislation.

Proposals to create new vacancies on the Supreme Court were the preferred method of Court-curbing for some members of Congress, whether by increasing the size of the Court to eleven or fifteen, mandating retirement at age 65 (or 70), or establishing a ten-year term for judges. Other bills addressed the issue of judicial review, including some that would have forbidden it altogether. Senator George Norris proposed an amendment that would require the agreement of seven justices in order to declare a federal law unconstitutional, then endorsed a bill mandating unanimity. La Follette wanted to empower the president to demand advisory opinions from the Court regarding the constitutionality of proposed federal statutes. At one time or another, Roosevelt was attracted by almost all of these ideas, including composite measures in one bill to allow the president and Congress to demand, receive, and reject advisory opinion from the Court, or in another to repass an overturned law after an intervening congressional election. Ultimately, he decided to adopt the essential elements of still another composite that Edward S. Corwin suggested in correspondence with Attorney-General Homer Cummings. It stipulated that whenever the Court included half or more justices who were 70 years or older, a new justice could be appointed for each justice in his seventies who declined to retire.

Not every suggestion to break the impasses between the justices and the New Deal involved an assault on the Court. Representative Hatton Sumners of Texas, the chairman of the House Committee on the Judiciary, proposed legislation to guarantee retirement pay for justices over 70. One effect of the Economy Act of 1933 had been to cut former Justice Oliver Wendell Holmes's benefits in half, and Sumners believed that at least two of the Four Horsemen, Van Devanter and Sutherland, were delaying their own retirements for fear of a similar fate. Another suggestion came from Arthur N. Holcombe of Harvard, who, in the spirit of Mr. Dooley's observation that "the Supreme Court follows th'illiction returns," urged that Roosevelt simply wait: "If these elections [of 1936] turn out satisfactorily, I cherish a strong hope that there will be a better prospect for liberal interpretation of the Constitution from the Supreme Court."

Elections.   In contrast to the elections of 1932 and 1934, the political implications of the 1936 results were ambiguous. Indisputably, the presidential landslide met one criterion for an empowering election—Roosevelt's margin of victory over Governor Alfred M. Landon was the largest in history. To interpret the congressional results was more difficult. Democrats gained only nine seats in the House, considerably less than the historical average. Their seven-seat gain in the Senate was smaller than in either 1932 or 1934, but it was impressive nonetheless. Certainly, few Democrats could deny that the main explanation for their party's rapid rise to majority status lay with Roosevelt. Some doubtless began to wonder, however, whether their personal political fortunes still were joined to the President, especially since the general assumption was that he was beginning his last term.

The aspect of the 1936 elections that was least empowering for the second term was the campaign Roosevelt waged. Early in the year, he made very few requests to Congress for new legislation. Then, after a fighting acceptance speech to the Democratic convention, he carefully struck a president-above-the-fray pose in public appearances during the late summer and early fall. And even when he sharpened his rhetoric in October, records Burns, "Roosevelt talked very little about the future . . . . He was making the New Deal record, not the New Deal promises, the issue."

Roosevelt's inattention to the Court controversy during the 1936 campaign warrants special mention. At the Republican convention, former President Hoover and the Republican platform had pledged to defend the judiciary and dared Roosevelt to state his own position. Landon and other party leaders made much of the issue. But Roosevelt was convinced that any intimation of his intention to confront the Court would create confusion and controversy among voters. Delegates to the Democratic convention, responding to Roosevelt's explicit instructions, fuzzed the Court issue: to the extent that the platform suggested that any action might be needed, it spoke of "clarifying amendments" that would allow government intervention in the economy.

Privately, Roosevelt had ambitious plans for the second term. "Wait until next year, Henry," he told Secretary of the Treasury Henry Morgenthau in May 1936, "I am really going to be radical." Certainly he had decided that a drastic remedy for the Court impasse was required, although he did not know specifically what it would be. But publicly the campaign urged voters to treat the election as a referendum on the first term. The Court issue continued to be ducked; Roosevelt never spoke of it during the fall campaign. Harold Ickes, who had urged Roosevelt to raise the issue as far back as January, later remarked ruefully that "the groundwork had not been laid," recognizing at least that some groundwork was required in the election campaign before taking the issue to Congress.

Skill.   Of the three main elements that make possible dramatic presidential leadership of Congress—suitable policy ideas, an empowering election, and the adroit exercise of presidential leadership skill—the last took on particular importance in the Court fight. The abundance of available ideas about how to break the impasse between the Court and the administration was both an advantage and a disadvantage to Roosevelt; he had no shortage of approaches to choose from, but there was little consensus about which was best. The verdict of the 1936 election, overwhelming in its endorsement of the legislative achievements of Roosevelt's first term, was ambiguous in its implications for the second. In this uncertain situation, unusually skillful presidential leadership clearly was needed if there were to be any hope of success.

For this challenge Roosevelt seemed particularly well-suited. His strategic sense, capacity to manage administration lieutenants for the development and promotion of policy ideas, presentational abilities in persuading and mobilizing the general public, and shrewd use of tactics within the Washington community are unrivaled among modern presidents. Yet with few exceptions, these skills were notably absent in the Court fight of 1937.

Strategic Sense. In democratic polities, a leader's effort to discern the historical possibilities of the time requires above all an ability to interpret the public mood. On matters involving the judiciary, Roosevelt was ill-equipped to do so by experience or temperament and made few efforts to remedy these shortcomings.

Americans generally have regarded the judicial process as somehow outside and above politics. This underlying regard was challenged in the 1930s by the Supreme Court's rebuke of the New Deal, but other aspects of that decade seem to have made the public's appreciation of the Court all the more profound. Ironically, the depression was one: "The greater the insecurity of the times," Leuchtenburg notes, "the more people cling to the few institutions which seem changeless." The number of justices had been fixed at nine since 1869, long enough for many people to regard it as set by the Framers. The rise of Hitler and Mussolini in Europe also made some feel especially protective of the independence that the American judiciary enjoys. "Even many people who believe in President Roosevelt . . . ," said Senator Henry Ashurst, "were haunted by the terrible fear that some future President might, by suddenly enlarging the Supreme Court, suppress free speech, free assembly, and invade other Constitutional guarantees of citizens." Apprehension about tampering with the ability of the Court (which had a strong record on civil liberties) to protect minorities was greatest among ideological liberals and certain religious, racial, and regional groups, including for different reasons many blacks and white southerners. Interestingly, almost every Catholic senator opposed the Court-packing plan.

Roosevelt lacked an intuitive appreciation of the public's regard for the judiciary. He had come of age in politics during a period of court-bashing and, as a lawyer, was particularly receptive to the emerging realistic school of legal intellectual thought, which considered judges to be policy makers motivated in large part by their own opinions and prejudices. Once, delivering a 1932 campaign speech, Roosevelt spoke from a prepared text that read: "After March 4, 1929, the Republican party was in complete control of all branches of the government—the Legislature, with the Senate and Congress, and the executive departments." Then he improvised: "and, I may add, for full measure, to make it complete, the United States Supreme Court as well." Soon after his inauguration in 1933 Roosevelt judged Chief Justice Hughes one who "wouldn't cooperate" when the chief justice declined to give informal advisory opinions on proposed legislation.

Compounding Roosevelt's difficulty in intuitively grasping public sensitivities on issues involving judicial independence was his more general tendency to overinterpret his mandate from the 1936 election. Although he had made his first term the issue, Roosevelt evidently felt that in giving him a forty-six-state majority, the voters had written a blank check to take the government in any direction he chose, by any means. He was encouraged in this view by aides such as Thomas Corcoran, Benjamin Cohen, and Harry Hopkins. Campaigns can educate candidates as well as voters; by gauging audiences' responses to particular appeals in campaign speeches, for example, the candidate can gain a sense of which issues are working and which are not. But even though Roosevelt never mentioned the Court in 1936, he spoke to a Democratic victory dinner on 4 March 1937 as if he had: "We gave warning last November that we had only just begun to fight. Did some people really believe we did not mean it? Well, I mean it and you meant it."

After the election, Roosevelt closed himself off from sources of information that would have informed his reading of public opinion, and neglected or downplayed available evidence that seemed to contradict that reading. Although Roosevelt regarded the labor, farm, and liberal lobbies' support for Court reform as vital, he did not consult with their leaders before launching his attack. Had he done so, he probably would have learned that for various reasons (the narrowness of organized labor's concern, extending mainly to the Wagner Act; the farmers' general conservatism, except when the issue was their own government benefits; liberals' apprehensions about civil liberties) such support would be limited, especially if the object of reform was the Court itself. As for the general public, evidence was available that should have given the President pause before claiming a mandate for reformist legislation in general and Court-curbing in particular. A Gallup poll taken in November 1936 found that 50 percent of a sample of voters hoped the second term would be more conservative than the first; 15 percent hoped it would be more liberal. Occasional Gallup polls in late 1935 and 1936 showed public resistance to proposals to restrict the Court's power to invalidate laws. Yet even the harsh and massive influx of congressional mail after the Court plan was introduced in early 1937 and subsequent Gallup polls that consistently demonstrated the absence of public enthusiasm for Court-packing did not intrude into Roosevelt's oft-repeated belief that: "The people are with me. I know it." Instead he clung to straws such as Lyndon Johnson's April 1937 victory in a special congressional election in Texas, even though Johnson was the only candidate in an eight-man field who favored the Roosevelt plan, and he won with only 28 percent of the vote.

Lack of empathy with the public regard for the Supreme Court, inattentiveness to opinion leaders, neglect of disagreeable evidence, an overly expansive interpretation of the meaning of the 1936 election—of all these explanations of the President's dulled strategic sense in the Court-packing episode, the election seems to have been the most important. Roosevelt had maintained a shrewd and studied silence in 1935 and 1936 while the Court was overturning his New Deal legislation; from 31 May 1935, when he made his "horse-and-buggy" remark, until 2 June 1936, when the *Tipaldo* decision provoked him to complain that the justices had created a constitutional "no-man's-land," Roosevelt made no public comment about the Court, biding his time and letting anti-Court sentiment grow on its own. But when Ickes, Norris, and others encouraged Roosevelt to reap the harvest of his patient waiting by taking the Court issue to the voters, he declined. He wanted the election to be fought on the least controversial basis possible, even though such a strategy meant that little about the second term would be taught or learned in the campaign. To the extent that Roosevelt's purpose was to create the largest possible landslide on election day, he succeeded. But then, having chosen to seek no mandate for future action from the voters, he claimed one anyway. . . .

Public Presentation. Roosevelt's decision not to address the Court issue in the 1936 election made the task of convincing and rallying the public both more difficult and more essential when he introduced the Court-packing plan in early 1937. Yet despite occasional glimpses of the customary Rooseveltian flair for skillfully presenting himself and his policies to the citizenry, the President's persuasive efforts were notably unsuccessful. He never was able to undo the ill effects of the deceptive design that he and Cummings had given to the plan.

Part of Roosevelt's problem was his apparent but curious belief that people either would take the plan's age-and-efficiency rationale at face value or, if they saw through to its real Court-packing purpose, would share his delight at its clever indirection. Either assumption was dubious; together they were poison. Yet at the press conference in which he first told the public about his intention to reform the Court, Roosevelt mixed careful reading and explication of the bill with winks and smiles. "He seemed to be asking the assembled newspapermen to applaud the perfections of his scheme, to note its nicely calculated indirections and praise its effectiveness," wrote two journalists.

The effects of Roosevelt's deceptive presentation were disastrous. As he conceded four years later, "I made one major mistake when I first presented the plan. I did not place enough emphasis on the real mischief— the kind of decisions which, as a studied and continued policy, had been coming down from the Supreme Court." The trumpet call he had issued to rally the faithful sounded false and uncertain. Deceptiveness disgusted some potential allies, notably Norris. It left the Court plan open to simple refutation of the facts that were its purported rationale. "The Supreme Court is fully abreast of its work . . . ," wrote Chief Justice Hughes in a public letter that was addressed to Senator Burton K. Wheeler, signed by Brandeis and Van Devanter, and supported, Hughes implied, by all the justices. Having thus disposed, with accompanying statistics, of Roosevelt's public diagnosis of the Court's maladies, Hughes went on to challenge the efficacy of his prescription: "An increase in the number of justices of the Supreme Court . . . would not promote the efficiency of the Court. There would be more judges to hear, more judges to confer, more judges to be convinced and to decide." The age issue—raised by passages in the President's message like: "A lower mental or physical vigor leads men to avoid an examination of complicated and changed conditions"—offended many old people, including a goodly number of septuagenarian members of Congress and legions of liberal admirers of the 80-year-old Brandeis. And not the least of the problems with the administration's public presentation of its case was that it was all but impossible to maintain. Even Cummings succumbed to candor when asked at a Senate hearing whether "after the six additional members of the Supreme Court are appointed, the Court should divide seven to eight, this entire plan would fail." He replied, "It would depend upon which side the seven were on and upon which side the eight were."

Perhaps the worst thing about Roosevelt's presentation of the Court plan was that it made him seem ashamed of his best and truest argument for reform. In January 1935, he had been prepared to make a ringing radio speech if the Court ruled against the New Deal in the gold clause cases. Neither he nor Congress would "stand idly by," the President planned to say, "and . . . permit the decision of the Supreme Court to be carried through to . . . imperil the economic and political security of the nation." Yet in the 1936 election he eschewed open confrontation with the Court, which by then had overturned a dozen laws enacted by the elected branches in their effort to meet the national crisis. In 1937 he launched his assault with circumspection so complete that one could barely find evidence in Roosevelt's public statements that he found the Court's conservative defiance objectionable.

An about-face by the President in March helped his case somewhat. Realizing the ineffectiveness of his efforts to date, Roosevelt took dead aim at the Court's obstructiveness in a fighting speech to a Democratic victory dinner on 4 March and a quieter but no less pointed fireside chat on 9 March. He displayed his gifts for dramaturgy later that spring, stopping in Texas in April, for example, to draw attention to the public endorsement of Court-packing that Johnson's election seemed to indicate.

But coming as late in the game as they did, these gestures were of little consequence and the speeches, although probably the source of the Court-packing proposal's only advance in the Gallup poll, prompted no outpouring of mail to wavering legislators, which had been the speeches' main purpose. Strangely, Roosevelt's frank admission of the real rationale behind Court-packing in early March did not lead him to make a logical accompanying change in tactics—to abandon the bill that he and Cummings had drafted and settle for a readily obtainable compromise that would create two or three new justiceships and thus allow him to tip the balance on the Court in favor of the New Deal.

Tactics. In addition to his deficient exercise of strategic, managerial, and presentational skills, Roosevelt was tactically maladroit in his dealings with other Washington politicians during the Court-packing episode. Roosevelt's first misstep was to keep his intentions secret, even in their broadest outlines, from those whose support he would need. His announcement of the plan to a called meeting of the cabinet and congressional leaders on the morning of 5 February, a half-hour before he had scheduled a session with the press, was the first word of his purposes that any of them other than Cummings heard; Roosevelt actually had dissembled to the cabinet in January. Most students of the Court-packing episode have rightly noted the damaging effects of Roosevelt's arrogance in all this. Even when he did summon leaders from the cabinet and Congress, he did nothing more than brief them and send them on their way. The post-briefing reactions of certain participants have entered the realm of folklore: Sumners's "Boys, here's where I cash in my chips"; Garner holding his nose with one hand and pointing thumbs-down with the other; Sam Rayburn's conclusion that Roosevelt was becoming a tin god.

But there were further, equally damaging effects of Roosevelt's policy of secrecy. For one, it left him tactically unprepared for unexpected resistance. The consensus was that the House would be the best place to begin the battle for passage, but that possibility was effectively foreclosed when Speaker William Bankhead, Majority Leader Rayburn, and Sumners (chairman of the judiciary committee) surprised Roosevelt by indicating their opposition to Court-packing. Sumners quickly rallied a majority of his committee (the rules committee also was opposed), and Bankhead and Rayburn decided to forestall any effort to bring the bill to the floor by a discharge petition.

Roosevelt's decision to keep congressional leaders in the dark hurt his cause in other ways. Throughout 1936 and at the start of the 75th Congress in 1937, many Washington politicians made commitments on the Court issue that later were difficult to reverse. Senator Ashurst, for example, denied during the 1936 campaign (as did Senator Joseph Bailey) that the President had any intention of packing the Court and denounced the idea as "the prelude to tyranny." Bankhead, Norris, Sumners, and others introduced reform measures when Congress opened in 1937, usually explaining why their ideas were better than Court-packing or other alternatives would be. By bringing these legislators in on the policy development process (even at a late stage), Roosevelt could have taken advantage of their desire to do something about the Court. By locking them out, he all but guaranteed that they would go their own ways. Ashurst endorsed Roosevelt's plan, but did not give it the kind of enthusiastic support the President needed from the chairman of the Senate Judiciary Committee. Secrecy from congressional allies also hurt Roosevelt when Senator Hugo Black left the judiciary committee for reasons of his own at the start of the January session, thus denying Roosevelt his one staunch and effective supporter on the committee. Had Black known anything of Roosevelt's plans, he almost certainly would have stayed where he would have been of greatest service.

Secrecy was not Roosevelt's only tactical error in the Court-packing fight. He also seriously underestimated his opposition. In at least one case, this was unavoidable: who could have foreseen that Senate Republicans would maintain a conspiracy of silence after the plan was introduced, leaving Democrats to lead the opposition to Court-packing and denying Roosevelt the opportunity to portray its critics as bitter-end partisans? But for the most part, Roosevelt's errors in judging his opponents were careless. To discount, as Roosevelt did, the political wiles of former New York governor, former secretary of state, former Republican presidential nominee Charles Evans Hughes was to leave his plan wide open to the sort of subtle attack Hughes later launched with his letter to Wheeler. Similarly, for Roosevelt to think that corporate America was politically impotent just because he had overcome its opposition in 1936 was reckless. In truth, led by publisher Frank Gannett, the business-funded National Committee to Uphold Constitutional

Government fought Court-packing both ardently (sending out ten million mailings that urged recipients to write Congress) and skillfully (Gannet even advanced civil libertarian arguments against the plan to Jews and blacks).

How does one account for Roosevelt's deftless approach to both his allies and his foes prior to announcing the Court-packing plan? Fear of leaks that would provoke a preemptive attack by administration opponents and divide the ranks of its supporters was the stated reason for Roosevelt's policy of secrecy. Even putting aside both the obvious costs of excluding needed and demonstratedly loyal allies and the clear value of airing the issue among voters in the campaign, this explanation would be easier to credit if Roosevelt himself had not leaked his intention to pack the Court to George Creel, who promptly published the news in the 26 December issue of *Collier's*. . . .

Less attractive personality traits, notably the impulse to punish as well as to overcome administration opponents, may explain Roosevelt's blindness to the political skills of big business and the Court itself. Business, of course, had provoked his astonishing 1936 election-eve statement: "I welcome their hatred. . . . I should like to have it said that in the second term these forces met their master." . . .

. . . Roosevelt's 1936 election landslide figures prominently in any explanation of why he behaved so uncharacteristically in launching the Court fight. During the first term, his temperamental inclinations notwithstanding, political uncertainty and shrewd tactical sense kept Roosevelt cautious. He consulted with congressional, cabinet, and interest group leaders; allowed them at least the illusion of influence over the administration's policies and strategies; and gauged the opposition carefully. Now, after the election, convinced that "the people are with me," Roosevelt shrugged off these self-imposed restraints and gave full vent to his desire for mastery.

Even after he introduced the Court-packing plan, election-born over-confidence continued to blur Roosevelt's tactical decision making. Virtually from the week of the plan's introduction in February 1936 until the last week in May, offers and pleas to compromise by settling for a simple two or three-seat expansion of the Court came into the White House from the Senate. Roosevelt correctly saw no need to strike a deal quickly, although his loud laughter in the faces of Garner and some congressional leaders when they proposed a three-seat increase in February was unhelpful. Pressures to settle for two additional justices increased by mid-April. Hughes had written his letter (March 22); Robert's switch-in-time had effectively reversed the Court's nine-month-old *Tipaldo* ruling (March 29) and upheld the Wagner Act (April 12); and public support for the Court plan had severely waned. Senator Charles O. Andrews even provided a face-saving rationale: growth in the number of federal judicial circuits, which historically had been the main basis for increasing the Court's size, could be said to imply ten associate justiceships, one for each circuit, and a chief justice serving at-large.

Roosevelt was implacable. A reasoned worst-case scenario provides part of the explanation. If Roberts reverted to conservatism and Senate Majority Leader Joseph Robinson, to whom Roosevelt had promised the first vacancy on the Court, voted with the Four Horsemen, the New Deal still would be at a 5–6 deficit. Reason also dictated, however, that with chances for any sort of victory fading, the President would do well to take what he could get, not only to settle the Court issue but also to end the bitter fight that was splitting his party and tying up the rest of his legislative agenda. Yet even in late May, by which time Justice Van Devanter had announced his retirement (May 18) and the Court had upheld the Social Security Act (May 24), Roosevelt stood his ground. He still wanted to teach a lesson about the dangers of defying the President to congressional Democrats, whom he regarded as his political debtors, and to the Court, which he was certain had changed course just to deny him victory for his plan.

On 3 June, Roosevelt finally accepted Senator Robinson's plea to authorize him to work out the best compromise he could. Robinson latched on to a proposal by Senator Carl Hatch that would empower the President to nominate a new justice for every 75-year-old member of the Court, at a rate of one such appointment per year. This guaranteed Roosevelt at least two appointments in 1937 and one each in 1938, 1939, and 1940. Robinson, who had labored without ceasing for the original Court-packing plan, redoubled his efforts. Roosevelt helped matters by playing genial host to Democratic legislators at the Jefferson Island Club on the Chesapeake Bay.

The President's turnabout came too late. Robinson thought he had engineered a narrow majority for a time, but opposition leaders had both the will and, with more than forty senators in their ranks, the way to conduct and sustain a filibuster. Then there was the House to overcome, its leaders still implacable and well-positioned to resist. In any event, defections by freshmen Democrats probably lost Robinson his majority even in the Senate by 13 July. Ashurst told a Roosevelt aide, "If anyone's telling the president he can pass this Court bill he's doing him a great disservice." On 14 July Robinson died. Shortly after his funeral, the Senate voted to table the bill, and the Court-packing episode of 1937 was over.

Alternatives to Court-Packing

William Leuchtenburg has defined the challenge sensibly for students of the Court-packing episode. "Before they are allowed to dismiss [Roosevelt's] proposal out of hand," he argues, "they should be required to examine the difficult situation he faced and to indicate what alternative he might have adopted that was truly feasible." Stated differently, the challenge is this: given the knowledge that was available to the President and accepting his view that to win Supreme Court acquiescence in the New Deal was an important second-term goal, "What then was Roosevelt to do?"

The analysis of presidential leadership that is presented in this article suggests an answer to Leuchtenburg's challenge. During the 1936 election campaign, Roosevelt's best strategy was to attack the Court frontally in order to lay the groundwork for post-inauguration reform; after the election, considering that he had not done so, his best remaining alternative was simply to wait.

Before the Election: Attack Frontally.   The reasoning of the majority opinions in the anti–New Deal Court decisions had convinced Roosevelt, quite understandably, that social security, the Wagner act, and other achievements of the first term would be declared unconstitutional when the Court ruled on them, as would the sorts of proposals he had in mind for the second term, such as wages and hours legislation. Roosevelt had heard and discussed the many and varied ideas that members of Congress, White House advisers, and others had suggested to end the Court's resistance; as much as anything, this experience had shown him that there was growing support in Washington to do something. He had determined in the aftermath of his much-criticized horse-and-buggy attack on the Court that time and presidential self-restraint were needed for public opinion to come around. He even suggested to the cabinet in January 1936 that he hoped the justices would void enough bills so that, in Ickes's account, "a real issue will be joined on which we can campaign to the country." The justices had more than cooperated, and Ickes, Norris, and others had urged the President to reap the harvest sown with his public patience by raising the Court issue in his speeches. Finally, Roosevelt had concluded that he was going to win reelection—in January, June, August, and October, his tallies of electoral votes, always cautious, showed that he saw himself well in the lead.

The sensible decision for Roosevelt—given the obstacles and opportunities he confronted, as he saw them—was to make his intention to end the Court's obstruction of the New Deal clear during the campaign, then claim a mandate for action after he won. His own hindsight, not future scholars', should have led him to this strategy. Certainly the lesson of 1932 had been that a presidential candidate did not need to be specific in his proposals. Simply to raise high an issue and pledge to remedy it in office was sufficient if he won a large victory. The experience of the first term also gave clear guidance about what the President should do after the election— consult with trusted and experienced advisers to develop a plan, bring in his ever-reliable congressional allies to advise him on how to promote the plan, then let them take the lead in Congress while he took his case to the voters.

After the Election: Wait.   Roosevelt, of course, did not attack the Court frontally before the 1936 election. The desire for the largest reelection majority possible that kept him from raising controversial issues in the campaign, the fear of leaks that prevented him from consulting even with allies and advisers, the fondness for indirection that made coy approaches so appealing—considerations such as these governed Roosevelt's behavior and left him in a much-changed situation after the election. A direct assault on the Court still would be better than a deceptive one, consultation better than secrecy. But if a frontal attack remained a better post-election alternative than the Court plan, it no longer was a good one: the President had sought no mandate and could claim none. Nor did his best remaining strategy seem all that appealing: simply to wait in the hope that the justices would come to appreciate the improved craftsmanship that had gone into the more recent

New Deal laws that now were coming before them; that vacancies would occur on the Court; or that the Court would fulfill Mr. Dooley and yield to the voters' endorsement of the New Deal.

Improved Legal Craftsmanship.   The legislation of the first New Deal was not well drawn; it too often tied sweeping assertions of federal power to slap-dash justifications like the doctrine of emergency powers from the World War. By 1934, a new group of draftsmen had joined the administration. Trained by Felix Frankfurter at Harvard Law School and by Brandeis or Holmes in Supreme Court clerkships, [Thomas] Corcoran, [Benjamin] Cohen, James Landis, and their colleagues were far more attentive to the need when writing legislation to skirt the legal landmines that were sprinkled through the Court's decisions and to offer the justices a plausible constitutional rationale for voting to uphold. Few, if any, expected that craftsmanship alone would move the Supreme Court, but in the event that one or more justices were open to persuasion for other reasons, intelligent administration rationales based on the commerce clause or the taxing power could only make the task easier.

Vacancies.   "It will fall to your lot to nominate more justices of the Supreme Court than any other president since General Washington," Senator Ashurst told Roosevelt in 1936. "Father time, with his scythe, is on your side. Anno Domini is your invincible ally." American history writ large provided a basis for Ashurst's prophecy: presidents prior to Roosevelt had appointed an average of one justice every twenty-three months, and previous "old" Courts usually had broken up quickly. But American history writ small was of greater interest to Roosevelt: his first four years had produced no vacancies and the hostile decisions of 1935 and 1936 had convinced him that all of the conservative justices would postpone retirement as long as he was president and that none of them would die. (Metropolitan Life's actuarial tables gave even the oldest justice another five years.) In the meantime, the New Deal remained in constant jeopardy.

Others thought they had reason to be less pessimistic than the President about the prospect of judicial retirements. Frances Perkins, the secretary of labor, had been told by McReynolds that some of his colleagues would retire if their full pensions were guaranteed against the kind of action that had reduced Holmes's by half. Stone said the same thing to Irving Brant, the editorialist of the *St. Louis Star-Times* and a sure conduit to the White House. Stone also hinted to Representative Emmanuel Celler that passage of Sumners's retirement bill, which was designed to protect the justices' benefits, would prompt two members of the Court to depart in six months to a year. Sumners himself was certain that Van Devanter and Sutherland, two of the Four Horsemen, would step down soon after his bill was passed. Three days after Roosevelt introduced the Court-packing proposal, Ashurst tried to interest him in the Sumners bill as an alternative. Rather than respond favorably (he regarded retirement legislation as a useless diversion), Roosevelt took Ashurst's suggestion as cause to doubt the senator's loyalty.

Congressional leaders rushed the Sumners bill to passage on 1 March, even though they feared that Roosevelt's assault on the Court would discourage justices from retiring quickly for fear of seeming weak. But Van Devanter, coaxed by Senator William Borah, who thought that a quick retirement would help the anti-Court-packing cause, stepped down just three months later, and Sutherland followed in January. Brandeis's retirement and Butler's death in 1939 gave Roosevelt his third and fourth appointments of the second term; by the time he left office, he had appointed nine justices.

Election Aftershocks.   Incredible though it may seem in view of the results, until the 1936 election was over, conservatives on the Court had some reason to think that the public agreed with them about the New Deal and that Roosevelt might be defeated. The *Schechter* decision overturning the National Industrial Recovery Act had been widely applauded, and a poll printed in the *Washington Post* on the eve of *U.S.* v. *Butler* showed the public opposed to the Agriculture Adjustment Act. On 19 October, Van Devanter wrote to a friend that he thought the election would be close. Roosevelt could not have known how Van Devanter and perhaps some of his colleagues felt, but he was aware of information in the public record that might be leading the justices to that conclusion. The fledgling Gallup poll indicated that the Republicans had nominated by far their most popular candidate and placed Landon within four or five percentage points of Roosevelt all summer. The prestigious *Literary Digest* poll, which had come within three points of the final tally in 1932, predicted a Landon victory with 57 percent of the popular vote and 370 electoral votes.

After the election, Cummings and Roosevelt discussed the possibility that the President's landslide would convince the Court that it was isolated and should yield, however grudgingly, to political reality. Although they decided that McReynolds and the other three conservative justices were too stubborn to change, there was some reason to think that the election results really had made a difference. Government lawyers noticed, for example, that the Four Horsemen now treated them with respect rather than contempt when they argued before the Court. And Hughes was on record, in a just-published book, as arguing that when the Court departed from "its fortress in public opinion," it "suffered severely from self-inflicted wounds." Did this not give reason to think the chief justice might change course now that he knew which way the political wind was blowing? Stone thought so; he also thought that Roberts might desert the Four Horsemen after election day.

Roberts, in fact, did desert: it was his vote in *West Coast Hotel* v. *Parrish* and the Wagner act and social security cases that constituted the switch in time. That Roberts abandoned the conservatives in the aftermath of the election but before the President's Court plan was introduced is clear. He told Hughes in December that he would vote to affirm the Washington state minimum wage law. Curiously, however, one could argue just as plausibly that the election postponed Roberts's alliance with the moderates as that it hastened the switch. Roberts had shown an early willingness to sustain New

Deal–style programs. In 1934, for example, he wrote the majority opinion in *Nebbia* v. *New York*, strongly asserting the primacy of the public interest when in conflict with property rights, much to the fury of the Four Horsemen. But in 1935 Roberts's name began to be mentioned as a possible presidential nominee for the Republicans in 1936, in the spirit of the draft of then-Justice Hughes in 1916. In view of the party's conservative center of gravity at the time, a shift to the right to draw the contrast between himself and the New Deal would have been sensible. In summer 1936, however, Roberts saw not just his own chances dashed but the nomination of a centrist candidate and the adoption of an anti-*Tipaldo* platform by the Republican convention. The results in November only underscored how far the country had moved from conservatism.

In 1954, a then-retired Roberts appeared before a Senate committee to warn of Supreme Court justices who

> have had in the back of their minds a possibility that they might get the nomination for president. Now, that is not a healthy situation because, however strong a man's mentality and character, if he has this ambition in his mind it may tinge or color what he does . . . . I happen to have a personal knowledge of what that pressure is like, for twice ill-advised but enthusiastic friends of mine urged me to let my name go up as a candidate for president while I was on the Court.

Roberts added: "Of course I turned a hard face in that thing. I never had the notion in my mind."

For Roosevelt to attack the Supreme Court in the 1936 campaign would have been risky. What if the issue backfired and made his reelection so narrow that he could not persuasively claim a mandate for Court reform afterward? After the election, to wait, even if waiting included an endorsement of Sumners's retirement bill and offered the hope that one or more of the hoped-for changes in the Court would come about naturally, meant gambling that the justices would not continue on the course they had followed since 1935. But presidential power is never a sure thing. In this case, as in all cases, the most that one can conclude is that in view of the situation Roosevelt faced at the time, to fight or to wait were more likely to achieve his goals than any of the alternatives, including the Court-packing plan.

Conclusion

The Court-packing episode of 1937 may be understood well as a case study in presidential leadership, not just a unique historical event or an aspect of a particular presidency, and from the perspective of Roosevelt's political situation at the time, rather than in hindsight. But is there a larger issue as well? Roosevelt's dramatic first-term legislative accomplishments already have been analyzed as manifestations of a pattern of presidential leadership success that includes an empowering election, suitable ideas, and the adroit exercise of political leadership skills. His second-term failure on Court-packing may illustrate another, more destructive pattern of the modern presidency.

It seems more than coincidental that the four twentieth-century presidents who have won the largest reelection victories (thus demonstrating their sensitivity to public opinion) instantly breached the bounds of permissible political action in a way that brought down the public's wrath: Roosevelt's Court-packing proposal in 1937, Johnson's unilateral escalation of the Vietnam war in 1965, the cover-up of the Watergate scandal by Richard M. Nixon in late 1972 and 1973, and Reagan's Iran-contra affair in 1985 and 1986. Compounding their problems, each then circled up the wagons, all of them manned by deferential aides and cronies, to seal out unpleasant but necessary political knowledge when things went badly. From the heights of political unity and consensus in the reelection, each president and the nation descended into varying depths of stalemate and suspicion during the second term.

The common feature of each of these self-inflicted wounds seems to have been the reelected president's errant conclusion that the voters had handed him blanket authorization to rule during the second term as he saw fit, rather than, as was more likely, that they had endorsed his conduct during the first term, expressed a lack of confidence in his opponent, and shown some faith that he would continue to lead as the skillful head of one branch of a three-branch government. There is nothing inevitable about such a reaction from presidents who are landslide reelection winners, but the temptation to a "*L'état, c'est moi*" way of thinking in such an instance— and the need to resist it—are obvious.

✤ *F U R T H E R   R E A D I N G*

Leonard Baker, *Back to Back: The Duel Between FDR and the Supreme Court* (1967)
James MacGregor Burns, *Roosevelt: The Lion and the Fox* (1956)
John W. Chambers, "The Big Switch: Justice Roberts and the Minimum Wage Cases," *Labor History* 10 (1969): 44–73
Richard Cortner, *The Jones & Laughlin Case* (1970)
Edward S. Corwin, "The Schechter Case—Landmark or What?," *New York University Law Quarterly* 13 (1936): 151–190
Frank Friedel, "The Sick Chicken Case," in John Garraty, *Quarrels That Have Shaped the Constitution* (1975): 191–209
Ellis Hawley, *The New Deal and the Problem of Monopoly* (1966)
Peter Irons, *The New Deal Lawyers* (1982)
Robert H. Jackson, *The Struggle for Judicial Power* (1949)
Charles A. Leonard, *A Search for a Judicial Philosophy: Mr. Justice Roberts and the Constitutional Reovlution of 1937* (1971)
William D. Leuchtenburg, "FDR's Court-Packing Plan: A Second Life, A Second Death," *Duke Law Journal* (June–September 1985): 673–689
Stuart N. Nagel, "Court-Curbing Periods in American History," *Vanderbilt Law Review* 18 (March 1965): 925–944
Arthur M. Schlesinger, Jr., *The Crisis of the Old Order, 1919–1933* (1957)
———, *The Politics of Upheaval* (1960)

CHAPTER
6

The Cold War
and Civil Liberties

✠

The strident anticommunism of the Cold War had deep roots. In 1940 Congress passed the Smith Act, also known as the Alien Registration Act, which was directed primarily at communists. At that time, a real threat of communist sabotage of defense industries loomed because Hitler and the Soviet Union were allies. Following the Third Reich's invasion of the Soviet Union, however, Stalin switched sides. The resulting alliance was always uneasy; and shortly after the war's end, it collapsed altogether. John Bricker, the Republican vice-presidential candidate in 1944, captured American unease when he proclaimed that ''Communist forces have taken over the New Deal and will destroy the very Foundations of the Republic.''

No other political figure more fully stoked the anticommunist fires, however, than Republican senator Joseph McCarthy of Wisconsin, whose name became synonymous with the red scare hysteria of the 1950s. McCarthy hauled a long list of prominent and not-so-prominent Americans before his Senate investigating committee, charging them on the flimsiest of grounds with being communists or communist sympathizers. Anticommunism drew support from some Democrats as well, including President Harry S Truman. His Department of Justice in 1948 undertook systematic prosecutions of the Communist party's top leadership under the Smith Act. In a nation wrestling with the implications of thermonuclear war and Cold War, the question of balancing internal security against individual freedom assumed great significance. One of the basic principles of political democracy is that the majority can make just such decisions that bind the minority, and among the most important of these is the preservation of the nation's security. Yet the Bill of Rights also stands for a counter-majority principle: there are certain actions that majorities, even working through elected representatives, cannot take.

Truman's stalking of the communist leadership posed these issues in stark terms. Should the federal government quash internal dissent when the national security is threatened? What are the appropriate constitutional measures by which to balance individual expression against national salvation? How can the public adequately assess the threat to national security when much of the mili-

tary and intelligence information about that threat is, for understandable reasons, suppressed? Is it appropriate to punish political dissenters for what they believe as well as what they say and do? The federal government's invocation of the Smith Act and the 1950 McCarran Act (which required communists to register with the government) posed one of the central issues of the Cold War: what was the scope of civil liberty?

✠ D O C U M E N T S

The New Deal redefined the meaning of the words *liberal* and *conservative* as they applied to civil liberties. In the first document, dating from 1936, the social philosopher John Dewey points to a contradiction that then existed in liberal (that is, laissez-faire) thought: liberals opposed state intervention in economic matters but ignored or even welcomed it where civil liberties were involved. Franklin Roosevelt's New Deal Court generally broke this pattern; old liberals, who had opposed government regulation, were supplanted by new liberals, who supported government intervention in the economy but not with civil liberties. The strength of anticommunist sentiments challenged the Roosevelt Court's new liberalism. The Smith Act, reproduced as the second document, and the debate over it in Congress, the third document, shed light on the depth of anticommunist sentiment. The Roosevelt Court's most important encounter with the Smith Act was *Dennis et al.* v. *United States* (1951), the fourth document. The Truman administration in 1948 won the indictment and conviction of twelve national leaders of the Communist Party of the United States, including its general secretary, Eugene Dennis. A lengthy and bombastic political trial followed that culminated in the conviction of all twelve defendants for conspiring to advocate the overthrow of the government of the United States. The Supreme Court, speaking through Chief Justice Fred Vinson, sustained the convictions by relying on a transformed version of Holmes's once libertarian doctrine of clear and present danger. Following *Dennis,* the federal government brought a number of prosecutions against Communist party leaders.

The justices eventually began to backtrack. In *Yates* v. *United States* (1957), the sixth document, Justice John Marshall Harlan nullified the *Dennis* opinion without taking the then politically risky step of reversing it altogether. The larger pattern of development was made clear by the political scientist John P. Roche, who argued in the seventh document that the consolidation and growth of the federal government had enhanced the liberty that Americans enjoyed. The final event in the collapse of constitutional support for anticommunism came in *Brandenburg* v. *Ohio* (1969), reprinted here as the last selection. The Supreme Court, in a per curiam opinion (that is, an opinion by the whole Court rather than by a single justice for the Court), made freedom of expression, except where government could establish a direct connection between speech and illegal activity, the rule.

John Dewey on Liberalism and Civil Liberties, 1936

The idea of civil liberties developed step by step as the ideals of liberalism displaced the earlier practices of political autocracy, which subordinated subjects to the arbitrary will of governmental authorities. In tradition, rather than in historic fact, their origin for English-speaking people is associated with the Magna Carta. Civil liberties were definitely formulated in the Bill of Rights adopted by the British Parliament in 1689 after the exile of the Stuarts and the final overthrow of dynastic government in that country. At the time of the revolt of the American colonies against the mother country many of the state constitutions embodied clauses very similar to those in the Bill of Rights. They were not contained in the Federal Constitution adopted at a time of reaction against the more radical revolutionary ideas, Hamilton being especially opposed to their inclusion. But in order to secure ratification by the several states, constitutional guarantees of civil rights were added in the first ten amendments in 1789. They contained, however, little more than what had become commonplaces of the rights of citizens in Great Britain. The only novel features in our constitutional provisions were the denial to government of the right of establishing religion and a greater emphasis upon the right of individuals to complete freedom in choice of a form of religious worship. The gist of the civil rights, constitutionally guaranteed to individuals, was freedom of the press, of peaceful assemblage and discussion, and of petition.

Conflicting Theories of Civil Liberties

I have given this slight historic review because history throws much light on the present confused state of civil liberties. A consistent social philosophy of the various rights that go by this name has never existed. Upon the whole, the dominant philosophy has sprung from fear of government and of organized control, on the ground of their supposed inherent antagonism to the liberties of individuals. Hence, one theoretical justification of freedom of conscience, of choice of worship, of freedom of speech (which is what freedom of assembly amounts to practically) and of publication, has been based upon the theory of natural rights, rights that inhere in individuals prior to political organization and independent of political authority. From this point of view, they are like the rights of "life, liberty, and the pursuit of happiness" made familiar to us in the Declaration of Independence. They represent fixed and external limits set to political action.

This motif comes out most clearly in the last two articles of the amendments that form the Bill of Rights, articles which expressly reserve to the several states or to the people in general all powers not expressly granted by the Constitution to the Federal Government. The majority opinion in the A.A.A. decision used this clause of the Constitution as its authority for declaring the Agricultural Adjustment Act unconstitutional. On the face of things, there is no kinship between regulation of agriculture and the right, say, of free speech. But the two things have been brought together in the theory that there is an inherent opposition between political power and individual liberty.

The opposite strain in the theory of civil liberties is indicated by the contrast between the word "civil" on the one hand and the words "natural" and "political" on the other. The term *civil* is directly connected with the idea of citizenship. On this basis, civil liberties are those which belong to citizens as such and are different both from those which individuals are supposed to possess in a state of nature and from political rights such as the franchise and the right to hold office. Upon this basis, the justification for the various civil liberties is the contribution they make to the welfare of the community.

Untenability of the Notion of Absolute Individual "Rights"

I have intimated that the present confused and precarious condition of civil liberties, even in nominally democratic countries like our own, is due to the conflict of these two opposed ideas of the basis and purpose of civil liberties. As social relations have become more complicated and the problem of maintaining social order becomes more difficult, it is practically inevitable that whatever the nominal theory be, *merely* individual claims will be forced to give way in practice to social claims. The individualistic and laissez-faire conception of civil liberties (say of free inquiry and free discussion) has been put forward to an extent which largely accounts for the ease with which nominally constitutional guarantees of civil liberties are violated in fact and are explained away by the courts. It is a commonplace that they go into the discard when a nation is engaged in war. This is simply the crucial instance of the fact that *merely* individual claims will be lightly esteemed when they appear (or can be made to appear) in conflict with the general social welfare.

Moreover, civil liberties are never absolute nor is their precise nature in concrete situations self-evident. Only a philosophic anarchist holds, for example, that the freedom of speech includes the right to urge other men to engage in murder, arson, or robbery. Hence in the concrete, civil liberties mean what the courts construe them to mean. Courts, in all matters that have a general political or social bearing, are notoriously subject to social pressure and social currents, both those coming from without and those flowing from the education and political affiliations of judges. These facts give short shrift to civil liberties that are claimed upon a purely individualistic basis when judges are of the opinion that their exercise is dangerous to social ends which the judges set store by. Holmes and Brandeis are notable not only for their sturdy defense of civil liberties but even more for the fact that they based their defense on the indispensable value of free inquiry and free discussion to the normal development of public welfare, not upon anything inherent in the individual as such.

The Social Welfare Criterion of Civil Liberties

Anyone who views the situation impartially will not be surprised at the contradiction which is so marked in the conduct of liberals of the laissez-faire school. They constantly protest against any "interference" on the part of government with freedom of business enterprise, but are almost uniformly silent in the case of even flagrant violations of civil liberties—in spite of lip service to liberal ideas and professed adulation of the Constitution. The cause for the contradiction is obvious. Business interests have been and still are socially and politically dominant. In standing for laissez-faire liberalism in economic matters, these "liberals" are moving with the tide. On the other hand, only those individuals who are *opposing* the established order ever get into trouble by using the right to free inquiry and public discussion. In their case, the "liberals" who are vociferous against anything that looks like economic regimentation, are content to tolerate intellectual and moral regimentation on the ground that it is necessary for the maintenance of "law and order."

No genuine believer in the democratic ideals of universal distribution of equal liberties will find it necessary to argue at large in behalf of the maximum possible of intellectual liberty in the fullest sense of that term. He knows that freedom of thought in inquiry and in dissemination of the conclusions of inquiry is the vital nerve of democratic institutions. Accordingly, I have not indulged in a general eulogy of civil liberties but have tried to show that the first step in rescuing them from their present uncertain and perilous state is to insist upon their social basis and social justification.

Invasions of civil liberties have grown in pretty much all directions since the World War, in spite of alleged constitutional guarantees. This fact is an illustration of the principle set forth in an earlier article in this series. The only hope for liberalism is to surrender, in theory and practice, the doctrine that liberty is a full-fledged ready-made possession of individuals independent of social institutions and arrangements, and to realize that social control, especially of economic forces, is necessary in order to render secure the liberties of the individual, including civil liberties.

The Alien Registration Act (Smith Act), 1940

An Act to prohibit certain subversive activities; to amend certain provisions of law with respect to the admission and deportation of aliens; to require the fingerprinting and registration of aliens; and for other purposes.

Title I

Section 1. (a) It shall be unlawful for any person, with intent to interfere with, impair, or influence the loyalty, morale, or discipline of the military or naval forces of the United States—

(1) to advise, counsel, urge, or in any manner cause insubordination, disloyalty, mutiny, or refusal of duty by any member of the military or naval forces of the United States; or

(2) to distribute any written or printed matter which advises, counsels, or urges insubordination, disloyalty, mutiny, or refusal of duty by any member of the military or naval forces of the United States.

Sec. 2. (a) It shall be unlawful for any person—

(1) to knowingly or willfully advocate, abet, advise, or teach the duty, necessity, desirability, or propriety of overthrowing or destroying any gov-

ernment in the United States by force or violence, or by the assassination of any officer of any such government;

(2) with the intent to cause the overthrow or destruction of any government in the United States, to print, publish, edit, issue, circulate, sell, distribute, or publicly display any written or printed matter advocating, advising, or teaching the duty, necessity, desirability, or propriety of overthrowing or destroying any government in the United States by force or violence;

(3) to organize or help to organize any society, group, or assembly of persons who teach, advocate, or encourage the overthrow or destruction of any government in the United States by force or violence; or to be or become a member of, or affiliate with, any such society, group, or assembly of persons, knowing the purposes thereof.

Senate Judiciary Committee Hearings on the Smith Act, 1940

. . . Mr. Smith. Now, I will pass to title II. . . . That is the title that makes it unlawful for any person to advocate the overthrow of the Government of the United States by force, and I very much hope that that may be retained in the act, and I do not know that there will be any particular objection to it, over here. I think there was some, in the hearings in the House, by certain organizations. I do not know that it needs any further discussion from me. You gentlemen I think understand just what it means. . . .

Senator Danaher. I would like to ask one question if I may. In what particulars do you change existing law, in title II, Judge? . . . Do you, Judge Smith, see any violation of article I of the Constitution imposed by the provisions of section 7, insofar as you use the language, "to print, publish, edit, issue, or knowingly circulate, sell, distribute, or publicly display any book, paper, document . . ."? In other words, does that inveigh against the right of free press?

Mr. Smith. I do not think so. If it does, I think we ought to change the Constitution. I guess we pass a good many laws here that have to stand the test of constitutionality in the courts, and this provision would not be an exception to that rule. . . .

Statement of Mary E. Bodkin, Secretary, National Legislative Committee, Descendants of the American Revolution

Senator Connally. Just give your name to the reporter, and state whom you represent.

Miss Bodkin. Mary E. Bodkin; Descendants of the American Revolution.

Senator Connally. All right, Miss Bodkin.

Miss Bodkin. Mr. Chairman, members of the subcommittee, the Descendants of the American Revolution, an organization dedicated to the defense of those civil rights for which our forefathers fought, wishes to register its strong opposition to this bill. (H. R. 5138).

The bill represents a concerted attack on the civil rights and liberties of citizens as well as aliens, embodying as it does many of the objectionable provisions of several similar individual bills also considered at this session of Congress. One of its provisions (found in title III, section 11) making deportable any alien who has "admitted in writing" sabotage or espionage against the United States since his entry, is practically identical with the Russell-Starnes bill, which recently received a presidential veto.

Title II of the bill contains a Federal criminal syndicalism clause applicable to both citizens and aliens. This provision would have the effect of attaching criminality to mere advocacy or suggestion of violent change of the existing economic and political order.

Senator Connally. Right, there, may I ask you a question. Do you favor that?

Miss Bodkin. The advocacy or suggestion?

Senator Connally. Yes. Do you favor advocating the overthrow of the Government by force?

Miss Bodkin. No.

Senator Connally. Then, if you do not advocate it, why do you object to making it an offense for somebody else to do it?

Miss Bodkin. Well, I think a little bit later we differentiate between the advocacy or suggestion—that is, the oral expression or written expression of the overthrow of government, and the actual acts which might overthrow the government.

Senator Connally. I think the man who advocates it but who is not sufficiently courageous to go out and commit some overt act is a bigger coward than the fellow whom he deludes and persuades to go out and commit such an act. I think he is more dangerous, because he goes out and stirs up people to resist, to commit overt acts, and he, due to his cowardice, refrains from doing it, himself. I do not want to interrupt the line of your argument, but I just wanted to suggest that thought.

Miss Bodkin. Yes. In that connection, I think it is the idea here of interfering with the absolute freedom of expression, assembly, and of the press—this bill might serve as an entering wedge to infringe upon those basic rights.

Senator Connally. You do not believe that the absolute right of the press ought to be used as an instrumentality for overthrowing a government which is trying to maintain freedom of the press and freedom of expression?

Miss Bodkin. No; but we do not believe that it should be made a criminal offense merely to express such an opinion.

Senator Connally. You would, in a way, pass a resolution condemning it, and let it go at that, is that it?

Miss Bodkin. Shall I go on?

Senator Connally. All right.

Miss Bodkin. It seeks to punish by long prison terms and heavy fines not only provocation to the use of force, but also the promulgation of any ideas which might possibly, if accepted cause someone to use force. The difference between the expression of radical ideas and direct provocation is one of degree, but it is a difference which those of us who wish to maintain and safeguard the basic tradition of freedom of speech and press regard as all-important. It is the difference between treason, a crime already punishable by statute, and mere expression of opinion; a difference the criminal law has always regarded as all-important.

The provisions of title I would also interfere with freedom of speech and press. If this bill were enacted, any person with strong pacifist feelings, who made them known to members of the Army and Navy would run the risk of fine and imprisonment and, in addition, if an alien, deportation. Deportation would also be the penalty under title IV for membership at any time, that is, either before entry into the United States or subsequent to it, in a group or organization that could be construed as advocating overthrow of the Government by force or violence, or opposition to all organized government (irrespective of the place, time, length, or character of such membership). Surely, no useful purpose can be served by thus drastically penalizing an individual for past beliefs or affiliations, or even for present ones. Applying the doctrine of Mr. Justice Holmes that unless the advocacy of the overthrow of the Government by force and violence constitutes a "clear and present" danger to organized society, it is not treasonable, obviously past affiliations would be of no significance, and present ones would be of significance only insofar as they constituted this "clear and present" danger.

Since our present treason laws afford adequate protection in this latter type of case, the deportation provisions of this title cannot be considered as necessary to safeguard the welfare of our Government.

Another objectionable provision of the bill would require the fingerprinting of all immigrants.

A bill which thus opens the way to vigilantism, to the suppression of trade-unions, and to the violation of many of the liberties guaranteed by the Bill of Rights to both alien and citizen alike can but receive our wholehearted condemnation. This bill represents a further phase of the tendency apparent in recent years to sacrifice civil liberties to governmental control in the interests of what the organs of the State consider desirable public policy. This is a regrettable un-American tendency—wholly incompatible with the principles upon which this country was founded, and a tendency which the Descendants of the American Revolution therefore feel must be most strongly combated.

For these reasons, we strenuously oppose the present bill.

Senator Connally. May I ask you a question? You are talking about suppression of trade-unionism in this bill. Where is there anything about trade-unions? It is not even mentioned, is it?

Miss Bodkin. I believe it was the intention of the committee which drew up this statement—it was in their minds, that a bill of this sort which attempts to suppress any of our basic civil rights would inevitably affect the tradeunions. I realize there is no specific provision.

Senator Connally. It would not affect the unions unless they did some of these acts which are condemned here.

Miss Bodkin. No. I realize there is no specific provision in the bill.

Senator Connally. They would have no more right to do it than anybody else. Were you before the House committee?

Miss Bodkin. No.

Senator Connally. May I ask you a question or two about your organization, Miss Bodkin?

Miss Bodkin. Yes, sir; surely.

Senator Connally. You belong to the Descendants of the American Revolution?

Miss Bodkin. Yes.

Senator Connally. How are you financed?

Miss Bodkin. The Descendants is a membership group which has local councils throughout the counties which pay dues. There are no paid members. The work is purely volunteer work.

Senator Connally. In order to be a member do you have to be a descendant of some revolutionary?

Miss Bodkin. Yes; you have to trace your genealogy back to someone who fought in the Revolution.

Senator Connally. Are you related in any way or affiliated with the Daughters of the American Revolution?

Miss Bodkin. No.

Senator Connally. Or with the Sons of the American Revolution?

Miss Bodkin. No. The membership requirements are somewhat the same, in the matter of genealogy, but it is quite a different organization.

Senator Connally. In what respect? What are your objectives, and what are your purposes? Are there any bylaws or rules?

Miss Bodkin. If I might, I think there I should like to read our program of the Descendants, which I have here. We have a 10-point program. Would you care to listen to those?

Senator Connally. If it is not too long.

Miss Bodkin [reading]:

To bring within an organization all descendants of the American Revolution who desire to make the ideals of their ancestors a living force today.

To reaffirm the Bill of Rights, and again to defend the liberties guaranteed by the Constitution.

To combat the activities of extralegal bodies who set themselves up to administer law and order by threat or force in defiance of constitutional authority.

To defend the American principle of the right of asylum to the politically and religiously oppressed of other lands.

To foster academic freedom in schools and colleges.

Those are four or five of the points in the program. . . .

Senator Danaher. Do your notes show the opinion from which you quoted? You quoted Justice Holmes. Do you remember the name of the case in which he made that statement?

Miss Bodkin. I am sorry, I do not.

Senator Danaher. I think I do, but I wanted to verify my recollection. All right, thank you.

Mr. Finerty. The opinion referred to was in the case of *Schenck* v. *United States.* . . .

Dennis et al. v. *United States,* 341 U.S. 494 (1951)

[6–2: Vinson, Reed, Burton, Minton,
Frankfurter, Jackson; Black, Douglas]

. . . Mr. Chief Justice Vinson announced the judgment of the Court. . . .

. . . The trial of the case extended over nine months, six of which were devoted to the taking of evidence, resulting in a record of 16,000 pages. Our limited grant of the writ of certiorari has removed from our consideration any question as to the sufficiency of the evidence to support the jury's determination that petitioners are guilty of the offense charged. Whether on this record petitioners did in fact advocate the overthrow of the Government by force and violence is not before us, and we must base any discussion of this point upon the conclusions stated in the opinion of the Court of Appeals, which treated the issue in great detail. That court held that the record in this case amply supports the necessary finding of the jury that petitioners, the leaders of the Communist Party in this country, were unwilling to work within our framework of democracy, but intended to initiate a violent revolution whenever the propitious occasion appeared. Petitioners dispute the meaning to be drawn from the evidence, contending that the Marxist-Leninist doctrine they advocated taught that force and violence to achieve a Communist form of government in an existing democratic state would be necessary only because the ruling classes of that state would never permit the transformation to be accomplished peacefully, but would use force and violence to defeat any peaceful political and economic gain the Communists could achieve. But the Court of Appeals held that the record supports the following broad conclusions: By virtue of their control over the political apparatus of the Communist Political Association, petitioners were able to transform that organization into the Communist Party; that the policies of the Association were changed from peaceful cooperation with the United States and its economic and political structure to a policy which had existed before the United States and the Soviet Union were fighting a common enemy, namely, a policy which worked for the overthrow of the Government by force and violence; that the Communist Party is a highly disciplined organization, adept at infiltration into strategic positions, use of aliases, and double-meaning language; that the Party is rigidly controlled; that Communists, unlike other political parties, tolerate no dissension from the policy laid down by the guiding forces, but that the approved program is slavishly followed by the members of the Party; that the literature of the Party and the statements and activities of its leaders, petitioners here, advocate, and the general goal of the Party was, during the period in question, to achieve a successful overthrow of the existing order by force and violence.

I.

It will be helpful in clarifying the issues to treat next the contention that the trial judge improperly interpreted the statute by charging that the statute required an unlawful intent before the jury could convict. More specifically, he charged that the jury could not find the petitioners guilty under the indictment unless they found that petitioners had the intent to "overthrow . . . the Government of the United States by force and violence as speedily as circumstances would permit."

. . . Because of the fact that § 2 (a) (2) expressly requires a specific intent to overthrow the Government, and because of the absence of precise language in the foregoing subsections, it is claimed that Congress deliberately omitted any such requirement. We do not agree. It would require a far greater indication of congressional desire that intent not be made an element of the crime than the use of the disjunctive "knowingly *or* willfully" in § (2) (a) (1), or the omission of exact language in § 2 (a) (3). The structure and purpose of the statute demand the inclusion of intent as an element of the crime. Congress was concerned with those who advocate and organize for the overthrow of the Government. Certainly those who recruit and combine for the purpose of advocating overthrow intend to bring about that overthrow. We hold that the statute requires as an essential element of the crime proof of the intent of those who are charged with its violation to overthrow the Government by force and violence. . . .

Nor does the fact that there must be an investigation of a state of mind under this interpretation afford any basis for rejection of that meaning. . . . The existence of a *mens rea* is the rule of, rather than the exception to, the principles of Anglo-American criminal jurisprudence. . . .

It has been suggested that the presence of intent makes a difference in the law when an "act otherwise excusable or carrying minor penalties" is accompanied by such an evil intent. . . . If that precise mental state may be an essential element of a crime, surely an intent to overthrow the Government of the United States by advocacy thereof is equally susceptible of proof.

II.

The obvious purpose of the statute is to protect existing Government, not from change by peaceable, lawful and constitutional means, but from change by violence, revolution and terrorism. That it is within the *power* of the Congress to protect the Government of the United States from armed rebellion is a proposition which requires little discussion. Whatever theoretical merit there may be to the argument that there is a "right" to rebellion against dictatorial governments is without force where the existing structure of the government provides for peaceable and orderly change. We reject any principle of governmental helplessness in the face of preparation for revolution, which principle, carried to its logical conclusion, must lead to anarchy. No one could conceive that it is not within the power of Congress to prohibit acts intended to overthrow the Government by force and violence. The question with which we are concerned here is not whether Congress has such *power,* but whether the *means* which it has employed conflict with the First and Fifth Amendments to the Constitution.

One of the bases for the contention that the means which Congress has employed are invalid takes the form of an attack on the face of the statute on the grounds that by its terms it prohibits academic discussion of the merits of Marxism-Leninism, that it stifles ideas and is contrary to all concepts of a free speech and a free press. Although we do not agree that the language itself has that significance, we must bear in mind that it is the duty of the federal courts to interpret federal legislation in a manner not inconsistent with the demands of the Constitution. . . .

The very language of the Smith Act negates the interpretation which petitioners would have us impose on that Act. It is directed at advocacy, not discussion. Thus, the trial judge properly charged the jury that they could not convict if they found that petitioners did "no more than pursue peaceful studies and discussions or teaching and advocacy in the realm of ideas." He further charged that it was not unlawful "to conduct in an American college or university a course explaining the philosophical theories set forth in the books which have been placed in evidence." Such a charge is in strict accord with the statutory language, and illustrates the meaning to be placed on those words. Congress did not intend to eradicate the free discussion of political theories, to destroy the traditional rights of Americans to discuss and evaluate ideas without fear of governmental sanction. Rather Congress was concerned with the very kind of activity in which the evidence showed these petitioners engaged.

III.

But although the statute is not directed at the hypothetical cases which petitioners have conjured, its application in this case has resulted in convictions for the teaching and advocacy of the overthrow of the Government by force and violence, which, even though coupled with the intent to accomplish that overthrow, contains an element of speech. For this reason, we must pay special heed to the demands of the First Amendment marking out the boundaries of speech.

We pointed out in *Douds* [1950], that the basis of the First Amendment is the hypothesis that speech can rebut speech, propaganda will answer propaganda, free debate of ideas will result in the wisest governmental policies. It is for this reason that this Court has recognized the inherent value of free discourse. An analysis of the leading cases in this Court which have involved direct limitations on speech, however, will demonstrate that both the majority of the Court and the dissenters in particular cases have recognized that this is not an unlimited, unqualified right, but that the societal value of speech must, on occasion, be subordinated to other values and considerations.

No important case involving free speech was decided by this Court prior to *Schenck* v. *United States* . . . (1919). Indeed, the summary treatment accorded an argument based upon an individual's claim that the First Amendment protected certain utterances indicates that the Court at earlier dates placed no unique emphasis upon that right. It was not until the classic dictum of Justice Holmes in the *Schenck* case that speech *per se* received that emphasis in a majority opinion. That case involved a conviction under the Criminal Espionage Act. . . . The question the Court faced was whether the evidence was sufficient to sustain the conviction. Writing for a unanimous Court, Justice Holmes stated that the "question in every case is whether the words used are used in such circumstances and are of such a nature as to create a clear and present danger that they will bring about the substantive evils that Congress has a right to prevent." . . .

In several later cases involving convictions under the Criminal Espionage Act, the nub of the evidence the Court held sufficient to meet the "clear and present danger" test [was also] enunciated in *Schenck.* . . . Justice Holmes wrote the opinions for a unanimous Court in *Schenck, Frohwerk* and *Debs.* He and Justice Brandeis dissented in *Abrams, Schaefer* and *Pierce.* The basis of these dissents was that, because of the protection which the First Amendment gives to speech, the evidence in each case was insufficient to show that the defendants had created the requisite danger under *Schenck.* But these dissents did not mark a change of principle. The dissenters doubted only the probable effectiveness of the puny efforts toward subversion. In *Abrams,* they wrote, "I do not doubt for a moment that by the same reasoning that would justify punishing persuasion to murder, the United States constitutionally may punish speech that produces or is intended to produce a clear and imminent danger that it will bring about forthwith certain substantive evils that the United States constitutionally may seek to prevent." . . . And in *Schaefer* the test was said to be one of "degree" . . . , although it is not clear whether "degree" refers to clear and present danger or evil. Perhaps both were meant.

The rule we deduce from these cases is that where an offense is specified by a statute in nonspeech or nonpress terms, a conviction relying upon speech or press as evidence of violation may be sustained only when the speech or publication created a "clear and present danger" of attempting or accomplishing the prohibited crime, *e.g.,* interference with enlistment. The dissents, we repeat, in emphasizing the value of speech, were addressed to the argument of the sufficiency of the evidence.

The next important case before the Court in which free speech was the crux of the conflict was *Gitlow* v. *New York* . . . (1925). There New York had made it a crime to advocate "the necessity or propriety of overthrowing . . . organized government by force. . . ." The evidence of violation of the statute was that the defendant had published a Manifesto attacking the Government and capitalism. The convictions were sustained, Justices Holmes and Brandeis dissenting. The majority refused to apply the "clear and present danger" test to the specific utterance. Its reasoning was as follows: The "clear and present danger" test was applied to the utterance itself in *Schenck* because the question was merely one of sufficiency of evidence under an admittedly constitutional statute. *Gitlow*, however, presented a different question. There a legislature had found that a certain kind of speech was, itself, harmful and unlawful. The constitutionality of such a state statute had to be adjudged by this Court just as it determined the constitutionality of any state statute, namely, whether the statute was "reasonable." Since it was entirely reasonable for a state to attempt to protect itself from violent overthrow, the statute was perforce reasonable. The only question remaining in the case became whether there was evidence to support the conviction, a question which gave the majority no difficulty. Justices Holmes and Brandeis refused to accept this approach, but insisted that wherever speech was the evidence of the violation, it was necessary to show that the speech created the "clear and present danger" of the substantive evil which the legislature had the right to prevent. Justices Holmes and Brandeis, then, made no distinction between a federal statute which made certain acts unlawful, the evidence to support the conviction being speech, and a statute which made speech itself the crime. This approach was emphasized in *Whitney* v. *California . . .* (1927), where the Court was confronted with a conviction under the California Criminal Syndicalist statute. The Court sustained the conviction, Justices Brandeis and Holmes concurring in the result. In their concurrence they repeated that even though the legislature had designated certain speech as criminal, this could not prevent the defendant from showing that there was no danger that the substantive evil would be brought about.

Although no case subsequent to *Whitney* and *Gitlow* has expressly overruled the majority opinions in those cases, there is little doubt that subsequent opinions have inclined toward the Holmes-Brandeis rationale. . . . But . . . neither Justice Holmes nor Justice Brandeis ever envisioned that a shorthand phrase should be crystallized into a rigid rule to be applied inflexibly without regard to the circumstances of each case. Speech is not an absolute, above and beyond control by the legislature when its judgment, subject to review here, is that certain kinds of speech are so undesirable as to warrant criminal sanction. Nothing is more certain in modern society than the principle that there are no absolutes, that a name, a phrase, a standard has meaning only when associated with the considerations which gave birth to the nomenclature. . . . To those who would paralyze our Government in the face of impending threat by encasing it in a semantic straitjacket we must reply that all concepts are relative.

In this case we are squarely presented with the application of the "clear and present danger" test, and must decide what that phrase imports. We first note that many of the cases in which this Court has reversed convictions by use of this or similar tests have been based on the fact that the interest which the State was attempting to protect was itself too insubstantial to warrant restriction of speech. . . . Overthrow of the Government by force and violence is certainly a substantial enough interest for the Government to limit speech. Indeed, this is the ultimate value of any society, for if a society cannot protect its very structure from armed internal attack, it must follow that no subordinate value can be protected. If, then, this interest may be protected, the literal problem which is presented is what has been meant by the use of the phrase "clear and present danger" of the utterances bringing about the evil within the power of Congress to punish.

Obviously, the words cannot mean that before the Government may act, it must wait until the *putsch* is about to be executed, the plans have been laid and the signal is awaited. If Government is aware that a group aiming at its overthrow is attempting to indoctrinate its members and to commit them to a course whereby they will strike when the leaders feel the circumstances permit, action by the Government is required. The argument that there is no need for Government to concern itself, for Government is strong, it possesses ample powers to put down a rebellion, it may defeat the revolution with ease needs no answer. For that is not the question. Certainly an attempt to overthrow the Government by force, even though doomed from the outset because of inadequate numbers or power of the revolutionists, is a sufficient evil for Congress to prevent. The damage which such attempts create both physically and politically to a nation makes it impossible to measure the validity in terms of the probability of success, or the immediacy of a successful attempt. In the instant case the trial judge charged the jury that they could not convict unless they found that petitioners intended to overthrow the Government "as speedily as circumstances would permit." This does not mean, and could not properly mean, that they would not strike until there was certainty of success. What was meant was that the revolutionists would strike when they thought the time was ripe. We must therefore reject the contention that success or probability of success is the criterion.

The situation with which Justices Holmes and Brandeis were concerned in *Gitlow* was a comparatively isolated event, bearing little relation in their minds to any substantial threat to the safety of the community. . . . They were not confronted with any situation comparable to the instant one—the development of an apparatus designed and dedicated to the overthrow of the Government, in the context of world crisis after crisis.

Chief Judge Learned Hand, writing for the majority below, interpreted the phrase as follows: "In each case [courts] must ask whether the gravity of the 'evil,' discounted by its improbability, justifies such invasion of free speech as is necessary to avoid the danger." . . . We adopt this statement of the rule. As articulated by Chief Judge Hand, it is as succinct and inclusive as any other we might devise at this time. It takes into consideration those factors which we deem relevant, and relates their significances. More we cannot expect from words.

Likewise, we are in accord with the court below, which affirmed the trial court's finding that the requisite danger existed. The mere fact that from the period 1945 to 1948 petitioners' activities did not result in an attempt to overthrow the Government by force and violence is of course no answer to the fact that there was a group that was ready to make the attempt. The formation by petitioners of such a highly organized conspiracy, with rigidly disciplined members subject to call when the leaders, these petitioners, felt that the time had come for action, coupled with the inflammable nature of world conditions, similar uprisings in other countries, and the touch-and-go nature of our relations with countries with whom petitioners were in the very least ideologically attuned, convince us that their convictions were justified on this score. And this analysis disposes of the contention that a conspiracy to advocate, as distinguished from the advocacy itself, cannot be constitutionally restrained, because it comprises only the preparation. It is the existence of the conspiracy which creates the danger. . . . If the ingredients of the reaction are present, we cannot bind the Government to wait until the catalyst is added.

IV.

Although we have concluded that the finding that there was a sufficient danger to warrant the application of the statute was justified on the merits, there remains the problem of whether the trial judge's treatment of the issue was correct. . . .

When facts are found that establish the violation of a statute, the protection against conviction afforded by the First Amendment is a matter of law. The doctrine that there must be a clear and present danger of a substantive evil that Congress has a right to prevent is a judicial rule to be applied as a matter of law by the courts. The guilt is established by proof of facts. Whether the First Amendment protects the activity which constitutes the violation of the statute must depend upon a judicial determination of the scope of the First Amendment applied to the circumstances of the case.

Petitioners' reliance upon Justice Brandeis' language in his concurrence in *Whitney* . . . is misplaced. In that case Justice Brandeis pointed out that the defendant could have made the existence of the requisite danger the important issue at her trial, but that she had not done so. In discussing this failure, he stated that the defendant could have had the issue determined by the court *or* the jury. No realistic construction of this disjunctive language could arrive at the conclusion that he intended to state that the question was *only* determinable by a jury. Nor is the incidental statement of the majority in *Pierce, supra.* of any more persuasive effect. There the issue of the probable effect of the publication had been submitted to the jury, and the majority was apparently addressing its remarks to the contention of the dissenters that the jury could not reasonably have returned a verdict of guilty on the evidence. Indeed, in the very case in which the phrase was born, *Schenck*, this Court itself examined the record to find whether the requisite danger appeared, and the issue was not submitted to a jury. And in every later case in which the Court has measured the validity of a statute by the "clear and present danger" test, that determination has been by the Court, the question of the danger not being submitted to the jury.

The question in this case is whether the statute which the legislature has enacted may be constitutionally applied. In other words, the Court must examine judicially the application of the statute to the particular situation, to ascertain if the Constitution prohibits the conviction. We hold that the statute may be applied where there is a "clear and present danger" of the substantive evil which the legislature had the right to prevent. Bearing, as it does, the marks of a "question of law," the issue is properly one for the judge to decide.

V.

There remains to be discussed the question of vagueness—whether the statute as we have interpreted it is too vague, not sufficiently advising those who would speak of the limitations upon their activity. It is urged that such vagueness contravenes the First and Fifth Amendments. This argument is particularly nonpersuasive when presented by petitioners, who, the jury found, intended to overthrow the Government as speedily as circumstances would permit. . . .

We agree that the standard as defined is not a neat, mathematical formulary. Like all verbalizations it is subject to criticism on the score of indefiniteness. But petitioners themselves contend that the verbalization "clear and present danger" is the proper standard. We see no difference, from the standpoint of vagueness, whether the standard of "clear and present danger" is one contained *in haec verba* within the statute, or whether it is the judicial measure of constitutional applicability. We have shown the indeterminate standard the phrase necessarily connotes. We do not think we have rendered that standard any more indefinite by our attempt to sum up the factors which are included within its scope. We think it well serves to indicate to those who would advocate constitutionally prohibited conduct that there is a line beyond which they may not go—a line which they, in full knowledge of what they intend and the circumstances in which their activity takes place, will well appreciate and understand. . . . Where there is doubt as to the intent of the defendants, the nature of their activities, or their power to bring about the evil, this Court will review the convictions with the scrupulous care demanded by our Constitution. But we are not convinced that because there may be borderline cases at some time in the future, these convictions should be reversed because of the argument that these petitioners could not know that their activities were constitutionally proscribed by the statute.

We have not discussed many of the questions which could be extracted from the record, although they were treated in detail by the court below. Our limited grant of the writ of certiorari has withdrawn from our consideration at this date those questions, which include, *inter alia,* sufficiency of the evidence, composition of jury, and conduct of the trial.

We hold that § § 2 (a) (1), 2 (a) (3) and 3 of the Smith Act do not inherently, or as construed or applied in the instant case, violate the First Amendment and other provisions of the Bill of Rights, or the First and Fifth Amendments because of indefiniteness. Petitioners intended to overthrow the Government of the United States as speedily as the circumstances would permit. Their conspiracy to organize the Communist Party and to teach and advocate the overthrow of the Government of the United States by force and violence created a "clear and present danger" of an attempt to overthrow the Government by force and violence. They were properly and constitutionally convicted for violation of the Smith Act. The judgments of conviction are *Affirmed.*

Mr. Justice Douglas, dissenting.

If this were a case where those who claimed protection under the First Amendment were teaching the techniques of sabotage, the assassination of the President, the filching of documents from public files, the planting of bombs, the art of street warfare, and the like, I would have no doubts. The freedom to speak is not absolute; the teaching of methods of terror and other seditious conduct should be beyond the pale along with obscenity and immorality. This case was argued as if those were the facts. The argument imported much seditious conduct into the record. That is easy and it has popular appeal, for the activities of Communists in plotting and scheming against the free world are common knowledge. But the fact is that no such evidence was introduced at the trial. There is a statute which makes a seditious conspiracy unlawful. Petitioners, however, were not charged with a "conspiracy to overthrow" the Government. They were charged with a conspiracy to form a party and groups and assemblies of people who teach and advocate the overthrow of our Government by force or violence and with a conspiracy to advocate and teach its overthrow by force and violence. It may well be that indoctrination in the techniques of terror to destroy the Government would be indictable under either statute. But the teaching which is condemned here is of a different character.

So far as the present record is concerned, what petitioners did was to organize people to teach and themselves teach the Marxist-Leninist doctrine contained chiefly in four books: Foundations of Leninism by Stalin (1924), The Communist Manifesto by Marx and Engels (1848), State and Revolution by Lenin (1917), History of the Communist Party of the Soviet Union (B) (1939). Those books are to Soviet Communism what Mein Kampf was to Nazism. If they are understood, the ugliness of Communism is revealed, its deceit and cunning are exposed, the nature of its activities becomes apparent, and the chances of its success less likely. That is not, of course, the reason why petitioners chose these books for their classrooms. They are fervent Communists to whom these volumes are gospel. They preached the creed with the hope that some day it would be acted upon.

The opinion of the Court does not outlaw these texts nor condemn them to the fire, as the Communists do literature offensive to their creed. But if the books themselves are not outlawed, if they can lawfully remain on library shelves, by what reasoning does their use in a classroom become a crime? [The] Act, as construed, requires the element of intent—that those who teach the creed believe in it. The crime then depends not on what is taught but on who the teacher is. That is to make freedom of speech turn not on *what is said,* but on the *intent* with which it is said. Once we start down that road we enter territory dangerous to the liberties of every citizen. . . .

There comes a time when even speech loses its constitutional immunity. Speech innocuous one year may at another time fan such destructive flames that it must be halted in the interests of the safety of the Republic. That is the meaning of the clear and present danger test. When conditions are so critical that there will be no time to avoid the evil that the speech threatens, it is time to call a halt. Otherwise, free speech which is the strength of the Nation will be the cause of its destruction. Yet free speech is the rule, not the exception. The restraint to be constitutional must be based on more than fear, on more than passionate opposition against the speech, on more than a revolted dislike for its contents. There must be some immediate injury to society that is likely if speech is allowed. . . .

The nature of Communism as a force on the world scene would, of course, be relevant to the issue of clear and present danger of petitioners' advocacy within the United States. But the primary consideration is the strength and tactical position of petitioners and their converts in this country. On that there is no evidence in the record. If we are to take judicial notice of the threat of Communists within the nation, it should not be difficult to conclude that *as a political party* they are of little consequence. Communism in the world scene is no bogeyman; but Communism as a political faction or party in this country plainly is. Communism has been so thoroughly exposed in this country that it has been crippled as a political force. Free speech has destroyed it as an effective political party. How it can be said that there is a clear and present danger that this advocacy will succeed is, therefore, a mystery. In America [Communists] are miserable merchants of unwanted ideas; their wares remain unsold. If we are to proceed on the basis of judicial notice, it is impossible for me to say that the Communists in this country are so potent or so strategically deployed that they must be suppressed for their speech. This is my view if we are to act on the basis of judicial notice. But the mere statement of the opposing views indicates how important it is that we know the facts before we act. Neither prejudice nor hate nor senseless fear should be the basis of this solemn act. Free speech should not be sacrificed on anything less than plain and objective proof of danger that the evil advocated is imminent.

Political Scientist John P. Roche Argues That We've Never Had More Freedom, 1956

. . . I [suggest] that the United States is today a freer nation, from the standpoint of the individual non-conformist, than ever before in its history. [T]hat American perennial, the reign of terror, [with] the situation today, when compared with the reigns of terror that have on a local basis bloodied up the American past, augurs well for the life-expectancy of the non-conformist. The bulk of punishments for non-conformity today are less severe

"We've Never Had More Freedom" by John P. Roche, *The New Republic* 134, February 6, 1956, pp. 13–15. Reprinted by permission of *The New Republic*, © 1956 The New Republic, Inc.

than was the case in the 19th Century: typically deviations are punished on a bureaucratic rather than on a direct level, *i.e.*, a "security risk" is dismissed from his job, not hanged to a lamppost or tarred and feathered.

The literature about individual violations of rights is abundant, so I shall not attempt an instance by instance, area by area, study. What I plan to do is investigate two major tendencies in American public policy. First, the enlargement of the political sector; and, second, the withering of decency. However, before I begin the discussion of these trends, it is essential that I define what I mean by democracy, for this definition is fundamental to my subsequent analysis.

Democratic government is by far the most difficult system to implement and operate yet conceived. The supreme danger that confronts it is a perpetual tendency to drift in the direction of majoritarianism. But majority rule is not democracy; to identify the two is to confuse the instrument with the premise. Once one identifies the two, he divorces himself from the democratic tradition and enters another which either overtly or covertly asserts that power is its own justification. The essence of this approach to democracy is that the fists of the majority, like Frederick the Great's cannon, are inscribed *ultima ratio regnum*—the ultimate justification of the state.

To the democrat, power is not self-legitimatizing. On the contrary, power is only legitimate to the extent that it forwards certain ethical, philosophical or religious ends. The basic purpose of power is to make possible a maximum development of human potentialities, and this purpose is in turn founded upon the unverifiable assumption that men are capable of rising to a level of unselfish dedication to each other and to the common weal.

Moreover, the democrat is denied the comforting crutch of certainty. While he holds his convictions *on the level of action* firmly enough to die for them on occasion, *on the level of thought* he is constantly engaged in questioning, in searching for better answers. It is his fate to be constantly battling for what he knows to be at best a half-truth, to be making a full action commitment on the basis of incomplete evidence.

To achieve working answers to everyday problems, the democrat accepts majority decisions as binding on the actions of the community. However, no decision is ever final. In the event that new evidence appears, a new trial is in order, and it is the dynamic function of the non-conformist to urge new trials, to submit new evidence, to demand a public hearing for a different view. Thus in a healthy democracy the majority and the nonconformist depend upon each other, and each supplies a vital component to the whole. Stability is provided by the majority, while vitality flows from the nonconformist. Consequently, the democrat protects the rights of the nonconformist not merely as an act of decency, but more significantly as an imperative for himself and the whole society.

This is the idea, and if, as I have suggested, we in the United States have tarnished it somewhat, even tarnished it has a grandeur which no elitist theory can approach. It is toward this great dream of power as the ethical instrument of a self-governing community—not as the whim of a prince, a priest or a proletariat, nor the passions of a majority—that I believe American public policy must be directed.

A major threat to the achievement of this goal seems to me to stem from the enlargement of the political sector. It is characteristic of totalitarian states that no sector of national life can exist free from political control. Everything from stamp clubs and bowling leagues to political parties and pressure groups must pay obeisance to political objectives, must if demanded, purge themselves of Jews, kulaks, Trotskyites or other deviants. The state becomes the only *real* organization, and all other groups are subservient to it. When this occurs, political criteria are injected into judgments where they have no rational meaning: chess players are evaluated in terms of their politics, not their chess; great physicists are condemned for their religion, while their scientific merit goes unevaluated.

The Soviet Union has pushed this tendency almost to its logical conclusion, and faced with worldwide assault from Communism, free societies have been forced to review their own definition of "political." For example, it is patent that 19th Century clichés about freedom of organization cannot suffice to deal with a political party that is also a foreign intelligence service and a potential rebel army. Similarly, insurance companies, sport clubs, trade unions, children's camps, have turned up which defy the classic definition of these organizations by having political rather than private objectives.

Faced with this strange and frightening phenomenon, the American people have moved in two directions to counteract the dangers they fear: first, they have rushed to set up a security program, or programs, based more on principles of vengeance than security; and, second, they have injected political criteria into areas where these principles have no meaning. In short, they have tended to defend themselves by imitating the tactics of the enemy, by enlarging the political sector.

Governments have the right to protect themselves from disloyal servants and I heartily approve of rigid standards of loyalty for all persons in sensitive positions. But our national security programs proceed, by methods that vary from careful scrutiny to malevolent idiocy (*cf.*, Wolf Ladejinsky), to dismiss from governmental positions of every description persons of "doubtful" loyalty.

This is "Getting Commies" with a vengeance, but it does not necessarily add one iota to the security of the United. States. The great bulk of government jobs are of a non-sensitive character and it seems to me that a meaningful security program with respect to these posts would require only old-fashioned civil service techniques with the burden of proof on the United States to demonstrate the malfeasance of the individual.

The second direction in which we have moved is toward applying political criteria in areas where they are senseless, if not pernicious. Many examples of this sort can be found on the American scene: harmonica players are denied a hall because of alleged subversive connections, boxers are required to take loyalty oaths before putting on the gloves, unemployed workers are refused compensation because of ties with Communist unions, etc. Most actions of this sort are merely silly and . . . there is certainly no reign of terror loose in the nation, but silly or not, their cumulative effect is dangerous.

Consequently we should make all possible efforts to limit the political sector. In dealing, for example, with Communist public school teachers, I feel the key level of examination is not that of Party membership, but that of teaching. It is my personal conviction that Communists make bad teachers because of the closed quality of their minds, to say nothing of their penchant for illegitimate extra-curricular activities such as organizing secret student cells, but this proposition is a matter to be tested and adjudicated in individual instances.

The second broad tendency which seems to me to threaten our liberties is what I have called the withering of decency. The assault against Communism has in the United States begun to resemble a campaign against rabid foxes—in word, if not in deed—and many seem to have forgotten a basic truth that can only be overlooked at great peril to an individual and a national soul: that Communists are human beings.

It has always been characteristic of public hysteria, reigns of terror, purges and the like that the enemy is dehumanized; he becomes a *thing*. The basic philosophical and theological case for human slavery from Aristotle down to our own times has rested on the premise that slaves are sub-human, and Hannah Arendt has pointed out the use to which modern totalitarianism has put this sophistry. How totalitarian regimes strip their opposition groups of humanity has also been recorded in such superb literary works as Koestler's *Darkness at Noon*, Orwell's *1984*, and Milosz's *Captive Mind*. Viewed from this perspective, the Moscow Trials were merely the disposal by the Stalinist state of some inadequate tools, that had not fulfilled their tasks properly.

Let us take a case with which I have some personal experience, the "Fifth Amendment librarian" of Plymouth Meeting, Pennsylvania. The background of this case is well known: Mary Knowles pleaded the Fifth Amendment before a Congressional committee some years ago in Boston after having been named by Herbert Philbrick as a Communist. She was dismissed from a public library in Massachusetts, but no indictment was lodged against her for any criminal offense. Moving to Wayne, Pennsylvania, she took a position with a little library run by a Quaker organization, and also in part subsidized from public funds. Her performance as librarian has been from all accounts excellent—there has been no evidence adduced to suggest that she has been using her job to forward the Communist Party.

However, in the neighboring area a group has organized to "get" Mrs. Knowles with the engaging title of "Citizens for Philbrick." I surely have no objections to citizens organizing peacefully for anything they choose, but this group has instituted a real campaign of hate against the librarian—a campaign which was intensified when the Fund for the Republic announced a $5,000 grant to the Quaker Meeting for standing fast against the lynch mob—and will apparently be satisfied with nothing less than her head on a platter. In the course of the affair, it has apparently been overlooked that Mrs. Knowles, a person against whom no criminal accusations have been lodged, is a human being who must eat.

On a broader level, probably no episode has left such a spoor of hate in its wake as the Rosenberg case. When human beings talk of other human beings as "rats"—"Kill the Rats!"—I feel an overpowering urge to abdicate from the human race.

We all know from personal experience how easy it is to be carried away by frenzy and join the haters—the human capacity to hate is proof of a sort for the doctrine of Original Sin—and we all have regretted our dalliance. It is probably to prevent our hasty judgments from haunting us forever that we have built elaborate procedural labyrinths into our law, and it is to prevent such frenzied aberrations from poisoning the future that we have built delay into our political institutions. As the Massachusetts *Body of Liberties* (1641) succinctly put the matter: "Our duty and desire is to do nothing suddainlie which fundamentally concerne us."

However, we cannot expect our institutions alone to preserve our spiritual chastity; on the contrary, these institutions can in the long haul be no stronger than the morality that supports them. This is why it is so important that our political leaders *be* leaders, be willing to stick their necks out in the cause of decency. While I have never been a devotee of Dean Acheson's foreign policy, he stands at the top of my list for his courageous decency. Tactically it was a blunder to state that he would not "turn his back on Alger Hiss," but in a moral sense it was an affirmation of humanity against the blood cultists.

A final aspect of this withering of decency that deserves mention is the tendency that accompanies it to turn life into a conspiracy: No blunder is ever accidental, no policy-maker is ever stupid. This approach to life supplies logical justification for exorcising decency from political relations, for if one assumes that individuals are mere instruments of alien forces, ideological automata, as it were, he is consistent when he treats his enemies as objects to be destroyed. A blunderer in the State Department loses his character as a fallible human being, perhaps deserving dismissal for incompetence, and becomes an enemy Knight on a cosmic chessboard, an object to be eliminated.

In evaluating errors in policy, we should always assume that bad judgment is at fault until it can be conclusively demonstrated to the contrary. In general, we should act upon the assumption that in politics, as in interpersonal relations, the simplest explanation is usually the best. If we abandon this common-sense rule, we enter a universe in which logic triumphs over life and decency is a superfluous, if not a dangerous, quality.

I have concentrated in this article on the two main trends in contemporary American life that seem to me to threaten the long-run development of our liberties. There are, of course, others which a longer analysis would have to take into account, notably the resurgence of direct democracy in the South since the Supreme Court's desegregation holding. It is my conviction that the law-abiding majority in the South will eventually rally to the Constitution and that, perhaps with great delays, white and Negro children will at last be granted full equality. However, before that day dawns, the Negro community in the South is going to have some rough sledding at the hands of the local forces of "law and order." To the extent that "Citizen's Councils" merely agitate against the Constitution—even if their agitation is of a despicable character—they are within their rights, but every resource that the national government can legitimately command should be employed against them if they employ force and violence to subvert the Constitution.

I have attempted an over-all appraisal of the state of American liberties as of 1956. Perhaps because I do not share the conviction of many American historians that the history of the United States has been the unfolding of Anglo-Saxon virtues and the assimilation to them of benighted Irish, Jews, Poles or Asians, I take a somewhat more jaundiced view in these articles of the American past than is customary. As a descendant of immigrants who were *not* greeted by Grover Whalen, but by signs reading "No Irish Need Apply," I may have an unduly prejudiced view of intergroup relations in the 19th Century. But whatever biases I may have, I submit that the evidence is clear: in the United States today, ethnic, political, religious non-conformists have more leeway, have a better life-expectancy, than was ever before the case. As the United States has emerged from the radical internal transformations that accompanied the industrial revolution, we seem to have achieved a new maturity, a willingness to live and let live, and a growing acceptance of legal procedures. As I have suggested . . . , great dangers confront us and those who cherish liberty must fight a many-fronted war if we are to maintain and enlarge our heritage. But in these fights we can draw some comfort from looking back at the great distance we have travelled and from the knowledge that while the American standard may be tattered, we have achieved a level of individual freedom that hundreds of millions of human beings can only conceive of as a remote, impossible aspiration.

Yates v. *United States,* 354 U.S. 298 (1957)

[6–1: Harlan, Douglas, Frankfurter, Warren,
Black, Burton; Clark]

Mr. Justice Harlan delivered the opinion of the Court.

We brought these cases here to consider certain questions arising under the Smith Act which have not heretofore been passed upon by this Court, and otherwise to review the convictions of these petitioners for conspiracy to violate that Act. Among other things, the convictions are claimed to rest upon an application of the Smith Act which is hostile to the principles upon which its constitutionality was upheld in *Dennis* v. *United States.* . . .

II. Instructions to the Jury

Petitioners contend that the instructions to the jury were fatally defective in that the trial court refused to charge that, in order to convict, the jury must find that the advocacy which the defendants conspired to promote was of a kind calculated to "incite" persons to action for the forcible overthrow of the Government. It is argued that advocacy of forcible overthrow as mere *abstract doctrine* is within the free speech protection of the First Amendment; that the Smith Act, consistently with that constitutional provision, must be taken as proscribing only the sort of advocacy which incites to illegal *action;* and that the trial court's charge, by permitting conviction for mere advocacy, unrelated to its tendency to produce forcible action, resulted in an unconstitutional application of the Smith Act. The Government, which at the trial also requested the court to charge in terms of "incitement," now takes the position, however, that the true constitutional dividing line is not between inciting and abstract advocacy of forcible overthrow, but rather between advocacy as such, irrespective of its inciting qualities, and the mere discussion or exposition of violent overthrow as an abstract theory. . . .

There can be no doubt from the record that in so instructing the jury the court regarded as immaterial, and intended to withdraw from the jury's consideration, any issue as to the character of the advocacy in terms of its capacity to stir listeners to forcible action. Both the petitioners and the Government submitted proposed instructions which would have required the jury to find that the proscribed advocacy was not of a mere abstract doctrine of forcible overthrow, but of action to that end, by the use of language reasonably and ordinarily calculated to incite persons to such action. The trial court rejected these proposed instructions on the ground that any necessity for giving them which may have existed at the time the *Dennis* case was tried was removed by this Court's subsequent decision in that case. The court made it clear in colloquy with counsel that in its view the illegal advocacy was made out simply by showing that what was said dealt with forcible overthrow and that it was uttered with a specific intent to accomplish that purpose, insisting that all such advocacy was punishable "whether it is language of incitement or not." . . .

We are thus faced with the question whether the Smith Act prohibits advocacy and teaching of forcible overthrow as an abstract principle, divorced from any effort to instigate action to that end, so long as such advocacy or teaching is engaged in with evil intent. We hold that it does not.

The distinction between advocacy of abstract doctrine and advocacy directed at promoting unlawful action is one that has been consistently recognized in the opinions of this Court. . . .

We need not, however, decide the issue before us in terms of constitutional compulsion, for our first duty is to construe this statute. In doing so we should not assume that Congress chose to disregard a constitutional danger zone so clearly marked, or that it used the words "advocate" and "teach" in their ordinary dictionary meanings when they had already been construed as terms of art carrying a special and limited connotation. . . .

The legislative history of the Smith Act and related bills shows beyond all question that Congress was aware of the distinction between the advocacy or teaching of abstract doctrine and the advocacy or teaching of action, and that it did not intend to disregard it. The statute was aimed at the advocacy and teaching of concrete action for the forcible overthrow of the Government, and not of principles divorced from action. . . .

In failing to distinguish between advocacy of forcible overthrow as an abstract doctrine and advocacy of action to that end, the District Court appears to have been led astray by the holding in *Dennis* that advocacy of violent action to be taken at some future time was enough. It seems to have considered that, since "inciting" speech is usually thought of as something calculated to induce immediate action, and since *Dennis* held advocacy of action for future overthrow sufficient, this meant that advocacy, irrespective of its tendency to generate action, is punishable, provided only that it is uttered with a specific intent to accomplish overthrow. In other words, the District Court apparently thought that *Dennis* obliterated the traditional dividing line between advocacy of abstract doctrine and advocacy of action.

This misconceives the situation confronting the Court in *Dennis* and what was held there. Although the jury's verdict, interpreted in light of the trial court's instructions, did not justify the conclusion that the defendants' advocacy was directed at, or created any danger of, immediate overthrow, it did establish that the advocacy was aimed at building up a seditious group and maintaining it in readiness for action at a propitious time. In such circumstances, said Chief Justice Vinson, the Government need not hold its hand "until the *putsch* is about to be executed, the plans have been laid and the signal is awaited. If Government is aware that a group aiming at its overthrow is attempting to indoctrinate its members and to commit them to a course whereby they will strike when the leaders feel the circumstances permit, action by the Government is required." . . . The essence of the *Dennis* holding was that indoctrination of a group in preparation for future violent action, as well as exhortation to immediate action, by advocacy found to be directed to "action for the accomplishment" of forcible overthrow, to violence as "a rule or principle of action," and employing "language of incitement," . . . is not constitutionally protected when the group is of sufficient size and cohesiveness, is sufficiently oriented towards action, and other circumstances are such as reasonably to justify apprehension that action will occur. This is quite a different thing from the view of the District Court here that mere doctrinal justification of forcible overthrow, if engaged in with the intent to accomplish overthrow, is punishable *per se* under the Smith Act. That sort of advocacy, even though uttered with the hope that it may ultimately lead to violent revolution, is too remote from concrete action to be regarded as the kind of indoctrination preparatory to action which was condemned in *Dennis*. . . .

In light of the foregoing we are unable to regard the District Court's charge upon this aspect of the case as adequate. The jury was never told that the Smith Act does not denounce advocacy in the sense of preaching abstractly the forcible overthrow of the Government. We think that the trial court's statement that the proscribed advocacy must include the "urging," "necessity," and "duty" of forcible overthrow, and not merely its "desirability" and "propriety," may not be regarded as a sufficient substitute for charging that the Smith Act reaches only advocacy of action for the overthrow of government by force and violence. The essential distinction is that those to whom the advocacy is addressed must be urged to *do* something, now or in the future, rather than merely to *believe* in something. At best the expressions used by the trial court were equivocal, since in the absence of any instructions differentiating advocacy of abstract doctrine from advocacy of action, they were as consistent with the former as they were with the latter. Nor do we regard their ambiguity as lessened by what the trial court had to say as to the right of the defendants to announce their beliefs as to the inevitability of violent revolution, or to advocate other unpopular opinions. Especially when it is unmistakable that the court did not consider the urging of action for forcible overthrow as being a necessary element of the proscribed advocacy, but rather considered the crucial question to be whether the advocacy was uttered with a specific intent to accomplish such overthrow, we would not be warranted in assuming that the jury drew from these instructions more than the court itself intended them to convey. . . .

We recognize that distinctions between advocacy or teaching of abstract doctrines, with evil intent, and that which is directed to stirring people to action, are often subtle and difficult to grasp, for in a broad sense, as Mr. Justice Holmes said in his dissenting opinion in *Gitlow*, . . . "Every idea is an incitement." But the very subtlety of these distinctions required the most clear and explicit instructions with reference to them, for they concerned an issue which went to the very heart of the charges against these petitioners. The need for precise and understandable instructions on this issue is further emphasized by the equivocal character of the evidence in this record, with which we deal in Part III of this opinion. Instances of speech that could be considered to amount to "advocacy of action" are so few and far between as to be almost completely overshadowed by the hundreds of instances in the record in which overthrow, if mentioned at all, occurs in the course of doctrinal disputation so remote from action as to be almost wholly lacking in probative value. Vague references to "revolutionary" or "militant" action of an unspecified character, which are found in the evidence, might in addition be given too great weight by the jury in the absence of more precise instructions. Particularly in light of this record, we must regard the trial court's charge in this respect as furnishing wholly inadequate guidance to the jury on this central point in the case. We cannot allow a conviction to stand on such "an equivocal direction to the jury on a basic issue." . . .

III. The Evidence

The determinations already made require a reversal of these convictions. Nevertheless, in the exercise of our power under 28 U.S.C. § 2106 to "direct the entry of such appropriate judgment . . . as may be just under the circumstances," we have conceived it to be our duty to scrutinize this lengthy record with care, in order to determine whether the way should be left open for a new trial of all or some of these petitioners. Such a judgment, we think, should, on the one hand, foreclose further proceedings against those of the petitioners as to whom the evidence in this record would be palpably insufficient upon a new trial, and should, on the other hand, leave the Government free to retry the other petitioners under proper legal standards, especially since it is by no means clear that certain aspects of the evidence against them could not have been clarified to the advantage of the Government had it not been under a misapprehension as to the burden cast upon it by the Smith Act. . . .

Brandenburg v. *Ohio,* 395 U.S. 444 (1969)

(Per Curiam)

The record shows that a man, identified at trial as the appellant, telephoned an announcer-reporter on the staff of a Cincinnati television station and invited him to come to a Ku Klux Klan "rally" to be held at a farm in Hamilton County. With the cooperation of the organizers, the reporter and a cameraman attended the meeting and filmed the events. Portions of the films were later broadcast on the local station and on a national network. The prosecution's case rested on the films and on testimony identifying the appellant as the person who communicated with the reporter and who spoke at the rally. . . .

One film showed 12 hooded figures, some of whom carried firearms. They were gathered around a large wooden cross, which they burned. No one was present other than the participants and the newsmen who made the film. Most of the words uttered during the scene were incomprehensible when the film was projected, but scattered phrases could be understood that were derogatory of Negroes and, in one instance, of Jews. Another scene on the same film showed the appellant, in Klan regalia, making a speech. The speech, in full, was as follows: "This is an organizers' meeting. We have had quite a few members here today which are—we have hundreds, hundreds of members throughout the State of Ohio. I can quote from a newspaper clipping from the Columbus, Ohio Dispatch, five weeks ago Sunday morning. The Klan has more members in the State of Ohio than does any other organization. We're not a revengent organization, but if our President, our Congress, our Supreme Court, continues to suppress the white, Caucasian race, it's possible that there might have to be some re-vengeance taken. We are marching on Congress July the Fourth, four hundred thousand strong. From there we are dividing into two groups, one group to march on St. Augustine, Florida, the other group to march into Mississippi. Thank you."

The second film showed six hooded figures one of whom, later identified as the appellant, repeated a speech very similar to that recorded on the first film. The reference to the possibility of "revengeance" was omitted, and one sentence was added: "Personally, I believe the nigger should be returned to Africa, the Jew returned to Israel." Though some of the figures in the films carried weapons, the speaker did not.

The Ohio Criminal Syndicalism Statute was enacted in 1919. From 1917 to 1920, identical or quite similar laws were adopted by 20 States and two territories. [In *Whitney* v. *California* (1927)], this Court sustained the constitutionality of California's Criminal Syndicalism Act, the text of which is quite similar to that of the laws of Ohio. . . . The Court upheld the statute on the ground that, without more, "advocating" violent means to effect political and economic change involves such danger to the security of the State that the State may outlaw it. . . . But *Whitney* has been thoroughly discredited by later decisions. . . . These later decisions have fashioned the principle that the constitutional guarantees of free speech and free press do not permit a State to forbid or proscribe advocacy of the use of force or of law violation except where such advocacy is directed to inciting or producing imminent lawless action and is likely to incite or produce such action. As we said, . . . "the mere abstract teaching of the moral propriety or even moral necessity for a resort to force and violence, is not the same as preparing a group for violent action and steeling it to such action." . . . A statute which fails to draw this distinction impermissibly intrudes upon the freedoms guaranteed by the First and Fourteenth Amendments. It sweeps within its condemnation speech which our Constitution has immunized from governmental control. . . .

Measured by this test, Ohio's Criminal Syndicalism Act cannot be sustained. The Act punishes persons who "advocate or teach the duty, necessity, or propriety" of violence "as a means of accomplishing industrial or political reform"; or who publish or circulate or display any book or paper containing such advocacy; or who "justify" the commission of violent acts "with intent to exemplify, spread or advocate the propriety of the doctrines of criminal syndicalism"; or who "voluntarily assemble" with a group formed "to teach or advocate the doctrines of criminal syndicalism." Neither the indictment nor the trial judge's instructions to the jury in any way refined the statute's bald definition of the crime in terms of mere advocacy not distinguished from incitement to imminent lawless action.

Accordingly, we are here confronted with a statute which, by its own words and as applied, purports to punish mere advocacy and to forbid, on pain of criminal punishment, assembly with others merely to advocate the described type of action. Such a statute falls within the condemnation of the First and Fourteenth Amendments. The contrary teaching of [*Whitney*] cannot be supported, and that decision is therefore overruled. *Reversed.*

⊞ *E S S A Y S*

The question of whether or not the federal government acted properly in the Cold War communist prosecutions has divided scholars. Most of them, including Michal Belknap, a professor of law at California Western School of Law, have argued that political expediency had much more to do with the anticommunist hysteria than did a legitimate concern with the nation's welfare. Given the recent collapse of communism in the Soviet Union and Eastern Europe, this interpretation, which is advanced in the first essay, has an intuitive appeal because it suggests that the communists were never really a threat.

The political scientist Walter Berns, now a fellow at the American Enterprise Institute, puts the issues of security and liberty differently in the second essay. He suggests that the real lesson to be learned from the anticommunist hysteria is that some persons, Eugene Dennis among them, cannot be trusted to exercise the freedom given to them. From this perspective, the constitutional issue emerges as a question of virtue. Berns differs from Belknap in arguing that some forms of censorship are necessary and that the *right* of anyone to speak depends on his or her ability to promote virtue through that speech. In short, according to Berns, there is not and cannot be an absolute right of individual expression.

Anticommunist Hysteria and Political Persecution

MICHAL BELKNAP

Convinced that the Korean conflict did not justify the ruling against them, [Eugene Dennis and the ten other Communists] quickly informed authorities that they would appeal [their conviction in federal district court] to the Supreme Court. Apparently within the Party leadership there were some who considered mass pressure more likely than further litigation to produce positive results, and the confusing signals sent out by the legal system only complicated this internal debate. First the court of appeals voted two to one to grant a government request for revocation of the convicted Communists' bail. Then Robert Jackson, the Supreme Court justice with responsibility for the Second Circuit, reversed that ruling, allowing the Eleven to remain free while they pressed their appeal. Jackson's colleagues quickly crushed whatever hopes his ruling might have inspired among Stalinists by granting a writ of certiorari to the Eleven but refusing to examine any of the many issues which they had raised except the constitutionality of the Smith Act. Now certain that the high tribunal was just "an instrument in the not-so-cold war," the Party sought to delay final determination of its leaders' fate, focus international attention on the case, and perhaps discredit the Court by asking permission for a British barrister, who already had a conflicting trial date in India, to participate in the oral arguments. The Supreme Court refused to grant the necessary postponement. Unable to turn the case into a labor defense spectacular and apparently convinced that, although capitalist judges were unreliable, the Eleven's only hope now lay in a favorable judicial ruling, the Party finally decided to depend on conventional constitutional adjudication but to bombard the Court with reminders of how "the people" felt the judges ought to rule.

Although its threats that mass protest would greet the wrong decision alienated at least one justice, the Communists had good reason to try some-

Reprinted by permission of Greenwood Publishing Group, Inc., Westport, CT, from Michal R. Belknap, *Cold War Political Justice: The Smith Act, the Communist Party, and American Civil Liberties*, pp. 132–140, 145–146, 240–241, 244–248, 281–282.

thing more than a traditional nonpolitical litigation strategy. Within the past year the Court had handed down the *Douds* decision and also refused to reverse Dennis's contempt-of-Congress conviction. Like its recent rulings, the composition of the high tribunal boded ill for the Communists' cause. Fourteen times during the period 1937–48 the Supreme Court had decided cases on the basis of the clear-and-present-danger test, always ruling against the challenged governmental action, but in the summer of 1949 death had claimed Frank Murphy and Wiley Rutledge, half of the four-man liberal phalanx around which the majorities in those cases had formed. As replacements Truman had named Sherman Minton, a former New Deal Democratic senator from Indiana, grown conservative during eight years on the U.S. Seventh Circuit Court of Appeals, and Tom Clark, the attorney general who had initiated the prosecution of the CPUSA [Communist Party of the United States of America]. Both new justices were far less committed to the protection of civil liberties than the men they replaced, and although Clark would have to disqualify himself in the *Dennis* case, the Communists' chances would have been far better had Murphy and Rutledge still held the seats that he and Minton now occupied.

Sitting with the newcomers were two other Truman appointees unlikely to respond favorably to the appeal, Harold Burton, a former mayor of Cleveland and a buddy of the President during his Senate days, was a moderately conservative Republican who supported libertarian claims more often than Clark and Minton but less frequently than a majority of the Court. Fred Vinson, secretary of the treasury when named chief justice in 1946, was a former Kentucky congressman who had held several lesser economic posts in the executive branch as well as a seat on the Court of Appeals for the District of Columbia. Highly indulgent toward loyalty programs, he was, with respect to civil liberties claims, among the most negative members of the Court, rejecting challenges to federal action in this area more than 90 percent of the time.

Vinson's views contrasted sharply with those of the two remaining members of the once-dominant liberal bloc. Hugo Black, a former senator from Alabama, had joined the Court in 1937 having no judicial experience other than that gained during a brief term on a police court, and under a cloud of suspicion because of his one-time membership in the Ku Klux Klan. But he proved to be both an able judge and a vigorous defender of the Bill of Rights. His liberal associate, William O. Douglas, who had taught law at Yale and served on the Securities and Exchange Commission before ascending to the bench in 1939, had enough status as a Democratic politician to receive serious consideration for the vice-presidential nomination in 1940, 1944, and 1948. Although hostile to communism, he believed passionately in free speech and was likely to give even members of the CPUSA a sympathetic hearing if they raised claims of its denial.

On the ideological ground between Black and Douglas and the four conservatives stood three other survivors of the "Roosevelt Court" of 1937–48: Justices Stanley Reed, Felix Frankfurter, and Robert Jackson. Reed, a Kentuckian, had come to Washington as an attorney for the Hoover administration and had stayed to serve the New Deal, first as counsel for the Reconstruction Finance Corporation and later as solicitor general. Appointed to the Court in 1938, he became a swing man between the liberal and conservative blocs. But in cases involving efforts to combat subversive activities, Reed consistently supported the government.

His ideological position was far easier to define than that of Frankfurter, a former Harvard Law School professor who had helped to found the ACLU [American Civil Liberties Union] and whose personal views on individual rights were so liberal that during his academic days some had considered him a radical. He had joined with other prominent lawyers in publishing a scathing indictment of the Justice Department's conduct during the Palmer raids and later nearly lost his professorial position for championing the cause of Sacco and Vanzetti. Despite his background, on the bench, where he had served since 1939, Frankfurter compiled a distinctly antilibertarian record. The reason was his devotion to the principle of judicial restraint. Believing it was not a judge's place to impose his will on the popularly elected branches of government, he often suppressed his personal feelings and voted to sustain laws he would have opposed had he been a legislator.

Jackson, too, defied easy classification. A justice since 1941, he had joined the Court after service as solicitor general and attorney general. His voting pattern resembled Frankfurter's, but his written opinions were erratic. Likely to influence Jackson's thinking on the Communist case was a deep concern about the capacity of totalitarian groups to seize power in democratic countries, which he had developed while prosecuting Nazi war criminals at Nuremberg.

If the Eleven were to achieve reversal, they needed Jackson's vote, as well as the votes of Black, Douglas, Frankfurter, and Reed. Because Reed seems to have been committed to affirmance from the beginning, the Communist leaders never really had a chance, but their lawyers made a determined effort. Around 20 November they filed a lengthy brief which argued that no one could make it a crime to advocate ideas and exercise the rights of speech, press, and assembly and that, even if advocacy was part of an effort to bring about a substantive evil, the First Amendment protected it, unless there was a clear and present danger. Petitioners went on to argue that the conspiracy section of the Smith Act was independently unconstitutional because, by making it a crime to agree to exercise civil rights at some unspecified time in the future, that provision imposed prior restraint on speech, press, and assembly. Their lawyers also challenged [Judge Harold] Medina's refusal to let the jury consider the clear-and-present-danger question and attacked Hand for changing the meaning of Holmes's classic constitutional test. In addition, petitioners accused the prosecution of attempting to convert the statute, the indictment, and indeed the entire case, from one involving speech, press, and assembly into one involving conduct. Their contention was that the Justice Department had suddenly "discovered," *after* Vinson declared in *Douds* that, although the government might not censor political views, it could impose some incidental burdens on free expression in order to regulate dangerous conduct, that the Eleven's conviction was really not for radical advocacy at all, but for forming fifth columns and recruiting revolutionaries to overthrow the government. Petitioners also insisted that their sympathy for the Soviet Union should not deprive them of the constitutional protection to which they would otherwise be entitled, and asserted that "Affirmance here would merely be a confession of our unwillingness to take the risk of permitting political dissent to be heard. This is a suppression of the democratic process itself." Both the ACLU and the National Lawyers Guild echoed this theme in motions requesting permission to file friend-of-the-court briefs.

The Justice Department, on the other hand, denied that freedom of expression was at issue, maintaining that the Smith Act punished not speech but the formation of fifth columns serving the aggressive purposes of foreign nations. Requiring the government to establish the existence of an imminent and immediate danger, even after Congress had explicitly prohibited utterances of this kind, might be appropriate in dealing with unorganized and irresponsible agitators, the government acknowledged. But, "Applied to these petitioners and their Communist Party, it would mean that the First Amendment protects their preparations until they are ready to attempt a seizure of power, or to act as a fifth column in time of crisis." The Justice Department argued that Soviet-sponsored Communist "aggression and disruption" made the highly disciplined CPUSA a clear and present danger, and denied both that the Smith Act was unconstitutionally vague and that it punished conduct excessively distant from actual armed revolt.

The petitioners countered with a devastating reply brief, which charged the Justice Department with falsely representing this as a case involving a conspiracy to overthrow the government rather than one to teach and advocate doctrine. In talking as if recruitment was the target and subject matter of the Smith Act, the Eleven charged, their opponents had misrepresented the nature of that statute and had ignored its legislative history. They bluntly accused the government of dishonesty.

Three days after receiving their reply brief, the Court heard oral arguments in the case. Solicitor General Philip B. Perlman told the justices that Congress had modeled the Smith Act on the New York statute upheld in *Gitlow* and contended that, because the Court had never overruled that decision, the federal law was obviously constitutional. Resorting to a complete non sequitur, he argued that because Communists would eliminate free speech if they gained power, it was not an issue in this case. Perlman sarcastically brushed aside the clear-and-present-danger test, contending that it applied only when the threat from suppression of speech exceeded that of the evil legislated against. His side did not have to establish the existence of a clear and present danger, the Solicitor General argued, as long as it showed that the Communists intended to overthrow the government when the time was ripe. Perlman's colleague, Irving Shapiro, reiterated the contention that the Eleven had been convicted, not for teaching philosophy and organizing a political party, but for training revolutionaries.

After Irving Saypol, John McGohey's replacement as U.S. attorney in the Southern District, and two Justice Department lawyers also argued for the government, George Crockett, Harry Sacher, and Abraham Isserman replied. Isserman contended that the Smith Act deprived petitioners of their right to due process of law and warned ominously that if the Supreme Court endorsed this statute, federal authorities would employ it against 500,000 Americans. Crockett argued that Medina's failure to submit the clear-and-present-danger issue to the jury violated the Eleven's Sixth Amendment rights. The heart of the Communists' case, however, was Sacher's summation, rated "excellent" by Justice Burton. The meaning of the clear-and-present-danger test, he argued, was that only an immediately threatening emergency could justify the government in abridging freedom of speech.

Sacher's chances of prevailing with this argument were slight, for in Korea Chinese "volunteers" had crossed the Yalu River in strength, smashing General MacArthur's Home-by-Christmas Offensive and sending American troops streaming south in disordered retreat. At home hysteria ran high. Senator Joe McCarthy, the anti-Communist demagogue, was a national hero. When Elizabeth Gurley Flynn's defense committee attempted to buy advertising space for an attack on the Smith Act, even such liberal organs as the *New York Post, New York Times,* and *New Republic* turned it down. This was a bad time to ask the Supreme Court for a dispassionate application of the clear-and-present-danger rule.

On 4 June 1951 the justices announced their decision. The CPUSA had lost badly, beaten by a vote of six to two. Vinson read the official opinion of the Court, a plurality one in which he spoke only for Burton, Minton, Reed, and himself. Although the case apparently had given his clerks some problems, the Chief Justice had not found it a difficult one to decide. To Vinson's way of thinking, "The government had to protect itself against communism. . . . " Consequently, as his former clerk, Howard Trienens, recalls, "if these guys were communists . . . those were not tough decisions for him." "This was the height of the Cold War," and Vinson, who had come to the Court from a wartime administration, still thought like a man mobilizing America for a struggle against the nation's enemies. Decisions involving Communists were for him "Foregone conclusions."

In justifying his disposition of the *Dennis* case, the Chief Justice followed the lead of Learned Hand. Like the court of appeals judge, he approved Medina's instruction that the defendants' conduct was punishable only if they had intended to bring about the violent overthrow of the government as speedily as circumstances would permit. The structure and purpose of the Smith Act, he said, demanded the inclusion of such intent as an element of the crime.

Vinson agreed with Hand that, as interpreted by Medina, the Smith Act was constitutional. Congress, he argued, had an undoubted right to prevent overthrow of the government by violent revolution. The only question was whether the means it had selected—the Smith Act—violated the First and Fifth Amendments. Vinson acknowledged that the statute punished communication but maintained that in previous cases neither the majority nor the dissenters had ever classified free speech as an unlimited and unqualified right. All justices had regarded it as sometimes subordinate to other societal values and considerations. Saving the government from violent overthrow, Vinson believed, was an interest substantial enough to warrant limiting expression. Had the Chief Justice been willing to rely on *Gitlow* and *Whitney*, he could simply have ruled that in passing the Smith Act Congress had recognized this fact and proscribed those utterances which would produce that result, but, like Hand, he felt compelled by recent decisions to employ the clear-and-present-danger rule.

As far as Vinson was concerned, the Holmes test could not mean that before the government might act, it had to wait "until the *putsch* is about to be executed, the plans have been laid and the signal is awaited." If legitimate authority was aware that a group aiming at its destruction was indoctrinating members and committing them to act when the leaders felt circumstances were right, surely the time to deal with the situation had arrived. Whether the proposed rebellion had any chance of success was irrelevant, Vinson said, for an attempt to overthrow the government by force, even if doomed to failure from the outset, was, because of the physical and political danger it would cause, an evil great enough for Congress to combat. The Chief Justice quoted and endorsed as "succinct and inclusive" the words of Learned Hand: "In each case [courts] must ask whether the gravity of the 'evil' discounted by its improbability, justifies such invasion of free speech as is necessary to avoid the danger." Vinson agreed with the courts below that during the period 1945–1948 a situation had existed which met the requirements of the rule. Like Hand, he found the danger in the conspiratorial nature of the Communist Party and the existence of the Cold War. These factors, he felt, had created a situation quite different from anything Holmes and Brandeis had ever confronted.

> The formation by petitioners of such a highly organized conspiracy, with rigidly disciplined members subject to call when the leaders, these petitioners, felt that the time had come for action, coupled with the inflammable nature of world conditions, similar uprisings in other countries, and the touch-and-go nature of our relations with countries with whom petitioners were in the very least ideologically attuned, convince us that their convictions were justified on this score.

Or, as Justice Reed, who endorsed Vinson's opinion, put it, "a teaching of force and violence by such a group as this, . . . is enough at this period of the world's history to make the protection of the First Amendment inapplicable." In other words, it was not so much *what* the Communist leaders planned to say that created a clear and present danger, as it was *who* they were.

Because the conspiracy itself created the threat, the Chief Justice added, there could be no merit in the petitioners' contention that conspiring to advocate, as distinguished from advocacy itself, was constitutionally protected. He then upheld Medina's refusal to refer the clear-and-present-danger question to the jury. As the Chief Justice saw it, whether activities that constituted a violation of the Smith Act fell within an area protected by the Constitution, as opposed to whether the defendants had broken the law or not, was an issue for a judge to decide. Because that was what determining whether a clear and present danger existed involved, the job was obviously a judicial one.

While Frankfurter agreed with Vinson's conclusion that the Communist leaders had been "properly and constitutionally convicted for violation of the Smith Act," he did not wish to associate himself with his colleague's reasoning. Frankfurter disagreed strongly with the policy decisions embodied in the Smith Act, fearing that such a law would silence critics of the government who did not advocate violent revolution but who feared authorities might misinterpret their remarks. Only his rigid devotion to judicial restraint enabled him to uphold the statute. In a concurring opinion Frankfurter proclaimed: "Free speech cases are not an exception to the principle that we are not legislators, that direct policymaking is not our province." He did not like the Smith Act, but that law was within the bounds of reason, and therefore, in his eyes, constitutional.

By acknowledging that a statute, even if valid on its face, might be applied in such a way as to violate the First Amendment, Frankfurter kept the door to judicial review open, but only at the cost of making his deference to legislative policy making look a little threadbare. Like Hand and Vinson, he took judicial notice of the Cold War and concluded that it could "amply justify a legislature in concluding that recruitment of additional members for the Party would create a substantial danger to national security." Perhaps the conspiratorial nature of the CPUSA and the Soviet-American conflict constituted a clear and present peril which could furnish constitutional justification for passage of a law punishing the solicitation of new members for such an organization. But it is hard to see how Frankfurter could rationalize as deference to the legislative will a decision upholding the application of the Smith Act to the Party's activities of the period 1945–48, in view of the fact that the statute did not explicitly mention recruitment and that it had been passed by Congress at a time when both world conditions and Communist policies differed considerably from those of the years covered by the indictment. Another problem with Frankfurter's restraint was that it ignored the great prestige of the Supreme Court and the power of the body to influence the thinking of a nation which worshiped its fundamental charter. By declaring the Smith Act constitutional, he and his colleagues had given that law a prestigious stamp of approval, which could not fail to hinder any legislative efforts to remove it from the statute books.

Jackson, like Frankfurter, filed a concurring opinion. Unable to accept what Vinson had done to the clear-and-present-danger rule, he advocated dismissing Holmes's test as inapplicable and upholding the convictions as though they were not for a speech offense at all, but for conspiring to overthrow the government. Jackson began with the proposition that the clear-and-present-danger test did not apply to conspiracies such as communism. Because Stalinists regarded force as only one of many means to the end they sought, laws that dealt with violent overthrow and were designed to combat anarchists could not, if prosecutors had to establish the existence of a clear and present danger, ever reach them. Homes's rule, Jackson argued, should be preserved pure and unmodified for the kind of situations, involving isolated actions by a few individuals, that had inspired it. Meanwhile, authorities could punish Communists for conspiring against the government. Although Jackson's opinion possessed a certain refreshing candor, his contention that the clear-and-present-danger test had developed out of cases which did not involve conspiracy was demonstrably incorrect. Also, the kind of law he endorsed for use against the CPUSA had a long and an inglorious history as an instrument for the oppression of unpopular groups. Even the justice himself, although convinced it was constitutional, acknowledged that this was an awkward and inept remedy for communism.

Besides the concurring opinions of Jackson and Frankfurter, the *Dennis* case produced two dissents. One, by Justice Black, contended that, in order to uphold the Smith Act and the convictions of eleven radicals, the majority had distorted the clear-and-present-danger test, thus constricting the First Amendment. Far from being too restrictive of governmental power, Black thought, Holmes's test did not go far enough. The Supreme Court, he asserted, had no more right to use its own notions of reasonableness to sustain laws suppressing freedom of speech than to employ those of Congress for that purpose.

Black's fellow libertarian, William O. Douglas, complained that, although this case had been argued as though it involved the teaching of sabotage, espionage, street warfare, and the like, the prosecution had neither introduced evidence of such advocacy nor prosecuted the defendants for seditious conspiracy. Douglas was sharply critical of the majority for rendering freedom of speech dependent, not on what was said, but on the identity of the speaker, and for making intent, rather than content, the crucial element in determining guilt. He found Jackson's opinion even more horrifying than Vinnson's, observing that never until today had anyone seriously thought that the law of conspiracy could be used to turn speech into seditious conduct. Freedom of expression was the rule, he said, and only the likelihood of immediate injury to society could justify its restriction. Whether such a clear and present danger existed was obviously a matter for a jury to decide, but regardless of who made the determination, there should be evidence in the record. There was none here. Of Vinson's efforts to establish the existence of a clear and present danger by taking judicial notice of the Cold War, Douglas remarked acidly that the Court might as well say the petitioners speech was illegal because the USSR and its army were a threat to world peace. What really mattered was the strength and tactical position of the Communists in this country. After recent assaults on them by everyone from labor unions to the attorney general, it was hard for him to see how they could now be so potent and strategically deployed as to necessitate suppressing them for their speech. The CPUSA constituted in his opinion "the most beset, and the least thriving of any fifth column in history." . . .

The Party had suffered a crushing defeat, and so had the First Amendment. The Supreme Court's "revolutionary departure from all previous interpretations of freedom of speech" had created what Aubrey Williams recognized as "a situation fraught with great danger and hazard. . . . " The possibilities for politically motivated abuse of *Dennis* were immense, and as Frankfurter realized, the Hand-Vinson modification of the clear-and-present-danger test could produce harmful results in future cases which had nothing to do with communism. In 1951 the First Amendment no longer meant what it once had. Because of judicial deliberations conducted in a Cold War climate, the right of each American to express his political beliefs now depended rather largely on who he was. As long as the emotions unleashed by Truman's crusade against international communism gripped the country, the legal principle which *Dennis* had established would threaten the liberties of all citizens. Those who realized that communism did not endanger freedom half so much as overreaction to it could only hope with Justice Black "that in calmer times, when present pressures, passions and fears subside, this or some later Court will restore the First Amendment liberties to the high preferred place where they belong in a free society." . . .

[In *Yates* v. *United States*], Communists convicted in Los Angeles had appealed the outcome of a trial which was in almost all respects a happy contrast to the riotous monstrosity at [the federal district court trial] Foley Square. It had generated no warfare between court and counsel, and, at least until after the jury returned a verdict, Judge Mathes had treated the defendants quite fairly. After reviewing his conduct of the trial, the Ninth Circuit Court of Appeals pronounced it impeccable and upheld the convictions in almost mechanical fashion.

According to that tribunal's Judge James Alger Fee, whose disposition of the case ignited Communist protests in Berkeley, San Francisco, and Los Angeles, the most impressive thing about *Yates* . . . was the fact that the Supreme Court had already ruled on almost all of the assignments of error presented by appellants. The principles that the main and concurring opinions in *Dennis* had laid down were, he felt, virtually conclusive in this case. Although the court of appeals saw no new issues in *Yates*, the Supreme Court nevertheless agreed to review the case, largely because it offered a way for justices concerned about the excesses of the anti-Communist crusade to limit the Smith Act prosecutions without having to take the embarrassing step of directly overruling *Dennis*. . . .

The Court's decision did not come until the following spring. On 17 June, "Red Monday" to some, the justices electrified the country with a cluster of opinions striking hard at McCarthyism. . . . By a six-to-one vote, it freed five of the California Communists and ordered new trials for the rest. Justice Brennan and an even more recent Eisenhower appointee, Charles E. Whittaker, both of whom had ascended to the high bench too late to participate in all stages of the case, took no part in the decision. Only Justice Clark dissented.

The official opinion of the Court, written by Harlan, had the complete support of only two other justices, Earl Warren and Felix Frankfurter. The votes of Harland and the Chief Justice were predictable products of their growing personal reaction against McCarthyism. That of Frankfurter was more surprising, for he had, of course, been part of the majority in *Dennis*.

But, while voting with Vinson in the earlier case, Frankfurter had not considered his opinion a binding precedent for the future. By 1957 the excesses of the anti-Communist crusade, so disturbing to Warren and Harlan, had shaken him too, converting his reluctant support for the Smith Act into quiet opposition. In an early 1955 exchange of letters with Erwin Griswold, Frankfurter revealed how upsetting he found the activities of Senator McCarthy. The fact that the rest of the federal judiciary had responded to *Dennis* by enlisting in the Justice Department's war on the CPUSA also disturbed him. By the fall of 1951, Frankfurter had become convinced of the need to impress upon the lower courts the fact that they "must not treat defendants even under the Smith Act prosecutions as though they were an indiscriminate lump, and especially as though their guilt were already assumed." Although he apparently agreed with his colleagues' refusal to grant certiorari in the *Flynn* and Baltimore cases, by the time the Pittsburgh and Los Angeles defendants requested review, his attitude had changed. The Pennsylvania record struck him as completely inadequate to justify conviction, particularly as it gave little indication that the Party had any immediate plans to overthrow the government by force and violence; thus Frankfurter decided that reversal was in order. The problem was singling out "any specific point" that would justify it. He set his clerks to work on this problem, and, after examining several possibilities, they and the justice apparently decided that the admission of certain statements by alleged co-conspirators offered the most plausible basis for the decision he wished to make. When the government raised the issue of possible perjury, it became possible to dispose of the case without reaching its merits. While welcoming this opportunity, Frankfurter, along with Burton and Harlan, opposed granting the defendants a new trial. What they wanted was a district court investigation of the perjury allegations. Frankfurter remained deeply concerned about the type of evidence the Justice Department was using in Smith Act cases and wanted stiffer standards imposed upon it.

In *Yates* Harlan produced an opinion that satisfied his desires. Long, complex, and painfully dull, it made difficult reading, even for a lawyer, but it was a model of scholarship and technical precision. With this opinion, Harlan managed to erect new safeguards for freedom of expression, while avoiding a wrenching reversal of *Dennis*. He and Frankfurter were judicial conservatives who earlier had defended the Smith Act; therefore, although they wished to reverse the convictions and check abusive use of that law, they could not employ short simple constitutional arguments to accomplish their objectives. Frankfurter and his clerks had discussed the possibility of reversing the Pittsburgh convictions because of the absence of an immediate revolutionary threat, but they had to reject the idea, because such a decision would have involved a retreat from *Dennis*. Just as Frankfurter's earlier insistence that the Smith Act represented a permissible congressional policy choice limited what he could do not, Harlan, as the author of the Second Circuit's *Flynn* decision, also worked in the shadow of his past professions. Whatever its stylistic weaknesses, his *Yates* opinion was a masterful piece of reasoning, admirably suited to disguise a change in outlook and allow its author and Frankfurter to maintain at least the illusion of consistency.

Harlan began his discussion with the organization issue and determined that "since the Communist Party came into being in 1945, and the indictment was not returned until 1951, the three-year statute of limitations had run on the 'organizing' charge and required the withdrawal of that part of the indictment from the jury's consideration." Under this interpretation, at the time of its adoption a key provision of the Smith Act would not have applied to the CPUSA, but Harlan insisted that the legislative history of the statute did not indicate that Congress had written the clause in question with particular reference to the Party. The justice rejected the contention that Mathes's misinterpretation of "organize"was a harmless error, because the trial judge's charge was not, in his opinion, clear and specific enough to support the conclusion that the jury had found the defendants guilty of conspiring to teach and advocate, as well as to organize. There was no way to determine, Harlan said, whether the jurors had believed the overt act which they were legally required to find was in furtherance of one objective or the other. Hence the Court had to set aside the verdict.

Harlan found another reason for reversal in Mathes's failure to instruct the jury that in order to convict it must find the defendants had conspired to promote advocacy aimed at producing conduct rather than commitment. The question was, he said, "whether the Smith Act prohibits advocacy and teaching of forcible overthrow as an abstract principle, divorced from any effort to instigate action to that end, so long as such advocacy or teaching is engaged in with evil intent. We hold," he announced for the Court, "that it does not." Although the government claimed to have relied on *Dennis*, Harlan contended that it had misinterpreted the 1951 decision, for although Vinson had said the Smith Act was directed at advocacy, rather than discussion, "it is clear that the reference was to advocacy of action, not ideas. . . . " A speaker might violate that law by urging his listeners to act at some distant time, Harlan said, but, while immediacy was not a necessary element of the crime, incitement was. "The essential distinction is that those to whom the advocacy is addressed must be urged to *do* something, now or in the future, rather than merely to *believe* in something." In the massive record before him, he found few instances of speech which would amount to advocacy of action.

Having made two determinations, each of which required reversal, the Supreme Court could simply have remanded the case for a new trial. Instead, the justices scrutinized the record to determine whether they should leave the way open for the government to retry some or all of the defendants. The result of this examination was a conclusion that against Richmond, Connelly, Rose Chernin Kusnitz, Frank Spector, and Henry Steinberg the evidence was clearly insufficient. The Smith Act prosecutions had always depended upon an equation between the teaching of Marxism-Leninism and advocacy of violent overthrow of the government as a principle of action, but, in Harlan's opinion, the evidence here proved only that the CPUSA taught abstract doctrine. The government had established nothing about these five defendants other than that they were officers and members of the Communist Party. Given the terms of section 4(f) of the Internal Security Act, there was simply no legal proof that could link them to a conspiracy to teach and advocate revolution as a rule of action. The Court, therefore, ordered their acquittal. According to Harlan, the record did contain evidence of incidents involving the other nine defendants which might be shown to constitute such teaching and advocacy. While doubtful that this could be done, he was not prepared to say at this stage of the case that it was impossible, nor to forbid the retrial of those Communists under proper legal standards. Clearly, though, his expectation was that the Justice Department would not again obtain convictions.

Although joining Harlan in voting to reverse, Harold Burton and Hugo Black filed separate opinions. Burton, like Frankfurter, had moved from the *Dennis* majority to the *Yates* one, but he had done so only because of his exasperation with Mathes's charge, and he wanted to make it clear that in his view the Court had misinterpreted "organize." Black, speaking also for Douglas, agreed with Harlan's treatment of that issue, but not with his handling of the advocacy problem. As far as the Alabama libertarian was concerned, any conviction for agreeing to advocate, as distinguished from agreeing to act, violated the First Amendment, even if the conspirators planned to urge action, rather than merely belief. In Black's opinion, the Court should have freed all fourteen defendants.

The only dissenter, Tom Clark, argued that the evidence in this case paralleled and was just as strong as that in *Dennis* and—doubtless a reminder to Justice Harlan—*Flynn* as well. He believed the Court should affirm the convictions, but if his colleagues insisted upon reversing them, Clark contended, they ought not arrogate to themselves the responsibility for acquitting defendants. That was a jury's job. Although convinced that the government should have another chance to make a case against the California Communists, the former attorney general conceded that, under the theories which the Court had announced, it was doubtful whether on remand the prosecution could muster sufficient evidence to obtain new convictions.

It was clear to the man who had launched the Smith Act prosecutions nine years earlier that his colleagues had dealt a devastating blow to the Justice Department's war on the Communist Party. In 1951 the Supreme Court had given federal prosecutors a green light; now the high tribunal had changed the color to red. "It is difficult," wrote University of Illinois political scientist Jack Peltason, "not to agree with Justice Clark's intimation that in fact the decision reverses, or at least severely restricts the sweep of, the *Dennis* Doctrine." This was something of an overstatement, for the new opinion was not legally inconsistent with the old, and, had the Court applied its 1957 standards to the 1951 case, the result could still have been affirmance. Yet history would validate the judgment of the student commentator for the *University of Minnesota Law Review,* who concluded after *Yates* that "little remains of the Smith Act with reference to Communists."

The Supreme Court had wrecked the instrument which six years earlier it had honed into a potent weapon for war against the CPUSA. The reason for its change of outlook was readily apparent at that time. The Sunday after Harlan read his opinion, E. W. Kenworthy of the *New York Times* reported from Washington that observers there agreed the decision reflected "the great changes in political climate at home and abroad, since Chief Justice Vinson wrote the Dennis opinion." To most of those who sat on the Supreme Court, methods used to attack domestic communism, which were regarded as appropriate and even necessary at a time when the Cold War between the United States and Russia was at its most frigid, now seemed far more menacing to American democracy than did the CPUSA. Even those justices committed to judicial restraint felt compelled to resist such tactics. By relying upon statutory interpretation, the Court avoided an open constitutional attack upon the Smith Act, but Harlan's subtleties were nearly as lethal as outright invalidation. The Smith Act still lived, but it was now a helpless cripple. . . .

Fortunately for the nation, despite the dangerous potential of the *Dennis* decision, American liberty managed to survive the challenge of a bad law. Even though the emotions generated by the Cold War were powerful and made the Smith Act for a time irresistible, in the end the nation's devotion to its fundamental values proved even stronger. The bar and the Supreme Court, official guardians of the Constitution, were slow to rise to its defense, but when they did, the public responded favorably, following their lead rather than that of the national security alarmists in Congress and the professional anti-Communists in the Department of Justice.

Although the Smith Act is still on the statute books, because of the *Yates* [decision] there is little likelihood that the government will again employ its conspiracy, advocacy, or membership provisions against a dissident organization. But America has not renounced political justice, and the attitudes that produced this law and demanded its use against a hapless radical sect are fully capable of fashioning other instruments of repression. As long as the devotion to fundamental freedoms which thwarted the Smith Act remains strong, there is little cause for concern, but whenever it fades, other Americans will surely share the fate of the Cold War Communist Party.

Free Speech Belongs to the Virtuous

WALTER BERNS

Dennis v. *United States*

Speech itself has not only become a problem in the United States, but, with the passage in 1940 of the Smith Act, a new dimension has been added to the law of the Constitution. Not only has Congress made some speech illegal,

From *Freedom, Virtue & the First Amendment* by Walter Berns, pp. 200–207, 247–253, 255–257. Copyright © 1957 by Louisiana State University Press.

but the Supreme Court has now blessed a statute that outlaws the mere advocacy of ideas. In effect, Congress has legislated against the expression of certain *beliefs*, against disloyalty as an idea; it is now a crime to be disloyal in thought as well as deed. Or in Professor Meiklejohn's terms, it is a criminal offense to hold certain "ideas about the common good." The people's representatives have so ruled. In its opinion in *Dennis* v. *United States,* which upheld the validity of the Smith Act, the Court attempted to merge past and present in a new version of the danger test and thus provide a semblance of continuity to the law of the First Amendment, but no one was deceived by this maneuver, least of all the libertarians who joined in a chorus of indignant protest against the decision.

Eugene Dennis, General Secretary of the American Communist Party, and ten other leaders of the Party were indicted for violation of the conspiracy provisions of the Smith Act of 1940. They were charged with willfully and knowingly conspiring "(1) to organize as the Communist Party of the United States of America a society, group and assembly of persons who teach and advocate the overthrow and destruction of the Government of the United States by force and violence, and (2) knowingly and willfully to advocate and teach the duty and necessity of overthrowing and destroying the Government of the United States by force and violence." They were found guilty and with one exception sentenced to five years in prison and a fine of $10,000 each. This conviction was affirmed by the Court of Appeals for the Second Circuit in an opinion in which Judge Learned Hand wrote still another version of the danger test, a version which was to be accepted by the Supreme Court.

In reviewing the case, the Supreme Court limited its consideration to two questions: whether Sections 2 and 3 of the Smith Act, inherently or as construed and applied, violate the First Amendment and other provisions of the Bill of Rights, and secondly, whether either section inherently or as construed and applied violates the First and Fifth Amendments because of indefiniteness.

Thus, the Court did not review the sufficiency of the evidence against the petitioners or the conduct of the trial; its concern lay solely with the constitutionality of Sections 2 and 3 of the Smith Act. There can be no quarrel with this, for, if the activity of the Communist Party leaders does not violate this statute, it is only because our legislators lacked the necessary skill to draft such a statute. The intent of the law is to make Communism a crime, because it is impossible to be a leader of the Communist Party, or for that matter, a rank and file member who knows what Communism is, and not advocate the desirability of overthrowing the government by force and violence.

It is, for our purposes, relatively unimportant to consider the character of the trial or the sufficiency of the evidence adduced by the government: Congress intended the law to be used against such men as these. "It shall be unlawful for *any* person to knowingly and willfully advocate . . . the desirability . . . of overthrowing or destroying any government in the United States by force and violence." Whatever the evidence produced by the government in the trial court, and that is no concern of ours here, anyone who knows anything about Communism knows that no person, except a fool, can be a Communist without violating this statute.

If the Smith Act had made it illegal to conspire to overthrow the government by force and violence, it would have been relevant to consider the conspiratorial and seditious activities of the Communist Party; but the Smith Act does not do this. It makes it illegal to *teach* and *advocate* the desirability of overthrowing the government by force and violence, which means that a Communist is guilty merely because of his adherence to Communism. Not only Party leaders, but rank and file members as well can be reached with this law. Are they not all part of the vanguard of the proletariat? Is it not a necessary tenet of faith with them that no ruling class ever abdicates willingly, and that the dictatorship of the proletariat can only follow a revolution? Did not Lenin denounce Kautsky for bourgeois deviation on this very point?

The only question presented in the Dennis case is whether Congress can outlaw political beliefs, which in the case of Communism, cannot be separated from the necessity of political action. This is the question raised by the Dennis case. In Frankfurter's words: "In enacting a statute which makes it a crime for the defendants to conspire to do what they have been found to have conspired to do, did Congress exceed its constitutional power?" This is not the sort of question raised in *Schenck* v. *United States*, the case that gave birth to the danger test.

The Espionage Act of 1917 under which Schenck was sentenced did not declare any belief illegal, or even any speech illegal; it declared it illegal to "obstruct the recruiting or enlistment service." Schenck's leaflets were deemed to constitute a clear and present danger of bringing about the event which Congress sought to prevent and had a right to prevent. But the Smith Act declares mere advocacy illegal; in effect, Congress has officially declared a permanent state of clear and present danger. In the light of such facts, how is it possible for the courts to weigh the constitutionality of the Smith Act with the danger test?

For all those who have protested its distortion in the Dennis case, it is necessary to recall what the test was originally: "The question in every case is whether the words used are used in such circumstances and are of such a nature as to create a clear and present danger *that they will bring about the substantive evils that Congress has a right to prevent.*" The constitutionality of the statute was assumed so far as the danger test was concerned. In the Schenck case Congress sought to prevent obstruction of the recruiting service, and no one denied this power to Congress. *Then* the danger test was applied and it was found that Schenck's leaflets created a clear and present danger of such obstruction. The test was not a test of the constitutionality of the statute, and when, in their Gitlow dissent, a case involving a state law almost identical with the Smith Act, Holmes and Brandeis urged the use of the danger test, they paved the way for the subsequent misapplication of the test in *Thornhill* v. *Alabama*. It was the effect of this misapplication that plagued the Court in the Dennis case.

Consider the situation. Suppose either a jury or the trial court had found no clear and present danger, would it have been possible to make such a finding without declaring the Smith Act unconstitutional? It is not likely. And the only way this conclusion can be escaped is to argue that Congress passed the Act in order to have it available in dangerous times, and that one part of the judicial function is to see to it that the Act is not applied in nondangerous times or circumstances: " . . . the Holmes-Brandeis philosophy insisted that where there was a direct restriction upon speech, a 'clear and present danger' that the substantive evil would be caused was necessary before the statute in question could be constitutionally applied." As we indicated earlier in discussing the rationale by which the literal meaning of the First Amendment is avoided, it is possible to make this argument in the case of some statutes, but to do so with the Smith Act would require a distortion of the plain meaning of the Act. What is the evil that Congress sought to prevent when it passed the Smith Act? It is *not* the overthrow of the government by force and violence; it *is* the advocacy of this idea. The Act does not say that such advocacy is bad only when there is a danger that it will lead to the overthrow, but it does say that such advocacy, like heresy of old, is always bad. Congress has legislated against certain beliefs, and the only question left for legal consideration in a case in which the defendants hold these beliefs is whether Congress has exceeded its powers by outlawing these beliefs.

But even if the Supreme Court or one of the lower courts applied the danger test and found no danger and the statute therefore invalid, such a function is no part of a jury's job. Juries are not supposed to find acts of Congress unconstitutional. The only possible use, therefore, to which the danger test can be put in this situation is to rule against the application of the Act to these particular defendants at this particular time, but to do this with the Smith Act would contravene the plain intent of the Act. Critics of the decision who have insisted that the application of the danger test is a function of the jury have not considered this fact. These petitioners were guilty of violating the Smith Act; the only question is whether the Smith Act violates the Constitution. Justice Black faced up to this when he said: "I would hold Section 3 of the Smith Act . . . unconstitutional on its face and as applied."

This, very briefly, is the case of *Dennis* v. *United States*, in which for the first time in our history it has been declared unlawful to hold certain ideas concerning the common good. The case represents the end of a one-way street for our liberal justices who have regarded free speech as a right of American citizenship, for it is difficult (although not impossible) to conceive of the Court after the Dennis decision invalidating any act of Congress touching the First Amendment. Much has been written about the decision, mostly in disagreement with it, and only a few benighted persons have seen fit to praise it. There is very little worthy of any man's praise in *Dennis* v. *United States*, to say nothing of the situation that gave rise to it; the five opinions written in the course of disposing of the case reveal subterfuge, confusion, anger, and sorrow, but hardly a flickering of wisdom. But *Dennis*

v. *United States* might possibly contain a lesson worth our while to find and reflect upon.

Certainly this decision is a restriction on the freedoms heretofore enjoyed by American citizens of all political persuasions; it is quite possible, although not necessary, that it will result in less freedom for non-Communist citizens. But before venting our accumulated spleen on the Court majority that permitted this result, it is wise to remember with Frankfurter that "on any scale of values which we have hitherto recognized, speech of this sort ranks low." It ought to rank low, and does in fact rank low on any "scale of values" except that which ranks freedom first.

> Full and free discussion has indeed been the first article of our faith. We have founded our political system on it. It has been the safeguard of every religious, political, philosophical, economic, and racial group amongst us. . . . This has been the one single outstanding tenet that has made our institutions the symbol of freedom and equality. . . . We have wanted a land where our people can be exposed to all the diverse creeds and cultures of the world.

Such a "faith" can be admired; so can the undoubted sincerity and the consistency with which Justice Douglas has stated and fought for it. But as with all faiths unsupported by reason, the libertarian faith in full and free discussion is vulnerable to being contradicted by practice as well as by reflection upon its unwarranted presuppositions. It may be that by taking one's bearings from a past in which, happily, perhaps unhappily, this nation was spared the necessity of raising fundamental questions, Justice Douglas, as well as other professors of the liberal faith, has reached conclusions untenable in the light of our present situation; and it is possible that these fundamental questions are more readily visible in our time. . . .

There is of course no necessity that law will succeed; success will depend on many factors, not the least important of which is the character of the men who make the law, who govern. To get good government means to get consent to good governors, and this is *the* political problem. To recognize it is not to solve it, but our ability to maintain freedom depends on the extent to which we do solve it.

From Hobbes and Locke and their successors, we have inherited a method of looking at political problems that obscures these problems while replacing political insight with partisan commitment. But the particular objects of this commitment have become problems in themselves; the once clear goals of liberal, or bourgeois, partisanship are questioned today: freedom of speech, as well as freedom of contract, and partiuclarly the idea of progress. It is time that our jurisprudence question them.

Conclusion

American constitutional law regarding free speech and press has tended to proceed on the assumptions that free speech and press is a *right* and that virtue could be ignored by the Court, that the rightness or wrongness of speech or of the beliefs it expressed was immaterial to a just solution of controversies. The practice has been to assert that the danger test should be applied to wide categories of cases regardless of the merits or dignity of the speech involved. Speech bad by any reasonable standard would be accorded the same constitutional standing as the best speech, and the two extremes, the best and the worst, would be subject to the same limitations, limitations related to the danger of the overthrow of American government.

At this writing, however, the status, even the meaning of the danger test is uncertain. What had been a judicial principle used with moderation by its originators, a kind of reminder to the Court to be prudent, became a shibboleth in the hands of the extreme libertarians. . . .

The fault of judicial practice lies in its being based on faulty theory: the theory that freedom of speech is a basic right, or even a natural right, which is everyman's birthright simply because he is born into the world. Whereas the first liberal took his departure from the right of self-preservation and constructed his idea of the only just civil society on this foundation stone; and John Locke added to the Hobbesian right of self-preservation the idea of comfortable self-preservation, which was expressed as the natural right to acquire property; the libertarians argue that the only just civil society is based on a quasi-natural right to speak and publish freely. The very men who make this assertion were among the most vociferous opponents of the late nineteenth- and early twentieth-century version of Lockean natural right.

Now it would seem that every argument they used against the laissez-faire attitude exhibited by the property Courts and the generally acknowledged injustices produced by these Courts, would be equally applicable, *mutatis mutandis,* to their assertions that the freedoms of speech, press, and religion are basic and absolute rights. This question should not be examined by comparing the importance of speech and property to the American democracy, although such a comparison is by no means irrelevant, but by asking whether citizens may hold absolute rights of any sort against government.

In practice, of course, the Court has generally acknowledged that the freedom of speech is not absolute—contrary assertions are generally made under the immunity afforded by the dissenting position. But, and this is the decisive point, the liberals have proceeded *as if* the First Amendment freedoms were absolute. This is the basis of the preferred position doctrine, and it means that all limitations on the freedoms of speech and press are, in effect, movements away from the absolute right position, but never so far from that position to escape the gravitational pull of the absolutist sun. The effect of this has been to regard the facts in speech case, if not with a bias, at least with attention so diverted that relevant aspects of the cases escape adequate consideration.

So long as the judge holds that freedom of speech, press, and religion are basic rights or matters in which government cannot concern itself, there is no room for a consideration of the dignity and value of the particular speech, press, or religion. Prudence is excluded; justice difficult to obtain;

and decency irrelevant. Instead, "the character of the *right* involved" determines the standards governing the case.

Even the danger test was influenced by the absolute right idea, and lent itself to subsequent misusage at the hands of doctrinaire judges. The difficulty with even the original formulation of the test is twofold: in the first place, it cannot be adapted to a time fraught with continual danger, such as the present situation. In such a time the government must overprotect itself. In the second place, by not distinguishing between good and bad speech, the legal rules and precedents are couched in "value-free" terms, to use the modern vernacular; and when that case arrives, as arrive it will, when speech must be limited, the resulting decision may act as a precedent against freedom for good speech even though the limitation was necessitated by bad speech. All this is merely to say that, try as they will, judges are not and cannot be aloof from moral considerations. Judges cannot be amoral because law is not amoral. Amoral law is bad law. Law that attempts to regulate the distribution of power without regard to the use to which that power is put is law for automatons, not people. One cannot say that a law that grants people the freedom to speak is a good law unless he examines what people do with that freedom. Or, a legal principle that defines justice as the maximum amount of personal freedom compatible with security ignores, what common sense does not ignore, that a secure nation may not be worth living in—no matter how much freedom exists.

Eugene Dennis has no *right* to free speech simply because he is a citizen of the United States: no citizen has a *right* to free speech, whatever the Court has said to the contrary in the past or will say in the future. The Court has taken its bearings from speech as a right because, no doubt, of the words of the First Amendment, which seem to require such an interpretation, but this procedure led the Court to a *cul de sac* in the Dennis case from which no member was able to extricate them. That decision cannot be squared with any interpretation yet given the First Amendment, for Dennis had not incited to riot, used fighting words, indulged in obscenity or defamatory speech, or uttered anything that could be said to constitute a clear and present danger to the nation. But he went to jail. To send him to jail the Court had to change the meaning of the First Amendment, but, if we continue to insist that the First Amendment is more than a prohibition of previous censorship, its only reasonable definition would read: Congress shall extend freedom to all good speech. For the guiding question should not be, from whom and under what circumstances is a "right" to be free speech withdrawn, but rather, *to whom is the freedom of speech granted.* The most immediately forthcoming answer to this question is: freedom is extended to those we can trust not to misuse the privilege. And it would be our problem, just as it is our problem today, to see to it that the government provides the terms "good speech" and "good use" with reasonable definitions. But since the First Amendment no longer lends itself readily to this interpretation, perhaps the best we can do is to interpret it to read: Congress shall make no law abridging the freedom of *good* speech. The basic point is that the purpose of law is and must be to promote virtue, not to guarantee rights of *any* description.

The complete absence of all forms of censorship, as well as the complete absence of any legislation touching the free use of private property, is theoretically untenable and practically infeasible. Men do live together, and living together, to say nothing of living well together, carries certain responsibilities. One Thoreau serves a salutary purpose; many more than one may require intervention by government. We must be clear about the duty of government to intervene; that neither nonpayment of taxes nor disloyalty, nor freedom of contract, is a right that the government must honor. Where these privileges exist, it is with the sufferance of government.

Civil society is possible under a system of absolute suppression of all heretical opinion. We have seen it. Civil society is impossible if every man retains an absolute freedom of opinion. The proper course for government, once we are clear on these extremes, is to follow the advice of ancient wisdom and so educate our citizens that suppression and persecution become unnecessary and, since moral education requires some censorship, to avoid rulers who appoint censors like Herr Goebbels the tyrant and John Winthrop the bigot. The virtuous man, no matter how convinced he is of his own wisdom, acts on it with moderation; bigotry is also a vice. Censors are not likely to be any more virtuous than the men who appoint them, and if the men who appoint them—the elected officials in a democracy—are bigots or demagogues, bigotry and demagoguery will prevail over virtue and freedom, no matter what the Supreme Court does.

This study has been critical of the manner in which the Supreme Court has handled First Amendment cases, and critical too of the liberal notion of law, which is the basis of our jurisprudence. If this criticism is justified and if the liberal approach to the problem of freedom and virtue has lacked true political knowledge, what is to be done? If not the danger test and preferred position, what? If the principles and rules used by the Court should be discarded, with what are they to be replaced?

The purpose of this study has not been to offer answers to replace the answers of the liberals. The purpose has been to show that the liberals have been answering without knowing what the true questions are. The liberals' questions (that is, how can we save our liberties in the Cold War era?) are not the right questions; they assume answers to more basic questions; they are partisan answers to unexamined questions. Much will have been achieved if instead of these partisan questions we provide better questions, for to ask the right questions is to understand the problem. To understand a problem truly is a legitimate goal of political inquiry, and the results of this particular inquiry are not wholly negative.

It is worth remembering, for example, that the problem of freedom cannot be severed from *the* political problem. The political problem, more visible at some times than at others, is how to get consent to wise decisions or wise leadership. In a democracy this means how to educate, how to form the characters of citizens so that they will give their consent to wise leadership and withhold it from fools, bigots, and demagogues. The solution to the problem of freedom cannot be found in a test to replace the danger test; the solution to the problem of maintaining free government, government under which men are permitted to speak freely, lies in citizenship education, moral education. It is ironic that liberals, who argue so vehemently for free government and free speech, cut themselves off from the very means by which they can attain them and maintain them. They do this by denying that government may legitimately concern itself with moral education. They should study the reasons once given for the knowledge that the formation of character is the principal duty of government. The right education is ultimately much more decisive for good government, for free government, than any of the mechanical arrangements, such as the separation of powers, in which we Americans have traditionally placed our trust. But the separation of powers can be made to play its part. . . .

The problem we have discussed in these pages is not really the problem of free speech at all; it is the problem of virtue. Under the influence of liberal theory, we have denied or overlooked what ancient wisdom declares to be the primary function of law: the formation of character. For, not only are the liberal efforts to devise legal formulas, such as the clear and present danger test, ignorant of the dimensions of the problem, but liberalism compounds the error by attempting to deny the law of its primary function. . . . The fact is, freedom is not enough—even Rousseau knew that. Civil society requires mutual trust, and if the community is made up of citizens who trust one another, there can be freedom of speech and opinion. But only if the community is made up predominantly of citizens of *good character* who trust one another, is freedom not only possible but desirable. It is not always desirable, for, to refer again to Professor Latham's analogy, Gresham's Law can operate in the area of speech and opinion as well as in the area of money. We have seen it. It can operate to the extent to which a community lacks the moral character to reject demagogic and vicious speech.

In saying that government should seek to attain justice and promote the virtue of citizens as a part of attaining justice, we are not unaware of the practical difficulties involved. There is the danger that censors are much the same now as they were in Milton's day. Nor, it should be clear, do we disagree with the Holmes-Brandeis dissent in the Abrams case; limitations on the freedom to speak easily become persecution. . . .

Life would be insufferable if we were permitted to preach only what we could practise, or even consistently practise. We cannot practise everything we preach all the time, but this in no way detracts from the validity of freedom as a goal, freedom to do good and speak the truth, freedom in this sense as a "standard maxim" for American society: a maxim "familiar to all and revered by all; constantly looked to, constantly labored for, and even though never perfectly attained, constantly approximated, and thereby constantly spreading and deepening its influence and augmenting the happiness and value of life to all people of all colors everywhere." . . .

⊞ *F U R T H E R   R E A D I N G*

Henry J. Abraham, *Freedom and the Court: Civil Liberties and Civil Rights in the United States*, 5th ed. (1988)

Chester J. Antieu, "*Dennis* v. *United States:* Precedent, Principle, or Perversion?" *Vanderbilt Law Review* 5 (1952): 141–149

Michal Belknap, ed., *American Political Trials* (1981)

David Carter, *The Great Fear: The Anti-Communist Purge Under Truman and Eisenhower* (1978)

Walter Goodman, *The Committee: The Extraordinary Career of the House Committee on Un-American Activities* (1968)

Morton Grodzins, *The Loyal and the Disloyal* (1956)

Gerald Gunther, "Learned Hand and the Origins of Modern First Amendment Doctrine: Some Fragments of History," *Stanford Law Review* 27 (1975): 719–773

Alan Harper, *The Politics of Loyalty: The White House and the Communist Issue, 1946–1952* (1968)

Stanley I. Kutler, *The American Inquisition: Justice and Injustice in the Cold War* (1982)

Charles Martin, *The Angelo Herndon Case and Southern Justice* (1976)

Wallace Mendelson, "Clear and Present Danger—From *Schenck* to *Dennis*," *Columbia Law Review* 52 (1952): 313–333

Robert Mollen, "Smith Act Prosecutions," *University of Pittsburg Law Review* 26 (1965): 705–748

Paul Murphy, *The Constitution in Crisis Times, 1918–1969* (1972)

C. Herman Pritchett, *Civil Liberties and the Vinson Court* (1954)

Frank R. Strong, "Fifty Years of 'Clear and Present Danger': From Schenck to Branderburg—and Beyond," *Supreme Court Review* (1969): 41–80

CHAPTER
7

The Modern Presidency

"Taken by and large," the political scientist Edward S. Corwin once observed, "the history of the presidency is a history of aggrandizement, but the story is a highly discontinuous one." Corwin argued that of the individuals who have filled the office, not more than one in three has contributed significantly to its development. He pointed, for example, only to Thomas Jefferson, Andrew Jackson, James K. Polk, and Abraham Lincoln as strong nineteenth-century presidents. In this century, we might include Theodore Roosevelt, Woodrow Wilson, and Franklin D. Roosevelt. FDR was particularly important; over the course of his four terms, he gave the presidency its modern character. His responses to the crises of the Great Depression and World War II fixed the presidential office as the center of national leadership. The ensuing Cold War between the United States and the Soviet Union accentuated the emergence of the modern presidency, creating a climate, according to historian Lawrence M. Friedman, in which it was possible to have weak presidents but not a weak presidency.

Since the nation's beginnings, the chief executive has enjoyed broad powers to conduct foreign affairs based on his role as commander-in-chief and his constitutional right to negotiate treaties. Congress has generally acquiesced in the expansion of these powers, accepting on pragmatic grounds that the president is in the best position to make quick decisions about national security. The traditional power of Congress to declare war has faded; instead, Congress has resorted to exercising its diminished powers by passing resolutions of support and holding the purse strings of U.S. military forces engaged in hostilities, as in the Korean and Vietnam wars.

New questions about the scope of the chief executive's privilege to keep information from Congress have attended the president's growing role in foreign and military affairs. The conflict between presidential powers and the oversight function of Congress crested in the Watergate scandal of 1973 and 1974. Before the 1972 presidential election, in which President Richard M. Nixon overwhelmingly won reelection, several burglars who later were found to be associated with the president's committee for reelection had been arrested in the office of the Democratic National Committee in Washington, D.C.'s Watergate office complex. Nixon tried to cover up the details of the break-in on finding out about them. The president's deceit was made more damaging by the fact that he was already under attack for his misuse of authority to bomb Cambodia secretly and to use the Internal Revenue Service and other governmental agencies for revenge on his alleged political enemies. Nixon's refusal to supply tape recordings of meetings with his aides over the Watergate incident shattered what little credibility he had left. The president ultimately surrendered the tapes after the Supreme Court ordered him to do so, but the disclosure of their contents forced Nixon to resign rather than face certain impeachment. Nonetheless, the questions raised by the Nixon presidency—the independence of the chief executive from Congress, the power of Congress to participate in foreign affairs—persisted into the administrations of Jimmy Carter and Ronald Reagan.

✠ *D O C U M E N T S*

The Cold War spawned numerous situations in which the president was called on to deploy U.S. military forces to protect national security. Such actions invariably raised questions, however, about the power of Congress to declare war, the scope of the president's authority under the commander-in-chief clause of the Constitution, the extent of the president's inherent (that is, implied rather than specified) powers, and the scope of executive privilege. When North Korean troops invaded South Korea in 1950, President Harry S Truman committed U.S. forces under the authority of a United Nations resolution. Senator Robert Taft of Ohio, while confirming the necessity of the action, argues in the first selection that it was also unconstitutional.

Truman's administration marked a milestone in presidential authority in another way. When steelworkers went on strike in 1952, the president cited the Korean War as the basis for ordering a government takeover of American steel plants pending a labor settlement. Truman invoked the concept of "inherent" executive powers and his role as commander-in-chief of the armed forces to support the seizure. By a 6–3 vote, the Supreme Court rejected this view in the *Youngstown Sheet and Tube Co.* case, reprinted as the second document. Later President Lyndon B. Johnson faced his own "Korea" in Vietnam. Following an alleged attack by North Vietnamese gunboats on U.S. destroyers in the Gulf of Tonkin in 1964, Congress passed the Tonkin Resolution, the third document. It amounted to a de facto declaration of war, especially because Congress continued to appropriate ever larger amounts of money to pay for the build-up of U.S. forces in Southeast Asia.

Quick victory, however, eluded Johnson. Consequently, when Richard M. Nixon entered the White House in 1969, he encountered serious domestic and international criticism of the war, as the fourth document, an excerpt from his memoirs, reveals. Nixon's unilateral exercise of power stirred Congress to reclaim some of its lost constitutional authority. The decisive event was the president's decision to bomb Hanoi and Haiphong on Christmas, 1972. Congress then began in earnest the process that culminated in the War Powers Resolution of 1973, the fifth document. Nixon continued to overplay his hand at home as well as abroad, and his attempt to cover up the Watergate break-in brought the principle of executive privilege before the Supreme Court. In *United States* v. *Nixon* (1974), the sixth document, the Court unanimously ordered Nixon to turn over the audiotapes of his conversations with his close advisers. North Carolina Senator Sam Ervin, Jr., who chaired the Senate Select Committee on Presidential Campaign Activities, sums up the meaning of the Watergate affair and, more generally, the rise of the "imperial" presidency, in the last document. In light of the Iran-contra scandal during Ronald Reagan's presidential administration and the deployment of

U.S. armed forces to Saudi Arabia in 1990, is presidential and governmental power any more secure today than it was when Senator Ervin spoke these words?

Senator Robert A. Taft on President Harry S Truman's Power to Make War, 1950

The Korean War Situation

Mr. Taft. Mr. President, I desire to speak with reference to the Korean crisis. . . .

Early on Sunday morning, June 25, the Communist-dominated Republic of North Korea launched an unprovoked aggressive military attack on the Republic of Korea, recognized as an independent nation by the United Nations. On the same day the Security Council of the United Nations adopted a resolution noting with grave concern the armed attack upon the Republic of Korea from forces from North Korea, and determining that this action constituted a breach of the peace. The resolution called for the immediate cessation of hostilities, for the withdrawal of the armed forces of North Korea to the thirty-eighth parallel, and for the United Nations Commission on Korea to make informational reports; and called "upon all members to render every assistance to the United Nations in the execution of this resolution and to refrain from giving assistance to the North Korean authorities." This resolution was adopted by a vote of nine members, Russia being absent, and Yugoslavia abstaining.

The attack did not cease, and on Tuesday, June 27, the President issued a statement announcing that he had "ordered United States air and sea forces to give the Korean Government troops cover and support." He also announced that he had ordered the Seventh Fleet to prevent any attack on Formosa, and that he had directed that United States forces in the Philippines be strengthened, and that military assistance to the Philippine Government and the forces of France and the associated states in Indochina be accelerated.

On the same day, last night, the United Nations adopted another resolution definitely recommending "that the members of the United Nations furnish such assistance to the Republic of Korea as may be necessary to repel the armed attack and restore international peace and security in the area." This vote was adopted by seven members of the Security Council; I am informed, I am not absolutely certain, Yugoslavia voting "no," and India and Egypt refraining from voting, Russia still being absent. American air and sea forces have moved into Korea and are partaking in the war against the northern Korea Communists.

No one can deny that a serious crisis exists. The attack was as much a surprise to the public as the attack at Pearl Harbor, although, apparently, the possibility was foreseen by all our intelligence forces, and should have been foreseen by the administration. We are now actually engaged in a de facto war with the northern Korean Communists. That in itself is serious, but nothing compared to the possibility that it might lead to war with Soviet

Russia. It is entirely possible that Soviet Russia might move in to help the North Koreans and that the present limited field of conflict might cover the entire civilized world. Without question, the attack of the North Koreans is an outrageous act of aggression against a friendly independent nation, recognized by the United Nations, and which we were instrumental in setting up. The attack in all probability was instigated by Soviet Russia. We can only hope that the leaders of that country have sufficient judgment to know that a world war will result in their own destruction, and will therefore refrain from such acts as might bring about such a tragic conflict.

Mr. President, Korea itself is not vitally important to the United States. It is hard to defend. We have another instance of communism picking out a soft spot where the Communists feel that they can make a substantial advance and can obtain a moral victory without risking war. From the past philosophy and declarations of our leaders, it was not unreasonable for the North Koreans to suppose that they could get away with it and that we would do nothing about it.

The President's statement of policy represents a complete change in the programs and policies heretofore proclaimed by the administration. I have heretofore urged a much more determined attitude against communism in the Far East, and the President's new policy moves in that direction. It seems to me that the time had to come, sooner or later, when we would give definite notice to the Communists that a move beyond a declared line would result in war. That has been the policy which we have adopted in Europe. Whether the President has chosen the right time or the right place to declare this policy may be open to question. He has information which I do not have.

It seems to me that the new policy is adopted at an unfortunate time, and involves the attempt to defend Korea, which is a very difficult military operation indeed. I sincerely hope that our Armed Forces may be successful in Korea. I sincerely hope that the policy thus adopted will not lead to war with Russia. In any event, I believe the general principle of the policy is right, and I see no choice except to back up wholeheartedly and with every available resource the men in our Armed Forces who have been moved into Korea.

If we are going to defend Korea, it seems to me that we should have retained our Armed Forces there and should have given, a year ago, the notice which the President has given today. With such a policy, there never would have been such an attack by the North Koreans. In short, this entirely unfortunate crisis has been produced first, by the outrageous, aggressive attitude of Soviet Russia, and second, by the bungling and inconsistent foreign policy of the administration.

I think it is important to point out, Mr. President, that there has been no pretense of any bipartisan foreign policy about this action. The leaders of the Republican Party in Congress have never been consulted on the Chinese policy or Formosa or Korea or Indochina. Republican members of the Foreign Relations Committee and of the Armed Forces Committee were called to the White House at 10:30 A.M. on June 27, and were informed with regard to the President's statement, but, of course, they had no opportunity to change it or to consult Republican policy committees in either the House of Representatives or the Senate.

I hope at a later time to put into the Record a historical statement of the position of various Republican leaders on the general question of China policy, showing that it is very different, indeed, from what the President has heretofore advocated, and that, in general, it is more in accord with what he is now proposing.

Furthermore, it should be noted that there has been no pretense of consulting the Congress. No resolution has ever been introduced asking for the approval of Congress for the use of American forces in Korea. I shall discuss later the question of whether the President is usurping his powers as Commander in Chief. My own opinion is that he is doing so; that there is no legal authority for what he has done. But I may say that if a joint resolution were introduced asking for approval of the use of our Armed Forces already sent to Korea and full support of them in their present venture, I would vote in favor of it. . . .

Although I should be willing to vote to approve the President's new policy as a policy, and give support to our forces in Korea, I think it is proper and essential that we discuss at this time the right and power of the President to do what he has done. I hope others will discuss it, because I have not thoroughly investigated the question of the right and the power of the President to do what he has done.

His action unquestionably has brought about a de facto war with the Government of northern Korea. He has brought that war about without consulting Congress and without congressional approval. We have a situation in which in a far distant part of the world one nation has attacked another, and if the President can intervene in Korea without congressional approval, he can go to war in Malaya or Indonesia or Iran or South America. Presidents have at times intervened with American forces to protect American lives or interests, but I do not think it has been claimed that, apart from the United Nations Charter or other treaty obligations, the President has any right to precipitate any open warfare.

It is claimed that the Korean situation is changed by the obligations into which we have entered under the Charter of the United Nations. I think this is true, but I do not think it justifies the President's present action without approval by Congress. I stated when we were discussing the bill to implement the United Nations Charter that I felt that once the American representative on the Security Council voted in favor of using armed forces then the President was entitled to go ahead and use those forces without further action by Congress. I objected to the bill because it gave the President unlimited power to tell our representative on the Security Council how he must vote so that he could commit the country to the use of armed forces without congressional authority. I felt that giving the President the right to tell our representative on the Security Council how he should or should not vote, in effect gave him the right to put the United States into war, provided the other sections of the bill were complied with.

Section 6, however, dealt particularly with the time in which armed forces may be used to support the United Nations. What it says is this:

> The President is authorized to negotiate a special agreement or agreements with the Security Council which shall be subject to the approval of the Congress by appropriate act or joint resolution, providing for the numbers and types of armed forces, their degree of readiness and general location, and the nature of facilities and assistance, including rights of passage, to be made available to the Security Council on its call for the purpose of maintaining international peace and security in accordance with article 43 of said Charter. The President shall not be deemed to require the authorization of the Congress to make available to the Security Council on its call in order to take action under article 42 of said Charter and pursuant to such special agreement or agreements the armed forces, facilities, or assistance provided for therein: *Provided,* That nothing herein contained shall be construed as an authorization to the President by the Congress to make available to the Security Council for such purpose armed forces, facilities, or assistance in addition to the forces, facilities, and assistance provided for in such special agreement or agreements.

So, we have enacted the circumstances under which the President may use armed forces in support of a resolution of the Security Council of the United Nations. The first requisite is that we negotiate an agreement to determine what forces shall be used, and in what quantity, and that the agreement be approved by Congress. No agreement has ever been negotiated, of course, and no agreement has ever been presented to Congress. So far as I can see, and so far as I have studied the matter, I would say that there is no authority to use armed forces in support of the United Nations in the absence of some previous action by Congress dealing with the subject and outlining the general circumstances and the amount of the forces that can be used.

Other questions arise out of the United Nations Charter which I think should be explored. At least, they should be debated by this body.

Article 27 provides that decisions of the Security Council on all matters shall be made by an affirmative vote of seven members, including the concurring votes of the permanent members. The word "veto" was never used in the United Nations Charter. It simply provides that there must be the concurring votes of the five permanent members. In this case Soviet Russia has not voted. They never even appeared at the meeting. It is suggested, I understand, that gradually, under the practice adopted, a veto must be expressed by a negative vote; even though that seems directly contrary to the language of article 27. I am not a student of that subject. I merely suggest that the question, and the fact that Korea is not a member of the United Nations, ought to be explored and debated very fully by the Senate. I do not think there is any immediate rush about it. I merely do not like to have this action go by with the approval of the Senate, if it is what it seems to me, namely, a complete usurpation by the President of authority to use the Armed Forces of this country. If the incident is permitted to go by without protest, at least from this body, we would have finally terminated for all time the right of Congress to declare war, which is granted to Congress alone by the Constitution of the United States. . . .

Youngstown Sheet & Tube Co. et al. v. Sawyer, 343 U.S. 579 (1952)

[6–3: Black, Clark, Douglas, Frankfurter,
Jackson, Rutledge; Reed, Minton, Vinson]

Mr. Justice Black delivered the opinion of the Court.

We are asked to decide whether the President was acting within his constitutional power when he issued an order directing the Secretary of Commerce to take possession of and operate most of the Nation's steel mills. The mill owners argue that the President's order amounts to lawmaking, a legislative function which the Constitution has expressly confided to the Congress and not to the President. The Government's position is that the order was made on findings of the President that his action was necessary to avert a national catastrophe which would inevitably result from a stoppage of steel production, and that in meeting this grave emergency the President was acting within the aggregate of his constitutional powers as the Nation's Chief Executive and the Commander in Chief of the Armed Forces of the United States. . . .

The President's power, if any, to issue the order must stem either from an act of Congress or from the Constitution itself. There is no statute that expressly authorizes the President to take possession of property as he did here. Nor is there any act of Congress to which our attention has been directed from which such a power can fairly be implied. Indeed, we do not understand the Government to rely on statutory authorization for this seizure. There are two statutes which do authorize the President to take both personal and real property under certain conditions. However, the Government admits that these conditions were not met and that the President's order was not rooted in either of the statutes. The Government refers to the seizure provisions of one of these statutes (§ 201 (b) of the Defense Production Act) as "much too cumbersome, involved, and time-consuming for the crisis which was at hand."

Moreover, the use of the seizure technique to solve labor disputes in order to prevent work stoppages was not only unauthorized by any congressional enactment; prior to this controversy, Congress had refused to adopt that method of settling labor disputes. When the Taft-Hartley Act was under consideration in 1947, Congress rejected an amendment which would have authorized such governmental seizures in cases of emergency. Apparently it was thought that the technique of seizure, like that of compulsory arbitration, would interfere with the process of collective bargaining. Consequently, the plan Congress adopted in that Act did not provide for seizure under any circumstances. Instead, the plan sought to bring about settlements by use of the customary devices of mediation, conciliation, investigation by boards of inquiry, and public reports. In some instances temporary injunctions were authorized to provide cooling-off periods. All this failing, unions were left free to strike after a secret vote by employees as to whether they wished to accept their employers' final settlement offer.

It is clear that if the President had authority to issue the order he did, it must be found in some provisions of the Constitution. And it is not claimed that express constitutional language grants this power to the President. The contention is that presidential power should be implied from the aggregate of his powers under the Constitution. Particular reliance is placed on provisions in Article II which say that "the executive Power shall be vested in a President . . . "; that "he shall take Care that the Laws be faithfully executed"; and that he "shall be Commander in Chief of the Army and Navy of the United States."

The order cannot properly be sustained as an exercise of the President's military power as Commander in Chief of the Armed Forces. The Government attempts to do so by citing a number of cases upholding broad powers in military commanders engaged in day-to-day fighting in a theater of war. Such cases need not concern us here. Even though "theater of war" be an expanding concept, we cannot with faithfulness to our constitutional system hold that the Commander in Chief of the Armed Forces has the ultimate power as such to take possession of private property in order to keep labor disputes from stopping production. This is a job for the Nation's lawmakers, not for its military authorities.

Nor can the seizure order be sustained because of the several constitutional provisions that grant executive power to the President. In the framework of our Constitution, the President's power to see that the laws are faithfully executed refutes the idea that he is to be a lawmaker. The Constitution limits his functions in the lawmaking process to the recommending of laws he thinks wise and the vetoing of laws he thinks bad. And the Constitution is neither silent nor equivocal about who shall make laws which the President is to execute. The first section of the first article says that "All legislative Powers herein granted shall be vested in a Congress of the United States. . . . " After granting many powers to the Congress, Article I goes on to provide that Congress may "make all Laws which shall be necessary and proper for carrying into Execution the foregoing Powers and all other Powers vested by this Constitution in the Government of the United States, or in any Department or Officer thereof."

The President's order does not direct that a congressional policy be executed in a manner prescribed by Congress—it directs that a presidential policy be executed in a manner prescribed by the President. The preamble of the order itself, like that of many statutes, sets out reasons why the President believes certain policies should be adopted, proclaims these policies as rules of conduct to be followed, and again, like a statute, authorizes a government official to promulgate additional rules and regulations consistent with the policy proclaimed and needed to carry that policy into execution. The power of Congress to adopt such public policies as those proclaimed by the order is beyond question. It can authorize the taking of private property for public use. It can make laws regulating the relationships between employers and employees, prescribing rules designed to settle labor disputes, and fixing wages and working conditions in certain fields of our economy. The Constitution did not subject this lawmaking power of Congress to presidential or military supervision or control.

It is said that other Presidents without congressional authority have taken possession of private business enterprises in order to settle labor disputes. But even if this be true, Congress has not thereby lost its exclusive constitutional authority to make laws necessary and proper to carry out the powers vested by the Constitution "in the Government of the United States, or in any Department or Officer thereof."

The founders of this Nation entrusted the lawmaking power to the Congress alone in both good and bad times. It would do no good to recall the historical events, the fears of power and the hopes for freedom that lay behind their choice. Such a review would but confirm our holding that this seizure order cannot stand.

The judgment of the District Court is *Affirmed*.

Mr. Justice Jackson, concurring in the judgment and opinion of the Court.

That comprehensive and undefined presidential powers hold both practical advantages and grave dangers for the country will impress anyone who has served as legal adviser to a President in time of transition and public anxiety. While an interval of detached reflection may temper teachings of that experience, they probably are a more realistic influence on my views than the conventional materials of judicial decision which seem unduly to accentuate doctrine and legal fiction. But as we approach the question of presidential power, we half overcome mental hazards by recognizing them. The opinions of judges, no less than executives and publicists, often suffer the infirmity of confusing the issue of a power's validity with the cause it is invoked to promote, of confounding the permanent executive office with its temporary occupant. The tendency is strong to emphasize transient results upon policies—such as wages or stabilization—and lose sight of enduring consequences upon the balanced power structure of our Republic.

A judge, like an executive adviser, may be surprised at the poverty of really useful and unambiguous authority applicable to concrete problems of executive power as they actually present themselves. Just what our forefathers did envision, or would have envisioned had they foreseen modern conditions, must be divined from materials almost as enigmatic as the dreams Joseph was called upon to interpret for Pharaoh. A century and a half of partisan debate and scholarly speculation yields no net result but only supplies more or less apt quotations from respected sources on each side of any question. They largely cancel each other. And court decisions are indecisive because of the judicial practice of dealing with the largest questions in the most narrow way.

The actual art of governing under our Constitution does not and cannot conform to judicial definitions of the power of any of its branches based on isolated clauses or even single Articles torn from context. While the Constitution diffuses power the better to secure liberty, it also contemplates that practice will integrate the dispersed powers into a workable government. It enjoins upon its branches separateness but interdependence, autonomy but reciprocity. Presidential powers are not fixed but fluctuate, depending upon their disjunction or conjunction with those of Congress. We may well begin by a somewhat over-simplified grouping of practical situations in which a President may doubt, or others may challenge, his powers, and by distinguishing roughly the legal consequences of this factor of relativity.

1. When the President acts pursuant to an express or implied authorization of Congress, his authority is at its maximum, for it includes all that he possesses in his own right plus all that Congress can delegate. In these circumstances, and in these only, may he be said (for what it may be worth) to personify the federal sovereignty. If his act is held unconstitutional under these circumstances, it usually means that the Federal Government as an undivided whole lacks power. A seizure executed by the President pursuant to an Act of Congress would be supported by the strongest of presumptions and the widest latitude of judicial interpretation, and the burden of persuasion would rest heavily upon any who might attack it.

2. When the President acts in absence of either a congressional grant or denial of authority, he can only rely upon his own independent powers, but there is a zone of twilight in which he and Congress may have concurrent authority, or in which its distribution is uncertain. Therefore, congressional inertia, indifference or quiescence may sometimes, at least as a practical matter, enable, if not invite, measures on independent presidential responsibility. In this area, any actual test of power is likely to depend on the imperatives of events and contemporary imponderables rather than on abstract theories of law.

3. When the President takes measures incompatible with the expressed or implied will of Congress, his power is at its lowest ebb, for then he can rely only upon his own constitutional powers minus any constitutional powers of Congress over the matter. Courts can sustain exclusive presidential control in such a case only by disabling the Congress from acting upon the subject. Presidential claim to a power at once so conclusive and preclusive must be scrutinized with caution, for what is at stake is the equilibrium established by our constitutional system.

Into which of these classifications does this executive seizure of the steel industry fit? It is eliminated from the first by admission, for it is conceded that no congressional authorization exists for this seizure. That takes away also the support of the many precedents and declarations which were made in relation, and must be confined, to this category.

Can it then be defended under flexible tests available to the second category? It seems clearly eliminated from that class because Congress has not left seizure of private property an open field but has covered it by three statutory policies inconsistent with this seizure. In cases where the purpose is to supply needs of the Government itself, two courses are provided: one, seizure of a plant which fails to comply with obligatory orders placed by the Government; another, condemnation of facilities, including temporary use under the power of eminent domain. The third is applicable where it is the general economy of the country that is to be protected rather than exclusive governmental interests. None of these were invoked. In choosing a different and inconsistent way of his own, the President cannot claim that it is necessitated or invited by failure of Congress to legislate upon the occasions, grounds and methods for seizure of industrial properties.

This leaves the current seizure to be justified only by the severe tests under the third grouping, where it can be supported only by any remainder of executive power after subtraction of such powers as Congress may have over the subject. In short, we can sustain the President only by holding that seizure of such strike-bound industries is within his domain and beyond control by Congress. Thus, this Court's first review of such seizures occurs under circumstances which leave presidential power most vulnerable to attack and in the least favorable of possible constitutional postures.

I did not suppose, and I am not persuaded, that history leaves it open to question, at least in the courts, that the executive branch, like the Federal Government as a whole, possesses only delegated powers. The purpose of the Constitution was not only to grant power, but to keep it from getting out of hand. However, because the President does not enjoy unmentioned powers does not mean that the mentioned ones should be narrowed by a niggardly construction. Some clauses could be made almost unworkable, as well as immutable, by refusal to indulge some latitude of interpretation for changing times. I have heretofore, and do now, give to the enumerated powers the scope and elasticity afforded by what seem to be reasonable, practical implications instead of the rigidity dictated by a doctrinaire textualism. . . .

The clause on which the Government next relies is that "The President shall be Commander in Chief of the Army and Navy of the United States. . . ." These cryptic words have given rise to some of the most persistent controversies in our constitutional history. Of course, they imply something more than an empty title. But just what authority goes with the name has plagued presidential advisers who would not waive or narrow it by nonassertion yet cannot say where it begins or ends. It undoubtedly puts the Nation's armed forces under presidential command. Hence, this loose appellation is sometimes advanced as support for any presidential action, internal or external, involving use of force, the idea being that it vests power to do anything, anywhere, that can be done with an army or navy.

That seems to be the logic of an argument tendered at our bar—that the President having, on his own responsibility, sent American troops abroad derives from that act "affirmative power" to seize the means of producing a supply of steel for them. To quote, "Perhaps the most forceful illustration of the scope of Presidential power in this connection is the fact that American troops in Korea, whose safety and effectiveness are so directly involved here, were sent to the field by an exercise of the President's constitutional powers." Thus, it is said, he has invested himself with "war powers."

I cannot foresee all that it might entail if the Court should indorse this argument. Nothing in our Constitution is plainer than that declaration of a war is entrusted only to Congress. Of course, a state of war may in fact exist without a formal declaration. But no doctrine that the Court could promulgate would seem to me more sinister and alarming than that a President whose conduct of foreign affairs is so largely uncontrolled, and often even is unknown, can vastly enlarge his mastery over the internal affairs of the country by his own commitment of the Nation's armed forces to some foreign venture. I do not, however, find it necessary or appropriate to consider the legal status of the Korean enterprise to discountenance argument based on it.

Assuming that we are in a war *de facto*, whether it is or is not a war *de jure*, does that empower the Commander in Chief to seize industries he thinks necessary to supply our army? The Constitution expressly places in Congress power "to raise and *support* Armies" and "to *provide* and *maintain* a Navy." (Emphasis supplied.) This certainly lays upon Congress primary responsibility for supplying the armed forces. Congress alone controls the raising of revenues and their appropriation and may determine in what manner and by what means they shall be spent for military and naval procurement. I suppose no one would doubt that Congress can take over war supply as a Government enterprise. On the other hand, if Congress sees fit to rely on free private enterprise collectively bargaining with free labor for support and maintenance of our armed forces, can the Executive, because of lawful disagreements incidental to that process, seize the facility for operation upon Government-imposed terms?

There are indications that the Constitution did not contemplate that the title Commander in Chief *of the Army and Navy* will constitute him also Commander in Chief of the country, its industries and its inhabitants. He has no monopoly of "war powers," whatever they are. While Congress cannot deprive the President of the command of the army and navy, only Congress can provide him an army or navy to command. It is also empowered to make rules for the "Government and Regulation of land and naval Forces," by which it may to some unknown extent impinge upon even command functions.

That military powers of the Commander in Chief were not to supersede representative government of internal affairs seems obvious from the Constitution and from elementary American history. Time out of mind, and even now in many parts of the world, a military commander can seize private housing to shelter his troops. Not so, however, in the United States, for the Third Amendment says, "No Soldier shall, in time of peace be quartered in any house, without the consent of the Owner, nor in time of war, but in a manner to be prescribed by law." Thus, even in war time, his seizure of needed military housing must be authorized by Congress. It also was expressly left to Congress to "provide for calling forth the Militia to execute the Laws of the Union, suppress Insurrections and repel Invasions. . . ." Such a limitation on the command power, written at a time when the militia rather than a standing army was contemplated as the military weapon of the Republic, underscores the Constitution's policy that Congress, not the Executive, should control utilization of the war power as an instrument of domestic policy. Congress, fulfilling that function, has authorized the President to use the army to enforce certain civil rights. On the other hand, Congress has forbidden him to use the army for the purpose of executing general laws except when *expressly* authorized by the Constitution or by Act of Congress.

While broad claims under this rubric often have been made, advice to the President in specific matters usually has carried overtones that powers, even under this head, are measured by the command functions usual to the topmost officer of the army and navy. Even then, heed has been taken of any efforts of Congress to negative his authority.

We should not use this occasion to circumscribe, much less to contract, the lawful role of the President as Commander in Chief. I should indulge the widest latitude of interpretation to sustain his exclusive function to command the instruments of national force, at least when turned against the outside world for the security of our society. But, when it is turned inward, not because of rebellion but because of a lawful economic struggle between industry and labor, it should have no such indulgence. His command power is not such an absolute as might be implied from that office in a militaristic system but is subject to limitations consistent with a constitutional Republic whose law and policy-making branch is a representative Congress. The purpose of lodging dual titles in one man was to insure that the civilian would control the military, not to enable the military to subordinate the presidential office. No penance would ever expiate the sin against free government of holding that a President can escape control of executive powers by law through assuming his military role. What the power of command may include I do not try to envision, but I think it is not a military prerogative, without support of law, to seize persons or property because they are important or even essential for the military and naval establishment. . . .

In view of the ease, expedition and safety with which Congress can grant and has granted large emergency powers, certainly ample to embrace this crisis, I am quite unimpressed with the argument that we should affirm possession of them without statute. Such power either has no beginning or it has no end. If it exists, it need submit to no legal restraint. I am not alarmed that it would plunge us straightway into dictatorship, but it is at least a step in that wrong direction.

As to whether there is imperative necessity for such powers, it is relevant to note the gap that exists between the President's paper powers and his real powers. The Constitution does not disclose the measure of the actual controls wielded by the modern presidential office. That instrument must be understood as an Eighteenth-Century sketch of a government hoped for, not as a blueprint of the Government that is. Vast accretions of federal power, eroded from that reserved by the States, have magnified the scope of presidential activity. Subtle shifts take place in the centers of real power that do not show on the face of the Constitution.

Executive power has the advantage of concentration in a single head in whose choice the whole Nation has a part, making him the focus of public hopes and expectations. In drama, magnitude and finality his decisions so far overshadow any others that almost alone he fills the public eye and ear. No other personality in public life can begin to compete with him in access to the public mind through modern methods of communications. By his prestige as head of state and his influence upon public opinion he exerts a leverage upon those who are supposed to check and balance his power which often cancels their effectiveness.

Moreover, rise of the party system has made a significant extraconstitutional supplement to real executive power. No appraisal of his necessities is realistic which overlooks that he heads a political system as well as a legal system. Party loyalties and interests, sometimes more binding than law, extend his effective control into branches of government other than his own and he often may win, as a political leader, what he cannot command under the Constitution. Indeed, Woodrow Wilson, commenting on the President as leader both of his party and of the Nation, observed, "If he rightly interpret the national thought and boldly insist upon it, he is irresistible. . . . His office is anything he has the sagacity and force to make it." I cannot be brought to believe that this country will suffer if the Court refuses further to aggrandize the presidential office, already so potent and so relatively immune from judicial review, at the expense of Congress.

But I have no illusion that any decision by this Court can keep power in the hands of Congress if it is not wise and timely in meeting its problems. A crisis that challenges the President equally, or perhaps primarily, challenges Congress. If not good law, there was worldly wisdom in the maxim attributed to Napoleon that "The tools belong to the man who can use them." We may say that power to legislate for emergencies belongs in the hands of Congress, but only Congress itself can prevent power from slipping through its fingers.

The essence of our free Government is "leave to live by no man's leave, underneath the law"—to be governed by those impersonal forces which we call law. Our Government is fashioned to fulfill this concept so far as humanly possible. The Executive, except for recommendation and veto, has no legislative power. The executive action we have here originates in the individual will of the President and represents an exercise of authority without law. No one, perhaps not even the President, knows the limits of the power he may seek to exert in this instance and the parties affected cannot learn the limit of their rights. We do not know today what powers over labor or property would be claimed to flow from Government possession if we should legalize it, what rights to compensation would be claimed or recognized, or on what contingency it would end. With all its defects, delays and inconveniences, men have discovered no technique for long preserving free government except that the Executive be under the law, and that the law be made by parliamentary deliberations.

Such institutions may be destined to pass away. But it is the duty of the Court to be last, not first, to give them up.

Mr. Chief Justice Vinson, with whom Mr. Justice Reed and Mr. Justice Minton join, dissenting.

. . . Some members of the Court are of the view that the President is without power to act in time of crisis in the absence of express statutory authorization. Other members of the Court affirm on the basis of their reading of certain statutes. Because we cannot agree that affirmance is proper on any ground, and because of the transcending importance of the questions presented not only in this critical litigation but also to the powers the President and of future Presidents to act in time of crisis, we are compelled to register this dissent. . . .

In passing upon the question of Presidential powers in this case, we must first consider the context in which those powers were exercised.

Those who suggest that this is a case involving extraordinary powers should be mindful that these are extraordinary times. A world not yet recovered from the devastation of World War II has been forced to face the threat of another and more terrifying global conflict.

Accepting in full measure its responsibility in the world community, the United States was instrumental in securing adoption of the United Nations Charter, approved by the Senate by a vote of 89 to 2. The first purpose of the United Nations is to "maintain international peace and security, and to that end: to take effective collective measures for the prevention and removal of threats to the peace, and for the suppression of acts of aggression or other breaches of the peace, ..." In 1950 when the United Nations called upon member nations "to render every assistance" to repel aggression in Korea, the United States furnished its vigorous support. For almost two full years, our armed forces have been fighting in Korea, suffering casualties of over 108,000 men. Hostilities have not abated. The "determination of the United Nations to continue its action in Korea to meet the aggression" has been reaffirmed. Congressional support of the action in Korea has been manifested by provisions for increased military manpower and equipment and for economic stabilization, as hereinafter described.

Further efforts to protect the free world from aggression are found in the congressional enactments of the Truman Plan for assistance to Greece and Turkey and the Marshall Plan for economic aid needed to build up the strength of our friends in Western Europe. In 1949, the Senate approved the North Atlantic Treaty under which each member nation agrees that an armed attack against one is an armed attack against all. Congress immediately implemented the North Atlantic Treaty by authorizing military assistance to nations dedicated to the principles of mutual security under the United Nations Charter. The concept of mutual security recently has been extended by treaty to friends in the Pacific.

Our treaties represent not merely legal obligations but show congressional recognition that mutual security for the free world is the best security against the threat of aggression on a global scale. The need for mutual security is shown by the very size of the armed forces outside the free world. Defendant's brief informs us that the Soviet Union maintains the largest air force in the world and maintains ground forces much larger than those presently available to the United States and the countries joined with us in mutual security arrangements. Constant international tensions are cited to demonstrate how precarious is the peace.

Even this brief review of our responsibilities in the world community discloses the enormity of our undertaking. Success of these measures may, as has often been observed, dramatically influence the lives of many generations of the world's peoples yet unborn. Alert to our responsibilities, which coincide with our own self preservation through mutual security, Congress has enacted a large body of implementing legislation. . . .

Congress also directed the President to build up our own defenses. Congress, recognizing the "grim fact . . . that the United States is now engaged in a struggle for survival" and that "it is imperative that we now take those necessary steps to make our strength equal to the peril of the hour," granted authority to draft men into the armed forces. As a result, we now have over 3,500,000 men in our armed forces. . . .

Congress recognized the impact of these defense programs upon the economy. Following the attack in Korea, the President asked for authority to requisition property and to allocate and fix priorities for scarce goods. In the Defense Production Act of 1950, Congress granted the powers requested and, *in addition,* granted power to stabilize prices and wages and to provide for settlement of labor disputes arising in the defense program. The Defense Production Act was extended in 1951, a Senate Committee noting that in the dislocation caused by the programs for purchase of military equipment "lies the seed of an economic disaster that might well destroy the military might we are straining to build." . . .

The President has the duty to execute the foregoing legislative programs. Their successful execution depends upon continued production of steel and stabilized prices for steel. Accordingly, when the collective bargaining agreements between the Nation's steel producers and their employees, represented by the United Steel Workers, were due to expire on December 31, 1951, and a strike shutting down the entire basic steel industry was threatened, the President acted to avert a complete shutdown of steel production. . . .

One is not here called upon even to consider the possibility of executive seizure of a farm, a corner grocery store or even a single industrial plant. Such considerations arise only when one ignores the central fact of this case—that the Nation's entire basic steel production would have shut down completely if there had been no Government seizure. Even ignoring for the moment whatever confidential information the President may possess as "the Nation's organ for foreign affairs," the uncontroverted affidavits in this record amply support the finding that "a work stoppage would immediately jeopardize and imperil our national defense." . . .

Accordingly, if the President has any power under the Constitution to meet a critical situation in the absence of express statutory authorization, there is no basis whatever for criticizing the exercise of such power in this case. . . .

Admitting that the Government could seize the mills, plaintiffs claim that the implied power of eminent domain can be exercised only under an Act of Congress; under no circumstances, they say, can that power be exercised by the President unless he can point to an express provision in enabling legislation. . . .

Under this view, the President is left powerless at the very moment when the need for action may be most pressing and when no one, other than he, is immediately capable of action. Under this view, he is left powerless because a power not expressly given to Congress is nevertheless found to rest exclusively with Congress. . . .

A review of executive action demonstrates that our Presidents have on many occasions exhibited the leadership contemplated by the Framers when they made the President Commander in Chief, and imposed upon him the trust to "take Care that the Laws be faithfully executed." With or without explicit statutory authorization, Presidents have at such times dealt with national emergencies by acting promptly and resolutely to enforce legislative programs, at least to save those programs until Congress could act. Congress and the courts have responded to such executive initiative with consistent approval.

. . . And many of the examples of Presidential practice go far beyond the extent of power necessary to sustain the President's order to seize the steel mills. The fact that temporary executive seizures of industrial plants to meet an emergency have not been directly tested in this Court furnishes not the slightest suggestion that such actions have been illegal. Rather, the fact that Congress and the courts have consistently recognized and given their support to such executive action indicates that such a power of seizure has been accepted throughout our history.

History bears out the genius of the Founding Fathers, who created a Government subject to law but not left subject to inertia when vigor and initiative are required. . . .

Focusing now on the situation confronting the President on the night of April 8, 1952, we cannot but conclude that the President was performing his duty under the Constitution to "take Care that the Laws be faithfully executed"—a duty described by President Benjamin Harrison as "the central idea of the office."

The President reported to Congress the morning after the seizure that he acted because a work stoppage in steel production would immediately imperil the safety of the Nation by preventing execution of the legislative programs for procurement of military equipment. And, while a shutdown could be averted by granting the price concessions requested by plaintiffs, granting such concessions would disrupt the price stabilization program also enacted by Congress. Rather than fail to execute either legislative program, the President acted to execute both. . . .

The absence of a specific statute authorizing seizure of the steel mills as a mode of executing the laws—both the military procurement program and the anti-inflation program—has not until today been thought to prevent the President from executing the laws. Unlike an administrative commission confined to the enforcement of the statute under which it was created, or the head of a department when administering a particular statute, the President is a constitutional officer charged with taking care that a "mass of legislation" be executed. Flexibility as to mode of execution to meet critical situations is a matter of practical necessity. This practical construction of the "Take Care" clause, advocated by John Marshall, was adopted by this Court in In re Neagle, In re Debs and other cases cited supra. . . .

There is no statute prohibiting seizure as a method of enforcing legislative programs. Congress has in no wise indicated that its legislation is not to be executed by the taking of private property (subject of course to the payment of just compensation) if its legislation cannot otherwise be executed. . . . Where Congress authorizes seizure in instances not necessarily crucial to the defense program, it can hardly be said to have disclosed an intention to prohibit seizures where essential to the execution of that legislative program.

Whatever the extent of Presidential power on more tranquil occasions, and whatever the right of the President to execute legislative programs as he sees fit without reporting the mode of execution to Congress, the single Presidential purpose disclosed on this record is to faithfully execute the laws by acting in an emergency to maintain the status quo, thereby preventing collapse of the legislative programs until Congress could act. The President's action served the same purposes as a judicial stay entered to maintain the status quo in order to preserve the jurisdiction of a court. In his Message to Congress immediately following the seizure, the President explained the necessity of his action in executing the military procurement and anti-inflation legislative programs and expressed his desire to cooperate with any legislative proposals approving, regulating or rejecting the seizure of the steel mills. Consequently, there is no evidence whatever of any Presidential purpose to defy Congress or act in any way inconsistent with the legislative will. . . .

. . . The Framers knew, as we should know in these times of peril, that there is real danger in Executive weakness. There is no cause to fear Executive tyranny so long as the laws of Congress are being faithfully executed. Certainly there is no basis for fear of dictatorship when the Executive acts, as he did in this case, only to save the situation until Congress could act. . . .

The Gulf of Tonkin Resolution, 1964

Joint Resolution to Promote the Maintenance of International Peace and Security in Southeast Asia

Whereas naval units of the Communist regime in Vietnam, in violation of the principles of the Charter of the United Nations and of international law, have deliberately and repeatedly attacked United States naval vessels lawfully present in international waters, and have thereby created a serious threat to international peace; and

Whereas these attacks are part of a deliberate and systematic campaign of aggression that the Communist regime in North Vietnam has been waging against its neighbors and the nations joined with them in the collective defense of their freedom; and

Whereas the United States is assisting the peoples of southeast Asia to protect their freedom and has no territorial, military or political ambitions in that area, but desires only that these peoples should be left in peace to work out their own destinies in their own way: Now, therefore, be it

Resolved by the Senate and House of Representatives of the United States of America in Congress assembled, That the Congress approves and supports the determination of the President, as Commander in Chief, to take all necessary measures to repel any armed attack against the forces of the United States and to prevent further aggression.

Sec. 2. The United States regards as vital to its national interest and to world peace the maintenance of international peace and security in southeast Asia. Consonant with the Constitution of the United States and the Charter of the United Nations and in accordance with its obligations under the Southeast Asia Collective Defense Treaty, the United States is, therefore, prepared, as the President determines, to take all necessary steps, including the use of armed force, to assist any member or protocol state of the Southeast Asia Collective Defense Treaty requesting assistance in defense of its freedom.

Sec. 3. This resolution shall expire when the President shall determine that the peace and security of the area is reasonably assured by international conditions created by action of the United Nations or otherwise, except that it may be terminated earlier by concurrent resolution of the Congress.

Approved August 10, 1964.

President Richard M. Nixon Views the Problems Before Him, 1969

[A]n element of desperation entered into the planning of the November Vietnam Moratorium, known as the New Mobe. We received alarming reports that several militant groups involved in the New Mobe now felt that only a violent confrontation could adequately dramatize their concerns. Because of the radical background of some of the New Mobe organizers, many congressmen who had supported the October Moratorium managed to be unavailable for comment before the New Mobe began and out of town while it was going on.

On November 15 the New Mobe arrived. In San Francisco, while some of the crowd of 125,000 yelled "Peace!" Black Panther leader David Hilliard insisted, "We will kill Richard Nixon. We will kill any [one] that stands in the way of our freedom."

In Washington, 250,000 demonstrators surged into the city, causing the Washington *Post* to rhapsodize: "To dig beneath the rhetoric is to discover something extraordinary, and quite beautiful. Those who were here . . . are here in support of what is best about this country." At the Washington Monument, Dick Gregory brought the crowd to its feet when he said, "The President says nothing you kids do will have any effect on him. Well, I suggest he make one long distance call to the LBJ Ranch." And later in the day came scattered episodes of violence. A group of protesters battled with police as they made their way through the streets knocking out windows. At the Justice Department protesters shouting "Smash the state!" stormed the building, tore down the American flag, burned it, and raised the Vietcong flag in its place.

I had never imagined that at the end of my first year as President I would be contemplating two more years of fighting in Vietnam. But the unexpected success of the November 3 speech had bought me more time, and, bolstered by Sir Robert Thompson's optimistic estimate that within two years we would be able to achieve a victory—either in the sense of an acceptable negotiated settlement or of having prepared the South Vietnamese to carry the burden of the fighting on their own—I was prepared to continue the war despite the serious strains that would be involved on the home front. Two years would bring us to the end of 1971 and the beginning of the 1972 campaign, and if I could hold the domestic front together until then, winning an honorable peace would redeem the interim difficulties.

As 1970 began, I envisioned a year of limited and even diminishing battlefield activity. I also envisioned the continuation of Kissinger's activity in the secret channel. I was rather less optimistic than Kissinger regarding the prospect of a breakthrough in the secret negotiations but I agreed that we must continue to pursue them as long as there was even a possibility they would be successful. Kissinger and I agreed that at the very least they would provide an indisputable record of our desire for peace and our efforts to achieve it.

I was disappointed but not surprised by the apparent ineffectiveness of our attempts in 1969 to get the Soviets to apply pressure on North Vietnam. But I understood the pressures placed on Moscow by the rivalry with Peking for ascendancy in the Communist world, and I felt that the important thing was to keep the Soviets aware that while we might recognize their inability to decrease their support of Hanoi or to apply pressure on the North Vietnamese to negotiate a settlement, we would not tolerate any major increase in aid or belligerent encouragement. Not surprisingly, the greatest incentive for Soviet cooperation in Vietnam was our new relationship with the Chinese, but that would not become a major factor until the middle of 1971.

I do not know whether or how I would have acted differently if at the end of 1969 I had known that within less than four months I would be forced to order an attack on the Communist sanctuaries in Cambodia, or that the next two years would once again bring America to the brink of internal disruption over Vietnam. At the same time I would have to walk a constantly higher tightrope trying to support our allies and our fighting men while not pushing the increasingly powerful antiwar forces in Congress into passing legislation that would cut off funds for the war or require our withdrawal.

All this lay ahead. As I sat in my study in San Clemente on New Year's Day thinking about these problems, I actually allowed myself a feeling of cautious optimism that we had weathered the worst blows from Vietnam and had only to hold firm until time began to work in our favor. I suppose that in some respects the Vietnam story is one of mutual miscalculation. But if I underestimated the willingness of the North Vietnamese to hang on and resist a negotiated settlement on any other than their own terms, they also underestimated my willingness to hold on despite the domestic and international pressures that would be ranged against me. . . .

The War Powers Resolution, 1973

Joint Resolution Concerning the War Powers of Congress and the President

Resolved by the Senate and House of Representatives of the United States of America in Congress assembled,

Short Title

Section 1. This joint resolution may be cited as the "War Powers Resolution."

Purpose and Policy

Sec. 2. (a) It is the purpose of this joint resolution to fulfill the intent of the framers of the Constitution of the United States and insure that the collective judgment of both the Congress and the President will apply to the introduction of United States Armed Forces into hostilities, or into situations where imminent involvement in hostilities is clearly indicated by the circumstances, and to the continued use of such forces in hostilities or in such situations.

(b) Under article I, section 8, of the Constitution, it is specifically provided that the Congress shall have the power to make all laws necessary and proper for carrying into execution, not only its own powers but also all other powers vested by the Constitution in the Government of the United States, or in any department or officer thereof.

(c) The constitutional powers of the President as Commander-in-Chief to introduce United States Armed Forces into hostilities, or into situations where imminent involvement in hostilities is clearly indicated by the circumstances, are exercised only pursuant to (1) a declaration of war, (2) specific statutory authorization, or (3) a national emergency created by attack upon the United States, its territories or possessions, or its armed forces.

Consultation

Sec. 3. The President in every possible instance shall consult with Congress before introducing United States Armed Forces into hostilities or into situations where imminent involvement in hostilities is clearly indicated by the circumstances, and after every such introduction shall consult regularly with the Congress until United States Armed Forces are no longer engaged in hostilities or have been removed from such situations.

Reporting

Sec. 4. (a) In the absence of a declaration of war, in any case in which United States Armed Forces are introduced—

(1) into hostilities or into situations where imminent involvement in hostilities is clearly indicated by the circumstances;

(2) into the territory, airspace or waters of a foreign nation, while equipped for combat, except for deployments which relate solely to supply, replacement, repair, or training of such forces; or

(3) in numbers which substantially enlarge United States Armed Forces equipped for combat already located in a foreign nation;

the President shall submit within 48 hours to the Speaker of the House of Representatives and to the President pro tempore of the Senate a report, in writing, setting forth—

(A) the circumstances necessitating the introduction of United States Armed Forces;

(B) the constitutional and legislative authority under which such introduction took place; and

(C) the estimated scope and duration of the hostilities or involvement.

(b) The President shall provide such other information as the Congress may request in the fulfillment of its constitutional responsibilities with respect to committing the Nation to war and to the use of United States Armed Forces abroad.

(c) Whenever United States Armed Forces are introduced into hostilities or into any situation described in subsection (a) of this section, the President shall, so long as such armed forces continue to be engaged in such hostilities or situation, report to the Congress periodically on the status of such hostilities or situation as well as on the scope and duration of such hostilities or situation, but in no event shall he report to the Congress less often than once every six months.

Congressional Action

Sec. 5. (a) Each report submitted pursuant to section 4(a)(1) shall be transmitted to the Speaker of the House of Representatives and to the President pro tempore of the Senate on the same calendar day. Each report so transmitted shall be referred to the Committee on Foreign Affairs of the House of Representatives and to the Committee on Foreign Relations of the Senate for appropriate action. If, when the report is transmitted, the Congress has adjourned sine die or has adjourned for any period in excess of three calendar days, the Speaker of the House of Representatives and the President pro tempore of the Senate, if they deem it advisable (or if petitioned by at least 30 percent of the membership of their respective Houses) shall jointly request the President to convene Congress in order that it may consider the report and take appropriate action pursuant to this section.

(b) Within sixty calendar days after a report is submitted or is required to be submitted pursuant to section 4(a)(1), whichever is earlier, the President shall terminate any use of United States Armed Forces with respect to which such report was submitted (or required to be submitted), unless the Congress (1) has declared war or has enacted a specific authorization for such use of United States Armed Forces, (2) has extended by law such sixty-day period, or (3) is physically unable to meet as a result of an armed attack upon the United States. Such sixty-day period shall be extended for not more than an additional thirty days if the President determines and certifies to the Congress in writing that unavoidable military necessity respecting the safety of United States Armed Forces requires the continued use of such armed forces in the course of bringing about a prompt removal of such forces.

(c) Notwithstanding subsection (b), at any time that United States Armed Forces are engaged in hostilities outside the territory of the United States, its possessions and territories without a declaration of war or specific statutory authorization, such forces shall be removed by the President if the Congress so directs by concurrent resolution.

Congressional Priority Procedures
for Joint Resolution or Bill

Sec. 6. (a) Any joint resolution or bill introduced pursuant to section 5(b) at least thirty calendar days before the expiration of the sixty-day period specified in such section shall be referred to the Committee on Foreign Affairs of the House of Representatives or the Committee on Foreign Relations of the Senate, as the case may be, and such committee shall report one such joint resolution or bill, together with its recommendations, not later than twenty-four calendar days before the expiration of the sixty-day period specified in such section, unless such House shall otherwise determine by the yeas and nays.

(b) Any joint resolution or bill so reported shall become the pending business of the House in question (in the case of the Senate the time for debate shall be equally divided between the proponents and the opponents), and shall be voted on within three calendar days thereafter, unless such House shall otherwise determine by yeas and nays.

(c) Such a joint resolution or bill passed by one House shall be referred to the committee of the other House named in subsection (a) and shall be reported out not later than fourteen calendar days before the expiration of the sixty-day period specified in section 5(b). The joint resolution or bill so reported shall become the pending business of the House in question and shall be voted on within three calendar days after it has been reported, unless such House shall otherwise determine by yeas and nays.

(d) In the case of any disagreement between the two Houses of Congress with respect to a joint resolution or bill passed by both Houses, conferees shall be promptly appointed and the committee of conference shall make and file a report with respect to such resolution or bill not later than four calendar days before the expiration of the sixty-day period specified in section 5(b). In the event the conferees are unable to agree within 48 hours, they shall report back to their respective Houses in disagreement. Notwithstanding any rule in either House concerning the printing of conference reports in the Record or concerning any delay in the consideration of such reports, such report shall be acted on by both Houses not later than the expiration of such sixty-day period.

Congressional Priority Procedures for Concurrent Resolution

Sec. 7. (a) Any concurrent resolution introduced pursuant to section 5(c) shall be referred to the Committee on Foreign Affairs of the House of Representatives or the Committee on Foreign Relations of the Senate, as the case may be, and one such concurrent resolution shall be reported out by such committee together with its recommendations within fifteen calendar days, unless such House shall otherwise determine by the yeas and nays.

(b) Any concurrent resolution so reported shall become the pending business of the House in question (in the case of the Senate the time for debate shall be equally divided between the proponents and the opponents) and shall be voted on within three calendar days thereafter, unless such House shall otherwise determine by yeas and nays.

(c) Such a concurrent resolution passed by one House shall be referred to the committee of the other House named in subsection (a) and shall be reported out by such committee together with its recommendations within fifteen calendar days and shall thereupon become the pending business of such House and shall be voted upon within three calendar days, unless such House shall otherwise determine by yeas and nays.

(d) In the case of any disagreement between the two Houses of Congress with respect to a concurrent resolution passed by both Houses, conferees shall be promptly appointed and the committee of conference shall make and file a report with respect to such concurrent resolution within six calendar days after the legislation is referred to the committee of conference. Notwithstanding any rule in either House concerning the printing of conference reports in the Record or concerning any delay in the consideration of such reports, such report shall be acted on by both Houses not later than six calendar days after the conference report is filed. In the event the conferees are unable to agree within 48 hours, they shall report back to their respective Houses in disagreement.

Interpretation of Joint Resolution

Sec. 8. (a) Authority to introduce United States Armed Forces into hostilities or into situations wherein involvement in hostilities is clearly indicated by the circumstances shall not be inferred—

(1) from any provision of law (whether or not in effect before the date of the enactment of this joint resolution), including any provision contained in any appropriation Act, unless such provision specifically authorizes the introduction of United States Armed Forces into hostilities or into

such situations and states that it is intended to constitute specific statutory authorization within the meaning of this joint resolution; or

(2) from any treaty heretofore or hereafter ratified unless such treaty is implemented by legislation specifically authorizing the introduction of United States Armed Forces into hostilities or into such situations and stating that it is intended to constitute specific statutory authorization within the meaning of this joint resolution.

(b) Nothing in this joint resolution shall be construed to require any further specific statutory authorization to permit members of United States Armed Forces to participate jointly with members of the armed forces of one or more foreign countries in the headquarters operations of high-level military commands which were established prior to the date of enactment of this joint resolution and pursuant to the United Nations Charter or any treaty ratified by the United States prior to such date.

(c) For purposes of this joint resolution, the term "introduction of United States Armed Forces" includes the assignment of members of such armed forces to command, coordinate, participate in the movement of, or accompany the regular or irregular military forces of any foreign country or government when such military forces are engaged, or there exists an imminent threat that such forces will become engaged, in hostilities.

(d) Nothing in this joint resolution—

(1) is intended to alter the constitutional authority of the Congress or of the President, or the provisions of existing treaties; or

(2) shall be construed as granting any authority to the President with respect to the introduction of United States Armed Forces into hostilities or into situations wherein involvement in hostilities is clearly indicated by the circumstances which authority he would not have had in the absence of this joint resolution.

Separability Clause

Sec. 9. If any provision of this joint resolution or the application thereof to any person or circumstance is held invalid, the remainder of the joint resolution and the application of such provision to any other person or circumstance shall not be affected thereby.

Effective Date

Sec. 10. This joint resolution shall take effect on the date of its enactment.

United States v. *Nixon*, 418 U.S. 683 (1974)

(Unanimous)

Mr. Chief Justice Burger delivered the opinion of the Court.

This litigation presents for review the denial of a motion, filed in the District Court on behalf of the President of the United States, in the case of *United States* v. *Mitchell* . . . , to quash a third-party subpoena *duces tecum* issued by the United States District Court for the District of Columbia. . . . The subpoena directed the President to produce certain tape recordings and documents relating to his conversations with aides and advisers. The court rejected the President's claims of absolute executive privilege, of lack of jurisdiction, and of failure to satisfy the requirements of Rule 17 (c). The President appealed to the Court of Appeals. We granted both the United States' petition for certiorari before judgment . . . , and also the President's cross-petition for certiorari before judgment . . . , because of the public importance of the issues presented and the need for their prompt resolution. . . .

On March 1, 1974, a grand jury of the United States District Court for the District of Columbia returned an indictment charging seven named individuals with various offenses, including conspiracy to defraud the United States and to obstruct justice. Although he was not designated as such in the indictment, the grand jury named the President, among others, as an unindicted co-conspirator. On April 18, 1974, upon motion of the Special Prosecutor . . . , a subpoena *duces tecum* was issued pursuant to Rule 17 (c) to the President by the United States District Court and made returnable on May 2, 1974. This subpoena required the production, in advance of the September 9 trial date, of certain tapes, memoranda, papers, transcripts, or other writings relating to certain precisely identified meetings between the President and others. The Special Prosecutor was able to fix the time, place, and persons present at these discussions because the White House daily logs and appointment records had been delivered to him. On April 30, the President publicly released edited transcripts of 43 conversations; portions of 20 conversations subject to subpoena in the present case were included. On May 1, 1974, the President's counsel filed a "special appearance" and a motion to quash the subpoena under Rule 17 (c). This motion was accompanied by a formal claim of privilege. At a subsequent hearing, further motions to expunge the grand jury's action naming the President as an unindicted co-conspirator and for protective orders against the disclosure of that information were filed or raised orally by counsel for the President.

On May 20, 1974, the District Court denied the motion to quash and the motions to expunge and for protective orders. . . . It further ordered "the President or any subordinate officer, official, or employee with custody or control of the documents or objects subpoenaed" . . . to deliver to the District Court, on or before May 31, 1974, the originals of all subpoenaed items, as well as an index and analysis of those items, together with tape copies of those portions of the subpoenaed recordings for which transcripts had been released to the public by the President on April 30. The District Court rejected jurisdictional challenges based on a contention that the dispute was nonjusticiable because it was between the Special Prosecutor and the Chief Executive and hence "intra-executive" in character; it also rejected the contention that the Judiciary was without authority to review an assertion of executive privilege by the President. . . .

The District Court held that the judiciary, not the President, was the final arbiter of a claim of executive privilege. The court concluded that, under the circumstances of this case, the presumptive privilege was overcome by the Special Prosecutor's prima facie "demonstration of need sufficiently compelling to warrant judicial examination in chambers. . . . " . . . The court held, finally, that the Special Prosecutor had satisfied the requirements of Rule 17 (c). . . .

Justiciability

In the District Court, the President's counsel argued that the court lacked jurisdiction to issue the subpoena because the matter was an intra-branch dispute between a subordinate and superior officer of the Executive Branch and hence not subject to judicial resolution. That argument has been renewed in this Court with emphasis on the contention that the dispute does not present a "case" or "controversy" which can be adjudicated in the federal courts. The President's counsel argues that the federal courts should not intrude into areas committed to the other branches of Government. He views the present dispute as essentially a "jurisdictional" dispute within the Executive Branch which he analogizes to a dispute between two congressional committees. Since the Executive Branch has exclusive authority and absolute discretion to decide whether to prosecute a case . . . , it is contended that a President's decision is final in determining what evidence is to be used in a given criminal case. Although his counsel concedes that the President has delegated certain specific powers to the Special Prosecutor, he has not "waived nor delegated to the Special Prosecutor the President's duty to claim privilege as to all materials . . . which fall within the President's inherent authority to refuse to disclose to any executive officer." . . . The Special Prosecutor's demand for the items therefore presents, in the view of the President's counsel, a political question under *Baker* v. *Carr* . . . , since it involves a "textually demonstrable" grant of power under Art. II. . . .

Our starting point is the nature of the proceeding for which the evidence is sought—here a pending criminal prosecution. It is a judicial proceeding in a federal court alleging violation of federal laws and is brought in the name of the United States as sovereign. . . . Under the authority of Art. II, § 2, Congress has vested in the Attorney General the power to conduct the criminal litigation of the United States Government. . . . It has also vested in him the power to appoint subordinate officers to assist him in the discharge of his duties. . . . Acting pursuant to those statutes, the Attorney General has delegated the authority to represent the United States in these particular matters to a Special Prosecutor with unique authority and tenure. The regulation gives the Special Prosecutor explicit power to contest the invocation of executive privilege in the process of seeking evidence deemed relevant to the performance of these specially delegated duties. . . .

The demands of and the resistance to the subpoena present an obvious controversy in the ordinary sense, but that alone is not sufficient to meet constitutional standards. In the constitutional sense, controversy means more than disagreement and conflict; rather it means the kind of controversy courts traditionally resolve. Here at issue is the production or nonproduction of specified evidence deemed by the Special Prosecutor to be relevant and admissible in a pending criminal case. It is sought by one official of the Executive Branch within the scope of his express authority; it is resisted by the Chief Executive on the ground of his duty to preserve the confidentiality of the communications of the President. Whatever the correct answer on the merits, these issues are "of a type which are traditionally justiciable." . . . The independent Special Prosecutor with his asserted need for the subpoenaed material in the underlying criminal prosecution is opposed by the President with his steadfast assertion of privilege against disclosure of the material. This setting assures there is "that concrete adverseness which sharpens the presentation of issues upon which the court so largely depends for illumination of difficult constitutional questions." . . . Moreover, since the matter is one arising in the regular course of a federal criminal prosecution, it is within the traditional scope of Art. III power. . . .

In light of the uniqueness of the setting in which the conflict arises, the fact that both parties are officers of the Executive Branch cannot be viewed as a barrier to justiciability. It would be inconsistent with the applicable law and regulation, and the unique facts of this case to conclude other than that the Special Prosecutor has standing to bring this action and that a justiciable controversy is presented for decision. . . .

The Claim of Privilege

A. Having determined that the requirements of Rule 17 (c) were satisfied, we turn to the claim that the subpoena should be quashed because it demands "confidential conversations between a President and his close advisors that it would be inconsistent with the public interest to produce." . . . The first contention is a broad claim that the separation of powers doctrine precludes judicial review of a President's claim of privilege. The second contention is that if he does not prevail on the claim of absolute privilege, the court should hold as a matter of constitutional law that the privilege prevails over the subpoena *duces tecum.*

In the performance of assigned constitutional duties each branch of the Government must initially interpret the Constitution, and the interpretation of its powers by any branch is due great respect from the others. The President's counsel, as we have noted, reads the Constitution as providing an absolute privilege of confidentiality for all Presidential communications. Many decisions of this Court, however, have unequivocally reaffirmed the holding of *Marbury* v. *Madison* . . . that "[i]t is emphatically the province and duty of the judicial department to say what the law is." . . .

No holding of the Court has defined the scope of judicial power specifically relating to the enforcement of a subpoena for confidential Presidential communications for use in a criminal prosecution, but other exercises of power by the Executive Branch and the Legislative Branch have been found invalid as in conflict with the Constitution. . . . *Youngstown Sheet & Tube Co.* v. *Sawyer* . . . (1952). . . .

Our system of government "requires that federal courts on occasion interpret the Constitution in a manner at variance with the construction given the document by another branch." . . . Notwithstanding the deference each branch must accord the others, the "judicial Power of the United States" vested in the federal courts by Art. III, § 1, of the Constitution can no more be shared with the Executive Branch than the Chief Executive, for example, can share with the Judiciary the veto power, or the Congress share with the Judiciary the power to override a Presidential veto. Any other conclusion would be contrary to the basic concept of separation of powers and the checks and balances that flow from the scheme of a tripartite government. . . . We therefore reaffirm that it is the province and duty of this Court "to say what the law is" with respect to the claim of privilege presented in this case. . . .

B. In support of his claim of absolute privilege, the President's counsel urges two grounds, one of which is common to all governments and one of which is peculiar to our system of separation of powers. The first ground is the valid need for protection of communications between high Government officials and those who advise and assist them in the performance of their manifold duties; the importance of this confidentiality is too plain to require further discussion. Human experience teaches that those who expect public dissemination of their remarks may well temper candor with a concern for appearances and for their own interests to the detriment of the decision-making process. Whatever the nature of the privilege of confidentiality of Presidential communications in the exercise of Art. II powers, the privilege can be said to derive from the supremacy of each branch within its own assigned area of constitutional duties. Certain powers and privileges flow from the nature of enumerated powers; the protection of the confidentiality of Presidential communications has similar constitutional underpinnings.

The second ground asserted by the President's counsel in support of the claim of absolute privilege rests on the doctrine of separation of powers. Here it is argued that the independence of the Executive Branch within its own sphere . . . insulates a President from a judicial subpoena in an ongoing criminal prosecution, and thereby protects confidential Presidential communications.

However, neither the doctrine of separation of powers, nor the need for confidentiality of high-level communications, without more, can sustain an absolute, unqualified Presidential privilege of immunity from judicial process under all circumstances. The President's need for complete candor and objectivity from advisers calls for great deference from the courts. However, when the privilege depends solely on the broad, undifferentiated claim of public interest in the confidentiality of such conversations, a confrontation with other values arises. Absent a claim of need to protect military, diplomatic, or sensitive national security secrets, we find it difficult to accept the argument that even the very important interest in confidentiality of

Presidential communications is significantly diminished by production of such material for *in camera* inspection with all the protection that a district court will be obliged to provide.

The impediment that an absolute, unqualified privilege would place in the way of the primary constitutional duty of the Judicial Branch to do justice in criminal prosecutions would plainly conflict with the function of the courts under Art. III. In designing the structure of our Government and dividing and allocating the sovereign power among three co-equal branches, the Framers of the Constitution sought to provide a comprehensive system, but the separate powers were not intended to operate with absolute independence. . . . To read the Art. II powers of the President as providing an absolute privilege as against a subpoena essential to enforcement of criminal statutes on no more than a generalized claim of the public interest in confidentiality of nonmilitary and nondiplomatic discussions would upset the constitutional balance of "a workable government" and gravely impair the role of the courts under Art. III.

C. . . . The expectation of a President to the confidentiality of his conversations and correspondence, like the claim of confidentiality of judicial deliberations, for example, has all the values to which we accord deference for the privacy of all citizens and, added to those values, is the necessity for protection of the public interest in candid, objective, and even blunt or harsh opinions in Presidential decisionmaking. A President and those who assist him must be free to explore alternatives in the process of shaping policies and making decisions and to do so in a way many would be unwilling to express except privately. These are the considerations justifying a presumptive privilege for Presidential communications. The privilege is fundamental to the operation of Government and inextricably rooted in the separation of powers under the Constitution. . . .

But this presumptive privilege must be considered in light of our historic commitment to the rule of law. This is nowhere more profoundly manifest than in our view that "the twofold aim [of criminal justice] is that guilt shall not escape or innocence suffer." . . . We have elected to employ an adversary system of criminal justice in which the parties contest all issues before a court of law. The need to develop all relevant facts in the adversary system is both fundamental and comprehensive. The ends of criminal justice would be defeated if judgments were to be founded on a partial or speculative presentation of the facts. The very integrity of the judicial system and public confidence in the system depend on full disclosure of all the facts, within the framework of the rules of evidence. To ensure that justice is done, it is imperative to the function of courts that compulsory process be available for the production of evidence needed either by the prosecution or by the defense. . . .

In this case the President challenges a subpoena served on him as a third party requiring the production of materials for use in a criminal prosecution; he does so on the claim that he has a privilege against disclosure of confidential communications. He does not place his claim of privilege on the ground they are military or diplomatic secrets. As to these areas of Art. II duties the courts have traditionally shown the utmost deference to Presidential responsibilities. . . . No case of the Court, however, has extended this high degree of deference to a President's generalized interest in confidentiality. Nowhere in the Constitution, as we have noted earlier, is there any explicit reference to a privilege of confidentiality, yet to the extent this interest relates to the effective discharge of a President's powers, it is constitutionally based.

The right to the production of all evidence at a criminal trial similarly has constitutional dimensions. The Sixth Amendment explicitly confers upon every defendant in a criminal trial the right "to be confronted with the witnesses against him" and "to have compulsory process for obtaining witnesses in his favor." Moreover, the Fifth Amendment also guarantees that no person shall be deprived of liberty without due process of law. It is the manifest duty of the courts to vindicate those guarantees, and to accomplish that it is essential that all relevant and admissible evidence be produced.

In this case we must weigh the importance of the general privilege of confidentiality of Presidential communications in performance of the President's responsibilities against the inroads of such a privilege on the fair administration of criminal justice. The interest in preserving confidentiality is weighty indeed and entitled to great respect. However, we cannot conclude that advisers will be moved to temper the candor of their remarks by the infrequent occasions of disclosure because of the possibility that such conversations will be called for in the context of a criminal prosecution.

On the other hand, the allowance of the privilege to withhold evidence that is demonstrably relevant in a criminal trial would cut deeply into the guarantee of due process of law and gravely impair the basic function of the courts. A President's acknowledged need for confidentiality in the communications of his office is general in nature, whereas the constitutional need for production of relevant evidence in a criminal proceeding is specific and central to the fair adjudication of a particular criminal case in the administration of justice. Without access to specific facts a criminal prosecution may be totally frustrated. The President's broad interest in confidentiality of communications will not be vitiated by disclosure of a limited number of conversations preliminarily shown to have some bearing on the pending criminal cases.

We conclude that when the ground for asserting privilege as to subpoenaed materials sought for use in a criminal trial is based only on the generalized interest in confidentiality, it cannot prevail over the fundamental demands of due process of law in the fair administration of criminal justice. The generalized assertion of privilege must yield to the demonstrated, specific need for evidence in a pending criminal trial.

D. . . . Since this matter came before the Court during the pendency of a criminal prosecution, and on representations that time is of the essence, the mandate shall issue forthwith. *Affirmed.*

Senator Sam Ervin on Watergate and the Presidency, 1974

Since the Senate Select Committee on Presidential Campaign Activities is filing with the Senate its final report concerning the investigation that body authorized and directed it to make, I deem it appropriate to state as succinctly as possible some of my personal observations respecting the tragic events known collectively as the Watergate, which disgraced the Presidential election of 1972.

In doing this, I ask and endeavor to answer these questions: What was Watergate? Why was Watergate? Is there an antidote which will prevent future Watergates? If so, what is that antidote?

Before attempting to answer these questions, I wish to make these things plain:

1. I am not undertaking to usurp and exercise the power of impeachment, which the Constitution confers upon the House of Representatives alone. As a consequence, nothing I say should be construed as an expression of an opinion in respect to the question of whether or not President Nixon is impeachable in connection with the Watergate or any other matter.

2. Inasmuch as its Committee on the Judiciary is now studying whether or not it ought to recommend to the House the impeachment of the President, I shall also refrain from making any comment on the question of whether or not the President has performed in an acceptable manner his paramount constitutional obligation "to take care that the laws be faithfully executed."

3. Watergate was not invented by enemies of the Nixon administration or even by the news media. On the contrary, Watergate was perpetrated upon America by White House and political aides, whom President Nixon himself had entrusted with the management of his campaign for reelection to the Presidency, a campaign which was divorced to a marked degree from the campaigns of other Republicans who sought election to public office in 1972. I note at this point without elaboration that these White House and political aides were virtually without experience in either Government or politics apart from their association with President Nixon.

4. Life had not subjected these White House and political aides to the disadvantaged conditions which are glibly cited as the causes of wrongdoing. On the contrary, fortune had smiled upon them. They came from substantial homes, possessed extraordinary talents, had had unusual educational opportunities, and occupied high social positions.

5. Watergate was unprecedented in the political annals of America in respect to the scope and intensity of its unethical and illegal actions. To be sure, there had been previous milder political scandals in American history. That fact does not excuse Watergate. Murder and stealing have occurred in every generation since Earth began, but that fact has not made murder meritorious or larceny legal.

What Was Watergate?

President Nixon entrusted the management of his campaign for reelection and his campaign finances to the Committee for the Re-Election of the President, which was headed by former Attorney General John N. Mitchell, and the Finance Committee To Re-Elect the President, which was headed by former Secretary of Commerce, Maurice Stans. Since the two committees occupied offices in the same office building in Washington and worked in close conjunction, it seems proper to call them for ease of expression the Nixon reelection committees.

Watergate was a conglomerate of various illegal and unethical activities in which various officers and employees of the Nixon reelection committees and various White House aides of President Nixon participated in varying ways and degrees to accomplish these successive objectives:

1. To destroy, insofar as the Presidential election of 1972 was concerned, the integrity of the process by which the President of the United States is nominated and elected.

2. To hide from law enforcement officers, prosecutors, grand jurors, courts, the news media, and the American people the identities and wrong-doing of those officers and employees of the Nixon reelection committees, and those White House aides who had undertaken to destroy the integrity of the process by which the President of the United States is nominated and elected.

To accomplish the first of these objectives, the participating officers and employees of the reelection committees and the participating White House aides of President Nixon engaged in one or more of these things:

1. They exacted enormous contributions—usually in cash—from corporate executives by impliedly implanting in their minds the impressions that the making of the contributions was necessary to insure that the corporations would receive governmental favors, or avoid governmental disfavors, while President Nixon remained in the White House. A substantial portion of the contributions were made out of corporate funds in violation of a law enacted by Congress a generation ago.

2. They hid substantial parts of these contributions in cash in safes and secret deposits to conceal their sources and the identities of those who had made them.

3. They disbursed substantial portions of these hidden contributions in a surreptitious manner to finance the bugging and the burglary of the offices of the Democratic National Committee in the Watergate complex in Washington for the purpose of obtaining political intelligence; and to sabotage by dirty tricks, espionage, and scurrilous and false libels and slanders the campaigns and the reputations of honorable men, whose only offenses were that they sought the nomination of the Democratic Party for President and the opportunity to run against President Nixon for that office in the Presidential election of 1972.

4. They deemed the departments and agencies of the Federal Govern-

ment to be the political playthings of the Nixon administration rather than impartial instruments for serving the people, and undertook to induce them to channel Federal contracts, grants, and loans to areas, groups, or individuals so as to promote the reelection of the President rather than to further the welfare of the people.

5. They branded as enemies of the President individuals and members of the news media who dissented from the President's policies and opposed his reelection, and conspired to urge the Department of Justice, the Federal Bureau of Investigation, the Internal Revenue Service, and the Federal Communications Commission to pervert the use of their legal powers to harass them for so doing.

6. They borrowed from the Central Intelligence Agency disguises which E. Howard Hunt used in political espionage operations, and photographic equipment which White House employees known as the "Plumbers" and their hired confederates used in connection with burglarizing the office of a psychiatrist which they believed contained information concerning Daniel Ellsberg which the White House was anxious to secure.

7. They assigned to E. Howard Hunt, who was at the time a White House consultant occupying an office in the Executive Office Building, the gruesome task of falsifying State Department documents which they contemplated using in their altered state to discredit the Democratic Party by defaming the memory of former President John Fitzgerald Kennedy, who as the hapless victim of an assassin's bullet had been sleeping in the tongueless silence of the dreamless dust for 9 years.

8. They used campaign funds to hire saboteurs to forge and disseminate false and scurrilous libels of honorable men running for the Democratic Presidential nomination in Democratic Party primaries.

During the darkness of the early morning of June 17, 1972, James W. McCord, the security chief of the John Mitchell committee, and four residents of Miami, Fla., were arrested by Washington police while they were burglarizing the offices of the Democratic National Committee in the Watergate complex to obtain political intelligence. At the same time, the four residents of Miami had in their possession more than fifty $100 bills which were subsequently shown to be a part of campaign contributions made to the Nixon reelection committees.

On September 15, 1972, these five burglars, E. Howard Hunt, and Gordon Liddy, general counsel of the Stans committee, were indicted by the grand jury on charges arising out of the bugging and burglary of the Watergate.

They were placed on trial upon these charges before Judge John Sirica, and a petit jury in the U.S. District Court for the District of Columbia in January 1973. At that time, Hunt and the four residents of Miami pleaded guilty, and McCord and Liddy were found guilty by the petit jury. None of them took the witness stand during the trial.

The arrest of McCord and the four residents of Miami created consternation in the Nixon reelection committees and the White House. Thereupon, various officers and employees of the Nixon reelection committees and various White House aides undertook to conceal from law-enforcement officers, prosecutors, grand jurors, courts, the news media, and the American people the identities and activities of those officers and employees of the Nixon reelection committees and those White House aides who had participated in any way in the Watergate affair.

Various officers and employees of the Nixon reelection committees and various White House aides engaged in one or more of these acts to make the concealment effective and thus obstruct the due administration of justice:

1. They destroyed the records of the Nixon reelection committees antedating the bugging and the burglary.

2. They induced the Acting Director of the FBI, who was a Nixon appointee, to destroy the State Department documents which E. Howard Hunt had been falsifying.

3. They obtained from the Acting Director of the FBI copies of scores of interviews conducted by FBI agents in connection with their investigation of the bugging and the burglary, and were enabled thereby to coach their confederates to give false and misleading statements to the FBI.

4. They sought to persuade the FBI to refrain from investigating the sources of the campaign funds which were used to finance the bugging and the burglary.

5. They intimidated employees of the Nixon reelection committees and employees of the White House by having their lawyers present when these employees were being questioned by agents of the FBI, and thus deterred these employees from making full disclosures to the FBI.

6. They lied to agents of the FBI, prosecutors, and grand jurors who undertook to investigate the bugging and the burglary, and to Judge Sirica and the petit jurors who tried the seven original Watergate defendants in January 1973.

7. They persuaded the Department of Justice and the prosecutors to take out-of-court statements from Maurice Stans, President Nixon's chief campaign fundraiser, and Charles Colson, Egil Krogh, and David Young, White House aides, and Charles Colson's secretary, instead of requiring them to testify before the grand jury investigating the bugging and the burglary in conformity with the established procedures governing such matters, and thus denied the grand jurors the opportunity to question them.

8. They persuaded the Department of Justice and the prosecutors to refrain from asking Donald Segretti, their chief hired saboteur, any questions involving Herbert W. Kalmbach, the President's personal attorney, who was known by them to have paid Segretti for dirty tricks he perpetrated upon honorable men seeking the Democratic Presidential nomination, and who was subsequently identified before the Senate Select Committee as one who played a major role in the secret delivery of hush money to the seven original Watergate defendants.

9. They made cash payments totaling hundreds of thousands of dollars out of campaign funds in surreptitious ways to the seven original Watergate

defendants as hush money to buy their silence and keep them from revealing their knowledge of the identities of the officers and employees of the Nixon reelection committees and the White House aides who had participated in the Watergate.

10. They gave assurances to some of the original seven defendants that they would receive Presidential clemency after serving short portions of their sentences if they refrained from divulging the identities and activities of the officers and employees of the Nixon reelection committees and the White House aides who had participated in the Watergate affair.

11. They made arrangements by which the attorneys who represented the seven original Watergate defendants received their fees in cash from moneys which had been collected to finance President Nixon's reelection campaign.

12. They induced the Department of Justice and the prosecutors of the seven original Watergate defendants to assure the news media and the general public that there was no evidence that any persons other than the seven original Watergate defendants were implicated in any way in any Watergate-related crimes.

13. They inspired massive efforts on the part of segments of the news media friendly to the administration to persuade the American people that most of the members of the Select Committee named by the Senate to investigate the Watergate were biased and irresponsible men motivated solely by desires to exploit the matters they investigated for personal or partisan advantage, and that the allegations in the press that Presidential aides had been involved in the Watergate were venomous machinations of a hostile and unreliable press bent on destroying the country's confidence in a great and good President.

One shudders to think that the Watergate conspiracies might have been effectively concealed and their most dramatic episode might have been dismissed as a "third-rate" burglary conceived and committed solely by the seven original Watergate defendants had it not been for the courage and penetrating understanding of Judge Sirica, the thoroughness of the investigative reporting of Carl Bernstein, Bob Woodward, and other representatives of a free press, the labors of the Senate Select Committee and its excellent staff, and the dedication and diligence of Special Prosecutors Archibald Cox and Leon Jaworski and their associates.

Why Was Watergate?

Unlike the men who were responsible for Teapot Dome, the Presidential aides who perpetrated Watergate were not seduced by the love of money, which is sometimes thought to be the root of all evil. On the contrary, they were instigated by a lust for political power, which is at least as corrupting as political power itself.

They gave their allegiance to the President and his policies. They had stood for a time near to him, and had been entrusted by him with great governmental and political power. They enjoyed exercising such power, and longed for its continuance.

They knew that the power they enjoyed would be lost and the policies to which they adhered would be frustrated if the President should be defeated.

As a consequence of these things, they believed the President's reelection to be a most worthy objective, and succumbed to an age-old temptation. They resorted to evil means to promote what they conceived to be a good end.

Their lust for political power blinded them to ethical considerations and legal requirements; to Aristotle's aphorism that the good of man must be the end of politics; and to Grover Cleveland's conviction that a public office is a public trust.

They had forgotten, if they ever knew, that the Constitution is designed to be a law for rulers and people alike at all times and under all circumstances; and that no doctrine involving more pernicious consequences to the commonweal has ever been invented by the wit of man than the notion that any of its provisions can be suspended by the President for any reason whatsoever.

On the contrary, they apparently believed that the President is above the Constitution, and has the autocratic power to suspend its provisions if he decides in his own unreviewable judgment that his action in so doing promotes his own political interests or the welfare of the Nation. As one of them testified before the Senate Select Committee, they believed that the President has the autocratic power to suspend the fourth amendment whenever he imagines that some indefinable aspect of national security is involved.

I digress to reject this doctrine of the constitutional omnipotence of the President. As long as I have a mind to think, a tongue to speak, and a heart to love my country, I shall deny that the Constitution confers any autocratic power on the President, or authorizes him to convert George Washington's America into Gaius Caesar's Rome.

The lust for political power of the Presidential aides who perpetrated Watergate on America blinded them to the laws of God as well as to the laws and ethics of man.

As a consequence, they violated the spiritual law which forbids men to do evil even when they think good will result from it, and ignored these warnings of the King James version of the Bible:

> There is nothing covered, that shall not be revealed; neither hid, that shall not be known.
>
> Be not deceived; God is not mocked: For whatsoever a man soweth, that shall he also reap.

I find corroboration for my conclusion that lust for political power produced Watergate in words uttered by the most eloquent and learned of all the Romans, Marcus Tullius Cicero, about 2100 years ago. He said:

Most men, however, are inclined to forget justice altogether, when once the craving for military power or political honors and glory has taken possession of them. Remember the saying of Ennius, "When crowns are at stake, no friendship is sacred, no faith shall be kept."

As one after another of the individuals who participated in Watergate goes to prison, we see in action an inexorable spiritual law which Rudyard Kipling phrased in this fashion in his poem about Tomlinson's Ghost:

> "For the sin ye do by two and two,
> You must pay for one by one."

As we contemplate the motives that inspired their misdeeds, we acquire a new awareness of the significance of Cardinal Wolsey's poignant lament:

> "Had I but serv'd my God with half
> The zeal I serv'd my King,
> He would not in mine age have left me
> Naked to mine enemies."

The Antidote for Future Watergates

Is there an antidote which will prevent future Watergates? If so, what is it?

The Senate Select Committee is recommending the enactment of new laws which it believes will minimize the danger of future Watergates and make more adequate and certain the punishment of those who attempt to perpetrate them upon our country.

Candor compels the confession, however, that law alone will not suffice to prevent future Watergates. In saying this, I do not disparage the essential role which law plays in the life of our Nation. As one who has labored as a practicing lawyer, a judge, and a legislator all of my adult years, I venerate the law as an instrument of service to society. At the same time, however, I know the weakness of the law as well as its strength.

Law is not self-executing. Unfortunately, at times its execution rests in the hands of those who are faithless to it. And even when its enforcement is committed to those who revere it, law merely deters some human beings from offending, and punishes other human beings for offending. It does not make men good. This task can be performed only by ethics or religion or morality.

Since politics is the art or science of government, no man is fit to participate in politics or to seek or hold public office unless he has two characteristics.

The first of these characteristics is that he must understand and be dedicated to the true purpose of government, which is to promote the good of the people, and entertain the abiding conviction that a public office is a public trust, which must never be abused to secure private advantage.

The second characteristic is that he must possess that intellectual and moral integrity, which is the priceless ingredient in good character.

When all is said, the only sure antidote for future Watergates is understanding of fundamental principles and intellectual and moral integrity in the men and women who achieve or are entrusted with governmental or political power.

Josiah Gilbert Holland, a poet of a bygone generation, recognized this truth in a poem which he called "The Day's Demand," and which I like to call "America's Prayer." I quote his words:

> "God give us men! A time like this demands
> Strong minds, great hearts, true faith and ready hands;
> Men whom the lust of office does not kill;
> Men whom the spoils of office cannot buy;
> Men who possess opinions and a will;
> Men who have honor—men who will not lie;
> Men who can stand before a demagogue
> And damn his treacherous flatteries without winking;
> Tall men, sun-crowned, who live above the fog
> In public duty, and in private thinking."

✠ E S S A Y S

The critical question raised by the modern presidency is whether the scheme of separation of powers crafted by the framers in 1787 still has meaning. The presidential role in the Korean and Vietnam conflicts as well as the Watergate affair has suggested to some observers the need for reform to strike a balance between Congress and the chief executive. Arthur M. Schlesinger, Jr., a Pulitzer Prize–winning historian at the City College of New York and a former adviser to President John F. Kennedy, argues in the first essay that the "imperial presidency" has been more the creation of the particular persons who have occupied the White House than the product of an inherently flawed constitutional system. In the specific case of war powers, the late Alexander Bickel, who taught at the Yale Law School, suggests in the second essay that much of the onus for the Vietnam War must rest with Congress, which failed to exercise its express powers forcefully. In the final selection, Philip B. Kurland of the University of Chicago Law School suggests, contrary to Schlesinger, that Watergate is best understood as the consequence of a systemic failure rather than of the shortcomings of Richard M. Nixon.

The Influence of Presidential Personality

ARTHUR M. SCHLESINGER, JR.

[T]he Korean War brought about a new national emergency, formally proclaimed by Truman in December 1950, and thereby injected new life into the war power and its personification, the Commander in Chief. By bringing the nation into war without congressional authorization and by then successfully defending his exercise of independent presidential initiative, Truman enormously expanded assumptions of presidential prerogative. "The acquisition of a dozen bases and gift of fifty destroyers that President Roosevelt moved on so cautiously less than fifteen years ago," Harold Stein, an eminent government-official-turned-political-scientist, wrote in the wake of Korea, "would be a routine, indeed a minor transaction today." And, where independent power exercised in domestic affairs did not necessarily produce equivalent power in foreign affairs, as the case of Roosevelt in the 1930s had shown, independent power exercised in foreign affairs was very likely to strengthen and embolden the Presidency at home.

In April 1952, fearing that a nationwide strike would shut down the steel industry and stop the flow of military material to the troops in Korea, Truman directed the Secretary of Commerce to seize and operate the steel mills. This was not done with particular relish or sweep. Truman emphasized his "distaste" for government operation of the steel industry. Presidential intervention was announced as temporary. Assurance was given that the mills would return as soon as possible to private ownership. Truman reported his action without delay to Congress and conceded its power to supersede his policy if it wished to do so. Subsequently he wrote the Senate requesting that Congress act, preferably in support of the seizure but, if it so judged, in rejection of "the course of action that I have followed." Truman's own summary was accurate enough: "I have twice sent messages to the Congress asking it to prescribe a course . . . if the Congress disagreed with the action I was taking. The Congress has not done so." In short, there was an emergency of a sort, the President's action was neither unreasonable nor irreversible, and Congress declined repeated invitations to veto the President's policy and enact one of its own.

Yet behind the moderate action lay an immoderate theory. Truman set forth the theory with typical bluntness. "The President of the United States," he said, "has very great inherent powers to meet great national emergencies"; indeed, "it was the duty of the President under the Constitution to act to preserve the safety of the Nation." In a somewhat garbled historical excursion he lectured to a press conference about "a gentleman by the name of Jefferson" who had used such powers to buy Louisiana ("they tried to impeach him for that, if I remember correctly"), "a gentleman by the name of Tyler . . . a gentleman by the name of Polk . . . Mr. Lincoln . . . President Roosevelt." As for the present situation, "We are in one of the greatest emergencies the country has ever been in." It would be "unthinkable" to let a steel strike block "our efforts to support our armed forces and to protect our national security." "I feel sure," the President said, "that the Constitution does not require me to endanger our national safety by letting all the steel mills shut down." In the name of emergency, in short, Truman was asserting the power to rule by decree in a field—industrial seizure—customarily controlled by Congress. Nor was it clear what he thought the limits on his emergency authority were. If he could seize steel mills under his inherent powers, could he also seize newspapers and radio stations? Asked this question, Truman made a direct, imprudent and characteristic response,

"Under similar circumstances the President of the United States has to act for whatever is for the best of the country. That's the answer."

This was Lockean prerogative with a vengeance. The steel companies promptly sued to get their property back, and the Truman thesis thereupon underwent judicial scrutiny. In the lower court an Assistant Attorney General defended the seizure in Trumanesque terms, claiming that the President had inherent and independent power, limited only by impeachment or by defeat in the next election, to save the nation from catastrophe. The district judge denied this spacious claim; and, when the case moved up to the Supreme Court, the government offered a more circumspect argument. It now said that the acuteness of the emergency required the President to act, and "the aggregate of his constitutional powers" as President and Commander in Chief authorized him to act, until Congress was prepared to act for itself. Both sides thus acknowledged ultimate legislative supremacy. The difference was that, where the government contended that the President had the right to act in an emergency unless or until Congress expressly denied his power to take the action, the steel companies contended the President had no power to act without prior congressional authorization or against earlier congressional instruction.

The Court delivered its judgment eight weeks after the President's intervention. It pronounced the seizure unconstitutional by a 6 to 3 vote. The nine justices, however, elaborated their views in seven separate opinions. The result was a confusing, if intermittently dazzling, examination of the presidential claim to emergency prerogative. The import of the verdict must be divined (to borrow the phrase Justice Jackson applied in his own opinion to the mystery of the Founding Fathers and the war-making power) from materials almost as enigmatic as the dreams Joseph was called on to interpret for Pharaoh.

There is no question that the idea of independent presidential power received a severe rebuke. But the rebuke was by no means total. It was confined, in the first place, to domestic abuse of presidential power. Neither the majority nor even the minority saw the case as involving in any primary sense the President's authority in foreign affairs. Jackson scouted the government's suggestion that, because Truman had sent troops to Korea in an exercise of "the President's constitutional powers," he was therefore justified in taking over the steel plants. "No doctrine that the Court could promulgate would seem to me more sinister and alarming," Jackson said,

> than that a President whose conduct of foreign affairs is so largely uncontrolled, and often even is unknown, can vastly enlarge his mastery over the internal affairs of the country by his own commitment of the Nation's armed forces to some foreign venture.

Justices were particularly caustic about the notion that the Commander in Chief clause conferred domestic powers on the Presidency. "Even though 'theater of war' be an expanding concept," Justice Black said dryly for the Court, "we cannot with faithfulness to our constitutional system hold that the Commander in Chief . . . has the ultimate power as such to take possession of private property in order to keep labor disputes from stopping production. This is a job for the Nation's lawmakers, not for its military authorities." Jackson dismissed the Commander in Chief thesis as a "loose appellation" unjustifiably advanced as support for any presidential action, internal or external, involving the use of force, "the idea being that it vests power to do anything, anywhere, that can be done with an army or navy." The Constitution, Jackson said, in making the President Commander in Chief of the Army and Navy, did not also constitute him "Commander in Chief of the country, its industries and its inhabitants." His powers as Commander in Chief were to be "measured by the command functions usual to the topmost officer of the army and navy." He added, "No penance would ever expiate the sin against free government of holding that a President can escape control of executive powers by law through assuming his military role."

The Court's rebuke to independent presidential power was further narrowed by the argument, advanced more carefully by some justices than others, that the steel seizure was invalid because undertaken in disregard of remedies already laid down by Congress for industrial emergencies. In this connection Jackson set forth an analysis, brilliant then and classic now, of the American separation of powers. Speaking for the Court, Black had given a rigid and rather unrealistic account of the equal and coordinate branches of government. Jackson, while agreeing that the Constitution had divided power in order to secure liberty, added that it had also supposed that practice would unite the divided powers into a workable government. The Constitution, he said, therefore enjoined upon the branches of government "separateness but interdependence, autonomy but reciprocity."

As for the Presidency and Congress, the two branches in contention over the steel seizure, they, Jackson continued, had three distinguishable levels of interdependence. The first was when the President acted in accordance with the express or implied authorization of Congress. Then, Jackson said, "his authority is at its maximum." Only in such a case could the President be said "to personify the federal sovereignty." When the Presidency and Congress acted together, they would be supported "by the strongest of presumptions and the widest latitude of judicial interpretation." The second level was a "zone of twilight" where the Presidency and Congress shared authority or where the distribution of authority was uncertain. In the twilight zone "congressional inertia, indifference or quiescence may sometimes, at least as a practical matter, enable, if not invite, measures on independent presidential responsibility." Acceptance of such presidential initiative would depend "on the imperatives of events and contemporary imponderables" rather than on abstract theories of law.

The third level, in which Jackson included the case at hand, was when the Presidency took measures "incompatible with the expressed or implied will of Congress." In this case presidential power was "at its lowest ebb," and the Court could sustain exclusive presidential control only by disqualifying Congress from acting upon the subject. "Presidential claim to a power at once so conclusive and preclusive must be scrutinized with caution, for what is at stake is the equilibrium established by our constitutional system." The steel seizure was therefore illegal because Congress had already covered the situation in statutes inconsistent with the President's action. Had Congress not pre-empted the field, then presumably the seizure would have fallen in the "zone of twilight" and would be validated or not by contemporary imperatives and imponderables rather than by abstract theories of law. . . .

Jackson's twilight zone thus seemed to admit a possibility of presidential emergency power. On the other hand, Jackson also took care to attack "the unarticulated assumption . . . that necessity knows no law." The Founding Fathers, he said, had known emergencies; they were children of revolution. But they had known too that emergency might be the pretext for usurpation. That was why, aside from a single exception, the suspension of *habeas corpus* in time of rebellion or invasion, they had made no express provision for exercise of extraordinary authority. "I do not think," Jackson said with a certain force, "we rightfully may so amend their work." Here Jackson disagreed with Lincoln, who, less convincingly, had claimed the *habeas corpus* clause as a precedent for broad suspension of constitutional rights in the presidential interest in time of rebellion or invasion.

In any case, Jackson felt that presidential claims to act beyond Congress required the most suspicious examination. For one thing, Congress itself had long since evolved a technique by which normal executive powers could be enlarged to embrace an emergency; "under this procedure we retain Government by law—special, temporary law, perhaps, but law none the less." Jackson pointed out that Franklin Roosevelt, though confronted by no less a catastrophe than the imminent collapse of the economic system, had not taken this as a justification for rule by decree; the New Deal had been founded on delegated congressional power, not on inherent presidential power. So too Frankfurter: "The fact that power exists in the Government does not vest it in the President. The need for new legislation does not enact it." It was an illuminating commentary on the changes in the Presidency since the Second World War that the four justices who had been closest to Roosevelt—Frankfurter, Douglas, Black, Jackson, fervent New Dealers all fifteen years before—saw no precedent in the New Deal for the steel seizure and united in voting against Truman's enlargement of independent presidential authority.

Where did all this leave Locke, Jefferson and Lincoln? Here the materials for divination grow more enigmatic than ever. Jackson was evidently against the law of necessity, except when Congress was silent and contemporary imperatives and imponderables might sustain presidential initiative. This was quite an exception. Justice Douglas said, "What a President may do as a matter of expediency or extremity may never reach a definitive constitutional decision." Justice Burton said, "The present situation is not comparable to that of an imminent invasion or threatened attack. We do not face the issue of what might be the President's constitutional power to meet such catastrophic situations." Justice Clark, who agreed with the majority in result but not in argument, went even farther. The Constitution in his view *did* "grant to the President extensive authority in time of grave and imperative national emergency. In fact, to my thinking such a grant may well be necessary to the very existence of the Constitution itself." In describing this authority, Clark said he did not care whether it was called "inherent," "residual," "implied," "emergency," "aggregate" or whatever; it existed, and had to exist. But having gone so far toward Lockean prerogative, Clark pulled back. In the case of the steel seizure, he said, Congress had laid down specific procedures, and Truman should have followed them. Yet "in the absence of such action by Congress, the President's independent power to act depends upon the gravity of the situation confronting the nation."

Clark's concern with the gravity of the particular emergency made the essential point. Truman claimed the strike as one of the greatest emergencies the country had ever faced, and Chief Justice Vinson wrote in his dissent that "the survival of the Republic itself might be at stake." But the opinions of the Court majority registered the sense of Congress and the nation, volubly expressed in the two months since the seizure, that Truman and Vinson had it wrong, and that this was simply not an emergency calling for drastic recourse to inherent presidential power. Had Congress not pre-empted the field and had the nation seen the necessity as truly imperious, a majority of justices—perhaps, as one counts the escape clauses in their opinions, all save Black—would probably have upheld the President.

The decision thus by no means excluded presidential initiative in authentic and indisputable crisis. But the Court made it clear that such initiative could not be exerted every time a President proclaimed a crisis not readily visible to the rest of the nation. In 1807 the judicial and public response to Jefferson's overreaction to the Burr conspiracy had disclosed certain practical limits on presidential claims of emergency power. In 1952 the judicial and public response to Truman's overreaction to the steel strike helped further define the conditions in which Presidents might persuasively invoke the Lockean prerogative. . . .

If the Court did not deny the Presidency the resort to emergency power in all circumstances, it did valuably challenge the presidential mystique in vogue among historians and political scientists. Executive power, as Jackson observed, had the advantage of concentration in a single person chosen by the whole nation, who became in consequence the unique focus of public hope and expectation. "In drama, magnitude and finality his decisions so far overshadow any other that almost alone he fills the public eye and ear." His prestige as chief of state and his command of public opinion blotted out those supposed to check and balance his power. "I cannot be brought to believe," Jackson said, "that this country will suffer if the Court refuses further to aggrandize the presidential office, already so potent and so relatively immune from judicial review, at the expense of Congress."

The Presidency, in short, was not the only source of wisdom in government. This very proposition, however, sent Congress an urgent message— a most solemn judicial reminder that congressional default was a large cause of presidential aggrandizement and that Congress, not the Court, had the key role to play in restoring the constitutional balance. Again Jackson made the point most vividly. "I have no illusion," he wrote, "that any decision by this Court can keep power in the hands of Congress if it is not wise and timely in meeting its problems." When a crisis challenged the President, it challenged Congress equally, or perhaps primarily. Recalling Napoleon's maxim that the tools belonged to the man who could use them, Jackson issued his own challenge to Congress: "We (the Court) may say that power to legislate for emergencies belongs in the hands of Congress, but only Congress itself can prevent power from slipping through its fingers." As for Truman, he yielded at once to the Court and ordered the government out of the mills. . . .

Lyndon Johnson came to the Presidency with an old and honest belief in spacious presidential authority to deploy force abroad in the service of American foreign policy. He had defended Truman's decision of 1950; and, while he had come to believe that Truman made a mistake in not asking for a congressional resolution, he saw this as political, not constitutional, error. A resolution could protect an administration's flanks, but the President already had the legal power. In 1954, with Eisenhower in the White House, Johnson had disclaimed any desire to take the responsibility out of the hands of "the constitutional leader." Now that he was the constitutional leader himself, it could not be supposed that he would take a narrower view of presidential prerogative. "There are many, many, who can recommend, advise and sometimes a few of them consent," he said in a speech in 1966. "But there is only one that has been chosen by the American people to decide." American history had traveled a long distance from Lincoln's proposition that "*no one man* should hold the power" of bringing the nation into war.

So in the spring of 1965 Johnson ordered 22,000 American troops to the Dominican Republic without seeking congressional authorization. His pretext was the protection of American lives. This was a traditional usage of executive power and did not require congressional consent. But 22,000 troops were about a hundred times more than were necessary for the specified purpose. Johnson's real reason, as he soon revealed, was that "we don't propose to sit here in our rocking chair with our hands folded and let the Communists set up any government in the Western Hemisphere." Armed intervention for political purposes clearly raised questions which under the Constitution, if not in the mind of the President, called for congressional participation.

With the same confidence in exclusive presidential prerogative, Johnson in early 1965 decreed the Americanization of the war in Vietnam, sending American combat units for the first time to the south and American bombers for the first time on a continuing basis to the north. This brought about a major change in the nature of the American involvement. What Kennedy on September 3, 1963, had called "their war" ("They are the ones who have to win it or lose it") had become, and remained for many years thereafter, "our war." It was a momentous decision—one that brought the United States into a war lasting longer than any other in American history, a war causing more American deaths in combat than any except the Civil War and the two World Wars, a war costing more money than any except the Second World War. "If this decision was not for Congress under the Constitution," Alexander Bickel of the Yale Law School has well said, "then no decision of any consequence in matters of war and peace is left to Congress."

There were no serious precedents for this decision. Unlike Roosevelt's Atlantic policy in 1941, Johnson was ordering American troops into immediate and calculated combat. Unlike Truman's decision in Korea, there were no UN resolutions to confer international legality, nor had there been clear-cut invasion across frontiers. Unlike the Cuban missile crisis, there was no emergency threat to the United States itself to compel secret and unilateral presidential decision. Unlike the Dominican Republic, there were no American civilians to be rescued.

There was of course the Tonkin Gulf resolution (officially the Southeast Asia resolution), rushed through Congress in August 1964 in a stampede of misinformation and misconception, if not of deliberate deception. After the alleged attacks on American destroyers off the coast of North Vietnam, Johnson called in the congressional leaders. Reminding himself, and them, of Taft's criticism of Truman for not seeking congressional ratification of the Korea decision, he asked their judgment about getting something this time that, as he cautiously put it, "would give us the opinion of Congress." The leaders thought it a fine idea, and the administration pulled out a draft resolution, prepared months before and awaiting the occasion.

The resolution passed the House unanimously. In the Senate only Wayne Morse and Ernest Gruening voted no, though Gaylord Nelson and others raised penetrating questions. The constitutional import of the resolution was by no means clear. The main reference to Congress held that Congress "approves and supports the determination of the President, as Commander in Chief, to take all necessary measures to repel any armed attack against the forces of the United States and to prevent further aggression." Did this last phrase mean further aggression against American forces or further aggression anywhere in Southeast Asia? Was Congress delegating *its* war-making authority to the President or was it acknowledging *his* pre-existing authority to do whatever he found necessary? Another section said that "the United States"—the United States government, Congress and President together? the United States as a whole, all 193,526,000 people?—was "prepared, as the President determines, to take all necessary steps, including the use of armed force, to assist any member or protocol state of the Southeast Asia Collective Defense Treaty requesting assistance in defense of its freedom."

Whatever the exact significance, the language on its face gave the President remarkable scope. When Senator John Sherman Cooper asked whether, "if the President decided that it was necessary to use such force as could lead into war, we will give that authority by this resolution?" Senator Fulbright, who was managing the bill, responded, "That is the way I would interpret it." He added optimistically, "I have no doubt that the President will consult with Congress in case a major change in present policy becomes necessary."

A resolution giving the President authority to use force as he saw fit in vague future contingencies was precisely the sort of resolution rejected as unacceptable in the early republic. The vagueness created a variety of congressional views as to what, in fact, Congress had authorized. Senator Sam Ervin, the North Carolina constitutionalist, observed in 1970 that the resolution was "clearly a declaration of war," and a good thing too. The legislative history leaves little doubt, however, that others who voted for it did *not* suppose they were authorizing a large and protracted war on the Asian mainland—"the last thing we would want to do," as Fulbright said in the debate. Indeed, President Johnson's defenders assert that, when he requested the resolution in August 1964, he did not himself suppose he would Americanize the war six months later, though some students of the Pentagon Papers dispute this assertion.

But there can be no doubt at all what Johnson thought Congress was doing. He had not used the phrase "the opinion of Congress" lightly. In his view, the Tonkin Gulf resolution was that, and nothing more. "We stated then," he said in 1967 of his conference with the leaders, "and we repeat now, we did not think the resolution was necessary to what we did and what we're doing." The significance of the resolution in Johnson's view was exclusively political. "Part of being ready, to me," he wrote in his memoirs, "was having the advance support of Congress for anything that might prove to be necessary. It was better to have a firm congressional resolution, and not need it, than some day to need it and not have it." Though it amused him to taunt members of Congress by pulling the Tonkin Gulf resolution out of his pocket and flourishing it as proof that Congress had authorized the escalation of American involvement, he did not believe for a moment that the resolution provided the legal basis for his action.

The role of Congress under the Johnson theory of the warmaking power was not to sanction but to support the war—a role that nearly all of Congress, except for the indomitable Morse and Gruening, accepted till 1966, and that most accepted for a long time afterward. In practice, Johnson could certainly have obtained congressional authorization beyond the Tonkin Gulf resolution for a limited war in Vietnam in 1965. He might even, had he wished (but no one wished), have obtained a declaration of war. Neither he nor most of Congress thought formal congressional action necessary.

Johnson's conception of presidential prerogative was somewhat overlaid by his protestations of an inexhaustible desire to "consult" with his old friends on Capitol Hill. But presidential consultation had become something of a mirage. If ordinary mortals fell into confused silence in any presidential presence, even senators, constrained less perhaps by awe than by a concern for future benefits, tended to repress their innermost thoughts, especially when confronted by so demanding and unrelenting a President as Lyndon Johnson. "The wise senator," George Reedy, who served as Johnson's press secretary, has written, " . . . enters cautiously, dressed in his Sunday best and with a respectful, almost pious, look on his face." If for any reason, he must express a dissent, "it is most deferential, almost apologetic." The aura of reverence surrounding a President, Reedy observed, was "so universal that the slightest hint of criticism automatically labels a man as a colossal lout."

Nor was consultation between lesser officials of the executive branch and members of Congress much more satisfactory. Such consultation usually meant, in effect, for one side to give and the other to receive a briefing; it was a form of political cajolery, serving no constitutional or substantive purpose. "The distinction between solicitation of advice in advance of a decision and the provision of information in the wake of a decision would seem to be a significant one," the Senate Foreign Relations Committee finally commented in 1969. Pointing out that in the cases of the Cuban missile crisis and the Dominican intervention congressional leaders were informed what was to be done only a few hours before the decisions were carried out, the Committee added dryly, "Such acts of courtesy are always to be welcomed; the Constitution, however, envisages something more." As for Vietnam, one searches in vain through the Pentagon Papers for mention of Congress except, in Fulbright's bitter remark, "as an appropriate object of manipulation, or as a troublesome nuisance to be disposed of." In the consciousness of the executive branch, the legislative branch existed as an irrational force, to be ignored as long as possible, then to be humored, managed or circumvented, never to be sought out as a possible source of intelligent advice. . . .

[Watergate] was a very near thing. In the months after the exposure, Americans tended to preen themselves on the virtues of the American form of government: "the system worked." But it came terribly close to not working. If, for example, that forgotten hero Frank Wills, the twenty-four-year-old security guard, had not noticed tape over the latches of two doors on the bottom level of the Watergate on June 17, 1972, the burglary would have remained undetected. Even when Wills called police and the burglars were arrested, nothing much happened. Public opinion could hardly have been less concerned. Despite Senator McGovern's efforts to rouse the conscience of the electorate, most Americans regarded "the Watergate caper" with indifference if not with complacency till well into 1973, and then began to react only after the issue had changed from the original depredation to the subsequent obstruction of justice.

As for President Nixon, he responded to growing congressional and public curiosity by enlarging his claims of presidential prerogative. Thus he wholly rejected any idea of personal appearance before a congressional committee or grand jury as incompatible with presidential dignity and the separation of powers. Actually Presidents more dignified than Nixon had failed to perceive so vast a barrier. Washington went to Congress to ask its advice about a treaty. Lincoln appeared before the House Judiciary Committee in 1862 to discuss the leak of his State of the Union message to the *New York Herald* and before the Committee on the Conduct of the War on other occasions, once, according to legend, to deny that his wife was a Confederate spy. Numerous Presidents, among them Lincoln, Wilson and Franklin Roosevelt, invited committees of Congress to meet them at the White House. Truman, as Nixon pointed out, did after his Presidency turn back a subpoena from the House Un-American Activities Committee; but the subpoena did not even specify the matter on which the Committee sought the former President's testimony, and the newspapers had indicated that it was in an area—his reasons for making executive appointments—that was exclusively a presidential responsibility. Ulysses S. Grant even thought it would be appropriate for himself, as President, to appear in a courtroom as a witness for the defense when his private secretary, General Orville Babcock, was under prosecution by his own Department of Justice.

Nixon, in short, wanted to make absolute what some of his predecessors had plainly regarded as less than absolute. It is true that, as he mentioned several times to Ervin, he was prepared to waive the lawyer-client privilege and let his former White House counsels testify. But here he was waiving something none of his predecessors had ever claimed; no previous President seems to have supposed that the White House counsel, whose job was to deal with public issues and whose salary was paid by the taxpayer, was equivalent to the President's personal attorney. As for papers, Nixon had contended that executive privilege covered everything that went in, through or out of the White House in connection with official duties. Then it developed that he himself had systematically taped conversations and meetings at the White House over a considerable time. Much of the discussion on the tapes unquestionably had to do with official business; but some of the tapes no doubt contained evidence pertinent to both judicial and congressional inquiries into the Watergate affair. Accordingly both Professor Archibald Cox, the Special Prosecutor, and the Senate Select Committee on the Watergate case chaired by Sam Ervin of North Carolina requested release of specified tapes.

These requests raised tangled constitutional problems. Nixon's first reaction was to tell Ervin that even controlled and selective disclosure would "inevitably" result in the destruction of "the indispensable principle of confidentiality." In a second letter to Ervin, however, he seemed to retreat for a moment from the claim of absolute privilege. If the release of the tapes would settle the question at issue, he now said, "then their disclosure might serve a substantial public interest," but, since he himself found the evidence on the tapes inconclusive, he would keep them under his "sole personal control." A few days later, he returned to the idea of absolute privilege. The issue, he wrote Judge John Sirica, who had presided over the trial of the Watergate burglars and who now, at the Special Prosecutor's behest, was seeking the tapes, went to the independence of the three branches of government: "It would be wholly inadmissible for the President to seek to compel some particular action by the courts. It is equally inadmissible for the courts to seek to compel some particular action from the President." This was a peculiar statement. From the time of *Marbury* v. *Madison* the other branches had conceded to the courts the power to construe the Constitution; and, pursuant to that power, the Supreme Court had repeatedly compelled particular actions from Presidents, such as requiring Truman to divest himself of the steel industry and Franklin Roosevelt to divest himself of much of the early New Deal.

In any case, the court served a subpoena *duces tecum* on the President—

the first since Marshall's to Jefferson 166 years before. Nixon's lawyers now claimed the issue as "starkly simple: will the Presidency be allowed to continue to function?" If the courts could command the disclosure of presidential conversations, the damage to the Presidency would be "severe and irreparable." Nor did executive privilege vanish simply because the grand jury was looking into charges of criminal conduct. Executive privilege "would be meaningless if it were to give way whenever there is reason to suspect that disclosure might reveal criminal acts." The decision about the tapes was the President's. "He—and he alone—must weigh the interest in prosecuting a wrongdoer against the interest in keeping all Presidential conversations confidential." He had "absolute power to decide what may be disclosed to others." . . .

Nixon continued thereafter to insist that "the principle of confidentiality of Presidential conversations" was at stake. Yet some wondered why, if he cared so much about the principle of confidentiality, he had taped everything in the first place. "The way to insure the confidentiality of future presidential conversations," as the *Wall Street Journal* sensibly said, "is to stop recording them on tape." While no one doubted the right to protect presidential conversations connected with the performance of official duties, the cover-up of crimes hardly rated as an official duty, and the claim that the President in discussing the cover-up was seeing that the laws were faithfully executed could only be substantiated if he had taken strong action against the lawbreakers. In any case, as Nixon's own lawyers conceded in their brief, "Quite commonly Presidents have voluntarily made available information for which a claim of privilege could have been made. That happens very often." Why did it not happen this time? Nixon, in the manner of his predecessors, could easily have affirmed the sacred principle while waiving it in this particular case. The answer, as murkily indicated in the presidential brief, was evidently that in this particular case Nixon felt that disclosure would do concrete harm to the public interest. The *public* interest?

The profounder question was whether any President could place himself beyond the process of law in a case involving not, like the case of *Mississippi v. Johnson,* the performance of official duties but criminal conduct as well as the President's own personal and political fortunes. "The privilege," as Justice Cardozo had said in another connection, "takes flight when abused." Woodrow Wilson surely stated the common sense of the Constitution when he said that "no peculiar dignity or sanctity attaches amongst us to any officer of government. The theory of our law is that an officer is an officer only so long as he acts within his powers; that when he transcends his authority he ceases to be an officer and is only a private individual, subject to be sued and punished for his offense."

Nixon's series of claims represented a last fling of the revolutionary Presidency. His conceded ability to make a one-time waiver without abandoning the principle led some to wonder whether his action was a defense of principle or of himself. If his claims were sustained by the courts, it would have the effect of confirming the President as judge in his own case and thereby giving him an immunity denied all other American citizens. The result could come close to establishing what Chief Justice Marshall had rejected so long ago—the view that the American President, like the English King, could do no wrong. . . .

The congressional performance in the second year of Watergate illustrates the problem. [The War Powers Act] was widely acclaimed, especially by the bill's supporters, as a triumph of congressional self-assertion. If it was a triumph of anything, it was at best of symbol over substance.

The War Powers Act of 1973 began by yielding the President power to commit the armed forces to hostilities. The preamble did suggest that this power could be properly exercised only pursuant to a declaration of war, to a specific statutory authorization or to a national emergency created by attack upon the United States, its possessions or its armed forces. But the conference report said that the rest of the act was "not dependent" upon this section, thereby leaving the language, which was in any case dangerously restrictive, as pious rhetoric, not binding law. The statute went on to direct the President to terminate what the Senate-House conferees interestingly called "unauthorized use of the Armed Forces" within 60 days (in practice, 90 days, since the act offered Presidents 30 additional days if they thought it necessary in the interests of disengagement) *unless* Congress explicitly provided otherwise. Congress, moreover, could order the withdrawal of American forces at any time by concurrent resolution, which was, of course, not subject to presidential veto.

This proved a richly ambiguous statute. Legislators argued bitterly as to whether it was an expansion or limitation of presidential warmaking power, whether it weakened or strengthened congressional participation in the decisions of war and peace. Some liberals, looking at the early sections of the act, denounced it as an unconstitutional delegation of the congressional warmaking power to the executive. Senator Thomas Eagleton of Missouri called the act "an undated, 90 day declaration of war." Congressman John Culver of Iowa said it would give the President "a blank check to wage war anywhere in the world for any reason of his choosing for a period of 60 to 90 days." Conservatives, looking at the later sections of the act, denounced it as an intolerable restriction of presidential authority. Barry Goldwater called it "destructive of America's credibility in any future crisis." Nixon, the final arbiter, solemnly pronounced it an unconstitutional infringement on his powers. He added ominously that, since these powers could be altered only by constitutional amendment, "any attempt to make such alterations by legislation alone is clearly without force"—a statement that, taken literally, appeared to serve notice that, because he personally found the law unconstitutional, he would not be bound by it. This, like so much else, showed the direction in which, even in the second year of Watergate, Nixon was still seeking to move the Presidency.

Plainly both sides exaggerated the significance of a rather feeble statute. Those who felt that it strengthened presidential warmaking power more than it strengthened congressional control of presidential initiatives probably had the better of the argument. For up to the passage of the act the concession to the Presidency of the power of military initiative had been, in some sense, a matter of usurpation. Now, at least for the first 90 days, it was a surrender of law. Within three weeks after the overriding of the veto, Nixon's Secretary of Defense, verifying the liberal criticism of the act rather than his own President's veto message, claimed that the act made it legally permissible for Nixon to order new bombing in Indochina in the event of a North Vietnamese offensive.

The Secretary of Defense no doubt claimed too much in this particular case. But it was a fact that the War Powers Act of 1973 gave the President legal authority to go to war. It also gave new authority to Congress. However, the chance that Congress would use its authority to terminate warlike presidential initiatives was not a fact but a speculation. Once American soldiers had been saving the republic for 60 or 90 days, it seemed unlikely, with presidential domination of information and command of public opinion, that Congress would turn down a President determined to keep a war going.

Beyond all this, and despite the background music about the great historic significance of this alleged reassertion of congressional partnership in national policy, the War Powers Act in fact assumed that the President would make all the vital decisions by himself. It had no serious provision for advance congressional participation while Presidents pondered whether to go to war or not. It accepted the imperial mythology, in short, and did not try to grapple with the harder problem. In consequence, one would be surprised if the act made any substantial difference to anything except (briefly) to congressional self-esteem. The obligations laid on the President to report and defend any commitment of force were useful, though excessively gentle. But the efficacy of the statute depended altogether on the presence of a congressional *will* to bring fighting to an end. When such a will existed, Congress could gain the same result, as it finally did in effect in Indochina, by using the power of the purse to cut off appropriations for the war. . . .

The Vietnam War as a Failure of Congress to Act

ALEXANDER M. BICKEL

. . . The Founding Fathers were no visionaries. They did not believe that in terms of formulating and executing the policy of a great nation, it is in fact easier to make peace than to make war. It is in fact, as Ellsworth was careful to say, harder to make peace and simpler to make war. But the Framers of the Constitution intended that our nation's institutions and processes should be so arranged as to make it harder to do the easy thing, and easier to achieve the difficult. For this reason, they insisted that the declaration of war not be an executive prerogative, as it had been under the British Crown. They insisted also that it not be left to the Senate, a single, less numerous chamber which they viewed as capable of more expeditious action than the House or than Congress as a whole. Rather they provided

"Congress, the President and the Power to Wage War" by Alexander M. Bickel, *Chicago-Kent Law Review* 48, pp. 131–147 (Fall/Winter 1971). Reprinted by special permission of IIT Chicago-Kent College of Law.

that Congress, acting through both Houses, should have the power to declare war.

The Convention earlier had thought of using another, more comprehensive word, and empowering Congress to *make* war. But this term seemed to vest in the Congress the function of conducting a war once it had started, and also possibly to deny the power of the Commander-in-Chief to repel attacks against the United States. Hence the Framers said, "declare," not "make." The President was to be Commander-in-Chief, exercise independent tactical control over the armed forces, and see to their safety. Congress, as the Framers knew and as Congress itself has on occasion discovered— for example during the Civil War—cannot well exercise command, and should not attempt to do so. The President was to have power also to repel attacks, and we must say in modern times, to respond to the threat of attacks against the United States or against our forces, when instant action is of the essence.

Yet the Framers were extraordinarily wary of standing armies and of their use by the Executive. They authorized Congress to "raise and support Armies," and then tried to ensure that the exclusive power of Congress would be jealously guarded, by providing that no appropriation of money to raise and support armies "shall be for a longer Term than two Years." Moreover, Congress was given the overall, comprehensive "necessary-and-proper" power.

The "necessary-and-proper" clause of article I of the Constitution authorizes Congress to make "all Laws which shall be necessary and proper for carrying into Execution the foregoing Powers. . . . " The reference is to the previously enumerated powers of Congress. But there is another portion of the necessary-and-proper clause, not so often cited, which is of the greatest consequence. The clause also charges Congress to make all laws which shall be necessary and proper for carrying into execution "all other Powers vested by this Constitution in the Government of the United States, or in any Department or Officer thereof"—a phrase that includes the President! The implied powers of the federal government, most of the unstated powers that inhere in nationhood, most everything that went without saying or that is residual—all that belongs to Congress.

Against this roster of congressional functions stand the summary provisions of article II of the Constitution, vesting the executive power in the President, declaring that he shall be Commander-in-Chief, and authorizing him, with the advice and consent of the Senate, to make treaties and appoint ambassadors.

The text of the Constitution and its history thus plainly limit the President. Yet the law of the Constitution under our system is not only defined by the text, but influenced by usage long indulged. The earliest practice conformed to the division of war-making powers intended by the Framers. Later practice, however, in this century, and on occasion in the nineteenth, has tended to enlarge the scope of independent presidential initiatives. . . .

The Korean action, no doubt, stretched presidential emergency power to a prior extreme. But the invasion of South Korea from the North was sudden, and it did threaten to succeed quite rapidly and irrevocably, thus affecting the position of our own forces in neighboring Japan. I am not maintaining that President Truman's independent action in Korea should necessarily be viewed as falling within the President's legitimate power. I am not attempting to adjudicate the Korean case. I merely emphasize the sudden nature of the emergency to which President Truman responded, and consequently the measure of plausibility, however faint, with which his action can be made to fit the established sudden-attack theory of presidential power. Again, there is a measure of plausibility in the attempt to fit the dispatch of troops to Lebanon by President Eisenhower before 1965, as well as President Johnson's intervention in the Dominican Republic later, into the neutral-interposition theory. But no such fits are possible for the round-the-clock bombing of North Vietnam, which began in February, 1965, or for the sending of 50,000 troops to fight in South Vietnam, by a single decision that President Johnson announced on July 28, 1965, commenting, "this is really war."

It was really war. It raised the American troop level to over 100,000, soon of course to be multiplied five times over, and it committed, as President Johnson had said some two weeks earlier, on July 9, "our power and our national honor"—by a deliberate decision, considered over an extended period of time, not forced by sudden events; a decision functionally and in every other way amounting to an initiative for war. If this decision was not for Congress under the Constitution, then no decision of any consequence in matters of war and peace is left to Congress. This time, no justifications drawn from sophisticated theories would do. The constitutional division of powers had been repudiated in the sincere, but I believe grievously misguided, conviction that it no longer suited modern conditions.

I may add that if the exercise of presidential power in 1965 was valid, then of course so were the march into Cambodia in April, 1970, and the use of American air power in Laos in 1971. Indeed, taken in isolation, and assuming that American forces are lawfully in Vietnam and that no act of Congress at the time forbade the incursions into Cambodia and Laos, these actions, I would say, fall within the ordinary powers of the Commander-in-Chief, like the decisions to invade North Africa in 1942, Europe in 1944, or North Korea in 1951. But in truth these episodes were the culminating moves in a series of presidential initiatives which, if we continue to accept them, will have totally stripped Congress of any power to choose between war and peace. Let us not forget, the Indochina war is no maneuver on our own border, as when President Polk prodded the Mexicans into war. Nor did it all begin, as in Korea, with a response by the Commander-in-Chief to an attack that had to be stemmed, if at all, within a matter of days. Deliberately, following an extended decision-making process behind closed doors, President Johnson committed, as he said, "our power and our national honor" to full-scale war thousands of miles away—entirely on his own authority. . . .

President Johnson relied heavily on the Tonkin Gulf resolution of August, 1964, as a source of authority, although the Nixon Administration abandoned it, and Congress repealed it in December, 1970. The language of that resolution is so extraordinarily broad that it can be read to have given away anything and everything. Although the text does express the intention to make the resolution "consonant with the Constitution of the United States" as well as with the Southeast Asia treaty and although portions of the brief debate that attended passage of the resolution support this intention, other passages in the debate do sound as if Congress had indeed given away anything and everything. Yet the first wisdom in the construction of statutes is that the intent of the legislature is to be understood against the background of facts and circumstances existing at the time of enactment, to which the legislature was addressing itself. Congress addressed itself immediately to the relatively trivial Tonkin Gulf incident. One would presume, therefore, that Congress intended to approve presidential reactions commensurate with that incident and with incidents of that sort, and not necessarily an undertaking of the magnitude of the Vietnam ground and air war.

If the resolution is read to have done more, the question arises whether it is within the power of Congress to give prospective approval to actions that would not, without such approval, conform to the Constitution. If without the Tonkin Gulf resolution the President had no constitutional authority to commit the nation to war in circumstances then undefined and unforeseen, could Congress prospectively, by blank check, give him that authority? . . .

The Tonkin Gulf Resolution declared itself to be "consonant with the Constitution." The sum of it is that, consonant with the Constitution, there was no need to come to Congress for authority the President has, as for example, to fire back when attacked. And it was no use coming to Congress for authority the Congress cannot constitutionally confer at large, for prospective use in indefinite circumstances. It is claimed further that Congress ratified the executive action by appropriating monies to support and steadily enlarge it. Congress assuredly did so, and assuredly it did so partly under a misapprehension that it was in principle obliged to extend general support, even if free to make its own judgments on questions of detail, and that in any event it was assuming no general responsibility by extending support. This is precisely the misapprehension it is necessary now to dispel.

It is asserted also in defense of independent presidential action that Congress is authorized by the Constitution only to declare war; and in modern circumstances, that is, after all, often not what is wanted. It is too much, and since too much is all that Congress has authority to do, it must be for the President to do anything somewhat less, which in present world conditions is generally what is required. The argument is altogether fallacious. There may actually be some sort of difference between the war we have waged in Vietnam and a war that Congress might have declared, although the difference, if any, is metaphysical. But there is utterly no reason to think that Congress has only the megapower to declare war in the exact terms of the constitutional clause that authorizes declarations of war and no mini- or intermediate power to commit the country to something less than a declared war. Congress, as I have emphasized, has the necessary-and-proper power, the power to do anything that is necessary and proper to carry out the functions conferred upon it and upon any other department or officer of the government. If in the conditions of our day it is necessary to carry out the power to declare war by taking measures short of a declaration of war, everything in the scheme of government set up by the Constitution indicates that Congress has the needed authority.

The strongest and most searching argument that is made in support of the constitutional power of the President to do what President Johnson did in 1965 relies on the practice which has steadily eroded the original constitutional scheme and on assessments of modern conditions which, it is contended, require a revised conception of presidential power. Granted that President Johnson carried the practice of a century forward, granted even that he extended it by some additional degrees, but usage, gradual changes by successive degrees to a point where a change in kind may be perceived— these, it is said, have been the life of the American Constitution. "Our Constitution," Justice Brandeis once wrote, "is not a strait-jacket. It is a living organism. As such it is capable of growth—of expansion and of adaptation to new conditions."

Now, Brandeis was talking about the growth of the great open-ended provisions of the Constitution—chiefly the Bill of Rights and the fourteenth amendment—which were intentionally framed in general terms, precisely so as to leave open the possibility of their evolution over time in light of new conditions. Constitutionalism also implies, however, the stability of certain structural arrangements, the stability and binding nature of the rules of the game, so to speak, which may be changed only by express amendment. We would not think, for example, that we could change the length of the President's term, as fixed in the Constitution, or abolish the electoral college, otherwise than by reaching a new consensus through the difficult amendment process and writing new provisions into the Constitution. Moreover, if the Constitution is a living organism, it grows and adapts itself without losing its essential shape. It does not undergo radical mutations, except by the process of amendment. There is a considerable difference, therefore, between extending the President's war-making power by another degree and leaping over the brink to a change in kind, to an explicit, notorious, inexpiable alteration in the shape of the original structure.

Be that as it may, it is useful to ask, as the argument about growth in the constitutional organism bids us ask, putting aside the constitutional text and its history, whether the change in the division of war-making power between President and Congress, resulting in what is at the least a marked imbalance in favor of the President, has been an element of beneficial growth in the Constitution, a necessary consequence of changes in the world about us, and justified by them. If this is the question, it makes a difference, obviously, whether one thinks that the Indochina war has been a noble effort on our part in the service of peace and freedom, which we will rue not carrying to a successful conclusion, or a moral and practical disaster. It is no accident that the constitutional issue has drawn so much lively interest these past couple of years. Nothing so enlightens us on the rights and wrongs of institutional arrangements as the wrong practical and moral results of an institutional arrangement.

For myself, I formed the opinion some years ago that the war has been a moral and practical disaster, and I believe further that we might have avoided it, or might at least avoid its repetition, if our institutional arrangements were such as to foreclose presidential wars. Many of us who hold this opinion are prone to join to it attitudes which I consider deplorably sentimental, or self-righteous, or both; and I digress for a moment on this point.

The country was awash with sentimentality just a few months ago as it contemplated the conviction of Lieutenant Calley. There was sentimentality to the left and sentimentality to the right. One should, of course, have compassion for the man, but he is, on the evidence, guilty of a vicious deed, and there is no basis for identifying most of his fellow soldiers with him, or all his superiors in the Army and the government, or all of us as Americans. "I do not know the method," said Burke, "of drawing up an indictment against an whole people." We might remember that. (He said it about us, incidentally.) It is sheer sentimentality, in my view, to hesitate about punishing the perpetrator of a vicious crime because some others may have committed similar crimes and gone unpunished and, beyond that, because of some vague feeling, not grounded in evidence, that none of us is fit to throw the first stone at anyone. The retribution visited by the criminal law is never perfect, and need not be. It is just nonetheless, and fulfills its function of vindicating the moral order. As for the vague feeling of common guilt— there is common guilt, no doubt, but for what and in what degree? Even indiscriminate air-bombardment, wrong as it may be, is not the same, after all, as the wild and willful shooting, face to face, of harmless women and children.

On the other hand, it is self-righteousness and moral arrogance, I think, to condemn as criminal policies that were wrong, that constituted, indeed, moral error, but whose intent and origin were those of our Indochina policy. What propelled us into this war, in my judgment, was a corruption of the generous, idealistic impulse which, together with a sense of legitimate self-interest, informed and sustained this country's foreign policy through the Second World War and in the years after. I use the word corruption not to connote evil, but merely decay. Our self-interest began to be invoked mechanically rather than realistically, and the altruistic impulse decayed into self-assurance and self-righteousness; it became, as generosity and idealism assuredly can, oppressive and in the end cruel. All sorts of ideologies, humanitarian and generous at the source, have a way of decaying in this fashion, as do religious ideas. Of course, they often draw to themselves authoritarian, sadistic and otherwise morally deficient personalities. But the seeds of decay are in the ideologies themselves, in their pretensions to universality, in their over-confident assaults on the variety and unruliness of the human condition, and in the intellectual and emotional imperialism of concepts such as freedom, equality, and, yes, even peace.

Well, though begun and continued by men with a normal moral endowment, the war has been a grievous error, in my opinion. It has been wrong too, I believe, for another reason, which is of particular interest from an institutional point of view. A democracy cannot well—compare the War of 1812 and the Mexican War—and should not, wage a war which a substantial and intense body of opinion—whether amounting to 35 or 45 or 51 per cent of the electorate—resolutely opposes on both political and moral grounds. Even autocracies cannot effectively wage wars in such circumstances. Of course the Constitution provides for no special majority, two-thirds or the like, and certainly not for any kind of referendum, before the country can go to war. Congress may declare war by the narrowest of majorities, and no individual is entitled to nullify application to himself of a declaration of war because he disagrees with it, any more than he can refuse to render unto Caesar the things which are Caesar's when it comes to other disagreeable laws passed by narrow divisions. This is not a question of law. It is a question of the forebearance and continence of those who govern, without which law cannot be effective, or on some occasions just. To revert again to Burke: "It is not," he said to the King's government in the second speech on conciliation with America, "it is not what a lawyer tells me I *may* do; but what humanity, reason, and justice, tell me I ought to do." Making war is not the same as enacting many another law, and it cannot be done effectively by a narrow majority, and should not be.

Now, I suggest that the double error of this terrible war is a product in good part of the imbalance we have permitted in the division of war-making power between the President and the Congress. To this sort of double error, the President as an institution is all too prone. I make bold to suggest even that something of this sort is what the Framers of our Constitution . . . had in mind when they built as they did, not as Lyndon Johnson, extending the blueprints of other Presidents, rearranged the architecture. Something of this sort is what George Mason had in mind when he urged that we should clog war and facilitate peace.

The President represents a distinct constituency, of course, and ought properly, therefore, to speak with an independent voice and to have considerable leverage. But the President is a single official, in many ways a distant and regal personage. The discipline of the democratic process plays on him only grossly, at wholesale. He commands attention and he communicates with greater impact than any other institution of government, but he is not equally communicated with. His policy-making process is necessarily private, almost like that of a court. The large results become known, and on these he can be judged and held to account. But the process by which he reaches them is seldom open to much scrutiny and, consequently, little open to influence.

Congress, on the other hand, is institutionalized communication access. Congress reflects in its very membership varieties of views and represents most groupings of opinion, to each of which it parcels out a share of power, at least negative power. It is subject, therefore, to being disabled by a minority of its membership from deciding too much, too soon, or even at all. Congress, in short, is the institution where we do not merely hold our government to account, but take part in it. It isn't always, but it can be. The Presidency by its nature rarely is.

The Presidency can speak for an existing broad consensus, and its genius is action. But its antennae are blunt, and it can mistake silence for consensus. Its errors are active ones, like the Indochina war—sins of commission. The genius of Congress lies precisely in its antennae, in its differentiated sensitivity. Its errors generally are those of irresolution, sins of omission; and we have learned, I trust, that these are, by and large, the less grave sins—in government, at any rate. The Tonkin Gulf resolution and the congressional war hawks of 1812 to the contrary notwithstanding, I do not believe the Congress, if it had been conscious of its own responsibility, would have plunged us into the Indochina war, or let it run as it has.

If, as I believe, we have permitted a serious imbalance to arise between President and Congress, which is bad for the country and reduces the capability of our government to devise and to implement effectively, policies that serve the national interest—if so, then what is to be done? The imbalance is not only bad in practice and wrong in theory. It runs counter to the constitutional text and to its history. . . .

[T]he answer [does not lie] with Congress. Whatever aggrandizement of presidential power we have witnessed, the practice of recent decades or of a century cannot have worked a reduction of the residual legislative power of Congress, if Congress should but exercise it. The power of Congress may have lain in disuse, but it is as legitimate as the day it was conferred. From it flows the duty to act. Congress should prescribe the mission of our troops in the field in accordance with a foreign and war policy of the United States which it is for Congress to set when it chooses to do so. And Congress should equally review and settle upon an appropriate foreign policy elsewhere than in Vietnam and reorder the deployment of our forces accordingly. It should finally, by statute, as Senator Javits has suggested, reassert its own general authority in matters of war and peace and redefine the President's.

I recognize that the United States remains a world power in a tense and nuclear world and as such must retain credible capability to act in a crisis. And while American power has, no doubt, been spread too thin, and mutual security treaties have proliferated beyond the likely limits of credibility, it does remain true that our security and the peace of the world still rest in some measure on international commitments undertaken by the United States. If we redefine presidential power, will we in effect be dismantling all that we have built in the world, by declaring that the United States could not lawfully react with the adequately speedy use of force in a crisis?

The answer, it seems to me, is that no one should ever reasonably have assumed that the United States could go to war by presidential say-so, contrary to our domestic constitutional arrangements, in pursuance of a treaty or like commitment; and our commitments, including the North Atlantic Alliance and the Southeast Asia Treaty, were not understood so to provide. All that commitments of this sort can do is affect the reaction to a crisis of the President and of Congress, each functioning as the Constitution envisions.

The President under our Constitution has power in an emergency to guard against attack or the threat of attack on the United States, or on lawfully deployed forces of the United States. If, in the event of an attack on a friend or ally, there is implicit the threat of an imminent attack also on us, the President can react. The existence of a mutual security commitment will enter into his decision. If there is an attack on a nation with which we have no mutual security arrangement, it will ordinarily be quite obviously far-fetched to deduce that a threat of an attack upon ourselves has thus arisen. If, on the other hand, there is an attack on a nation with which we do have a mutual security treaty, circumstances are certainly imaginable in which the President may deduce that the attack on our ally signals the danger of an imminent attack upon ourselves. In such a case, he may react. This is the difference that a commitment can make and will continue to make. Constitutionally it is the only way even a treaty could ever enhance the President's independent war-making power.

Again, as has been the case all along, if an attack on a friendly nation creates an adequate consensus in the country that we should spring to the help of our friend, Congress can be persuaded to act and act fast enough. If Congress will not act, or if our friend is devoured within a day or two, then it is surely evident that we could not have helped effectively anyway. That should be quite plain to any realistic foreign head of government. De Gaulle knew it. A mutual security treaty can only make it more likely than it might otherwise be that Congress will wish to commit American forces.

The one thing we and the world have learned from the Vietnam experience is that without understanding why we fight, and without the will to fight as a nation, we cannot fight effectively. Hence if the conditions are such that the threat of an attack upon ourselves cannot be deduced, and if Congress won't take the country into war, Presidents attempting what Lyndon Johnson attempted are only heading for failure. This much friend and foe alike surely know about us by now. We do well to recognize it ourselves and redefine our domestic institutional arrangements accordingly.

Watergate and Reform of the Presidency

PHILIP B. KURLAND

The primary evil revealed by the events of Watergate was the presidency: not the man but the office. It was and is bloated with unrestrained power, available for use for good or evil, with little or no accountability for the use to which it is put. . . .

. . . Watergate was an executive branch disaster, an outcome of the imperial presidency.

Arthur Schlesinger was more wont to place the blame on the occupant of the office than on the inherent defects of an office that had become overgrown with powers not subject to limitation. His explanation of the problem, nevertheless, affords us insight into the difficulties:

From *Watergate and the Constitution* by Philip B. Kurland, 1978 pp. 153, 169–172, 176, 179. Reprinted by permission of the University of Chicago Press.

The imperial Presidency, born in the 1940s and 1950s to save the outer world from perdition, thus began in the 1960s and 1970s to find nurture at home. Foreign policy had given the President the command of peace and war. Now the decay of the parties left him in command of the political scene, and the Keynesian revelation placed him in command of the economy. At this extraordinary historical moment, when foreign and domestic lines of force converged, much depended on whether the occupant of the White House was moved to ride the new tendencies of power or to resist them. . . .

With Nixon there came, whether by weird historical accident or by unconscious national response to historical pressure and possibility, a singular confluence of the job with the man. The Presidency, as enlarged by international delusions and domestic propulsions, found a President whose inner mix of vulnerability and ambition impelled him to push the historical logic to its extremity.

Some years earlier, Schlesinger had written of Nixon: "He is the only major American politician in our history who came to prominence by techniques which, if generally adopted, would destroy the whole fabric of mutual confidence on which democracy rests." That statement was written in 1960, before the campaigns of 1968 and 1972, which are adequately, if more in admiration than distaste, described by T. H. White in his *Making of the President* books. White had to write still another book explaining what he considered Nixon's treachery to those who had thought so highly of him.

It was, however, not only the President but the presidency that was at fault in the Watergate affair. The witnesses at the Senate hearings who were most revealing of the functioning of the office rather than the man were, not the President, who declined the invitation to appear, but Haldeman and Ehrlichman, Dean and Magruder, Butterfield and Moore.

The Watergate problem has its parallel in English history during the period of the American Revolution. The historical analogy is described by Bernard Bailyn, speaking of the discontent with British government of that time:

The most common explanation, however—an explanation that rose from the deepest sources of British political culture, that was a part of the very structure of British political thought—located "the spring and cause of all the distresses and complaints of the people in England or in America" in "a kind of fourth power that the constitution knows nothing of, or has not provided against." This "overruling arbitrary power, which absolutely controls the King, Lords, and Commons," was composed, it was said, of the "ministers and favorites" of the King, who, in defiance of God and man alike, "extend their usurped authority infinitely too far," and throwing off the balance of the constitution, make their "despotic will" the authority of the nation. . . . This "junto of courtiers and state-jobbers," these "court locusts," whispering in the royal ear, "instill in the King's mind a divine right of authority to command his subjects" at the same time as they advance their "detestable scheme" by misinforming and misleading the people.

This is a most fitting description of the Executive Office of the President under Nixon, and particularly of the branch of that office called the White

House. This perversion of the English balanced government was called the "corruption of the constitution." . . .

Part of the problem has been that which the French historian Guizot noted more than one hundred and thirty years ago:

> The disposition of the most eminent men, and of the best among the most eminent, to keep aloof from public affairs, in a free democratic society, is a serious fact. . . . It would seem as if, in this form of society, the tasks of government were too severe for men who are capable of comprehending its extent, and desirous of discharging the trust in a proper manner.

This tendency toward abstention has been exacerbated by the post-Watergate mentality. Because the structural problems of Watergate have never been addressed, but only the shades of these problems, the conditions now imposed on men who would undertake public office are so burdensome that talented and sensitive persons, who do not seek power for the sake of exerting power, are not readily recruited for any administration. The recent notion that the exaltation of the forms of ethical conduct over its substance will avoid "mal-administration" is ingenuous or disingenuous. But then we live in a society in which the symbolic is all and substance nothing. This, too, is a lesson of the Nixon years, but it has not prevented his successors from emulating him, on this score at least.

The structure that gave rise in the United States to the corruption of the Constitution reached in Watergate, strangely enough, derived from the need for an additional, an extraconstitutional, form of checks and balances. With the growth of government and governmental functions came . . . judicial constructions of the Constitution that effectively licensed the executive branch to secure the dominant voice in our society with the acquiescence of the legislature, which has been forthcoming. . . .

During the New Deal period, the Court called a temporary halt to this willy-nilly abdication of responsibility by the Congress. In a series of cases concerned with the framing of the National Industrial Recovery Act codes, the Court, unanimously or with strong majorities, held that the power delegated to frame governing codes had been invalidly surrendered by Congress. After Roosevelt's Court-packing plan failed, but his court-packing itself succeeded, the doctrine of invalid delegation fell out of sight and has since showed only feeble signs of life. There have been recent stirrings in the academic world for the restoration of some semblance of integrity to the legislative function. But there yet is no indication that these have had or will have any serious effect on limiting congressional abdication.

The separation of powers as a doctrine restraining the exercise of power by the executive branch has all but disappeared. There are still some old checks and one or two new ones, the latter of dubious constitutional validity. Thus, theoretically Congress still has the power over the purse as a limit on executive power, but the budget—in spite of modern innovations in the Congress—remains largely an executive budget and in its appropriations bills only minor variations are made by the Congress from the demands of the executive departments. The power of congressional inquisition remains, but subject to the still undefined scope of the newly recognized, constitutionally founded, "executive privilege." The comptroller general, an official responsible to Congress, still has auditing authority. And there is a provision for the required reporting of expenditures that may burgeon though it is still largely unused.

The result of this Supreme Court license and congressional irresponsibility is that the nation is now governed essentially, not by laws enacted by Congress, but by rules and regulations promulgated by the executive branch and by independent agency actions, purporting to be in compliance with the congressional will, *i.e.*, where congressional will can be derived from something besides silence, but frequently in opposition to it. With this greatly expanded governmental function, the executive branch has become a series of bureaucracies uncontrolled even by the upper echelons of executive officials and only occasionally subjected to judicial scrutiny. . . .

The ancient concept of separation of powers and checks and balances has been reduced to a slogan, to be trotted out by the Supreme Court from time to time as a substitute for a reasoned judgment. The concentration of power has certainly reached the point that made the Founding Fathers fear the necessary consequent tyranny. If it is not to be expected that the constitutional balances can be restored, if it is clear that the Congress has neither the will nor the capacity to act as a strong counterbalance to the executive authority, it is equally clear that some alternatives must be sought. I doubt . . . whether . . . movement to a cabinet government is either possible or desirable. But we need reform. . . .

✣ *F U R T H E R   R E A D I N G*

Raoul Berger, *Executive Privilege: A Constitutional Myth* (1974)
——— , *Impeachment: The Constitutional Problem* (1973)
Barton J. Bernstein, "The Road to Watergate and Beyond: The Growth and Abuse of Executive Power Since 1940," *Law & Contemporary Problems* 40 (1976): 58–86
Charles L. Black, Jr., *Impeachment: A Handbook* (1974)
Thomas Cronin, *The State of the Presidency* (1975)
William M. Goldsmith, *The Growth of Presidential Power: A Documentary History*, 3 vols. (1974)
Warren W. Hassler, Jr., *The President as Commander in Chief* (1971)
Leon Jaworski, *The Right and the Power: The Prosecution of Watergate* (1976)
Stanley I. Kutler, *The Wars of Watergate* (1990)
Harvey Mansfield, ed., *Congress Against the President* (1976)
Maeva Marcus, *Truman and the Steel Seizure Case: The Limits of Presidential Power* (1977)
James L. Sundquist, *The Decline and Resurgence of Congress* (1981)
Ralph K. Winter, *Watergate and the Law: Political Campaigns and Presidential Power* (1974)
Robert Woodward and Carl Bernstein, *All the President's Men* (1974)

CHAPTER
8

Affirmative Action

Beginning in the mid-1930s, the National Association for the Advancement of Colored People (NAACP) mounted an ultimately successful campaign to secure racial equality before the law for all U.S. citizens. Its Legal Defense Fund persuaded the Supreme Court, in Brown v. Board of Education of Topeka, Kansas *(1954/1955), to order an end ''with all deliberate speed'' to the principle of separate-but-equal established in* Plessy v. Ferguson *(1896). Southerners hunkered down in resistance to* Brown *for a decade more, claiming that the federal mandate to integrate public schools would result in violence. Not until Congress passed the Civil Rights Act of 1964, which threatened institutions practicing discrimination with the loss of federal funds, and not until a 1965 federal measure that pumped millions of dollars into public education, did the South's political leaders accept the futility of further defiance.*

The initial objective of school desegregation was a color-blind legal order in which government disregarded race. By the mid-1960s the vast majority of Americans rejected as morally wrong the sort of racial discrimination practiced by law in the South. Americans could not agree, however, about what remedies to take in response to past racial injustice. In part because of the intransigence of southerners, and in part because of the new aggressiveness of African-American leaders, the constitutional debate over racial equality gradually shifted from providing equal opportunity to giving minorities a share of society's benefits, a development that the Supreme Court encouraged. In fact, the beginning of affirmative action can be traced to the Court's decision in Green v. County Board of New Kent County *(1968). Justice William Brennan's opinion for the Court in the* Green *case imposed on school districts ''an affirmative duty'' not only to eliminate legal barriers that kept blacks and whites apart but also to promote integration actively. Busing emerged as the preferred method by which federal district courts imposed this affirmative duty to integrate. Busing stirred heated controversy, however, because in giving black students access to good schools, some white students had to be sent elsewhere.*

The real impetus for affirmative-action programs came from Congress and state legislatures, not the Supreme Court. Legislators increasingly built into employment statutes requirements intended to remedy discriminatory practices by hiring minority-group members based on existing population percentages involving race, color, and sex. These programs were controversial because they involved giving minorities preferential access to college and professional education, hiring policies, and the use of federal funds to support minority contractors. The affirmative-action programs also collided with traditional arrangements, such as laying off the most junior persons first in hard economic times and promoting persons with the best test scores to positions of increased responsibility—and salary. Critics of affirmative action argue that the policy does exactly what the Civil Rights Act of 1964 sought to prevent: it discriminates based on race and sex.

The Supreme Court has relied on the equal-protection clause of the Fourteenth Amendment and—where federal action is involved—the due-process clause of the Fifth Amendment to measure the constitutionality of affirmative-action programs. The equal-protection clause in the Fourteenth Amendment is preceded by the phrase that "no state shall" make any law denying a person the equal protection of the laws. The Court, in Bolling v. Sharpe *(1954) (the companion case from the federally controlled District of Columbia to* Brown v. Board of Education of Topeka, Kansas) *declared that, although the Fifth Amendment did "not contain an equal protection clause as does the Fourteenth Amendment which applies only to the states . . . the concepts of equal protection and due process . . . are not mutually exclusive . . . and . . . discrimination may be so unjustifiable as to be violative of due process." Equal protection of the law has emerged as one of the most important—and controversial—features of modern constitutional history. Liberals argue that the amendment's equal protection clause promises to make more equal in law the less equal in life. Conservatives complain that the justices have used the clause to unfairly benefit minorities at the expense of the majority.*

✠ D O C U M E N T S

In the 1896 decision of *Plessy* v. *Ferguson*, which is reproduced as the first document, the Court (with only Justice John Marshall Harlan dissenting) sustained the constitutionality of segregation by race as long as separate public facilities were equal. A later Court overturned that provision in *Brown* v. *Board of Education of Topeka, Kansas* (1954), the second document. The following year, in *Brown II* (1955), the third selection, the Court charged lower federal-court judges to proceed with "all deliberate speed" in dismantling the existing system of segregation. Southerners pleaded their case in the fourth document, the Southern Manifesto. Real progress toward desegregation did not begin until the passage of the Civil Rights Act of 1964, of which Titles IV, VI, and VII are excerpted in the fifth selection.

After 1964, efforts to deal with discrimination turned increasingly affirmative and controversial. In 1978, the justices struck a compromise on affirmative-action admissions programs to professional schools in *Regents of the University of California* v. *Bakke*, which is the sixth document. This somewhat confusing decision accepted the argument of Allan Bakke, a white male, that he had been unconstitutionally denied admission to the medical school at the University of California, Davis, while also finding that properly constructed affirmative-action programs were still acceptable. In 1980, the justices underscored their support for government policies giving preference to minority contractors in *Fullilove* v. *Klutznick*, the seventh document. Such policies have come under attack, however, on the grounds cited by Thomas Sowell, an African-American economics professor. Sowell's essay, "Are Quotas Good for Blacks?" (the last document) summarizes the case against affirmative-action programs.

Plessy v. Ferguson, 163 U.S. 537 (1896)

[8–1: Brown, Brewer, Field, Fuller, Gray,
Peckham, Shiras, White; Harlan]

Mr. Justice Brown . . . delivered the opinion of the court.

This case turns upon the constitutionality of an act of the General Assembly of the State of Louisiana, passed in 1890, providing for separate railway carriages for the white and colored races. . . .

The first section of the statute enacts "that all railway companies carrying passengers in their coaches in this State, shall provide equal but separate accommodations for the white, and colored races, by providing two or more passenger coaches for each passenger train, or by dividing the passenger coaches by a partition so as to secure separate accommodations: *Provided,* That this section shall not be construed to apply to street railroads. No person or persons, shall be admitted to occupy seats in coaches, other than, the ones, assigned, to them on account of the race they belong to." . . .

The information filed in the criminal District Court charged in substance that Plessy, being a passenger between two stations within the State of Louisiana, was assigned by officers of the company to the coach used for the race to which he belonged, but he insisted upon going into a coach used by the race to which he did not belong. . . .

The petition for the writ of prohibition averred that petitioner was seven eighths Caucasian and one eighth African blood; that the mixture of colored blood was not discernible in him, and that he was entitled to every right, privilege and immunity secured to citizens of the United States of the white race; and that, upon such theory, he took possession of a vacant seat in a coach where passengers of the white race were accommodated, and was ordered by the conductor to vacate said coach and take a seat in another assigned to persons of the colored race, and having refused to comply with such demand he was forcibly ejected with the aid of a police officer, and imprisoned in the parish jail to answer a charge of having violated the above act.

The constitutionality of this act is attacked upon the ground that it conflicts both with the Thirteenth Amendment of the Constitution, abolishing slavery, and the Fourteenth Amendment, which prohibits certain restrictive legislation on the part of the States.

1. That it does not conflict with the Thirteenth Amendment, which abolished slavery and involuntary servitude, except as a punishment for crime, is too clear for argument. Slavery implies involuntary servitude—a state of bondage; the ownership of mankind as a chattel, or at least the control of the labor and services of one man for the benefit of another, and the absence of a legal right to the disposal of his own person, property and services. . . .

A statute which implies merely a legal distinction between the white and colored races—a distinction which is founded in the color of the two races, and which must always exist so long as white men are distinguished from the other race by color—has no tendency to destroy the legal equality of the two races, or reëstablish a state of involuntary servitude. Indeed, we do not understand that the Thirteenth Amendment is strenuously relied upon by the plaintiff in error in this connection.

2. By the Fourteenth Amendment, all persons born or naturalized in the United States, and subject to the jurisdiction thereof, are made citizens of the United States and of the State wherein they reside; and the States are forbidden from making or enforcing any law which shall abridge the privileges or immunities of citizens of the United States, or shall deprive any person of life, liberty or property without due process of law, or deny to any person within their jurisdiction the equal protection of the laws.

The proper construction of this amendment was first called to the attention of this court in the *Slaughter-house cases* . . . , which involved, however, not a question of race, but one of exclusive privileges. The case did not call for any expression of opinion as to the exact rights it was intended to secure to the colored race, but it was said generally that its main purpose was to establish the citizenship of the negro; to give definitions of citizenship of the United States and of the States, and to protect from the hostile legislation of the States the privileges and immunities of citizens of the United States, as distinguished from those of citizens of the States.

The object of the amendment was undoubtedly to enforce the absolute equality of the two races before the law, but in the nature of things it could not have been intended to abolish distinctions based upon color, or to enforce social, as distinguished from political equality, or a commingling of the two races upon terms unsatisfactory to either. Laws permitting, and even requiring, their separation in places where they are liable to be brought into contact do not necessarily imply the inferiority of either race to the other, and have been generally, if not universally, recognized as within the competency of the state legislatures in the exercise of their police power. The most common instance of this is connected with the establishment of separate schools for white and colored children, which has been held to be a valid exercise of the legislative power even by courts of States where the political rights of the colored race have been longest and most earnestly enforced. . . .

While we think the enforced separation of the races, as applied to the internal commerce of the State, neither abridges the privileges or immunities of the colored man, deprives him of his property without due process of law, nor denies him the equal protection of the laws, within the meaning of the Fourteenth Amendment, we are not prepared to say that the conductor, in assigning passengers to the coaches according to their race, does not act at his peril, or that the provision of the second section of the act, that denies to the passenger compensation in damages for a refusal to receive him into the coach in which he properly belongs, is a valid exercise of the legislative power. . . .

So far, then, as a conflict with the Fourteenth Amendment is concerned, the case reduces itself to the question whether the statute of Louisiana is a reasonable regulation, and with respect to this there must necessarily be a large discretion on the part of the legislature. In determining the question of reasonableness it is at liberty to act with reference to the established usages, customs and traditions of the people, and with a view to the promotion of their comfort, and the preservation of the public peace and good order. Gauged by this standard, we cannot say that a law which authorizes or even requires the separation of the two races in public conveyances is unreasonable, or more obnoxious to the Fourteenth Amendment than the acts of Congress requiring separate schools for colored children in the District of Columbia, the constitutionality of which does not seem to have been questioned, or the corresponding acts of state legislatures.

We consider the underlying fallacy of the plaintiff's argument to consist in the assumption that the enforced separation of the two races stamps the colored race with a badge of inferiority. If this be so, it is not by reason of anything found in the act, but solely because the colored race chooses to put that construction upon it. The argument necessarily assumes that if, as has been more than once the case, and is not unlikely to be so again, the colored race should become the dominant power in the state legislature, and should enact a law in precisely similar terms, it would thereby relegate the white race to an inferior position. We imagine that the white race, at least, would not acquiesce in this assumption. The argument also assumes that social prejudices may be overcome by legislation, and that equal rights cannot be secured to the negro except by an enforced commingling of the two races. We cannot accept this proposition. If the two races are to meet upon terms of social equality, it must be the result of natural affinities, a mutual appreciation of each other's merits and a voluntary consent of individuals. . . . Legislation is powerless to eradicate racial instincts or to abolish distinctions based upon physical differences, and the attempt to do so can only result in accentuating the difficulties of the present situation. If the civil and political rights of both races be equal one cannot be inferior to the other civilly or politically. If one race be inferior to the other socially, the Constitution of the United States cannot put them upon the same plane.

It is true that the question of the proportion of colored blood necessary to constitute a colored person, as distinguished from a white person, is one upon which there is a difference of opinion in the different States, some holding that any visible admixture of black blood stamps the person as belonging to the colored race . . . ; others that it depends upon the preponderance of blood . . . ; and still others that the predominance of white blood must only be in the proportion of three fourths. . . . But these are questions to be determined under the laws of each State and are not properly put in issue in this case. Under the allegations of his petition it may undoubtedly become a question of importance whether, under the laws of Louisiana, the petitioner belongs to the white or colored race.

The judgment of the court below is, therefore, *Affirmed.*

Mr. Justice Harlan dissenting.

. . . While there may be in Louisiana persons of different races who are not citizens of the United States, the words in the act, "white and colored races," necessarily include all citizens of the United States of both races residing in that State. So that we have before us a state enactment that compels, under penalties, the separation of the two races in railroad passenger coaches, and makes it a crime for a citizen of either race to enter a coach that has been assigned to citizens of the other race.

Thus the State regulates the use of a public highway by citizens of the United States solely upon the basis of race.

However apparent the injustice of such legislation may be, we have only to consider whether it is consistent with the Constitution of the United States. . . .

In respect of civil rights, common to all citizens, the Constitution of the United States does not, I think, permit any public authority to know the race of those entitled to be protected in the enjoyment of such rights. Every true man has pride of race, and under appropriate circumstances when the rights of others, his equals before the law, are not to be affected, it is his privilege to express such pride and to take such action based upon it as to him seems proper. But I deny that any legislative body or judicial tribunal may have regard to the race of citizens when the civil rights of those citizens are involved. Indeed, such legislation, as that here in question, is inconsistent not only with that equality of rights which pertains to citizenship, National and State, but with the personal liberty enjoyed by every one within the United States.

The Thirteenth Amendment does not permit the withholding or the deprivation of any right necessarily inhering in freedom. It not only struck down the institution of slavery as previously existing in the United States, but it prevents the imposition of any burdens or disabilities that constitute badges of slavery or servitude. It decreed universal civil freedom in this country. This court has so adjudged. But that amendment having been found inadequate to the protection of the rights of those who had been in slavery, it was followed by the Fourteenth Amendment, which added greatly to the dignity and glory of American citizenship, and to the security of personal liberty, by declaring that "all persons born or naturalized in the United States, and subject to the jurisdiction thereof, are citizens of the United States and of the State wherein they reside," and that "no State shall make or enforce any law which shall abridge the privileges or immunities of citizens of the United States; nor shall any State deprive any person of life, liberty or property without due process of law, nor deny to any person within its jurisdiction the equal protection of the laws." These two amendments, if enforced according to their true intent and meaning, will protect all the civil rights that pertain to freedom and citizenship. . . .

These notable additions to the fundamental law were welcomed by the friends of liberty throughout the world. They removed the race line from our governmental systems. They had, as this court has said, a common purpose, namely, to secure "to a race recently emancipated, a race that through many generations have been held in slavery, all the civil rights that the superior race enjoy." They declared, in legal effect, this court has further said, "that the law in the States shall be the same for the black as for the white; that all persons, whether colored or white, shall stand equal before the laws of the States, and, in regard to the colored race, for whose protection the amendment was primarily designed, that no discrimination shall be made against them by law because of their color." . . .

The white race deems itself to be the dominant race in this country. And so it is, in prestige, in achievements, in education, in wealth and in power. So, I doubt not, it will continue to be for all time, if it remains true to its great heritage and holds fast to the principles of constitutional liberty. But in view of the Constitution, in the eye of the law, there is in this country no superior, dominant, ruling class of citizens. There is no caste here. Our Constitution is color-blind, and neither knows nor tolerates classes among citizens. In respect of civil rights, all citizens are equal before the law. The humblest is the peer of the most powerful. The law regards man as man, and takes no account of his surroundings or of his color when his civil rights as guaranteed by the supreme law of the land are involved. It is, therefore, to be regretted that this high tribunal, the final expositor of the fundamental law of the land, has reached the conclusion that it is competent for a State to regulate the enjoyment by citizens of their civil rights solely upon the basis of race.

In my opinion, the judgment this day rendered will, in time, prove to be quite as pernicious as the decision made by this tribunal in the *Dred Scott case*. . . . The present decision, it may well be apprehended, will not only stimulate aggressions, more or less brutal and irritating, upon the admitted rights of colored citizens, but will encourage the belief that it is possible, by means of state enactments, to defeat the beneficent purposes which the people of the United States had in view when they adopted the recent amendments of the Constitution, by one of which the blacks of this country were made citizens of the United States and of the States in which they respectively reside, and whose privileges and immunities, as citizens, the States are forbidden to abridge. Sixty millions of whites are in no danger from the presence here of eight millions of blacks. The destinies of the two races, in this country, are indissolubly linked together, and the interests of both require that the common government of all shall not permit the seeds of race hate to be planted under the sanction of law. What can more certainly arouse race hate, what more certainly create and perpetuate a feeling of distrust between these races, than state enactments, which, in fact, proceed on the ground that colored citizens are so inferior and degraded that they cannot be allowed to sit in public coaches occupied by white citizens? That, as all will admit, is the real meaning of such legislation as was enacted in Louisiana. . . .

If evils will result from the commingling of the two races upon public highways established for the benefit of all, they will be infinitely less than those that will surely come from state legislation regulating the enjoyment of civil rights upon the basis of race. We boast of the freedom enjoyed by our people above all other peoples. But it is difficult to reconcile that boast with a state of the law which, practically, puts the brand of servitude and degradation upon a large class of our fellow-citizens, our equals before the law. . . .

I am of opinion that the statute of Louisiana is inconsistent with the personal liberty of citizens, white and black, in that State, and hostile to both the spirit and letter of the Constitution of the United States. If laws of like character should be enacted in the several States of the Union, the effect would be in the highest degree mischievous. Slavery, as an institution tolerated by law would, it is true, have disappeared from our country, but there would remain a power in the States, by sinister legislation, to interfere with the full enjoyment of the blessings of freedom; to regulate civil rights, common to all citizens, upon the basis of race; and to place in a condition of legal inferiority a large body of American citizens, now constituting a part of the political community called the People of the United States, for whom, and by whom through representatives, our government is administered.

Brown v. *Board of Education of Topeka, Kansas,* 347 U.S. 483 (1954)

(Unanimous)

Mr. Chief Justice Warren delivered the opinion of the Court.

These cases come to us from the States of Kansas, South Carolina, Virginia, and Delaware. They are premised on different facts and different local conditions, but a common legal question justifies their consideration together in this consolidated opinion.

In each of the cases, minors of the Negro race, through their legal representatives, seek the aid of the courts in obtaining admission to the public schools of their community on a nonsegregated basis. In each instance, they had been denied admission to schools attended by white children under laws requiring or permitting segregation according to race. This segregation was alleged to deprive the plaintiffs of the equal protection of the laws under the Fourteenth Amendment. In each of the cases other than the Delaware case, a three-judge federal district court denied relief to the plaintiffs on the so-called "separate but equal" doctrine announced by this Court in *Plessy* v. *Ferguson*. . . . Under that doctrine, equality of treatment is accorded when the races are provided substantially equal facilities, even though these facilities be separate. In the Delaware case, the Supreme Court of Delaware adhered to that doctrine, but ordered that the plaintiffs be admitted to the white schools because of their superiority to the Negro schools.

The plaintiffs contend that segregated public schools are not "equal" and cannot be made "equal," and that hence they are deprived of the equal protection of the laws. Because of the obvious importance of the question presented, the Court took jurisdiction. Argument was heard in the 1952 Term, and reargument was heard this Term on certain questions propounded by the Court.

Reargument was largely devoted to the circumstances surrounding the adoption of the Fourteenth Amendment in 1868. It covered exhaustively consideration of the Amendment in Congress, ratification by the states, then existing practices in racial segregation, and the views of proponents and opponents of the Amendment. This discussion and our own investigation convince us that, although these sources cast some light, it is not enough to resolve the problem with which we are faced. At best, they are inconclusive. The most avid proponents of the post-War Amendments undoubtedly intended them to remove all legal distinctions among "all persons born or naturalized in the United States." Their opponents, just as certainly, were antagonistic to both the letter and the spirit of the Amendments and wished them to have the most limited effect. What others in Congress and the state legislatures had in mind cannot be determined with any degree of certainty.

An additional reason for the inconclusive nature of the Amendment's history, with respect to segregated schools, is the status of public education at that time. In the South, the movement toward free common schools, supported by general taxation, had not yet taken hold. Education of white children was largely in the hands of private groups. Education of Negroes was almost nonexistent, and practically all of the race were illiterate. In fact, any education of Negroes was forbidden by law in some states. Today, in contrast, many Negroes have achieved outstanding success in the arts and sciences as well as in the business and professional world. It is true that public school education at the time of the Amendment had advanced further in the North, but the effect of the Amendment on Northern States was generally ignored in the congressional debates. Even in the North, the conditions of public education did not approximate those existing today. The curriculum was usually rudimentary; ungraded schools were common in rural areas; the school term was but three months a year in many states; and compulsory school attendance was virtually unknown. As a consequence, it is not surprising that there should be so little in the history of the Fourteenth Amendment relating to its intended effect on public education.

In the first cases in this Court construing the Fourteenth Amendment, decided shortly after its adoption, the Court interpreted it as proscribing all state-imposed discriminations against the Negro race. The doctrine of "separate but equal" did not make its appearance in this Court until 1896 in the case of *Plessy* v. *Ferguson* . . . , involving not education but transportation. American courts have since labored with the doctrine for over half a century. . . .

In the instant cases . . . , there are findings below that the Negro and white schools involved have been equalized, or are being equalized, with respect to buildings, curricula, qualifications and salaries of teachers, and other "tangible" factors. Our decision, therefore, cannot turn on merely a comparison of these tangible factors in the Negro and white schools involved in each of the cases. We must look instead to the effect of segregation itself on public education.

In approaching this problem, we cannot turn the clock back to 1868 when the Amendment was adopted, or even to 1896 when *Plessy* v. *Ferguson* was written. We must consider public education in the light of its full development and its present place in American life throughout the Nation.

Only in this way can it be determined if segregation in public schools deprives these plaintiffs of the equal protection of the laws.

Today, education is perhaps the most important function of state and local governments. Compulsory school attendance laws and the great expenditures for education both demonstrate our recognition of the importance of education to our democratic society. It is required in the performance of our most basic public responsibilities, even service in the armed forces. It is the very foundation of good citizenship. Today it is a principal instrument in awakening the child to cultural values, in preparing him for later professional training, and in helping him to adjust normally to his environment. In these days, it is doubtful that any child may reasonably be expected to succeed in life if he is denied the opportunity of an education. Such an opportunity, where the state has undertaken to provide it, is a right which must be made available to all on equal terms.

We come then to the question presented: Does segregation of children in public schools solely on the basis of race, even though the physical facilities and other "tangible" factors may be equal, deprive the children of the minority group of equal educational opportunities? We believe that it does.

In *Sweatt* v. *Painter* . . . , in finding that a segregated law school for Negroes could not provide them equal educational opportunities, this Court relied in large part on "those qualities which are incapable of objective measurement but which make for greatness in a law school." In *McLaurin* v. *Oklahoma State Regents* . . . , the Court, in requiring that a Negro admitted to a white graduate school be treated like all other students, again resorted to intangible considerations: ". . . his ability to study, to engage in discussions and exchange views with other students, and, in general, to learn his profession." Such considerations apply with added force to children in grade and high schools. To separate them from others of similar age and qualifications solely because of their race generates a feeling of inferiority as to their status in the community that may affect their hearts and minds in a way unlikely ever to be undone. The effect of this separation on their educational opportunities was well stated by a finding in the Kansas case by a court which nevertheless felt compelled to rule against the Negro plaintiffs:

> Segregation of white and colored children in public schools has a detrimental effect upon the colored children. The impact is greater when it has the sanction of the law; for the policy of separating the races is usually interpreted as denoting the inferiority of the negro group. A sense of inferiority affects the motivation of a child to learn. Segregation with the sanction of law, therefore, has a tendency to [retard] the educational and mental development of negro children and to deprive them of some of the benefits they would receive in a racial[ly] integrated school system.

Whatever may have been the extent of psychological knowledge at the time of *Plessy* v. *Ferguson,* this finding is amply supported by modern authority. Any language in *Plessy* v. *Ferguson* contrary to this finding is rejected.

We conclude that in the field of public education the doctrine of "separate but equal" has no place. Separate educational facilities are inherently unequal. Therefore, we hold that the plaintiffs and others similarly situated for whom the actions have been brought are, by reason of the segregation complained of, deprived of the equal protection of the laws guaranteed by the Fourteenth Amendment. This disposition makes unnecessary any discussion whether such segregation also violates the Due Process Clause of the Fourteenth Amendment.

Because these are class actions, because of the wide applicability of this decision, and because of the great variety of local conditions, the formulation of decrees in these cases presents problems of considerable complexity. On reargument, the consideration of appropriate relief was necessarily subordinated to the primary question—the constitutionality of segregation in public education. We have now announced that such segregation is a denial of the equal protection of the laws. In order that we may have the full assistance of the parties in formulating decrees, the cases will be restored to the docket, and the parties are requested to present further argument. . . . The Attorney General of the United States is again invited to participate. The Attorneys General of the states requiring or permitting segregation in public education will also be permitted to appear as *amici curiae* upon request to do so by September 15, 1954, and submission of briefs by October 1, 1954. *It is so ordered.*

Brown v. *Board of Education of Topeka, Kansas,* 349 U.S. 294 (1955)

(Unanimous)

Mr. Chief Justice Warren delivered the opinion of the Court.

These cases were decided on May 17, 1954. The opinions of that date, declaring the fundamental principle that racial discrimination in public education is unconstitutional, are incorporated herein by reference. All provisions of federal, state, or local law requiring or permitting such discrimination must yield to this principle. There remains for consideration the manner in which relief is to be accorded. Because these cases arose under different local conditions and their disposition will involve a variety of local problems, we requested further argument on the question of relief. In view of the nationwide importance of the decision, we invited the Attorney General of the United States and the Attorneys General of all states requiring or permitting racial discrimination in public education to present their views on that question. The parties, the United States, and the States of Florida, North Carolina, Arkansas, Oklahoma, Maryland, and Texas filed briefs and participated in the oral argument. . . .

Full implementation of these constitutional principles may require solution of varied local school problems. School authorities have the primary responsibility for elucidating, assessing, and solving these problems; courts will have to consider whether the action of school authorities constitutes good faith implementation of the governing constitutional principles. Because of their proximity to local conditions and the possible need for further hearings, the courts which originally heard these cases can best perform this judicial appraisal. Accordingly, we believe it appropriate to remand the cases to those courts.

In fashioning and effectuating the decrees, the courts will be guided by equitable principles. Traditionally, equity has been characterized by a practical flexibility in shaping its remedies and by a facility for adjusting and reconciling public and private needs. These cases call for the exercise of these traditional attributes of equity power. At stake is the personal interest of the plaintiffs in admission to public schools as soon as practicable on a nondiscriminatory basis. To effectuate this interest may call for elimination of a variety of obstacles in making the transition to school systems operated in accordance with the constitutional principles set forth in our May 17, 1954, decision. Courts of equity may properly take into account the public interest in the elimination of such obstacles in a systematic and effective manner. But it should go without saying that the vitality of these constitutional principles cannot be allowed to yield simply because of disagreement with them.

While giving weight to these public and private considerations, the courts will require that the defendants make a prompt and reasonable start toward full compliance with our May 17, 1954, ruling. Once such a start has been made, the courts may find that additional time is necessary to carry out the ruling in an effective manner. The burden rests upon the defendants to establish that such time is necessary in the public interest and is consistent with good faith compliance at the earliest practicable date. To that end, the courts may consider problems related to administration, arising from the physical condition of the school plant, the school transportation system, personnel, revision of school districts and attendance areas into compact units to achieve a system of determining admission to the public schools on a nonracial basis, and revision of local laws and regulations which may be necessary in solving the foregoing problems. They will also consider the adequacy of any plans the defendants may propose to meet these problems and to effectuate a transition to a racially nondiscriminatory school system. During this period of transition, the courts will retain jurisdiction of these cases. [L]ower courts are to take such proceedings and enter such orders and decrees consistent with this opinion as are necessary and proper to admit to public schools on a racially nondiscriminatory basis with all deliberate speed the parties to these cases.

The Southern Manifesto, 1956

We regard the decision of the Supreme Court in the school cases as clear abuse of judicial power. It climaxes a trend in the Federal judiciary undertaking to legislate, in derogation of the authority of Congress, and to encroach upon the reserved rights of the states and the people.

The original Constitution does not mention education. Neither does the Fourteenth Amendment nor any other amendment. The debates preceding the submission of the Fourteenth Amendment clearly show that there was no intent that it should affect the systems of education maintained by the states.

The very Congress which proposed the amendment subsequently provided for segregated schools in the District of Columbia.

When the amendment was adopted in 1868, there were thirty-seven states of the Union. Every one of the twenty-six states that had any substantial racial differences among its people either approved the operation of segregated schools already in existence or subsequently established such schools by action of the same law-making body which considered the Fourteenth Amendment.

As admitted by the Supreme Court in the public school case (*Brown* v. *Board of Education*), the doctrine of separate but equal schools "apparently originated in *Roberts* v. *City of Boston* (1849), upholding school segregation against attack as being violative of a state constitutional guarantee of equality." This constitutional doctrine began in the North—not in the South—and it was followed not only in Massachusetts but in Connecticut, New York, Illinois, Indiana, Michigan, Minnesota, New Jersey, Ohio, Pennsylvania and other northern states until they, exercising their rights as states through the constitutional processes of local self-government, changed their school systems.

In the case of *Plessy* v. *Ferguson* in 1896 the Supreme Court expressly declared that under the Fourteenth Amendment no person was denied any of his rights if the states provided separate but equal public facilities. This decision has been followed in many other cases. It is notable that the Supreme Court, speaking through Chief Justice Taft, a former President of the United States, unanimously declared in 1927 in *Lum* v. *Rice* that the "separate but equal" principle is ". . . within the discretion of the state in regulating its public schools and does not conflict with the Fourteenth Amendment."

This interpretation, restated time and again, became a part of the life of the people of many of the states and confirmed their habits, customs, traditions and way of life. It is founded on elemental humanity and common sense, for parents should not be deprived by Government of the right to direct the lives and education of their own children.

Though there has been no constitutional amendment or act of Congress changing this established legal principle almost a century old, the Supreme Court of the United States, with no legal basis for such action, undertook to exercise their naked judicial power and substituted their personal political and social ideas for the established law of the land.

This unwarranted exercise of power by the court, contrary to the Constitution, is creating chaos and confusion in the states principally affected. It is destroying the amicable relations between the white and Negro races that have been created through ninety years of patient effort by the good people of both races. It has planted hatred and suspicion where there has been heretofore friendship and understanding.

Without regard to the consent of the governed, outside agitators are threatening immediate and revolutionary changes in our public school systems. If done, this is certain to destroy the system of public education in some of the states.

With the gravest concern for the explosive and dangerous condition created by this decision and inflamed by outside meddlers:

We reaffirm our reliance on the Constitution as the fundamental law of the land.

We decry the Supreme Court's encroachments on rights reserved to the states and to the people, contrary to established law and to the Constitution.

We commend the motives of those states which have declared the intention to resist forced integration by any lawful means.

We appeal to the states and people who are not directly affected by these decisions to consider the constitutional principles involved against the time when they too, on issues vital to them, may be the victims of judicial encroachment.

Even though we constitute a minority in the present Congress, we have full faith that a majority of the American people believe in the dual system of government which has enabled us to achieve our greatness and will in time demand that the reserved rights of the states and of the people be made secure against judicial usurpation.

We pledge ourselves to use all lawful means to bring about a reversal of this decision which is contrary to the Constitution and to prevent the use of force in its implementation.

In this trying period, as we all seek to right this wrong, we appeal to our people not to be provoked by the agitators and troublemakers invading our states and to scrupulously refrain from disorder and lawless acts.

The Civil Rights Act of 1964

Title IV—Desegregation of Public Education

Survey and Report of Educational Opportunities

Sec. 402. The Commissioner shall conduct a survey and make a report to the President and the Congress, within two years of the enactment of this title, concerning the lack of availability of equal educational opportunities for individuals by reason of race, color, religion, or national origin in public educational institutions at all levels in the United States, its territories and possessions, and the District of Columbia.

Technical Assistance

Sec. 403. The Commissioner is authorized, upon the application of any school board, State, municipality, school district, or other governmental unit legally responsible for operating a public school or schools, to render technical assistance to such applicant in the preparation, adoption, and implementation of plans for the desegregation of public schools. Such technical assistance may, among other activities, include making available to such agencies information regarding effective methods of coping with special educational problems occasioned by desegregation, and making available to such agencies personnel of the Office of Education or other persons specially equipped to advise and assist them in coping with such problems.

Training Institutes

Sec. 404. The Commissioner is authorized to arrange, through grants or contracts, with institutions of higher education for the operation of short-term or regular session institutes for special training designed to improve the ability of teachers, supervisors, counselors, and other elementary or secondary school personnel to deal effectively with special educational problems occasioned by desegregation. Individuals who attend such an institute on a full-time basis may be paid stipends for the period of their attendance at such institute in amounts specified by the Commissioner in regulations, including allowances for travel to attend such institute.

Grants

Sec. 405. (a) The Commissioner is authorized, upon application of a school board, to make grants to such board to pay, in whole or in part, the cost of—

(1) giving to teachers and other school personnel inservice training in dealing with problems incident to desegregation, and
(2) employing specialists to advise in problems incident to desegregation.

(b) In determining whether to make a grant, and in fixing the amount thereof and the terms and conditions on which it will be made, the Commissioner shall take into consideration the amount available for grants under this section and the other applications which are pending before him; the financial condition of the applicant and the other resources available to it; the nature, extent, and gravity of its problems incident to desegregation; and such other factors as he finds relevant. . . .

Title VI—Nondiscrimination in Federally Assisted Programs

Sec. 601. No person in the United States shall, on the ground of race, color, or national origin, be excluded from participation in, be denied the benefits of, or be subjected to discrimination under any program or activity receiving Federal financial assistance.

Sec. 602. Each Federal department and agency which is empowered to extend Federal financial assistance to any program or activity, by way of grant, loan, or contract other than a contract of insurance or guaranty, is authorized and directed to effectuate the provisions of section 601 with respect to such program or activity by issuing rules, regulations, or orders of general applicability which shall be consistent with achievement of the objectives of the statute authorizing the financial assistance in connection with which the action is taken. No such rule, regulation, or order shall become effective unless and until approved by the President. Compliance with any requirement adopted pursuant to this section may be effected (1) by the termination of or refusal to grant or to continue assistance under such program or activity to any recipient as to whom there has been an express finding on the record, after opportunity for hearing, of a failure to comply with such requirement, but such termination or refusal shall be limited to the particular political entity, or part thereof, or other recipient as to whom such a finding has been made and, shall be limited in its effect to the particular program, or part thereof, in which such noncompliance has been so found, or (2) by any other means authorized by law: *Provided, however,* That no such action shall be taken until the department or agency concerned has advised the appropriate person or persons of the failure to comply with the requirement and has determined that compliance cannot be secured by voluntary means. In the case of any action terminating, or refusing to grant or continue, assistance because of failure to comply with a requirement imposed pursuant to this section, the head of the Federal department or agency shall file with the committees of the House and Senate having legislative jurisdiction over the program or activity involved a full written report of the circumstances and the grounds for such action. No such action shall become effective until thirty days have elapsed after the filing of such report. . . .

Title VII—Equal Employment Opportunity

Discrimination Because of Race, Color, Religion, Sex, or National Origin
Sec. 703. (a) It shall be an unlawful employment practice for an employer—

(1) to fail or refuse to hire or to discharge any individual, or otherwise to discriminate against any individual with respect to his compensation, terms, conditions, or privileges of employment, because of such individual's race, color, religion, sex, or national origin; or
(2) to limit, segregate, or classify his employees in any way which would deprive or tend to deprive any individual of employment opportunities or otherwise adversely affect his status as an employee, because of such individual's race, color, religion, sex, or national origin.

(b) It shall be an unlawful employment practice for an employment agency to fail or refuse to refer for employment, or otherwise to discriminate against, any individual because of his race, color, religion, sex, or national origin, or to classify or refer for employment any individual on the basis of his race, color, religion, sex, or national origin.
(c) It shall be unlawful employment practice for a labor organization—

(1) to exclude or to expel from its membership, or otherwise to discriminate against, any individual because of his race, color, religion, sex, or national origin;

(2) to limit, segregate, or classify its membership, or to classify or fail or refuse to refer for employment any individual, in any way which would deprive or tend to deprive any individual of employment opportunities, or would limit such employment opportunities or otherwise adversely affect his status as an employee or as an applicant for employment, because of such individual's race, color, religion, sex, or national origin; or

(3) to cause or attempt to cause an employer to discriminate against an individual in violation of this section.

(d) It shall be an unlawful employment practice for any employer, labor organization, or joint labor-management committee controlling apprenticeship or other training or retraining, including on-the-job training programs to discriminate against any individual because of his race, color, religion, sex, or national origin in admission to, or employment in, any program established to provide apprenticeship or other training.

(e) Notwithstanding any other provision of this title, (1) it shall not be an unlawful employment practice for an employer to hire and employ employees, for an employment agency to classify, or refer for employment any individual, for a labor organization to classify its membership or to classify or refer for employment any individual, or for an employer, labor organization, or joint labor-management committee controlling apprenticeship or other training or retraining programs to admit or employ any individual in any such program, on the basis of his religion, sex, or national origin in those certain instances where religion, sex, or national origin is a bona fide occupational qualification reasonably necessary to the normal operation of that particular business or enterprise, and (2) it shall not be an unlawful employment practice for a school, college, university, or other educational institution or institution of learning to hire and employ employees of a particular religion if such school, college, university, or other educational institution or institution of learning is, in whole or in substantial part, owned, supported, controlled, or managed by a particular religion or by a particular religious corporation, association, or society, or if the curriculum of such school, college, university, or other educational institution or institution of learning is directed toward the propagation of a particular religion.

(f) As used in this title, the phrase "unlawful employment practice" shall not be deemed to include any action or measure taken by an employer, labor organization, joint labor-management committee, or employment agency with respect to an individual who is a member of the Communist Party of the United States or of any other organization required to register as a Communist-action or Communist-front organization by final order of the Subversive Activities Control Board pursuant to the Subversive Activities Control Act of 1950.

(g) Notwithstanding any other provision of this title, it shall not be an unlawful employment practice for an employer to fail or refuse to hire and employ any individual for any position, for an employer to discharge any individual from any position, or for an employment agency to fail or refuse to refer any individual for employment in any position, or for a labor organization to fail or refuse to refer any individual for employment in any position, if—

(1) the occupancy of such position, or access to the premises in or upon which any part of the duties of such position is performed or is to be performed, is subject to any requirement imposed in the interest of the national security of the United States under any security program in effect pursuant to or administered under any statute of the United States or any Executive order of the President; and

(2) such individual has not fulfilled or has ceased to fulfill that requirement.

(h) Notwithstanding any other provision of this title, it shall not be an unlawful employment practice for an employer to apply different standards of compensation, or different terms, conditions, or privileges of employment pursuant to a bona fide seniority or merit system, or a system which measures earnings by quantity or quality of production or to employees who work in different locations, provided that such differences are not the result of an intention to discriminate because of race, color, religion, sex, or national origin, nor shall it be an unlawful employment practice for an employer to give and to act upon the results of any professionally developed ability test provided that such test, its administration or action upon the results is not designed, intended or used to discriminate because of race, color, religion, sex or national origin. It shall not be an unlawful employment practice under this title for any employer to differentiate upon the basis of sex in determining the amount of the wages or compensation paid or to be paid to employees of such employer if such differentiation is authorized by the provisions of section 6(d) of the Fair Labor Standards Act of 1938, as amended (29 U.S.C. 206(d)).

(i) Nothing contained in this title shall apply to any business or enterprise on or near an Indian reservation with respect to any publicly announced employment practice of such business or enterprise under which a preferential treatment is given to any individual because he is an Indian living on or near a reservation.

(j) Nothing contained in this title shall be interpreted to require any employer, employment agency, labor organization, or joint labor-management committee subject to this title to grant preferential treatment to any individual or to any group because of the race, color, religion, sex, or national origin of such individual or group on account of an imbalance which may exist with respect to the total number or percentage of persons of any race, color, religion, sex, or national origin employed by any employer, referred or classified for employment by any employment agency or labor organization, admitted to membership or classified by any labor organization, or admitted to, or employed in, any apprenticeship or other training program, in comparison with the total number or percentage of persons of such race, color, religion, sex, or national origin in any community, State, section, or other area, or in the available work force in any community, State, section, or other area. . . .

Regents of the University of California v. Bakke,
438 U.S. 265 (1978)

[5–4: multiple opinions]

Mr. Justice Powell announced the judgment of the Court.

The concept of "discrimination," like the phrase "equal protection of the laws," is susceptible of varying interpretations, for as Mr. Justice Holmes declared, "[a] word is not a crystal, transparent and unchanged, it is the skin of a living thought and may vary greatly in color and content according to the circumstances and the time in which it is used." . . . Examination of the voluminous legislative history of Title VI reveals a congressional intent to halt federal funding of entities that violate a prohibition of racial discrimination similar to that of the Constitution. Although isolated statements of various legislators, taken out of context, can be marshaled in support of the proposition that § 601 enacted a purely color-blind scheme, without regard to the reach of the Equal Protection Clause, these comments must be read against the background of both the problem that Congress was addressing and the broader view of the statute that emerges from a full examination of the legislative debates.

The problem confronting Congress was discrimination against Negro citizens at the hands of recipients of federal moneys. . . .

In view of the clear legislative intent, Title VI must be held to proscribe only those racial classifications that would violate the Equal Protection Clause or the Fifth Amendment. . . .

En route to this crucial battle over the scope of judicial review, the parties fight a sharp preliminary action over the proper characterization of the special admissions program. Petitioner prefers to view it as establishing a "goal" of minority representation in the Medical School. Respondent, echoing the courts below, labels it a racial quota.

This semantic distinction is beside the point: The special admissions program is undeniably a classification based on race and ethnic background. To the extent that there existed a pool of at least minimally qualified minority applicants to fill the 16 special admissions seats, white applicants could compete only for 84 seats in the entering class, rather than the 100 open to minority applicants. Whether this limitation is described as a quota or a goal, it is a line drawn on the basis of race and ethnic status. . . .

It is settled beyond question that the "rights created by the first section of the Fourteenth Amendment are, by its terms, guaranteed to the individual." . . . The guarantee of equal protection cannot mean one thing when applied to one individual and something else when applied to a person of another color. If both are not accorded the same protection, then it is not equal.

Nevertheless, petitioner argues that the court below erred in applying strict scrutiny to the special admissions program because white males, such as respondent, are not a "discrete and insular minority" requiring extraordinary protection from the majoritarian political process. . . . This rationale, however, has never been invoked in our decisions as a prerequisite to subjecting racial or ethnic distinctions to strict scrutiny. Nor has this Court held that discreteness and insularity constitute necessary preconditions to a holding that a particular classification is invidious. . . .

Racial and ethnic classifications, however, are subject to stringent examination without regard to these additional characteristics. . . . Racial and ethnic distinctions of any sort are inherently suspect and thus call for the most exacting judicial examination. . . .

Although many of the Framers of the Fourteenth Amendment conceived of its primary function as bridging the vast distance between members of the Negro race and the white "majority," . . . the Amendment itself was framed in universal terms, without reference to color, ethnic origin, or condition of prior servitude. . . .

Petitioner urges us to adopt for the first time a more restrictive view of the Equal Protection Clause and hold that discrimination against members of the white "majority" cannot be suspect if its purpose can be characterized as "benign." The clock of our liberties, however, cannot be turned back to 1868. . . . It is far too late to argue that the guarantee of equal protection to *all* persons permits the recognition of special wards entitled to a degree of protection greater than that accorded others. . . .

[T]he white "majority" itself is composed of various minority groups, most of which can lay claim to a history of prior discrimination at the hands of the State and private individuals. Not all of these groups can receive preferential treatment and corresponding judicial tolerance of distinctions drawn in terms of race and nationality, for then the only "majority" left would be a new minority of white Anglo-Saxon Protestants. There is no principled basis for deciding which groups would merit "heightened judicial solicitude" and which would not. . . .

If it is the individual who is entitled to judicial protection against classifications based upon his racial or ethnic background because such distinctions impinge upon personal rights, rather than the individual only because of his membership in a particular group, then constitutional standards may be applied consistently. Political judgments regarding the necessity for the particular classification may be weighed in the constitutional balance, *Korematsu* v. *United States* . . . (1944), but the standard of justification will remain constant. This is as it should be, since those political judgments are the product of rough compromise struck by contending groups within the democratic process. When they touch upon an individual's race or ethnic background, he is entitled to a judicial determination that the burden he is asked to bear on that basis is precisely tailored to serve a compelling governmental interest. The Constitution guarantees that right to every person regardless of his background. . . .

Petitioner contends that on several occasions this Court has approved preferential classifications without applying the most exacting scrutiny. . . .

The school desegregation cases are inapposite. Each involved remedies for clearly determined constitutional violations. . . . Racial classifications thus were designed as remedies for the vindication of constitutional entitlement. . . . But we have never approved preferential classifications in the absence of proved constitutional or statutory violations. . . .

In this case, . . . there has been no determination by the legislature or a responsible administrative agency that the University engaged in a discriminatory practice requiring remedial efforts. Moreover, the operation of petitioner's special admissions program is quite different from the remedial measures approved in those cases. It prefers the designated minority groups at the expense of other individuals who are totally foreclosed from competition for the 16 special admissions seats in every Medical School class. Because of that foreclosure, some individuals are excluded from enjoyment of a state-provided benefit—admission to the Medical School—they otherwise would receive. When a classification denies an individual opportunities or benefits enjoyed by others solely because of his race or ethnic background, it must be regarded as suspect. . . .

The special admissions program purports to serve the purposes of: (i) "reducing the historic deficit of traditionally disfavored minorities in medical schools and in the medical profession," Brief for Petitioner 32; (ii) countering the effects of societal discrimination; (iii) increasing the number of physicians who will practice in communities currently underserved; and (iv) obtaining the educational benefits that flow from an ethnically diverse student body. It is necessary to decide which, if any, of these purposes is substantial enough to support the use of a suspect classification.

If petitioner's purpose is to assure within its student body some specified percentage of a particular group merely because of its race or ethnic origin, such a preferential purpose must be rejected not as insubstantial but as facially invalid. Preferring members of any one group for no reason other than race or ethnic origin is discrimination for its own sake. This the Constitution forbids. . . .

The State certainly has a legitimate and substantial interest in ameliorating, or eliminating where feasible, the disabling effects of identified discrimination. The line of school desegregation cases, commencing with *Brown*, attests to the importance of this state goal and the commitment of the judiciary to affirm all lawful means toward its attainment. In the school cases, the States were required by court order to redress the wrongs worked by specific instances of racial discrimination. That goal was far more focused than the remedying of the effects of "societal discrimination," an amorphous concept of injury that may be ageless in its reach into the past.

We have never approved a classification that aids persons perceived as members of relatively victimized groups at the expense of other innocent individuals in the absence of judicial, legislative, or administrative findings of constitutional or statutory violations. . . . Without such findings of constitutional or statutory violations, it cannot be said that the government has any greater interest in helping one individual than in refraining from harming another. Thus, the government has no compelling justification for inflicting such harm.

Petitioner does not purport to have made, and is in no position to make, such findings. . . .

Hence, the purpose of helping certain groups whom the faculty of the Davis Medical School perceived as victims of "societal discrimination" does not justify a classification that imposes disadvantages upon persons like respondent, who bear no responsibility for whatever harm the beneficiaries of the special admissions program are thought to have suffered. To hold otherwise would be to convert a remedy heretofore reserved for violations of legal rights into a privilege that all institutions throughout the Nation could grant at their pleasure to whatever groups are perceived as victims of societal discrimination. That is a step we have never approved. . . .

Petitioner identifies, as another purpose of its program, improving the delivery of health-care services to communities currently underserved. It may be assumed that in some situations a State's interest in facilitating the health care of its citizens is sufficiently compelling to support the use of a suspect classification. But there is virtually no evidence in the record indicating that petitioner's special admissions program is either needed or geared to promote that goal. . . .

The fourth goal asserted by petitioner is the attainment of a diverse student body. This clearly is a constitutionally permissible goal for an institution of higher education. Academic freedom, though not a specifically enumerated constitutional right, long has been viewed as a special concern of the First Amendment. The freedom of a university to make its own judgments as to education includes the selection of its student body. . . . The atmosphere of "speculation, experiment and creation"—so essential to the quality of higher education—is widely believed to be promoted by a diverse student body. . . .

Thus, in arguing that its universities must be accorded the right to select those students who will contribute the most to the "robust exchange of ideas," petitioner invokes a countervailing constitutional interest, that of the First Amendment. In this light, petitioner must be viewed as seeking to achieve a goal that is of paramount importance in the fulfillment of its mission. . . .

Ethnic diversity, however, is only one element in a range of factors a university properly may consider in attaining the goal of a heterogeneous student body. Although a university must have wide discretion in making the sensitive judgments as to who should be admitted, constitutional limitations protecting individual rights may not be disregarded. Respondent urges—and the courts below have held—that petitioner's dual admissions program is a racial classification that impermissibly infringes his rights under the Fourteenth Amendment. As the interest of diversity is compelling in the context of a university's admissions program, the question remains whether the program's racial classification is necessary to promote this interest. . . .

It may be assumed that the reservation of a specified number of seats in each class for individuals from the preferred ethnic groups would contribute to the attainment of considerable ethnic diversity in the student body. But petitioner's argument that this is the only effective means of serving the interest of diversity is seriously flawed. In a most fundamental sense the argument misconceives the nature of the state interest that would justify consideration of race or ethnic background. It is not an interest in simple ethnic diversity, in which a specified percentage of the student body is in effect guaranteed to be members of selected ethnic groups, with the remaining percentage an undifferentiated aggregation of students. The diversity that furthers a compelling state interest encompasses a far broader array of qualifications and characteristics of which racial or ethnic origin is but a single though important element. Petitioner's special admissions program, focused *solely* on ethnic diversity, would hinder rather than further attainment of genuine diversity. . . .

The experience of other university admissions programs, which take race into account in achieving the educational diversity valued by the First Amendment, demonstrates that the assignment of a fixed number of places to a minority group is not a necessary means toward that end. An illuminating example is found in the Harvard College program:

> In recent years Harvard College has expanded the concept of diversity to include students from disadvantaged economic, racial and ethnic groups. Harvard College now recruits not only Californians or Louisianans but also blacks and Chicanos and other minority students. . . .
>
> In practice, this new definition of diversity has meant that race has been a factor in some admission decisions. When the Committee on Admissions reviews the large middle group of applicants who are "admissible" and deemed capable of doing good work in their courses, the race of an applicant may tip the balance in his favor just as geographic origin or a life spent on a farm may tip the balance in other candidates' cases. A farm boy from Idaho can bring something to Harvard College that a Bostonian cannot offer. Similarly, a black student can usually bring something that a white person cannot offer. . . .
>
> In Harvard College admissions the Committee has not set target-quotas for the number of blacks, or of musicians, football players, physicists or Californians to be admitted in a given year. . . . It means only that in choosing among thousands of applicants who are not only "admissible" academically but have other strong qualities, the Committee, with a number of criteria in mind, pays some attention to distribution among many types and categories of students. . . .

This kind of program treats each applicant as an individual in the admissions process. The applicant who loses out on the last available seat to another candidate receiving a "plus" on the basis of ethnic background will not have been foreclosed from all consideration for that seat simply because he was not the right color or had the wrong surname. It would mean only that his combined qualifications, which may have included similar nonobjective factors, did not outweigh those of the other applicant. His qualifications would have been weighed fairly and competitively, and he would have no basis to complain of unequal treatment under the Fourteenth Amendment.

It has been suggested that an admissions program which considers race only as one factor is simply a subtle and more sophisticated—but no less effective—means of according racial preference than the Davis program. A facial intent to discriminate, however, is evident in petitioner's preference program and not denied in this case. No such facial infirmity exists in an admissions program where race or ethnic background is simply one element—to be weighed fairly against other elements—in the selection process. . . . And a court would not assume that a university, professing to employ a facially nondiscriminatory admissions policy, would operate it as a cover for the functional equivalent of a quota system. In short, good faith would be presumed in the absence of a showing to the contrary in the manner permitted by our cases. . . .

In summary, it is evident that the Davis special admissions program involves the use of an explicit racial classification never before countenanced by this Court. It tells applicants who are not Negro, Asian, or Chicano that they are totally excluded from a specific percentage of the seats in an entering class. No matter how strong their qualifications, quantitative and extracurricular, including their own potential for contribution to educational diversity, they are never afforded the chance to compete with applicants from the preferred groups for the special admissions seats. At the same time, the preferred applicants have the opportunity to compete for every seat in the class.

The fatal flaw in petitioner's preferential program is its disregard of individual rights as guaranteed by the Fourteenth Amendment. . . . Such rights are not absolute. But when a State's distribution of benefits or imposition of burdens hinges on ancestry or the color of a person's skin, that individual is entitled to a demonstration that the challenged classification is necessary to promote a substantial state interest. Petitioner has failed to carry this burden. For this reason, that portion of the California court's judgment holding petitioner's special admissions program invalid under the Fourteenth Amendment must be affirmed.

In enjoining petitioner from ever considering the race of any applicant, however, the courts below failed to recognize that the State has a substantial interest that legitimately may be served by a properly devised admissions program involving the competitive consideration of race and ethnic origin. For this reason, so much of the California court's judgment as enjoins petitioner from any consideration of the race of any applicant must be reversed.

With respect to respondent's entitlement to an injunction directing his admission to the Medical School, petitioner has conceded that it could not carry its burden of proving that, but for the existence of its unlawful special admissions program, respondent still would not have been admitted. Hence, respondent is entitled to the injunction, and that portion of the judgment must be affirmed.

Fullilove v. *Klutznick*, 448 U.S. 448 (1980)

[6–3: Burger, Blackmun, Brennan, Marshall,
Powell, White; Rehnquist, Stevens, Stewart]

Mr. Chief Justice Burger announced the judgment of the Court. . . .

. . . A program that employs racial or ethnic criteria, even in a remedial context, calls for close examination; yet we are bound to approach our task with appropriate deference to the Congress, a co-equal branch charged by the Constitution with the power to "provide for the . . . general Welfare of the United States" and "to enforce, by appropriate legislation," the equal protection guarantees of the Fourteenth Amendment. . . .

The clear objective of the [Minority Business Enterprise] (MBE) provision [of the Local Public Works Capital Development and Investment Act of 1976] is disclosed by our necessarily extended review of its legislative and administrative background. The program was designed to ensure that, to the extent federal funds were granted under the Public Works Employment Act of 1977, grantees who elect to participate would not employ procurement practices that Congress had decided might result in perpetuation of the effects of prior discrimination which had impaired or foreclosed access by minority businesses to public contracting opportunities. The MBE program does not mandate the allocation of federal funds according to inflexible percentages solely based on race or ethnicity. . . .

In enacting the MBE provision, it is clear that Congress employed an amalgam of its specifically delegated powers. The Public Works Employment Act of 1977, by its very nature, is primarily an exercise of the Spending Power. . . . Congress has frequently employed the Spending Power to further broad policy objectives by conditioning receipt of federal moneys upon compliance by the recipient with federal statutory and administrative directives. This Court has repeatedly upheld against constitutional challenge the use of this technique to induce governments and private parties to cooperate voluntarily with federal policy. . . .

The legislative history of the MBE provision shows that there was a rational basis for Congress to conclude that the subtracting practices of prime contractors could perpetuate the prevailing impaired access by minority businesses to public contracting opportunities, and that this inequity has an effect on interstate commerce. Thus Congress could take necessary and proper action to remedy the situation. . . .

It is not necessary that these prime contractors be shown responsible for any violation of antidiscrimination laws. Our cases dealing with application of Title VII of the Civil Rights Act of 1964, 78 Stat. 253, as amended, express no doubt of the congressional authority to prohibit practices "challenged as perpetuating the effects of [not unlawful] discrimination occurring prior to the effective date of the Act." . . .

With respect to the MBE provision, Congress had abundant evidence from which it could conclude that minority businesses have been denied effective participation in public contracting opportunities by procurement practices that perpetuated the effects of prior discrimination. . . . Although much of this history related to the experience of minority businesses in the area of federal procurement, there was direct evidence before the Congress that this pattern of disadvantage and discrimination existed with respect to state and local construction contracting as well. In relation to the MBE provision, Congress acted within its competence to determine that the problem was national in scope. . . .

Insofar as the MBE program pertains to the actions of state and local grantees, Congress could have achieved its objectives by use of its power under § 5 of the Fourteenth Amendment. We conclude that in this respect the objectives of the MBE provision are within the scope of the Spending Power. . . .

We now turn to the question whether, as a *means* to accomplish these plainly constitutional objectives, Congress may use racial and ethnic criteria, in this limited way, as a condition attached to a federal grant. . . . However, Congress may employ racial or ethnic classifications in exercising its Spending or other legislative powers only if those classifications do not violate the equal protection component of the Due Process Clause of the Fifth Amendment. We recognize the need for careful judicial evaluation to assure that any congressional program that employs racial or ethnic criteria to accomplish the objective of remedying the present effects of past discrimination is narrowly tailored to the achievement of that goal. . . .

Our review of the regulations and guidelines governing administration of the MBE provision reveals that Congress enacted the program as a strictly remedial measure; moreover, it is a remedy that functions prospectively, in the manner of an injunctive decree. Pursuant to the administrative program, grantees and their prime contractors are required to seek out all available, qualified, bona fide MBE's; they are required to provide technical assistance as needed, to lower or waive bonding requirements where feasible, to solicit the aid of the Office of Minority Business Enterprise, the SBA [Small Business Administration], or other sources for assisting MBE's to obtain required working capital, and to give guidance through the intricacies of the bidding process. . . . The program assumes that grantees who undertake these efforts in good faith will obtain at least 10% participation by minority business enterprises. It is recognized that, to achieve this target, contracts will be awarded to available, qualified, bona fide MBE's even though they are not the lowest competitive bidders, so long as their higher bids, when challenged, are found to reflect merely attempts to cover costs inflated by the present effects of prior disadvantage and discrimination. . . . There is available to the grantee a provision authorized by Congress for administrative waiver on a case-by-case basis should there be a demonstration that, despite affirmative efforts, this level of participation cannot be achieved without departing from the objectives of the program. . . . There is also an administrative mechanism, including a complaint procedure, to ensure that only bona fide MBE's are encompassed by the remedial program, and to prevent unjust participation in the program by those minority firms whose access to public contracting opportunities is not impaired by the effects of prior discrimination. . . .

As a threshold matter, we reject the contention that in the remedial context the Congress must act in a wholly "color-blind" fashion. In *Swann v. Charlotte-Mecklenburg Board of Education* . . . (1971), we rejected this argument in considering a court-formulated school desegregation remedy on the basis that examination of the racial composition of student bodies was an unavoidable starting point and that racially based attendance assignments were permissible so long as no absolute racial balance of each school was required. . . .

Here we deal, as we noted earlier, not with the limited remedial powers of a federal court, for example, but with the broad remedial powers of Congress. It is fundamental that in no organ of government, state or federal, does there repose a more comprehensive remedial power than in the Congress, expressly charged by the Constitution with competence and authority to enforce equal protection guarantees. Congress not only may induce voluntary action to assure compliance with existing federal statutory or constitutional antidiscrimination provisions, but also, where Congress has authority to declare certain conduct unlawful, it may, as here, authorize and induce state action to avoid such conduct. . . .

A more specific challenge to the MBE program is the charge that it impermissibly deprives nonminority businesses of access to at least some portion of the government contracting opportunities generated by the Act. It must be conceded that by its objective of remedying the historical impairment of access, the MBE provision can have the effect of awarding some contracts to MBE's which otherwise might be awarded to other businesses, who may themselves be innocent of any prior discriminatory actions. Failure of nonminority firms to receive certain contracts is, of course, an incidental consequence of the program, not part of its objective; similarly, past impairment of minority-firm access to public contracting opportunities may have been an incidental consequence of "business as usual" by public contracting agencies and among prime contractors.

It is not a constitutional defect in this program that it may disappoint the expectations of nonminority firms. When effectuating a limited and properly tailored remedy to cure the effects of prior discrimination, such "a sharing of the burden" by innocent parties is not impermissible. . . . The actual "burden" shouldered by nonminority firms is relatively light in this connection when we consider the scope of this public works program as compared with overall construction contracting opportunities. Moreover, although we may assume that the complaining parties are innocent of any discriminatory conduct, it was within congressional power to act on the assumption that in the past some nonminority businesses may have reaped competitive benefit over the years from the virtual exclusion of minority firms from these contracting opportunities. . . .

The history of governmental tolerance of practices using racial or ethnic criteria for the purpose or with the effect of imposing an invidious discrimination must alert us to the deleterious effects of even benign racial or ethnic classifications when they stray from narrow remedial justifications. Even in the context of a facial challenge such as is presented in this case, the MBE provision cannot pass muster unless, with due account for its administrative program, it provides a reasonable assurance that application of racial or ethnic criteria will be limited to accomplishing the remedial objectives of Congress and that misapplications of the program will be promptly and adequately remedied administratively.

It is significant that the administrative scheme provides for waiver and exemption. Two fundamental congressional assumptions underlie the MBE program: (1) that the present effects of past discrimination have impaired the competitive position of businesses owned and controlled by members of minority groups; and (2) that affirmative efforts to eliminate barriers to minority-firm access, and to evaluate bids with adjustment for the present effects of past discrimination, would assure that at least 10% of the federal funds granted under the Public Works Employment Act of 1977 would be accounted for by contracts with available, qualified, bona fide minority business enterprises. Each of these assumptions may be rebutted in the administrative process. . . .

Grantees are given the opportunity to demonstrate that their best efforts will not succeed or have not succeeded in achieving the statutory 10% target for minority firm participation within the limitations of the program's remedial objectives. In these circumstances a waiver or partial waiver is available once compliance has been demonstrated. A waiver may be sought and granted at any time during the contracting process, or even prior to letting contracts if the facts warrant. . . .

That the use of racial and ethnic criteria is premised on assumptions rebuttable in the administrative process gives reasonable assurance that application of the MBE program will be limited to accomplishing the remedial objectives contemplated by Congress and that misapplications of the racial and ethnic criteria can be remedied. . . .

Any preference based on racial or ethnic criteria must necessarily receive a most searching examination to make sure that it does not conflict with constitutional guarantees. This case is one which requires, and which has received, that kind of examination. This opinion does not adopt, either expressly or implicitly, the formulas of analysis articulated in such cases as *University of California Regents* v. *Bakke* . . . (1978). However, our analysis demonstrates that the MBE provision would survive judicial review under either "test" articulated in the several *Bakke* opinions. The MBE provision of the Public Works Employment Act of 1977 does not violate the Constitution. *Affirmed.*

Black Economist Thomas Sowell Asks, "Are Quotas Good for Blacks?" 1978

Race has never been an area noted for rationality of thought or action. Almost every conceivable form of nonsense has been believed about racial or ethnic groups at one time or another. Theologians used to debate whether black people had souls (today's terminology might suggest that *only* black people have souls). As late as the 1920s, a leading authority on mental tests claimed that test results disproved the popular belief that Jews are intelligent.

"Are Quotas Good for Blacks?" by Thomas Sowell. Reprinted from *Commentary*, June 1978, pp. 39–43 by permission; all rights reserved.

Since then, Jewish IQ's have risen above the national average and more than one-fourth of all American Nobel Prize-winners have been Jewish.

Today's grand fallacy about race and ethnicity is that the statistical "representation" of a group—in jobs, schools, etc.—shows and measures *discrimination*. This notion is at the center of such controversial policies as affirmative-action hiring, preferential admissions to college, and public-school busing. But despite the fact that far-reaching judicial rulings, political crusades, and bureaucratic empires owe their existence to that belief, it remains an unexamined assumption. Tons of statistics have been collected, but only to be interpreted in the light of that assumption, never to test the assumption itself. Glaring facts to the contrary are routinely ignored. Questioning the "representation" theory is stigmatized as not only inexpedient but immoral. It is the noble lie of our time.

Affirmative-Action Hiring

"Representation" or "underrepresentation" is based on comparisons of a given group's percentage in the population with its percentage in some occupation, institution, or activity. This might make sense if the various ethnic groups were even approximately similar in age distribution, education, and other crucial variables. But they are not.

Some ethnic groups are a whole decade younger than others. Some are two decades younger. The average age of Mexican Americans and Puerto Ricans is under twenty, while the average age of Irish Americans or Italian Americans is over thirty—and the average age of Jewish Americans is over forty. This is because of large differences in the number of children per family from one group to another. Some ethnic groups have more than twice as many children per family as others. Over half of the Mexican American and Puerto Rican population consists of teenagers, children, and infants. These two groups are likely to be underrepresented in any adult activity, whether work or recreation, whether controlled by others or entirely by themselves, and whether there is discrimination or not.

Educational contrasts are also great. More than half of all Americans over thirty-five of German, Irish, Jewish, or Oriental ancestry have completed at least four years of high school. Less than 20 per cent of all Mexican Americans in the same age bracket have done so. The disparities become even greater when you consider quality of school, field of specialization, postgraduate study, and other factors that are important in the kind of high-level jobs on which special attention is focused by those emphasizing representation. Those groups with the most education—Jews and Orientals—also have the highest quality education, as measured by the rankings of the institutions from which they receive their college degrees, and specialize in the more difficult and remunerative fields, such as science and medicine. Orientals in the United States are so heavily concentrated in the scientific area that there are more Oriental scientists than there are black scientists in absolute numbers, even though the black population of the United States is more than twenty times the size of the Oriental population.

Attention has been focused most on high-level positions—the kind of jobs people reach after years of experience or education, or both. There is no way to get the experience or education without also growing older in the process, so when we are talking about top-level jobs, we are talking about the kind of positions people reach in their forties and fifties rather than in their teens and twenties. Representation in such jobs cannot be compared to representation in a population that includes many five-year-olds—yet it is.

The general ethnic differences in age become extreme in some of the older age brackets. Half of the Jewish population of the United States is forty-five years old or older, but only 12 per cent of the Puerto Rican population is that old. Even if Jews and Puerto Ricans were identical in every other respect, and even if no employer ever had a speck of prejudice, there would still be huge disparities between the two groups in top-level positions, just from age differences alone.

Virtually every underrepresented racial or ethnic group in the United States has a lower than average age and consists disproportionately of children and inexperienced young adults. Almost invariably these groups also have less education, both quantitatively and qualitatively. The point here is not that we should "blame the victim" or "blame society." The point is that we should, first of all, *talk sense*! "Representation" talk is cheap, easy, and misleading; discrimination and opportunity are too serious to be discussed in gobbledy-gook.

The idea that preferential treatment is going to "compensate" people for past wrongs flies in the face of two hard facts:

1. Public-opinion polls have repeatedly shown most blacks opposed to preferential treatment either in jobs or college admissions. A Gallup Poll in March 1977, for example, found only 27 per cent of non-whites favoring "preferential treatment" over "ability as determined by test scores," while 64 per cent preferred the latter and 9 per cent were undecided. (The Gallup breakdown of the U.S. population by race, sex, income, education, etc. found that "not a single population group supports affirmative action.")

How can you compensate people by giving them something they have explicitly rejected?

2. The income of blacks relative to whites reached its peak *before* affirmative-action hiring and has *declined* since. The median income of blacks reached a peak of 60.9 per cent of the median income of whites in 1970— the year before "goals" and "timetables" became part of the affirmative-action concept. "In only one year of the last six years," writes Andrew Brimmer, "has the proportion been as high as 60 per cent."

Before something can be a "compensation," it must first be a benefit.

The repudiation of the numerical or preferential approach by the very people it is supposed to benefit points out the large gap between illusion and reality that is characteristic of affirmative action. So does the cold fact that there are few, if any, benefits to offset all the bitterness generated by this heavy-handed program. The bitterness is largely a result of a deeply resented principle, galling bureaucratic processes, and individual horror sto-

ries. Overall, the program has changed little for minorities or women. Supporters of the program try to cover up its ineffectiveness by comparing the
position of minorities today with their position many years ago. This ignores
all the progress that took place under straight equal-treatment laws in the
1960s—progress that has not continued at anywhere near the same pace
under affirmative action.

Among the reasons for such disappointing results is that hiring someone
to fill a quota gets the government off the employer's back for the moment,
but buys more trouble down the road whenever a disgruntled employee
chooses to go to an administrative agency or a court with a complaint based
on nothing but numbers. Regardless of the merits, or the end result, a very
costly process for the employer must be endured, and the threat of this is
an incentive *not* to hire from the groups designated as special by the government. The affirmative-action program has meant mutually canceling incentives to hire and not to hire—and great bitterness and cost from the
process, either way.

If blacks are opposed to preferential treatment and whites are opposed
to it, who then is in favor of it, and how does it go on? The implications
of these questions are even more far-reaching and more disturbing than the
policy itself. They show how vulnerable our democratic and constitutional
safeguards are to a relative handful of determined people. Some of those
people promoting preferential treatment and numerical goals are so convinced of the rightness of what they are doing that they are prepared to
sacrifice whatever needs to be sacrificed—whether it be other people, the
law, or simple honesty in discussing what they are doing (note "goals,"
"desegregation," and similar euphemisms). Other supporters of numerical
policies have the powerful drive of self-interest as well as self-righteousness.
Bureaucratic empires have grown up to administer these programs, reaching
into virtually every business, school, hospital, or other organization. The
rulers and agents of this empire can order employers around, make college
presidents bow and scrape, assign schoolteachers by race, or otherwise gain
power, publicity, and career advancement—regardless of whether minorities
are benefited or not.

While self-righteousness and self-interest are powerful drives for those
who have them, they can succeed only insofar as other people can be persuaded, swept along by feelings, or neutralized. Rhetoric has accomplished
this with images of historic wrongs, visions of social atonement, and a horror
of being classed with bigots. These tactics have worked best with those most
affected by words and least required to pay a price personally: non-elected
judges, the media, and the intellectual establishment.

The "color-blind" words of the Civil Rights Act of 1964, or even the
protections of the Constitution, mean little when judges can creatively rein-
terpret them out of existence. It is hard to achieve the goal of an informed
public when the mass media show only selective indignation about power
grabs and a sense of pious virtue in covering up the failures of school
integration. Even civil libertarians—who insist that the Fifth Amendment
protection against self-incrimination is a sacred right that cannot be denied

Nazis, Communists, or criminals—show no concern when the government routinely forces employers to confess "deficiencies" in their hiring processes, without a speck of evidence other than a numerical pattern different from the government's preconception.

Preferential Admissions

Preferential admissions to colleges and universities are "justified" by similar rhetoric and the similar assumption that statistical underrepresentation means institutional exclusion. Sometimes this assumption is buttressed by notions of "compensation" and a theory that (1) black communities need more black practitioners in various fields; and that (2) black students will ultimately supply that need. The idea that the black community's doctors, lawyers, etc. should be black is an idea held by white liberals, but no such demand has come from the black community, which has rejected preferential admissions in poll after poll. Moreover, the idea that an admissions committee can predict what a youth is going to do with his life years later is even more incredible—even if the youth is one's own son or daughter, much less someone from a wholly different background.

These moral or ideological reasons for special minority programs are by no means the whole story. The public image of a college or university is often its chief financial asset. Bending a few rules here and there to get the right body count of minority students seems a small price to pay for maintaining an image that will keep money coming in from the government and the foundations. When a few thousand dollars in financial aid to students can keep millions of tax dollars rolling in, it is clearly a profitable investment for the institution. For the young people brought in under false pretense, it can turn out to be a disastrous and permanently scarring experience.

The most urgent concern over image and over government subsidies, foundation grants, and other donations is at those institutions which have the most of all these things to maintain—that is, at prestigious colleges and universities at the top of the academic pecking order. The Ivy League schools and the leading state and private institutions have the scholarship money and the brand-name visibility to draw in enough minority youngsters to look good statistically. The extremely high admissions standards of these institutions usually cannot be met by the minority students—just as most students in general cannot meet them. But in order to have a certain minority body count, the schools bend (or disregard) their usual standards. The net result is that thousands of minority students who would normally qualify for good, non-prestigious colleges where they could succeed, are instead enrolled in famous institutions where they fail. For example, at Cornell during the guns-on-campus crisis, fully half of the black students were on academic probation, despite easier grading standards for them in many courses. Yet these students were by no means unqualified. Their average test scores put them in the top quarter of all American college students—but the other Cornell students ranked in the top *1 per cent*. In other words, minority students with every prospect of success in a normal college environment were artificially turned into failures by being mismatched with an institution with standards too severe for them.

When the top institutions reach further down to get minority students, then academic institutions at the next level are forced to reach still further down, so that they too will end up with a minority body count high enough to escape criticism and avoid trouble with the government and other donors. Each academic level, therefore, ends up with minority students underqualified for that level, though usually perfectly qualified for some other level. The end result is a systematic mismatching of minority students and the institutions they attend, even though the wide range of American colleges and universities is easily capable of accommodating those same students under their normal standards.

Proponents of "special" (lower) admissions standards argue that without such standards no increase in minority enrollment would have been possible. But this blithely disregards the fact that when more *money* is available to finance college, more low-income people go to college. The GI Bill after World War II caused an even more dramatic increase in the number of people going to college who could never have gone otherwise—and without lowering admissions standards. The growth of special minority programs in recent times has meant both a greater availability of money and lower admissions standards for black and other designated students. It is as ridiculous to ignore the role of money in increasing the numbers of minority students in the system as a whole as it is to ignore the effect of double standards on their maldistribution among institutions. It is the double standards that are the problem, and they can be ended without driving minority students out of the system. Of course, many academic hustlers who administer special programs might lose their jobs, but that would hardly be a loss to anyone else.

As long as admission to colleges and universities is not unlimited, someone's opportunity to attend has to be sacrificed as the price of preferential admission for others. No amount of verbal sleight-of-hand can get around this fact. None of those sacrificed is old enough to have had anything to do with historic injustices that are supposedly being compensated. Moreover, it is not the offspring of the privileged who are likely to pay the price. It is not a Rockefeller or a Kennedy who will be dropped to make room for quotas; it is a DeFunis or a Bakke. Even aside from personal influence on admissions decisions, the rich can give their children the kind of private schooling that will virtually assure them test scores far above the cut-off level at which sacrifices are made.

Just as the students who are sacrificed are likely to come from the bottom of the white distribution, so the minority students chosen are likely to be from the top of the minority distribution. In short, it is a forced transfer of benefits from those least able to afford it to those least in need of it. In some cases, the loose term "minority" is used to include individuals who are personally from more fortunate backgrounds than the average American. Sometimes it includes whole groups, such as Chinese or Japanese Americans, who have higher incomes than whites. One-fourth of all employed Chinese in this country are in professional occupations—nearly double the national average. No amount of favoritism to the son or daughter of a Chinese doctor or mathematician today is going to compensate some Chinese of the past who was excluded from virtually every kind of work except washing clothes or washing dishes.

The past is a great unchangeable fact. *Nothing* is going to undo its sufferings and injustices, whatever their magnitude. Statistical categories and historic labels may seem real to those inspired by words, but only living flesh-and-blood people can feel joy or pain. Neither the sins nor the sufferings of those now dead are within our power to change. Being honest and honorable with the people living in our own time is more than enough moral challenge, without indulging in illusions about rewriting moral history with numbers and categories.

School Busing

It is chilling to hear parents say that the worst racists they know are their own children. Yet such statements have been made by black and white parents, liberals and conservatives, and without regard to geographical location. It is commonplace to hear of integrated schools where no child of either race would dare to enter a toilet alone. The fears and hatreds of these schoolchildren are going to be part of the American psyche long after the passing of an older generation of crusading social experimenters. It is quite a legacy to leave.

The ringing principles of equal rights announced in the 1954 Supreme Court decision in *Brown* v. *Board of Education* have been transformed by twenty years of political and judicial jockeying into a nightmare pursuit of elusive statistical "balance." The original idea that the government should not classify children by race was turned around completely to mean that the government must classify children by race. The fact that the racial integration of youngsters from similar backgrounds has worked under voluntary conditions was seized upon as a reason for forcing statistical integration of schoolchildren, without regard to vast contrasts of income, way of life, or cultural values. Considerations of cost, time, feelings, or education all give way before the almighty numbers. As more and more evidence of negative consequences to the children has piled up, the original notion that this was going to benefit somebody has given way to the idea that "the law of the land" has to be carried out, even if the skies fall. Less grandly, it means that judges cannot back off from the can of worms they have opened, without admitting that they have made asses of themselves.

The civil-rights establishment has a similar investment of ego and self-interest to protect. The NAACP Legal Defense Fund now insists that the issue is not "educational" but "constitutional." This might be an understandable position for an academic association of legal theorists, but not for an organization claiming to speak in the name of flesh-and-blood black people—people who reject busing in nationwide polls and who reject it by large majorities in cities where it has been tried. The head of the NAACP

Legal Defense Fund brushes this aside by saying that they cannot ask "each and every black person" his opinion before proceeding, but the real question is whether they can consistently go counter to the majority opinions of the very people in whose name they presume to speak.

The tragic Boston busing case shows all these institutional ego forces at work. Local black organizations urged Judge Garrity *not* to bus their children to South Boston, where educational standards were notoriously low and racial hostility notoriously high. Both the NAACP and the judge proceeded full-speed-ahead anyway. Black children were forced to run a gauntlet of violence and insults for the greater glory of institutional grand designs. In Detroit, Atlanta, and San Francisco the NAACP also opposed local blacks on busing—including local chapters of its own organization in the last two cities. The supreme irony is that Linda Brown, of *Brown* v. *Board of Education,* has now gone into court to try to keep her children from being bused.

That "a small band of willful men" could inflict this on two races opposed to it is a sobering commentary on the fragility of democracy. Moreover, what is involved is not merely mistaken zealotry. What is involved is an organization fueled by money from affluent liberals whose own children are safely tucked away in private schools, and a crusade begun by men like Thurgood Marshall and Kenneth B. Clark whose own children were also in private schools away from the storms they created for others. The very real educational problems of black children, and the early hopes that desegregation would solve them, provided the impetus and the support for a crusade that has now degenerated into a numerical fetish and a judicial unwillingness to lose face. What actually happens to black children, or white children, has been openly relegated to a secondary consideration in principle, and less than that in practice.

The 1954 *Brown* decision did not limit itself to ruling that it is unconstitutional for a state to segregate by race. It brought in sociological speculation that separate schools are inherently inferior. Yet within walking distance of the Supreme Court was an all-black high school whose eighty-year history would have refuted that assumption—if anyone had been interested in facts. As far back as 1939, the average IQ at Dunbar High School was 11 per cent above the national average—fifteen years before the Court declared this impossible. The counsel for the NAACP in that very case came from a similar quality all-black school in Baltimore. There are, and have been, other schools around the country where black children learned quite well without white children (or teachers) around, as well as other schools where each race failed to learn, with or without the presence of the other. The most cursory look at the history of all-Jewish or all-Oriental schools would have reduced the separate-is-inferior doctrine to a laughingstock instead of the revered "law of the land."

The Court's excursion into sociology came back to haunt it. When the end of state-enforced segregation did not produce any dramatic change in the racial makeup of neighborhood schools, or any of the educational benefits anticipated, the civil-rights establishment pushed on for more desegregation—now stretched to mean statistical balance, opposition to ability grouping, and even the hiring and assignment of teachers by race. If the magic policy of integration had not worked, it could only be because there had not yet been enough of it! Meanwhile, the real problems of educating real children were lost in the shuffle.

However futile the various numerical approaches have been in their avowed goal of advancing minorities, their impact has been strongly felt in other ways. The message that comes through loud and clear is that minorities are losers who will never have anything unless someone gives it to them. The destructiveness of this message—on society in general and minority youth in particular—outweighs any trivial gains that may occur here and there. The falseness of the message is shown by the great economic achievements of minorities during the period of equal-rights legislation before numerical goals and timetables muddied the waters. By and large, the numerical approach has achieved nothing, and has achieved it at great cost.

Underlying the attempt to move people around and treat them like chess pieces on a board is a profound contempt for other human beings. To ignore or resent people's resistance—on behalf of their children or their livelihoods—is to deny our common humanity. To persist dogmatically in pursuit of some abstract goal, without regard to how it is reached, is to despise freedom and reduce three-dimensional life to cardboard pictures of numerical results. The false practicality of results-oriented people ignores the fact that the ultimate results are in the minds and hearts of human beings. Once personal choice becomes a mere inconvenience to be brushed aside by bureaucrats or judges, something precious will have been lost by all people from all backgrounds.

A multi-ethnic society like the United States can ill-afford continually to build up stores of inter-group resentments about such powerful concerns as one's livelihood and one's children. It is a special madness when tensions are escalated between groups who are basically in accord in their opposition to numbers games, but whose legal establishments and "spokesmen" keep the fires fueled. We must never think that the disintegration and disaster that has hit other multi-ethnic societies "can't happen here." The mass internment of Japanese Americans just a generation ago is a sobering reminder of the tragic idiocy that stress can bring on. We are not made of different clay from the Germans, who were historically more enlightened and humane toward Jews than many other Europeans—until the generation of Hitler and the Holocaust.

The situation in America today is, of course, not like that of the Pearl Harbor period, nor of the Weimar republic. History does not literally repeat, but it can warn us of what people are capable of, when the stage has been set for tragedy. We certainly do not need to let emotionally combustible materials accumulate from ill-conceived social experiments.

⊞ *E S S A Y S*

While a broad consensus exists that discrimination based on race is both immoral and unconstitutional, there is no agreement about the wisdom of affirmative-action programs. Judge J. Harvie Wilkinson of the Fourth United States Court of Appeals argues in the first essay that the Supreme Court's original goal of providing equality of opportunity in the *Brown* decision has become perverted to mean the establishment of quotas for blacks and other minorities. Given this development, white males face the same kind of government-imposed discrimination that blacks once did, Wilkinson maintains. Judge J. Skelly Wright, formerly of the United States Court of Appeals for the District of Columbia Circuit, argues the opposite point of view in the second essay. He believes not only that affirmative-action programs are in the best traditions of American constitutionalism, but also that the elimination of discrimination is necessary to the success of the nation's entire democratic experiment. Judges and legislators, Wright argues, must do more than simply outlaw discrimination; they must also redress old wrongs against persons of color. Do you agree?

The Luminous but Flawed Goal of Racial Justice

J. HARVIE WILKINSON III

Thrust and parry, charge and counter-charge, a duel of minds and morals dominated the long year before *Bakke*. Yet no decisive advantage was ever won. Perhaps there has never been a case before the Supreme Court with opposing arguments of more equal legitimacy. The Court's own task in *Bakke* was to avoid a conclusive outcome. It must not, in this most divisive of cases, hoist the arms of a victorious contestant. Meg Greenfield of the Washington *Post* prayed the Supreme Court "will find a way to blur the edges of the controversy and reaffirm the important values raised by both sides. You say that is fudging the issue? Fine. It ought to be fudged."

The Court did just that. If *Brown* was a great moral blow, *Bakke* was a brokered judgment. The Supreme Court offered "a Solomonic compromise," in which "the nine justices spoke in many voices, a chorus of competing viewpoints adding up to a well-modulated counterpoint." The Court struck down the Davis program with its "specified number of [minority] seats" but upheld the use of race or ethnicity as "a 'plus' in a particular applicant's file" so long as "it does not insulate the individual from comparison with all other candidates for the available seats." QUOTAS: NO / RACE: YES capsuled the cover of *Time* magazine. Because Bakke's exclusion was to all appearances the result of Davis's unlawful program, the Court ordered his admission. "Mr. Bakke won, but so did the general principle of affirmative action," wrote Anthony Lewis. "That was the comforting paradox communicated to the world."

The Court in *Bakke* tried to keep faith with *Brown*. To the university, *Brown* stood for minority educational opportunity, "but implementation of the commitment expressed in *Brown* has taken years and is even today not complete." To others, *Brown* stood for the ideal of color blindness: "It must be the exclusion on racial grounds which offends the Constitution, and not

From *"From Brown" to "Bakke": The Supreme Court and School Integration 1954–1978* by J. Harvie Wilkinson III, pp. 298–306. Copyright © 1979 by Oxford University Press, Inc. Reprinted by permission.

the particular skin color of the person excluded." *Bakke* stood for both, perhaps, or for neither. It attempted, at least, to bridge the unbridgeable: the disparate legacies of *Brown.*

Many were left vaguely uneasy, few bitterly displeased. Most disconsolate was Thurgood Marshall, who found it "more than a little ironic that after several hundred years of class-based discrimination against Negroes, the Court is unwilling to hold that a class-based remedy for that discrimination is permissible." Other black leaders were more sanguine. Benjamin Hooks, executive director of the NAACP, termed *Bakke* "a mixed bag, both a victory and a defeat." Vernon Jordan of the National Urban League, while deploring the loss of Davis-style admissions, felt the Court's judgment "should constitute a green light to go forward with acceptable affirmative-action programs." All sides combed the 154 pages of opinions for language they liked. For the Court, once again, political diplomacy prevailed; its decision "gave almost everyone—Bakke, the government, civil rights groups, and most universities—a victory, if a small one."

Bakke himself had spent the week avoiding reporters, even to the point of covering his face with a newspaper. "Hi, I heard the news," his secretary beamed the morning of the decision. Bakke smiled, nodded slightly, then ducked into his office. The Court, for all of its power, could not make men whole. For Bakke at age thirty-eight, the dream came true, but five years late. The dream had also come dear. For the sake of medicine, Bakke had forsaken anonymity. "People aren't going to forget what he represents," said one second year student at Davis. "He will never not be Allan Bakke," Dr. Morton Levitt, the medical school's associate dean, remarked.

To say that the Court as a whole "fudged" in *Bakke* is really misleading. Eight justices took polar positions. Four—Stevens, Stewart, Rehnquist, and Chief Justice Burger—argued that the Davis program violated Title VI of the 1964 Civil Rights Act by excluding Bakke because of his race. There is, of course, that venerable bromide of restraint that statutory grounds of decision are to be preferred to constitutional ones. Its application to *Bakke,* however, was questionable. The parties had argued and the courts below had ruled on constitutional grounds alone. Thus the Court had to request supplemental briefing on the statutory issue, i.e., it stretched for restraint. Though the language of Title VI when read literally did cover Bakke's case, how could a Congress preoccupied with the evils of segregation have addressed the much later issue of minority preferences as well? To hold for Bakke on Title VI was to postpone the constitutional issue in a case where the Court's constitutional competence was clear. . . . It was also to throw the onus of decision on Congress—an evasive course of action for the Court of last resort. Finally, and by all odds most important, to discover in Title VI requirements of color blindness risked re-estranging minorities and rolling back much of the long progress since *Brown.*

The statutory foursome lent *Bakke* itself an air of impermanence. Since a majority of the Court held Title VI did permit race to be considered in admissions, the statutory foursome may face the constitutional issue in some later case. Their views on this question are by no means certain. It is not impossible that one or more of the four will one day join with the justices advocating affirmative action to uphold sweeping and far-reaching programs.

The justices most supportive of affirmative action also numbered four—Brennan, White, Marshall, and Blackmun. Together they found that Title VI permitted the adoption of race-conscious means to overcome past societal discrimination. The Constitution was no less generous. Racial remedies were quite permissible where, as in medicine, "minority underrepresentation is substantial and chronic" and where there was reason to believe past societal discrimination was the cause. These justices thus adopted the broadest and most permissive view of compensatory justice. A particular entity, such as Davis, itself free of past discrimination, might repent the sins of society at large. Their formulation was as timeless as it was universal. Davis might consider, as part of the basis for its program, the experience of "slavery, [where] penal sanctions were imposed upon anyone attempting to educate Negroes." When the age of compensation might end was likewise left open. The choice of means was left also to Davis's discretion. Inclusion of academically successful Asian Americans in its program went unquestioned. As long as Davis's purpose was benign and its program nonstigmatic, the reservation of "a predetermined number of places" for minority applicants was quite acceptable.

The most heartfelt pleas for affirmative action came individually, from Justices Marshall and Blackmun. "The experience of Negroes in America has been different in kind, not just in degree, from that of other ethnic groups," Marshall declared. "It is not merely the history of slavery alone but also that a whole people were marked as inferior by the law. And that mark has endured. The dream of America as the great melting pot has not been realized for the Negro; because of his skin color he never even made it into the pot." Justice Blackmun was scarcely less moving. "I yield to no one," he confessed, "in my earnest hope that the time will come when an 'affirmative action' program is unnecessary and is, in truth, only a relic of the past. . . . [But] in order to get beyond racism, we must first take account of race. There is no other way." Such sentiments, unfortunately, framed but half the picture. The factional hostilities aroused by admission by the numbers, the stereotypes encouraged, the caprice, insult and treacherousness of sorting by race all appeared to have left little mark. Such dangers were paid lip service, and little more.

Thus *Bakke*'s noted compromise was largely the making of the Court's "ninth man." Between the statutory foursome of Burger, Stevens, Stewart, and Rehnquist, and the permissive foursome of Brennan, White, Marshall, and Blackmun was Justice Powell. "Powell took his position at the outset and never got anyone to go along with him," one Court insider was quoted as saying. Because the swing judgment was Powell's alone, the Court may yet shift from him.

To some, Powell's vote came as a surprise. An irony of *Bakke*, wrote Washington attorney and Civil Rights activist Joseph Rauh, was that "affirmative action was saved by a conservative Southern justice." Yet the result was typical of Powell the diplomat, Powell the balancer, Powell the quiet man of the middle way. Law, he believed, had to serve the cause of social stability. Instinctively he dreaded chaos and upheaval; the 1960s had been a most unnerving decade. Back then he had denounced civil disobedience as "a heresy which could weaken the foundations of our system of government," part of "the disquieting trend—so evident in our country—toward organized lawlessness and even rebellion." Yet rebellion was never just something to stamp out by fiat and force; the causes of unrest, he recognized, "involve[d] complex and deep-seated social and economic problems."

Bakke, too, was a rebellious case, menacing to social peace, the most volatile case of Powell's time on the Court. A compromise would have to be struck. Affirmative action plans were now the status quo; Powell did not wish to upend them. But he distrusted quotas, "those direct and provocative approaches which stir so much envy and distemper in the society." The solution was typically Powellian: a sober opinion with words precise but pale; a narrow result that allowed the employment and sex discrimination cases to continue their own separate channels; and, above all, a compromise that majorities of both races might abide.

Since Powell's was the swing vote in *Bakke*, his opinion was naturally the most scrutinized. What did it mean for the future of affirmative action? Powell certainly disapproved Davis's program not only because it reserved "a fixed number of [minority] places" but because it insulated minorities "from comparison with all other candidates" for the reserved spots. But a program "where race or ethnic background is simply one element—to be weighed fairly against other elements—in the selection process" would meet Powell's approval. What, one wondered, was the difference? The admissions process at Harvard College, which Powell acclaimed as a model because of its "flexible" use of race, produced much the same minority enrollments as those at Davis: 8.1 percent black, 4.6 percent Hispanic, 5.7 percent Asian American, and 0.4 percent American Indian for the freshman class of 1978. Nor was it clear that these percentages varied much from year to year.

Citation of Harvard was an important cue. Simply by hearing *DeFunis* and *Bakke*, the Court had thrown affirmative action into limbo. Powell meant to remove the cloud, dispel the doubt, in short, to legitimate. His tone, in fact, was more permissive than not. It will be "the very rare affirmative action program that is disqualified under the *Bakke* standards," the *New Republic* predicted. Educators guessed that 90 percent of existing admissions programs—all but the crasser varieties—would satisfy Justice Powell. "It's music to our ears," said John Harding, counsel to Columbia University. "Now we can continue to do what we are already doing."

By approving a plethora of factors in admissions decisions—"exceptional personal talents, unique work or service experience, leadership potential, maturity, demonstrated compassion, a history of overcoming disadvantage, ability to communicate with the poor, or other qualifications"—Powell enthroned the discretion and biases of admissions deans everywhere. "Institutionally and practically," noted Norman Dorsen of the ACLU [American Civil Liberties Union], "it is the school admissions officers and administrators who will be crucial in determining what the impact of the *Bakke* decision will be." Powell had sanctioned not only taking race into account but a subjective approach to admissions as well. Intellectual aptitude, he implied, need not be the only ticket to academic life. Character, personality, motivation—that cluster of attributes known as the "intangibles"—might count as well. Whether subjective systems would actually produce exceptional people or simply reward the well-connected remained an open question.

Powell's approach and that of the four justices to his left differed markedly. Powell rejected unbounded notions of compensatory justice as a basis for affirmative action plans. That, said he, only created "a privilege that all institutions throughout the Nation could grant at their pleasure to whatever groups are perceived as victims of societal discrimination." What justified the "flexible" use of race and, indeed, subjective admissions generally was educational diversity. Indeed, noted Powell, "it is not too much to say that 'the nation's future depends upon leaders trained through wide exposure' to the ideas and mores of students as diverse as this Nation of many peoples." Diversity, he even felt, was of constitutional origin: the First Amendment and its promise of broad traffic in ideas.

Invocation of diversity was Powell's master stroke. It was also his healing gesture. Diversity was the most acceptable public rationale for affirmative action, because it has been, historically, clearly related to a university's function. It was the most traditional justification, because the most analogous to geographical preference. Diversity, to be real, implied more than token minority numbers. But it supposed also that minority students had something genuine to contribute to higher education; they had not been let in simply to avenge ancestral sins. Diversity, as such, was a narrower rationale than compensatory justice; it applied obviously to education, not so clearly to employment. And it skirted the sticky questions of compensatory justice: whom do we compensate, how much, and for how long. For the need for diversity will continue forever, as long as race matters to men. But diversity, though color-conscious, was also color-blind. Working class whites might one day be seen as capable of bringing more diversity to middle-class havens of higher education than well-off blacks. All, in fact, can be diverse, because all are different: the Alaskan or Greek American, the oboist or naturalist, all, said Powell, who "exhibit qualities more likely to promote beneficial educational pluralism."

Powell was predictably criticized by both sides for doing nothing more than chasing "reverse racism" underground. Opponents of special admissions complained that universities "will be able to continue almost all their current efforts to help minorities, especially if they're willing to engage in a bit of dissembling to satisfy Justice Powell, the swing vote." Allan Bakke at least knew what was up. The Harvard model was more subtle than Davis's and thus more sinister. Applicants—black and white—might distrust all the more what they could not see. Diversity itself was idiosyncratic, dependent on the eye of the beholding institution. The four justices supporting the Davis program were as reluctant as opponents to embrace covertness as a constitutional goal. "[T]here is no basis for preferring a particular preference program," they argued, "simply because . . . it proceeds in a manner that is not immediately apparent to the public."

Yet to call Powell's approach dissembling is not quite fair. The great pretense would have been to insist upon color blindness but then allow some proxy characteristic—disadvantage, cultural bias—to subtly substitute for race in admissions decisions. Powell did not do that. He said, quite openly, that race *qua* race could be used. Perhaps charges of dissembling and concealment are the inevitable cost of any approach that bans prior numerical reliance. If so, it is a cost to bear. Preset numbers stain any affirmative action plan, whether they be goals, targets, quotas, guideposts or other labels Powell might decide to dismiss as "semantic distinction[s]." Numbers divide; numbers demean; numbers dehumanize by subordinating personhood to race. Numbers recall most vividly historical villainy and abuse. Numbers create the incentives to divvy up the admissions pie. The value of Justice Powell's approach depends largely on avoiding prefixed numbers based on ethnicity or race.

That will not be easy. Numbers attract, because they assure minimum minority representation. But *Bakke,* of course, made the numbers game more dangerous to play. After *Bakke,* numerical guideposts are likely to be so subtle, so tacit, so internalized and unwritten as to defy judicial discernment. And the line between prior numerical reliance and the "individualized, case by case" review urged by Justice Powell is so fine as to make future litigation a certainty. Powell himself would give admissions officers the benefit of good faith. But at what point do unvarying percentages of annual minority enrollments create the presumption of a de facto quota? What of numerical objectives much more flexible than that of Davis? What of the admissions officer who feels true educational diversity requires a student body roughly 10 to 15 percent black? Or one who, after surveying low minority enrollment percentages for the past several years, announces openly a need to "improve?" What of an otherwise objective admissions system that, to ensure racial diversity, adds 12 percent to minority test scores? Would courts proscribe such mechanical use of race? Borderline cases are legion. The volume of subsequent litigation might force a closer relationship between courts and university admissions than Justice Powell himself would prefer.

Bakke, for all Justice Powell's distaste for numbers, contained a large loophole that may yet make racial percentages commonplace. Numerical preference for blacks, Justice Powell conceded, might be necessary in the event of "judicial, legislative, or administrative findings of constitutional or statutory violations." Proof of past discrimination against minorities, in other words, might justify remedial quotas; "the legal rights of the victim must be vindicated." Because Davis Medical School began only in 1968, it had little chance to engage in such past practices. But how many institutional histories were as spotless?

This exception, so Powell thought, was necessary to explain those busing and employment precedents in which racial percentages formed part of the remedy. But it threatened to swallow the rule and to reduce *Bakke* to insignificance. A scenario similar to busing might emerge, whereby racial quotas could yet be achieved through ingenious incursions into institutional pasts. What kind of prior discrimination on the part of a university justified preferential numbers now? De jure segregation in 1954? Past admissions preferences for sons of alumni, wealthy donors, influential legislators from which whites but not blacks stood to benefit? Past recruitment efforts at white, but not black schools? Past discrimination in fraternities or extra-curriculars? A past absence of black faculty, curricular neglect of black history and culture, all of which made black students reluctant to apply? Or any past admissions policy, in violation of federal statute, with a "disparate and unjustified racial impact?" How far into the past must we peer? Who may determine historical wrongdoing? A university clearly could not. "Its broad mission," noted Powell, "is education, not the formulation of any legislative policy or the adjudication of particular claims of illegality." But a court, a legislature, or a legislatively authorized administrative body could. All this suggested to Davis's supporters on the Court how the Powell approach might yet be undercut. Violations necessary to justify numerical minority preferences might even be collusively rigged.

Answers to such questions will determine how significant a legal mile-stone *Bakke* really is. "The very fact that [*Bakke*] is somewhat fuzzy," noted Professor Freund, "leaves room for development, and on the whole that's a good thing." Congress and the Department of Health, Education, and Welfare were virtually invited by the Court to share in this development, both in defining violations and shaping affirmative action plans. How much *Bakke* itself would influence the future remained to be seen. Contemporaries knew *Brown* to be a landmark case. "But none," noted Professor Kurland, "could really say in 1954 just how important it was to be." So it was in 1978. *Bakke*, as *Brown* had been, was only a beginning. Where, one has to wonder, will it end?

The Morality of Affirmative Action

J. SKELLY WRIGHT

Color-blind theory has proven to be the main tribute inequality pays to the principle of equality in our national life. At the nation's founding, the assertion that "all men are created equal" was used to justify establishment of a regime in which enslavement of the black population was given constitutional sanction. In 1857 the Supreme Court managed to harmonize the principle of equality of all citizens with the continued existence of slavery by simply declaring that black persons are not citizens. In 1896 the Supreme Court placed its imprimatur on a ghastly system of apartheid, but in doing so, felt it necessary to declare the policy "separate but equal." It is a tribute

"Color-Blind Theories and Color-Conscious Remedies" by J. Skelly Wright. *The University of Chicago Law Review* 47, 1980, pp. 213–221, 225, 229–231, 245. Reprinted by permission.

to the American ideal of equality that the High Court was driven to *lie* rather than to admit what it was doing.

Today, many decry affirmative attempts to remedy the continued social and economic deprivation of blacks and other minority group members. Once again, people tip their hats in tribute to the principle of equality and insist that their sole object is to ensure that everyone is treated equally without regard to race. I suggest that this version of equality, which permits the continuation, indeed the exacerbation, of grave disparities in the opportunities and advantages available to persons of different races, ignores the context in which the problem of inequality has persisted in this country, and ultimately endangers our democratic institutions.

I do not suggest that everyone who opposes affirmative action on behalf of persons of disadvantaged background is motivated by racism or ill will. Quite the contrary: many are sincere and idealistic. Moreover, it is easy to understand the distaste many feel for programs that allocate burdens or benefits on the basis of race. Nevertheless, I believe that such persons focus too narrowly on the importance of formally neutral rules, and thereby inhibit achievement of the equality necessary to our political system. No one can deny that race is, and has always been, the most serious, the most divisive, and the most persistent problem in the United States. [T]he lesson of race relations in this country has been the same since the Founding; inequality between the races is "illegal, immoral, unconstitutional, inherently wrong, and destructive of democratic society." If we come to understand why this is so, then it may become more clear what we must do about it.

I

Equality and egalitarian justice have animated political movements in countries around the globe through much of recent history. Yet nowhere is the principle of equality so central to the proper functioning of the political system as it is in the United States. This is partly the product of historical and geographical circumstance: the United States—more than most nations—comprises a profusion of races and ethnic groups. It is not surprising that racial equality is a vital issue to so heterogeneous a people. But in saying that racial equality is central to our political institutions, I am referring not to historical happenstance, but rather to political theory and practice.

People often assert that equality is antithetical to liberty, and that promotion of equality is antidemocratic. Properly understood, these concepts are in harmony. This understanding is best captured by the ideal of self-rule, by which I mean a system of government in which a large measure of control is vested in each citizen over his own life, and in which social control is exercised with the consent of, and through the representatives of, the citizens. Equality, far from being antithetical to this understanding of liberty, is indispensable to it. The essential equality of the citizens is a fundamental precondition to the operation of the liberal democratic regime as established in this country.

The genius of the American system has been to mold out of the conflicting private interests of its individual citizens a common interest of the community. The system requires a particular type of citizen, and it emphasizes a particular type of interest. The citizen must have a stake in his country: he must feel that his country's prosperity is his prosperity, that his country's woe is his woe. Unless he feels this bond of community, he will—no matter what his legal status—consider himself an alien in his own land. Moreover, the individual citizens must pursue interests that are flexible and open to compromise, lest they be unable to reach mutually advantageous agreements with citizens who have conflicting interests. Thus, our politics must be based upon the shifting alliances of economic and social interest, rather than the immutable and uncompromising lines of race, clan, or religion. With respect to each of these requirements, racial inequality destroys the operation of the political system.

How can we expect blacks and other members of disadvantaged minority groups to feel they have a stake in the present system? They are denied the fruits of the nation's bounty. They are crowded together in the nation's slums; they suffer widespread unemployment; they receive the worst of most social services; they bear the brunt of the nation's brutalities. As they survey our white legislatures and congresses, our white courtrooms and bureaucracies, must they not feel that their citizenship is second-rate—that, no matter what the Constitution may say about their equality as citizens, they are unequal and ruled from above? And if this *objective* inequality undermines the bonds of community felt by black Americans, the fact that it was the *deliberate* product of oppression by the white majority should make white Americans marvel at the continued patience and patriotism of their black countrymen. Plainly, the disadvantaged position of blacks and members of other minority groups is a structural flaw in our political system, and an abomination.

Moreover, so long as the disadvantaged groups of the United States remain outside of the mainstream of our social and economic life, they will be driven to the very race-based politics feared by many opponents of affirmative action. A poor black man will often vote for black candidates espousing black causes, just as any other citizen may sometimes vote on the basis of racial or ethnic identity. But unlike his more prosperous fellow citizens, whose ethnic identity is diluted and usually overwhelmed by interests grounded in economic or other concerns, the poor black man often has no faction to support other than one based on race. Because he plays no other role in the economy or society, he has no conflicting allegiance. Hence, affirmative action may be the only way to dismantle racial politics in the long run. Only when the divisions of race and ethnicity cease to correspond, and begin to conflict, with divisions along economic, social, and other shifting lines will racial politics be subordinated. When there are large numbers of black doctors, shopkeepers, corporate executives, developers, engineers, shareholders, and so on, the problem will be solved. This must be the goal of the United States, if the clash of private interests is to continue to serve as our means of approaching the common good.

II

America's tragedy has been her failure to guarantee the equality among the races so manifestly required by the structure and theory of her government. The country has paid a price. It took a bloody civil war to extirpate slavery, and an acrimonious Reconstruction attempt, unsuccessfully, to eradicate the gross inequality that remained. More recently there has been disorder in our cities and elsewhere, which has subsided into squabbling among races and ethnic groups for larger shares of an economic pie now perceived by many to be shrinking. Obviously, the problem of inequality has not been solved, and we can expect further racial troubles in the future until its solution. A nation preconditioned on equality among its major groups cannot function with such a contradiction in its midst.

Unfortunately, inequality among the races is extraordinarily difficult to eradicate. Many persons expected that, once formal discrimination had been curbed, members of deprived minorities would have little difficulty in entering into the mainstream of American economic and social life. It has not been so—even assuming optimistically that most formal discrimination has now ceased. We should have known that inequality would continue until we took active steps to end it. As de Tocqueville predicted long before slavery was abolished, "[a] natural prejudice leads a man to scorn anybody who has been his inferior, long after he has become his equal; the real inequality . . . is always followed by an imagined inequality rooted in mores." This "imagined inequality rooted in mores" plagues our civic life with a vengeance, and will continue to do so until experience proves that blacks can serve competently in all levels of society.

Inequality and disadvantage do not end simply because we pass laws against them. For a member of a deprived minority group to succeed, he must develop the discipline, drive, and skills demanded by the marketplace. Unfortunately, schools and job training programs cannot effectively impart such attributes, or our task would be relatively easy. Rather, the most basic education needed by a person entering the economic and social mainstream of this country must usually be provided in the home. And although many disadvantaged parents try very hard to train their children for productive lives, they succeed too rarely. A black mother and father, deprived by past discrimination of an adequate education, and inured because of past experience to second-class status, may often be unable to help their children to develop their academic skills and self-confidence. Their despair, compounded by the cruelties of the welfare system as it is administered, may indeed cause a breakdown in the family structure altogether—to the severe detriment of their children's chances to take advantage of opportunities now open by law to them. Discrimination, having once taken its toll, can in this manner perpetuate its effects long after the society has adopted formal equality in its racial practices.

Moreover, poverty and race, acting in conjunction, tend to produce prejudice. So long as most blacks are poor, they will continue to exhibit the work habits and other characteristics of the poor that often impede success in the employment and society of middle-class America. And so long as white persons associate being black with being poor, they will tend to discriminate against blacks, no matter how open-minded they may imagine themselves to be. This places the poor black in a situation far more desperate than that of his poor white counterpart. Both must overcome severe educational handicaps, but the black must in addition overcome the obstacles of racial prejudice.

It has become increasingly evident that this cycle of discrimination, deprivation, inadequate education, and renewed discrimination must be broken if a genuine equality is to emerge. Doing nothing—or doing nothing but prohibiting the more obvious forms of racial discrimination—will avail little against the momentum of poverty and discrimination that we have allowed to build. To break this cycle requires, as a matter of common sense, special treatment for the victims of past discrimination. Such special treatment may appear unnatural—even unfair in the short run—but the only alternative is to allow the effects of our history of discrimination to plague our civic life in perpetuity.

Oddly, affirmative efforts designed to remedy the effects of past racial or ethnic discrimination have aroused far more heated opposition, both in the public and in the Supreme Court, than have efforts to remedy other forms of discrimination. Even though it is now well established, as a matter of either constitutional or statutory law, that discrimination *against* older persons, handicapped persons, and women is illegal, we find that private and governmental efforts *on their behalf* are largely considered unobjectionable. Who doubts that Social Security for the aged and special programs for the handicapped are legal and constitutional? Affirmative action on behalf of women is more controversial, at least in some settings, but the Supreme Court—with the acquiescence of some opponents of racial affirmative action—has sustained special benefits to women on the ground that such benefits are needed to remedy the relative economic deprivation of women caused by economic discrimination. . . .

III

Rarely do opponents of affirmative action on behalf of racial or ethnic minorities squarely confront the undeniable need of those minorities for special assistance, or the grave consequences of continuing to deny such assistance. Rather, they immediately retreat to the abstract ground of high principle. They assert the necessity of strict neutrality between the races, and urge the courts to adopt what they invariably describe as a "color-blind" theory of the Constitution and laws. They argue that such neutrality is required by the equal protection clause, thereby giving a new twist to Justice Holmes's disparaging characterization of equal protection claims as "the usual last resort of constitutional arguments." In fact, strict "color-blindness" of a sort was frequently urged by opponents of the Civil Rights Act of 1964. This strict neutrality would require that the government not interfere with the decisions made by its citizens, whatever their basis. Just as the government has no business telling its citizens that they should treat ballet the same way that they treat roller derby, so also should it permit its citizens to prefer whites to blacks, blacks to whites, or whatever. In this way, the government could remain aloof from the matter of color; it would treat all citizens exactly alike.

Whether or not we fully realize it, this nation has irrevocably rejected the strict "color-blind" theory of government. Now it is agreed and solemnly enacted into law that racism—both governmental and private—is wrong, and that the government should employ its power to eradicate it. The purpose of this legislation cannot be denied: to help blacks and members of other minority groups overcome the prejudice that oppresses them. Its effect is to give special advantage to those minority groups. To call such legislation "color-blind" is a meaningless abstraction. Legislation against invidious discrimination helps one race and not the other because one race and not the other needs such help. Blacks and members of other minority groups receive special protection against the irrational or malevolent decisions of states, schools, or employers, because they need it. *Equal* protection for them is not the *same* protection accorded others. . . .

B.   Racial discrimination must not only be detected, but it must also be remedied. In practice, this requires that the courts and other institutions engaged in remedying past discrimination begin to prefer minority groups to the majority. Even if they adopt a "color-blind" theory, they will find that preferential methods are the only effective means of executing it. . . .

IV

Few parties in litigation now question the broad discretion of courts to remedy proven past discrimination, even using preferential goals and quotas, however controversial the practice may still be in academia or among the public. Although the Supreme Court has never authoritatively approved racial hiring or promotion quotas imposed by court decree, the lower federal courts have uniformly done so. But controversy still rages over the seemingly subsidiary issue of *who* may determine when race-conscious remedies are needed. Some argue that such remedies are appropriate *only* when particular acts of past discrimination have been proven in some authoritative public forum: by court decree if possible, or maybe by administrative or congressional determination.

On the surface, this purported limitation on the freedom of institutions to remedy the effects of past misdeeds seems curious. It seems to suggest that affirmative action is forbidden unless it is required: an unusual proposition under our jurisprudence. Moreover, in an age when moderates and conservatives are usually heard to praise the virtues of voluntarism and to decry coercion, it is surprising that on this issue they should forbid uncoerced acts to remedy injustice. In an age when moderates and conservatives are quick to point out the inefficiencies and perversities of decision making by bureaucrats, politicians, and judges, it is peculiar to hear them say that *only* such officials have the ability accurately to discern racial discrimination. In an age when moderates and conservatives frequently express concern that businesses are unfairly throttled by unclear and inconsistent governmental pronouncements, it is odd that they should be willing to impose antidiscrimination laws on employers and unions, but deny them the only clear and manageable way of ensuring compliance with the law. . . .

Were it not for Justice Powell's opinion in *Regents of the University of California* v. *Bakke,* I would have thought the matter settled in other statutory or constitutional areas as well. In *Bakke,* however, Justice Powell said that a racially based classification cannot be upheld on the ground that it "aids persons perceived as members of relatively victimized groups at the expense of other innocent individuals in the absence of judicial, legislative, or administrative findings of constitutional or statutory violations."

Does Justice Powell really mean to limit constructive efforts to remedy the effects of past discrimination to those aimed at specific discriminatory acts identified by a governmental tribunal? In the face of the past treatment of this nation's black citizens by the white majority, it takes no special expertise to see that the present disadvantaged position of blacks can be traced directly to that unfair treatment. Why is a governmental tribunal needed to tell us what we already know? The only effect such a requirement could have would be to slow the process by preventing persons of goodwill from helping to remedy this pressing inequality. If we must wait for governmental tribunals, we may wait forever.

The appeal to the expertise of a governmental tribunal seems especially strained in the context of *Bakke.* Justice Powell stated that the University of California at Davis was "not competent" to make findings concerning past discrimination. The "broad mission" of the University, the Justice said, "is education, and not the formulation of any legislative policy or the adjudication of particular claims of illegality." Were it not for this pronouncement, most persons probably would think that education professionals are the most "competent" to judge the effects of various causes on the educational attainments of students—certainly in a better position than judges or bureaucrats. One would also think that education professionals are the most "competent" to decide what sort of remedial program would be most effective in counteracting past discrimination. Moreover, as an agency receiving federal funds, the University was explicitly authorized by HEW [Department of Health, Education, and Welfare] regulations to "take affirmative action to overcome the effects of conditions which resulted in limiting participation by persons of a particular race, color, or national origin." Apparently HEW did not think any special "competence" necessary to perceive that blacks and members of other minorities have suffered discrimination in the past; the Regents of the University of California obviously were not disabled on that score. So long as the remedial purpose of the program was clear, what difference did it make that the need for it was perceived by the University and not by the courts? Allan Bakke is equally disadvantaged either way, and there is no reason to suppose that one way of making the necessary determinations is more or less accurate than the other. The primary effect of imposing the hurdle of "judicial, legislative, or administrative findings" is to make affirmative action programs rarer by making them procedurally more complicated to obtain.

In short, vigilance in the detection and remedy of racial discrimination requires race-consciousness, and such race-consciousness can be legitimate in a variety of circumstances, on the part of a variety of institutions. In the last few years the Supreme Court, albeit haltingly, has approved the use of race-conscious remedies by both public and private institutions on the basis of a number of rationales. In my view, this means that a significant victory against discrimination has been won, a victory that "color-blind" theory could never have achieved. . . .

Conclusion

Affirmative action programs are now firmly entrenched in our public law as a means of eradicating the gross disparities in opportunity between the white majority and the nonwhite minorities. . . . Indeed, such remedies are the necessary result of this nation's belated decision to cease its course of racial discrimination in favor of a regime of equality among the races. That principle, in turn, can be traced to the Civil War, and still farther to the Founding itself. The task now is not to justify remedies for the centuries of oppression of blacks by whites, but rather to ensure that the remedies we choose will create a nation of genuine equality in the future. For who are we to accept the bounty that this country presents us, if we do not seek to share that bounty with our fellow citizens?

It is time for the legal community to stop its squabbling: to admit that the Constitution and the Civil Rights Act permit us to remedy the wrongs of the past. It is time to abandon the abstractions of "color-blind" theory and admit that there can be no such thing as a "color-blind" approach to achieving racial equality. It is time now to concentrate our efforts on ensuring that the remedies we construct are humane and effective, that they respect, so much as is possible, the rights of all. Most important, we must be sure that—for the first time in history—we do the job right, so that succeeding generations will not still be faced with the odious sight of institutionalized racial injustice.

✣ *F U R T H E R   R E A D I N G*

Numan Bartley, *The Rise of Massive Resistance* (1969)
Alexander Bickel, *The Morality of Consent* (1975)
Boris I. Bittker, *The Case for Black Reparations* (1973)
Carl N. Brauer, *John F. Kennedy and the Second Reconstruction* (1977)
Tony A. Freyer, *The Little Rock Crisis: A Constitutional Interpretation* (1984)
Robert K. Fullinwider, *The Reverse Discrimination Controversy* (1980)
Lino Graglia, *Disaster by Decree: The Supreme Court Decisions on Race and the Schools* (1976)

Richard Kluger, *Simple Justice: The History of Brown v. Board of Education and Black America's Struggle for Equality* (1976)

C. M. Lytle, "History of the Civil Rights Bill of 1964," *Journal of Negro History* 51 (1966): 275–292

George R. Metcalf, *From Little Rock to Boston: The History of School Desegregation* (1983)

Gary Orfield, *Must We Bus? Segregated Schools and National Policy* (1978)

Bernard Schwartz, *Behind Bakke: Affirmative Action and the Supreme Court* (1988)

———, *Swann's Way: The School Busing Case and the Supreme Court* (1986)

Allan P. Sindler, *Bakke, DeFunis, and Minority Admissions: The Quest for Equal Opportunity* (1978)

Mark V. Tushnet, *The NAACP's Legal Strategy Against Segregated Education, 1925–1950* (1987)

Raymond Wolters, *The Burden of Brown: Thirty Years of School Desegregation* (1984)

CHAPTER
9

Women and Equal Rights

The women's rights movement in the early twentieth century sought to secure both the vote and constitutional equality for women. It gained the former, through the adoption of the Nineteenth Amendment, but not the latter. Even the later Warren Court (1953–1969), which extended new constitutional protection to African-Americans under the equal-protection clause of the Fourteenth Amendment, declined to do the same for women. Old cultural traditions died hard. In Hoyt v. *Florida (1961), for example, the Warren Court concluded that women could be legally excluded from jury service because their place was properly at "the center of home and family."*

Such stereotypical notions eroded, however, before the unrelenting pressures of economic and demographic change in the 1960s and 1970s. First, women's economic role shifted dramatically in these years. The employment of white and married women became the norm; by 1987 almost 80 percent of the wives from families with incomes of more than $10,000 worked outside the home. As women poured into the employment market, the birthrate dropped to record lows. Second, the black civil-rights movement gave a new boost to a tradition of female activism dating back to the 1848 Declaration of the Seneca Falls Convention. Although women held few leadership positions in the civil-rights movement, the tactics and moral tone of the movement provided women with a model for mobilization. It is not coincidental, for example, that Betty Friedan published The Feminine Mystique—*the early gospel of the women's movement—in 1963, the same year as the great March on Washington for civil rights.*

The Civil Rights Act of 1964 reflected the growing urgency surrounding gender discrimination. Title VII of that statute banned discrimination in employment on the basis of sex. When the federal government balked at enforcing it, women activists formed the National Organization of Women (NOW) in 1966. NOW fashioned a stronger legislative foundation for women's rights while pursuing a litigation strategy designed to persuade federal judges to treat gender-based discrimination with the same degree of searching judicial inquiry that they accorded racial discrimination.

NOW's leaders also wanted to broaden the constitutional protection of women through the adoption of the Equal Rights Amendment (ERA) to the Constitution. The amendment was originally the idea of Alice Paul, the leader of the National Woman's party in the 1920s. The new ERA, which Congress sent to the states for ratification in 1972, fell just short of the three-quarters majority

407

required for ratification. Some opponents claimed that the measure was unnecessary because the equal-protection clause of the Fourteenth Amendment provided all the constitutional protection women needed. Proponents of the amendment replied that the High Court had refused to provide the same level of constitutional protection to women that it conferred on minority racial groups. The ERA lost also because women differed among themselves, with critics of the amendment, such as Phyllis Schlafly, insisting that the traditional place assigned women in the constitutional order was altogether appropriate.

The debate over women's rights grew even more heated with Roe v. Wade *(1973), the Supreme Court's highly controversial abortion decision. At the time, Chief Justice Warren Burger, an appointee of Republican president Richard Nixon, presided over the Court; ironically, the sitting justices expanded the constitutional rights of women to a degree almost as far reaching as that established by the Warren Court for African-Americans. These advances for women notwithstanding, women activists worried by the early 1990s that the gains made in the previous two decades, especially on matters of abortion, would be impaired by an increasingly conservative Supreme Court, even though that Court counted a woman — the United States' first female justice, Sandra Day O'Connor — among its members.*

⊕ D O C U M E N T S

The first document, *Griswold* v. *Connecticut* (1964), involved an 1879 Connecticut statute prohibiting the use of any drug or device to prevent contraception. Justice William O. Douglas's opinion in *Griswold* expanded the list of rights that were not specifically enumerated in the Constitution, in this instance the right of privacy. The impact of the Burger Court on the rights of women is reflected clearly in *Frontiero* v. *Richardson* (1973), the next document. In their decision, the justices invalidated a provision of the Equal Pay Act, which permitted the military to extend automatically housing allowances and health-care benefits to the wives of male soldiers but required female soldiers to prove that they provided three-quarters of their families' support to qualify. The Court stopped short, however, of designating sex a suspect classification as it already had designated race. Proponents of full equality for women pointed somewhat ironically to the *Frontiero* decision as evidence that the Equal Rights Amendment, reprinted here as the third document, was necessary.

The reasons for the amendment's rejection can be gleaned from the statements of Phyllis Schlafly and Marlow Cook, the fourth and fifth selections, respectively. Antifeminist and fundamentalist evangelicals, among them the Reverend Jerry Falwell, whose observations are excerpted as the sixth document, denounced the ERA on moral grounds. The same year that the ERA went to the states, the justices decided *Roe* v. *Wade*, the seventh document, in which the Court overturned a Texas statute limiting abortions. Justice Harry Blackmun's opinion in the *Roe* case established a limited right to an abortion, a finding that gradually has been chipped away, most recently in *Webster* v. *Reproductive Health Services et al.* (1989), the last document. Many legal commentators believe that the Court will soon overturn *Roe* and return the question of regulating abortion to the states.

Griswold v. *Connecticut,* 381 U.S. 419 (1965)

[7–2: Douglas, Brennan, Clark, Goldberg,
Harlan, Warren, Whittaker; Black, Stewart]

Mr. Justice Douglas delivered the opinion of the Court.

We have had many controversies over these penumbral rights of "privacy and repose." . . . [This case bears] witness that the right of privacy which presses for recognition here is a legitimate one.

The present case, then, concerns a relationship lying within the zone of privacy created by several fundamental constitutional guarantees. And it concerns a law which, in forbidding the *use* of contraceptives rather than regulating their manufacture or sale, seeks to achieve its goals by means having a maximum destructive impact upon that relationship. Such a law cannot stand in light of the familiar principle, so often applied by this Court, that a "governmental purpose to control or prevent activities constitutionally subject to state regulation may not be achieved by means which sweep unnecessarily broadly and thereby invade the area of protected freedoms." . . . Would we allow the police to search the sacred precincts of marital bedrooms for telltale signs of the use of contraceptives? The very idea is repulsive to the notions of privacy surrounding the marriage relationship.

We deal with a right of privacy older than the Bill of Rights—older than our political parties, older than our school system. Marriage is a coming together for better or for worse, hopefully enduring, and intimate to the degree of being sacred. It is an association that promotes a way of life, not causes; a harmony in living, not political faiths; a bilateral loyalty, not commercial or social projects. Yet it is an association for as noble a purpose as any involved in our prior decisions. *Reversed.*

Mr. Justice Black, with whom Justice Stewart joined, dissenting.

. . . The Court talks about a constitutional "right of privacy" as though there is some constitutional provision or provisions forbidding any law ever to be passed which might abridge the "privacy" of individuals. But there is not. There are, of course, guarantees in certain specific constitutional provisions which are designed in part to protect privacy at certain times and places with respect to certain activities. Such, for example, is the Fourth Amendment's guarantee against "unreasonable searches and seizures." But I think it belittles that Amendment to talk about it as though it protects nothing but "privacy." To treat it that way is to give it a niggardly interpretation, not the kind of liberal reading I think any Bill of Rights provision should be given. The average man would very likely not have his feelings soothed any more by having his property seized openly than by having it seized privately and by stealth. He simply wants his property left alone. And a person can be just as much, if not more, irritated, annoyed and injured by an unceremonious public arrest by a policeman as he is by a seizure in the privacy of his office or home.

One of the most effective ways of diluting or expanding a constitutionally guaranteed right is to substitute for the crucial word or words of a constitutional guarantee another word, more or less flexible and more or less restricted in its meaning. This fact is well illustrated by the use of the term "right of privacy" as a comprehensive substitute for the Fourth Amendment's guarantee against "unreasonable searches and seizures." "Privacy" is a broad, abstract and ambiguous concept which can easily be shrunken in meaning but which can also, on the other hand, easily be interpreted as a constitutional ban against many things other than searches and seizures. I have expressed the view many times that First Amendment freedoms, for example, have suffered from a failure of the courts to stick to the simple language of the First Amendment in construing it, instead of invoking multitudes of words substituted for those the Framers used. . . . For these reasons I get nowhere in this case by talk about a constitutional "right of privacy" as an emanation from one or more constitutional provisions. I like my privacy as well as the next one, but I am nevertheless compelled to admit that government has a right to invade it unless prohibited by some specific constitutional provision. For these reasons I cannot agree with the Court's judgment and the reasons it gives for holding this Connecticut law unconstitutional. . . .

Frontiero v. *Richardson*, 411 U.S. 677 (1973)

[8–1: Brennan, Burger, Blackmun, Douglas,
Marshall, Powell, Stewart, White; Rehnquist]

Mr. Justice Brennan announced the judgment of the Court. . . .

The question before us concerns the right of a female member of the uniformed service to claim her spouse as a "dependent" for the purposes of obtaining increased quarters allowances and medical and dental benefits on an equal footing with male members. Under the statutes, a serviceman may claim his wife as a "dependent" without regard to whether she is in fact dependent upon him for any part of her support but a servicewoman may not claim her husband as a "dependent" unless he is in fact dependent upon her for over one-half of his support. . . .

At the outset, appellants contend that classifications based upon sex, like classifications based upon race, alienage, and national origin, are inherently suspect and must therefore be subjected to close judicial scrutiny. We agree. . . .

There can be no doubt that our Nation has had a long and unfortunate history of sex discrimination. Traditionally, such discrimination was rationalized by an attitude of "romantic paternalism" which, in practical effect put women, not on a pedestal, but in a cage. As a result of notions such as these, our statute books gradually became laden with gross, stereotyped distinctions between the sexes and, indeed, throughout much of the 19th century the position of women in our society was, in many respects, comparable to that of blacks under the pre–Civil War slave codes. Neither slaves nor women could hold office, serve on juries, or bring suit in their own names, and married women traditionally were denied the legal capacity to hold or convey property or to serve as legal guardians of their own children. And although blacks were guaranteed the right to vote in 1870, women were denied even that right until adoption of the 19th Amendment half a century later.

It is true, of course, that the position of women in America has improved markedly in recent decades. Nevertheless, it can hardly be doubted that, in part because of the high visibility of the sex characteristic, women still face pervasive, although at times more subtle, discrimination in our educational institutions, in the job market and, perhaps most conspicuously, in the political arena. Moreover, since sex, like race and national origin, is an immutable characteristic determined solely by the accident of birth, the imposition of special disabilities upon the members of a particular sex because of their sex would seem to violate "the basic concept of our system that legal burdens should bear some relationship to individual responsibility." And what differentiates sex from such nonsuspect statuses as intelligence or physical disability, and aligns it with the recognized suspect criteria, is that the sex characteristic frequently bears no relation to ability to perform or contribute to society. As a result, statutory distinctions between the sexes often have the effect of invidiously relegating the entire class of females to inferior legal status without regard to the actual capabilities of its individual members. . . . We can only conclude that classifications based upon sex, like classifications based upon race, alienage, or national origin, are inherently suspect, and must therefore be subjected to strict judicial scrutiny. Applying the analysis mandated by that stricter standard of review, it is clear that the statutory scheme now before us is constitutionally invalid.

The Government concedes that the differential treatment accorded men and women under these statutes serves no purpose other than mere "administrative convenience." It maintains that, as an empirical matter, wives in our society frequently are dependent upon their husbands, while husbands rarely are dependent upon their wives. Thus, the Government argues that Congress might reasonably have concluded that it would be both cheaper and easier simply conclusively to presume that wives of male members are financially dependent upon their husbands, while burdening female members with the task of establishing dependency in fact. The Government offers no concrete evidence, however, tending to support its view that such differential treatment in fact saves the Government any money. In order to satisfy the demands of strict judicial scrutiny, the Government must demonstrate, for example, that it is actually cheaper to grant increased benefits with respect to *all* male members, than it is to determine which male members are in fact entitled to such benefits and to grant increased benefits only to those members whose wives actually meet the dependency requirement. In any case, our prior decisions make clear that, although efficacious administration of governmental programs is not without some importance, "the Constitution recognizes higher values than speed and efficiency." When we enter the realm of "strict judicial scrutiny," there can be no doubt that "administrative convenience" is not a shibboleth. On the contrary, any statutory scheme which draws a sharp line between the sexes, *solely* for the purpose of achieving administrative convenience, necessarily commands "dissimilar treatment for men and women who are similarly situated," and therefore involves the "very kind of arbitrary legislative choice forbidden by the Constitution." *Reversed.* . . .

Mr. Justice Powell . . . concurred in the judgment.

It is unnecessary for the Court in this case to characterize sex as a suspect classification, with all of the far-reaching implications of such a holding. *Reed,* which abundantly supports our decision today, did not add sex to the narrowly limited group of classifications which are inherently suspect. In my view, we can and should decide this case on the authority of *Reed* and reserve for the future any expansion of its rationale.

There is another, and I find compelling, reason for deferring a general categorizing of sex classifications as invoking the strictest test of judicial scrutiny. The Equal Rights Amendment, which if adopted will resolve the substance of this precise question, has been approved by the Congress. By acting prematurely and unnecessarily, as I view it, the Court has assumed a decisional responsibility at the very time when state legislatures, functioning within the traditional democratic process, are debating the proposed Amendment. It seems to me that this reaching out to preempt by judicial action a major political decision which is currently in process of resolution does not reflect appropriate respect for duly prescribed legislative process. . . .

The Equal Rights Amendment, 1972

The Senate and House Joint Resolution containing the proposed Equal Rights Amendment provides as follows:

Resolved by the Senate and House of Representatives of the United States of America in Congress assembled (two-thirds of each House concurring therein), That the following article is proposed as an amendment to the Constitution of the United States, which shall be valid to all intents and purposes as part of the Constitution when ratified by the legislatures of three-fourths of the several States within seven years from the date of its submission by the Congress:

Section 1   Equality of rights under the law shall not be denied or abridged by the United States or by any State on account of sex.

Section 2   The Congress shall have the power to enforce, by appropriate legislation, the provisions of this article.

Section 3   This amendment shall take effect two years after the date of ratification.

Phyllis Schlafly Opposes the ERA, 1973

The Equal Rights Amendment will not give women anything which they do not already have, or have a way of getting, but it will take away from women some of their most important legal rights, benefits and exemptions. It is like trying to kill a fly with a sledgehammer; you probably won't kill the fly, but you surely will break up some of the furniture.

Most people who supported ERA as it sailed through Congress by big margins did so because they believed it would give women "equal pay for equal work." The fact is, however, that ERA will not do anything whatsoever for women in the field of employment. In not a single one of the 15 state legislative hearings where I have testified have the pro-ERA lawyers claimed that ERA will help women in this vital area. When I stated that ERA will do nothing for women in the field of employment, in a live debate with the leading Congressional proponent of ERA, Congresswoman Martha Griffiths, on the Lou Gordon television show in Detroit, she replied, "I never claimed it would."

One of the reasons why this is so is the existence of the Equal Employment Opportunity Act of 1972, a law which is very specific in requiring equality for women in hiring, pay and promotions. There is nothing more, constitutionally or legislatively, that women could reasonably want. The only thing remaining is implementation, and this is proceeding rapidly. For example, the $38 million settlement which the Equal Employment Opportunity Act forced on American Telephone and Telegraph required back payments not only to women who hadn't been paid as much as they should have been, but also to women who hadn't been promoted as they thought they should have been, and even to women who never applied for jobs because they didn't think they would get them!

In the various state legislative hearings, the pro-ERA lawyers have not cited any state laws which adversely discriminate against women which ERA will remedy. In state after state, the proponents say: There is nothing wrong with the laws in *this* state, but we want to help those poor discriminated-against women in other states. Those "other" states have never been identified.

Congresswoman Leonor Sullivan, distinguished member of Congress for some 20 years, who voted against ERA in Congress, answered this point very well. She said: "What is the matter with women in any state who permit a state law to remain on the books which is clearly discriminatory? Missouri has no such laws. Our women were instrumental in eliminating them. I suggest the women in other states do likewise."

The women in Illinois have just done exactly this. On September 13, 1973, the Governor signed ten bills which eliminate every vestige of discrimination against women in Illinois, including such areas as credit cards, home loans, housing and bigamy. These bills went through the General Assembly quickly and without controversy, and they take effect immediately, without the two-year waiting period ERA would require. These new laws prove that specific legislation to meet particular problems is the practical, proper, and prompt procedure—rather than the blunderbuss language of the Federal Equal Rights Amendment which would, at the same time, deprive women of the legal rights, benefits, and exemptions they now possess.

ERA will not even do anything for women in the field of education.

Women are already fully guaranteed equality in educational opportunities, admissions, and employment through Title VII of the Civil Rights Act of 1964, the Equal Pay Act of 1963, the Education Amendments of June 1972, and Executive Order 11246 which authorizes broad administrative power to enforce corrective goals, timetables and affirmative action plans.

The major effort of ERA in the field of family relations is that it will invalidate the state laws which impose the obligation on the husband to support his wife. These laws are fundamental to the institution of the family and an essential part of the marriage contract. They give the wife her legal right to be a full-time wife and mother, in her own home, taking care of her own babies. . . .

Typical of the state laws guaranteeing the wife her legal right to be supported is the Ohio statute: "The husband must support himself, his wife, and his minor children out of his property or by his labor. If he is unable to do so, the wife must assist him so far as she is able. If he neglects to support his wife, any other person, in good faith, may supply her with necessaries for her support, and recover the reasonable value thereof from the husband unless she abandons him without cause." . . .

These are the present rights which wives will lose if ERA is ratified because ERA will mandate a doctrinaire legal equality between the sexes, and will make unconstitutional any law which imposes an obligation on one sex that it does not impose on the other. Under ERA, all laws which say the *husband* must support his *wife* will immediately become unconstitutional. Either the state legislatures will be forced to rewrite the state laws on marital support and make them "sex-neutral," (that is, replace "husband" and "wife" with the word "spouse"), or, if the legislatures fail to act, the courts will nullify the present wording. Pro-ERA lawyers have not denied this in testimony at the state legislative hearings around the country.

Pro-ERA lawyers have attempted to answer this point by claiming that "sex-neutral" language could still impose an obligation on the "wage-earning spouse" to support the spouse who remains at home. However, this would reduce the wife's legal rights even further. This would mean that, if the husband is lazy and wants to watch television all day, and the wife conscientiously takes a job to feed her hungry children, then she, as the "principal wage-earning spouse," would acquire the obligation to support her lazy husband, subject to criminal penalties if she failed to support him and pay all his debts!

ERA proponents usually try to divert the argument from the rights of the wife to the plight of the divorced woman, which is a different matter altogether. A divorced woman does not have the rights of a wife, but only the rights given in the divorce decree. There is, however, one dramatic way that ERA will reduce the rights of a divorced woman: She will lose her present presumption of custody of the children. Pro-ERA lawyers admit that the divorce court will be required to award custody of the children on the new constitutional principle of equality between the sexes—instead of on the present presumption (in the absence of evidence of bad character) that the mother should keep her children, which is enshrined in custom.

ERA proponents claim that the courts will not interfere in an on-going marriage to guarantee a wife's right to support. In most cases, a wife does not need to go to court to get support from her husband. The husband knows that he is responsible to pay for his wife's necessaries according to their standard of living, and that, to fulfill this obligation, his wages may be garnisheed, his bank account attached, he may have to post a bond, or ultimately go to jail. Case law proves that the courts will require a husband in an on-going marriage to pay his wife's bills even though he tries to get out of it by saying that the credit is extended without his knowledge or consent, and even though the wife has separate funds of her own and can afford to pay the bill. . . .

The second large area of legal rights enjoyed by women which ERA would take away pertains to the draft and military service. The majority US House Judiciary Committee *Report on the Equal Rights Amendment* states: "Not only would women, including mothers, be subject to the draft, but the military would be compelled to place them in combat units alongside the men."

The ERA proponents say that they want women to serve in the military on an absolutely equal basis with men. . . .

At the state legislative hearings around the country, ERA proponents have confirmed this and stated that this is what they want. For example, at the Virginia General Assembly's Task Force Hearings on September 18, 1973, an ERA proponent claimed that it would be unfair discrimination if women were kept out of combat or off warships because this might prevent them from winning Congressional Medals of Honor!

The present exemption for women does prevent them from having to fight a jungle war in Vietnam, or from being POWs or MIAs. There are a few radicals who think this is "discrimination," but not many.

One of the favorite dodges of the ERA proponents is to say that Congress *now* has the power to draft women. This is true—but Congress has used its power to exempt women, and that is the way the overwhelming majority of American men and women want it. If ERA is ratified, Congress will no longer have this option. If we have a national emergency and ERA is in effect, Congress will be constitutionally compelled to draft women on the same basis as men. If the emergency requires the drafting of fathers, as it did during World War II, then Congress would be compelled to draft mothers. There can, of course, be exemptions on the basis of age, physical disability, etc., but not on the basis of sex.

The third group of rights and benefits which ERA will take away from women concerns protective labor legislation, that is, the various state laws designed to give women employees particular benefits and protections not granted to men. These laws include such provisions as protecting women from being compelled to work too many hours a day or week or at night, the weight-lifting restrictions, provisions which mandate rest areas, rest periods, protective equipment, or a chair for a woman who stands on her feet all day, laws which protect women from being forced to work in dangerous jobs such as mining, and the laws which grant more generous workmen's compensation for injuries to a woman than to a man.

Women have worked hard over many generations to achieve such legislation to protect and benefit women whom economic necessity requires to work in a paying job. If ERA is ratified, all these laws will be wiped out with one stroke of the pen. ERA proponents cannot, and do not, dispute this fundamental fact.

Some ERA proponents argue that protective labor legislation is already outlawed by Title VII of the Civil Rights Act of 1964. It is true that *some* labor legislation in *some* states has been invalidated by the courts, but this is no reason to use the sledgehammer approach and knock it all out. To any extent that labor legislation has been knocked out by the Civil Rights Act, it can be restored by another amendment to the Civil Rights Act. But if it is knocked out by the Constitution, it cannot be restored except by the long and laborious process of repealing a constitutional amendment.

The business and professional women who have appeared as witnesses for ERA before state legislatures usually argue that protective labor legislation doesn't "protect" but instead discriminates adversely, and that protective legislation is obsolete and unnecessary in this modern technological age. This is the attitude of a business or professional woman who sits at a comfortable desk in a clean office and finds intellectual fulfillment in her job.

Only if ERA is permanently rejected will women be protected in their right to have overtime on a voluntary basis and their right to reject heavy and dangerous work without penalty.

One part of the Equal Rights Amendment which the proponents seldom, if ever, mention is Section 2, which states, "The Congress shall have the power to enforce, by appropriate legislation, the provisions of this article." Section 2 will transfer jurisdiction over women's rights, domestic relations, and criminal law and property law pertaining to women, out of the hands of the state legislatures and into the hands of the federal government: the Congress, the Executive branch, and the federal courts.

This grab of power by the federal government would involve matters that heretofore have been generally acknowledged to be the primary and, in some cases, the exclusive legislative responsibility of the states. These would include family law, divorce, child custody, alimony, minimum marriageable age limits, dower rights, inheritance, survivor's benefits, insurance rates, welfare, prison regulations, and protective labor legislation. All state and local laws, policies and regulations involving any difference of treatment between the sexes will be over-ridden by federal legislation, which means, ultimately, administrative regulations.

During most of the time that the Equal Rights Amendment was being considered by the US Congress, it had attached to it the Hayden Modification which stated: "The provisions of this article shall not be construed to impair any rights, benefits or exemptions conferred by law upon persons of the female sex." The Hayden Modification was deleted under pressure from the women's liberationists who lobbied for ERA.

Professor Paul A. Freund of the Harvard Law School, whose study of the Equal Rights Amendment covers 25 years, wrote in the March 1971 issue of the *Harvard Civil Rights-Civil Liberties Law Review:* "The real issue is not the legal status of women. The issue is the integrity and responsibility of the law-making process itself." Professor Philip B. Kurland of the University of Chicago Law School told the Illinois General Assembly on June 5, 1972: "I think that it is largely misrepresented as a women's rights amendment when in fact the primary beneficiary will be men."

Thus it is clear, that ERA will do absolutely nothing for women in the field of employment, but will take away from women their present superior rights, benefits, and exemptions. The devastating effects of ERA on women's rights were forecast on September 19, 1973, when the Pennsylvania Superior Court held that Pennsylvania's new state equal rights amendment invalidates Pennsylvania laws giving special marital rights and remedies to women only. The court specifically rejected the argument that ERA was meant to apply only to jobs, wages, and education, and stated that the "plain meaning" of ERA does not permit any exemptions.

The tally on the Equal Rights Amendment is impressive. Thirty states ratified, most of those very quickly, without the debate and study which a constitutional amendment deserves. Twenty states have refused to ratify. Of the 30 states which ratified, the Nebraska Legislature has already rescinded its previous ratification, and resolutions to rescind have been introduced in 12 other states. Wisconsin, which passed ERA early and without much debate, subsequently resoundingly defeated an ERA amendment to the state constitution in a statewide referendum. Since it takes 38 states to put a new amendment in the Constitution, ERA can be considered a terminal case.

Marlow W. Cook Supports the ERA, 1973

In a 1776 letter to her husband, Abigail Adams requested that US laws be formulated to no longer treat women as "vassals." She wrote:

". . . and by the way in the new Code of Laws which I suppose it will be necessary for you to make I desire you would Remember the Ladies, and be more generous and favourable to them than your ancestors. Do not put such unlimited power into the hands of the Husbands. Remember all Men would be tyrants if they could. If particular care and attention is not paid to the Ladies we are determined to foment a Rebellion, and will not hold ourselves bound by any Laws in which we have no voice, or Representation."

Two hundred years later, America has finally begun to take Mrs. Adams' request seriously. Congress has proposed, and 30 states have ratified the Equal Rights Amendment, which simply states:

"Equality of rights under the law shall not be denied or abridged by the United States or by any State on account of sex."

To become law, the Amendment must be ratified by 38 states.

A number of state legislatures will decide, when they reconvene in

"In Support of the ERA" by Marlow W. Cook from *Trial Magazine* (November/December 1973). Reprinted with permission of TRIAL. Copyright The Association of Trial Lawyers of America.

January, whether to ratify the Equal Rights Amendment. In so deciding, two basic questions must be faced once the effects of the Amendment are understood.

First is the threshold question of whether we want to eliminate sex discrimination in federal, state and local law and governmental actions. The second is whether we want a constitutional amendment to accomplish this equalization. The two are interrelated, in view of recent Supreme Court decisions and the trend toward equality in America. But let us try to explore them separately.

I believe there is practical unanimity among Americans that women should be extended equality of status, rights and opportunities in our laws. What controversy there is concerns extending equal responsibilities to women. As a matter of simple justice and common sense, equal rights and *responsibilities* must be extended to all citizens without discrimination.

I say this for a number of reasons, the primary being that one is not possible without the other. Any exceptions used to escape the responsibilities of citizenship can be just as easily used to deny equality of rights of citizenship.

Another reason that equal rights and responsibilities should be extended to women is the psychology of inferiority that results when classes of persons otherwise equally capable are not treated equally. The Supreme Court recognized this psychological effect in *Brown* v. *Board of Education* with regard to race. Others have explored the phenomenon with regard to sex.

But the equalization that is so necessary is the coming trend in this country in any event. America has already recognized that its women citizens have not been receiving equality of treatment under the law. The Supreme Court in its most recent statement on this issue, has stated:

"There can be no doubt that our Nation has had a long and unfortunate history of sex discrimination. Traditionally, such discrimination was rationalized by an attitude of "romantic paternalism" which, in practical effect, put women not on a pedestal, but in a cage." . . .

Thus, I think it safe to say that sex is no longer considered a rational classification, reasonably related to any legitimate state interest. Four members of the Court in *Frontiero* went further to find that sex, like race, alienage and national origin, is a "suspect classification," requiring close judicial scrutiny and a compelling state interest to uphold. This is the test that I believe should be used under the 14th Amendment for classifications based on sex. But this test has not yet been accepted by a majority of the Court in regard to sex classifications in our laws.

The important point is that the current trend in formulating and interpreting our laws is that the sex characteristic bears no relation to ability to perform or contribute to society. This means that nearly every argument opposing the Equal Rights Amendment overlooks the present trend toward equality which could accomplish much of what the ERA will. Those who would opt for "protecting" women have already lost the war.

Although current developments in the law are very favorable toward women gaining equality of rights, I must stress how far those developments are from the idea of total equality for women.

The majority of the Supreme Court may have found that sex is an "invidious" classification, but *not* that sex is a "suspect" classification. Thus, the constitutional test to be used in judging future cases is in doubt. No one knows how important a governmental interest is needed to uphold a statute or governmental practice that discriminates on the basis of sex.

We need a more definite standard by which judges, legislatures and public officials can act. We need a standard which cannot be abrogated by future courts or public officials. We need a constitutional amendment, particularly in view of the legislative history of the Equal Rights Amendment, which elucidates with specificity how its requirements can be met.

The ERA would become effective two years after the date of ratification. During those two years, the federal and state legislatures would have a tremendous incentive to re-examine their laws in light of the new and definite standard of equality for women and men. Judges would have to take judicial notice of the new standard rather than follow the concededly bad history of discriminatory precedents adhered to in the past. . . .

There is confusion on the part of some, as to how the declaration of equality, ordered by the ERA, will be translated into statutes, court decisions and governmental actions.

The purpose of the amendment is simply to end the unequal treatment under the law to which women have been subjected since the Constitution was first adopted. It is important to note that the only kind of sex discrimination which this would forbid is that which exists in law. Interpersonal relationships and customs of chivalry will, of course, remain as they always have been, a matter of individual choice. The adoption of this amendment will neither make a man a gentleman nor will it require him to stop being one.

It has been stated by some, that the ERA would deny women the "automatic" right to support, custody and alimony in the area of domestic relations law. These rights under present law are often illusory if they are granted at all. The Senate Judiciary Committee *Report on the Equal Rights Amendment* in explaining the effect of the ERA in family law, quoted the report of the Association of the Bar of the City of New York:

"The Amendment would bar a state from imposing a greater liability on one spouse than on the other merely because of sex. It is clear that the Amendment would not require both a husband and wife to contribute identical amounts of money to a marriage. The support obligation of each spouse would be defined in functional terms based, for example, on each spouse's earning power, current resources and nonmonetary contributions to the family welfare.

"Thus, if spouses have equal resources and earning capacities, each would be equally liable for the support of the other—or in practical effect, neither would be required to support the other. On the other hand, where one spouse is the primary wage earner and the other runs the home, the wage earner would have a duty to support the spouse who stays at home in compensation for the performance of her or his duties." . . .

The Equal Rights Amendment will require laws that discriminate on the basis of sex to be rewritten, but not drastically changed. Rather, the rights of spouses and parents will simply be viewed more equitably under the ERA than under present laws.

In other areas of domestic relations law, women stand to gain a great deal: the right of a separate domicile, the right to contract when married, the right to consortium, the right to one's own name, and the right to marry or divorce on an equal basis with men.

In community property states the power of management and control over the community property could not remain with the husband alone, as is the present case in all community property states except Texas. In the forty-two common law property states, a greater deference would be given the contribution to common property by a spouse who works in the home.

Thus, it can be seen that no great change in the American social structure would follow from adoption of the Equal Rights Amendment. No women who wish to remain in the home would be driven out, and the legal obligations persons assume upon marriage would remain. The only change would be a more equitable treatment for persons under the law.

A second area of supposed "protections" that women would lose under the Equal Rights Amendment concerns the draft-exempt status that women have held up to this time. This is indeed a policy question, just as drafting of men is. The Senate Report and Senate floor debate in defeating riders to the Equal Rights Amendment make clear that any draft law under the ERA could not discriminate on the basis of sex.

As in the past, only those qualified would be drafted, and exemptions for parents could be implemented. Service to one's country in the armed services is an obligation of citizenship. In return, many benefits of service are extended to veterans and servicemen and women: training, education, medical care, G.I. benefits, upward mobility for the poor, and preference in hiring.

Much of the wind has been sucked from the sails of the opponents of the ERA by the outstanding performance of our military women in combat areas of Southeast Asia. The *Frontiero* decision and the new assignment policies of the services point in the direction toward increased equality for women in the military.

Without a draft, women would have to be allowed to volunteer for service on an equal basis with men. Assignments of personnel would remain as they always have been, on the basis of individual capability and the needs of the service.

One recurring "red herring" opponents have argued is in the area of the right to privacy. As the Senate Report states and floor debate further attests to, the legislative intent of the ERA is that the right to privacy in private bodily functions such as sleeping, disrobing, and bathing will remain, even if this means separation of the sexes in state dormitories, prisons, military barracks or ships.

This is a narrow exception to the rule of equality laid down by the Equal Rights Amendment.

It has been said that women will forfeit "protective" labor legislation under the Equal Rights Amendment, such as hours, weight-lifting and mandatory rest period laws. Just as the Supreme Court has already recognized, some such protective laws do not protect, but in reality, restrain working women from progressing in their employment. Progress is already being made in this area under federal legislation, state law and court decisions.

Under the ERA, any state would be free to enact legislation that truly protects persons from dangerous working conditions and courts could extend benefits to discriminated classes of workers, rather than denying benefits (if they are truly beneficial) to men.

In the area of criminal law, it has been said that women will lose the protection of rape laws under the ERA. The legislative history of the Amendment is clearly contrary to that opinion.

The Senate Committee *Report* states, "But the Amendment will not invalidate laws which punish rape, for such laws are designed to protect women in a way that they are uniformly distinct from men." Senate floor debate also made this point clear. The Senate was satisfied as to the effect of the Equal Rights Amendment, and voted down a change to the Amendment's wording, with regard to sexual offenses.

Women stand to gain a great deal in the criminal law area under the ERA, and such discriminatory treatment as outlined in the Senate Committee Report below, could no longer be perpetrated:

"There is also invidious discrimination against women in the criminal laws of some states. One state has a statute allowing women to be jailed for three years for habitual drunkenness, while a man can receive only 30 days for the same offense. In two states, the defense of "passion killing" is allowed to the wronged husband, but not to the deceived wife. And in another state, female juvenile offenders can be declared "persons in need of supervision" for non-criminal acts until they are 18, while males are covered by the statute only until age 16.

Women have faced widespread discrimination in the area of education and stand to lose no "protections" here. Discrimination in admission to college, graduate and professional schools is widespread, as is discrimination against women in every level of the teaching profession.

The Senate Committee *Report* explained the effect of the ERA in this area as follows:

"With respect to education, the Equal Rights Amendment will require that state supported schools at all levels eliminate laws of regulations or official practices which exclude women or limit their numbers. The Amendment would not require quotas for men and women, nor would it require that schools accurately reflect the sex distribution of the population; rather admission would turn on the basis of ability or other relevant characteristics, and not on the basis of sex."

The Report also stated that scholarship funds would have to be distributed on a nondiscriminatory basis; state schools limited to one sex would have to allow both sexes to attend; and employment and promotion in public schools would, as in other cases of governmental action, have to be free from sex discrimination.

Congress, through legislation, has already taken steps to assure equality in schools receiving federal funds, with limited exceptions. But it is time to assure, through a constitutional amendment, that no one will be denied equal educational opportunity by the state.

The policy question of eliminating sex discrimination from federal and state law and governmental acts is being answered affirmatively with greater certainty with each passing day. Women are anxious to share in the fullness of citizenship, and have been since our country was founded. As a matter of simple justice and common sense, equality of rights and responsibilities must be shared by all.

Once the effects of the ERA are understood, it can be readily seen that no real "protections" will be lost by women, but many rights and opportunities will be gained.

As our country prepares to celebrate our second century of existence, I think it most fitting to rededicate ourselves to the principle of equality of all citizens. It is unfortunate that equal rights for men and women is a cause whose time has come. For, as Abigail Adams pointed out, this is a cause that should have always been.

The Reverend Jerry Falwell on the ERA, 1980

I believe that at the foundation of the women's liberation movement there is a minority core of women who were once bored with life, whose real problems are spiritual problems. Many women have never accepted their God-given roles. They live in disobedience to God's laws and have promoted their godless philosophy throughout our society. God Almighty created men and women biologically different and with differing needs and roles. He made men and women to complement each other and to love each other. Not all the women involved in the feminist movement are radicals. Some are misinformed, and some are lonely women who like being housewives and helpmeets and mothers, but whose husbands spend little time at home and who take no interest in their wives and children. Sometimes the full load of rearing a family becomes a great burden to a woman who is not supported by a man. Women who work should be respected and accorded dignity and equal rewards for equal work. But this is not what the present feminist movement and equal rights movement are all about.

The Equal Rights Amendment is a delusion. I believe that women deserve more than equal rights. And, in families and in nations where the Bible is believed, Christian women are honored above men. Only in places where the Bible is believed and practiced do women receive more than equal rights. Men and women have differing strengths. The Equal Rights Amendment can never do for women what needs to be done for them. Women need to know Jesus Christ as their Lord and Savior and be under His Lordship. They need a man who knows Jesus Christ as his Lord and Savior, and they need to be part of a home where their husband is a godly leader and where there is a Christian family.

The Equal Rights Amendment strikes at the foundation of our entire

From *Listen America* by Jerry Falwell. Doubleday, 1980.

social structure. If passed, this amendment would accomplish exactly the opposite of its outward claims. By mandating an absolute equality under the law, it will actually take away many of the special rights women now enjoy. ERA is not merely a political issue, but a moral issue as well. A definite violation of holy Scripture, ERA defies the mandate that "the husband is the head of the wife, even as Christ is the head of the church" (Ep. 5:23). In 1 Peter 3:7 we read that husbands are to give their wives honor as unto the weaker vessel, that they are both heirs together of the grace of life. Because a woman is weaker does not mean that she is less important.

Roe v. *Wade*, 410 U.S. 113 (1973)

[7–2: Blackmun, Brennan, Burger, Douglas,
Marshall, Stewart, Powell; Rehnquist, White]

Mr. Justice Blackmun delivered the opinion of the Court. . . .

We forthwith acknowledge our awareness of the sensitive and emotional nature of the abortion controversy, of the vigorous opposing views, even among physicians, and of the deep and seemingly absolute convictions that the subject inspires. One's philosophy, one's experiences, one's religious training, one's attitudes toward life and family and their values, and the moral standards one establishes and seeks to observe, are all likely to influence and to color one's thinking and conclusions about abortion.

In addition, population growth, pollution, poverty, and racial overtones tend to complicate and not to simplify the problem.

Our task, of course, is to resolve the issue by constitutional measurement, free of emotion and of predilection. We seek earnestly to do this, and, because we do, we have inquired into, and in this opinion place some emphasis upon, medical and medical-legal history and what that history reveals about man's attitudes toward the abortion procedure over the centuries. . . .

V

The principal thrust of appellant's attack on the Texas statutes is that they improperly invade a right, said to be possessed by the pregnant woman, to choose to terminate her pregnancy. Appellant would discover this right in the concept of personal "liberty" embodied in the Fourteenth Amendment's Due Process Clause; or in personal, marital, familial, and sexual privacy said to be protected by the Bill of Rights or its penumbras. . . . Before addressing this claim, we feel it desirable briefly to survey, in several aspects, the history of abortion, for such insight as that history may afford us, and then to examine the state purposes and interests behind the criminal abortion laws.

VI

It perhaps is not generally appreciated that the restrictive criminal abortion laws in effect in a majority of States today are of relatively recent vintage.

Those laws, generally proscribing abortion or its attempt at any time during pregnancy except when necessary to preserve that pregnant woman's life, are not of ancient or even of common-law origin. Instead, they derive from statutory changes effected, for the most part, in the latter half of the nineteenth century.

1. *Ancient attitudes.* These are not capable of precise determination. . . . [A]bortion was practiced in Greek times as well as in the Roman Era, and . . . "it was resorted to without scruple." . . . If abortion was prosecuted in some places, it seems to have been based on a concept of a violation of the father's right to his offspring. Ancient religion did not bar abortion.

2. *The Hippocratic Oath.* What then of the famous Oath that has stood so long as the ethical guide of the medical profession and that bears the name of the great Greek (460?–377? B.C.), who has been described as the Father of Medicine . . . ? The Oath was not uncontested even in Hippocrates' day; only the Pythagorean school of philosophers frowned upon the related act of suicide. Most Greek thinkers, on the other hand, commended abortion, at least prior to viability. . . . For the Pythagoreans, however, it was a matter of dogma. For them the embryo was animate from the moment of conception, and abortion meant destruction of a living being. The abortion clause of the Oath, therefore, "echoes Pythagorean doctrines," and "[i]n no other stratum of Greek opinion were such views held or proposed in the same spirit of uncompromising austerity." . . . But with the end of antiquity a decided change took place. Resistance against suicide and against abortion became common. The Oath came to be popular. The emerging teachings of Christianity were in agreement with the Pythagorean ethic. The Oath "became the nucleus of all medical ethics" and "was applauded as the embodiment of truth." . . .

This . . . enables us to understand, in historical context, a long-accepted and revered statement of medical ethics.

3. *The common law.* It is undisputed that at common law, abortion performed *before* "quickening"—the first recognizable movement of the fetus *in utero,* appearing usually from the 16th to the 18th week of pregnancy—was not an indictable offense. . . . Christian theology and the canon law came to fix the point of animation at 40 days for a male and 80 days for a female, a view that persisted until the 19th century, [but] there was otherwise little agreement about the precise time of formation or animation. There was agreement, however, that prior to this point the fetus was to be regarded as part of the mother, and its destruction, therefore, was not homicide. Due to continued uncertainty about the precise time when animation occurred, to the lack of any empirical basis for the 40–80-day view, and perhaps to Aquinas' definition of movement as one of the two first principles of life, Bracton focused upon quickening as the critical point. The significance of quickening was echoed by later common-law scholars and found its way into the received common law in this country.

Whether abortion of a *quick* fetus was a felony at common law, or even a lesser crime, is still disputed. . . . A recent review of the common-law precedents argues . . . that those precedents contradict Coke and that even post-quickening abortion was never established as a common-law crime. . . . [I]t now appear[s] doubtful that abortion was ever firmly established as a common-law crime even with respect to the destruction of a quick fetus.

4. *The English statutory law.* England's first criminal abortion statute, Lord Ellenborough's Act, 43 Geo. 3, ch. 58, came in 1803. It made abortion of a quick fetus, § 1, a capital crime, but in § 2 it provided lesser penalties for the felony of abortion before quickening, and thus preserved the "quickening" distinction. . . . [J. Blackmun traces British abortion law up to the present. As of 1967 British law was similar to the Georgia statute treated in *Doe* v. *Bolton.*]

5. *The American law.* In this country, the law in effect in all but a few States until mid-nineteenth century was the pre-existing English common law. Connecticut, the first State to enact abortion legislation, adopted in 1821 that part of Lord Ellenborough's Act that related to a woman "quick with child." The death penalty was not imposed. Abortion before quickening was made a crime in that State only in 1860. In 1828, New York enacted legislation that, in two respects, was to serve as a model for early anti-abortion statutes. First, while barring destruction of an unquickened fetus as well as a quick fetus, it made the former only a misdemeanor, but the latter second-degree manslaughter. Second, it incorporated a concept of therapeutic abortion by providing that an abortion was excused if it "shall have been necessary to preserve the life of such mother, or shall have been advised by two physicians to be necessary for such purpose." By 1840, when Texas had received the common law, only eight American States had statutes dealing with abortion. It was not until after the War Between the States that legislation began generally to replace the common law. Most of those initial statutes dealt severely with abortion after quickening but were lenient with it before quickening. Most punished attempts equally with completed abortions. While many statutes included the exception for an abortion thought by one or more physicians to be necessary to save the mother's life, that provision soon disappeared and the typical law required that the procedure actually be necessary for that purpose.

Gradually, in the middle and late nineteenth century the quickening distinction disappeared from the statutory law of most States and the degree of the offense and the penalties were increased. By the end of the 1950s, a large majority of the jurisdictions banned abortion, however and whenever performed, unless done to save or preserve the life of the mother. . . . In the past several years, however, a trend toward liberalization of abortion statutes has resulted in adoption, by about one-third of the States, of less stringent laws, most of them patterned after the ALI Model Penal Code. . . .

It is thus apparent that at common law, at the time of the adoption of our Constitution, and throughout the major portion of the nineteenth century, abortion was viewed with less disfavor than under most American statutes currently in effect. Phrasing it another way, a woman enjoyed a substantially broader right to terminate a pregnancy than she does in most States today. At least with respect to the early stage of pregnancy, and very possibly without such a limitation, the opportunity to make this choice was present in this country well into the nineteenth century. Even later, the law continued for some time to treat less punitively an abortion procured in early pregnancy.

6. *The position of the American Medical Association.* [J. Blackmun recapitulates AMA committee reports of 1857 and 1871 condemning abortion and calling "the attention of the clergy of all denominations to the perverted views of morality entertained by a large class of females—aye, and men also, on this important question." He then describes the liberalization of AMA positions in 1967 and 1970.]

7. *The position of the American Public Health Association.* In October 1970, the Executive Board of the APHA adopted Standards for Abortion Services. These [urged that:]

> Rapid and simple abortion referral must be readily available through state and local public health departments, medical societies, or other nonprofit organizations. . . . (Recommended Standards for Abortion Services, 61 Am. J. Pub. Health 396 [1971].)

. . . It was said that at present abortions should be performed by physicians or osteopaths who are licensed to practice and who have "adequate training." . . .

8. *The position of the American Bar Association.* At its meeting in February 1972 the ABA House of Delegates approved, with 17 opposing votes, the Uniform Abortion Act. . . . We set forth the Act in full in the margin.* . . .

---

* Uniform Abortion Act

Section 1. [*Abortion Defined: When Authorized.*]

(a) "Abortion" means the termination of human pregnancy with an intention other than to produce a live birth or to remove a dead fetus.

(b) An abortion may be performed in this state only if it is performed:

(1) by a physician licensed to practice medicine [or osteopathy] in this state or by a physician practicing medicine [or osteopathy] in the employ of the government of the United States or of this state, [and the abortion is performed [in the physician's office or in a medical clinic, or] in a hospital approved by the [Department of Health] or operated by the United States, this state, or any department, agency, or political subdivision of either;] or by a female upon herself upon the advice of the physician; and

(2) within [20] weeks after the commencement of the pregnancy [or after [20] weeks only if the physician has reasonable cause to believe (i) there is a substantial risk that continuance of the pregnancy would endanger the life of the mother or would gravely impair the physical or mental health of the mother, (ii) that the child would be born with grave physical or mental defect, or (iii) that the pregnancy resulted from rape or incest, or illicit intercourse with a girl under the age of 16 years].

Section 2. [*Penalty.*] Any person who performs or procures an abortion other than authorized by this Act is guilty of a [felony] and, upon conviction thereof, may be sentenced to pay a fine not exceeding [$1,000] or to imprisonment [in the state penitentiary] not exceeding [5 years], or both.

Section 3. [*Uniformity of Interpretation.*] This Act shall be construed to effectuate its general purpose to make uniform the law with respect to the subject of this Act among those states which enact it.

Section 4. [*Short Title.*] This Act may be cited as the Uniform Abortion Act.

Section 5. [*Severability.*] If any provision of this Act or the application thereof to any person or circumstance is held invalid, the invalidity does not affect other provisions or applications of this Act which can be given effect without the invalid provision or application, and to this end the provisions of this Act are severable.

VII

Three reasons have been advanced to explain historically the enactment of criminal abortion laws in the nineteenth century and to justify their continued existence.

It has been argued occasionally that these laws were the product of a Victorian social concern to discourage illicit sexual conduct. Texas, however, does not advance this justification in the present case, and it appears that no court or commentator has taken the argument seriously. The appellants and *amici* contend, moreover, that this is not a proper state purpose at all and suggest that, if it were, the Texas statutes are overbroad in protecting it since the law fails to distinguish between married and unwed mothers.

A second reason is concerned with abortion as a medical procedure. When most criminal abortion laws were first enacted, the procedure was a hazardous one for the woman. This was particularly true prior to the development of antisepsis. Antiseptic techniques . . . were not generally accepted and employed until about the turn of the century. Abortion mortality was high. Even after 1900, and perhaps until as late as the development of antibiotics in the 1940s, standard modern techniques such as dilation and curettage were not nearly so safe as they are today. Thus, it has been argued that a State's real concern in enacting a criminal abortion law was to protect the pregnant woman, that is, to restrain her from submitting to a procedure that placed her life in serious jeopardy.

Modern medical techniques have altered this situation. Appellants and various *amici* refer to medical data indicating that abortion in early pregnancy, that is, prior to the end of the first trimester, although not without its risk, is now relatively safe. Mortality rates for women undergoing early abortions, where the procedure is legal, appear to be as low or lower than the rates for normal childbirth. Consequently, any interest of the State in protecting the woman from an inherently hazardous procedure, except when it would be equally dangerous for her to forgo it, has largely disappeared. Of course, important state interests in the areas of health and medical standards do remain. The State has a legitimate interest in seeing to it that abortion, like any other medical procedure, is performed under circumstances that insure maximum safety for the patient. This interest obviously extends at least to the performing physician and his staff, to the facilities involved, to the availability of after-care, and to adequate provision for any complication or emergency that might arise. . . . Moreover, the risk to the woman increases as her pregnancy continues. Thus, the State retains a definite interest in protecting the woman's own health and safety when an abortion is proposed at a late stage of pregnancy.

The third reason is the State's interest—some phrase it in terms of duty—in protecting prenatal life. Some of the argument for this justification rests on the theory that a new human life is present from the moment of conception. The State's interest and general obligation to protect life then extends, it is argued, to prenatal life. Only when the life of the pregnant mother herself is at stake, balanced against the life she carries within her, should the interest of the embryo or fetus not prevail. Logically, of course, a legitimate state interest in this area need not stand or fall on acceptance of the belief that life begins at conception or at some other point prior to live birth. In assessing the State's interest, recognition may be given to the less rigid claim that as long as at least *potential* life is involved, the State may assert interests beyond the protection of the pregnant woman alone.

Parties challenging state abortion laws have sharply disputed in some courts the contention that a purpose of these laws, when enacted, was to protect prenatal life . . . [and] they claim that most state laws were designed solely to protect the woman. Because medical advances have lessened this concern, at least with respect to abortion in early pregnancy, they argue that with respect to such abortions the laws can no longer be justified by any state interest. There is some scholarly support for this view of original purpose. The few state courts called upon to interpret their laws in the late nineteenth and early twentieth centuries did focus on the State's interest in protecting the woman's health rather than in preserving the embryo and fetus. Proponents of this view point out that in many States, including Texas, by statute or judicial interpretation, the pregnant woman herself could not be prosecuted for self-abortion or for cooperating in an abortion performed upon her by another. They claim that adoption of the "quickening" distinction through received common law and state statutes tacitly recognizes the greater health hazards inherent in the late abortion and impliedly repudiates the theory that life begins at conception. . . .

VIII

The Constitution does not explicitly mention any right of privacy. In a line of decisions, however, . . . the Court has recognized that a right of personal privacy, or a guarantee of certain areas or zones of privacy, does exist under the Constitution. In varying contexts, the Court or individual Justices have, indeed, found at least the roots of that right in the First Amendment, . . . ; in the Fourth and Fifth Amendments, . . . ; in the penumbras of the Bill of Rights, *Griswold* v. *Connecticut,* 381 U.S., at 484–885; in the Ninth Amendment, *id.* at 486 (Goldberg, J., concurring); or in the concept of liberty guaranteed by the first section of the Fourteenth Amendment. . . . These decisions made it clear that only personal rights that can be deemed "fundamental" or "implicit in the concept of ordered liberty," *Palko* v. *Connecticut* . . . (1937), are included in this guarantee of personal privacy. They also make it clear that the right has some extension to activities relating to marriage. . . .

This right of privacy, whether it be founded in the Fourteenth Amendment's concept of personal liberty and restrictions upon state action, as we feel it is, or, as the District Court determined, in the Ninth Amendment's reservation of rights to the people, is broad enough to encompass a woman's decision whether or not to terminate her pregnancy. The detriment that the State would impose upon the pregnant woman by denying this choice altogether is apparent. Specific and direct harm medically diagnosable even in early pregnancy may be involved. Maternity, or additional offspring, may force upon the woman a distressful life and future. Psychological harm may be imminent. Mental and physical health may be taxed by child care. There is also the distress, for all concerned, associated with the unwanted child, and there is the problem of bringing a child into a family already unable, psychologically and otherwise, to care for it. In other cases, as in this one, the additional difficulties and continuing stigma of unwed motherhood may be involved. All these are factors the woman and her responsible physician necessarily will consider in consultation.

On the basis of elements such as these, appellant and some *amici* argue that the woman's right is absolute and that she is entitled to terminate her pregnancy at whatever time, in whatever way, and for whatever reason she alone chooses. With this we do not agree. Appellant's arguments that Texas either has no valid interest at all in regulating the abortion decision, or no interest strong enough to support any limitation upon the woman's sole determination, are unpersuasive. The Court's decisions recognizing a right of privacy also acknowledge that some regulation in areas protected by that right is appropriate. As noted above, a State may properly assert important interests in safeguarding health, in maintaining medical standards, and in protecting potential life. At some point in pregnancy, these respective interests become sufficiently compelling to sustain regulation of the factors that govern the abortion decision. The privacy right involved, therefore, cannot be said to be absolute. In fact, it is not clear to us that the claim asserted by some *amici* that one has an unlimited right to do with one's body as one pleases bears a close relationship to the right of privacy previously articulated in the Court's decisions. The Court has refused to recognize an unlimited right of this kind in the past. . . .

We, therefore, conclude that the right of personal privacy includes the abortion decision, but that this right is not unqualified and must be considered against important state interests in regulation. . . . [This] right, nonetheless, is not absolute and is subject to some limitations; and . . . at some point the state interests as to protection of health, medical standards, and prenatal life, become dominant. . . .

Where certain "fundamental rights" are involved, the Court has held that regulation limiting these rights may be justified only by a "compelling state interest," . . . and that legislative enactments must be narrowly drawn to express only the legitimate state interests at stake. . . .

In the recent abortion cases, . . . courts have recognized these principles. Those striking down state laws have generally scrutinized the State's interests in protecting health and potential life, and have concluded that neither interest justified broad limitations on the reasons for which a physician and his pregnant patient might decide that she should have an abortion in the early stages of pregnancy. Courts sustaining state laws have held that the State's determinations to protect health or prenatal life are dominant and constitutionally justifiable.

IX

The District Court held that the appellee failed to meet his burden of demonstrating that the Texas statute's infringement upon Roe's rights was necessary to support a compelling state interest, and that, although the appellee presented "several compelling justifications for state presence in the area of abortions," the statutes outstripped these justifications and swept "far beyond any areas of compelling state interest." . . . Appellant and appellee both contest that holding. Appellant, as has been indicated, claims an absolute right that bars any state imposition of criminal penalties in the area. Appellee argues that the State's determination to recognize and protect prenatal life from and after conception constitutes a compelling state interest. As noted above, we do not agree fully with either formulation.

A. The appellee and certain *amici* argue that the fetus is a "person" within the language and meaning of the Fourteenth Amendment. In support of this, they outline at length and in detail the well-known facts of fetal development. If this suggestion of personhood is established, the appellant's case, of course, collapses, for the fetus' right to life would then be guaranteed specifically by the Amendment . . . [but] no case [can] be cited that holds that a fetus is a person within the meaning of the Fourteenth Amendment.

The Constitution does not define "person" in so many words. Section 1 of the Fourteenth Amendment contains three references to "person." The first, in defining "citizens," speaks of "persons born or naturalized in the United States." . . . "Person" is used in other places in the Constitution. . . . But in nearly all these instances, the use of the word is such that it has application only postnatally. None indicates, with any assurance, that it has any possible prenatal application.

All this, together with our observation, *supra,* that throughout the major portion of the nineteenth century prevailing legal abortion practices were far freer than they are today, persuades us that the word "person," as used in the Fourteenth Amendment, does not include the unborn. This is in accord with the results reached in those few cases where the issue has been squarely presented. . . .

B. The pregnant woman cannot be isolated in her privacy. She carries an embryo and, later, a fetus. . . . The situation therefore is inherently different from marital intimacy, or bedroom possession of obscene material, or marriage, or procreation, or education. . . . As we have intimated above, it is reasonable and appropriate for a State to decide that at some point in time another interest, that of health of the mother or that of potential human life, becomes significantly involved. The woman's privacy is no longer sole and any right of privacy she possesses must be measured accordingly.

Texas urges that, apart from the Fourteenth Amendment, life begins at conception and is present throughout pregnancy, and that, therefore, the State has a compelling interest in protecting that life from and after conception. We need not resolve the difficult question of when life begins. When those trained in the respective disciplines of medicine, philosophy, and theology are unable to arrive at any consensus, the judiciary, at this point in the·development of man's knowledge, is not in a position to speculate as to the answer.

It should be sufficient to note briefly the wide divergence of thinking on this most sensitive and difficult question. There has always been strong support for the view that life does not begin until live birth. This was the belief of the Stoics. It appears to be the predominant, though not the unanimous, attitude of the Jewish faith. It may be taken to represent also the position of a large segment of the Protestant community, insofar as that can be ascertained; organized groups that have taken a formal position on the abortion issue have generally regarded abortion as a matter for the conscience of the individual and her family. As we have noted, the common law found greater significance in quickening. Physicians and their scientific colleagues have regarded that event with less interest and have tended to focus either upon conception, upon live birth, or upon the interim point at which the fetus becomes "viable," that is, potentially able to live outside the mother's womb, albeit with artificial aid. Viability is usually placed at about seven months (28 weeks) but may occur earlier, even at 24 weeks. . . . [The Roman Catholic Church] would recognize the existence of life from the moment of conception. . . . As one brief *amicus* discloses, this is a view strongly held by many non-Catholics as well, and by many physicians. Substantial problems for precise definition of this view are posed, however, by new embryological data that purport to indicate that conception is a "process" over time, rather than an event, and by new medical techniques such as menstrual extraction, the "morning-after" pill, implantation of embryos, artificial insemination, and even artificial wombs.

In areas other than criminal abortion, the law has been reluctant to endorse any theory that life, as we recognize it, begins before live birth or to accord legal rights to the unborn except in narrowly defined situations and except when the rights are contingent upon live birth. For example, the traditional rule of tort law denied recovery for prenatal injuries even though the child was born alive. That rule has been changed in almost every jurisdiction. In most States, recovery is said to be permitted only if the fetus is viable, or at least quick, when the injuries were sustained, though few courts have squarely so held. In a recent development, generally opposed by the commentators, some States permit the parents of a stillborn child to maintain an action for wrongful death because of prenatal injuries. Such an action, however, would appear to be one to vindicate the parents' interest and is thus consistent with the view that the fetus, at most, represents only the potentiality of life. . . .

X

In view of all this, we do not agree that, by adopting one theory of life, Texas may override the rights of the pregnant woman that are at stake. We repeat, however, that the State does have an important and legitimate interest in preserving and protecting the health of the pregnant woman, whether she be a resident of the State or a nonresident who seeks medical consultation and treatment there, and that it has still *another* important and legitimate interest in protecting the potentiality of human life. These interests are separate and distinct. Each grows in substantiality as the woman approaches term and, at a point during pregnancy, each becomes "compelling."

With respect to the State's important and legitimate interest in the health of the mother, the "compelling" point, in the light of present medical knowledge, is at approximately the end of the first trimester. This is so because of the now-established medical fact, referred to above, that until the end of the first trimester mortality in abortion may be less than mortality in normal childbirth. It follows that, from and after this point, a State may regulate the abortion procedure to the extent that the regulation reasonably relates to the preservation and protection of maternal health. Examples of permissible state regulation in this area are requirements as to the qualifications of the person who is to perform the abortion; as to the licensure of that person; as to the facility in which the procedure is to be performed, that is, whether it must be a hospital or may be a clinic or some other place of less-than-hospital status; as to the licensing of the facility; and the like.

This means, on the other hand, that, for the period of pregnancy prior to this "compelling" point, the attending physician, in consultation with his patient, is free to determine, without regulation by the State, that, in his medical judgment, the patient's pregnancy should be terminated. If that decision is reached, the judgment may be effectuated by an abortion free of interference by the State.

With respect to the State's important and legitimate interest in potential life, the "compelling" point is at viability. This is so because the fetus then presumably has the capability of meaningful life outside the mother's womb. State regulation protective of fetal life after viability thus has both logical and biological justifications. If the State is interested in protecting fetal life after viability, it may go so far as to proscribe abortion during that period, except when it is necessary to preserve the life or health of the mother.

Measured against these standards, Article 1196 of the Texas Penal Code, in restricting legal abortions to those "procured or attempted by medical advice for the purpose of saving the life of the mother," sweeps too broadly. The statute made no distinction between abortions performed early in pregnancy and those performed later, and it limits to a single reason, "saving" the mother's life, the legal justification for the procedure. The statute, therefore, cannot survive the constitutional attack made upon it here. . . .

XI

To summarize and to repeat:

1. A state criminal abortion statute of the current Texas type, that excepts from criminality only a *life-saving* procedure on behalf of the mother, without regard to pregnancy stage and without recognition of the other interests involved, is violative of the Due Process Clause of the Fourteenth Amendment.

(a) For the stage prior to approximately the end of the first trimester, the abortion decision and its effectuation must be left to the medical judgment of the pregnant woman's attending physician.

(b) For the stage subsequent to approximately the end of the first trimester, the State, in promoting its interest in the health of the mother, may, if it chooses, regulate the abortion procedure in ways that are reasonably related to maternal health.

(c) For the stage subsequent to viability, the State in promoting its interest in the potentiality of human life may, if it chooses, regulate, and even proscribe, abortion except where it is necessary, in appropriate medical judgment, for the preservation of the life or health of the mother.

2. The State may define the term "physician," as it has been employed in the preceding paragraphs of this part XI of this opinion, to mean only a physician currently licensed by the State, and may proscribe any abortion by a person who is not a physician as so defined.

In *Doe* v. *Bolton, post,* procedural requirements contained in one of the modern abortion statutes are considered. That opinion and this one, of course, are to be read together. . . .

Mr. Justice Rehnquist, dissenting. . . .

The Court's opinion brings to the decision of this troubling question both extensive historical fact and a wealth of legal scholarship. While the opinion thus commands my respect, I find myself nonetheless in fundamental disagreement with those parts of it that invalidate the Texas statute in question, and therefore dissent.

I

The Court's opinion decides that a State may impose virtually no restriction on the performance of abortions during the first trimester of pregnancy. Our previous decisions indicate that a necessary predicate for such an opinion is a plaintiff who was in her first trimester of pregnancy at some time during the pendency of her lawsuit. While a party may vindicate his own constitutional rights, he may not seek vindication for the rights of others. . . . The Court's statement of facts in this case makes clear, however, that the record in no way indicates the presence of such a plaintiff. We know only that plaintiff Roe at the time of filing her complaint was a pregnant woman; for aught that appears in this record, she may have been in her *last* trimester of pregnancy as of the date the complaint was filed.

Nothing in the Court's opinion indicates that Texas might not constitutionally apply its proscription of abortion as written to a woman in that stage of pregnancy. Nonetheless, the Court uses her complaint against the Texas statute as a fulcrum for deciding that States may impose virtually no restrictions on medical abortions performed during the *first* trimester of pregnancy. In deciding such a hypothetical lawsuit, the Court departs from the long-standing admonition that it should never "formulate a rule of constitutional law broader than is required by the precise facts to which it is to be applied." . . .

II

Even if there were a plaintiff in this case capable of litigating the issue which the Court decides, I would reach a conclusion opposite to that reached by the Court. I have difficulty in concluding, as the Court does, that the right of "privacy" is involved in this case. Texas, by the statute here challenged, bars the performance of a medical abortion by a licensed physician on a plaintiff such as *Roe.* A transaction resulting in an operation such as this is not "private" in the ordinary usage of the word. Nor is the "privacy" that the Court finds here even a distant relative of the freedom from searches and seizures protected by the Fourth Amendment to the Constitution, which the Court has referred to as embodying a right to privacy. . . .

If the Court means by the term "privacy" no more than that the claim of a person to be free from unwanted state regulation of consensual transactions may be a form of "liberty" protected by the Fourteenth Amendment, there is no doubt that similar claims have been upheld in our earlier decisions on the basis of that liberty. I agree with the statement of Mr. Justice Stewart in his concurring opinion that the "liberty," against deprivation of which without due process the Fourteenth Amendment protects, embraces more than the rights found in the Bill of Rights. But that liberty is not guaranteed absolutely against deprivation, only against deprivation without due process of law. The test traditionally applied in the area of social and economic legislation is whether or not a law such as that challenged has a rational relation to a valid state objective. . . . The Due Process Clause of the Fourteenth Amendment undoubtedly does place a limit, albeit a broad one, on legislative power to enact laws such as this. If the Texas statute were to prohibit an abortion even where the mother's life is in jeopardy, I have little doubt that such a statute would lack a rational relation to a valid state objective under the test stated in *Williamson.* But the Court's sweeping invalidation of any restrictions on abortion during the first trimester is impossible to justify under that standard, and the conscious weighing of competing factors that the Court's opinion apparently substitutes for the established test is far more appropriate to a legislative judgment than to a judicial one. . . .

As in *Lochner* and similar cases applying substantive due process standards to economic and social welfare legislation, the adoption of the compelling state interest standard will inevitably require this Court to examine the legislative policies and pass on the wisdom of these policies in the very process of deciding whether a particular state interest put forward may or may not be "compelling." The decision here to break pregnancy into three distinct terms and to outline the permissible restrictions the State may impose in each one, for example, partakes more of judicial legislation than it does of a determination of the intent of the drafters of the Fourteenth Amendment.

The fact that a majority of the States reflecting, after all, the majority sentiment in those States, have had restrictions on abortions for at least a century is a strong indication, it seems to me, that the asserted right to an abortion is not "so rooted in the traditions and conscience of our people as to be ranked as fundamental," . . . . Even today, when society's views on abortion are changing, the very existence of the debate is evidence that the "right" to an abortion is not so universally acceptable as the appellant would have us believe.

To reach its result, the Court necessarily has had to find within the scope of the Fourteenth Amendment a right that was apparently completely unknown to the drafters of the Amendment. As early as 1821, the first state law dealing directly with abortion was enacted by the Connecticut Legislature. . . . By the time of the adoption of the Fourteenth Amendment in 1868, there were at least 36 laws enacted by state or territorial legislatures limiting abortion. While many States have amended or updated their laws, 21 of the laws on the books of 1868 remain in effect today. . . .

There apparently was no question concerning the validity of this provision or of any of the other state statutes when the Fourteenth Amendment was adopted. The only conclusion possible from this history is that the drafters did not intend to have the Fourteenth Amendment withdraw from the States the power to legislate with respect to this matter.

III

Even if one were to agree that the case that the court decides were here, and that the enunciation of the substantive constitutional law in the Court's opinion were proper, the actual disposition of the case by the Court is still difficult to justify. The Texas statute is struck down in *toto,* even though the Court apparently concedes that at later periods of pregnancy Texas might impose these selfsame statutory limitations on abortion. My understanding of past practice is that a statute found to be invalid as applied to a particular plaintiff, but not unconstitutional as a whole, is not simply "struck down" but is, instead, declared unconstitutional as applied to the fact situation before the Court. . . .

For all of the foregoing reasons, I respectfully dissent.

Webster v. *Reproductive Health Services et al.,* 57 L.W. 5023 (1989)

(Multiple opinions)

Mr. Chief Justice Rehnquist announced the judgment of the Court and delivered the opinion of the Court with respect to Parts I, II-A, II-B, and II-C, and an opinion with respect to Parts II-D and III, in which Justice White and Justice Kennedy join.

This appeal concerns the constitutionality of a Missouri statute regulating the performance of abortions. The United States Court of Appeals for the Eighth Circuit struck down several provisions of the statute on the ground that they violated this Court's decision in *Roe* v. *Wade,* 410 U.S. 113 (1973), and cases following it. We . . . now reverse.

I

In June 1986, the Governor of Missouri signed into law Missouri Senate Committee Substitute for House Bill No. 1596 (hereinafter Act or statute), which amended existing state law concerning unborn children and abortions. The Act consisted of 20 provisions, 5 of which are now before the Court. The first provision, or preamble, contains "findings" by the state legislature that "[t]he life of each human being begins at conception," and that "unborn children have protectable interests in life, health, and well-being." . . . The Act further requires that all Missouri laws be interpreted to provide unborn children with the same rights enjoyed by other persons, subject to the Federal Constitution and this Court's precedents. . . .

We think that the doubt cast upon the Missouri statute is not so much a flaw in the statute as it is a reflection of the fact that the rigid trimester analysis of the course of a pregnancy enunciated in *Roe* has resulted in subsequent cases . . . making constitutional law in this area a virtual Procrustean bed. Statutes specifying elements of informed consent to be provided abortion patients, for example, were invalidated if they were thought to "structur[e] . . . the dialogue between the woman and her physician." . . .

Stare decisis is a cornerstone of our legal system, but it has less power in constitutional cases, where, save for constitutional amendments, this Court is the only body able to make needed changes. . . . We have not refrained from reconsideration of a prior construction of the Constitution that has proved "unsound in principle and unworkable in practice." . . . We think the *Roe* trimester framework falls into that category.

In the first place, the rigid *Roe* framework is hardly consistent with the notion of a Constitution cast in general terms, as ours is, and usually speaking in general principles, as ours does. The key elements of the *Roe* framework—trimesters and viability—are not found in the text of the Constitution or in any place else one would expect to find a constitutional principle. Since the bounds of the inquiry are essentially indeterminate, the result has been a web of legal rules that have become increasingly intricate, resembling a code of regulations rather than a body of constitutional doctrine. As Justice White has put it, the trimester framework has left this Court to serve as the country's "*ex officio* medical board with powers to approve or disapprove medical and operative practices and standards throughout the United States." . . .

In the second place, we do not see why the State's interest in protecting potential human life should come into existence only at the point of viability, and that there should therefore be a rigid line allowing state regulation after viability but prohibiting it before viability. . . .

The tests that § 188.029 requires the physician to perform are designed to determine viability. The State here has chosen viability as the point at which its interest in potential human life must be safeguarded. . . . ("No abortion of a viable unborn child shall be performed unless necessary to preserve the life or health of the woman"). It is true that the tests in question increase the expense of abortion, and regulate the discretion of the physician in determining the viability of the fetus. Since the tests will undoubtedly show in many cases that the fetus is not viable, the tests will have been performed for what were in fact second-trimester abortions. But we are satisfied that the requirement of these tests permissibly furthers the State's interest in protecting potential human life, and we therefore believe § 188.029 to be constitutional.

The dissent takes us to task for our failure to join in a "great issues" debate as to whether the Constitution includes an "unenumerated" general right to privacy as recognized in cases such as *Griswold* v. *Connecticut* . . . and *Roe*. But *Griswold* v. *Connecticut,* unlike *Roe,* did not purport to adopt a whole framework, complete with detailed rules and distinctions, to govern the cases in which the asserted liberty interest would apply. As such, it was far different from the opinion, if not the holding, of *Roe* v. *Wade,* which sought to establish a constitutional framework for judging state regulation of abortion during the entire term of pregnancy. That framework sought to deal with areas of medical practice traditionally subject to state regulation, and it sought to balance once and for all by reference only to the calendar the claims of the State to protect the fetus as a form of human life against the claims of a woman to decide for herself whether or not to abort a fetus she was carrying. The experience of the Court in applying *Roe* v. *Wade* in later cases . . . suggests to us that there is wisdom in not unnecessarily attempting to elaborate the abstract differences between a "fundamental right" to abortion, . . . a "limited fundamental constitutional right," which Justice Blackmun's dissent today treats *Roe* as having established, . . . or a liberty interest protected by the Due Process Clause, which we believe it to be. The Missouri testing requirement here is reasonably designed to ensure that abortions are not performed where the fetus is viable—an end which all concede is legitimate—and that is sufficient to sustain its constitutionality.

The dissent also accuses us, *inter alia,* of cowardice and illegitimacy in dealing with "the most politically divisive domestic legal issue of our time." . . . There is no doubt that our holding today will allow some governmental regulation of abortion that would have been [previously] prohibited. . . . But the goal of constitutional adjudication is surely not to remove inexorably "politically divisive" issues from the ambit of the legislative process, whereby the people through their elected representatives deal with matters of concern to them. The goal of constitutional adjudication is to hold true the balance between that which the Constitution puts beyond the reach of the democratic process and that which it does not. We think we have done that today. The dissent's suggestion . . . that legislative bodies, in a Nation where more than half of our population is women, will treat our decision today as an invitation our views but does scant justice to those who serve in such bodies and the people who elect them.

III

Both appellants and the United States as *Amicus Curiae* have urged that we overrule our decision in *Roe* v. *Wade.* . . . The facts of the present case, however, differ from those at issue in *Roe.* Here, Missouri has determined that viability is the point at which its interest in potential human life must be safeguarded. In *Roe,* on the other hand, the Texas statute criminalized the performance of *all* abortions, except when the mother's life was at stake. . . . This case therefore affords us no occasion to revisit the holding of *Roe,* which was that the Texas statute unconstitutionally infringed the right to an abortion derived from the Due Process Clause, . . . and we leave it undisturbed. To the extent indicated in our opinion, we would modify and narrow *Roe* and succeeding cases.

Because none of the challenged provisions of the Missouri Act properly before us conflict with the Constitution, the judgment of the Court of Appeals is *Reversed.*

✣ E S S A Y S

The Supreme Court has treated gender discrimination and the right to an abortion as separate matters. Considering that the Constitution nowhere mentions abortion or privacy as a fundamental right, should the justices use their offices to create such a right? John Hart Ely, a Stanford Law School professor, argues in the opening essay that they should not, and maintains that the *Roe* decision was an inappropriate use of judicial power that resulted in bad constitutional law. Sylvia Law, a law professor at the New York University Law School, takes the opposite position in the second essay. She believes that a constitutional standard of sex-based equality must, of necessity, take into account the real biological differences separating men and women. Only when these differences (such as women's exclusive ability to bear children) are understood will women enjoy meaningful constitutional equality. Law's approach—which is also strongly critical of the paternalistic legislation that sought to protect women on the grounds that they were physically and emotionally infirm—combines the abortion and gender-equality issues in novel and controversial ways. In the closing essay, Deborah Rhode, professor of law and director of the Institute for Research on Women and Gender at Stanford University, explains how these contradictory visions of equality shaped the debate over the ERA.

Why *Roe* v. *Wade* Was a Mistake

JOHN HART ELY

. . . In *Roe* v. *Wade*, decided January 22, 1973, the Supreme Court—Justice Blackmun speaking for everyone but Justices White and Rehnquist—held unconstitutional Texas's (and virtually every other state's) criminal abortion statute. The broad outlines of its argument are not difficult to make out:

1. The right to privacy, though not explicitly mentioned in the Constitution, is protected by the Due Process Clause of the Fourteenth Amendment.

2. This right "is broad enough to encompass a woman's decision whether or not to terminate her pregnancy."

3. This right to an abortion is "fundamental" and can therefore be regulated only on the basis of a "compelling" state interest.

4. The state does have two "important and legitimate" interests here, the first in protecting maternal health, the second in protecting the life (or potential life) of the fetus. But neither can be counted "compelling" throughout the entire pregnancy: Each matures with the unborn child.

These interests are separate and distinct. Each grows in substantiality as the woman approaches term and, at a point during pregnancy, each becomes "compelling."

5. During the first trimester of pregnancy, neither interest is sufficiently compelling to justify any interference with the decision of the woman and her physician. Appellants have referred the Court to medical data indicating that mortality rates for women undergoing early abortions, where abortion is legal, "appear to be as low as or lower than the rates for normal childbirth." Thus the state's interest in protecting maternal health is not compelling during the first trimester. Since the interest in protecting the fetus is not yet compelling either, during the first trimester the state can neither prohibit an abortion nor regulate the conditions under which one is performed.

6. As we move into the second trimester, the interest in protecting the fetus remains less than compelling, and the decision to have an abortion thus continues to control. However, at this point the health risks of abortion begin to exceed those of childbirth. "It follows that, from and after this point, a State may regulate the abortion procedure to the extent that the regulation reasonably relates to the preservation and protection of maternal health." Abortion may not be prohibited during the second trimester, however.

7. At the point at which the fetus becomes viable the interest in protecting it becomes compelling, and therefore from that point on the state can prohibit abortions *except*—and this limitation is also apparently a constitutional command, though it receives no justification in the opinion—when they are necessary to protect maternal life or health.

"The Wages of Crying Wolf: A Comment on Roe v. Wade" by John Hart Ely *The Yale Law Journal* 82 (1973). Reprinted by permission of The Yale Law Journal Company and Fred B. Rothman & Company from *The Yale Law Journal*, Vol. 82, pp. 920–949.

I

A number of fairly standard criticisms can be made of *Roe.* A plausible narrower basis of decision, that of vagueness, is brushed aside in the rush toward broader ground. The opinion strikes the reader initially as a sort of guidebook, addressing questions not before the Court and drawing lines with an apparent precision one generally associates with a commissioner's regulations. On closer examination, however, the precision proves largely illusory. Confusing signals are emitted, particularly with respect to the nature of the doctor's responsibilities and the permissible scope of health regulations after the first trimester. The Court seems, moreover, to get carried away on the subject of remedies: Even assuming the case can be made for an unusually protected constitutional right to an abortion, it hardly seems necessary to have banned during the first trimester *all* state regulation of the conditions under which abortions can be performed.

By terming such criticisms "standard," I do not mean to suggest they are unimportant, for they are not. But if they were all that was wrong with *Roe,* it would not merit special comment.

II

Let us not underestimate what is at stake: Having an unwanted child can go a long way toward ruining a woman's life. And at bottom *Roe* signals the Court's judgment that this result cannot be justified by any good that anti-abortion legislation accomplishes. This surely is an understandable conclusion—indeed it is one with which I agree—but ordinarily the Court claims no mandate to second-guess legislative balances, at least not when the Constitution has designated neither of the values in conflict as entitled to special protection. But even assuming it would be a good idea for the Court to assume this function, *Roe* seems a curious place to have begun. Laws prohibiting the use of "soft" drugs or, even more obviously, homosexual acts between consenting adults can stunt "the preferred life styles" of those against whom enforcement is threatened in very serious ways. It is clear such acts harm no one besides the participants, and indeed the case that the participants are harmed is a rather shaky one. Yet such laws survive, on the theory that there exists a societal consensus that the behavior involved is revolting or at any rate immoral. Of course the consensus is not universal but it is sufficient, and this is what is counted crucial, to get the laws passed and keep them on the books. Whether anti-abortion legislation cramps the life style of an unwilling mother more significantly than anti-homosexuality legislation cramps the life style of a homosexual is a close question. But even granting that it does, the *other* side of the balance looks very different. For there is more than simple societal revulsion to support legislation restricting abortion: Abortion ends (or if it makes a difference, prevents) the life of a human being other than the one making the choice.

The Court's response here is simply not adequate. It agrees, indeed it holds, that after the point of viability (a concept it fails to note will become even less clear than it is now as the technology of birth continues to develop) the interest in protecting the fetus is compelling. Exactly why that is the magic moment is not made clear: Viability, as the Court defines it, is achieved some six to twelve weeks after quickening. (Quickening is the point at which the fetus begins discernibly to move independently of the mother and the point that has historically been deemed crucial—to the extent *any* point between conception and birth has been focused on.) But no, it is *viability* that is constitutionally critical: the Court's defense seems to mistake a definition for a syllogism.

> With respect to the State's important and legitimate interest in potential life, the "compelling" point is at viability. This is so because the fetus then presumably has the capacity of meaningful life outside the mother's womb.

With regard to why the state cannot consider this "important and legitimate interest" prior to viability, the opinion is even less satisfactory. The discussion begins sensibly enough: The interest asserted is not necessarily tied to the question whether the fetus is "alive," for whether or not one calls it a living being, it is an entity with the potential for (and indeed the likelihood of) life. But all of arguable relevance that follows are arguments that fetuses (a) are not recognized as "persons in the whole sense" by legal doctrine generally and (b) are not "persons" protected by the Fourteenth Amendment.

To the extent they are not entirely inconclusive, the bodies of doctrine to which the Court adverts respecting the protection of fetuses under general legal doctrine tend to undercut rather than support its conclusion. And the argument that fetuses (unlike, say, corporations) are not "persons" under the Fourteenth Amendment fares little better. The Court notes that most constitutional clauses using the word "persons"—such as the one outlining the qualifications for the Presidency—appear to have been drafted with postnatal beings in mind. (It might have added that most of them were plainly drafted with *adults* in mind, but I suppose that wouldn't have helped.) In addition, "the appellee conceded on reargument that no case can be cited that holds that a fetus is a person within the meaning of the Fourteenth Amendment." (The other legal contexts in which the question could have arisen are not enumerated.)

The canons of construction employed here are perhaps most intriguing when they are contrasted with those invoked to derive the constitutional right to an abortion. But in any event, the argument that fetuses lack constitutional rights is simply irrelevant. For it has never been held or even asserted that the state interest needed to justify forcing a person to refrain from an activity, *whether or not that activity is constitutionally protected*, must implicate either the life or the constitutional rights of another person. Dogs are not "persons in the whole sense" nor have they constitutional rights, but that does not mean the state cannot prohibit killing them: It does not even mean the state cannot prohibit killing them in the exercise of the First Amendment right of political protest. Come to think of it, draft cards aren't persons either.

Thus even assuming the Court ought generally to get into the business of second-guessing legislative balances, it has picked a strange case with which to begin. Its purported evaluation of the balance that produced anti-abortion legislation simply does not meet the issue: That the life plans of the mother must, not simply may, prevail over the state's desire to protect the fetus simply does not follow from the judgment that the fetus is not a person. Beyond all that, however, the Court has no business getting into that business.

III

Were I a legislator I would vote for a statute very much like the one the Court ends up drafting. I hope this reaction reflects more than the psychological phenomenon that keeps bombardiers sane—the fact that it is somehow easier to "terminate" those you cannot see—and am inclined to think it does: that the mother, unlike the unborn child, has begun to imagine a future for herself strikes me as morally quite significant. But God knows I'm not *happy* with that resolution. Abortion is too much like infanticide on the one hand, and too much like contraception on the other, to leave one comfortable with any answer; and the moral issue it poses is as fiendish as any philosopher's hypothetical.

Of course, the Court often resolves difficult moral questions, and difficult questions yield controversial answers. I doubt, for example, that most people would agree that letting a drug peddler go unapprehended is morally preferable to letting the police kick down his door without probable cause. The difference, of course, is that the Constitution, which legitimates and theoretically controls judicial intervention, has some rather pointed things to say about this choice. There will of course be difficult questions about the applicability of its language to specific facts, but at least the document's special concern with one of the values in conflict is manifest. It simply says nothing, clear or fuzzy, about abortion.

The matter cannot end there, however. The Burger Court, like the Warren Court before it, has been especially solicitous of the right to travel from state to state, demanding a compelling state interest if it is to be inhibited. Yet nowhere in the Constitution is such a right mentioned. It is, however, as clear as such things can be that this right was one the framers intended to protect, most specifically by the Privileges and Immunities Clause of Article IV. The right is, moreover, plausibly inferable from the system of government, and the citizen's role therein, contemplated by the Constitution. The Court in *Roe* suggests an inference of neither sort—from the intent of the framers, or from the governmental system contemplated by the Constitution—in support of the constitutional right to an abortion.

What the Court does assert is that there is a general right of privacy granted special protection—that is, protection above and beyond the baseline requirement of "rationality"—by the Fourteenth Amendment, and that that right "is broad enough to encompass" the right to an abortion. The general right of privacy is inferred, as it was in *Griswold* v. *Connecticut*, from various provisions of the Bill of Rights manifesting a concern with privacy, notably the Fourth Amendment's guarantee against unreasonable searches, the Fifth Amendment's privilege against self-incrimination, and the right, inferred from the First Amendment, to keep one's political associations secret.

One possible response is that all this proves is that the things explicitly mentioned are forbidden, if indeed it does not actually demonstrate a disposition *not* to enshrine anything that might be called a general right of privacy. In fact the Court takes this view when it suits its purposes. (On the *same day* it decided *Roe,* the Court held that a showing of reasonableness was not needed to force someone to provide a grand jury with a voice exemplar, reasoning that the Fifth Amendment was not implicated because the evidence was not "testimonial" and that the Fourth Amendment did not apply because there was no "seizure.") But this approach is unduly crabbed. Surely the Court is entitled, indeed I think it is obligated, to seek out the sorts of evils the framers meant to combat and to move against their twentieth century counterparts.

Thus it seems to me entirely proper to infer a general right of privacy, *so long as some care is taken in defining the sort of right the inference will support.* Those aspects of the First, Fourth and Fifth Amendments to which the Court refers all limit the ways in which, and the circumstances under which, the government can go about gathering information about a person he would rather it did not have. *Katz* v. *United States,* limiting governmental tapping of telephones, may not involve what the framers would have called a "search," but it plainly involves this general concern with privacy. *Griswold* is a long step, even a leap, beyond this, but at least the connection is discernible. Had it been a case that purported to discover in the Constitution a "right to contraception," it would have been *Roe*'s strongest precedent. But the Court in *Roe* gives no evidence of so regarding it, and rightly not. Commentators tend to forget, though the Court plainly has not, that the Court in *Griswold* stressed that it was invalidating only that portion of the Connecticut law that proscribed the *use,* as opposed to the manufacture, sale, or other distribution of contraceptives. That distinction (which would be silly were the right to contraception being constitutionally enshrined) makes sense if the case is rationalized on the ground that the section of the law whose constitutionality was in issue was such that *its enforcement would have been virtually impossible without* the most outrageous sort of governmental prying into the privacy of the home. . . . Thus even assuming (as the Court surely seemed to) that a state can constitutionally seek to minimize or eliminate the circulation and use of contraceptives, Connecticut had acted unconstitutionally by selecting a means, that is a direct ban on use, that would generate intolerably intrusive modes of data-gathering. No such rationalization is attempted by the Court in *Roe*—and understandably not, for whatever else may be involved, it is not a case about governmental snooping.

The Court reports that some amici curiae argued for an unlimited right to do as one wishes with one's body. This theory holds, for me at any rate, much appeal. However, there would have been serious problems with its invocation in this case. In the first place, more than the mother's own body is involved in a decision to have an abortion; a fetus may not be a "person in the whole sense," but it is certainly not nothing. Second, it is difficult to find a basis for thinking that the theory was meant to be given constitutional sanction: Surely it is no part of the "privacy" interest the Bill of Rights suggests. . . . Unfortunately, having thus rejected the amici's attempt to define the bounds of the general constitutional right of which the right to an abortion is a part, on the theory that the general right described has little to do with privacy, the Court provides neither an alternative definition nor an account of why *it* thinks privacy is involved. It simply announces that the right to privacy "is broad enough to encompass a woman's decision whether or not to terminate her pregnancy." Apparently this conclusion is thought to derive from the passage that immediately follows it:

> The detriment that the State would impose upon the pregnant woman by denying this choice altogether is apparent. Specific and direct harm medically diagnosable even in early pregnancy may be involved. Maternity, or additional offspring, may force upon the woman a distressful life and future. Psychological harm may be imminent. Mental and physical health may be taxed by child care. There is also the distress, for all concerned, associated with the unwanted child, and there is the problem of bringing a child into a family already unable, psychologically and otherwise, to care for it. In other cases, as in this one, the additional difficulties and continuing stigma of unwed motherhood may be involved.

All of this is true and ought to be taken very seriously. But it has nothing to do with privacy in the Bill of Rights sense or any other the Constitution suggests. I suppose there is nothing to prevent one from using the word "privacy" to mean the freedom to live one's life without governmental interference. But the Court obviously does not so use the term. Nor could it, for such a right is at stake in *every* case. Our life styles are constantly limited, often seriously, by governmental regulation; and while many of us would prefer less direction, granting that desire the status of a preferred constitutional right would yield a system of "government" virtually unrecognizable to and only slightly more recognizable to our forefathers. The Court's observations concerning the serious, life-shaping costs of having a child prove what might to the thoughtless have seemed unprovable: That even though a human life, or a potential human life, hangs in the balance, the moral dilemma abortion poses is so difficult as to be heartbreaking. What they fail to do is even begin to resolve that dilemma so far as our governmental system is concerned by associating either side of the balance with a value inferable from the Constitution.

But perhaps the inquiry should not end even there. In his famous *Carolene Products* footnote, Justice Stone suggested that the interests to which the Court can responsibly give extraordinary constitutional protection include not only those expressed in the Constitution but also those that are unlikely to receive adequate consideration in the political process, specifically the interests of "discrete and insular minorities" unable to form effective political alliances. There can be little doubt that such considerations have influenced the direction, if only occasionally the rhetoric, of the recent Courts. My repeated efforts to convince my students that sex should be treated as a "suspect classification" have convinced me it is no easy matter to state such considerations in a "principled" way. But passing that problem, *Roe* is not an appropriate case for their invocation.

Compared with men, very few women sit in our legislatures, a fact I believe should bear some relevance—even without an Equal Rights Amendment—to the appropriate standard of review for legislation that favors men over women. But *no* fetuses sit in our legislatures. Of course they have their champions, but so have women. The two interests have clashed repeatedly in the political arena, and had continued to do so up to the date of the opinion, generating quite a wide variety of accommodations. By the Court's lights virtually all of the legislative accommodations had unduly favored fetuses; by its definition of victory, women had lost. Yet in every legislative balance one of the competing interests loses to some extent; indeed usually, as here, they both do. On some occasions the Constitution throws its weight on the side of one of them, indicating the balance must be restruck. And on others—and this is Justice Stone's suggestion—it is at least arguable that, constitutional directive or not, the Court should throw *its* weight on the side of a minority demanding in court more than it was able to achieve politically. But even assuming this suggestion can be given principled content, it was clearly intended and should be reserved for those interests which, *as compared with the interests to which they have been subordinated,* constitute minorities unusually incapable of protecting themselves. Compared with men, women may constitute such a "minority"; compared with the unborn, they do not. I'm not sure I'd know a discrete and insular minority if I saw one, but confronted with a multiple choice question requiring me to designate (a) women or (b) fetuses as one, I'd expect no credit for the former answer.

Of course a woman's freedom to choose an abortion is part of the "liberty" the Fourteenth Amendment says shall not be denied without due process of law, as indeed is anyone's freedom to do what he wants. But "due process" generally guarantees only that the inhibition be procedurally fair and that it have some "rational" connection—though plausible is probably a better word—with a permissible governmental goal. What is unusual about *Roe* is that the liberty involved is accorded a far more stringent protection, so stringent that a desire to preserve the fetus's existence is unable to overcome it—a protection more stringent, I think it fair to say, than that the present Court accords the freedom of the press explicitly guaranteed by the First Amendment. What is frightening about *Roe* is that this super-protected right is not inferable from the language of the Constitution, the framers' thinking respecting the specific problem in issue, any general value derivable from the provisions they included, or the nation's governmental structure. Nor is it explainable in terms of the unusual political impotence of the group judicially protected vis-à-vis the interest that legislatively prevailed over it. And that, I believe—the predictable early re-

action to *Roe* notwithstanding ("more of the same Warren-type activism")—
is a charge that can responsibly be leveled at no other decision of the past
twenty years. At times the inferences the Court has drawn from the values
the Constitution marks for special protection have been controversial, even
shaky, but never before has its sense of an obligation to draw one been so
obviously lacking.

IV

. . . I am aware the Court cannot simply "lay the Article of the Constitution
which is invoked beside the statute which is challenged and . . . decide
whether the latter squares with the former." That is precisely the reason
commentators are needed.

> [P]recisely because it is the Constitution alone which warrants judicial in-
> terference in sovereign operations of the State, the basis of judgment as to
> the Constitutionality of state action must be a rational one, approaching
> the text which is the only commission for our power not in a literalistic
> way, as if we had a tax statute before us, but as the basic charter of our
> society, setting out in spare but meaningful terms the principles of
> government.
>
> No matter how imprecise in application to specific modern fact situations,
> the constitutional guarantees do provide a direction, a goal, an ideal citizen-
> government relationship. They rule out many alternative directions, goals,
> and ideals.

And they fail to support the ruling out of others.

Of course that only begins the inquiry. Identification and definition of
the values with which the Constitution is concerned will often fall short of
indicating with anything resembling clarity the deference to be given those
values when they conflict with others society finds important. (Though even
here the process is sometimes more helpful than the commentators would
allow.) Nor is it often likely to generate, fullblown, the "neutral" principle
that will avoid embarrassment in future cases. But though the identification
of a constitutional connection is only the beginning of analysis, it is a necessary beginning. The point that often gets lost in the commentary, and
obviously got lost in *Roe,* is that *before* the Court can get to the "balancing"
stage, *before* it can worry about the next case and the case after that (or
even about its institutional position) it is under an obligation to trace its
premises to the charter from which it derives its authority. A neutral and
durable principle may be a thing of beauty and a joy forever. But if it lacks
connection with any value the Constitution marks as special, it is not a
constitutional principle and the Court has no business imposing it. I hope
that will seem obvious to the point of banality. Yet those of us to whom it
does seem obvious have seldom troubled to say so. And because we have
not, we must share in the blame for this decision.

The Reality of Biological Differences
for Gender Equality

SYLVIA LAW

[My] central thesis is that the development of modern constitutional sex equality doctrine has suffered from a lack of focus on biological reproductive differences between men and women. The reality of sex-based physical differences poses a significant problem for a society committed to ideals of individual human freedom and equality of opportunity.

To the extent that constitutional doctrine shapes culture and individual identity, an equality doctrine that denies the reality of biological difference in relation to reproduction reflects an idea about personhood that is inconsistent with people's actual experience of themselves and the world. The constitutional ideal alienates people from their own experience. Given our history in which the idea of "man" is the linguistic and legal equivalent of "person," a concept of equality that denies biological difference has particularly adverse effects upon women.

The central biological difference between men and women is that only women have the capacity to create a human being. For many people, the decision to bear a child is jointly made by a man and a woman and is the occasion for joyous commitment to one another, to the child, and to the future. But it is not always so. Only women can grow a human being, and, although sperm is also needed, it is easily obtainable. The power to create people is awesome. Men are profoundly disadvantaged by the reality that only women can produce a human being and experience the growth of a child in pregnancy. Pregnancy and childbirth are also burdensome to health, mobility, independence, and sometimes to life itself, and women are profoundly disadvantaged in that they alone bear these burdens. And although men may be disadvantaged by their relatively minor role in reproduction, we have constructed a society in which men are advantaged, relative to women, in important material and spiritual ways.

The focus here is exclusively on a relatively narrow point of constitutional sex equality doctrine. I do not deal comprehensively with the critical equality issues of state action and the public/private split, or with the question when discrimination can be proved by showing that state policy in fact has discriminatory effects, or with the issue of affirmative programs to redress the disabilities of past discrimination. Further, I make no effort to describe an affirmative program to promote greater sex-based equality. The judicial enforcement of constitutional norms, even when broadly conceived and applied, is not likely to produce sex-based equality. Achieving sex-based equality requires social movement for transformation of the family, child rearing arrangements, the economy, the wage labor market, and human consciousness. No constitutional principle mandates or allows courts to effectuate the range of changes needed to allow actual equality between men and women.

From "Rethinking Sex in the Constitution" by Sylvia A. Law. *University of Pennsylvania Law Review*, 132, 1984, pp. 955–963, 970–977, 979–982, 1036–1040. Reprinted by permission.

Nonetheless, constitutional concepts of equality are important both because of their concrete impact on legislative power and individual right and because constitutional ideas reflect and shape culture.

The relationship between constitutional concepts and culture is reciprocal. The rise of the women's movement in the early 1970s provided impetus for Supreme Court revision of constitutional standards applicable to laws controlling reproduction and incorporating sex-based classifications. The ideas of equality reflected both in Supreme Court decisions under the fourteenth amendment and in the recently defeated Equal Rights Amendment in turn generate more general thought about sex-based equality. Contemporary ideas of equality are also reciprocal in relation to our past in two significant ways. First, historically, biology provided a central justification for the subjugation of women. That history partially explains the lack of focus on reproductive difference in contemporary equality doctrine and also suggests the need for close attention to such differences in developing new ideas of equality. Second, "protection" of women—construction of the pedestal/cage—was a core mechanism for oppression of women. Contemporary feminists are hence rightly skeptical of measures that protect women by providing them with special treatment.

At various periods the law has embodied different ideas about sex-based differences. Prior to the mid-nineteenth century, culture and religion required women to marry, and the law declared the married woman dead. The law denied married women both identity and power. With the enactment of the married women's property acts in the late 1800s, the law recognized women's existence. But two legal constructs enforced the subservience of women and the dominance of men in the home and wage market: first, the creation of separate spheres for men and women and, second, enactment of limits on women's power to control reproductive capacity.

Assumptions about biological difference and destiny provided the prime justification for creating a separate, inferior legal status for women. The law denied women equal opportunity for wage work and participation in public life. It reinforced social and religious commitment to family-centered child rearing. Women were required, by law and custom, to care for men and children. Although women and children were and are entitled to look to men for financial support, that expectation was and is not theoretically enforceable during an ongoing marriage nor as a practical matter when marriage ends.

For most of the twentieth century, the law also preserved the dominance of men by creating obstacles to women's ability to control their reproductive capacity. Beginning in the mid-1800s the law restricted access to contraception and abortion. Sex outside of marriage was condemned, by society and the law, much more harshly and consistently for women than for men. If an unmarried woman became pregnant, she needed to persuade a man to marry her. The law did not compel a man to take responsibility for the pregnancy he had helped to cause or the child he had helped to create. The law condemned the child as a bastard and subjected the child to significant legal disabilities. Laws disfavoring the children of an unmarried woman encouraged her sexual purity and made the social and economic status of both the child and mother "ultimately dependent upon the male."

Legal structures that support the dominance of men and subservience of women are fundamentally inconsistent with constitutional ideals of individual worth and equality of opportunity. It is crucial to understand, then, why contemporary constitutional sex equality doctrine evidences a lack of concern about the implications of state regulations that are based on biological differences and have been prominent in establishing and perpetuating the inequality of women. . . .

Legal concepts of equality are informed by social vision. A growing literature attempts to give concrete content to social visions of sexual equality. In legal doctrine the dominant vision of sex equality is an assimilationist one, which conceives of a society in which sex would be a wholly unimportant characteristic of individuals, having no greater significance than eye color has in our own society. The assimilationist ideal posits that some characteristics—race, sex, eye color—do not describe differences that should ever be allowed to matter in any significant way. Even in the most personal social relations, an individual who selected friends on the basis of eye color would be regarded as idiosyncratic. The assimilationist vision asserts that it is unjust to distribute rights or responsibilities on the basis of distinctions that do not ever describe relevant differences—sex, race, or eye color. This vision is best developed in relation to race. The assimilationist view of sex equality is attractive to constitutional lawyers because it builds upon analogies between race- and sex-based discrimination.

The analogies between race- and sex-based discrimination are powerful. Blacks and women share a similar history of oppression; prior to the Civil War the laws defining the status of blacks and women borrowed freely from one another. Sex, like race, is an immutable characteristic. . . .

During the 1960s, the civil rights movement inspired many Americans to grapple with the ideal of equality and the difficulty of achieving it. Millions of blacks and whites saw the pervasiveness and subtlety of racism. It is quite astonishing that throughout the decade, as the Supreme Court decided cases that addressed issues of race discrimination and expanded concepts of constitutional equality beyond their historic racial core, the Court never applied ideals of equality to sex-based limitations. Through most of the 1960s few observed the parallels between racism and sexism that Gunnar Myrdal had so trenchantly documented in 1944. Nonetheless, the growth of consciousness supporting the aspiration of racial equality and the externally imposed and internally accepted stereotypes that prevented its achievement facilitated perception of the injustice of sex-defined legal and social constraints on human freedom.

By the late 1960s many women had participated in the civil rights and antiwar movements and had learned new political skills. Also of invaluable importance to the struggle for women's rights were the consciousness-raising groups of the late 1960s. Through these groups women discovered that their most intimate personal concerns were shared by other women and that their private, individual lives were shaped by deep social and cultural structures.

These groups provided women with the solidarity and strength to seek transformation of themselves and society. The contemporary revision of constitutional doctrine in relation to sex equality and reproduction is the product of these radical shifts in women's consciousness and behavior.

When women began challenging legal restraints on human liberty, their central focus was on laws denying women access to abortion. . . . These women, in cooperation with medical, family-planning, and religious groups, persuaded many state legislatures to liberalize criminal statutes prohibiting abortions.

In 1969 women began integrating constitutional litigation into this organizational and educational effort. Suits often named hundreds and sometimes thousands of women as individual plaintiffs. Live testimony educated judges, lawyers, and the public about the impact of unwanted pregnancy upon women's lives. Women filled courtrooms, bringing babies and the coat hangers that symbolize illegal abortions. Despite women's paramount concern for the right to obtain abortions, the constitutionality of government restrictions on the right was not presented to the courts as a clear issue of sex equality. Rather, women challenged the abortion restrictions on two other grounds: first, the fourteenth amendment's guarantee of liberty, as explicated by the Supreme Court in *Griswold* v. *Connecticut,* protected the right to an abortion; second, the fourteenth amendment's guarantee of equality precluded certain limits on the availability of abortions because they discriminated against poor and non-white women. In addition, in several major cases, these claims by women were joined by physicians' challenges to the abortion restrictions based on claims that the laws were impermissibly vague and violated the privacy of the doctor/patient relationship. . . .

The Supreme Court did not apply the fourteenth amendment's guarantee of equality to invalidate a sex classification until 1971, near the beginning of the Burger Court era. In *Reed* v. *Reed* the Court struck down an Idaho law that gave men a blanket preference over women as administrators of estates. . . . Thus, the unanimous decision in *Reed* v. *Reed* signified that classifications based on sex would be treated less deferentially by reviewing courts, but it failed to explain why or how.

Another major development in relation to sex-based equality came in 1971. The United States Congress held hearings on the Equal Rights Amendment (ERA), which was submitted to the states for ratification in 1972. A centerpiece of the ratification hearings was a *Yale Law Journal* article, written by several young feminist legal scholars and Thomas Emerson, perhaps the nation's leading scholar of constitutional civil rights and liberties. This article was intended to provide an interpretative guide to the meaning of the proposed ERA, and it was widely regarded as such, both in the Senate debate and in the subsequent ratification debates in the states. The Yale ERA article established as the "basic principle" of the amendment that "sex is not a permissible factor in determining the legal rights of women, or of men. . . . In short, sex is a prohibited classification." The article also concluded, however, that the ERA would not prohibit all legislative distinctions between the sexes: The authors wrote that the fundamental legal principle underlying the ERA "does not preclude legislation (or other official action) which regulates, takes into account, or otherwise deals with a physical characteristic unique to one sex. . . . This subsidiary principle is limited to *physical* characteristics . . . ."

The article argued that laws regulating these physical characteristics should be scrutinized by courts in the same way that sex-neutral rules that have a disparate impact on women would be scrutinized. The authors contended that the ERA would prohibit both such laws when they served as a subterfuge for sex-based discrimination, but they did not advocate any independent principle for laws regulating physical characteristics unique to one sex. Most interestingly, the article's discussion and application of its test to regulations of physical characteristics made no mention of laws restricting access to abortions. Nor did the article mention laws excluding pregnant women from health insurance programs. These two omissions are especially striking because abortion rights and pregnancy benefits are much more central to the goal of sex equality than the examples discussed in the article, such as laws that regulate wet nurses, sperm donors, medical leave for childbearing, and determination of fatherhood. . . .

The possibility of greater judicial sensitivity to issues of sex equality was, however, suggested by the Court's decision in *Reed.* Two years later, ACLU [American Civil Liberties Union] counsel Ruth Bader Ginsburg urged, in *Frontiero* v. *Richardson,* that the Court's scrutiny of sex-based classifications be formalized and that such classifications, like those based on race, be treated as constitutionally suspect. The task confronting the appellants in *Frontiero* was formidable. At that time, the prevailing constitutional law still included *Bradwell* v. *Illinois, Muller* v. *Oregon, Goesaert* v. *Cleary,* and *Hoyt* v. *Florida.* The ACLU brief discussed these cases under the consummately understated banner, "Precedent in Need of Reevaluation." The argument urging that sex-based classifications be treated as constitutionally suspect incorporated three themes. First, historically women have been subjugated, their essential humanity denied, and the pedestal upon which they have been placed has all too often been a cage. Second, women seek to be judged on their individual merits; the stereotypes of married women as economically dependent are inaccurate generally and particularly as applied to the Frontieros. And third, sex is an immutable characteristic that frequently bears no relation to ability to perform or contribute. Historical oppression, the value of individuality, and the presumptive inaccuracy of sex-based stereotypes all supported vigorous scrutiny of sex-based classifications.

Like the Yale ERA article, the ACLU brief in *Frontiero* did not focus on the reality of biological difference. It mentioned biological difference only once, stating that legislative "discrimination grounded on sex, for purposes unrelated to any biological difference between the sexes, ranks with legislative discrimination based on race." The failure to address the issue of biological difference is justifiable in relation to the specific claim presented by Sharon Frontiero, who was challenging a law that required that male spouses—but not female spouses—be actually dependent, in order to receive military benefits. Biological differences had no relation to the sex discriminatory military pay policy at issue in the case. But if the *Frontiero* briefs are examined not simply as an individual family's challenge to a sex discriminatory pay policy but as an attempt to articulate a coherent scheme for addressing issues of sex equality, the failure to address in any detail the relation between equality and biological difference is puzzling. It is also troubling that the brief's only reference to biological difference suggests that laws based on such difference may not raise equality concerns and, consequently, may not need to be scrutinized as carefully.

In *Frontiero*, four Justices ruled that sex-based classifications should be regarded as constitutionally suspect. Four Justices concurred in the result but thought it sufficient to invalidate the classification as unreasonable, without addressing the general issue of the appropriate constitutional standard for judging sex-based classifications.

On January 23, 1973, just after the argument in *Frontiero*, the Court held in *Roe* v. *Wade* that the constitutional right to privacy protects the right of women and their physicians to determine whether or not to terminate pregnancy. Nothing the Supreme Court has ever done has been more concretely important for women. Laws denying access to abortion have a sex-specific impact. Although both men and women seek to control reproduction, only women become pregnant. Only women have abortions. Laws restricting access to abortion have a devastating sex-specific impact. Despite the decision's overwhelming importance to women, it was not grounded on the principle of sex equality. The plaintiffs in *Roe* v. *Wade* and *Doe* v. *Bolton* had not challenged the abortion restrictions as sex discriminatory, and the Supreme Court did not rely upon the sex-specific impact of laws restricting access to abortion.

Thus, during the early 1970s the constitutional rights of women began to be recognized by the Supreme Court, but several forces encouraged the Court to avoid addressing the relationship between sex-based equality and biological differences. First, those primarily responsible for developing a constitutional doctrine of sex-based equality, including the ACLU and the proponents of the ERA, adopted what amounted to an assimilationist vision of sex equality, which minimized the significance of biological differences. Second, many who worked to develop constitutional doctrine to support reproductive freedom emphasized rights of privacy, physician discretion, and the vagueness and uncertainty of the criminal laws prohibiting abortions. The decision to deemphasize sex discrimination in the reproductive freedom cases reflected a judgment that privacy was a more conservative and, hence, stronger constitutional tool than sex-based equality. . . .

The Supreme Court's doctrine of sex-based equality under the fourteenth amendment is exceedingly unstable. This instability is manifest in the sharp divisions in analysis and result in cases such as *Parham* v. *Hughes, Caban* v. *Mohammed, Lehr* v. *Robertson,* and *Michael M.* v. *Superior Court.* The core principles of the Court's equality doctrine—the requirement that men and women be treated as individuals rather than stereotypes and the recognition that laws based on stereotypical assumptions are self-fulfilling as well as inaccurate in particular cases—are inconsistent with the approach that various members of the Court have taken in these cases. An unstable present necessarily implies an uncertain future.

The fourteenth amendment guarantees equal treatment under the law and recognition of the injustice of denying men and women opportunities solely on the basis of sex is broad and deep. It would be possible to achieve greater strength and stability in sexual equality doctrine through the approach advocated here, which focuses directly on the reality and myth of biological differences. The Court could draw a sharp distinction between laws creating sex-based classifications and laws regulating sex-specific physical character-istics and still recognize that laws regulating sex-specific physical character-istics implicate the core concerns of sex-based equality.

For the most part the argument advanced here builds upon equality and privacy doctrine. Courts are skilled at the manipulation of doctrine. When doctrine develops quickly, in response to large changes in consciousness, modification in the light of experience and insight seems particularly appropriate. . . .

The Equal Rights Amendment has been defeated, but it is certain to rise again. What is not so certain is whether we will continue to regard laws regulating reproductive biology as tangential to the constitutional guarantee of sex-based equality. The direction in which the Court will move under the fourteenth amendment and the vision of sex-based equality reflected in the next ERA depend in large part upon the vision of equality adopted by those who shape claims of sex-based equality and reproductive freedom under existing constitutional guarantees and those who fight for the new ERA.

The ideas developed here are simply one woman's thoughts about the meaning of sex equality, under either the fourteenth amendment or the ERA. Although I support the Equal Rights Amendment, its major congres-sional proponents and the leaders of the struggle to enact it have expressed a different vision of sex-based equality. Strong reasons, both political and conceptual, support separation of doctrines of sex equality and reproductive freedom. The political reality is that extreme conservative religious and political groups have made opposition to abortion an organizing issue—a *sine qua non* political test. Although there is wide political support for equal pay for equal work and the claims of individual aspirational women seeking access to traditional male power, women's claims for control of their bodies present a more profound challenge to prevailing structures of male domi-nance, and are less widely accepted. Conceptual support for the separation of sex-based equality and reproductive freedom rests on skepticism whether courts are able to implement, with good faith and good sense, a concept of sex equality that recognizes the reality of biological difference. Further, privacy doctrine is richly developed in relation to reproductive freedom, and a shift to sex equality analysis in these cases seems, to many, unlikely.

Nonetheless, . . . a strong concept of sex-based equality will require that we come to grips with the reality of sex-based biological differences, either through the approach proposed here or in some other way. A political struggle that embraces recognition that men and women are both limited by biology and able to transcend it may be stronger than one that ignores the core reality of sex difference in relation to reproductive biology.

Are we locked into the road we have taken? Are the two lines of constitutional doctrine—reproductive freedom and sex-based equality—which began as a unified whole to preserve male dominance and diverged in the early 1970s, now on fixed projections that move ineluctably further apart? I think not. The law is a social creation that produced the legal structure that made biology destiny and enforced the subjugation of women. In the 1970s we began the divergent movements to create a different social construct of sex equality and reproductive freedom. We can, if we choose, move toward a more unified understanding of the ways in which the law perpetuates sex-based restraints on human equality and liberty.

Gender as Disadvantage Rather Than Difference

DEBORAH L. RHODE

Instrumental Claims

[The proponents of the Equal Rights Amendment argued] that it would provide the most effective means of combating sex-based classifications in areas such as employment, education, welfare, credit, pensions, domestic relations, and military service. To seek piecemeal legislative or judicial remedies against each discriminatory action could result in interminable delay and inordinate expense, while offering no protection against future abuses. It would, as one supporter put it, be like "enforcing the Emancipation Proclamation plantation by plantation."

Moreover, court decisions under existing statutory and constitutional provisions had produced "uneven developments marked by sharply divided opinions." According to many proponents, that result stemmed from the Supreme Court's unwillingness to view sex, like race, as a "suspect classification" triggering "strict scrutiny." Such scrutiny requires that the challenged classification serve a "compelling" state interest that cannot be achieved by less burdensome means. Few discriminatory practices have survived this test. Accordingly, proponents hoped that an equal-rights amendment would mandate a comparable level of scrutiny for sex-based classifications and thus promote a more egalitarian social order.

There were a number of difficulties with this argument. As opponents often pointed out, the volume of antidiscrimination legislation, administrative regulation, and judicial intervention was already increasing without a constitutional catalyst. Many legal developments that anticipated the consequences of an equal-rights amendment were making it appear less essential and less worthy of political struggle. Moreover, passage of the ERA [Equal Rights Amendment] would not eliminate the need for piecemeal litigation to interpret its meaning and secure its enforcement. Analogies to the Eman-

Reprinted by permission of the publishers from *Justice and Gender: Sex Discrimination and the Law* by Deborah L. Rhode. Cambridge, MA: Harvard University Press, pp. 65–72. Copyright © 1989 by the President and Fellows of Harvard College.

cipation Proclamation also missed the mark. By the 1970s, the evils of slavery were self-evident. The need for an equal-rights amendment was not. According to one representative public-opinion survey of the early seventies, 75 percent of male respondents and 71 percent of females considered the position of women in American society to be either "excellent or good." Once Schlafly and her followers raised concerns about the ERA's effects on laws advantaging women, doubts about the necessity of constitutional change grew stronger.

The loss of preferential treatment was one of the opposition's most effective themes. While supporters appealed to women's aspirations, opponents appealed to women's fears. According to Schlafly, a constitutional mandate of equal treatment would jeopardize a host of "precious rights," particularly those related to family and military service obligations. Opponents claimed, for example, that wives would lose entitlement to support during or after marriage and would have a "*legal obligation* to go out to work to provide half the family income." Such predictions evoked broad concerns. Wives with unstable marriages or few marketable skills complained that the amendment might be "all right for a younger woman," but that they were unsure how to support themselves and their children under an equal-rights amendment. To traditional homemakers, a constitutional mandate seemed to offer an unnecessary and unwelcome exchange: they would pay the price of expanding some abstract set of opportunities that they had never experienced and would never enjoy.

Opposition arguments concerning family law were among those most irritating to ERA proponents. Given Schlafly's training as a lawyer, her claims appeared somewhat disingenuous. As supporters pointed out, the amendment would cover only state action; it would not dictate families' private financial arrangements or require wives to work. Nor would it materially alter husbands' support obligations. Under current laws, courts virtually never enforced such obligations in ongoing marriages; and once a marriage terminated, judges would still be free under sex-blind provisions to require support for dependent homemakers. Even without the ERA, most state legislatures were already enacting gender-neutral family laws, and judicial decisions barring sex-based alimony statutes were accelerating that trend. As proponents noted, such statutory modifications had not produced the "radical" upheavals in family life that Schlafly predicted.

These rejoinders were not entirely effective in allaying public concerns. [T]raditional homemakers have not always fared well under gender-neutral family law reforms. Although such provisions have avoided sex-based stereotyping, they have also failed to address sex-based disadvantages. The real weakness in Schlafly's claim was that most wives already were, and always had been, less secure than she implied, and gender-neutral mandates were not the cause. The difficulty was not with reforms such as those replacing "wife" with "spouse" in alimony statutes that authorized "equitable" awards. Rather the difficulty lay in decisionmakers' interpretations of what "equity" meant, interpretations that undervalued domestic work and its effect on an individual's earning potential. Such judicial biases were as apparent under sex-specific statutes as under their gender-neutral replacements. But that message was unwelcome in many quarters. Many homemakers were more inclined to reject the messenger than to acknowledge their own vulnerability.

Opponents' other most effective argument involved military service. Equality in the workplace was one thing; equality in the trenches was quite another. Throughout state capitols, legislators visualized their daughters sharing barracks, bunkers, or latrines with hardened combat troops, and having their "fair forms blasted into fragments" by "bayonets, bombs, [and] bullets." The issue was not only the future of womanhood but the security of the nation. According to politicians such as Illinois Representative Webber Borchers, women's "inadequate hip structure . . . tender [feet]," and inability "to press the attack" would "hamstring" the infantry.

On this issue, proponents never developed a consistent response. The most common rejoinder—that Congress already had power to draft women—was hardly adequate to the occasion. According to Schlafly, the ERA would require women to assume the same military obligations as men, including combat service. The legal basis for that assertion was, however, open to dispute, as a subsequent Supreme Court decision permitting sex-based draft registration suggested. Thus, some proponents took the position that the ERA would not mandate women in combat; under the Constitution's War Powers clause, judges could properly defer to military leaders' resolution of the issue.

Other ERA supporters, including the authors of a highly influential *Yale Law Journal* article, maintained that the amendment would mandate sex-neutral treatment in the armed forces. This position was consistent with Congress' refusal on several occasions to endorse an equal-rights amendment with exemptions for military service. Proponents also cited evidence indicating that women were capable of performing many combat jobs and that their exclusion from such positions had adverse effects on military and civilian opportunities. From this perspective, until women were prepared to accept the full responsibilities of citizenship, including the draft, they would have difficulty claiming its full entitlements. Most Americans, however, took a different view. According to public-opinion polls, a majority of respondents opposed equal treatment for men and women in the military, and state legislators did not appear to be an exception.

A final cluster of arguments that proved effective with some groups involved sexuality, reproduction, and privacy. Catholic and fundamentalist leaders often linked the ERA with legalized abortion, homosexual marriage, and the related evils of a "singles society." Although proponents generally denied those connections, their position was not unproblematic. Supporters were, of course, correct in noting that the Supreme Court had based abortion rights on considerations of privacy rather than equality. However, as opponents also pointed out, feminists had invoked state equal-rights amendments and federal equal-protection guarantees as a justification for governmental funding of abortion. On issues of sexual preference, proponents often noted that courts generally had not interpreted legal mandates against gender discrimination to bar discrimination against gays or lesbians as long as males and females were treated similarly. But some feminists opposed those rulings and were reluctant to relinquish the ERA as a potential ground for challenging them.

Opponents' privacy arguments had less legal substance, though many members of their audience may not have recognized as much. The most notorious example involved Schlafly's account of the ERA's effects on public bathrooms. In her view, "the only reason that this nation has separate restrooms for men and women and boys and girls is sex. Consequently, being a distinction based on sex, the ERA would abolish the power of the Federal Government and the power of the 50 states to require separate facilities of this nature for persons of different sexes." With comparable logic, other opponents projected the demise of sex-segregated locker rooms, saunas, hospital facilities, and homes for wayward girls.

Such arguments ignored the legislative history of the amendment, which clearly preserved an exception for privacy-related regulation. Moreover, the triviality of the argument invited ridicule. Within some constituencies, opponents' resort to "potty politics" was counterproductive. ERA supporters capitalized on the fact that Schlafly herself had apparently managed to survive the ordeal of undifferentiated restrooms during her frequent airline excursions to testify against the amendment. Other proponents claimed that women's greatest risk concerning single-sex bathrooms was that women would be cleaning them. Yet the persistence of some privacy-related claims suggests that they may have touched deeper nerves than proponents generally acknowledged. Although the particular examples opponents cited may not have had great independent significance, when taken together, they evoked a vision of androgyny that threatened core American values.

Symbolic Underpinnings

For both sides in the ratification campaign, the ERA became a stand-in for more fundamental concerns and a battleground for symbolic politics. To proponents, the amendment represented a significant affirmation of equality as well as a means for attaining it. To opponents, the ERA appeared as a "unisex" mandate, a tool to "nullify . . . distinction[s] between the sexes," and to transform the United States into a "gender-free society." Thus, Ronald Reagan maintained, "I do not want to see sex and sexual differences treated as casually and amorally as dogs and other beasts treat them. I believe this could happen under the ERA." From opponents' perspective, the amendment's egalitarian premises ignored sex-linked characteristics that were biologically determined or culturally desirable.

Once again, the nineteenth-century cult of domesticity found adherents. In the world as ERA opponents conceived it, men and women assumed unique roles, dictated by nature and sanctified by scripture. Or, as Schlafly succinctly put it, "Women have babies so men should support them." Despite the fact that over half of all women were in the workforce, "marriage and the home [remained] the greatest liberation for women."

The claim was not without irony, particularly given the source. The

Supreme Court had, a century earlier, invoked precisely the same argument about women's maternal mission when it denied female applicants entry to Schlafly's chosen profession. Indeed, as ERA supporters occasionally noted, America's preeminent defender of woman's "God-given right to stay home" rarely exercised that right. Schlafly was a lawyer with a Harvard master's degree, the author of several books, the editor of a prominent conservative newsletter, and a political organizer with a national following.

Other ERA opponents were in less anomalous positions. Many of these women were traditional homemakers who felt embattled and embittered by feminist rhetoric. Once "women's libbers" had been cast as the driving force behind the amendment, opponents were often preaching to the converted. Public-opinion polls throughout the 1970s indicated that most Americans did not view the organized feminist movement in a favorable light, even though many supported certain central feminist objectives. Opposition to that movement galvanized opposition to constitutional change. To members of groups such as the Feminine Anti-Feminists, Gigi Gals Galore Against the ERA, Winsome Wives and Homemakers, and Women Who Want to Be Women, Schlafly's message appeared flattering and reassuring. It exalted their values and ennobled their station. By contrast, much feminist rhetoric implied that these women had made the wrong choices and demanded reappraisal of their self-image, priorities, and daily lives.

That message was understandably unwelcome in many quarters. For some, it seemed to come too late. Those who had followed traditional paths resented the assault, and the anti-ERA campaign offered a way to vent their frustration and reaffirm their sense of importance in a changing social order. Once family and feminism were fixed as the symbolic poles of debate, many women would be expected to rally around the symbol by which they had ordered their own priorities.

For other women whose lives were less traditional, but whose opportunities appeared limited, the assumptions of the women's movement appeared to be out of touch with daily realities. Among those who lacked adequate skills, mobility, or employment opportunities, the feminist agenda seemed elitist and irrelevant. Particularly among minority women, many of whom confronted constant problems of racism, poverty, and violence, a campaign for constitutional symbols seemed largely beside the point.

Women with unsatisfactory employment opportunities often measured their status and self-worth by traditional feminine standards. By devaluing these standards, the "liberation" movement appeared to endorse an alternative as limited as the domestic stereotypes it sought to supplant. According to one New York opponent, "I know [feminists] are intelligent women but I don't [think] they put enough value on the feminine role in the home. The woman who stays home is preparing the next generation but that's not respected. They don't even value volunteer work. I just don't [think] they've tried to reach women in general."

These problems in the equal-rights campaign mirrored the problems of feminism over the last two decades. While radical rhetoric played an important role in expanding public consciousness on women's issues, it also alienated some constituencies who were most in need of assistance. For many women, it was Schlafly who gave dignity and significance to a domestic role that society as a whole has undervalued.

Other grounds for opposition included resistance to change in general and to women's advancement in particular. Within some conservative constituencies, the amendment became an all-purpose symbolic scapegoat. According to many opponents, the ERA, by weakening women's traditional role, would also weaken traditional values. In tones reminiscent of anti-suffragist rhetoric, opponents predicted that the ultimate result of equal rights would be an array of social problems including increased "divorce . . . desertion . . . alcoholism, suicide, and possible deviation." The principal beneficiaries of constitutional change would be "offbeats and deadbeats": the "homosexual who wants the same rights as husbands, the husband who wants to escape supporting his wife and children, the coward who wants to get out of military service by giving his place to a woman."

Extremist right-wing organizations imbued the amendment with even more subversive overtones. Despite the Communist Party's long-standing opposition to the ERA, the John Birch Society perceived the amendment as an integral part of "Communist plans . . . at work in a now vast effort to reduce human beings to living at the same level as animals." Other opponents, less certain about the ERA's conspiratorial origins, nonetheless perceived it as promoting a "communistic way of life." In Southern states, conservative leaders also identified the amendment as yet another assault on states' rights and recalled the federal government's enforcement of comparably open-textured mandates in civil rights cases.

Although proponents often dismissed these claims as pretextual, their underpinnings may have been more complex. For example, while arguments regarding states' rights may not have been decisive for many legislators, neither were such claims as patently disingenuous as was sometimes assumed. Schlafly and her associates framed the question as one of power: "Who's going to have it, the states or the feds?" To some state legislators, the amendment represented yet another blow to their declining status.

Among conservative constituencies the ERA fell victim to a general backlash against the radicalism of the 1960s. Calls for emancipation rekindled fears, if not of revolution, of severe dislocations in a congenial way of life. Some legislators found the amendment threatening in a more fundamental sense. To conservative male politicians, it often loomed as the embodiment of an ideology that was personally offensive and socially pernicious. Women's liberation, with its claims of oppression, challenged not only these legislators' values, but also their self-esteem. Under the more radical feminist view, many of the domestic arrangements and professional achievements of these politicians were neither desirable nor deserved but rather a product of illicit subjugation and false consciousness. Not surprisingly, some legislators viewed the ERA as an opportunity to respond in kind, to vent their spleen against the "bra-less brainless broads" who had demeaned their status and relationships.

Of course antifeminist sentiments were also common among women opposed to the ERA. But the rhetoric issuing from state capitols had a different resonance. On the whole, Schlafly and her female allies depicted a social order in which women were separate but equal. Many conservative legislators seemed less certain about the "equal." A surprising number were quite explicit on the point. One Montana legislator informed his colleagues that if God had wanted "women to be equal," he would have had "six female apostles." A wife's destiny was to "serve her husband"; she would rather be "loved than liberated." According to a poem read into the record by one Illinois lawmaker with literary aspirations,

> Just to be needed is more sweet says she
> Than any freedom in this world could be.

Such sentiments did not receive universal critical acclaim. In the view of the *Chicago Daily News* editors, the ERA was blocked by a "prim little covey of legislators convinced that females were put on this earth for kuchen and kinder and, by cracky, not much else." These press accounts, if somewhat simplistic, nonetheless captured a significant point about political discourse. Tributes built on group stereotypes carry different symbolic baggage depending on their source. When mothers exalt the mystique of motherhood, it appears as an affirmation of personal identity and group status. When such tributes originate with males opposed to equal rights, the stereotypes may be the same but the effect is different. As Simone de Beauvoir suggested, we should regard with some skepticism the "enthusiasm for women's destiny manifested by men who would not for the world have any part of it."

What is revealing about the anti-ERA rhetoric is not only what it discloses about the biases of particular legislators but also what it suggests about the ideological climate in state capitols. The record hardly reaffirms the Founding Fathers' vision of the ratification process as "the most likely means of drawing forth the best men in the states" to resolve fundamental issues of constitutional governance. That so many politically accountable officials felt free to couch their objections in phrases like "loved not liberated" or "bra-less brainless broads" demonstrates more than a flair for alliteration or a facility for grandstanding. Rather, it testifies to the perceived legitimacy of certain core attitudes about women's roles and feminist ideology. By the 1970s it would have been difficult to visualize even the most racist politician publicly objecting to civil rights legislation on the grounds that blacks would rather "serve than be served," or that proponents were "nagging noxious Negroes." Sensitivities to racism and sexism remained on qualitatively different levels.

Yet ironically enough, the candor of conservative legislators proved one of proponents' most effective organizational assets. It was the rhetoric as well as the results of the state ERA campaigns that enlisted large numbers of supporters. Sexist sentiments generated a backlash of financial and lobbying support that gave proponents enormous organizational advantages. A recurring question is why supporters could not capitalize on those advantages and convince enough legislators that equal rights, if not ideologically congenial, were at least politically expedient. . . .

✜ *F U R T H E R   R E A D I N G*

Charles H. Baron, "Abortion and Legal Process in the United States: An Overview of the Post-Webster Legal Landscape," *Journal of Law, Medicine & Health Care* 17 (Winter 1989): 368–375

Mary Frances Berry, *Why the ERA Failed* (1986)

Janet Boles, *The Politics of the Equal Rights Amendment* (1979)

Jane DeHart-Matthews and Donald Matthews, *The Equal Rights Amendment and the Politics of Cultural Conflict* (1988)

Richard A. Epstein, "Substantive Due Process by Any Other Name: The Abortion Cases," *Supreme Court Review* (1973): 159–185

Sara Evans, *Born for Liberty: A History of Women in America* (1990)

Marian Faux, *Roe v. Wade* (1988)

Ann E. Freedman, "Sex Equality, Sex Differences, and the Supreme Court," *Yale Law Journal* 92 (1983): 913–968

Leslie Friedman Goldstein, *The Constitutional Rights of Women,* rev. ed. (1988)

Jane Mansbridge, *Why We Lost the ERA* (1986)

James Mohr, *Abortion in America* (1980)

Rosalind Pollack Pechesky, "Antiabortion, Antifeminism, and the Rise of the New Right," *Feminist Studies,* 7 (Summer 1981): 206–246

Alan F. Westin, *Privacy and Freedom* (1967)

Tinsley E. Yarbrough, "The Burger Court and Unspecified Rights," *Duke Law Review,* (1977): 143–170

CHAPTER
10

Freedom of and Freedom
from Religion

Contradictory themes pervaded the history of religious freedom in early America, and those contradictions are still with us today. Although Europeans immigrated to the New World in quest of liberty, many were intolerant of the religious views of others. Puritans persecuted Quakers in Massachusetts; Anglicans attacked Baptists in Virginia. Most colonies provided for an "established church," which their citizens were required to attend and pay taxes to support.

By the Revolution, the wisdom of such practices came under attack. In Virginia, for example, where Patrick Henry favored the continued establishment of the Anglican church, Thomas Jefferson and James Madison argued for its abolition; Jefferson insisted that a high wall of separation between church and state was necessary to guarantee individual religious freedom. Most early state constitutions followed Jefferson's lead, although several states continued to provide direct support to churches. The Continental Congress appeared to promote religion through the declaration in the Northwest Ordinance of 1787 that "religion, morality, and knowledge [are] necessary to good government and the happiness of mankind." The Anti-Federalists complained that the Constitution, drafted that same year, left open the possibility that the new government could establish a national church, for the document mentioned religion only once—in its prohibition on religious tests for those seeking government office. James Madison in 1790 addressed these concerns with the First Amendment provision that "Congress shall make no law respecting an establishment of religion, or prohibiting the free exercise thereof."

Throughout the nineteenth and early twentieth centuries, the Supreme Court had little occasion to interpret the Constitution's so-called free-exercise and establishment clauses. Rather, state governments regularly treated questions of religious liberty under their own constitutions. By the 1940s, however, the cumulative effects of successive waves of immigration begun a half-century earlier wrought an unprecedented degree of religious diversity. Some groups, among them the Jehovah's Witnesses and the Jews, expected the Supreme Court to protect them from state interference with their religious practices; other groups, notably Catholics, demanded that state and local governments finance their schools.

Religious freedom became a subject of profound constitutional struggle in the

Supreme Court. Atheists and religious minorities (such as Jews and Jehovah's Witnesses) wanted the justices to sustain Jefferson's high wall of separation. They claimed that any effort by government to require certain religious practices of them, such as through a requirement that their children recite prayers in public schools, breached that wall. When most schoolchildren were Protestant in the nineteenth century, reciting the Lord's Prayer or verses from the King James version of the Bible offended few persons. As America became an ethnic and religious polyglot, however, the Christian consensus that supported these practices evaporated. Most American religious leaders agreed that the expression of faith should be free from government interference, but some of them nonetheless believed that in certain ways the wall of separation should be lowered to permit government the opportunity to support religion. Confronted with the soaring costs of education, the Catholic church, for example, clamored for public financing of some of the operating costs of parochial schools, such as the expense of transporting students by bus. Some public officials embraced limited aid to parochial schools as a way of reducing the overall burden on public-education facilities. The relationship between church and state became even more tense in the 1970s and 1980s as religious fundamentalists, reacting to the counterculture of the 1960s, demanded that government switch from a merely supporting role to one in which it would directly encourage the teaching of moral and religious beliefs through prayer and creation science.

Contemporary debate about the Constitution's religion clauses has also raised questions about the proper scope of the Supreme Court's powers. One of the most controversial areas of dispute has involved the incorporation doctrine. This is the process by which the justices apply provisions of the Bill of Rights against the states by bringing those provisions under the umbrella of the due process clause of the Fourteenth Amendment. This practice has been particularly disturbing to critics of the Court, since the religion clauses of the First Amendment are explicitly addressed to Congress. The Court, however, has incorporated the free exercise and no-establishment clauses through the Fourteenth Amendment and, in the process, struck down a host of state legislation involving religion.

Conservative critics of the Court argue that the framers of the Fourteenth Amendment never intended such incorporation; on the other side, liberal supporters of the justices' religion-clause decisions insist that incorporation was essential to making the concept of religious liberty truly national. Beginning in the 1940s, the Court has held that these provisions occupy a "preferred position," meaning that state governments have carried a heavy burden in justifying interference with religion.

Is the High Court's prohibition of the states' involvement with religion absolute? The answer is clearly no, for the justices have accepted that, given certain guidelines, the states can provide financial support to parochial schools, permit the display of Christmas scenes on public property, and provide tax exemptions for churches. In sum, the modern Court has favored a high wall of separation, but its position has never been altogether consistent. It has been unable to reconcile the Constitution's command that the American people enjoy at once both freedom of and freedom from religion.

✧ D O C U M E N T S

The documents in this chapter concentrate on the establishment clause, with special emphasis on the issue of school prayer, although in many instances the clause's meaning is tied to the free-exercise clause. For example, the first document, James Madison's "Memorial and Remonstrance Against Religious Assessments," argues that religion is a private, voluntary affair not subject to government in any way; any establishment therefore violates the free exercise of religion and threatens public liberty. The establishment controversy did not reach the Supreme Court until 1947, when the justices handed down their decision in *Everson* v. *Board of Education*, the second document. The Board of Education of Ewing, New Jersey, had provided free transportation for all students to and from school as a means of assisting parochial and independent schools. The High Court, speaking through Justice Hugo Black, upheld the measure, but Black nonetheless erected a high wall of separation between church and state. Justices Robert H. Jackson and Felix Frankfurter dissented, arguing that Black's reasoning should have led him to overturn the New Jersey law.

No decision by the High Court in the area of religion stirred greater controversy than *Engel* v. *Vitale* (1962), the third document. Once again Justice Black spoke for the Court, but this time he struck down a state-mandated prayer used in New York to open each school day. This decision by the Warren Court evoked howls of political protest and unleashed banner headlines declaring COURT OUTLAWS GOD. President John F. Kennedy addressed the issue in his news conference of June 27, 1962, excerpted as the fourth document, in which he observed that children were already free to engage in silent prayer in schools.

The Alabama legislature borrowed Kennedy's reasoning when it fashioned a statute directing teachers to lead "willing students" in one minute of silent meditation and prayer. Ishmael Jaffree, an African-American who opposed the Alabama law, explains in the fifth document his reasons for feeling as he did. Judge W. Brevard Hand of the federal District Court for the Southern District of Alabama found in favor of the prayer in *Jaffree* v. *The Board of School Commissioners of Mobile County*, the sixth document. Religious right-wing factions embraced Hand's opinion. The Supreme Court, in *Wallace* v. *Jaffree* (1985), the seventh document, rejected Hand's constitutional and historical analysis outright. In the last document, Senator Jesse Helms of North Carolina, a longtime critic of the Supreme Court's treatment of school prayer, summarizes the current demands for congressional action.

James Madison Warns Against Religious Establishment, 1785

To the Honorable the General Assembly of the Commonwealth of Virginia

We, the subscribers, citizens of the said Commonwealth, having taken into serious consideration, a Bill printed by order of the last Session of General Assembly, entitled "A Bill establishing a provision for Teachers of the Christian Religion," and conceiving that the same, if finally armed with the sanctions of a law, will be a dangerous abuse of power, are bound as faithful members of a free State, to remonstrate against it, and to declare the reasons by which we are determined. We remonstrate against the said Bill,

1. Because we hold it for a fundamental and undeniable truth, "that Religion or the duty which we owe to our Creator and the Manner of

discharging it, can be directed only by reason and conviction, not by force or violence." The Religion then of every man must be left to the conviction and conscience of every man; and it is the right of every man to exercise it as these may dictate. This right is in its nature an unalienable right. It is unalienable; because the opinions of men, depending only on the evidence contemplated by their own minds, cannot follow the dictates of other men: It is unalienable also, because what is here a right towards men, is a duty towards the Creator. It is the duty of every man to render to the Creator such homage, and such only, as he believes to be acceptable to him. This duty is precedent both in order of time and degree of obligation, to the claims of Civil Society. Before any man can be considered as a member of Civil Society, he must be considered as a subject of the Governor of the Universe: And if a member of Civil Society, who enters into any subordinate Association, must always do it with a reservation of his duty to the general authority; much more must every man who becomes a member of any particular Civil Society, do it with a saving of his allegiance to the Universal Sovereign. We maintain therefore that in matters of Religion, no man's right is abridged by the institution of Civil Society, and that Religion is wholly exempt from its cognizance. True it is, that no other rule exists, by which any question which may divide a Society, can be ultimately determined, but the will of the majority; but it is also true, that the majority may trespass on the rights of the minority.

2. Because if religion be exempt from the authority of the Society at large, still less can it be subject to that of the Legislative Body. The latter are but the creatures and vicegerents of the former. Their jurisdiction is both derivative and limited: it is limited with regard to the co-ordinate departments, more necessarily is it limited with regard to the constituents. The preservation of a free government requires not merely, that the metes and bounds which separate each department of power may be invariably maintained; but more especially, that neither of them be suffered to overleap the great Barrier which defends the rights of the people. . . .

3. Because, it is proper to take alarm at the first experiment on our liberties. We hold this prudent jealousy to be the first duty of citizens, and one of [the] noblest characteristics of the late Revolution. The freemen of America did not wait till usurped power had strengthened itself by exercise, and entangled the question in precedents. They saw all the consequences in the principle, and they avoided the consequences by denying the principle. We revere this lesson too much, soon to forget it. . . .

4. Because, the bill violates that equality which ought to be the basis of every law, and which is more indispensable, in proportion as the validity or expediency of any law is more liable to be impeached. If "all men are by nature equally free and independent," all men are to be considered as entering into Society on equal conditions; as relinquishing no more, and therefore retaining no less, one than another, of their natural rights. Above all are they to be considered as retaining an "*equal* title to the free exercise of Religion according to the dictates of conscience." Whilst we assert for ourselves a freedom to embrace, to profess and to observe the Religion

which we believe to be of divine origin, we cannot deny an equal freedom to those whose minds have not yet yielded to the evidence which has convinced us. If this freedom be abused, it is an offence against God, not against man: To God, therefore, not to men, must an account of it be rendered. . . .

5. Because the bill implies either that the Civil Magistrate is a competent Judge of Religious truth; or that he may employ Religion as an engine of Civil policy. The first is an arrogant pretension falsified by the contradictory opinions of Rulers in all ages, and throughout the world: The second an unhallowed perversion of the means of salvation.

6. Because the establishment proposed by the Bill is not requisite for the support of the Christian Religion. To say that it is, is a contradiction to the Christian Religion itself; for every page of it disavows a dependence on the powers of this world: it is a contradiction to fact; for it is known that this Religion both existed and flourished, not only without the support of human laws, but in spite of every opposition from them; and not only during the period of miraculous aid, but long after it had been left to its own evidence, and the ordinary care of Providence: Nay, it is a contradiction in terms; for a Religion not invented by human policy, must have pre-existed and been supported, before it was established by human policy. It is moreover to weaken in those who profess this Religion a pious confidence in its innate excellence, and the patronage of its Author; and to foster in those who still reject it, a suspicion that its friends are too conscious of its fallacies, to trust it to its own merits.

7. Because experience witnesseth that ecclesiastical establishments, instead of maintaining the purity and efficacy of Religion, have had a contrary operation. . . .

8. Because the establishment in question is not necessary for the support of Civil Government. If it be urged as necessary for the support of Civil Government only as it is a means of supporting Religion, and it be not necessary for the latter purpose, it cannot be necessary for the former. . . . A just government, instituted to secure & perpetuate it, needs them not. Such a government will be best supported by protecting every citizen in the enjoyment of his Religion with the same equal hand which protects his person and his property; by neither invading the equal rights of any Sect, nor suffering any Sect to invade those of another.

9. Because the proposed establishment is a departure from that generous policy, which, offering an asylum to the persecuted and oppressed of every Nation and Religion, promised a lustre to our country, and an accession to the number of its citizens. What a melancholy mark is the Bill of sudden degeneracy? Instead of holding forth an asylum to the persecuted, it is itself a signal of persecution. It degrades from the equal rank of Citizens all those whose opinions in Religion do not bend to those of the Legislative authority. . . .

10. Because, it will have a likely tendency to banish our Citizens. The allurements presented by other situations are every day thinning their number. To superadd a fresh motive to emigration, by revoking the liberty which

they now enjoy, would be the same species of folly which has dishonoured and depopulated flourishing kingdoms.

11. Because, it will destroy that moderation and harmony which the forbearance of our laws to intermeddle with Religion, has produced amongst its several sects. Torrents of blood have been spilt in the old world, by vain attempts of the secular arm to extinguish Religious discord, by proscribing all difference in Religious opinions. Time has at length revealed the true remedy. Every relaxation of narrow and rigorous policy, wherever it has been tried, has been found to assuage the disease. . . .

12. Because, the policy of the bill is adverse to the diffusion of the light of Christianity. The first wish of those who enjoy this precious gift, ought to be that it may be imparted to the whole race of mankind. Compare the number of those who have as yet received it with the number still remaining under the dominion of false Religions; and how small is the former! Does the policy of the Bill tend to lessen the disproportion? No; it at once discourages those who are strangers to the light of [revelation] from coming into the Region of it; and countenances, by example the nations who continue in darkness, in shutting out those who might convey it to them. Instead of levelling as far as possible, every obstacle to the victorious progress of truth, the Bill with an ignoble and unchristian timidity would circumscribe it, with a wall of defence, against the encroachments of error.

13. Because attempts to enforce by legal sanctions, acts obnoxious to so great a proportion of Citizens, tend to enervate the laws in general, and to slacken the bands of Society. . . .

14. Because a measure of such singular magnitude and delicacy ought not to be imposed, without the clearest evidence that it is called for by a majority of citizens: and no satisfactory method is yet proposed by which the voice of the majority in this case may be determined, or its influence secured. . . .

15. Because, finally, "the equal right of every citizen to the free exercise of his Religion according to the dictates of conscience" is held by the same tenure with all our other rights. If we recur to its origin, it is equally the gift of nature; if we weigh its importance, it cannot be less dear to us; if we consult the Declaration of those rights which pertain to the good people of Virginia, as the "basis and foundation of Government," it is enumerated with equal solemnity, or rather studied emphasis. . . . We the subscribers say, that the General Assembly of this Commonwealth have no such authority: And that no effort may be omitted on our part against so dangerous an usurpation, we oppose to it, this remonstrance; earnestly praying, as we are in duty bound, that the Supreme Lawgiver of the Universe, by illuminating those to whom it is addressed, may on the one hand, turn their councils from every act which would affront his holy prerogative, or violate the trust committed to them: and on the other, guide them into every measure which may be worthy of his [blessing, may re]dound to their own praise, and may establish more firmly the liberties, the prosperity, and the Happiness of the Commonwealth.

Everson v. *Board of Education of the Township of Ewing*, 330 U.S. 1 (1947)

[5–4: Black, Douglas, Murphy, Reed, Vinson;
Burton, Frankfurter, Jackson, Rutledge]

Mr. Justice Black delivered the opinion of the Court.

The only contention here is that the state statute and the resolution, insofar as they authorized reimbursement to parents of children attending parochial schools, violate the Federal Constitution in these two respects, which to some extent overlap. *First.* They authorize the State to take by taxation the private property of some and bestow it upon others, to be used for their own private purposes. This, it is alleged, violates the due process clause of the Fourteenth Amendment. *Second.* The statute and the resolution forced inhabitants to pay taxes to help support and maintain schools which are dedicated to, and which regularly teach, the Catholic Faith. This is alleged to be a use of state power to support church schools contrary to the prohibition of the First Amendment which the Fourteenth Amendment made applicable to the states. . . .

. . . The New Jersey statute is challenged as a "law respecting an establishment of religion." The First Amendment, as made applicable to the states by the Fourteenth . . . commands that a state "shall make no law respecting an establishment of religion, or prohibiting the free exercise thereof. . . ." These words of the First Amendment reflected in the minds of early Americans a vivid mental picture of conditions and practices which they fervently wished to stamp out in order to preserve liberty for themselves and for their posterity. Doubtless their goal has not been entirely reached; but so far has the Nation moved toward it that the expression "law respecting an establishment of religion," probably does not so vividly remind present-day Americans of the evils, fears, and political problems that caused that expression to be written into our Bill of Rights. Whether this New Jersey law is one respecting an "establishment of religion" requires an understanding of the meaning of that language, particularly with respect to the imposition of taxes. Once again, therefore, it is not inappropriate briefly to review the background and environment of the period in which that constitutional language was fashioned and adopted.

A large proportion of the early settlers of this country came here from Europe to escape the bondage of laws which compelled them to support and attend government-favored churches. The centuries immediately before and contemporaneous with the colonization of America had been filled with turmoil, civil strife, and persecutions, generated in large part by established sects determined to maintain their absolute political and religious supremacy. With the power of government supporting them, at various times and places, Catholics had persecuted Protestants, Protestants had persecuted Catholics, Protestant sects had persecuted other Protestant sects, Catholics of one shade of belief had persecuted Catholics of another shade of belief, and all of these had from time to time persecuted Jews. In efforts to force loyalty to whatever religious group happened to be on top and in league with the government of a particular time and place, men and women had been fined, cast in jail, cruelly tortured, and killed. Among the offenses for which these punishments had been inflicted were such things as speaking disrespectfully of the views of ministers of government-established churches, non-attendance at those churches, expressions of non-belief in their doctrine, and failure to pay taxes and tithes to support them.

These practices of the old world were transplanted to and began to thrive in the soil of the new America. The very charters granted by the English Crown to the individuals and companies designated to make the laws which would control the destinies of the colonials authorized these individuals and companies to erect religious establishments which all, whether believers or non-believers, would be required to support and attend. An exercise of this authority was accompanied by a repetition of many of the old-world practices and persecutions. Catholics found themselves hounded and proscribed because of their faith; Quakers who followed their conscience went to jail; Baptists were peculiarly obnoxious to certain dominant Protestant sects; men and women of varied faiths who happened to be in a minority in a particular locality were persecuted because they steadfastly persisted in worshipping God only as their own consciences dictated. And all of these dissenters were compelled to pay tithes and taxes to support government-sponsored churches whose ministers preached inflammatory sermons designed to strengthen and consolidate the established faith by generating a burning hatred against dissenters.

These practices became so commonplace as to shock the freedom-loving colonials into a feeling of abhorrence. The imposition of taxes to pay ministers' salaries and to build and maintain churches and church property aroused their indignation. It was these feelings which found expression in the First Amendment. No one locality and no one group throughout the Colonies can rightly be given entire credit for having aroused the sentiment that culminated in adoption of the Bill of Rights' provisions embracing religious liberty. But Virginia, where the established church had achieved a dominant influence in political affairs and where many excesses attracted wide public attention, provided a great stimulus and able leadership for the movement. The people there, as elsewhere, reached the conviction that individual religious liberty could be achieved best under a government which was stripped of all power to tax, to support, or otherwise to assist any or all religions, or to interfere with the beliefs of any religious individual or group.

The movement toward this end reached its dramatic climax in Virginia in 1785–86 when the Virginia legislative body was about to renew Virginia's tax levy for the support of the established church. Thomas Jefferson and James Madison led the fight against this tax. Madison wrote his great Memorial and Remonstrance against the law. In it, he eloquently argued that a true religion did not need the support of law; that no person, either believer or non-believer, should be taxed to support a religious institution of any kind; that the best interest of a society required that the minds of men always be wholly free; and that cruel persecutions were the inevitable result of government-established religions. Madison's Remonstrance received strong support throughout Virginia, and the Assembly postponed consideration of the proposed tax measure until its next session. When the proposal came up for consideration at that session, it not only died in committee, but the Assembly enacted the famous "Virginia Bill for Religious Liberty" originally written by Thomas Jefferson. . . .

. . . Prior to the adoption of the Fourteenth Amendment, the First Amendment did not apply as a restraint against the states. Most of them did soon provide similar constitutional protections for religious liberty. But some states persisted for about half a century in imposing restraints upon the free exercise of religion and in discriminating against particular religious groups. In recent years, so far as the provision against the establishment of a religion is concerned, the question has most frequently arisen in connection with proposed state aid to church schools and efforts to carry on religious teachings in the public schools in accordance with the tenets of a particular sect. Some churches have either sought or accepted state financial support for their schools. Here again the efforts to obtain state aid or acceptance of it have not been limited to any one particular faith. The state courts, in the main, have remained faithful to the language of their own constitutional provisions designed to protect religious freedom and to separate religions and governments. Their decisions, however, show the difficulty in drawing the line between tax legislation which provides funds for the welfare of the general public and that which is designed to support institutions which teach religion. . . .

The "establishment of religion" clause of the First Amendment means at least this: Neither a state nor the Federal Government can set up a church. Neither can pass laws which aid one religion, aid all religions, or prefer one religion over another. Neither can force nor influence a person to go to or to remain away from church against his will or force him to profess a belief or disbelief in any religion. No person can be punished for entertaining or professing religious beliefs or disbeliefs, for church attendance or non-attendance. No tax in any amount, large or small, can be levied to support any religious activities or institutions, whatever they may be called, or what-ever form they may adopt to teach or practice religion. Neither a state nor the Federal Government can, openly or secretly, participate in the affairs of any religious organizations or groups and *vice versa*. In the words of Jefferson, the clause against establishment of religion by law was intended to erect "a wall of separation between church and State." . . .

Measured by these standards, we cannot say that the First Amendment prohibits New Jersey from spending tax-raised funds to pay the bus fares of parochial school pupils as a part of a general program under which it pays the fares of pupils attending public and other schools. It is undoubtedly true that children are helped to get to church schools. There is even a possibility that some of the children might not be sent to the church schools if the parents were compelled to pay their children's bus fares out of their own pockets when transportation to a public school would have been paid for by the State. The same possibility exists where the state requires a local transit company to provide reduced fares to school children including those attending parochial schools, or where a municipally owned transportation system undertakes to carry all school children free of charge. Moreover, state-paid policemen, detailed to protect children going to and from church schools from the very real hazards of traffic, would serve much the same purpose and accomplish much the same result as state provisions intended to guarantee free transportation of a kind which the state deems to be best for the school children's welfare. And parents might refuse to risk their children to the serious danger of traffic accidents going to and from parochial schools, the approaches to which were not protected by policemen. Similarly, parents might be reluctant to permit their children to attend schools which the state had cut off from such general government services as ordinary police and fire protection, connections for sewage disposal, public highways and sidewalks. Of course, cutting off church schools from these services, so separate and so indisputably marked off from the religious function, would make it far more difficult for the schools to operate. But such is obviously not the purpose of the First Amendment. That Amendment requires the state to be a neutral in its relations with groups of religious believers and non-believers; it does not require the state to be their adversary. State power is no more to be used so as to handicap religions than it is to favor them.

This Court has said that parents may, in the discharge of their duty under state compulsory education laws, send their children to a religious rather than a public school if the school meets the secular educational re-quirements which the state has power to impose. . . . It appears that these parochial schools meet New Jersey's requirements. The State contributes no money to the schools. It does not support them. Its legislation, as applied, does no more than provide a general program to help parents get their children, regardless of their religion, safely and expeditiously to and from accredited schools.

The First Amendment has erected a wall between church and state. That wall must be kept high and impregnable. We could not approve the slightest breach. New Jersey has not breached it here.

Mr. Justice Jackson, dissenting.

I find myself, contrary to first impressions, unable to join in this decision. I have a sympathy, though it is not ideological, with Catholic citizens who are compelled by law to pay taxes for public schools, and also feel constrained by conscience and discipline to support other schools for their own children. Such relief to them as this case involves is not in itself a serious burden to taxpayers and I had assumed it to be as little serious in principle. Study of this case convinces me otherwise. The Court's opinion marshals every ar-gument in favor of state aid and puts the case in its most favorable light, but much of its reasoning confirms my conclusions that there are no good grounds upon which to support the present legislation. In fact, the undertones of the opinion, advocating complete and uncompromising separation of Church from State, seem utterly discordant with its conclusion yielding support to their commingling in educational matters. The case which irresistibly comes to mind as the most fitting precedent is that of Julia who, according to Byron's reports, "whispering, 'I will ne'er consent,'—consented."

I

. . . If we are to decide this case on the facts before us, our question is simply this: Is it constitutional to tax this complainant to pay the cost of carrying pupils to Church schools of one specified denomination?

II

Whether the taxpayer constitutionally can be made to contribute aid to parents of students because of their attendance at parochial schools depends upon the nature of those schools and their relation to the Church. The Constitution says nothing of education. It lays no obligation on the states to provide schools and does not undertake to regulate state systems of education if they see fit to maintain them. But they cannot, through school policy any more than through other means, invade rights secured to citizens by the Constitution of the United States. . . . One of our basic rights is to be free of taxation to support a transgression of the constitutional command that the authorities "shall make no law respecting an establishment of religion, or prohibiting the free exercise thereof. . . ."

. . . It is no exaggeration to say that the whole historic conflict in temporal policy between the Catholic Church and non-Catholics comes to a focus in their respective school policies. The Roman Catholic Church, counseled by experience in many ages and many lands and with all sorts and conditions of men, takes what, from the viewpoint of its own progress and the success of its mission, is a wise estimate of the importance of education to religion. It does not leave the individual to pick up religion by chance. It relies on early and indelible indoctrination in the faith and order of the Church by the word and example of persons consecrated to the task.

Our public school, if not a product of Protestantism, at least is more consistent with it than with the Catholic culture and scheme of values. It is a relatively recent development dating from about 1840. It is organized on the premise that secular education can be isolated from all religious teaching so that the school can inculcate all needed temporal knowledge and also maintain a strict and lofty neutrality as to religion. The assumption is that after the individual has been instructed in worldly wisdom he will be better fitted to choose his religion. Whether such a disjunction is possible, and if possible whether it is wise, are questions I need not try to answer.

I should be surprised if any Catholic would deny that the parochial school is a vital, if not the most vital, part of the Roman Catholic Church. If put to the choice, that venerable institution, I should expect, would forego its whole service for mature persons before it would give up education of the young, and it would be a wise choice. Its growth and cohesion, discipline and loyalty, spring from its schools. Catholic education is the rock on which the whole structure rests, and to render tax aid to its Church school is indistinguishable to me from rendering the same aid to the Church itself.

III

. . . It seems to me that the basic fallacy in the Court's reasoning, which accounts for its failure to apply the principles it avows, is in ignoring the essentially religious test by which beneficiaries of this expenditure are selected. A policeman protects a Catholic, of course—but not because he is a Catholic; it is because he is a man and a member of our society. The fireman protects the Church school—but not because it is a Church school; it is because it is property, part of the assets of our society. Neither the fireman nor the policeman has to ask before he renders aid "Is this man or building identified with the Catholic Church?" But before these school authorities draw a check to reimburse for a student's fare they must ask just that question, and if the school is a Catholic one they may render aid because it is such, while if it is of any other faith or is run for profit, the help must be withheld. To consider the converse of the Court's reasoning will best disclose its fallacy. That there is no parallel between police and fire protection and this plan of reimbursement is apparent from the incongruity of the limitation of this Act if applied to police and fire service. Could we sustain an Act that said the police shall protect pupils on the way to or from public schools and Catholic schools but not while going to and coming from other schools, and firemen shall extinguish a blaze in public or Catholic school buildings but shall not put out a blaze in Protestant Church schools or private schools operated for profit? That is the true analogy to the case we have before us and I should think it pretty plain that such a scheme would not be valid. . . .

This policy of our Federal Constitution has never been wholly pleasing to most religious groups. They all are quick to invoke its protections; they all are irked when they feel its restraints. This Court has gone a long way, if not an unreasonable way, to hold that public business of such paramount importance as maintenance of public order, protection of the privacy of the home, and taxation may not be pursued by a state in a way that even indirectly will interfere with religious proselyting. . . .

But we cannot have it both ways. Religious teaching cannot be a private affair when the state seeks to impose regulations which infringe on it indirectly, and a public affair when it comes to taxing citizens of one faith to aid another, or those of no faith to aid all. If these principles seem harsh in prohibiting aid to Catholic education, it must not be forgotten that it is the same Constitution that alone assures Catholics the right to maintain these schools at all when predominant local sentiment would forbid them. . . . Nor should I think that those who have done so well without this aid would want to see this separation between Church and State broken down. If the state may aid these religious schools, it may therefore regulate them. . . .

But in any event, the great purposes of the Constitution do not depend on the approval or convenience of those they restrain. I cannot read the history of the struggle to separate political from ecclesiastical affairs . . . without a conviction that the Court today is unconsciously giving the clock's hands a backward turn. . . .

Engel v. *Vitale,* 370 U.S. 421 (1962)

[6–1: Black, Brennan, Clark, Douglas, Warren, Whittaker; Stewart]

Mr. Justice Black delivered the opinion of the Court.

The respondent Board of Education of Union Free School District No. 9, New Hyde Park, New York, acting in its official capacity under state law, directed the School District's principal to cause the following prayer to be said aloud by each class in the presence of a teacher at the beginning of each school day:

> Almighty God, we acknowledge our dependence upon Thee, and we beg
> Thy blessings upon us, our parents, our teachers and our Country.

This daily procedure was adopted on the recommendation of the State Board of Regents, a governmental agency created by the State Constitution to which the New York Legislature has granted broad supervisory, executive, and legislative powers over the State's public school system. These state officials composed the prayer, which they recommended and published as a part of their "Statement on Moral and Spiritual Training in the Schools," saying: "We believe that the Statement will be subscribed to by all men and women of good will, and we call upon all of them to aid in giving life to our program."

Shortly after the practice of reciting the Regents' prayer was adopted by the School District, the parents of ten pupils brought this action in a New York State Court insisting that use of this official prayer in the public schools was contrary to the beliefs, religions, or religious practices of both themselves and their children. Among other things, these parents challenged the constitutionality of both the state law authorizing the School District to direct the use of prayer in public schools and the School District's regulation ordering the recitation of this particular prayer on the ground that these actions of official governmental agencies violate that part of the First Amendment of the Federal Constitution which commands that "Congress shall make no law respecting an establishment of religion"—a command which was "made applicable to the State of New York by the Fourteenth Amendment of the said Constitution." . . . We granted certiorari to review this important decision involving rights protected by the First and Fourteenth Amendments.

We think that by using its public school system to encourage recitation of the Regents' prayer, the State of New York has adopted a practice wholly inconsistent with the Establishment Clause. There can, of course, be no doubt that New York's program of daily classroom invocation of God's blessings as prescribed in the Regents' prayer is a religious activity. It is a solemn avowal of divine faith and supplication for the blessings of the Almighty. The nature of such a prayer has always been religious, none of the respondents has denied this. . . .

It is a matter of history that this very practice of establishing governmentally composed prayers for religious services was one of the reasons which caused many of our early colonists to leave England and seek religious freedom in America. The Book of Common Prayer, which was created under governmental direction and which was approved by Acts of Parliament in 1548 and 1549, set out in minute detail the accepted form and content of prayer and other religious ceremonies to be used in the established, tax-supported Church of England. The controversies over the Book and what should be its content repeatedly threatened to disrupt the peace of that country as the accepted forms of prayer in the established church changed with the views of the particular ruler that happened to be in control at the time. Powerful groups representing some of the varying religious views of the people struggled among themselves to impress their particular views upon the Government and obtain amendments of the Book more suitable to their respective notions of how religious services should be conducted in order that the official religious establishment would advance their particular religious beliefs. Other groups, lacking the necessary political power to influence the Government on the matter, decided to leave England and its established church and seek freedom in America from England's governmentally ordained and supported religion.

It is an unfortunate fact of history that when some of the very groups which had most strenuously opposed the established Church of England found themselves sufficiently in control of colonial governments in this country to write their own prayers into law, they passed laws making their own religion the official religion of their respective colonies. Indeed, as late as the time of the Revolutionary War, there were established churches in at least eight of the thirteen former colonies and established religions in at least four of the other five. But the successful Revolution against English political domination was shortly followed by intense opposition to the practice of establishing religion by law. This opposition crystallized rapidly into an effective political force in Virginia where the minority religious groups such as Presbyterians, Lutherans, Quakers and Baptists had gained such strength that the adherents to the established Episcopal Church were actually a minority themselves. In 1785–1786, those opposed to the established Church, led by James Madison and Thomas Jefferson, who, though themselves not members of any of these dissenting religious groups, opposed all religious establishments by law on grounds of principle, obtained the enactment of the famous "Virginia Bill for Religious Liberty" by which all religious groups were placed on an equal footing so far as the State was concerned. Similar though less far-reaching legislation was being considered and passed in other States.

By the time of the adoption of the Constitution, our history shows that there was a widespread awareness among many Americans of the dangers of a union of Church and State. These people knew, some of them from bitter personal experience, that one of the greatest dangers to the freedom of the individual to worship in his own way lay in the Government's placing its official stamp of approval upon one particular kind of prayer or one particular form of religious services. They knew the anguish, hardship and bitter strife that could come when zealous religious groups struggled with one another to obtain the Government's stamp of approval from each King, Queen, or Protector that came to temporary power. The Constitution was intended to avert a part of this danger by leaving the government of this country in the hands of the people rather than in the hands of any monarch. But this safeguard was not enough. Our Founders were no more willing to let the content of their prayers and their privilege of praying whenever they pleased be influenced by the ballot box than they were to let these vital matters of personal conscience depend upon the succession of monarchs. The First Amendment was added to the Constitution to stand as a guarantee that neither the power nor the prestige of the Federal Government would be used to control, support or influence the kinds of prayer the American people can say—that the people's religions must not be subjected to the pressures of government for change each time a new political administration is elected to office. Under that Amendment's prohibition against governmental establishment of religion, as reinforced by the provisions of the Fourteenth Amendment, government in this country, be it state or federal, is without power to prescribe by law any particular form of prayer which is to be used as an official prayer in carrying on any program of governmentally sponsored religious activity.

There can be no doubt that New York's state prayer program officially establishes the religious beliefs embodied in the Regents' prayer. The respondents' argument to the contrary, which is largely based upon the contention that the Regents' prayer is "non-denominational" and the fact that the program, as modified and approved by state courts, does not require all pupils to recite the prayer but permits those who wish to do so to remain silent or be excused from the room, ignores the essential nature of the program's constitutional defects. Neither the fact that the prayer may be denominationally neutral nor the fact that its observance on the part of the students is voluntary can serve to free it from the limitations of the Establishment Clause, as it might from the Free Exercise Clause, of the First Amendment, both of which are operative against the States by virtue of the Fourteenth Amendment. Although these two clauses may in certain instances overlap, they forbid two quite different kinds of governmental encroachment upon religious freedom. The Establishment Clause, unlike the Free Exercise Clause, does not depend upon any showing of direct governmental compulsion and is violated by the enactment of laws which establish an official religion whether those laws operate directly to coerce nonobserving individuals or not. This is not to say, of course, that laws officially prescribing a particular form of religious worship do not involve coercion of such individuals. When the power, prestige and financial support of government is placed behind a particular religious belief, the indirect coercive pressure upon religious minorities to conform to the prevailing officially approved religion is plain. But the purposes underlying the Establishment Clause go much further than that. Its first and most immediate purpose rested on the belief that a union of government and religion tends to destroy government and to degrade religion. The history of governmentally established religion, both in England and in this country, showed that whenever government had allied itself with one particular form of religion, the inevitable result had been that it had incurred the hatred, disrespect and even contempt of those who held contrary beliefs. That same history showed that many people had lost their respect for any religion that had relied upon the support of government to spread its faith. The Establishment Clause thus stands as an expression of principle on the part of the Founders of our Constitution that religion is too personal, too sacred, too holy, to permit its "unhallowed perversion" by a civil magistrate. Another purpose of the Establishment Clause rested upon an awareness of the historical fact that governmentally established religions and religious persecutions go hand in hand. The Founders knew that only a few years after the Book of Common Prayer became the only accepted form of religious services in the established Church of England, an Act of Uniformity was passed to compel all Englishmen to attend those services and to make it a criminal offense to conduct or attend religious gatherings of any other kind—a law which was consistently flouted by dissenting religious groups in England and which contributed to widespread persecutions of people like John Bunyan who persisted in holding "unlawful [religious] meetings . . . to the great disturbance and distraction of the good subjects of this kingdom. . . ." And they knew that similar persecutions had received the sanction of law in several of the colonies in this country soon after the establishment of official religions in those colonies. It was in large part to get completely away from this sort of systematic religious persecution that the Founders brought into being our Nation, our Constitution, and our Bill of Rights with its prohibition against any governmental establishment of religion. The New York laws officially prescribing the Regents' prayer are inconsistent both with the purposes of the Establishment Clause and with the Establishment Clause itself.

It has been argued that to apply the Constitution in such a way as to prohibit state laws respecting an establishment of religious services in public schools is to indicate a hostility toward religion or toward prayer. Nothing, of course, could be more wrong. The history of man is inseparable from the history of religion. And perhaps it is not too much to say that since the beginning of that history many people have devoutly believed that "More things are wrought by prayer than this world dreams of." It was doubtless largely due to men who believed this that there grew up a sentiment that caused men to leave the cross-currents of officially established state religions and religious persecution in Europe and come to this country filled with the hope that they could find a place in which they could pray when they pleased to the God of their faith in the language they chose. And there were men of this same faith in the power of prayer who led the fight for adoption of our Constitution and also for our Bill of Rights with the very guarantees of religious freedom that forbid the sort of governmental activity which New York has attempted here. These men knew that the First Amendment, which tried to put an end to governmental control of religion and of prayer, was not written to destroy either. They knew rather that it was written to quiet well-justified fears which nearly all of them felt arising out of an awareness that governments of the past had shackled men's tongues to make them speak only the religious thoughts that government wanted them to speak and to pray only to the God that government wanted them to pray to. It is neither sacrilegious nor antireligious to say that each separate government in this country should stay out of the business of writing or sanctioning official prayers and leave that purely religious function to the people themselves and to those the people choose to look to for religious guidance.

It is true that New York's establishment of its Regents' prayer as an officially approved religious doctrine of that State does not amount to a total establishment of one particular religious sect to the exclusion of all others— that, indeed, the governmental endorsement of that prayer seems relatively insignificant when compared to the governmental encroachments upon religion which were commonplace 200 years ago. To those who may subscribe to the view that because the Regents' official prayer is so brief and general there can be no danger to religious freedom in its governmental establishment, however, it may be appropriate to say in the words of James Madison, the author of the First Amendment:

> [I]t is proper to take alarm at the first experiment on our liberties. . . .
> Who does not see that the same authority which can establish Christianity,
> in exclusion of all other Religions, may establish with the same ease any
> particular sect of Christians, in exclusion of all other Sects? That the same
> authority which can force a citizen to contribute three pence only of his
> property for the support of any one establishment, may force him to conform
> to any other establishment in all cases whatsoever?

The judgment of the Court of Appeals of New York is reversed and the cause remanded for further proceedings not inconsistent with this opinion. *Reversed and remanded.*

Mr. Justice Stewart, dissenting.

A local school board in New York has provided that those pupils who wish to do so may join in a brief prayer at the beginning of each school day, acknowledging their dependence upon God and asking His blessing upon them and upon their parents, their teachers, and their country. The Court today decides that in permitting this brief nondenominational prayer the school board has violated the Constitution of the United States. I think this decision is wrong.

The Court does not hold, nor could it, that New York has interfered with the free exercise of anybody's religion. For the state courts have made clear that those who object to reciting the prayer must be entirely free of any compulsion to do so, including any "embarrassments and pressures." . . . But the Court says that in permitting school children to say this simple prayer, the New York authorities have established "an official religion."

With all respect, I think the Court has misapplied a great constitutional principle. I cannot see how an "official religion" is established by letting those who want to say a prayer say it. On the contrary, I think that to deny the wish of these school children to join in reciting this prayer is to deny them the opportunity of sharing in the spiritual heritage of our Nation.

The Court's historical review of the quarrels over the Book of Common Prayer in England throws no light for me on the issue before us in this case. England had then and has now an established church. Equally unenlightening, I think, is the history of the early establishment and later rejection of an official church in our own States. For we deal here not with the establishment of a state church, which would, of course, be constitutionally impermissible, but with whether school children who want to begin their day by joining in prayer must be prohibited from doing so. Moreover, I think that the Court's task, in this as in all areas of constitutional adjudication, is not responsibly aided by the uncritical invocation of metaphors like the "wall of separation," a phrase nowhere to be found in the Constitution. What is relevant to the issue here is not the history of an established church in sixteenth century England or in eighteenth century America, but the history of the religious traditions of our people, reflected in countless practices of the institutions and officials of our government.

At the opening of each day's Session of this Court we stand, while one of our officials invokes the protection of God. Since the days of John Marshall our Crier has said, "God save the United States and this Honorable Court." Both the Senate and the House of Representatives open their daily Sessions with prayer. Each of our Presidents, from George Washington to John F. Kennedy, has upon assuming his Office asked the protection and help of God. . . .

The Court today says that the state and federal governments are without constitutional power to prescribe any particular form of words to be recited by any group of the American people on any subject touching religion. One of the stanzas of "The Star-Spangled Banner," made our National Anthem by Act of Congress in 1931, contains these verses:

> Blest with victory and peace, may the heav'n rescued land
> Praise the Pow'r that hath made and preserved us a nation!
> Then conquer we must, when our cause it is just,
> And this be our motto "In God is our Trust."

In 1954 Congress added a phrase to the Pledge of Allegiance to the Flag so that it now contains the words "one Nation *under God,* indivisible, with liberty and justice for all." In 1952 Congress enacted legislation calling upon the President each year to proclaim a National Day of Prayer. Since 1865 the words IN GOD WE TRUST have been impressed on our coins. . . .

I do not believe that this Court, or the Congress, or the President has by the actions and practices I have mentioned established an "official religion" in violation of the Constitution. And I do not believe the State of New York has done so in this case. What each has done has been to recognize and to follow the deeply entrenched and highly cherished spiritual traditions of our Nation—traditions which come down to us from those who almost two hundred years ago avowed their "firm Reliance on the Protection of divine Providence" when they proclaimed the freedom and independence of this brave new world.

I dissent.

President John F. Kennedy Discusses the Supreme Court and Public-School Prayer, 1962

. . . Q. Mr. President, in the furor over the Supreme Court's decision on prayer in the schools, some members of Congress have been introducing legislation for constitutional amendments specifically to sanction prayer or religious exercise in the schools. Can you give us your opinion of the decision itself and of these moves of the Congress to circumvent it?

The President. I haven't seen the measures in the Congress and you would have to make a determination of what the language was and what effect it would have on the first amendment. The Supreme Court has made its judgment, and a good many people obviously will disagree with it. Others will agree with it. But I think that it is important for us if we are going to maintain our constitutional principle that we support the Supreme Court decisions even when we may not agree with them.

In addition, we have in this case a very easy remedy and that is to pray ourselves. And I would think that it would be a welcome reminder to every American family that we can pray a good deal more at home, we can attend our churches with a good deal more fidelity, and we can make the true meaning of prayer much more important in the lives of all of our children. That power is very much open to us. And I would hope that as a result of this decision that all American parents will intensify their efforts at home, and the rest of us will support the Constitution and the responsibility of the Supreme Court in interpreting it, which is theirs, and given to them by the Constitution. . . .

Ishmael Jaffree Opposes Public-School Prayer, 1985

I was born on March 28, 1944, in a home for unwed mothers in Cleveland, Ohio, the first and only child of my mother. By reference to where I was born, she clearly was unwed at the time of my birth and she remained unwed. . . . I never did know my father. She told me that my father had died before I was born. It wasn't until I was grown that I found out that wasn't the truth. My mother was poor; she did domestic work for white people and she only made about $30 a week. In the early years of my life, I never had anything new. My clothes were purchased from Goodwill, and we ate mostly pork and beans and wieners. Unlike many only children, I didn't have everything that I wanted. I had very little of what I wanted because my mother couldn't afford it.

I started very early being different from other children—sort of a non-conformist in certain areas. . . . I didn't even conform to the behavior patterns of my mother. However, my mother did early-on influence me with respect to religious matters. She was a Baptist, but she was somewhat hypocritical in her religious precepts. Her being religious did not stop her from socializing with married men. Her being religious did not stop her from going into a restaurant and stealing the silverware. She claimed that she had paid for it in the cost of the meal and that justified her taking it. I observed this hypocrisy in my mother and vowed that I would never be a religious hypocrite.

Despite my mother's hypocrisy, she wanted me to be a minister. She promoted the idea that I was gifted or a God-chosen person. . . . In my early years I was very much a student of the Bible and I used to read it a lot. Very early in my childhood I used to go on the street corners and minister to the people and preach. I would take my Bible and tell people to repent and come right with God, that you are all sinners.

Even before my teenage years I sort of strayed from the straight and narrow. I became a petty thief and was stealing things from department stores. When I was only ten I was sent to a juvenile detention home for taking a machete from a truck. Later on I was judged to be a juvenile delinquent, and I served an eight-month term in a juvenile institution. . . .

But I continued to articulate strong religious views even after I enrolled in junior college. One incident that influenced my religious views occurred in a sociology class. The teacher was discussing how values are formed, how groups influence individuals. As part of that discussion she took a survey and asked all those who believed in God to raise their hand. Practically everyone did and I thought everyone had. Then she asked all those who don't believe in God, who are atheists, to raise their hand, and one female white student raised her hand. That was the first I came into face-to-face contact with someone who professed to be an atheist. And I remember that I instantly *hated* this woman and I couldn't understand her. I wondered how could she possibly raise her hand to deny the existence of a God that was responsible for her being here, responsible for her breathing. How could she turn her back on God and admit publicly that she did not believe? I felt she did not even have a right to live.

Some time later I started questioning why I was so angry just because this lady thought differently than I did. Later on I started taking courses in comparative religions, and all of a sudden my views started to change. As my views progressed, I adopted what we referred to as a black religion, a black theology. My concept of Jesus Christ became a black person, justified by passages in the Bible that suggested that Christ's hair was like wool. And from the country that he came from, he must have been black. I no longer believed that Jesus Christ had blue eyes and white skin. So I was part of a movement at this time, in the mid-sixties, that pushed the theory that Jesus Christ was black and therefore, of course, God was black. I wanted to encourage black people to accept that concept.

When I got into regular college in 1968, at Cleveland State University, I started to waver in that theology. I started thinking that maybe God is just an image, an energy force perhaps, and doesn't have to look like any particular person or be any particular color. And then I started questioning whether God exists at all, and started thinking about how I formed my ideas and how religious ideas got formulated in the first place. How an early Cro-Magnon person was afraid of fire because he couldn't understand it and ascribed supernatural qualities to it. I started thinking about how, through an evolutionary process, we got to where we are. Once I did that I became an agnostic, and I began to question everything. . . .

At the same time I was going through an evolution with respect to my religious beliefs, I was going through an evolution with respect to my racial attitudes. I went from having a complex about being black to being proud that I was black. As a result of the sixties and seventies, I also went through a political metamorphosis in the sense that I went from being supportive of the military complex system to being opposed to the military and the war in Vietnam. . . .

The way I became a lawyer goes back to when I was put out of high school. I worked after that for several years, at all kinds of jobs: I worked at restaurants as a busboy, and in an auto plant. Then I went back to an alternative-education school. What caused me to go back was that I used to watch Perry Mason on TV and became fascinated with him. And I thought, Gee, I'd like to be a lawyer, but in order to do that at least I have to finish high school. So I completed that and went on to junior college.

And about that time I got interested in politics, and I learned that a lot of politicians were attorneys, so that was further motivation to go to law school. I got involved in the campaign of Carl Stokes, a black man who ran for mayor of Cleveland. After he won, the second time he ran, I thought, Gee, I'd like to run for political office, and law would be a good stepping-stone. Also at that time, in 1972, I changed my name from Frederick Hobbs to Ishmael Jaffree. Most black people's names came from former slave owners, and I rejected the slave-master path. I chose Ishmael because it means "outcast," and Jaffree came from a Cleveland State professor that I admired.

While I was at Cleveland State University, I became active in trying to encourage law schools in Ohio to recruit blacks. And after I finished college, I applied to several and got turned down because my law-board score was so low. I applied to NYU, Cornell, Ohio State, Case Western Reserve. I finally got accepted at Cleveland—Marshall College of Law, principally because they had balked at admitting black students. I was a hell-raiser in college, and I was protesting, and I threatened to go to the media. I met with the dean, who fancied himself as a civil libertarian. So they started a special program at Cleveland—Marshall for disadvantaged youths, and I was in the first group they admitted.

Law school was easy for me. . . . I didn't have difficulty passing the Ohio bar exam. When I came to Alabama, I didn't even study for the bar; I just took it based on the Ohio bar.

What I wanted to do after I finished law school was constitutional law. That was what I enjoyed the most in law school. What I *didn't* want to do was criminal law, which I thought was too easy. . . .

When I was in law school I heard about a program called the Reggie fellowships, the Reginald Heber Smith fellowships to support law-school graduates in legal-services work for one year. I applied, and at the time I had recently been married and my wife had gone to school in Huntsville, Alabama. I was tired of Cleveland, and I thought the civil-rights movement was moving to the South, and that's where all the action was going to be. So I moved to Huntsville, which is an attractive city; but there weren't many black people there or much social or political activity going on. After a year in Huntsville I moved to the legal-services office in Mobile in 1977. I heard that they had a voting-rights case that was very active, and that they had a few black attorneys here.

The reason I brought the school prayer case is that I wanted my children to be free from programmed thinking, conditioned thinking. I wanted them to be free to explore a wide variety of ideas and not have to go through the long and painful metamorphosis that I went through. The case started in 1981 when my son Chioke, who was five and had just started kindergarten, came home from school one day and I asked him what's going on in school. He told me his teacher, Mrs. Boyd, was having the class line up before lunch and bow their heads and sing this grace.

Chioke was going to the same school where my wife, Mozelle, was teaching. My daughter Makeba was then seven, and she was in the second grade; and my son Aaki was eight, and he was in a special program because he had academic and emotional problems. They were all going to different schools in Mobile. When Chioke told me his teacher was leading the class in grace before meals, I remember telling him, Your teacher is doing something that's not legal. I want you to tell her that what she's doing is not legal. And he said, Okay.

I didn't think anything about it at the time. And about two weeks later, he said, Remember I told you my teacher was leading the class in prayer? She's still doing it. I said, Did you tell her what I said? He said, Yeah, but she's still doing it; she didn't care. So I wrote a letter for him to give his teacher, saying that my son has advised me that you are leading your class in a prayer before meals. You should know that this is unlawful; that the Supreme Court ruled some time ago that this is unconstitutional.

I gave Chioke the letter to his teacher, and I asked him when he got back from school did he give it to her, and he said, Yeah. Did she read it? Yeah. Did she stop? No. I then went down to the school and talked to Mrs. Boyd, who was a black teacher. I said, Chioke brought you a letter, and he said you're still leading the class in prayer. I don't really want to make a big issue out of this, but you really ought not to do that. I told her that I had reached an agreement with Mozelle that we are not trying to promote religion in our household. Mozelle is a Bahai and she's very religious, and I don't subscribe to any religion, but I don't influence the children to my way of thinking. Here you are undermining that neutrality in our household by promoting your brand of religion, and it's really unlawful. I'm not making any children say anything, she said. Her attitude was one of shock that I would even complain about it.

Then I talked with the principal, and she said that she would talk with the superintendent of schools and get back to me. By this time, my other two children told me that their classes were doing it, too. And I talked with *their* principals, and they said they would have to check with the superintendent as well. When I called them back, they said they were told the teachers could lead the children in prayer as long as they didn't make them take part. So I wrote a very long letter to the superintendent, whose name was Abe Hammons, complaining about the principals and telling him about the separation of church and state and how this is unlawful.

Superintendent Hammons told me he would check with his attorney and get back to me. But all the teachers kept doing it. I realized that it was getting close to the end of the school year. I was getting angry, so I decided to file a lawsuit. I contacted the ACLU and they said they didn't have the money to hire an attorney. Then I got a bright idea and contacted Ron Williams here in Mobile, and I told him that I didn't want to lose my job at Legal Services but that I would do all the work in the background. He used to work for Legal Services as well, and had recently gone into private practice. So we quickly dictated a complaint and filed it in federal court.

I was naive at the time and thought that once it reached the federal attorney, he'd say, Let's settle this case and stop this practice. I thought it wouldn't last more than two weeks. But the school-board president, Dan Alexander, had political ambitions. They had a meeting and he told them, Either we are going to have to say that what the teachers are doing is wrong and they will stop it, or we'll have to fight this all the way. The board voted to fight it.

The governor at the time, Fob James, heard about my lawsuit, and he called a special session of the Alabama state legislature. He called the media in advance and told them he was having a special news conference. So he went on statewide TV and criticized me by name and said I had sued these three brave teachers who were doing nothing more than teaching the children of our state to pray. The governor submitted legislation to permit teachers to lead willing students in prayer, and it was passed within a week. The legislation included a prayer that was written by the governor's son. They are both religious fanatics. So I quickly filed an amended complaint to challenge this new law as well, and I added the governor as a party.

That's when the publicity really started. The school-board president thought he could make political points and he started attacking me, and the local media just had a field day. I got a lot of hostile reaction. The black community was up in arms that some black person had done this. I got portrayed as a person who was trying to take God out of the public schools. The talk shows in Mobile were filled with people who said, Why doesn't he go back to Africa where he came from. I got all kinds of nasty letters, and I got nasty phone calls at all times of night. I used to talk with people and try to let them understand why I did this—that it was a matter of principle and the schools shouldn't be promoting anybody's religion. People in the neighborhood stopped their children from associating with my children. My children got jumped on, laughed at, talked about in school. My children started turning against me; they said it was a stupid lawsuit. They especially turned against me when Judge Hand ruled against me. They told me the judge had said what I was doing was stupid.

This case was originally assigned to Judge Cox, who was a new federal judge in Mobile. Cases were assigned on an even-number, odd-number basis. Judge Cox would get all the even-numbered cases and Judge Hand would get the odd-numbered cases. This was an even-numbered case. Judge Hand learned about the case and he wanted it, so he just took it from Judge Cox and put it on his own docket. . . .

All of a sudden, these people from the biggest Baptist church in Mobile, Cottage Hill Baptist Church, moved to intervene in my case. They wanted to be defendants and said they wanted prayer in the schools. They claimed it would be a denial of their rights of free exercise of religion to take prayer out of public schools. We objected to their presence, but Judge Hand said, I'll just let them stay in temporarily and hear what they have to say. We had a preliminary hearing and I subpoenaed Senator Holmes, who sponsored the law, and we got him to admit that he wanted to get prayer back into the schools.

Then the intervenors said, We have some people we want to testify—and they brought in this Baptist minister from Florida who said that our religion requires prayer to be said everywhere, including the schools. Then he mentioned secular humanism, which he had been talking about every Sunday on his television show. We objected, but Judge Hand said that it's about time the courts started looking at what he called the religion of secular humanism. So the other side got their clue, and they started making secular-humanism noises. And they said that if Jaffree is successful in getting an injunction against the Christian religion, we want an injunction against secular humanism as well. . . .

Judge Hand heard all of this testimony over our objections. Then he came out with this opinion saying that the teachers were promoting prayer but it didn't matter, because the states are free to establish a religion if they want to and the Supreme Court had erred; that he had studied some fresh historical analysis on this. And he put in this footnote that said if the Supreme Court overruled him, he had heard testimony that secular humanism was a religion and was being advanced in the schools. I'm going to hunker down, he said, and go through these books page by page, and you'll get censorship like you've never seen. I was really shocked! I had *no* idea he would come out from that angle.

As soon as Judge Hand ruled, *everybody* started having prayer sessions in school. The school-board president even called in the media and led children in prayer at lunch. This was all focused on my children. One of them used to bury his head when the media came around. We got more threats on my life. Some of the black people would see me at the mall and criticize me. I was considered a misfit. It wasn't until the court of appeals ruled in my favor that the attitude among blacks started to change slightly.

I didn't argue my case before the Supreme Court, but I knew the law so well that I programmed the attorney who did the argument. We had a session where I pretended that I was each of the members of the Supreme Court, and I put hypothetical questions to them. I studied opinions that all the justices had written, and when I wrote the brief I incorporated stuff they had said, to sort of lock them into positions on these issues. I tried to anticipate what they would say in light of what they had written before, and what kinds of questions they might possibly ask.

I had never been in the Supreme Court before, and I was aware of a sense of awe, the sense of serenity of the place, the power that these justices have. Everything was so solemn and quiet. It was like a church. . . .

I thought I was going to lose. I had studied the Supreme Court enough that I didn't think it would say that schools could not even set aside a moment and tell students they could pray or meditate in that moment. Teachers leading students in vocal prayer—of course not. But telling students that they could meditate or pray silently, which they could do anyway, I didn't think the Supreme Court would find that constitutionally infirm.

By the time the Supreme Court ruled for me, the mood of the community had tempered somewhat. When Judge Hand's ruling had sunk in, some people had been embarrassed, because he had gone too far. I mean, he had reversed the Supreme Court, which he had no power to do, and said that the Bill of Rights didn't apply to the states. And nobody in Mobile was really excited about the meditation issue. What they really wanted was vocal prayer! So that didn't create the hostile reaction that the case earlier had.

The Supreme Court decision created a great deal of joy in my children. They suddenly realized that I had won, and that the whole case was over. That was it! The teachers in my children's schools stopped saying the prayers, although I found out they were still praying in other schools. But they are very careful not to pray in *my* children's schools, because they know that I, more than any other person in Mobile, would raise the issue all over again.

Jaffree v. *The Board of School Commissioners of Mobile County,* 554 Fed. Supp. 1104 (1983)

United States District Court, S.D. Alabama

. . . The United States Supreme Court has previously addressed itself in many cases to the practice of prayer and religious services in the public schools. As courts are wont to say, this court does not write upon a clean slate when it addresses the issue of school prayer. . . .

In *Engel* v. *Vitale* parents of public school students filed suit to compel the board of education to discontinue the use of an official prayer in the public schools. The prayer was asserted to be contrary to the beliefs, religions, or religious practices of the complaining parents and their children. In *Engel* the board of education, acting in its official capacity under state law, directed the principals to cause the following prayer to be said aloud by each class at the beginning of the day in each homeroom: "Almighty God, we acknowledge our dependence upon Thee, and we beg Thy blessings upon us, our parents, our teachers and our Country." . . . This prayer was adopted by the school board because it believed the prayer would help instill the proper moral and spiritual training needed by the students. . . .

[U]nder present rulings the use of officially-authorized prayers or Bible readings for motivational purposes constitutes a direct violation of the establishment clause. Through a series of decisions, the courts have held that the establishment clause was designed to avoid any official sponsorship or approval of religious beliefs. Even though a practice may not be coercive, active support of a particular belief raises the danger, under the rationale of the Court, that state-approved religious views may be eventually established.

Although a given prayer or practice may not favor any one sect, the principle of neutrality in religious matters is violated under these decisions by any program which places tacit government approval upon religious views or practices. While the purpose of the program might be neutral or secular, the effect of the program or practice is to give government aid in support of the advancement of religious beliefs. Thus the programs are held invalid without any consideration as to whether they excessively entangle the state in religious affairs.

In contrast, the Supreme Court has permitted the use of the Bible in a literature course where the literary aspects of the Bible are emphasized over its religious contents. . . . So long as the study does not amount to prayer or the advancement of religious beliefs, a teacher may discuss the literary aspects of the Bible in a secular course of study. Finally, the Supreme Court permits religious references in official ceremonies, including some school exercises, on the basis that these references are part of our secularized traditions and thus will not advance religion. . . .

In the face of this precedent the defendants argue that school prayers as they are employed are constitutional. The historical argument which they advance takes two tacks. First, the defendants urge that the first amendment to the U.S. Constitution was intended only to prohibit the *federal government* from establishing a *national* religion. Read in its proper historical context, the defendants contend that the first amendment has no application to the states. The intent of the drafters and adoptors of the first amendment was to prevent the establishment of a national church or religion, and to prevent any single religious sect or denomination from obtaining a preferred position under the auspices of the federal government.

The corollary of this historical intent, according to the defendants, was to allow the states the freedom to address the establishment of religions as an individual prerogative of each state. Stated differently, the election by a state to establish a religion within its boundaries was intended by the framers of the Constitution to be a power reserved to the several states.

Second, the defendants argue that whatever prohibitions were initially placed upon the federal government by the first amendment that those prohibitions were not incorporated against the states when the fourteenth amendment became law on July 19, 1868. The defendants have introduced the Court to a mass of historical documentation which all point to the intent of the Thirty-ninth Congress to narrowly restrict the scope of the fourteenth amendment. In particular, these historical documents, according to the defendants, clearly demonstrate that the first amendment was never intended to be incorporated through the fourteenth amendment to apply against the states. The Court shall examine each historical argument in turn.

In the alternative, the defendant-intervenors argue that if the first amendment does bar the states from establishing a religion then the Mobile County schools have established or are permitting secular humanism . . . to be advanced in the curriculum and, being a religion, it must be purged also. Such a purge, maintain the defendant-intervenors, is nigh impossible because such teachings have become so entwined in every phase of the curriculum that it is like a pervasive cancer. If this must continue, say the defendant-intervenors, the only tenable alternative is for the public schools to allow the alternative religious views to be presented so that the students might better make more meaningful choices. . . .

More than any other provision of the Constitution, the interpretation by the United States Supreme Court of the establishment clause has been steeped in history. This Court's independent review of the relevant historical documents and its reading of the scholarly analysis convinces it that the United States Supreme Court has erred in its reading of history. Perhaps this opinion will be no more than a voice crying in the wilderness and this attempt to right that which this Court is persuaded is a misreading of history will come to nothing more than blowing in the hurricane, but be that as it may, this Court is persuaded as was Hamilton that "[e]very breach of the fundamental laws, though dictated by necessity impairs the sacred reverence which ought to be maintained in the breast of the rulers towards the constitution." . . .

. . . Because the establishment clause of the first amendment to the United States Constitution does not prohibit the state from establishing a religion, the prayers offered by the teachers in this case are not unconstitutional. Therefore, the Court holds that the complaint fails to state a claim for which relief could be granted.

Conclusion

There are pebbles on the beach of history from which scholars and judges might attempt to support the conclusions that they are wont to reach. That is what Professors Flack, Crosskey and the more modern scholars have done in attempting to establish a beachhead, as did Justice Black, that there is a basis for their conclusions that Congress and the people intended to alter the direction of the country by incorporating the first eight amendments to the Constitution. However, in arriving at this conclusion, they, and each of them, have had to revise established principles of constitutional interpretation by the judiciary. Whether the judiciary, inadvertently or eagerly, walked into this trap is not for discussion. The result is that the judiciary has, in fact, amended the Constitution to the consternation of the republic. As Washington pointed out in his Farewell Address, . . . this clearly is the avenue by which our government can and, ultimately, will be destroyed. We think we move in the right direction today, but in so doing we are denying to the people their right to express themselves. It is not what we, the judiciary want, it is what the people want translated into law pursuant to the plan established in the Constitution as the framers intended. This is the bedrock and genius of our republic. The mantle of office gives us no power to fix the moral direction that this nation will take. When we undertake such course we trample upon the law. In such instances the people have a right to complain. The Court loses its respect and our institution is brought low. This misdirection should be cured now before it is too late. We must give no future generation an excuse to use this same tactic to further their ends which they think proper under the then political climate as for instance did Adolph Hitler when he used the court system to further his goals.

What is past is prologue. The framers of our Constitution, fresh with recent history's teachings, knew full well the propriety of their decision to leave to the peoples of the several states the determination of matters religious. The wisdom of this decision becomes increasingly apparent as the courts wind their way through the maze they have created for themselves by amending the Constitution by judicial fiat to make the first amendment applicable to the states. Consistency no longer exists. Where you cannot recite the Lord's Prayer, you may sing his praises in God Bless America. Where you cannot post the Ten Commandments on the wall for those to read if they do choose, you can require the Pledge of Allegience. Where you cannot acknowledge the authority of the Almighty in the Regent's prayer, you can acknowledge the existence of the Almighty in singing the verses of America and Battle Hymn of the Republic. It is no wonder that the people perceive that justice is myoptic [*sic*], obtuse, and janus-like.

If the appellate courts disagree with this Court in its examination of history and conclusion of constitutional interpretation thereof, then this Court will look again at the record in this case and reach conclusions which it is not now forced to reach.

Order

It is therefore ordered that the complaint in this case be dismissed with prejudice. Costs are taxed against the plaintiffs. . . .

Wallace v. *Jaffree*, 472 U.S. 38 (1985)

[6–3: Stevens, Blackmun, Brennan, Marshall,
O'Connor, Powell; Burger, White, Rehnquist]

. . . Our unanimous affirmance of the Court of Appeals' judgment . . . makes it unnecessary to comment at length on the District Court's remarkable conclusion that the Federal Constitution imposes no obstacle to Alabama's establishment of a state religion. Before analyzing the precise issue that is presented to us, it is nevertheless appropriate to recall how firmly embedded in our constitutional jurisprudence is the proposition that the several States have no greater power to restrain the individual freedoms protected by the First Amendment than does the Congress of the United States.

As is plain from its text, the First Amendment was adopted to curtail the power of Congress to interfere with the individual's freedom to believe, to worship, and to express himself in accordance with the dictates of his own conscience. Until the Fourteenth Amendment was added to the Constitution, the First Amendment's restraints on the exercise of federal power simply did not apply to the States. But when the Constitution was amended to prohibit any State from depriving any person of liberty without due process of law, that Amendment imposed the same substantive limitations on the States' power to legislate that the First Amendment had always imposed on the Congress' power. This Court has confirmed and endorsed this elementary proposition of law time and time again.

Just as the right to speak and the right to refrain from speaking are complementary components of a broader concept of individual freedom of mind, so also the individual's freedom to choose his own creed is the counterpart of his right to refrain from accepting the creed established by the majority. At one time it was thought that this right merely proscribed the preference of one Christian sect over another, but would not require equal respect for the conscience of the infidel, the atheist, or the adherent of a non-Christian faith such as Mohammedism or Judaism. But when the underlying principle has been examined in the crucible of litigation, the Court has unambiguously concluded that the individual freedom of conscience protected by the First Amendment embraces the right to select any religious faith or none at all. This conclusion derives support not only from the interest in respecting the individual's freedom of conscience, but also from the conviction that religious beliefs worthy of respect are the product of free and voluntary choice by the faithful, and from recognition of the fact that the political interest in forestalling intolerance extends beyond intolerance among Christian sects—or even intolerance among "religions"—to encompass intolerance of the disbeliever and the uncertain. The State of Alabama, no less than the Congress of the United States, must respect that basic truth.

III. . . . The First Amendment requires that a statute must be invalidated if it is entirely motivated by a purpose to advance religion.

In applying the purpose test, it is appropriate to ask "whether government's actual purpose is to endorse or disapprove of religion." . . . In this case, the answer to that question is dispositive. For the record not only provides us with an unambiguous affirmative answer, but it also reveals that the enactment . . . was not motivated by any clearly secular purpose—indeed, the statute had *no* secular purpose.

IV. The sponsor of the bill . . . , Senator Donald Holmes, inserted into the legislative record—apparently without dissent—a statement indicating that the legislation was an "effort to return voluntary prayer" to the public schools. Later Senator Holmes confirmed this purpose before the District Court. In response to the question whether he had any purpose for the legislation other than returning voluntary prayer to public schools, he stated,

"No, I did not have no other purpose in mind." The State did not present evidence of *any* secular purpose. . . .

. . . The Legislature acted . . . for the sole purpose of expressing the State's endorsement of prayer activities for one minute at the beginning of each school day. The addition of "or voluntary prayer" indicates that the State intended to characterize prayer as a favored practice. Such an endorsement is not consistent with the established principle that the Government must pursue a course of complete neutrality toward religion.

The importance of that principle does not permit us to treat this as an inconsequential case involving nothing more than a few words of symbolic speech on behalf of the political majority. For whenever the State itself speaks on a religious subject, one of the questions that we must ask is "whether the Government intends to convey a message of endorsement or disapproval of religion." The well-supported concurrent findings of the District Court and the Court of Appeals—that [the statute] was intended to convey a message of State-approval of prayer activities in the public schools—make it unnecessary, and indeed inappropriate, to evaluate the practical significance of the addition of the words "or voluntary prayer" to the statute. Keeping in mind, as we must, "both the fundamental place held by the Establishment Clause in our constitutional scheme and the myriad, subtle ways in which Establishment Clause values can be eroded," . . . we conclude that [the statute] violates the First Amendment.

The judgment of the Court of Appeals is affirmed.

Senator Jesse Helms on Prayer in the Public Schools, 1985

Let's talk about reining in the Supreme Court. Lawyers and laymen alike today recognize that the Supreme Court has gone far beyond its constitutional role of interpreter of the law. In recent years, it has transformed itself from interpreter of law to lawmaker, a role neither authorized nor anticipated by the Constitution. The Supreme Court improperly makes law in two ways. First, it invades the prerogatives of the legislative branch, in effect, by amending federal statutes. A recent illustration is the *Bob Jones* case, in which the Internal Revenue Code was directly amended by court decree. Second, the Supreme Court regularly alters the Constitution itself without benefit of a constitutional amendment. This is the more dangerous of the two problems.

For example, in the early 1960s, contrary to all precedent and tradition and without any official change in the Constitution, the Supreme Court held unconstitutional voluntary group prayer in the public schools. I cannot comprehend how Congress could ever have directly achieved this sweeping result. The plain fact is that the Constitution does not confer upon any branch of the federal government the power to tell the states that they cannot conduct voluntary prayer in their own schools if they so choose. But the Supreme

"Prayer in the Public Schools" by Senator Jesse Helms. Reprinted by permission.

Court of the United States did not hesitate, in the now-famous *Engle* and *Schempp* cases, to tell the states just that. The theories used were novel and without historical basis. They were that the Establishment Clause of the First Amendment had been incorporated against the states and that its terms prohibited voluntary prayer in public classrooms. Thus the court in effect amended the Constitution in a way that Congress never could. By a simple majority vote of the nine Supreme Court Justices, voluntary school prayer was rendered unconstitutional throughout the United States.

Ironically, Congress had in fact tried in 1875 to bring about at least partially the result achieved by the Supreme Court in the prayer cases. But unlike the Court, Congress proceeded according to the Constitution, and considered proposing a constitutional amendment to the states for their ratification. That amendment, the so-called Blaine Amendment, would have applied the Establishment and Free Exercise Clauses of the First Amendment to the states. It was rejected, but no one even implied, as the modern Supreme Court has declared, that the Fourteenth Amendment incorporated the Establishment Clause against the states.

My point here—and it applies in other important areas of the law, such as abortion, forced busing, capital punishment, criminal procedure, pornography, and libel—is that the Supreme Court arrogantly has taken unto itself the power of amending the Constitution. It sits today virtually as a continuing constitutional convention with powers of ratification, even though the Constitution gives it no such status.

Instead of properly using the powers of judicial review to invalidate statutes repugnant to the Constitution in cases before it, the Supreme Court employs judicial review first to expand the Constitution according to the Justices' personal views, and then to declare unconstitutional laws otherwise valid. This exotic and extravagant latter-day jurisprudence threatens not only our Constitution but the rule of law itself.

Under these circumstances, Congress, in my judgment, has not only the power, but the duty, to rein in a wayward judiciary and thereby restore a proper balance of power among the three branches of our tripartite government.

What can Congress do? Well, the Framers of the Constitution had an original design of checks and balances, giving Congress significant powers over the judicial branch. The Senate, for example, is authorized to give advice and consent to the President's nominations to the federal bench. The House can impeach and the Senate can remove judges for misconduct. Congress holds the purse-strings for judicial appropriations. Congress has specific enforcement powers over the Fourteenth Amendment and other constitutional provisions. And finally, Congress can do two things that deserve special consideration: propose constitutional amendments and limit the appellate jurisdiction of the Supreme Court. . . .

In 1979, when the Democrats held a majority in the Senate, my bill to withdraw jurisdiction over school prayer passed twice by votes of 47–37 and 51–40, only to be killed in the House by Speaker O'Neill and Representative Peter Rodino and their allies. In 1982, the same bill survived a tabling motion, 53–57, before later being set aside to pave the way for passage of a federal debt-limit extension. The point is this: these votes demonstrate that the will is there, in the Senate of the United States, to apply the brakes on the federal judiciary by withdrawing jurisdiction. Not only should we pursue such means to restore the people's liberty on prayer and other fundamental issues, but also I believe that we in Congress will be delinquent in our duty to preserve and protect and defend the Constitution if we do not apply the brakes on the federal judiciary. It is Congress that was given the authority to check the Supreme Court, and it is to Congress that the American people should look to remedy judicial usurpation.

✣ E S S A Y S

The following essays present diametrically opposed interpretations of the Constitution's establishment clause. In the first selection, James McClellan, the founder and director of the Center for Judicial Studies and a former aide to Senator Jesse Helms of North Carolina, argues not only that the Supreme Court erred in incorporating the establishment clause into the Fourteenth Amendment's due-process clause but also that the framers of the Bill of Rights intended a low wall of separation between church and state. Professor Leonard W. Levy, a historian at the Claremont Graduate School, dismisses McClellan's arguments as "bizarre" in the second essay and insists that incorporation was both appropriate and in keeping with the intentions of the framers of the religion clauses to protect freedom of belief.

The Supreme Court's Usurpation of Freedom of Religion

JAMES MCCLELLAN

. . . To appreciate the significance of the *Jaffree* case, it is essential to begin where Judge Hand begins—with Justice Hugo Black's opinion for the Court in *Everson* v. *Board of Education,* decided in 1947. *Everson* is the key to an understanding of the issues involved and the foundation for every establishment clause case decided by the Supreme Court.

In *Everson* Black promulgated two revolutionary principles of constitutional construction. First, he held, *without supporting argument,* that the establishment clause applied to the states. By this radical innovation the Court overturned more than one hundred and fifty years of constitutional law that had regularly permitted the states to determine their own church-state relationships in accordance with their own state laws and constitutions.

Second—and equally novel—Black announced that the establishment clause erected a "wall of separation" between church and state that prohibited the states from giving any aid of any kind not merely to specific religious sects or denominations but to religion generally. "Neither a state

"Hand's Writing on the Wall of Separation: The Significance of *Jaffree* in Future Cases on Religious Establishment" by James McClellan, pp. 44–52, 59–64. Reprinted with the permission of the American Enterprise Institute for Public Policy Research, Washington, D.C.

nor the Federal Government," said Justice Black, "can set up a church. Neither can pass laws which aid one religion, *aid all religions,* or prefer one religion over another. . . . No tax in *any* amount, large or small, can be levied to support *any* religious activities or institutions." On the basis of these absolutist pronouncements in *Everson,* the Court subsequently ruled in *Engel* v. *Vitale* that the voluntary recitation of a state-composed prayer, though nondenominational, constituted an aid to, and thus an establishment of, religion.

As Judge Hand demonstrates rather convincingly in the *Jaffree* case, neither of the principles embraced by the Court in *Everson* is supported by the language or intent of the Constitution or by historical experience. Throughout most of this century, it would seem, the Supreme Court has been misreading the meaning and purpose of the Bill of Rights in general and the establishment clause in particular, to the extent that the first nine amendments of our Constitution are being used by the Court to establish total federal control over all civil and criminal rights disputes in the nation. This is the very result that the Bill of Rights was designed to prevent.

The Bill of Rights, according to Judge Hand, originally had a dual purpose. It was designed not merely to assure each individual that the federal government would not abridge the freedoms enumerated but also to assure each *state* that the federal government would not encroach upon the jurisdiction of the states over such matters. With regard to this second purpose, therefore, the Bill of Rights was conceived as a states' rights document. Each amendment was a guarantee to the individual *and* to the states.

A survey of constitutional development leading to the creation and adoption of the Bill of Rights during the formative era of American history lends considerable weight to Judge Hand's thesis. In the Federal Convention of 1787, one of the leading spokesmen for states' rights was George Mason of Virginia, who doggedly resisted the Nationalist plan at every turn. Shortly before the convention completed its work on September 17, Mason remarked that he "wished the plan had been prefaced with a Bill of Rights," adding that he "would second a motion if made for the purpose." Elbridge Gerry of Massachusetts, who had been fighting at Mason's side throughout the summer against the Nationalists, quickly obliged and moved the establishment of a committee to prepare the document.

Only one member of the convention, Roger Sherman of Connecticut, spoke against the motion, but his response ended the debate as abruptly as it had begun. A Bill of Rights would be redundant, Sherman explained, because "the State Declarations of Rights are not repealed by this Constitution; and being in force are sufficient." Mason feared that "the laws of the U.S. are to be paramount to State Bills of Rights," but the delegates agreed with Sherman that Mason's apprehensions were unfounded, and the motion was voted down unanimously.

This brief exchange on the need for a bill of rights is the only mention of the subject during the entire Federal Convention. The reasons for the lack of interest are rather obvious: First, the delegates were already agreed that the states would retain jurisdiction over most civil rights disputes between a state and its citizens under the new Constitution, and there had been no serious attempt to establish federal control in this area at any time during the convention. Second, it was generally assumed, as Sherman explained, that state bills of rights would remain the supreme law of each state; the new system of government did not call for uniformity of civil rights but preserved intact the diversity that existed under the Articles of Confederation. Third, the delegated and enumerated powers of the central government did not include the power to prescribe national standards or rules for the states in the field of civil liberties.

This also explains why the Federalists "bowed to the wishes of the Antifederalists in the ratification fight and, without much of a struggle, agreed to the adoption of a bill of rights. . . . The Bill of Rights changed nothing as far as the Constitutional structure was concerned and neither reduced federal power nor increased state power. It simply declared what was already understood." The issue, in other words, was not who would establish civil rights policies within the states but the proper wording of the Constitution that would ensure *state* enforcement of civil liberties in disputes between a state and its citizens. . . .

Likewise, the dominant theme of the Antifederalist critique of the Constitution was not civil rights but states' rights. During the ratification struggle Antifederalists placed far greater emphasis on the federalism of the Bill of Rights than on the substantive content or meaning of the liberties themselves. Six states proposed long lists of amendments before the Constitution was adopted. . . .

The task of sorting through the various constitutional amendments proposed by the states and reducing them to a coherent whole was given to James Madison. On June 7, 1789, Madison introduced two amendments dealing with the subject of religion. The first provided that "the Civil Rights of none shall be abridged on account of religious belief or worship, nor shall any *national* religion be established, nor shall the full and equal rights of conscience be in any manner, nor on any pretext infringed."

The wording of the amendment clearly indicated that the prohibition against religious establishment applied only to the federal government and that the states would retain exclusive control over church-state relations within their spheres of authority. This understanding prevailed in subsequent drafts and became a permanent feature of the First Amendment. The language finally approved exempted the states and declared only that "Congress shall make no law respecting an establishment of religion."

Madison's second amendment (his fifth resolution), which would have reversed the consensus of the convention and revolutionized the relationship between the federal and state governments, met a different fate. It provided—and no state had even hinted at the idea—that "no *State* shall violate the equal rights of conscience, or the freedom of the press, or trial by jury in criminal cases." Here, then, was the first and only attempt to apply any portion of what was to become the Bill of Rights to the states. The measure was referred to a select committee, whose membership included Madison, which recommended the part to limit the powers of the states respecting the equal rights of conscience. It passed the House after little debate but was defeated in the Senate. . . .

As finally approved, the relevant portions of the First Amendment provide that "Congress shall make no law respecting an establishment of religion, or prohibiting the free exercise thereof." It may thus be seen that the First Amendment to the Constitution that evolved out of these congressional proceedings was a stunning victory for states' rights. The amendment was framed, considered, and adopted with federalism in mind, and it applied only to the federal government. Not even Madison wished to apply the establishment clause to the states, and his attempt to restrict the state power under an early version of both the free exercise and the freedom of the press clauses was nipped in the bud.

In his *Jaffree* opinion, Judge Hand summarized the intent of the framers accordingly:

> The prohibition in the first amendment against the establishment of religion gave the states, by implication, full authority to determine church-state relations within their respective jurisdictions. "Thus the establishment clause actually had a dual purpose: to guarantee to each *individual* that Congress would not impose a national religion, and to each *state* that it was free to define the meaning of religious establishment under its own state constitution and laws. The Federal government, in other words, simply had no authority over the states respecting the matter of church-state relations." . . .

For more than a century the Supreme Court, with only a few scattered dissents, interpreted the Bill of Rights in conformity with this understanding. Speaking for a unanimous Court in *Barron* v. *Baltimore*, Chief Justice John Marshall declared in 1833 that the first eight amendments "contain no expression indicating an intention to apply them to the state governments." . . .

Even after the adoption in 1868 of the Fourteenth Amendment, which prohibited the *states* from denying a person life, liberty, or property without due process of law, an undivided Supreme Court continued to follow the *Barron* principle. Throughout the latter half of the nineteenth century and well into the twentieth, state and federal courts summarily dismissed the notion that the Bill of Rights applied to the states. . . .

Surely the most revolutionary decision handed down by the Supreme Court in its history, *Gitlow* v. *New York* prepared the way for a massive shift of power from the states to the federal judiciary. The ultimate power to define—and therefore to expand or restrict—civil liberties had silently slipped from the hands of the states to those of the central government, or more particularly the Supreme Court. A staggering blow had thus been inflicted at the very heart of federalism. Such a drastic and swift rupture with the past could only have succeeded through a profound misunderstanding of the constitutional structure by the members of the American legal profession. . . .

Through this rule of interpretation, it may now be seen, the Supreme Court has been engaged in a wholesome usurpation of state power for more than fifty years. As a result, nine individuals sitting on the Supreme Court for life now have virtually unlimited power to determine the scope and meaning of nearly every freedom that the American people possess. That the Court has met so little resistance in achieving this remarkable result demonstrates rather convincingly that few Americans, particularly in this century, have fully understood the meaning and purpose of the Bill of Rights or appreciated that it has been transformed into an instrument of minority rule by a handful of federal judges—the very essence of tyrannical government.

The enigmatic response of the American legal profession to the Court's incorporation of the establishment clause is a case in point. *Everson* . . . was the first instance in which the Court interpreted the establishment clause as a restriction on the states. The state law in question sought to reimburse the parents of parochial school children for school transportation costs and was challenged on the ground that it constituted an "establishment of religion." A majority of the justices found the law valid under the theory that it was a welfare measure benefiting the children rather than religion, but not one member of the Court challenged Justice Black's unsupported assumption of jurisdiction. To this day no member of the Supreme Court has ever questioned the application of the establishment clause to the states.

Even more astonishing is the fact that, until *Jaffree,* not a single attorney appearing before the Supreme Court during the past four decades ever challenged the incorporation of the establishment clause. During the course of their research, the intervenors in the *Jaffree* case examined all the oral arguments and all the briefs in the leading establishment and free exercise cases argued before the Court since 1940. . . .

Such is the level of understanding about the federalism of the Bill of Rights among the rising generation of American lawyers. The Constitution has largely been entrusted to their care. Their failure to explore the origins of the Constitution concerning so important a matter as the Bill of Rights, their resulting inability, it would seem, to grasp the theory and purpose of the system, and their proclivity to accept the Supreme Court's interpretation of the Constitution as gospel constitute a serious indictment of the profession. The problem is surely attributable in part to the case method of study in modern legal education, which emphasizes judicial interpretations of the Constitution rather than original sources and encourages lawyers to structure their arguments within the narrow framework of current case law and the crabbed learning of the judges. Nothing illustrates these points better than the fact that Judge Hand's landmark opinion in *Jaffree* is based almost exclusively on the accumulated research and writing of political scientists. Indeed, it is they and not the lawyers who have led the assault on the doctrine of incorporation and exposed its inherent fallacies, particularly as it applies to the establishment clause. . . .

Even if the Fourteenth Amendment were intended to apply the establishment clause against the states, it is clear that the Court's view of religious establishment has little basis in American history. In almost every establishment case the Supreme Court has been at pains to justify its absolutist interpretation of the establishment clause on historical grounds. From Justice

Black's opinion in *Everson* down to the present there are lengthy discourses on religious liberty purporting to demonstrate the universal acceptance throughout the American past of the Jeffersonian proposition that the First Amendment "erected a wall of separation between church and state," prohibiting the federal and state governments from giving aid of any kind not only to particular religious sects but to all religions or for general religious and moral purposes. . . .

The facts show . . . that no such wall was ever intended. Indeed, it never existed. A bare catalogue of church-state relations in all the states before and after the adoption of the Constitution would require many volumes. Suffice it to say that the overwhelming majority of states had clearly rejected the principle that there should be an absolute separation of church and state at the time they ratified the Bill of Rights. In 1791 there were three patterns of church-state relations in the United States: (1) quasi-establishment of Congregationalism in New England, where the church enjoyed direct and indirect benefits through state constitutions and statutes; (2) quasi-establishment of the Protestant religion in ten states; and (3) disestablishment of all religious sects in Rhode Island and Virginia.

The establishment clause preserved intact these various relationships and served two purposes. First, it served as a guarantee to the states that the federal government had no authority either to disestablish a sect or religion enjoying a preferred status or to pass a law *respecting* (that is, dealing with the subject of) the establishment of a religion. To suggest that any of the states ratified the First Amendment with the understanding that their assent cleared the way for federal interference in their internal religious affairs is to misunderstand the basic purpose of the establishment clause. The second purpose, as Justice Joseph Story explained in his *Commentaries on the Constitution*, was "to prevent any national ecclesiastical establishment that would give to an hierarchy the exclusive patronage of the *national* government."

The debates in the First Congress, which drafted the Bill of Rights, also reflect strong opposition to the view that the federal government should be prohibited from giving "any aid of any kind" to religion. In his analysis of documentary sources on the First Congress, including the notes of the reporter Thomas Lloyd, Michael Malbin has noted "that the members of the First Congress did not intend the establishment clause to mean anything remotely resembling what the Supreme Court has been saying it means, at least since 1947." Summarizing the debates, the various drafts of the amendment leading up to the final version, and the events surrounding the parliamentary struggle, Malbin concludes, "The legislative history of the establishment clause shows that the framers accepted nondiscriminatory aid to religion."

Turning finally to legislative proposals offered contemporaneously with the debate and adoption of the First Amendment and in the early years of the Republic, we again discern widespread acceptance of the principle that nondiscriminatory aid to religion generally and to Christianity in particular is consistent with the purposes of the First Amendment. One of the earliest acts of the House of Representatives, for example, was the election of a chaplain and an appropriation of $500 to pay his salary. Madison was a member of the committee that recommended the chaplain system.

While a member of the House, Madison endorsed Washington's presidential proclamations dealing with thanksgiving, fasting, and prayer. Later, while serving as president, Madison himself issued four prayer proclamations. Of the first four presidents of the United States, only Jefferson declined to issue executive religious proclamations; but his refusal derived not from the belief that such exercises constituted an establishment of religion but from his conviction as a states' rightist that the federal government had no authority to enter the field. . . .

[A] divided Court ruled in *Wallace* v. *Jaffree* that the Alabama "moment of silence" statute violated the establishment clause. The majority not only turned a deaf ear to Judge Hand's exposition of the incorporation doctrine but ignored as well his arguments disproving the separationist theory of construction. Like an incantation, the Court summarily recited its own decisions in reply to Hand's opinion, barely acknowledging the documentary evidence of original intent the judge had amassed to support his position. These are telltale signs of raw judicial power; and they reveal an uneasiness and uncertainty in that high tribunal, intimating self-doubt, not self-confidence.

We would be shortsighted, however, if we concluded from the holding in *Jaffree* that Hand's effort was an exercise in futility; for Hand has stirred a national debate of no small importance. He has found a convert on the Supreme Court—then-Justice William H. Rehnquist, who asserted for the first time in his judicial career that on the subject of religious establishment the Supreme Court has been laboring under a "mistaken understanding of constitutional history" during the past forty years. In a lengthy dissent that includes original source material cited by Hand, Rehnquist argued that the Court should promptly abandon the erroneous "wall of separation" theory. . . . "There is simply no historical foundation for the proposition that the Framers intended to build the 'wall of separation' that was constitutionalized in *Everson*." It is a "mischievous diversion of judges from the actual intentions of the drafters of the Bill of Rights," he observed, and "has no basis in the history of the [First] amendment." Justice Byron R. White also dissented, asserting that he "would support a basic reconsideration of our precedents." On the basis of Rehnquist's persuasive analysis of the religion clauses, said White, "it would be quite understandable if we undertook to reassess our cases dealing with these clauses, particularly those dealing with the Establishment Clause." But for Hand's challenge to the Court, these dissents would surely not have been written.

The influence of Judge Hand's opinion does not end in the pages of the Supreme Court reports. The incorporation doctrine, for example, has percolated to the surface of public debate since *Jaffree* and is now a common topic of discussion; and for the first time its legitimacy has been questioned by the attorney general of the United States. In a major address before the American Bar Association, Edwin Meese III spoke critically of the "bewildering" logic and "tangled case law" exhibited by the Supreme Court in establishment cases, pointing to *Jaffree* in particular. "Most Americans forget," he reminded the legal profession, "that it was not until 1925, in *Gitlow v. New York*, that *any* provision of the First Amendment was applied to the States. Nor was it until 1947 that the Establishment Clause was made applicable to the States through the Fourteenth Amendment." Noting further that the doctrine of incorporation was imposed "without any substantive argument" and that it rests on an "intellectually shaky foundation," the attorney general surmised that "nowhere else has the principle of federalism been dealt so politically violent and constitutionally suspect a blow as by the theory of incorporation." Without mentioning Brevard Hand by name, the attorney general endorsed his view that the wall of separation notion contravened the meaning and purpose of the establishment clause, concluding that there is "much merit in Justice Rehnquist's dissent in *Jaffree*."

In the final analysis, it seems clear that Judge Hand's opinion has left a deep and permanent scar on the face of the Supreme Court; for he has rather successfully challenged the Court's self-proclaimed infallibility, at least on the question of religious establishment, eliciting thereby a favorable response from two of its members. Moreover, he has laid bare the utter falsity of the incorporation and wall of separation theories. The study and practice of constitutional law in this country, notwithstanding Leonard Levy's chimerical writings on the establishment clause, will never be quite the same. Taken together, the Hand and Rehnquist opinions invigorate the legitimacy of a great body of scholarship that has been ignored by the Court, creating a haven for dissenters that will strengthen their position as never before. In these respects *Jaffree* may well mark an important turning point in American constitutional history. Truth is a stubborn adversary and has a way of haunting men—even those on the high court.

The Supreme Court's Defense of Freedom of Religion

LEONARD W. LEVY

The First Amendment bans laws respecting an establishment of religion. Most of the framers of that amendment very probably meant that government should not promote, sponsor, or subsidize religion because it is best left to private voluntary support for the sake of religion itself as well as for government, and above all for the sake of the individual. Some of the framers undoubtedly believed that government should maintain a close relationship with religion, that is, with Protestantism, and that public support should uphold even tax support for churches and their ministers. The framers who came from Massachusetts and Connecticut certainly believed this, as did the representatives of New Hampshire, but New Hampshire was the only one of these New England states that ratified the First Amendment. Of the eleven states that ratified the First Amendment, New Hampshire and Ver-

Reprinted with permission of Macmillan Publishing Company from *The Establishment Clause: Religion and the First Amendment* by Leonard W. Levy, pp. 121–127, 184–185. Copyright © 1986 by Macmillan Publishing Company, a division of Macmillan, Inc.

mont were probably the only ones in which a majority of the people believed that the government should support religion. In all the other ratifying states, a majority very probably opposed such support. But whether those who framed and ratified the First Amendment believed in government aid to religion or in its private voluntary support, the fact is that no framer believed that the United States had or should have power to legislate on the subject of religion, and no state supported that power either.

Those who framed and ratified the First Amendment meant that the establishment clause, like the rest of the Bill of Rights, should apply to the national government only. After all, the First Amendment explicitly levies a ban on Congress, in contrast to the later Fourteenth Amendment, which expressly limits the states. James Madison in 1789 proposed an amendment to the Constitution prohibiting the states from violating certain rights, including freedom of religion. Had that amendment been adopted, the federal courts could easily have construed it to prohibit the states from maintaining establishments of religion. Except, perhaps, for Congregational New England, most of the nation believed that an establishment of religion violated religious liberty. The House approved of Madison's proposal but the Senate voted it down. The fact that Congress considered an amendment other than the one that prohibited Congress from passing laws respecting an establishment of religion shows that the establishment clause could not have been meant to apply to the states. The fact that Congress considered and rejected a prohibition on the states showed, further, that so far as the United States Constitution was concerned, the states were free to re-create the Inquisition or to erect and maintain exclusive establishments of religion, at least until ratification of the Fourteenth Amendment in 1868.

According to the Fourteenth Amendment, no state may deprive any person of liberty without due process of law. Is a state law respecting an establishment of religion a deprivation of liberty? Does the word "liberty" include within its meaning a right to be free from a law respecting an establishment of religion? The preponderance of evidence suggests that the framers of the Fourteenth Amendment neither intended its provisions to incorporate any part of the Bill of Rights nor to impose on the states the same limitations previously imposed on the United States only. However, the language of the Fourteenth Amendment—no state denials of liberty—allowed for the possibility that the Constitution prevented the states, as well as the United States, from violating the First Amendment. A rule of constitutional interpretation known as the "incorporation doctrine" posits that the Fourteenth Amendment incorporates the rights protected by the First Amendment. In 1940, when the Supreme Court incorporated the free exercise of religion clause into the Fourteenth Amendment, the Court assumed that the establishment clause imposed upon the states the same restraints as upon the United States. In the 1947 *Everson* case that obiter dictum became a holding of constitutional law. The Court unanimously agreed that the Fourteenth Amendment incorporated the establishment clause. Consequently the principle embodied in the First Amendment separated government and religion throughout the land, outlawing government support of religion, or, rather, laws respecting an establishment of religion. But what constitutes an establishment of prohibited support, according to the Supreme Court?

In the *Everson* case the Court laid down principles for interpreting the establishment clause that it has never abandoned, despite its frequently perplexing application of those principles. One such principle is that an establishment of religion includes "aid to all religions" as well as aid to just one in preference to others; another principle is that no tax in any amount can be used "to support any religious activities or institutions." These principles express, in part, the broad interpretation of what the framers of the First Amendment intended by the establishment clause. Justice Hugo L. Black, speaking for the majority in *Everson*, stated the broad interpretation as follows:

> The "establishment of religion" clause of the First Amendment means at least this: Neither a state nor the Federal Government can set up a church. Neither can pass laws which aid one religion, aid all religions, or prefer one religion over another. Neither can force nor influence a person to go to or to remain away from church against his will or force him to profess a belief or disbelief in any religion. No person can be punished for entertaining or professing religious beliefs or disbeliefs, for church attendance or nonattendance. No tax in any amount, large or small, can be levied to support any religious activities or institutions, whatever they may be called, or whatever form they may adopt to teach or practice religion. Neither a state nor the Federal Government can, openly or secretly, participate in the affairs of any religious organizations or groups and vice versa. In the words of Jefferson, the clause against establishment of religion by laws was intended to erect a "wall of separation between Church and State."

The Court has frequently quoted these words, with approval, as recently as 1985.

The dissenting justices in the *Everson* case, while disagreeing with the majority on the question whether the "wall of separation" had in fact been breached by the practice at issue, concurred with the majority on the historical question of the intentions of the framers and the meaning of the establishment clause. The opinion of Justice Wiley B. Rutledge, which all the dissenting justices endorsed, declared: "The Amendment's purpose was not to strike merely at the official establishment of a single sect, creed or religion, outlawing only a formal relation such as had prevailed in England and some of the colonies. Necessarily it was to uproot all such relationships. But the object was broader than separating church and state in this narrow sense. It was to create a complete and permanent separation of the spheres of religious activity and civil authority by comprehensively forbidding every form of public aid or support for religion."

Thus the heart of this broad interpretation, endorsed by the entire *Everson* Court, is that the First Amendment does not even permit government aid impartially and equitably administered to all religious groups.

The second or narrow interpretation of the clause, which Justices Byron R. White and William H. Rehnquist espouse on the present Court, is that of nonpreferentialism or accommodation to religion. According to this interpretation, the First Amendment prevents the establishment by the government of a single state church that would have any sort of preference over other churches. Justice Rehnquist accepts the proposition that the historical and proper definition of an establishment of religion is "a formal, legal union of a single church or religion with government, giving the one church or religion an exclusive position of power and favor over all other churches or denominations." An advocate of this view rejects the contention that every form of public aid or support for religion is prohibited; he also rejects Justice Black's opinion that government cannot aid all religions nor levy a tax on behalf of religious activities or institutions. He might rephrase the debatable part of Justice Black's statement to read: The establishment of religion clause of the First Amendment means this: Neither can pass laws which aid one religion or prefer one religion over another. No tax can be levied to support any religious activities or institutions unless apportioned in some equitable form and without discrimination in any form or degree. Government participation in the affairs of any religious organization or groups is prohibited unless with the consent and approval of such. The very phrase "wall of separation between Church and State" is ambiguous and misleading.

According to this view, the wall of separation merely keeps the government from abridging religious liberty by discriminatory practices against religion generally, or against any particular sects or denominations; the wall was not intended, however, to enjoin the government from fostering religion generally or all such religious groups or institutions as are willing to accept government aid, whether in the form of tax support, promotional activities, or otherwise. Nor was the wall meant to deny the benefits of government services to school children or their parents for religious reasons. That point makes us confront the fact that absolutes are as absent from the constitutional law of the establishment clause as from the law of search and seizure, and the law of the establishment clause seems to be nearly as murky.

As early as 1930 the Supreme Court held that a state did not take property or deprive anyone of it by appropriating tax monies for the purchase of books for children in private sectarian schools. The Court announced the "child benefit" theory to support its decision. The free school books were meant for the benefit of the school children, not their schools. Similarly, as if to prove that not even the broadest interpretation of the establishment clause prevents all aid, the *Everson* Court, no less, saw nothing unconstitutional in state-subsidized bus rides for children attending parochial schools. *Everson* showed how the Court can agree, unanimously, on principle yet disagree as closely as possible, 5–4, on the application of that principle in an actual case. Justice Black, for the majority, insisted that the wall of separation "must be kept high and impregnable" and that the Court "could not approve the slightest breach," yet he sustained the state practice in question, as well he should have. The township of Ewing, New Jersey, had authorized reimbursement of money spent by parents for the transportation of their children on public buses to attend school. To have prohibited repayment to the parents of parochial school children would have denied a benefit extended for the safety and convenience of all children regardless of religion. They are as entitled to the bus service as they, their schools, and their church are entitled to such civic services as police and fire protection. In theory, then, free textbooks and free busrides constitute only indirect or incidental aids to religion.

But even seemingly direct aids that endorse or reflect religious beliefs honeycomb official practices, despite the fact that the Supreme Court holds that the establishment clause prevents government sponsorship of religion. Justice William J. Brennan once observed, in the single opinion on the establishment clause most worthy of study, that its framers meant to prohibit involvements between government and religion that serve religion, employ government organs for religious purposes, or use religious means to serve government ends when secular means would suffice. Yet witnesses in courts swear on the Bible and take an oath that concludes, "so help me God." The Supreme Court itself opens its sessions daily with the invocation, "God save the United States and this honorable Court." Both houses of Congress and also our state legislatures daily precede their work with a prayer uttered by a legislative chaplain paid from our taxes. Our currency carries the motto, "In God We Trust," and school children pledge allegiance to "one nation under God." Except for sustaining the constitutionality of legislative chaplains, the Supreme Court has had the good judgment to decline deciding cases that question whether such practices violate the establishment clause. If that question has to be decided, those practices should be held unconstitutional, but the Court has enough cunning to avoid rendering such judgments. Public opinion and historical custom dictate a prudent abstention. . . .

Separation has other bountiful results. Government and religion in America are mutually independent of each other, much as Jefferson and Madison hoped they would be. Government maintains a benign neutrality toward religion without promoting or serving religion's interests in any significant way except, perhaps, for the policy of tax exemption. To be sure, government's involvement with religion takes many forms. The joint chiefs of staff supposedly begin their meetings with prayer, as do our legislatures. The incantation, "God save the United States and this honorable Court" and the motto "In God We Trust" and its relatives are of trifling significance in the sense that they have little genuine religious content. Caesar exploits, secularizes, and trivializes, but leaves organized religion alone. Free of government influence, organized religion in turn does not use government for religious ends. Thus, history has made the wall of separation real. The wall is not just a metaphor. It has constitutional existence. . . .

✠ F U R T H E R   R E A D I N G

Henry J. Abraham, *Freedom and the Court: Civil Rights and Liberties in the United States* (1967)

Robert L. Cord, "Church-State Separation: Restoring the 'No-Preference' Doctrine of the First Amendment," *Harvard Journal of Law and Public Policy* 9 (1986): 129–172

————, *Separation of Church and State: Historical Fact and Current Fiction* (1982)

Thomas J. Curry, *The First Freedoms: Church and State in America to the Passage of the First Amendment* (1986)

Kenneth M. Dolbeare and Phillip E. Hammond, *The School Prayer Decision: From Court Policy to Local Practice* (1970)

Dean M. Kelley, *Why Conservative Churches Are Growing*, rev. ed. (1976)

John H. Laubach, *School Prayers: Congress, the Court, and the Public* (1969)

Michael W. McConnell, "Accommodation of Religion," *Supreme Court Review* (1985): 1–59

Michael Malbin, *Religion and Politics: The Intentions of the Authors of the First Amendment* (1978)

David Manwaring, *Render unto Caesar: The Flag Salute Controversy* (1962)

William L. Miller, *The First Liberty: Religion and the American Republic* (1986)

Robert E. Morgan, *The Supreme Court and Religion* (1972)

Frank J. Sorauf, *The Wall of Separation: The Constitutional Politics of Church and State* (1976)

CHAPTER
11

The Constitutionality
of the Death Penalty

Throughout American history, the purposes of punishment (retribution, deterrence, and rehabilitation) have progressed through alternate cycles. During the past thirty years, for example, the burst of enthusiasm in favor of rehabilitation through individualized treatment—an approach associated with the 1960s—has come into conflict with mounting demands that violent criminals be put to death. The number of nationwide executions peaked in 1933 at 199; it declined by 1967 to only 2. After 1967 the next execution did not take place until 1977, when Gary Gilmore died before a Utah firing squad. Since then, capital punishment has once again become a regular feature of the American criminal-justice system.

Throughout this period after 1977, the American Civil Liberties Union (ACLU) and the NAACP Legal and Educational Defense Fund, Inc. (LDF) attempted repeatedly to challenge the death penalty on constitutional grounds. The first of these grounds had to do with the Eighth Amendment provision barring "cruel and unusual punishment." Opponents of the death penalty argued that death is inherently the cruelest and most unusual of all punishments. The second challenge involved the equal-protection clause of the Fourteenth Amendment, in which opponents charged that the death penalty is inflicted disproportionately on African-Americans. In landmark decisions in 1972 and 1976, the Supreme Court disposed of the first, and in 1987 it rejected the second, although it continued to leave open the possibility that, if a condemned person could show a specific instance of discrimination, he or she could be spared from execution.

The constitutional debate over death as a punishment raged against a backdrop of soaring crime rates. The incidence of serious crime against persons and property began to climb at an alarming rate in 1963. Between 1960 and 1974, for example, the total volume of crime shot up by 203 percent. At the same time, the Supreme Court, especially during the tenure of Chief Justice Earl Warren from 1953 to 1969, dramatically expanded the scope of the rights of the accused. It did so by nationalizing various aspects of the Bill of Rights, including the Fourth, Fifth, and Sixth amendments. State and local authorities historically had controlled the criminal-justice system with little supervision from national officials.

Proponents of crime control attributed (incorrectly, it should be pointed out) the surge in crime to what they viewed as the twin evils of the Warren Court: a rigid concern with defendants' due-process rights and the collapse of local control through the incorporation doctrine. First President Richard Nixon, and later President Ronald Reagan, protested against the Court's coddling of criminals, and they fought, unsuccessfully, to reverse Court-mandated policies such as the exclusionary rule, which prohibited prosecutors from using at trial any evidence that had been seized illegally. The justices did acknowledge, however, in 1984 that evidence seized illegally could be used if the police had acted in good faith.

With the death penalty, though, the justices refused to nationalize the Eighth Amendment. The Court did tighten the administration of the death penalty, but the justices refused to declare capital punishment unconstitutional.

⳥ D O C U M E N T S

Louisiana ex rel. Francis v. *Resweber* (1947), the first document, posed the constitutional questions about the death penalty in strikingly human terms. Willie Francis, a black man, sought release from his death sentence when the Louisiana electric chair failed the first time the switch was thrown. By a 5–4 vote, the Court ruled that a second execution would not violate the Constitution's prohibitions of either double jeopardy or cruel and unusual punishment.

The Court returned to the second of these issues in 1972, when it decided the case of *Furman* v. *Georgia,* excerpted in the second document. The Court did not declare the death penalty unconstitutional per se; instead, it held that the states had to revise their sentencing guidelines. State legislatures immediately began to do so, and in the *Gregg* v. *Georgia* decision of 1976, the third document, the justices affirmed the death penalty in those states that had adopted adequate procedural safeguards. The thirty-seven state legislatures that successfully reinstated the death penalty did so by dividing capital cases into two phases. The jury in the first phase determined the guilt or innocence of the accused; if found guilty, the defendant then faced a jury hearing to set punishment. In *Gregg* a bare majority of the Court held that, with appropriate procedural safeguards, the death penalty was constitutional.

Murder, of course, involves real victims, as the fourth document shows in its recounting of various violent crimes in modern-day Georgia. At the same time, however, the ultimate penalty falls most harshly on minorities and poor people. The justices in *McCleskey* v. *Kemp* (1987) rejected a statistical demonstration of bias in the administration of the death penalty as a basis on which to overturn a death sentence in a particular case. Instead, a once again closely divided Court held that a condemned person had to show overt and purposely racial bias in his or her particular case to escape execution. *McCleskey* is noteworthy also because of the heavy use that the justices made of social-science evidence.

Louisiana ex rel. Francis v. *Resweber,*
329 U.S. 459 (1947)

[5–4: Reed, Black, Frankfurter, Jackson,
Vinson; Burton, Douglas, Murphy, Rutledge]

Mr. Justice Reed announced the judgment of the Court in an opinion in which The Chief Justice, Mr. Justice Black and Mr. Justice Jackson join.

This writ of certiorari brings before this Court a unique situation. The petitioner, Willie Francis, is a colored citizen of Louisiana. He was duly convicted of murder and in September, 1945, sentenced to be electrocuted for the crime. Upon a proper death warrant, Francis was prepared for execution and on May 3, 1946, pursuant to the warrant, was placed in the official electric chair of the State of Louisiana in the presence of the authorized witnesses. The executioner threw the switch but, presumably because of some mechanical difficulty, death did not result. He was thereupon removed from the chair and returned to prison where he now is. A new death warrant was issued by the Governor of Louisiana, fixing the execution for May 9, 1946.

Applications to the Supreme Court of the state were filed for writs of certiorari, mandamus, prohibition and habeas corpus, directed to the appropriate officials in the state. Execution of the sentence was stayed. By the applications petitioner claimed the protection of the due process clause of the Fourteenth Amendment on the ground that an execution under the circumstances detailed would deny due process to him because of the double jeopardy provision of the Fifth Amendment and the cruel and unusual punishment provision of the Eighth Amendment. These federal constitutional protections, petitioner claimed, would be denied because he had once gone through the difficult preparation for execution and had once received through his body a current of electricity intended to cause death. . . .

To determine whether or not the execution of the petitioner may fairly take place after the experience through which he passed, we shall examine the circumstances under the assumption, but without so deciding, that violation of the principles of the Fifth and Eighth Amendments, as to double jeopardy and cruel and unusual punishment, would be violative of the due process clause of the Fourteenth Amendment. As nothing has been brought to our attention to suggest the contrary, we must and do assume that the state officials carried out their duties under the death warrant in a careful and humane manner. Accidents happen for which no man is to blame. We turn to the question as to whether the proposed enforcement of the criminal law of the state is offensive to any constitutional requirements to which reference has been made.

First. Our minds rebel against permitting the same sovereignty to punish an accused twice for the same offense. . . . [But w]hen an accident, with no suggestion of malevolence, prevents the consummation of a sentence, the state's subsequent course in the administration of its criminal law is not affected on that account by any requirement of due process under the Fourteenth Amendment. We find no double jeopardy here which can be said to amount to a denial of federal due process in the proposed execution.

Second. We find nothing in what took place here which amounts to cruel and unusual punishment in the constitutional sense. The case before us does not call for an examination into any punishments except that of death. . . . The traditional humanity of modern Anglo-American law forbids the infliction of unnecessary pain in the execution of the death sentence. Prohibition against the wanton infliction of pain has come into our law from the Bill of Rights of 1688. The identical words appear in our Eighth Amendment. The Fourteenth would prohibit by its due process clause execution by a state in a cruel manner.

Petitioner's suggestion is that because he once underwent the psychological strain of preparation for electrocution, now to require him to undergo this preparation again subjects him to a lingering or cruel and unusual punishment. Even the fact that petitioner has already been subjected to a current of electricity does not make his subsequent execution any more cruel in the constitutional sense than any other execution. The cruelty against which the Constitution protects a convicted man is cruelty inherent in the method of punishment, not the necessary suffering involved in any method employed to extinguish life humanely. The fact that an unforeseeable accident prevented the prompt consummation of the sentence cannot, it seems to us, add an element of cruelty to a subsequent execution. There is no purpose to inflict unnecessary pain nor any unnecessary pain involved in the proposed execution. The situation of the unfortunate victim of this accident is just as though he had suffered the identical amount of mental anguish and physical pain in any other occurrence, such as, for example, a fire in the cell block. We cannot agree that the hardship imposed upon the petitioner rises to that level of hardship denounced as denial of due process because of cruelty. . . . *Affirmed.*

Mr. Justice Burton, with whom Mr. Justice Douglas, Mr. Justice Murphy and Mr. Justice Rutledge concur, dissenting.

Under circumstances unique in judicial history, the relator asks this Court to stay his execution on the ground that it will violate the due process of law guaranteed to him by the Constitution of the United States. We believe that the unusual facts before us require that the judgment of the Supreme Court of Louisiana be vacated and that this cause be remanded for further proceedings not inconsistent with this opinion. Those proceedings should include the determination of certain material facts not previously determined, including the extent, if any, to which electric current was applied to the relator during his attempted electrocution on May 3, 1946. Where life is to be taken, there must be no avoidable error of law or uncertainty of fact. . . .

The capital case before us presents an instance of the violation of constitutional due process that is more clear than would be presented by many lesser punishments prohibited by the Eighth Amendment or its state counterparts. Taking human life by unnecessarily cruel means shocks the most fundamental instincts of civilized man. It should not be possible under the constitutional procedure of a self-governing people. Abhorrence of the cruelty of ancient forms of capital punishment has increased steadily until, today, some states have prohibited capital punishment altogether. It is unthinkable that any state legislature in modern times would enact a statute expressly authorizing capital punishment by repeated applications of an electric current separated by intervals of days or hours until finally death shall result. The Legislature of Louisiana did not do so. The Supreme Court of Louisiana did not say that it did. The Supreme Court of Louisiana said merely that the pending petitions for relief in this case presented an executive rather than a judicial question and, by that mistake of law, it precluded itself from discussing the constitutional issue before us.

In determining whether the proposed procedure is unconstitutional, we must measure it against a lawful electrocution. The contrast is that between instantaneous death and death by installments—caused by electric shocks administered after one or more intervening periods of complete consciousness of the victim. Electrocution, when instantaneous, *can* be inflicted by a state in conformity with due process of law. . . .

The all-important consideration is that the execution shall be so instantaneous and substantially painless that the punishment shall be reduced, as nearly as possible, to no more than that of death itself. Electrocution has been approved only in a form that eliminates suffering. . . .

[The Louisiana statute] does not provide for electrocution by interrupted or repeated applications of electric current at intervals of several days or even minutes. It does not provide for the application of electric current of an intensity less than that sufficient to cause death. It prescribes expressly and solely for the application of a current of sufficient intensity to cause death and for the *continuance* of that application until death results. Prescribing capital punishment, it should be construed strictly. There can be no implied provision for a second, third or multiple application of the current. There is no statutory or judicial precedent upholding a delayed process of electrocution. . . .

Furman v. *Georgia*, 408 U.S. 238 (1972)

(Multiple Opinions)

Per Curiam.

The Court holds that the imposition and carrying out of the death penalty in these cases constitutes cruel and unusual punishment in violation of the Eighth and Fourteenth Amendments. The judgment in each case is therefore reversed insofar as it leaves undisturbed the death sentence imposed, and the cases are remanded for further proceedings. So ordered.

Judgment in each case reversed in part and cases remanded. . . .

Mr. Justice Douglas, concurring.

In these three cases the death penalty was imposed, one of them for murder, and two for rape. In each the determination of whether the penalty should be death or a lighter punishment was left by the State to the discretion of the judge or of the jury. In each of the three cases the trial was to a jury. . . .

In this country there was almost from the beginning a "rebellion against the common-law rule imposing a mandatory death sentence on all convicted murderers." The first attempted remedy was to restrict the death penalty to defined offenses such as "premeditated" murder. But juries took "the law into their own hands" and refused to convict on the capital offense.

> In order to meet the problem of jury nullification, legislatures did not try, as before, to refine further the definition of capital homicides. Instead they adopted the method of forthrightly granting juries the discretion which they had been exercising in fact.

The Court [in *McGautha* v. *California* (1971)] concluded, "In light of history, experience, and the present limitations of human knowledge, we find it quite impossible to say that committing to the untrammeled discretion of the jury the power to pronounce life or death in capital cases is offensive to anything in the Constitution."

The Court refused to find constitutional dimensions in the argument that those who exercise their discretion to send a person to death should be given standards by which that discretion should be exercised. . . . We are now imprisoned in the *McGautha* holding. Indeed the seeds of the present cases are in *McGautha*. Juries (or judges, as the case may be) have practically untrammeled discretion to let an accused live or insist that he die. . . .

A law that stated that anyone making more than $50,000 would be exempt from the death penalty would plainly fail, as would a law that in terms said that Blacks, those who never went beyond the fifth grade in school, or those who made less than $3,000 a year, or those who were unpopular or unstable should be the only people executed. A law which in the overall view reaches that result in practice has no more sanctity than a law which in terms provides the same.

Thus, these discretionary statutes are unconstitutional in their operation. They are pregnant with discrimination and discrimination is an ingredient not compatible with the idea of equal protection of the laws that is implicit in the ban on "cruel and unusual" punishments.

Any law which is nondiscriminatory on its face may be applied in such a way as to violate the Equal Protection Clause of the Fourteenth Amendment. Such conceivably might be the fate of a mandatory death penalty, where equal or lesser sentences were imposed on the elite, a harsher one on the minorities or members of the lower castes. Whether a mandatory death penalty would otherwise be constitutional is a question I do not reach. . . .

Mr. Justice Brennan, concurring.

At bottom, then, the Cruel and Unusual Punishments Clause prohibits the infliction of uncivilized and inhuman punishments. The State, even as it punishes, must treat its members with respect for their intrinsic worth as human beings. A punishment is "cruel and unusual," therefore, if it does not comport with human dignity.

This formulation, of course, does not of itself yield principles for assessing the constitutional validity of particular punishments. Nevertheless, even though "this Court has had little occasion to give precise content to the [Clause]," there are principles recognized in our cases and inherent in the clause sufficient to permit a judicial determination whether a challenged punishment comports with human dignity.

The primary principle is that a punishment must not be so severe as to be degrading to the dignity of human beings. . . .

In determining whether a punishment comports with human dignity, we are aided also by a second principle inherent in the Clause—that the State must not arbitrarily inflict a severe punishment. This principle derives from the notion that the State does not respect human dignity when, without reason, it inflicts upon some people a severe punishment that it does not inflict upon others. . . .

A third principle inherent in the Clause is that a severe punishment must not be unacceptable to contemporary society. . . .

The final principle inherent in the Clause is that a severe punishment must not be excessive. A punishment is excessive under this principle if it is unnecessary: the infliction of a severe punishment by the State cannot comport with human dignity when it is nothing more than the pointless infliction of suffering. If there is a significantly less severe punishment adequate to achieve the purposes for which the punishment is inflicted, the punishment inflicted is unnecessary and therefore excessive. . . .

When the punishment of death is inflicted in a trivial number of the cases in which it is legally available, the conclusion is virtually inescapable that it is being inflicted arbitrarily. Indeed, it smacks of little more than a lottery system. The States claim, however, that this rarity is evidence not of arbitrariness, but of informed selectivity: Death is inflicted, they say, only in "extreme" cases.

Informed selectivity, of course, is a value not to be denigrated. Yet presumably the State could make precisely the same claim if there were 10 executions per year, or five, or even if there were but one. That there may be as many as 50 per year does not strengthen the claim. When the rate of infliction is at this low level, it is highly implausible that only the worst criminals or the criminals who commit the worst crimes are selected for this punishment. No one has yet suggested a rational basis that could differentiate in those terms the few who die from the many who go to prison. Crimes and criminals simply do not admit of a distinction that can be drawn so finely as to explain, on that ground, the execution of such a tiny sample of those eligible. Certainly the laws that provide for this punishment do not attempt to draw that distinction; all cases to which the laws apply are necessarily "extreme." Nor is the distinction credible in fact. If, for example, petitioner Furman or his crime illustrates the "extreme," then nearly all murderers and their murders are also "extreme." Furthermore, our procedures in death cases, rather than resulting in the selection of "extreme" cases for this punishment, actually sanction an arbitrary selection. For this Court has held that juries may, as they do, make the decision whether to impose a death sentence wholly unguided by standards governing that decision. In other words, our procedures are not constructed to guard against the totally capricious selection of criminals for the punishment of death. . . .

Mr. Justice Stewart, concurring.

Legislatures—state and federal—have sometimes specified that the penalty of death shall be the mandatory punishment for every person convicted of engaging in certain designated criminal conduct. Congress, for example, has provided that anyone convicted of acting as a spy for the enemy in time of war shall be put to death. The Rhode Island Legislature has ordained the death penalty for a life term prisoner who commits murder. Massachusetts has passed a law imposing the death penalty upon anyone convicted of murder in the commission of a forcible rape. An Ohio law imposes the mandatory penalty of death upon the assassin of the President of the United States or the Governor of the State.

If we were reviewing death sentences imposed under these or similar laws, we would be faced with the need to decide whether capital punishment is unconstitutional for all crimes and under all circumstances. We would need to decide whether a legislature—state or federal—could constitutionally determine that certain criminal conduct is so atrocious that society's interest in deterrence and retribution wholly outweighs any considerations of reform or rehabilitation of the perpetrator, and that, despite the inconclusive empirical evidence, only the automatic penalty of death will provide maximum deterrence.

On that score I would say only that I cannot agree that retribution is a constitutionally impermissible ingredient in the imposition of punishment. The instinct for retribution is part of the nature of man, and channeling that instinct in the administration of criminal justice serves an important purpose in promoting the stability of a society governed by law. When people begin to believe the organized society is unwilling or unable to impose upon criminal offenders the punishment they "deserve," then there are sown the seeds of anarchy—of self-help, vigilante justice, and lynch law.

The constitutionality of capital punishment in the abstract is not, however, before us in these cases. For the Georgia and Texas legislatures have not provided that the death penalty shall be imposed upon all those who are found guilty of forcible rape. And the Georgia Legislature has not ordained that death shall be the automatic punishment for murder. In a word, neither State has made a legislative determination that forcible rape and murder can be deterred only by imposing the penalty of death upon all who perpetrate those offenses. . . .

Instead, the death sentences now before us are the product of a legal system that brings them, I believe, within the very core of the Eighth Amendment's guarantee against cruel and unusual punishments, a guarantee applicable against the States through the Fourteenth Amendment. In the first place, it is clear that these sentences are "cruel" in the sense that they excessively go beyond, not in degree but in kind, the punishments that the state legislatures have determined to be necessary. In the second place, it is equally clear that these sentences are "unusual" in the sense that the penalty of death is infrequently imposed for murder, and that its imposition for rape is extraordinarily rare. But I do not rest my conclusion upon these two propositions alone.

These death sentences are cruel and unusual in the same way that being struck by lightening [sic] is cruel and unusual. For, of all the people convicted of rapes and murders in 1967 and 1968, many just as reprehensible as these, the petitioners are among a capriciously selected random handful upon whom the sentence of death has in fact been imposed. My concurring Brothers have demonstrated that, if any basis can be discerned for the selection of these few to be sentenced to die, it is the constitutionally impermissible basis of race. But racial discrimination has not been proved, and I put it to one side. I simply conclude that the Eighth and Fourteenth Amendments cannot tolerate the infliction of a sentence of death under legal systems that permit this unique penalty to be so wantonly and so freakishly imposed. . . .

Mr. Justice White, concurring.

. . . I begin with what I consider a near truism: that the death penalty could so seldom be imposed that it would cease to be a credible deterrent or measurably to contribute to any other end of punishment in the criminal justice system. It is perhaps true that no matter how infrequently those convicted of rape or murder are executed, the penalty so imposed is not disproportionate to the crime and those executed may deserve exactly what they received. It would also be clear that executed defendants are finally and completely incapacitated from again committing rape or murder or any other crime. But when imposition of the penalty reaches a certain degree of infrequency, it would be very doubtful that any existing general need for retribution would be measurably satisfied. Nor could it be said with confidence that society's need for specific deterrence justifies death for so few when for so many in like circumstances life imprisonment or shorter prison terms are judged sufficient, or that community values are measurably re-enforced by authorizing a penalty so rarely invoked.

Most important, a major goal of the criminal law—to deter others by punishing the convicted criminal—would not be substantially served where the penalty is so seldom invoked that it ceases to be the credible threat essential to influence the conduct of others. For present purposes I accept the morality and utility of punishing one person to influence another. I accept also the effectiveness of punishment generally and need not reject the death penalty as a more effective deterrent than a lesser punishment. But common sense and experience tell us that seldom-enforced laws become ineffective measures for controlling human conduct and that the death penalty, unless imposed with sufficient frequency, will make little contribution to deterring those crimes for which it may be exacted. . . .

It is also my judgment that this point has been reached with respect to capital punishment as it is presently administered under the statutes involved in these cases. Concededly, it is difficult to prove as a general proposition that capital punishment, however administered, more effectively serves the ends of the criminal law than does imprisonment. But however that may be, I cannot avoid the conclusion that as the statutes before us are now administered, the penalty is so infrequently imposed that the threat of execution is too attenuated to be of substantial service to criminal justice.

I need not restate the facts and figures that appear in the opinion of my Brethren. Nor can I "prove" my conclusion from these data. But like my Brethren, I must arrive at judgment; and I can do no more than state a conclusion based on 10 years of almost daily exposure to the facts and circumstances of hundreds and hundreds of federal and state criminal cases involving crimes for which death is the authorized penalty. That conclusion, as I have said, is that the death penalty is exacted with great infrequency even for the most atrocious crimes and that there is no meaningful basis for distinguishing the few cases in which it is imposed from the many cases in which it is not. The short of it is that the policy of vesting sentencing authority primarily in juries—a decision largely motivated by the desire to mitigate the harshness of the law and to bring community judgment to bear on the sentence as well as guilt or innocence—has so effectively achieved its aims that capital punishment within the confines of the statutes now before us has for all practical purposes run its course. . . .

Mr. Justice Marshall, concurring.

A punishment may be deemed cruel and unusual for any one of four distinct reasons.

First, there are certain punishments which inherently involve so much physical pain and suffering that civilized people cannot tolerate them—e.g., use of the rack, the thumbscrew, or other modes of torture. Regardless of public sentiment with respect to imposition of one of these punishments in a particular case or at any one moment in history, the Constitution prohibits it. These are punishments that have been barred since the adoption of the Bill of Rights.

Second, there are punishments which are unusual, signifying that they were previously unknown as penalties for a given offense. . . .

Third, a penalty may be cruel and unusual because it is excessive and serves no valid legislative purpose. The decisions previously discussed are replete with assertions that one of the primary functions of the cruel and unusual punishments clause is to prevent excessive or unnecessary penalties. . . .

Fourth, where a punishment is not excessive and serves a valid legislative purpose, it still may be invalid if popular sentiment abhors it. . . .

There is but one conclusion that can be drawn from all of this—i.e., the death penalty is an excessive and unnecessary punishment which violates the Eighth Amendment. The statistical evidence is not convincing beyond all doubt, but it is persuasive. It is not improper at this point to take judicial notice of the fact that for more than 200 years men have labored to demonstrate that capital punishment serves no purpose that life imprisonment could not serve equally as well. And they have done so with great success. Little if any evidence has been adduced to prove the contrary. The point has now been reached at which deference to the legislatures is tantamount to abdication of our judicial roles as factfinders, judges, and ultimate arbiters of the Constitution. We know that at some point the presumption of constitutionality accorded legislative acts gives way to a realistic assessment of those acts. This point comes when there is sufficient evidence available so that judges can determine not whether the legislature acted wisely, but whether it had any rational basis whatsoever for acting. We have this evidence before us now. There is no rational basis for concluding that capital punishment is not excessive. It therefore violates the Eighth Amendment.

In addition, even if capital punishment is not excessive, it nonetheless violates the Eighth Amendment because it is morally unacceptable to the people of the United States at this time in their history. . . .

Chief Justice Burger, with whom Justices Blackmun, Powell, and Rehnquist join, dissenting.

While I cannot endorse the process of decisionmaking that has yielded today's result and the restraints which that result imposes on legislative action, I am not altogether displeased that legislative bodies have been given the opportunity, and indeed unavoidable responsibility, to make a thorough re-evaluation of the entire subject of capital punishment. If today's opinions demonstrate nothing else, they starkly show that this is an area where legislatures can act far more effectively than courts.

The legislatures are free to eliminate capital punishment for specific crimes or to carve out limited exceptions to a general abolition of the penalty, without adherence to the conceptual strictures of the Eighth Amendment. The legislatures can and should make an assessment of the deterrent influence of capital punishment, both generally and as affecting the commission of specific types of crimes. If legislatures come to doubt the efficacy of capital punishment, they can abolish it, either completely or on a selective basis. If new evidence persuades them that they have acted unwisely, they can reverse their field and reinstate the penalty to the extent it is thought warranted. An Eighth Amendment ruling by judges cannot be made with such flexibility or discriminating precision. . . .

The five opinions in support of the judgment differ in many respects, but they share a willingness to make sweeping factual assertions, unsupported by empirical data, concerning the manner of imposition and effectiveness of capital punishment in this country. Legislatures will have the opportunity to make a more penetrating study of these claims with the familiar and effective tools available to them as they are not to us.

Gregg v. *Georgia*, 428 U.S. 153 (1976)

[7–2: Stewart, Blackmun, Burger, Powell,
Rehnquist, Stevens, White; Brennan, Marshall]

Judgment of the Court, and opinion of Justices Stewart, Powell, and Stevens, announced by Justice Stewart.

The issue in this case is whether the imposition of the sentence of death for the crime of murder under the law of Georgia violates the Eighth and Fourteenth Amendments. . . .

Before considering the issues presented it is necessary to understand the Georgia statutory scheme for the imposition of the death penalty. The Georgia statute, as amended after our decision in *Furman* v. *Georgia* . . . (1972), retains the death penalty for six categories of crime: murder, kidnaping for ransom or where the victim is harmed, armed robbery, rape, treason, and aircraft hijacking. . . . The capital defendant's guilt or innocence is determined in the traditional manner, either by a trial judge or a jury, in the first stage of a bifurcated trial.

If trial is by jury, the trial judge is required to charge lesser included offenses when they are supported by any view of the evidence. . . . After a verdict, finding, or plea of guilty to a capital crime, a presentence hearing is conducted before whoever made the determination of guilt. The sentencing procedures are essentially the same in both bench and jury trials. . . .

In the assessment of the appropriate sentence to be imposed the judge is also required to consider or to include in his instructions to the jury "any mitigating circumstances or aggravating circumstances otherwise authorized by law and any of [10] statutory aggravating circumstances which may be supported by the evidence. . . ." The scope of the nonstatutory aggravating or mitigating circumstances is not delineated in the statute. Before a convicted defendant may be sentenced to death, however, except in cases of treason or aircraft hijacking, the jury, or the trial judge in cases tried without a jury, must find beyond a reasonable doubt one of the 10 aggravating circumstances specified in the statute. The sentence of death may be imposed only if the jury (or judge) finds one of the statutory aggravating circumstances and then elects to impose that sentence. . . . If the verdict is death, the jury or judge must specify the aggravating circumstance(s) found. . . . In jury cases, the trial judge is bound by the jury's recommended sentence. . . .

In addition to the conventional appellate process available in all criminal cases, provision is made for special expedited direct review by the Supreme Court of Georgia of the appropriateness of imposing the sentence of death in the particular case. The court is directed to consider "the punishment as well as any errors enumerated by way of appeal." . . . If the court affirms a death sentence, it is required to include in its decision reference to similar cases that it has taken into consideration. . . . Under its special review authority, the court may either affirm the death sentence or remand the case for resentencing. In cases in which the death sentence is affirmed there remains the possibility of executive clemency.

We address initially the basic contention that the punishment of death for the crime of murder is, under all circumstances, "cruel and unusual" in violation of the Eighth and Fourteenth Amendments of the Constitution. . . .

The Court on a number of occasions has both assumed and asserted the constitutionality of capital punishment. In several cases that assumption provided a necessary foundation for the decision, as the Court was asked to decide whether a particular method of carrying out a capital sentence would be allowed to stand under the Eighth Amendment. But until *Furman*

v. *Georgia* . . . the Court never confronted squarely the fundamental claim that the punishment of death always, regardless of the enormity of the offense or the procedure followed in imposing the sentence, is cruel and unusual punishment in violation of the Constitution. Although this issue was presented and addressed in *Furman,* it was not resolved by the Court. Four Justices would have held that capital punishment is not unconstitutional *per se;* two Justices would have reached the opposite conclusion; and three Justices, while agreeing that the statutes then before the Court were invalid as applied, left open the question whether such punishment may ever be imposed. We now hold that the punishment of death does not invariably violate the Constitution.

The history of the prohibition of "cruel and unusual" punishment already has been reviewed at length. . . . The American draftsmen, who adopted the English phrasing in drafting the Eighth Amendment, were primarily concerned, however, with proscribing "tortures" and other "barbarous" methods of punishment." . . .

In the earliest cases raising Eighth Amendment claims, the Court focused on particular methods of execution to determine whether they were too cruel to pass constitutional muster. The constitutionality of the sentence of death itself was not at issue, and the criterion used to evaluate the mode of execution was its similarity to "torture" and other "barbarous" methods. . . .

But the Court has not confined the prohibition embodied in the Eighth Amendment to "barbarous" methods that were generally outlawed in the 18th century. Instead, the Amendment has been interpreted in a flexible and dynamic manner. The Court early recognized that "a principle to be vital, must be capable of wider application than the mischief which gave it birth." . . . Thus the Clause forbidding "cruel and unusual" punishments "is not fastened to the obsolete but may acquire meaning as public opinion becomes enlightened by a humane justice." . . .

. . . Our cases also make clear that public perceptions of standards of decency with respect to criminal sanctions are not conclusive. A penalty also must accord with "the dignity of man," which is the "basic concept underlying the Eighth Amendment." . . . This means, at least, that the punishment not be "excessive." When a form of punishment in the abstract (in this case, whether capital punishment may ever be imposed as a sanction for murder) rather than in the particular (the propriety of death as a penalty to be applied to a specific defendant for a specific crime) is under consideration, the inquiry into "excessiveness" has two aspects. First, the punishment must not involve the unnecessary and wanton infliction of pain. . . . Second, the punishment must not be grossly out of proportion to the severity of the crime. . . .

Of course, the requirements of the Eighth Amendment must be applied with an awareness of the limited role to be played by the courts. This does not mean that judges have no role to play, for the Eighth Amendment is a restraint upon the exercise of legislative power. . . .

Therefore, in assessing a punishment selected by a democratically elected legislature against the constitutional measure, we presume its validity. We may not require the legislature to select the least severe penalty possible so long as the penalty selected is not cruelly inhumane or disproportionate to the crime involved. And a heavy burden rests on those who would attack the judgment of the representatives of the people.

This is true in part because the constitutional test is intertwined with an assessment of contemporary standards and the legislative judgment weighs heavily in ascertaining such standards. "[I]n a democratic society legislatures, not courts, are constituted to respond to the will and consequently the moral values of the people." . . .

A decision that a given punishment is impermissible under the Eighth Amendment cannot be reversed short of a constitutional amendment. The ability of the people to express their preference through the normal democratic processes, as well as through ballot referenda, is shut off. Revisions cannot be made in the light of further experience. . . .

In the discussion to this point we have sought to identify the principles and considerations that guide a court in addressing an Eighth Amendment claim. We now consider specifically whether the sentence of death for the crime of murder is a *per se* violation of the Eighth and Fourteenth Amendments to the Constitution. We note first that history and precedent strongly support a negative answer to this question. . . .

Four years ago, the petitioners in *Furman* and its companion cases predicated their argument primarily upon the asserted proposition that standards of decency had evolved to the point where capital punishment no longer could be tolerated. The petitioners in those cases said, in effect, that the evolutionary process had come to an end, and that standards of decency required that the Eighth Amendment be construed finally as prohibiting capital punishment for any crime regardless of its depravity and impact on society. This view was accepted by two Justices. Three other Justices were unwilling to go so far; focusing on the procedures by which convicted defendants were selected for the death penalty rather than on the actual punishment inflicted, they joined in the conclusion that the statutes before the Court were constitutionally invalid.

The petitioners in the capital cases before the Court today renew the "standards of decency" argument, but developments during the four years since *Furman* have undercut substantially the assumptions upon which their argument rested. Despite the continuing debate, dating back to the 19th century, over the morality and utility of capital punishment, it is now evident that a large proportion of American society continues to regard it as an appropriate and necessary criminal sanction.

The most marked indication of society's endorsement of the death penalty for murder is the legislative response to *Furman*. The legislatures of at least 35 States have enacted new statutes that provide for the death penalty for at least some crimes that result in the death of another person. And the Congress of the United States, in 1974, enacted a statute providing the death penalty for aircraft piracy that results in death. These recently adopted statutes have attempted to address the concerns expressed by the Court in *Furman* primarily (i) by specifying the factors to be weighed and the procedures to be followed in deciding when to impose a capital sentence, or (ii) by making the death penalty mandatory for specified crimes. But all of the post-*Furman* statutes make clear that capital punishment itself has not been rejected by the elected representatives of the people. . . .

In sum, we cannot say that the judgment of the Georgia Legislature that capital punishment may be necessary in some cases is clearly wrong. Considerations of federalism, as well as respect for the ability of a legislature to evaluate, in terms of its particular State, the moral consensus concerning the death penalty and its social utility as a sanction, require us to conclude, in the absence of more convincing evidence, that the infliction of death as a punishment for murder is not without justification and thus is not unconstitutionally severe.

Finally, we must consider whether the punishment of death is disproportionate in relation to the crime for which it is imposed. There is no question that death as a punishment is unique in its severity and irrevocability. . . . When a defendant's life is at stake, the Court has been particularly sensitive to insure that every safeguard is observed. . . . But we are concerned here only with the imposition of capital punishment for the crime of murder, and when a life has been taken deliberately by the offender, we cannot say that the punishment is invariably disproportionate to the crime. It is an extreme sanction, suitable to the most extreme of crimes.

We hold that the death penalty is not a form of punishment that may never be imposed, regardless of the circumstances of the offense, regardless of the character of the offender, and regardless of the procedure followed in reaching the decision to impose it. . . .

A Sample of Georgia Murder Cases, 1960–1978

Culpability Level 1 (Least Culpable)

a. The defendant is a 19-year-old male with a prior conviction for a violent crime against a person and a conviction for a nonviolent crime. He and three coperpetrators noticed that the victim, a 27-year-old male, was carrying a lot of money. They followed him until they reached a secluded road, where they blocked the road with their car. A coperpetrator, carrying a shotgun, approached the victim while the victim was still in his car and demanded his money. When the victim started to back up his vehicle, the gun discharged, killing the victim. . . .

From *Equal Justice and the Death Penalty: A Legal and Empirical Analysis* by David Baldus, George G. Woodworth, and Charles A. Pulaski, Jr., pp. 602–609. Copyright © 1990 by David C. Baldus, George G. Woodworth, and Charles A. Pulaski, Jr. Reprinted with the permission of Northeastern University Press.

Culpability Level 2

a. The defendant, a 21-year-old male with a prior conviction for a nonviolent crime, and three coperpetrators planned to rob the victim, a 41-year-old male. Two of the coperpetrators went to the victim's house, but the victim refused to go into a dark alley where the defendant and the other coperpetrator were hiding. The two coperpetrators then left, but later returned with a pistol. They had planned to hold the victim with the pistol, and then later kill him with a shotgun, but the victim struggled and one of the coperpetrators killed him with a shot to the chest. The defendant claimed he was at a party smoking marijuana when he heard the shots. The coperpetrators testified against him. . . .

Culpability Level 3

a. The defendant, a 36-year-old female with two prior convictions for nonviolent crimes, joined with four others in a plan to embarrass the victim, a 48-year-old male, by staging an armed robbery. The victim, an owner of a sporting-goods store, had allegedly made sexual advances toward the defendant. The plan was that one of the coperpetrators would lure the victim into the store by appearing to want to seduce him. While in the store, the other two coperpetrators planned to jump the victim, knock him unconscious, steal his money, and leave him half nude so that he would wake up embarrassed the next morning. However, as it happened, the victim suffered a serious beating and died three weeks later from head wounds. The defendant was not at the scene of the crime. She eventually made an admission to the police. . . .

b. The defendant is an 18-year-old male with no prior convictions. He raped and shot to death a 25-year-old woman in the presence of her 4-year-old daughter. The defendant claimed the death was an accident; however, the victim was shot twice. . . .

Culpability Level 4

a. The defendant is a male, aged 45, with over 85 arrests, almost all for drunkenness. Both victims and the defendant had been drinking heavily at the time of the homicide. Victim #1, a 45-year-old female, may have been dating both the defendant and victim #2, a 32-year-old male, who was the defendant's brother. The victims were found dead from multiple stab wounds in victim #1's trailer. Witnesses had seen the defendant at the trailer earlier that day. The police found the defendant's fingerprints in victim #1's trailer and clothes with the victim's blood type in the defendant's house. . . .

Culpability Level 5

a. The defendant, a male aged 16 with no prior criminal record, and two coperpetrators pulled into his stepfather's Amoco station and stole the money in the register at gunpoint. Then they drove the stepfather and an 11-year-old boy to a deserted field, where the defendant told the two to lie down on the ground. Somebody shot and killed both victims, but it is unclear who did the shooting. There was some evidence that the defendant did it. Just before the killing, the boy told the defendant that he did not want to die. After his arrest, the defendant admitted to being the ringleader of the group and said that he wanted to be the biggest black gangster that ever lived. . . .

Culpability Level 6 (Most Culpable)

. . . *b.* The defendant, a 35-year-old male with a prior conviction for burglary and two convictions for nonviolent crimes, and three coperpetrators planned to burglarize a home. While the three coperpetrators were in the house, three male victims came home and the perpetrators shot them. Three more victims then arrived, two of whom were shot. The perpetrators took the remaining victim, the only female, to the woods, where she was raped and sodomized. They then shot her twice and mutilated her breasts. The defendant claimed to be in another state at the time of the killings, but a coperpetrator testified that the defendant killed one of the victims. . . .

McCleskey v. *Kemp*, 481 U.S. 279 (1987)

[5–4: Powell, O'Connor, Rehnquist, Scalia,
White; Brennan, Blackmun, Marshall, Stevens]

Justice Powell delivered the opinion of the Court.

This case presents the question whether a complex statistical study that indicates a risk that racial considerations enter into capital sentencing determinations proves that petitioner McCleskey's capital sentence is unconstitutional under the Eighth or Fourteenth Amendment.

I

McCleskey, a black man, was convicted of two counts of armed robbery and one count of murder in the Superior Court of Fulton County, Georgia, on October 12, 1978. McCleskey's convictions arose out of the robbery of a furniture store and the killing of a white police officer during the course of the robbery. The evidence at trial indicated that McCleskey and three accomplices planned and carried out the robbery. All four were armed. McCleskey entered the front of the store while the other three entered the rear. McCleskey secured the front of the store by rounding up the customers and forcing them to lie face down on the floor. The other three rounded up the employees in the rear and tied them up with tape. The manager was forced at gunpoint to turn over the store receipts, his watch, and $6.00. During the course of the robbery, a police officer, answering a silent alarm, entered the store through the front door. As he was walking down the center aisle of the store, two shots were fired. Both struck the officer. One hit him in the face and killed him.

Several weeks later, McCleskey was arrested in connection with an unrelated offense. He confessed that he had participated in the furniture store robbery, but denied that he had shot the police officer. At trial, the State introduced evidence that at least one of the bullets that struck the officer was fired from a .38 caliber Rossi revolver. This description matched the description of the gun that McCleskey had carried during the robbery. The State also introduced the testimony of two witnesses who had heard McCleskey admit to the shooting.

The jury convicted McCleskey of murder. At the penalty hearing, the jury heard arguments as to the appropriate sentence. Under Georgia law, the jury could not consider imposing the death penalty unless it found beyond a reasonable doubt that the murder was accompanied by one of the statutory aggravating circumstances. . . . The jury in this case found two aggravating circumstances to exist beyond a reasonable doubt: the murder was committed during the course of an armed robbery, . . . and the murder was committed upon a peace officer engaged in the performance of his duties. . . . In making its decision whether to impose the death sentence, the jury considered the mitigating and aggravating circumstances of McCleskey's conduct. . . . McCleskey offered no mitigating evidence. The jury recommended that he be sentenced to death on the murder charge and to consecutive life sentences on the armed robbery charges. The court followed the jury's recommendation and sentenced McCleskey to death. . . .

McCleskey['s] petition raised 18 claims, one of which was that the Georgia capital sentencing process is administered in a racially discriminatory manner in violation of the Eighth and Fourteenth Amendments to the United States Constitution. In support of his claim, McCleskey proffered a statistical study performed by Professors David C. Baldus, George Woodworth, and Charles Pulaski (the Baldus study) that purports to show a disparity in the imposition of the death sentence in Georgia based on the race of the murder victim and, to a lesser extent, the race of the defendant. The Baldus study is actually two sophisticated statistical studies that examine over 2,000 murder cases that occurred in Georgia during the 1970s. The raw numbers collected by Professor Baldus indicate that defendants charged with killing white persons received the death penalty in 11% of the cases, but defendants charged with killing blacks received the death penalty in only 1% of the cases. The raw numbers also indicate a reverse racial disparity according to the race of the defendant: 4% of the black defendants received the death penalty, as opposed to 7% of the white defendants.

Baldus also divided the cases according to the combination of the race of the defendant and the race of the victim. He found that the death penalty was assessed in 22% of the cases involving black defendants and white victims; 8% of the cases involving white defendants and white victims; 1% of the cases involving black defendants and black victims; and 3% of the cases involving white defendants and black victims. Similarly, Baldus found that prosecutors sought the death penalty in 70% of the cases involving black defendants and white victims; 32% of the cases involving white defendants and white victims; 15% of the cases involving black defendants and black victims; and 19% of the cases involving white defendants and black victims.

Baldus subjected his data to an extensive analysis, taking account of 230 variables that could have explained the disparities on nonracial grounds. One of his models concludes that, even after taking account of 39 nonracial variables, defendants charged with killing white victims were 4.3 times as likely to receive a death sentence as defendants charged with killing blacks. According to this model, black defendants were 1.1 times as likely to receive a death sentence as other defendants. Thus, the Baldus study indicates that black defendants, such as McCleskey, who kill white victims have the greatest likelihood of receiving the death penalty. . . .

II

McCleskey's first claim is that the Georgia capital punishment statute violates the Equal Protection Clause of the Fourteenth Amendment. He argues that race has infected the administration of Georgia's statute in two ways: persons who murder whites are more likely to be sentenced to death than persons who murder blacks, and black murderers are more likely to be sentenced to death than white murderers. As a black defendant who killed a white victim, McCleskey claims that the Baldus study demonstrates that he was discriminated against because of his race and because of the race of his victim. In its broadest form, McCleskey's claim of discrimination extends to every actor in the Georgia capital sentencing process, from the prosecutor who sought the death penalty and the jury that imposed the sentence, to the State itself that enacted the capital punishment statute and allows it to remain in effect despite its allegedly discriminatory application. We agree with the Court of Appeals, and every other court that has considered such a challenge, that this claim must fail.

A.   Our analysis begins with the basic principle that a defendant who alleges an equal protection violation has the burden of proving "the existence of purposeful discrimination." . . . [T]o prevail under the Equal Protection Clause, McCleskey must prove that the decisionmakers in *his* case acted with discriminatory purpose. He offers no evidence specific to his own case that would support an inference that racial considerations played a part in his sentence. Instead, he relies solely on the Baldus study. McCleskey argues that the Baldus study compels an inference that his sentence rests on purposeful discrimination. McCleskey's claim that these statistics are sufficient proof of discrimination, without regard to the facts of a particular case, would extend to all capital cases in Georgia, at least where the victim was white and the defendant is black.

The Court has accepted statistics as proof of intent to discriminate in certain limited contexts. . . .

But the nature of the capital sentencing decision, and the relationship of the statistics to that decision, are fundamentally different from the corresponding elements in the venire-selection or Title VII cases. Most importantly, each particular decision to impose the death penalty is made by a petit jury selected from a properly constituted venire. Each jury is unique in its composition, and the Constitution requires that its decision rest on consideration of innumerable factors that vary according to the characteristics of the individual defendant and the facts of the particular capital offense. . . . Thus, the application of an inference drawn from the general statistics to a specific decision in a trial and sentencing simply is not comparable to the application of an inference drawn from general statistics to a specific venire-selection or Title VII case. In those cases, the statistics relate to fewer entities, and fewer variables are relevant to the challenged decisions. . . .

Finally, McCleskey's statistical proffer must be viewed in the context of his challenge. McCleskey challenges decisions at the heart of the State's criminal justice system. . . . Implementation of these laws necessarily requires discretionary judgments. Because discretion is essential to the criminal justice process, we would demand exceptionally clear proof before we would infer that the discretion has been abused. The unique nature of the decisions at issue in this case also counsel against adopting such an inference from the disparities indicated by the Baldus study. Accordingly, we hold that the Baldus study is clearly insufficient to support an inference that any of the decisionmakers in McCleskey's case acted with discriminatory purpose.

B.   McCleskey also suggests that the Baldus study proves that the State as a whole has acted with a discriminatory purpose. He appears to argue that the State has violated the Equal Protection Clause by adopting the capital punishment statute and allowing it to remain in force despite its allegedly discriminatory application. . . . For this claim to prevail, McCleskey would have to prove that the Georgia Legislature enacted or maintained the death penalty statute *because of* an anticipated racially discriminatory effect. In *Gregg* v. *Georgia* . . . (1976), this Court found that the Georgia capital sentencing system could operate in a fair and neutral manner. There was no evidence then, and there is none now, that the Georgia Legislature enacted the capital punishment statute to further a racially discriminatory purpose.

Nor has McCleskey demonstrated that the legislature maintains the capital punishment statute because of the racially disproportionate impact suggested by the Baldus study. As legislatures necessarily have wide discretion in the choice of criminal laws and penalties, and as there were legitimate reasons for the Georgia Legislature to adopt and maintain capital punishment . . . , we will not infer a discriminatory purpose on the part of the State of Georgia. Accordingly, we reject McCleskey's equal protection claims.

III

McCleskey also argues that the Baldus study demonstrates that the Georgia capital sentencing system violates the Eighth Amendment. We begin our analysis of this claim by reviewing the restrictions on death sentences established by our prior decisions under that Amendment.

A. The Eighth Amendment prohibits infliction of "cruel and unusual punishments." This Court's early Eighth Amendment cases examined only the "particular methods of execution to determine whether they were too cruel to pass constitutional muster." . . . Subsequently, the Court recognized that the constitutional prohibition against cruel and unusual punishments "is not fastened to the obsolete but may acquire meaning as public opinion becomes enlightened by a humane justice." . . . [T]he Court identified a second principle inherent in the Eighth Amendment, "that punishment for crime should be graduated and proportioned to offense." . . .

Chief Justice Warren, writing for the plurality in *Trop* v. *Dulles* . . . (1958), acknowledged the constitutionality of capital punishment. In his view, the "basic concept underlying the Eighth Amendment" in this area is that the penalty must accord with "the dignity of man." . . . In applying this mandate, we have been guided by his statement that "[t]he Amendment must draw its meaning from the evolving standards of decency that mark the progress of a maturing society." . . . Thus, our constitutional decisions have been informed by "contemporary values concerning the infliction of a challenged sanction" . . . . In assessing contemporary values, we have eschewed subjective judgment, and instead have sought to ascertain "objective indicia that reflect the public attitude toward a given sanction." . . . First among these indicia are the decisions of state legislatures, "because the . . . legislative judgment weighs heavily in ascertaining" contemporary standards. . . . We also have been guided by the sentencing decisions of juries, because they are "a significant and reliable objective index of contemporary values." . . . Most of our recent decisions as to the constitutionality of the death penalty for a particular crime have rested on such an examination of contemporary values. . . .

D. In sum, our decisions since *Furman* have identified a constitutionally permissible range of discretion in imposing the death penalty. First, there is a required threshold below which the death penalty cannot be imposed. In this context, the State must establish rational criteria that narrow the decisionmaker's judgment as to whether the circumstances of a particular defendant's case meet the threshold. Moreover, a societal consensus that the death penalty is disproportionate to a particular offense prevents a State from imposing the death penalty for that offense. Second, States cannot limit the sentencer's consideration of any relevant circumstance that could cause it to decline to impose the penalty. In this respect, the State cannot channel the sentencer's discretion, but must allow it to consider any relevant information offered by the defendant.

IV

A. In light of our precedents under the Eighth Amendment, McCleskey cannot argue successfully that his sentence is "disproportionate to the crime in the traditional sense." . . . He does not deny that he committed a murder in the course of a planned robbery, a crime for which this Court has determined that the death penalty constitutionally may be imposed. . . . His disproportionality claim "is of a different sort." . . . McCleskey argues that the sentence in his case is disproportionate to the sentence in other murder cases.

On the one hand, he cannot base a constitutional claim on an argument that his case differs from other cases in which defendants *did* receive the death penalty. On automatic appeal, the Georgia Supreme Court found that McCleskey's death sentence was not disproportionate to other death sentences imposed in the State. . . . The court supported this conclusion with an appendix containing citations to 13 cases involving generally similar murders. . . . Moreover, where the statutory procedure adequately channel the sentencer's discretion, such proportionality review is not constitutionally required. . . .

On the other hand, absent a showing that the Georgia capital punishment system operates in an arbitrary and capricious manner, McCleskey cannot prove a constitutional violation by demonstrating that other defendants who may be similarly situated did *not* receive the death penalty. . . .

Because McCleskey's sentence was imposed under Georgia sentencing procedures that focus discretion "on the particularized nature of the crime and the particularized characteristics of the individual defendant," . . . we lawfully may presume that McCleskey's death sentence was not "wantonly and freakishly" imposed . . . and thus that the sentence is not disproportionate within any recognized meaning under the Eighth Amendment.

B.   Although our decision in *Gregg* as to the facial validity of the Georgia capital punishment statute appears to foreclose McCleskey's disproportionality argument, he further contends that the Georgia capital punishment system is arbitrary and capricious in *application,* and therefore his sentence is excessive, because racial considerations may influence capital sentencing decisions in Georgia. We now address this claim.

To evaluate McCleskey's challenge, we must examine exactly what the Baldus study may show. Even Professor Baldus does not contend that his statistics *prove* that race enters into any capital sentencing decisions or that race was a factor in McCleskey's particular case. Statistics at most may show only a likelihood that a particular factor entered into some decisions. There is, of course, some risk of racial prejudice influencing a jury's decision in a criminal case. There are similar risks that other kinds of prejudice will influence other criminal trials. . . .

C.   At most, the Baldus study indicates a discrepancy that appears to correlate with race. Apparent disparities in sentencing are an inevitable part of our criminal justice system. The discrepancy indicated by the Baldus study is "a far cry from the major systemic defects identified in *Furman*." . . . As this Court has recognized, any mode for determining guilt or punishment "has its weaknesses and the potential for misuse." . . .

V

Two additional concerns inform our decision in this case. First, McCleskey's claim, taken to its logical conclusion, throws into serious question the principles that underlie our entire criminal justice system. The Eighth Amendment is not limited in application to capital punishment, but applies to all penalties. . . . Thus, if we accepted McCleskey's claim that racial bias has impermissibly tainted the capital sentencing decision, we could soon be faced with similar claims as to other types of penalty. Moreover, the claim that his sentence rests on the irrelevant factor of race easily could be extended to apply to claims based on unexplained discrepancies that correlate to membership in other minority groups, and even to gender. Similarly, since McCleskey's claim relates to the race of his victim, other claims could apply with equally logical force to statistical disparities that correlate with the race or sex of other actors in the criminal justice system, such as defense attorneys, or judges. Also, there is no logical reason that such a claim need be limited to racial or sexual bias. If arbitrary and capricious punishment is the touchstone under the Eighth Amendment, such a claim could—at least in theory— be based upon any arbitrary variable, such as the defendant's facial characteristics, or the physical attractiveness of the defendant or the victim, that some statistical study indicates may be influential in jury decisionmaking. As these examples illustrate, there is no limiting principle to the type of challenge brought by McCleskey. The Constitution does not require that a State eliminate any demonstrable disparity that correlates with a potentially irrelevant factor in order to operate a criminal justice system that includes capital punishment. . . .

Second, McCleskey's arguments are best presented to the legislative bodies. It is not the responsibility—or indeed even the right—of this Court to determine the appropriate punishment for particular crimes. It is the legislatures, the elected representatives of the people, that are "constituted to respond to the will and consequently the moral values of the people." . . . Legislatures also are better qualified to weigh and "evaluate the results of statistical studies in terms of their own local conditions and with a flexibility of approach that is not available to the courts." . . . Capital punishment is now the law in more than two thirds of our States. It is the ultimate duty of courts to determine on a case-by-case basis whether these laws are applied consistently with the Constitution. Despite McCleskey's wide ranging arguments that basically challenge the validity of capital punishment in our multi-racial society, the only question before us is whether in his case . . . the law of Georgia was properly applied. We agree with the District Court and the Court of Appeals for the Eleventh Circuit that this was carefully and correctly done in this case. . . .

Accordingly, we affirm the judgment of the Court of Appeals for the Eleventh Circuit. *It is so ordered.*

Justice Brennan, with whom Justice Marshall joins, and with whom Justice Blackmun and Justice Stevens join in all but Part I, dissenting.

I

Adhering to my view that the death penalty is in all circumstances cruel and unusual punishment forbidden by the Eighth and Fourteenth Amendments, I would vacate the decision below insofar as it left undisturbed the death sentence imposed in this case. . . .

Even if I did not hold this position, however, I would reverse the Court of Appeals, for petitioner McCleskey has clearly demonstrated that his death sentence was imposed in violation of the Eighth and Fourteenth Amendments. . . . I write . . . to emphasize how conclusively McCleskey has also demonstrated precisely the type of risk of irrationality in sentencing that we have consistently condemned in our Eighth Amendment jurisprudence.

II

At some point in this case, Warren McCleskey doubtless asked his lawyer whether a jury was likely to sentence him to die. A candid reply to this question would have been disturbing. First, counsel would have to tell McCleskey that few of the details of the crime or of McCleskey's past criminal conduct were more important than the fact that his victim was white. . . . Furthermore, counsel would feel bound to tell McCleskey that defendants charged with killing white victims in Georgia are 4.3 times as likely to be sentenced to death as defendants charged with killing blacks. . . . In addition, frankness would compel the disclosure that it was more likely than not that the race of McCleskey's victim would determine whether he received a death sentence: 6 of every 11 defendants convicted of killing a white person would not have received the death penalty if their victims had been black . . . while, among defendants with aggravating and mitigating factors comparable to McCleskey, 20 of every 34 would not have been sentenced to die if their victims had been black. . . . Finally, the assessment would not be complete without the information that cases involving black defendants and white victims are more likely to result in a death sentence than cases featuring any other racial combination of defendant and victim. . . . The story could be told in a variety of ways, but McCleskey could not fail to grasp its essential narrative line: there was a significant chance that race would play a prominent role in determining if he lived or died.

The Court today holds that Warren McCleskey's sentence was constitutionally imposed. It finds no fault in a system in which lawyers must tell their clients that race casts a large shadow on the capital sentencing process. The Court arrives at this conclusion by stating that the Baldus Study cannot "*prove* that race enters into any capital sentencing decisions or that race was a factor in McCleskey's particular case." . . . Since, according to Professor Baldus, we cannot say "to a moral certainty" that race influenced a decision, we can identify only "a likelihood that a particular factor entered into some decisions," . . . and "a discrepancy that appears to correlate with race." . . . This "likelihood" and "discrepancy," holds the Court, is insufficient to establish a constitutional violation. The Court reaches this conclusion by placing four factors on the scales opposite McCleskey's evidence: the desire to encourage sentencing discretion, the existence of "statutory safeguards" in the Georgia scheme, the fear of encouraging widespread challenges to other sentencing decisions, and the limits of the judicial role. The Court's evaluation of the significance of petitioner's evidence is fundamentally at odds with our consistent concern for rationality in capital sentencing, and the considerations that the majority invokes to discount that evidence cannot justify ignoring its force.

III

A. . . . The Court assumes the statistical validity of the Baldus study, . . . and acknowledges that McCleskey has demonstrated a risk that racial prejudice plays a role in capital sentencing in Georgia. . . . Nonetheless, it finds the probability of prejudice insufficient to create constitutional concern. . . . Close analysis of the Baldus study, however, in light of both statistical principles and human experience, reveals that the risk that race influenced McCleskey's sentence is intolerable by any imaginable standard.

B. The Baldus study indicates that, after taking into account some 230 nonracial factors that might legitimately influence a sentencer, the jury *more likely than not* would have spared McCleskey's life had his victim been black. The study distinguishes between those cases in which (1) the jury exercises virtually no discretion because the strength or weakness of aggravating factors usually suggests that only one outcome is appropriate; and (2) cases reflecting an "intermediate" level of aggravation, in which the jury has considerable discretion in choosing a sentence. McCleskey's case falls into the intermediate range. In such cases, death is imposed in 34% of white-victim crimes and 14% of black-victim crimes, a difference of 139% in the rate of imposition of the death penalty. . . . In other words, just under 59%—almost 6 in 10—defendants comparable to McCleskey would not have received the death penalty if their victims had been black.

Furthermore, even examination of the sentencing system as a whole, factoring in those cases in which the jury exercises little discretion, indicates the influence of race on capital sentencing. For the Georgia system as a whole, race accounts for a six percentage point difference in the rate at which capital punishment is imposed. Since death is imposed in 11% of all white-victim cases, the rate in comparably aggravated black-victim cases is 5%. The rate of capital sentencing in a white-victim case is thus 120% greater than the rate in a black-victim case. Put another way, over half—55%—of defendants in white-victim crimes in Georgia would not have been sentenced to die if their victims had been black. Of the more than 200 variables potentially relevant to a sentencing decision, race of the victim is a powerful explanation for variation in death sentence rates—as powerful as nonracial aggravating factors such as a prior murder conviction or acting as the principal planner of the homicide.

These adjusted figures are only the most conservative indication of the risk that race will influence the death sentences of defendants in Georgia. Data unadjusted for the mitigating or aggravating effect of other factors show an even more pronounced disparity by race. The capital sentencing rate for all white-victim cases was almost *11 times* greater than the rate for black-victim cases. . . . Furthermore, blacks who kill whites are sentenced to death at nearly *22 times* the rate of blacks who kill blacks, and more than *7 times* the rate of whites who kill blacks. . . . In addition, prosecutors seek the death penalty for 70% of black defendants with white victims, but for only 15% of black defendants with black victims, and only 19% of white defendants with black victims. . . . Since our decision upholding the Georgia capital-sentencing system in *Gregg,* the State has executed 7 persons. All of the 7 were convicted of killing whites, and 6 of the 7 executed were black. Such execution figures are especially striking in light of the fact that, during the period encompassed by the Baldus study, only 9.2% of Georgia homicides involved black defendants and white victims, while 60.7% involved black victims.

McCleskey's statistics have particular force because most of them are the product of sophisticated multiple-regression analysis. Such analysis is designed precisely to identify patterns in the aggregate, even though we may not be able to reconstitute with certainty any individual decision that goes to make up that pattern. Multiple-regression analysis is particularly well-suited to identify the influence of impermissible considerations in sentencing, since it is able to control for permissible factors that may explain an apparent arbitrary pattern. While the decision-making process of a body such as a jury may be complex, the Baldus study provides a massive compilation of the details that are most relevant to that decision. . . .

The statistical evidence in this case thus relentlessly documents the risk that McCleskey's sentence was influenced by racial considerations. This evidence shows that there is a better than even chance in Georgia that race will influence the decision to impose the death penalty: a majority of defendants in white-victim crimes would not have been sentenced to die if their victims had been black. In determining whether this risk is acceptable, our judgment must be shaped by the awareness that "[t]he risk of racial prejudice infecting a capital sentencing proceeding is especially serious in light of the complete finality of the death sentence." . . . In determining the guilt of a defendant, a state must prove its case beyond a reasonable doubt. That is, we refuse to convict if the chance of error is simply less likely than not. Surely, we should not be willing to take a person's life if the chance that his death sentence was irrationally imposed is *more* likely than not. In light of the gravity of the interest at stake, petitioner's statistics on their face are a powerful demonstration of the type of risk that our Eighth Amendment jurisprudence has consistently condemned. . . .

V

At the time our Constitution was framed 200 years ago this year, blacks "had for more than a century before been regarded as beings of an inferior

order, and altogether unfit to associate with the white race, either in social
or political relations; and so far inferior, that they had no rights which the
white man was bound to respect." *Dred Scott* v. *Sandford,* . . . (1857). Only
130 years ago, this Court relied on these observations to deny American
citizenship to blacks. . . . A mere three generations ago, this Court sanctioned racial segregation, stating that "[i]f one race be inferior to the other
socially, the Constitution of the United States cannot put them upon the
same plane." *Plessy* v. *Ferguson,* . . . (1896).

In more recent times, we have sought to free ourselves from the burden
of this history. Yet it has been scarcely a generation since this Court's first
decision striking down racial segregation, and barely two decades since the
legislative prohibition of racial discrimination in major domains of national
life. These have been honorable steps, but we cannot pretend that in three
decades we have completely escaped the grip of an historical legacy spanning
centuries. Warren McCleskey's evidence confronts us with the subtle and
persistent influence of the past. His message is a disturbing one to a society
that has formally repudiated racism, and a frustrating one to a Nation ac-
customed to regarding its destiny as the product of its own will. Nonetheless,
we ignore him at our peril, for we remain imprisoned by the past as long
as we deny its influence in the present.

It is tempting to pretend that minorities on death row share a fate in
no way connected to our own, that our treatment of them sounds no echoes
beyond the chambers in which they die. Such an illusion is ultimately cor-
rosive, for the reverberations of injustice are not so easily confined. "The
destinies of the two races in this country are indissolubly linked together,"
. . . and the way in which we choose those who will die reveals the depth
of moral commitment among the living.

The Court's decision today will not change what attorneys in Georgia
tell other Warren McCleskeys about their chances of execution. Nothing will
soften the harsh message they must convey, nor alter the prospect that race
undoubtedly will continue to be a topic of discussion. McCleskey's evidence
will not have obtained judicial acceptance, but that will not affect what is
said on death row. However many criticisms of today's decision may be
rendered, these painful conversations will serve as the most eloquent dissents
of all.

✤ E S S A Y S

The essays featured in this chapter emphasize how moral and social choices shape
constitutional argument. Walter Berns, a political scientist at the American Enterprise Institute, argues in the first essay that the death penalty is moral and therefore constitutional. Charles L. Black, a retired law professor who taught at Yale
University, disagrees sharply with Berns, contending in the second essay that,
given the inevitability of mistakes within a less-than-perfect legal system, the innocent will sometimes die. Finally, David C. Baldus, professor of law at the University of Iowa, and his collaborators argue in the third selection that social-scientific

evidence leaves little doubt that race figures disproportionately in who receives the death sentence. Should the Court consider such nonlegal material in reaching constitutional decisions, especially in cases where individual life weighs in the balance?

The Morality of the Death Penalty

WALTER BERNS

The opponents of capital punishment [in 1976] had good reason to believe they would win their case in the Supreme Court. They had come close in 1972 when the Court held that the death penalty had been administered in so discriminatory, capricious, or arbitrary a manner as to be a cruel and unusual punishment, and two members of the five-man majority in those cases regarded the death penalty as unconstitutional no matter how administered. It is true that public and legislative opinion seemed to be moving against them, but if Arthur Koestler's [American novelist] characterization of the public support of the death penalty is accurate—that it is based on "ignorance, traditional prejudice and repressed cruelty"—then it was likely that the penalty would continue to be imposed discriminatorily, capriciously, or arbitrarily, and that a majority of the Court would, sooner or later, come to the conclusion that it could be imposed in no other manner. This may yet happen. In 1976, however, seven members of the Court not only voted to uphold the death penalty statutes of three states and the sentences imposed under them, but, in the course of doing so, gave the sanction of the Constitution to the principle that criminals should be paid back for their crimes.

It was this sanctioning of the retributive principle that especially disturbed Justice Marshall, one of the two dissenters. He would apparently be willing to allow executions if it could be shown that they serve some useful purpose—for example, that they serve to deter others from committing capital crimes (and he was not persuaded by Ehrlich's study suggesting that they do deter)—but to execute someone simply because society thinks he deserves to be executed is, he said, to deny him his "dignity and worth." Why it would not deprive a man of his dignity and worth to use him (by executing him) in order to influence the behavior of other men, Marshall did not say; apparently he would be willing to accept society's calculations but not its moral judgments. Be that as it may, it cannot be denied that he and other abolitionists have a point: to say that someone deserves to be executed is to make a godlike judgment with no assurance that it can be made with anything resembling godlike perspicacity. In the extreme case, and some abolitionists make much of its possibility, society may execute an innocent person, and no one can assure us that this has never happened or that it will never happen in the future. Yet Bedau, probably the best known of America's abolitionists, refuses to credit it, or to rely on it as part of his case against the death penalty. He calls it "false sentimentality to argue that the death penalty ought to be abolished because of the abstract possibility that an innocent person might be executed, when the record fails to disclose that such cases occur." The more likely mistakes are of a different order of magnitude.

A recent study of the manner in which homicide was punished in Philadelphia in the year 1970 discloses great and apparently unjustifiable variations in the sentences handed down, the problem being not that the sentences are too lenient or too severe, but that they are both; as the authors say, "the going price of criminal homicide is two years or twenty." It was the apparently equally arbitrary imposition of the death penalty that the Court in 1972 found to be cruel and unusual, and that the statutes enacted after 1972—the so-called post-*Furman* statutes—were designed to prevent. The editors of the *Harvard Law Review,* in a careful review of these statutes, concluded that, if the 1972 decisions dictate strict limits on both sentencing and nonsentencing discretion in capital cases, none of the new laws is constitutional because none of them "fulfills these demands." Juries would, they argued, easily find ways of avoiding those limits when they impose sentences, prosecutors would continue to make their own judgments as to who should be prosecuted for what, and governors would continue to commute or not to commute death sentences in an arbitrary manner. Charles Black [a professor of constitutional law] goes so far as to insist that "caprice and mistake" are inevitable in capital cases, and that, however carefully written and whatever the language employed to force juries to follow statutory standards, no statute can prevent mistakes or reduce their incidence and magnitude to a point where they might be tolerated. Nevertheless, justice requires that juries be allowed to exercise discretion.

Not all murderers deserve to be executed; not even all first-degree murderers deserve to be executed, because not all first-degree murders are equally terrible. Yet, in reaction to the 1972 Supreme Court decisions, a number of states, determined to demonstrate that they could eliminate the injustice of arbitrary capital sentencing, enacted new statutes making death the mandatory sentence for persons convicted of first-degree murder. This is a mistake, and I think most of us know it. We can recognize the difference between the culpability of Jack Ruby, for example, the killer of Lee Harvey Oswald, and that of Lee Harvey Oswald himself (assuming, of course, that he was indeed the killer of President Kennedy); we could accept a prison term, perhaps even a relatively brief prison term, for Ruby because we could accept the prospect of his return to our community; but I doubt that we could accept the same sentence for Oswald or the prospect of *his* return to our community, even if he promised never again to assassinate a president. Black, with reference to the new Georgia statute which directs the jury to decide whether the charged offense was "outrageously or wantonly vile," insists that it is "impossible to imagine a murder" that cannot be so described, but surely this exaggerates; the typical jury is not that obtuse. Consider the recent case of Hamaas Abdul Khaalis and his Hanafi Muslim sect who in March 1977 seized hostages in the course of occupying three Washington, D.C., buildings and at this time stand charged with the murder of a reporter who was in one of them. The seizures were surely outrageous, irrational, and admixed with an element of bigotry; but they were provoked by a terrible event, the killing of Khaalis's children and grandchild. Five Black Muslims shot and killed two of the children, drowned three others in a bathtub, and, with its mother forced to look on, drowned a ten-day-old baby in a sink. That is an outrageous, wanton, and vile crime. Khaalis is reported as saying, "I'm waiting to see what my country is going to do about the gang in Chicago that killed my family." What his country did—this being during the period when capital punishment was in ill-repute—was to sentence the five killers to life imprisonment, which Khaalis, not unreasonably, regarded as wholly inadequate. But what of the killing of Maurice Williams, the reporter who had the misfortune to be in one of the buildings during its occupation by the Khaalis group? A grave offense, surely, and one that deserves to be severely punished; but it does not deserve to be classed with the murders of the Khaalis children, and, unlike Black, I think the typical jury would agree.* When it is informed that the term "outrageously or wantonly vile" is intended to differentiate among murders—all murders being grave offenses—a jury is capable of seeing the difference. Of course jury discretion should be limited, which is to say that statutes should provide standards to guide sentencing decisions, but it is unjust to deprive juries of all discretion. The jury is expected to exercise the community's moral judgment in a particular case involving a particular crime and a particular criminal, and no statutory language is capable of describing these particularities in advance. Besides, mandatory statutes do not in practice eliminate jury discretion: when juries are of the opinion that an offender does not deserve death, they simply do not convict him of the capital offense. It was to be expected, therefore, that the Supreme Court would, as it did, strike down the North Carolina and Louisiana statutes making death the mandatory sentence for first-degree murder.

The three statutes upheld on that same day in 1976 permit jury discretion but attempt to prevent its abuse, or, to speak more reasonably, attempt to reduce the possibility of this abuse to a tolerable minimum. It remains to be seen whether, contrary to the expectations of Charles Black and the editors of the *Harvard Law Review,* they will succeed in doing so. Carefully drafted, all three statutes, especially the one from Georgia, embody procedures intended to impress on judges and juries the gravity of the judgment they are asked to make in capital cases—for example, all three require the sentencing decision to be separated from the decision respecting guilt or innocence; and in one way or another, all three imply that the death sentence is not to be looked upon as ordinary. Thus, the Georgia law requires (except in cases of treason and aircraft hijacking) a finding beyond a reasonable doubt of the presence of at least one of the aggravating circumstances specified in the statute, and requires the judge or, as the case might be, the jury

---

* In the event, Khaalis was sentenced to 41 to 123 years imprisonment, and Abdul Muzikir, who shot Williams, the reporter, to 77 years to life. See *New York Times,* Sept. 7, 1977, p. 18.

to specify the circumstance found. Texas requires the jury, during the sentencing proceeding, to answer affirmatively three questions: whether the evidence established beyond a reasonable doubt that the murder was committed deliberately, whether the evidence established beyond a reasonable doubt that there was a probability that the defendant would commit criminal acts of violence in the future, and, when relevant, whether the defendant's conduct was an unreasonable response to any provocation by the deceased. The Florida statute requires a weighing of aggravating and mitigating circumstances, which are listed in the statute. Finally, all three statutes permit or require an expedited appeal to or review by their respective supreme courts, which are authorized to set aside a death sentence in order to ensure, for example, that similar results are reached in similar cases. (That this review is not perfunctory is indicated in the fact that the Florida supreme court had, at the time of the U.S. Supreme Court decisions, vacated eight of the twenty-one sentences to come before it under the new law.)

These statutes are surely improvements over the ones they replaced, but in one respect they do not, in my opinion, go far enough. The very awesomeness of condemning a man to death requires the punishment to be reserved for extraordinarily heinous crimes, but throughout most of modern history this has not been the case. The historical record is sprinkled with statements to the effect that no man's property will be safe unless death is the penalty for stealing it, even if the property is no more than that which is carried casually in a pocket and the theft is accomplished merely by picking that pocket. But retributive justice requires punishment to fit the crime, which requires a schedule of punishments, ranging from the most lenient through various degrees of severity to the most awful, death, because the moral sentiments of a just people recognize that crimes range from the most petty through various degrees of gravity to the most awful, which, as we understand these things, is the taking of a human life. The law cannot reinforce these moral sentiments (and its purpose is to do just that) if it executes the pickpocket or the shoplifter as well as the murderer; to do that is to equate petty theft with murder, and petty amounts of property with a human life, and to do that *is* to deny human dignity. The law that does it will lose, and will deserve to lose, the respect it must enjoy among the people, who will neither obey it nor, when serving on juries, enforce it. To reinforce the moral sentiments of a people, the criminal law must be made awful or awesome, and . . . the only way within our means to do that today is to impose the death sentence; but an execution cannot be awesome if it is associated with petty affairs or becomes a customary, familiar event. Thus, while the death penalty should not be seen as cruel, by the same token it should be seen as unusual, not in the techniques employed when carrying it out, but in the frequency with which it is carried out. It is this principle that should be embodied in statutes and impressed upon judge and jury; a properly drawn statute will allow the death penalty only for the most awful crimes: treason, some murders, and some particularly vile rapes. It is not beyond the skill of legislators to draft such a statute—for example, it could provide that the death sentence be imposed *only* for "outrageously or wantonly vile" offenses—one that defers to the jury's judgment in particular cases but, at the same time, impresses upon the jury the awesome character of the judgment it is asked to make. This is not incompatible with retributive sentencing; on the contrary, retribution, unlike deterrence, precisely because it derives from moral sensibilities, recognizes the justice of mercy, the injustice of punishing the irresponsible, and limits to the severity of punishment. (If the only purpose of punishment is deterrence, why not boil murderers in oil or chop off the hands of shoplifters?) It is also compatible with the purpose of capital punishment; only a relatively few executions are required to enhance the dignity of the criminal law, and that number is considerably smaller than the number of murderers and rapists. The other purpose of punishment can be more fully accomplished by a more rigorous enforcement of the other criminal statutes. . . .

It is simply an unhappy fact that blacks commit a disproportionate number of the known crimes in the United States, including capital crimes. In 1974, a typical year, 57 percent of the persons arrested for murder were black; but, what is sometimes forgotten, 50 percent of homicide victims were also black, and most black people, like most white people, are not criminals. What distinguishes them is that the law-abiding black population supplies a disproportionate number of the victims of crime; and it would be a cruel victory indeed if, having struggled so long and so hard, and, finally, so successfully against all the forms of injustice imposed on them by the white population, they were now to be exposed to what may be—in part, at least— preventable black crime because of the reluctance of white liberals to allow black criminals to be punished as they deserve to be punished. A country that does not punish its grave offenses severely thereby indicates that it does not regard them as grave offenses; and a country that does not punish severely its black murderers thereby indicates that it does not regard murder to be a grave offense when it is committed in the black community. This is what it would amount to, as the annual statistics on the proportion of black murder victims imply. Of course, the situation as it has existed historically in the United States can scarcely be described as one reflecting a reluctance to execute black men—on the contrary—and the future of capital punishment in America will probably depend on whether it can be imposed without regard to race and class, on white as well as black, on rich as well as poor. To execute black murderers or poor murderers because they are murderers is not unjust; to execute them because they are black or poor is unconscionable and unconstitutional. That much was decided in 1972.

There is, finally, the question of whether executions should be public. I have made much of the point that the anger that gives rise to the demand that criminals be paid back is not in principle selfish or otherwise reprehensible, and that it is a function of the law to tame that anger by satisfying and thereby justifying it. This it does when it punishes criminals; punishment, I have argued, serves to praise and reward law-abidingness even as it blames crime. But that anger has also to be tamed in the sense of being moderated. A proper criminal trial achieves this to some extent by forcing the jury to determine beyond a reasonable doubt that the accused is guilty as charged.

In order further to calm or moderate that anger, and to impress upon the population the awesomeness of the moral order and the awful consequences of its breach, I think it necessary that executions be public. There are obvious objections to public executions, even when they are not the sort of spectacle Mandeville was describing in the eighteenth century. No ordinary citizen can be required to witness them, and it would be better if some people not be permitted to witness them—children, for example, and the sort of person who would, if permitted, happily join a lynch mob. Executions should not be televised, both because of the unrestricted character of the television audience and the tendency of television to make a vulgar spectacle of the most dignified event. Yet executions must be witnessed, and witnessed by the public, which means not hidden from the view of all but prison personnel and a few others. The solution to this problem is to be found where the framers of the Constitution found part of the solution to the problem of democracy, namely, in the principle of representation. In addition to prison personnel and the others now attending them, executions should be witnessed by representatives of the people. Since the process of selecting them could not be controlled sufficiently to ensure that decorum attend every aspect of this ceremony (and I use that word advisedly), the representatives should not be specially selected for this purpose but should be those, or a part of those, already elected to the legislatures. They represent the people when they enact the statutes permitting the penalty of death, and they can represent the people when they witness its carrying out. As Madison said in the tenth *Federalist,* they are a "chosen body of citizens" who can be expected to "refine and enlarge the public views," and we have a right to expect them also to represent the public's moral indignation. If they cannot do this, they are not justified in enacting death penalty statutes. The abolitionists make this point and they are right. But executions solemnly witnessed and carried out are not barbaric; on the contrary, they enhance the awesome dignity of the law and of the moral order it serves and protects.

When abolitionists speak of the barbarity of capital punishment and when Supreme Court justices denounce expatriation in almost identical language, they ought to be reminded that men whose moral sensitivity they would not question have supported both punishments. Lincoln, for example, albeit with a befitting reluctance, authorized the execution of 267 persons during his presidency, and ordered the "Copperhead" Clement L. Vallandigham banished; and it was Shakespeare's sensitivity to the moral issue that required him to have Macbeth killed. They should also be given some pause by the knowledge that the man who originated the opposition to both capital and exilic punishment, Cesare Beccaria, was a man who argued that there is no morality outside the positive law and that it is reasonable to love one's property more than one's country. There is nothing exalted in these opinions, and there is nothing exalted in the versions of them that appear in today's judicial opinions. Capital punishment was said by Justice Brennan to be a denial of human dignity, but in order to reach this conclusion he had to reduce human dignity to the point where it became something possessed by "the vilest criminal." Expatriation is said by the Court to be unconstitutional because it deprives a man of his right to have rights, which *is* his citizenship, and no one, no matter what he does, can be dispossessed of the right to have rights. (Why not a right to the right to have rights?) Any notion of what Justice Frankfurter in dissent referred to as "the communion of our citizens," of a community that can be violated by murderers or traitors, is wholly absent from these opinions; so too is any notion that it is one function of the law to protect that community.

But, contrary to abolitionist hopes and expectations, the Court did not invalidate the death penalty. It upheld it. It upheld it on retributive grounds. In doing so, it recognized, at least implicitly, that the American people are entitled *as a people* to demand that criminals be paid back, and that the worst of them be made to pay back with their lives. In doing this, it gave them the means by which they might strengthen the law that makes them a people, and not a mere aggregation of selfish individuals.

The Whim and Caprice of the Death Penalty

CHARLES L. BLACK

[My] central thesis . . . is that the problems of mistake and caprice are ineradicable in the administration of the death penalty. In a narrow case, then, I am saying that these seemingly more "precise" statutes . . . do not cure the fundamental defect that was the basis of the Supreme Court's 1972 decision in the Furman case, outlawing capital punishment as it has been administered. Though the truth of this assertion can be established from the new statutes alone . . . , I want to make my case in a wider frame of reference. This widening will consist in opening to the reader's view the entire *series of decisions* made by the legal system as a person goes the road from freedom to the electric chair. Let us take an overview of these.

I will skip over the preliminary decision on arrest, and go on to the two-pronged decision made by the prosecutor. On the facts before him, he must first decide whether to *charge* an offense carrying the penalty of death, or a lesser offense. If he decides to charge the capital offense, he must quite commonly decide whether to *accept a plea of guilty* to a lesser (and therefore noncapital) offense, thus permitting the defendant to escape at this early stage the possibility of execution, at the price of going to prison without trial. . . .

If the *prosecutor,* having charged a capital crime, is nevertheless willing to accept a plea of guilty to a lesser offense, then the *defendant* has in turn the choice of accepting or rejecting this offer. This dreadful choice has to be made by a man in custody, often disoriented and frightened, and hence

Reprinted from *Capital Punishment: The Inevitability of Caprice and Mistake* by Charles L. Black, Jr., pp. 14–21 by permission of W.W. Norton & Company, Inc. Copyright © 1974 by W.W. Norton & Company, Inc.

dependent upon advice, and susceptible to following possibly bad advice; at this point, then, the choice is partly or wholly made by the *lawyer* for the defendant. With the best of intentions, this lawyer's decision is often a difficult one. . . .

If a "plea bargain" is not struck, then the defendant goes on trial for his life. At the end of this trial, the jury has a number of decisions or choices to make, most of them veiled by the secrecy of the jury-room. It must decide what the gross *physical* facts were: Did this defendant, for example, actually stab the deceased, or did somebody else do it? Did the defendant stab the victim at a time when the victim was trying to stab the defendant, or did he stab a man whose knife was sheathed? (I will now mention, not for the last time, that "mistake" as to these questions of physical fact seems to be what most people mean when they speak of "mistake" in criminal proceedings; I hope I shall be able to convince you that the range of possible "mistake" is much broader than that.) Having satisfied its mind as to the *physical* facts, the jury must then tackle the *psychological* facts. Did the defendant, who clearly (or admittedly) shot a man while that man was reaching for his handkerchief, *believe* that that man was reaching for a gun, or is the pretense that he so believed mere sham? Did the defendant *plan* this killing, or was it done in the heat of passion? Did he *intend* to kill at all?

The jury in a criminal case does not announce its decision on each of such points one by one. It simply comes in with a verdict of "not guilty," or "guilty of murder in the first degree," or of "manslaughter," or of some other offense known to the state's law. There is no question in the mind of anybody who has dealt with the criminal-law system that a jury sometimes comes in with a verdict of "guilty" of some offense lesser than the one strictly warranted by the evidence. All kinds of factors—sympathy, doubt of physical "guilt" in the narrow sense, doubt as to the other, less tangible factors going to make up "guilt," a feeling that extenuating circumstances exist, and so on—may motivate this behavior. But the pragmatic fact, visible from the outside, is that the jury, in finding a defendant guilty, let us say, of "second-degree" rather than of "first-degree" murder, is, for whatever reason and on whatever basis, *choosing* that this defendant not suffer death.

Very commonly, at this stage, the jury must rule on the "insanity defense." I single it out for special emphasis because it is so crucially important, particularly in cases of a revolting sort, likely to inflame a jury, and also because it plumbs the whole theory of criminal responsibility. A verdict of "not guilty by reason of insanity" is a jury's choice for some form of imprisonment rather than for death. . . .

If the jury, accepting the prosecutor's version of the facts and rejecting all defenses, convicts the defendant of an offense for which the death penalty is possible, the choice then has to be made as to *sentencing*. Under the old system, condemned in the 1972 Furman case, the usual procedure was for the jury, "in its discretion," to decide whether a death sentence was to be imposed. The form of words varied from state to state; sometimes the death sentence followed automatically unless the jury recommended mercy, while sometimes the affirmative recommendation of the jury was necessary for the sentence of death. Sometimes, indeed, the judge rather than the jury exercised this "discretion." In the newer statutes . . . a *second* hearing on sentencing often occurs, at the end of which, on the basis of mitigating or aggravating circumstances named in the new law, the sentence of death may or may not be imposed. In this initial survey, it is enough to note that this choice must usually be made. (Sometimes the sentence of death is "mandatory" on conviction of certain crimes—but note, above, that prosecutor and jury practically always retain control [by discretion in charging and in accepting a "plea," and by finding the defendant guilty of a less-than-capital offense] over the decision whether conviction of this "mandatorily" capital crime can occur.)

After conviction, sentencing, and appeal, we reach the possibility of executive clemency, or clemency exercised by a pardon board. In no state, as far as I know, is it the case that a death sentence, once imposed, *must* be carried out, without the possibility of there intervening an act of mercy by some authority. The national Constitution fixes this principle for federal crime, by giving the pardoning power to the President.

Now that is about the range, though some minor points may have been skipped, for later filling in. It becomes plainly visible that the choice of death as the penalty is the result not of just *one* choice—that of the trial judge or jury, dealt with in the Furman case—but of a *number* of choices, starting with the prosecutor's choice of a charge, and ending with the choice of the authority—the governor or a board—charged with the administration of clemency.

Regarding *each* of these choices, through all the range, one of two things, or perhaps both, may be true.

First, the choice made may be a *mistaken* one. The defendant may not have committed the act of which he is found guilty; the factors which ought properly to induce a prosecutor to accept a plea to a lesser offense may have been present, though he refused to do so; the defendant may have been "insane" in the way the law requires for exculpation, though the jury found that he was not. And so on.

Secondly, there may either be no legal standards governing the making of the choice, or the standards verbally set up by the legal system for the making of the choice may be so vague, at least in part of their range, as to be only *apparent* standards, in truth furnishing no direction and leaving the actual choice quite arbitrary.

These two possibilities have an interesting (and, in the circumstances, tragic) relationship. The concept of *mistake* fades out as the *standard* grows more and more vague and unintelligible. There is no vagueness problem about the question, "Did Y hit Z on the head with a piece of pipe?" It is, for just that reason, easily possible to conceive of what it means to be "mistaken" in answering this question; one is "mistaken" if one answers it "yes" when in fact Y did not hit Z with the pipe. It is even fairly clear what it means to be "mistaken" in answering the question "Did Y *intend* to kill Z?" Conscious intents are facts; the difference here really is that, for obvious reasons, *mistake is more likely* in the second case than in the first, for it is hard or impossible to be confident of coming down on the right side of a question about past psychological fact.

It is very different when one comes to the question, "Was the action of which the defendant was found guilty performed in such a manner as to evidence an 'abandoned and malignant heart'?" (This phrase figures importantly in homicide law.) This question has the same grammatical form as a clearcut factual question; actually, through a considerable part of its range, it is not at all clear what it means. It sets up, in this range, not a standard but a *pseudo-standard*. One cannot, strictly speaking, be *mistaken* in answering it, at least within a considerable range, because to be mistaken is to be on the wrong side of a line, and there is no real line here. But that, in turn, means that the "test" may often be no test at all, but merely an invitation to arbitrariness and passion, or even to the influence of dark unconscious factors.

"Mistake" and "arbitrariness" therefore are reciprocally related. As a purported "test" becomes less and less intelligible, and hence more and more a cloak for arbitrariness, "mistake" becomes less and less possible— not, let it be strongly emphasized, because of any certainty of one's being right, but for the exactly contrary reason that there is no "right" or "wrong" discernible.

Sometimes, there is a puzzling intermediate or hybrid case, where the "test," though expressed in exceedingly obscure language, may, in some metaphysical sense, have "meaning," so that one can, in theory, be right or wrong in some application of it. But so obscurely expressed a standard *invites* mistake, even if the standard itself, in some ideal sense, is meaningful. The truth is that we mortals cannot really tell whether such obscurely expressed standards have, in some arcane sense, any meaning, so we don't know whether, in trying to apply them, we are behaving quite arbitrarily or are making all the mistakes that are inevitable when the standards given us are all but totally unclear in expression. . . .

All of this sounds uncomfortably close to philosophy, and is not the kind of thing congenial to me or, I dare say, to most of you. I have one excuse for taking you through such dull stuff, and for having the nerve to insist that you must try to follow it, going back and reading it over if necessary. My excuse I urge as clearly sufficient, for it is no less than the fact that, within a year or two, several hundred men and women may have electric current passed through their bodies until their eyeballs pop out and their brains are cooked, as a result of choices made under standards vulnerable to the objections I have just rehearsed. Let us understand these issues. Let us spare ourselves no pain of consideration before we see that occur—before we commit our society yet again to the policy of officially sanctioned killing.

For it is my assertion . . . that, in one way or another, the official choices—by prosecutors, judges, juries, and governors—that divide those who are to die from those who are to live are on the whole not made, and cannot be made, under standards that are consistently meaningful and clear, but that they are often made, and in the foreseeable future will continue often to be made, under no standards at all or under pseudo-standards without discoverable meaning. My further (and closely connected) assertion is that *mistake* in these choices is fated to occur. . . .

Race and the Death Penalty

DAVID BALDUS et al.

. . . Justice Powell [of the U.S. Supreme Court] held that McCleskey's equal-protection claim [in *McCleskey* v. *Kemp*] failed because he did not prove "that the decisionmakers in his case acted with discriminatory purpose." The failure of proof, he said, stemmed from the absence of "evidence specific to his own case that would support an inference that racial considerations played a part in his sentence." Justice Powell implied that classwide statistical evidence alone was not relevant to the issue of discrimination in an individual defendant's case regardless of what it suggested about the policies of the state's prosecutors and jurors in general. By so limiting capital punishment equal-protection claims, the Court in *McCleskey* created a nearly insuperable barrier to proof. In order to secure relief, it now appears that capital defendants must demonstrate the existence of purposeful discrimination based upon admissions by biased prosecutors or jurors or by circumstantial evidence of discriminatory intent affecting their individual cases, without reference to evidence of classwide discrimination against their racial group.

Justice Powell's opinion recognized that the Supreme Court has previously held that statistical evidence is relevant as proof of intent to discriminate—both in jury cases brought under the Fourteenth Amendment and in classwide purposeful discrimination cases brought under Title VII of the 1964 Civil Rights Act, which prohibits intentional employment discrimination. He held, however, that to accept such a showing in capital cases "without regard to the facts of a particular case would extend [relief] to all capital cases in Georgia, at least where the victim was white and the defendant is black." This alternative appeared particularly objectionable since the statistical evidence presented in McCleskey's case indicated that, in many highly aggravated black-defendant/white-victim cases, the race of the defendant and victim played no role at all.

Justice Powell's analysis of the probative value of statistical proof suggested, in short, that the Court confronted an "all or nothing" choice. Either it could accept statistical evidence as proof of an equal-protection violation "without regard to the facts of a particular case," or it could deny completely the relevance of statistical evidence of classwide discrimination and insist that McCleskey demonstrate strictly on the basis of case-specific evidence that his prosecutor or jury acted with a racial animus.

From *Equal Justice and the Death Penalty: A Legal and Empirical Analysis* by David C. Baldus, George G. Woodworth, and Charles A. Pulaski, Jr., pp. 370–375, 386–387. Copyright © 1990 by David C. Baldus, George G. Woodworth, and Charles A. Pulaski, Jr. Reprinted with the permission of Northeastern University Press.

In fact, however, the Court's choice of methods of proof was not as limited as Justice Powell suggested. The Court had itself developed a modified approach, which combined elements of both the statistical and the case-specific models in *International Brotherhood of Teamsters* v. *United States,* a Title VII classwide purposeful discrimination case. This hybrid model relies initially on statistical proof to establish the existence of classwide, intentional discrimination but employs case-specific evidence of purposeful discrimination to fashion relief, thus retaining the advantages that statistical evidence can provide in discrimination cases. At the same time, however, by conditioning relief on some further, case-specific showing of purposeful discrimination, it avoids the injustice that might result from uniformly granting relief to all affected parties without regard to their particular situation.

Justice Powell employs three arguments to justify his explicit rejection of the purely statistical model of proof and his implicit rejection of the hybrid model. First, he suggests that the imposition of an essentially unattainable burden of proof is necessary to maintain the legitimate discretion of prosecutors and jurors in the death-sentencing context. Indeed, his opinion even asserts that permitting the type of statistical proof of systemwide racial disparities in death sentencing that McCleskey offered would jeopardize the very heart of the state's criminal justice system. But he does not really develop the argument.

Second, he rejects the strictly statistical model of proof on the ground that it would invalidate a significant number of death sentences without regard to whether they were a product of purposeful discrimination. This is a reasonable basis for rejecting the exclusively statistical model, since, as noted earlier, it is plain that many death sentences are imposed in highly aggravated cases in which the race of victim or defendant clearly has no effect on the outcome. This rationale does not, however, justify a rejection of the hybrid model, which contemplates a case-by-case inquiry into the specifics of each case as a basis for awarding relief.

Justice Powell's third and principal argument was based on methodological grounds that apply to both the purely statistical and hybrid models of proof. In essence, he held that the strength of the inference that could be drawn from evidence of classwide, purposeful discrimination was different in the death-sentencing context than it was in jury and employment cases: "[T]he nature of the capital sentencing decision, and the relationship of the statistics to that decision, are fundamentally different from the corresponding elements in the [jury] venire-selection or Title VII cases."

Justice Powell offered three reasons for this judgment. First, there are more distinct and autonomous decision-making entities involved in a death-sentencing system, and they operate without any "coordination." Second, many more characteristics of each case may influence death-sentencing decisions. Third, there is "no common standard" by which a court can "evaluate all defendants who have or have not received the death penalty." For these reasons, Justice Powell concluded that "the application of an inference drawn from the general statistics to a specific decision in a trial and sentencing simply is not comparable to the application of an inference drawn from general statistics to a specific venire-selection or Title VII case."

To the extent that Justice Powell's conclusion rests upon his presumptions about the capacity of statistical methodology in the death-sentencing context, it is quite unpersuasive. First, the capacity of a multivariate statistical analysis to identify the factors that are influencing a discretionary decision-making system is not a function of the number of decision makers in the system. If decision makers apply similar selection criteria, a regression analysis will identify those criteria no matter how many people participate in the processing of each case and no matter how many different cases each participant handles. A multiple-regression analysis has the same power to identify commonly applied selection criteria in a system that requires a series of people to process each case and that limits each person's participation to only a single case as it has in a system that requires the same person to process each case in a single decision.

It is, of course, true that the probability of identifying the selection criteria being applied is reduced as the number of autonomous participants in a process increases, since the more autonomous actors there are in a system, the less likely it is that they will apply common selection criteria. Indeed, a characteristic that constitutes an aggravating factor in a case for some prosecutors and juries may mitigate it for others; the inconsistent statistical effects thereby produced within each subset of cases will be muffled and obscured in an analysis including all of the cases. For example, our Georgia data show that black offenders are treated more leniently than white offenders in urban districts, but more punitively in rural areas. However, when we analyze the data statewide those independent effects cancel each other out and the statistics show no statewide race-of-defendant effect. Similarly, within a single jurisdiction we have seen the effects of more favorable treatment of white defendants at early stages in the process offset by more favorable treatment for black defendants in the penalty-trial stage. The result is that an analysis of the combined effects of all of the stages in the system shows no race-of-defendant effect at all.

Within a system as large and decentralized as the Georgia capital-sentencing system, therefore, it is not surprising that relatively few factors emerge as statistically important. Moreover, because of the substantial risk that the effects of many factors will be potentially or wholly obscured in a statistical analysis, we can be confident that those that do emerge as important have a strong and consistent influence in the system. In fact, the factors that do emerge as important tend to be those that we would reasonably expect all participants in the system to recognize as significant—for example, the defendant's role in the homicide and the number of victims in the case.

Moreover, the presence or absence of "coordination" between decision makers in the system has nothing whatever to do with the capacity of a statistical analysis to identify the policies revealed by their decisions. Heretofore, the policy that decision makers believed they were applying has not been determinative or even particularly important. The ultimate concern was with the policy that in fact was applied, and that policy is precisely what a properly designed multivariate statistical analysis can reveal.

We also found unpersuasive Justice Powell's argument about the number of variables that are relevant in the death-sentencing context and his concern about the absence of a "common standard" on which a court can determine whether the cases of two or more death-eligible defendants have similar levels of aggravation or blameworthiness. Justice Powell is correct in stating that there are common standards applied in employment cases. Examples would include economic worth, productivity, competence, and efficiency. Since these properties cannot be directly measured, proxies for them, which can be measured, are used to identify groups of cases that are similar and should be treated alike. Frequently used proxies in employment cases include such characteristics as years of prior experience, seniority, education, output, and supervisor evaluations. Variables for such case characteristics are then analyzed with cross-tabular and multiple-regression procedures to estimate sex and race disparities in treatment.

However, Justice Powell is unconvincing when he suggests that there exists "no common standard by which to evaluate" the treatment of death-eligible defendants. Indeed, his own characterization of the Georgia death-sentencing system belies his claim.

> The Baldus study in fact confirms that the Georgia system results in a reasonable level of proportionality among the class of murderers eligible for the death penalty. As Professor Baldus confirmed, the system sorts out cases where the sentence of death is highly likely and highly unlikely, leaving a mid-range of cases where the imposition of the death penalty in any particular case is less predictable.

Implicit in this statement is the proposition that considerations of blameworthiness and overall moral culpability do explain the distribution of death sentences in the Georgia system. Those defendants who are most morally culpable and blameworthy are the most likely to receive a death sentence. More to the point, if, in fact, no common standard could be discerned in the operation of Georgia's capital-sentencing system, then that system would still offend the Supreme Court's ruling in *Furman,* which condemned death sentences imposed by Georgia because they "could not be meaningfully distinguished" from the many cases that resulted in lesser punishments.

Justice Powell's third reason for imposing more exacting standards of proof in death-sentencing cases concerned the State's ability to respond to the claimant's statistical proof. In the death-sentencing context, stated Justice Powell, "the State has no practical opportunity to rebut" the evidence of classwide discrimination; this lack of opportunity stems both from " 'controlling considerations of . . . public policy,' " that prevent the testimony of jurors as witnesses, and from the impossibility of requiring prosecutors to defend decisions made years earlier.

This reasoning lacks force for several reasons. First, as Justice Blackmun's dissent correctly points out, prosecutors are not barred from giving testimony in the same way as jurors are. Indeed, such testimony by prosecutors is particularly apt in cases involving claims of racial discrimination. Nor is the reliability of such testimony any more suspect than is the testimony of employers in Title VII cases, who routinely testify about decisions made years earlier.

Second, Justice Powell fundamentally misperceives the importance of verbal testimony in rebutting statistical evidence of classwide discrimination in jury-selection and Title VII cases. Although he suggests that such evidence is key, in fact it plays only a minor role. In jury cases, the self-serving testimony of jury commissioners that racial factors played no role in their decisions carries little weight. The persuasive rebuttal evidence in such cases is objective data, the adjustment for which eliminates the racial disparities. Similarly, in employment cases alleging classwide intentional discrimination, defendants can rebut the plaintiff's case far more effectively by attacking the validity of the plaintiff's statistics or by introducing objective statistical evidence that explains away the disparities underlying the plaintiff's prima facie case than by offering the employer's self-serving denials of racial animus.

Similarly, in the death-sentencing context, we would expect the testimony of prosecutors to be of minor importance in rebutting statistical evidence of excessiveness or discrimination. Far more effective would be the rebuttal evidence of the general type the State presented in *McCleskey*—attacks on the validity of the petitioner's statistics and quantitative efforts to explain away the observed racial disparities. Indeed, in *McCleskey* the State made no effort even to call as a witness the assistant district attorney who prosecuted the case.

Similar considerations apply to the evidentiary disqualification of juror testimony. The state's inability to present such testimony would appear to be of little consequence, since, even if allowed, it would do little more in the great majority of cases than confirm which facts in the record were determinative for the jury. Furthermore, in most situations the party whom the juror-disqualification rule disadvantages is a prisoner seeking to establish juror misconduct or bias through juror testimony. Many prisoners are denied a decision on the merits of their claims for this reason. Thus, to deny prisoners the opportunity to assert statistically grounded claims of classwide discrimination in the capital-sentencing context because the juror-disqualification rule would disadvantage the State hardly seems to comport with parity of treatment. . . .

Justice Powell . . . feared a ruling for McCleskey under the Eighth Amendment would open the entire criminal justice system to a disruptive invasion of social scientists and statisticians. To be sure, a ruling favorable to McCleskey would have disrupted the death-sentencing systems of some states, at least for the short term; but Justice Powell's apprehension of a parade of social scientists disrupting the courts appears to be greatly exaggerated. In the first place, the only social science research relevant to judicial proceedings would be field research conducted in actual courts. Most of the social science studies cited by Justice Powell were not field studies but experiments that used students as mock jurors. Second, field research of the type Justice Powell fears is expensive, extremely time-consuming, and, because of its applied nature, generally not favored by funding sources. The relatively small amount of judicial field research done to date is suggestive of the few incentives that the system offers to produce it. Third, most of the field research conducted so far tends to undercut the farfetched claims that Justice Powell thinks social scientists would be inclined to support. That research does not suggest that the criminal justice system is systematically biased or invidious, or that it characteristically functions arbitrarily or irrationally. To be sure, there is substantial evidence of sentencing disparities among similarly situated offenders, but most of the available evidence does not suggest that these disparities are correlated with sex, physical appearance, or any of the other factors hypothesized by the Court. In fact, the literature suggests that, with respect to the issue of discrimination, further empirical inquiry may increase public confidence in the basic fairness of the system.

Finally, we find it distressing that a majority of the Supreme Court would choose to reject a claim based upon invidious racial discrimination because of the work load that a ruling in the claimant's favor might entail in later cases. Former Chief Justice Burger frequently urged Congress to conduct a "judicial impact study" before enacting new legislation. Justice Powell's avowed concerns in *McCleskey* have the same flavor but, given the constitutional character of the rights asserted, seem much less appropriate.

✠ F U R T H E R   R E A D I N G

Hugo Bedau, *The Courts, the Constitution, and Capital Punishment* (1977)
———, *Death Is Different: Studies in the Morality, Law, and Politics of Capital Punishment* (1987)
Jane C. England, "Capital Punishment in the Light of Constitutional Evolution: An Analysis of Distinctions Between *Furman* and *Gregg*," *Notre Dame Lawyer* 52 (1977): 596–610
Frank Graham, *The Due Process Revolution* (1970)
Jack Greenberg, "Capital Punishment as a System," *Yale Law Journal* 91 (1982): 908–936
Roger Hood, *The Death Penalty: A World-Wide Perspective* (1989)
Louis Masur, *Rites of Execution* (1990)
Barry Nakell and Kenneth A. Hardy, *The Arbitrariness of the Death Penalty* (1987)
Johan T. Sellin, *The Penalty of Death* (1980)
Ernest van den Haag and J. Conrad, *The Death Penalty: A Debate* (1983)
Samuel Walker, *Popular Justice: A History of American Criminal Justice* (1980)
Franklin E. Zimring and Gordon Hawkins, *Capital Punishment and the American Agenda* (1986)

Original Intent and

Constitutional Interpretation

The problem of how to interpret the Constitution has been debated throughout American history. In the past quarter-century, the debate assumed new energy as conservative critics of the Warren Court charged that its justices had substituted their wishes for the intentions of the Constitution's framers. Former attorney general Edwin Meese and Supreme Court justice William H. Rehnquist have argued, for example, that the High Court has become nothing more than a continuing constitutional convention. They urge the adoption of a jurisprudence of original intention as a means of curbing judicial excesses. The original purposes to which the framers of the Constitution and its amendments adhered should bind subsequent generations. The framers' wishes, according to this view, are not only the relevant but also the authoritative basis for constitutional interpretation.

Three important assumptions undergird this doctrine of original intent. First, legitimate authority in a democracy must rest on majority rule. When a judge exercises judicial review, he or she can overrule a legislature only when it has ignored majority will. A justice can exercise judicial review most appropriately when preserving majority sentiment. Second, because the justices interpret law, and the Constitution is law, they must take seriously the intentions of those who framed the document. Third, without the stern discipline of precedent and history to guide them, the justices would simply substitute their personal views for the majority will of the legislature.

Non-originalists disagree sharply with these assumptions. They believe that the legitimacy of constitutional law rests on the discretionary power of the justices. These critics of original intent, such as Senator Edward Kennedy of Massachusetts and former Supreme Court Justice William Brennan, insist that an active judiciary stands as the best bulwark against majority tyranny. Moreover, each generation must come to terms with the nation's ruling document based on existing social realities; the originalists' attempt at the judicial reconstruction of history is doomed to failure. Simply put, the justices are ill equipped to deal with the past. Even if they were exceedingly accurate historians, the non-originalists conclude, the documentary records with which they must work are often ambiguous and incomplete. The most skilled historians have trouble knowing precisely, for example, what the framers of the Bill of Rights intended with regard to freedom of speech and press because most of the debates in Congress over the Constitution's first ten amendments were not recorded. Non-originalists argue, moreover, that there are likely to be several sources from which to glean original intent. When we speak of original intent, do we mean the wishes of the framers of the Constitution and its amendments? Or should we turn instead to the intent of those persons who ratified all constitutional changes? Finally, critics of originalism complain that the task of a judge is to administer justice; the past should not prevent the Court from achieving that goal based on an understanding of present circumstances. To do otherwise would be to make the entire system of law appear ridiculous and illegitimate.

The current debate over original intent relates directly to the role of the Supreme Court within the constitutional system. Should the unelected officials who serve on the Court during good behavior possess the power that they do? Is not original intent only another means of rendering them even less accountable than they are presently? Or are the justices, through inept interpretation of history, as likely to stray from the goals of our constitutional system as they would be if they ignored history altogether? Should the justices act as policymakers? Do we want innovative justices? Or do they best fulfill our expectations when they follow tradition?

The reasonable conclusion is that we should expect from Supreme Court justices a mix of the pragmatic and the principled. History and original intent are the glue of our constitutional system; they link generation to generation in common constitutional understanding. To discard either would be to turn constitutional law into a free-for-all. After all, history has utility in helping us to rediscover old ideas that define our present and future constitutional aspirations. History also teaches—as the fate of women and blacks reveals—that for all of the framers' genius, the Court must be prepared to shake free of the past when the only purpose of precedent is to perpetuate that which we know to be unjust.

✠ D O C U M E N T S

Former attorney general Edwin Meese III emerged during the 1980s as the most vocal public official in support of original intent. His address to the American Bar Association on November 15, 1985, which is excerpted as the first document, forcefully presented the case for original intent. Recently retired Supreme Court justice William Brennan in that same year took a position sharply at odds with Meese, as the second document reveals. Justice Thurgood Marshall in 1987, the year of the Bicentennial of the Constitution, suggested that, from the perspective of African-Americans and women, homage to the founders was unwarranted. Justice Marshall's swipe against the founders (the final document) brings to mind Henry Ford's famous dictum that "history is bunk." Was Ford right?

Former Attorney General Edwin Meese III on the Wisdom of Relying on the Framers' Original Intentions, 1985

A large part of American history has been the history of constitutional debate. From the Federalists and the Anti-Federalists, to Webster and Calhoun, to Lincoln and Douglas, we find many examples. Now, as we approach the Bicentennial of the framing of the Constitution, we are witnessing another debate concerning our fundamental law. It is not simply a ceremonial debate, but one that promises to have a profound effect on the future of our Republic.

The current debate is a sign of a healthy nation. Unlike people of many other countries, we are free both to discover the defects of our laws and our government through open discussion and to correct them through our political system.

This debate on the Constitution involves great and fundamental issues. It invites the participation of the best minds the bar, the academy, and the bench have to offer. In recent weeks there have been important new contributions to this debate from some of the most distinguished scholars and jurists in the land. Representatives of the three branches of the federal government have entered the debate, journalistic commentators too.

A great deal has already been said, much of it of merit and on point. But occasionally there has been confusion and in some cases even distortion. Caricatures and straw men, as one customarily finds even in the greatest debates, have made appearances. I've been surprised at some of the hysterical shrillness that we've seen in editorials and other commentary. Perhaps this response is explained by the fact that what we've said defies liberal dogma.

Still, whatever the differences, most participants are agreed about the same high objective: fidelity to our fundamental law.

Today I would like to discuss further the meaning of constitutional fidelity. In particular, I would like to describe in more detail this administration's approach.

Before doing so, I would like to make a few commonplace observations about the original document itself.

It is easy to forget what a young country America really is. The bicentennial of our independence was just a few years ago, that of the Constitution still two years off.

The period surrounding the creation of the Constitution is not a dark and mythical realm. The young America of the 1780s and 90s was a vibrant place, alive with pamphlets, newspapers, and books chronicling and commenting upon the great issues of the day. We know how the Founding Fathers lived, and much of what they read, thought, and believed. The disputes and compromises of the Constitutional Convention were carefully recorded. The minutes of the Convention are a matter of public record. Several of the most important participants—including James Madison, the "father" of the Constitution—wrote comprehensive accounts of the Convention. Others, Federalists and Anti-Federalists alike, committed their arguments for and against ratification, as well as their understandings of the Constitution, to paper, so that their ideas and conclusions could be widely circulated, read, and understood.

In short, the Constitution is not buried in the mists of time. We know a tremendous amount of the history of its genesis. The Bicentennial is encouraging even more scholarship about its origins. We know who did what, when, and many times why. One can talk intelligently about a "founding generation."

With these thoughts in mind, I would like to discuss the administration's approach to constitutional interpretation which has been led by President Reagan and which we at the Department of Justice and my colleagues in other agencies have advanced. But to begin, it may be useful to say what it is not.

Our approach does not view the Constitution as some kind of super municipal code, designed to address merely the problems of a particular era—whether those of 1787, 1789, or 1868. There is no question that the Constitutional Convention grew out of widespread dissatisfaction with the Articles of Confederation. But the delegates at Philadelphia moved beyond the job of patching that document to write a *Constitution*. Their intention was to write a document not just for their times but for posterity.

The language they employed clearly reflects this. For example, they addressed *commerce*, not simply shipping or barter. Later the Bill of Rights spoke, through the fourth amendment, to "unreasonable searches and seizures," not merely the regulation of specific law enforcement practices of 1789. Still later, the Framers of the fourteenth amendment were concerned not simply about the rights of black citizens to personal security, but also about the equal protection of the law for all persons within the states.

The Constitution is not a legislative code bound to the time in which it was written. Neither, however, is it a mirror that simply reflects the thoughts and ideas of those who stand before it.

Our approach to constitutional interpretation begins with the document itself. The plain fact is, it exists. It is something that has been written down. Walter Berns of the American Enterprise Institute has noted that the central object of American constitutionalism was "the effort" of the Founders "to express fundamental governmental arrangements in a legal document—to 'get it in writing.' "

Indeed, judicial review has been grounded in the fact that the Constitution is a written, as opposed to an unwritten, document. In *Marbury* v. *Madison* John Marshall rested his rationale for judicial review on the fact that we have a written constitution with meaning that is binding upon judges. "[I]t is apparent," he wrote, "that the framers of the constitution contemplated that instrument as a rule for the government of *courts*, as well as of the legislature. Why otherwise does it direct the judges to take an oath to support it?"

The presumption of a written document is that it conveys meaning. . . .

We know that those who framed the Constitution chose their words carefully. They debated at great length the most minute points. The language they chose meant something. They proposed, they substituted, they edited, and they carefully revised. Their words were studied with equal care by state ratifying conventions.

This is not to suggest that there was unanimity among the Framers and ratifiers on all points. The Constitution and the Bill of Rights, and some of the subsequent amendments, emerged after protracted debate. Nobody got everything they wanted. What's more, the Framers were not clairvoyants— they could not foresee every issue that would be submitted for judicial review. Nor could they predict how all foreseeable disputes would be resolved under the Constitution. But the point is, the meaning of the Constitution can be known.

What does this written Constitution mean? In places it is exactingly specific. Where it says that Presidents of the United States must be at least thirty-five years of age it means exactly that. (I have not heard of any claim that thirty-five means thirty or twenty-five or twenty.) Where it specifies how the House and Senate are to be organized, it means what it says.

The Constitution, including its twenty-six amendments, also expresses particular principles. One is the right to be free of an unreasonable search or seizure. Another concerns religious liberty. Another is the right to equal protection of the laws.

Those who framed these principles meant something by them. And the meanings can be found, understood, and applied.

The Constitution itself is also an expression of certain general principles. These principles reflect the deepest purpose of the Constitution—that of establishing a political system through which Americans can best govern themselves consistent with the goal of securing liberty.

The text and structure of the Constitution are instructive. It contains very little in the way of specific political solutions. It speaks volumes on how problems should be approached, and by *whom.* For example, the first three articles set out clearly the scope and limits of three distinct branches of national government, the powers of each being carefully and specifically enumerated. In this scheme it is no accident to find the legislative branch described first, as the Framers had fought and sacrificed to secure the right of democratic self-governance. Naturally, this faith in republicanism was not unbounded. . . .

Yet the Constitution remains a document of powers and principles. And its undergirding premise remains that democratic self-government is subject only to the limits of certain constitutional principles. This respect for the political process was made explicit early on. When John Marshall upheld the act of Congress chartering a national bank in *McCulloch* v. *Maryland* he wrote: "The Constitution [was] intended to endure for ages to come, and, consequently, to be adapted to the various crises of human affairs." But to use *McCulloch,* as some have tried, as support for the idea that the Constitution is a protean, changeable thing is to stand history on its head. Marshall was keeping faith with the original intention that Congress be free to elaborate and apply constitutional powers and principles. He was not saying that the Court must invent some new constitutional value in order to keep pace with the times. In Walter Berns' words: "Marshall's meaning is not that the Constitution may be adapted to the 'various crises of human affairs,' but that the legislative powers granted by the Constitution are adaptable to meet these crises."

The approach this administration advocates is rooted in the text of the Constitution as illuminated by those who drafted, proposed, and ratified it. In his famous "Commentary on the Constitution of the United States" Justice Joseph Story explained that "[t]he first and fundamental rule in the interpretation of all instruments is, to construe them according to the sense of the terms, and the intention of the parties."

Our approach understands the significance of a written document and seeks to discern the particular and general principles it expresses. It recognizes that there may be debate at times over the application of these principles. But it does not mean these principles cannot be identified.

Constitutional adjudication is obviously not a mechanical process. It requires an appeal to reason and discretion. The text and intention of the Constitution must be understood to constitute the banks within which constitutional interpretation must flow. As James Madison said, if "the sense in which the Constitution was accepted and ratified by the nation . . . be not the guide in expounding it, there can be no security for a consistent and stable, more than for a faithful exercise of its powers."

Thomas Jefferson, so often cited incorrectly as a framer of the Constitution, in fact shared Madison's view: "Our peculiar security is in the possession of a written Constitution. Let us not make it a blank paper by construction."

Jefferson was even more explicit in his personal correspondence:

On every question of construction [we should] carry ourselves back to the time, when the constitution was adapted; recollect the spirit manifested in the debates; and instead of trying [to find] what meaning may be squeezed out of the text, or invented against it, conform to the probable one, in which it was passed.

In the main a jurisprudence that seeks to be faithful to our Constitution—a jurisprudence of original intention, as I have called it—is not difficult to describe. Where the language of the Constitution is specific, it must be obeyed. Where there is a demonstrable consensus among the Framers and ratifiers as to a principle stated or implied by the Constitution, it should be followed. Where there is ambiguity as to the precise meaning or reach of a constitutional provision, it should be interpreted and applied in a manner so as to at least not contradict the text of the Constitution itself.

Sadly, while almost everyone participating in the current constitutional debate would give assent to these propositions, the techniques and conclusions of some of the debaters do violence to them. What is the source of this violence? In large part I believe that it is the misuse of history stemming from the neglect of the idea of a written constitution.

There is a frank proclamation by some judges and commentators that what matters most about the Constitution is not its words but its so-called "spirit." These individuals focus less on the language of specific provisions than on what they describe as the "vision" or "concepts of human dignity" they find embodied in the Constitution. This approach to our jurisprudence has led to some remarkable and tragic conclusions.

In the 1850s, the Supreme Court under Chief Justice Roger B. Taney read blacks out of the Constitution in order to invalidate Congress' attempt to limit the spread of slavery. The *Dred Scott* decision, famously described as a judicial "self-inflicted wound," helped bring on the Civil War. There is a lesson in such history. There is danger in seeing the Constitution as an empty vessel into which each generation may pour its passion and prejudice.

Our own time has its own fashions and passions. In recent decades many have come to view the Constitution—more accurately, part of the Constitution, provisions of the Bill of Rights and the fourteenth amendment—as a charter for judicial activism on behalf of various constituencies. Those who hold this view often have lacked demonstrable textual or historical support for their conclusions. Instead they have grounded their rulings in appeals to social theories, to moral philosophies or personal notions of human dignity, or to "penumbras," somehow emanating ghostlike from various provisions—identified and not identified—in the Bill of Rights. The problem with this approach, as John Hart Ely, Dean of Stanford Law School, has observed with respect to one such decision, is not that it is bad constitutional law, but that it is not constitutional law in any meaningful sense at all.

Despite this fact, the perceived popularity of some results in particular cases has encouraged some observers to believe that any critique of the methodology of those decisions is an attack on the results. This perception is sufficiently widespread that it deserves an answer. My answer is to look at history.

When the Supreme Court, in *Brown* v. *Board of Education,* sounded the death knell for official segregation in the country, it earned all the plaudits it received. But the Supreme Court in that case was not giving new life to old words, or adapting a "living," "flexible" Constitution to new reality. It was restoring the original principle of the Constitution to constitutional law. The *Brown* Court was correcting the damage done fifty years earlier, when in *Plessy* v. *Ferguson* an earlier Supreme Court had disregarded the clear intent of the Framers of the civil war amendments to eliminate the legal degradation of blacks, and had contrived a theory of the Constitution to support the charade of "separate but equal" discrimination.

It is amazing how so much of what passes for social and political progress is really the undoing of old judicial mistakes.

Mistakes occur when the principles of specific constitutional provisions—such as those contained in the Bill of Rights—are taken by some as invitations to read into the Constitution values that contradict the clear language of other provisions.

Acceptances to this illusory invitation have proliferated in recent decades. One Supreme Court Justice identified the proper judicial standard as asking "what's best for this country." Another said it is important to "keep the Court out in front" of the general society. Various academic commentators have poured rhetorical gasoline on this judicial fire, suggesting that constitutional interpretation appropriately be guided by such standards as whether a public policy "personifies justice" or "comports with the notion of moral evolution" or confers "an identity" upon our society or was consistent with "natural ethical law" or was consistent with some "right of equal citizenship." These amorphous concepts, as opposed to the written Constitution, form a very poor base for judicial interpretation.

Unfortunately, as I've noted, navigation by such lodestars has in the past given us questionable economics, governmental disorder, and racism—all in the guise of constitutional law. Recently one of the distinguished judges of one of our federal appeals courts got it about right when he wrote: "The truth is that the judge who looks outside the Constitution always looks inside himself and nowhere else." Or, as we recently put it before the Supreme Court in an important brief: "The further afield interpretation travels from its point of departure in the text, the greater the danger that constitutional adjudication will be like a picnic to which the framers bring the words and the judges the meaning." . . .

Any true approach to constitutional interpretation must respect the document in all its parts and be faithful to the Constitution in its entirety.

What must be remembered in the current debate is that interpretation does not imply results. The Framers were not trying to anticipate every answer. They were trying to create a tripartite national government, within a federal system, that would have the flexibility to adapt to face new exigencies—as it did, for example, in chartering a national bank. Their great interest was in the distribution of power and responsibility in order to secure the great goal of liberty for all.

A jurisprudence that seeks fidelity to the Constitution—a jurisprudence of original intention—is not a jurisprudence of political results. It is very much concerned with process, and it is a jurisprudence that in our day seeks to depoliticize the law. The great genius of the constitutional blueprint is found in its creation and respect for spheres of authority and the limits it places on governmental power. In this scheme the Framers did not see the courts as the exclusive custodians of the Constitution. Indeed, because the document posits so few conclusions it leaves to the more political branches the matter of adapting and vivifying its principles in each generation. It also leaves to the people of the states, in the tenth amendment, those responsibilities and rights not committed to federal care. The power to declare acts of Congress and laws of the states null and void is truly awesome. This power must be used when the Constitution clearly speaks. It should not be used when the Constitution does not.

In *Marbury* v. *Madison*, at the same time he vindicated the concept of judicial review, Marshall wrote that the "principles" of the Constitution "are deemed fundamental and permanent," and except for formal amendment, "unchangeable." If we want a change in our Constitution or in our laws we must seek it through the formal mechanisms presented in that organizing document of our government.

In summary, I would emphasize that what is at issue here is not an agenda of issues or a menu of results. At issue is a way of government. A jurisprudence based on first principles is neither conservative nor liberal, neither right nor left. It is a jurisprudence that cares about committing and limiting to each organ of government the proper ambit of its responsibilities. It is a jurisprudence faithful to our Constitution.

By the same token, an activist jurisprudence, one which anchors the Constitution only in the consciences of jurists, is a chameleon jurisprudence, changing color and form in each era. The same activism hailed today may threaten the capacity for decision through democratic consensus tomorrow, as it has in many yesterdays. Ultimately, as the early democrats wrote into the Massachusetts state constitution, the best defense of our liberties is a government of laws and not men. . . .

As students of the Constitution are aware, the struggle for ratification was protracted and bitter. Essential to the success of the campaign was the outcome of the debate in the two most significant states: Virginia and New York. In New York that battle between Federalist and Anti-Federalist forces was particularly hard. Both sides eagerly awaited the outcome in Virginia, which was sure to have a profound effect on the struggle in the Empire State. When news that Virginia had voted to ratify came, it was a particularly bitter blow to the Anti-Federalist side. Yet on the evening the message reached New York an event took place that speaks volumes about the character of early America. The losing side, instead of grousing, feted the Federalist leaders in the taverns and inns of the city. There followed a night of good fellowship and mutual toasting. When the effects of the good cheer wore off, the two sides returned to their inkwells and presses, and the debate resumed.

There is a great temptation among those who view this debate from the outside to see in it a clash of personalities, a bitter exchange. But you and I, and I hope the other participants in this dialogue know better. We and our distinguished opponents carry on the old tradition, of free, uninhibited, and vigorous debate. Out of such arguments come no losers, only truth.

It's the American way. And the Founders wouldn't want it any other way.

Former Supreme Court Justice William J. Brennan, Jr., on the Failure of the Doctrine of Original Intent, 1985

. . . It will perhaps not surprise you that the text I have chosen for exploration is the amended Constitution of the United States, which, of course, entrenches the Bill of Rights and the Civil War amendments, and draws sustenance from the bedrock principles of another great text, the Magna Carta. So fashioned, the Constitution embodies the aspiration to social justice, brotherhood, and human dignity that brought this nation into being. The Declaration of Independence, the Constitution and the Bill of Rights solemnly committed the United States to be a country where the dignity and rights of all persons were equal before all authority. In all candor we must concede that part of this egalitarianism in America has been more pretension than realized fact. But we are an aspiring people, a people with faith in progress. Our amended Constitution is the lodestar for our aspirations. Like every text worth reading, it is not crystalline. The phrasing is broad and the limitations of its provisions are not clearly marked. Its majestic generalities and ennobling pronouncements are both luminous and obscure. This ambiguity of course calls forth interpretation, the interaction of reader and text. The encounter with the Constitutional text has been, in many senses, my life's work.

My approach to this text may differ from the approach of other participants in this symposium to their texts. Yet such differences may themselves stimulate reflection about what it is we do when we "interpret" a text. Thus I will attempt to elucidate my approach to the text as well as my substantive interpretation.

Perhaps the foremost difference is the fact that my encounters with the constitutional text are not purely or even primarily introspective; the Constitution cannot be for me simply a contemplative haven for private moral reflection. My relation to this great text is inescapably public. That is not to say that my reading of the text is not a personal reading, only that the personal reading perforce occurs in a public context, and is open to critical scrutiny from all quarters.

The Constitution is fundamentally a public text—the monumental charter of a government and a people—and a Justice of the Supreme Court must apply it to resolve public controversies. For, from our beginnings, a most important consequence of the constitutionally created separation of powers has been the American habit, extraordinary to other democracies, of casting social, economic, philosophical and political questions in the form of lawsuits, in an attempt to secure ultimate resolution by the Supreme Court. In this way, important aspects of the most fundamental issues confronting our democracy may finally arrive in the Supreme Court for judicial determination. Not infrequently, these are the issues upon which contemporary society is most deeply divided. They arouse our deepest emotions. The main burden of my twenty-nine Terms on the Supreme Court has thus been to wrestle with the Constitution in this heightened public context, to draw meaning from the text in order to resolve public controversies.

Two other aspects of my relation to this text warrant mention. First, constitutional interpretation for a federal judge is, for the most part, obligatory. When litigants approach the bar of court to adjudicate a constitutional dispute, they may justifiably demand an answer. Judges cannot avoid a definitive interpretation because they feel unable to, or would prefer not to, penetrate to the full meaning of the Constitution's provisions. Unlike literary critics, judges cannot merely savor the tensions or revel in the ambiguities inhering in the text—judges must resolve them.

Second, consequences flow from a Justice's interpretation in a direct and immediate way. A judicial decision respecting the incompatibility of Jim Crow with a constitutional guarantee of equality is not simply a contemplative exercise in defining the shape of a just society. It is an order—supported by the full coercive power of the State—that the present society change in a fundamental aspect. Under such circumstances the process of deciding can be a lonely, troubling experience for fallible human beings conscious that their best may not be adequate to the challenge. We Justices are certainly aware that we are not final because we are infallible; we know that we are infallible only because we are final. One does not forget how much may depend on the decision. More than the litigants may be affected. The course of vital social, economic and political currents may be directed.

These three defining characteristics of my relation to the constitutional text—its public nature, obligatory character, and consequentialist aspect— cannot help but influence the way I read that text. When Justices interpret the Constitution they speak for their community, not for themselves alone. The act of interpretation must be undertaken with full consciousness that it is, in a very real sense, the community's interpretation that is sought. Justices are not platonic guardians appointed to wield authority according to their personal moral predilections. Precisely because coercive force must attend any judicial decision to countermand the will of a contemporary majority, the Justices must render constitutional interpretations that are received as legitimate. The source of legitimacy is, of course, a wellspring of controversy in legal and political circles. At the core of the debate is what the late Yale Law School professor Alexander Bickel labeled "the counter-majoritarian difficulty." Our commitment to self-governance in a representative democracy must be reconciled with vesting in electorally unaccountable Justices the power to invalidate the expressed desires of representative bodies on the ground of inconsistency with higher law. Because judicial power resides in the authority to give meaning to the Constitution, the debate is really a debate about how to read the text, about constraints on what is legitimate interpretation.

There are those who find legitimacy in fidelity to what they call "the intentions of the Framers." In its most doctrinaire incarnation, this view demands that Justices discern exactly what the Framers thought about the question under consideration and simply follow that intention in resolving the case before them. It is a view that feigns self-effacing deference to the specific judgments of those who forged our original social compact. But in truth it is little more than arrogance cloaked as humility. It is arrogant to pretend that from our vantage we can gauge accurately the intent of the Framers on application of principle to specific, contemporary questions. All too often, sources of potential enlightenment such as records of the ratification debates provide sparse or ambiguous evidence of the original intention. Typically, all that can be gleaned is that the Framers themselves did not agree about the application or meaning of particular constitutional provisions, and hid their differences in cloaks of generality. Indeed, it is far from clear whose intention is relevant—that of the drafters, the congressional disputants, or the ratifiers in the states?—or even whether the idea of an original intention is a coherent way of thinking about a jointly drafted document drawing its authority from a general assent of the states. And apart from the problematic nature of the sources, our distance of two centuries cannot but work as a prism refracting all we perceive. One cannot help but speculate that the chorus of lamentations calling for interpretation faithful to "original intention"—and proposing nullification of interpretations that fail this quick litmus test—must inevitably come from persons who have no familiarity with the historical record.

Perhaps most importantly, while proponents of this facile historicism justify it as a depoliticization of the judiciary, the political underpinnings of such a choice should not escape notice. A position that upholds constitutional claims only if they were within the specific contemplation of the Framers in effect establishes a presumption of resolving textual ambiguities against the claim of constitutional right. It is far from clear what justifies such a presumption against claims of right. Nothing intrinsic in the nature of interpretation—if there is such a thing as the "nature" of interpretation—commands such a passive approach to ambiguity. This is a choice no less political than any other; it expresses antipathy to claims of the minority to rights against the majority. Those who would restrict claims of right to the values of 1789 specifically articulated in the Constitution turn a blind eye to social progress and eschew adaptation of overarching principles to changes of social circumstances.

Another, perhaps more sophisticated, response to the potential power of judicial interpretation stresses democratic theory: because ours is a government of the people's elected representatives, substantive value choices should by and large be left to them. This view emphasizes not the transcendent historical authority of the framers but the predominant contemporary authority of the elected branches of government. Yet it has similar consequences for the nature of proper judicial interpretation. Faith in the majoritarian process counsels restraint. Even under more expansive formulations of this approach, judicial review is appropriate only to the extent of ensuring that our democratic process functions smoothly. Thus, for example, we would protect freedom of speech merely to ensure that the people are heard by their representatives, rather than as a separate, substantive value. When, by contrast, society tosses up to the Supreme Court a dispute that would require invalidation of a legislature's substantive policy choice, the Court generally would stay its hand because the Constitution was meant as a plan of government and not as an embodiment of fundamental substantive values.

The view that all matters of substantive policy should be resolved through the majoritarian process has appeal under some circumstances, but I think it ultimately will not do. Unabashed enshrinement of majority will would permit the imposition of a social caste system or wholesale confiscation of property so long as a majority of the authorized legislative body, fairly elected, approved. Our Constitution could not abide such a situation. It is the very purpose of a Constitution—and particularly of the Bill of Rights—to declare certain values transcendent, beyond the reach of temporary political majorities. The majoritarian process cannot be expected to rectify claims of minority right that arise as a response to the outcomes of that very majoritarian process. As James Madison put it:

> The prescriptions in favor of liberty ought to be levelled against that quarter where the greatest danger lies, namely, that which possesses the highest prerogative of power. But this is not found in either the Executive or Legislative departments of Government, but in the body of the people, operating by the majority against the minority.

Faith in democracy is one thing, blind faith quite another. Those who drafted our Constitution understood the difference. One cannot read the text without admitting that it embodies substantive value choices; it places certain values beyond the power of any legislature. Obvious are the separation of powers; the privilege of the Writ of Habeas Corpus; prohibition of Bills of Attainder and ex post facto laws; prohibition of cruel and unusual punishments; the requirement of just compensation for official taking of property; the prohibition of laws tending to establish religion or enjoining the free exercise of religion; and, since the Civil War, the banishment of slavery and official race discrimination. With respect to at least such principles, we simply have not constituted ourselves as strict utilitarians. While the Constitution may be amended, such amendments require an immense effort by the People as a whole.

To remain faithful to the content of the Constitution, therefore, an approach to interpreting the text must account for the existence of these substantive value choices, and must accept the ambiguity inherent in the effort to apply them to modern circumstances. The Framers discerned fundamental principles through struggles against particular malefactions of the Crown; the struggle shapes the particular contours of the articulated principles. But our acceptance of the fundamental principles has not and should not bind us to those precise, at times anachronistic contours. Successive generations of Americans have continued to respect these fundamental choices and adopt them as their own guide to evaluating quite different historical practices. Each generation has the choice to overrule or add to the fundamental principles enunciated by the Framers; the Constitution can be amended or it can be ignored. Yet with respect to its fundamental principles, the text has suffered neither fate. Thus, if I may borrow the words of an esteemed predecessor, Justice Robert Jackson, the burden of judicial interpretation is to translate "the majestic generalities of the Bill of Rights, conceived as part of the pattern of liberal government in the eighteenth century, into concrete restraints on officials dealing with the problems of the twentieth century."

We current Justices read the Constitution in the only way that we can: as Twentieth Century Americans. We look to the history of the time of framing and to the intervening history of interpretation. But the ultimate question must be, what do the words of the text mean in our time? For the genius of the Constitution rests not in any static meaning it might have had in a world that is dead and gone, but in the adaptability of its great principles to cope with current problems and current needs. What the constitutional fundamentals meant to the wisdom of other times cannot be their measure to the vision of our time. Similarly, what those fundamentals mean for us, our descendants will learn, cannot be their measure to the vision of their time. . . . Interpretation must account for the transformative purpose of the text. Our Constitution was not intended to preserve a preexisting society but to make a new one, to put in place new principles that the prior political community had not sufficiently recognized. Thus, for example, when we interpret the Civil War Amendments to the charter—abolishing slavery, guaranteeing blacks equality under law, and guaranteeing blacks the right to vote—we must remember that those who put them in place had no desire to enshrine the status quo. Their goal was to make over their world, to eliminate all vestiges of slave caste.

Having discussed at some length how I, as a Supreme Court Justice, interact with this text, I think it time to turn to the fruits of this discourse. For the Constitution is a sublime oration on the dignity of man, a bold commitment by a people to the ideal of libertarian dignity protected through law. Some reflection is perhaps required before this can be seen.

The Constitution on its face is, in large measure, a structuring text, a blueprint for government. And when the text is not prescribing the form of government it is limiting the powers of that government. The original document, before addition of any of the amendments, does not speak primarily of the rights of man, but of the abilities and disabilities of government. When one reflects upon the text's preoccupation with the scope of government as well as its shape, however, one comes to understand that what this text is about is the relationship of the individual and the state. The text marks the metes and bounds of official authority and individual autonomy. When one studies the boundary that the text marks out, one gets a sense of the vision of the individual embodied in the Constitution.

As augmented by the Bill of Rights and the Civil War Amendments, this text is a sparkling vision of the supremacy of the human dignity of every individual. This vision is reflected in the very choice of democratic self-governance; the supreme value of a democracy is the presumed worth of each individual. And this vision manifests itself most dramatically in the specific prohibitions of the Bill of Rights, a term which I henceforth will apply to describe not only the original first eight amendments, but the Civil War amendments as well. It is a vision that has guided us as a people throughout our history, although the precise rules by which we have protected fundamental human dignity have been transformed over time in response to both transformations of social condition and evolution of our concepts of human dignity. . . .

It was in particular the Fourteenth Amendment's guarantee that no person be deprived of life, liberty or property without due process of law that led us to apply many of the specific guarantees of the Bill of Rights to the States. In my judgment, Justice Cardozo best captured the reasoning that brought us to such decisions when he described what the court has done as a process by which the guarantees "have been taken over from the earlier articles of the federal bill of rights and brought within the Fourteenth Amendment by a process of absorption . . . [that] has had its source in the belief that neither liberty nor justice would exist if [those guarantees] . . . were sacrificed." But this process of absorption was neither swift nor steady. As late as 1922 only the Fifth Amendment guarantee of just compensation for official taking of property had been given force against the states. Between then and 1956 only the First Amendment guarantees of speech and conscience and the Fourth Amendment ban of unreasonable searches and seizures had been incorporated—the latter, however, without the exclusionary rule to give it force. As late as 1961, I could stand before a distinguished assemblage of the bar at New York University's James Madison Lecture and list the following as guarantees that had not been thought to be sufficiently fundamental to the protection of human dignity so as to be enforced against the states: the prohibition of cruel and unusual punishments, the right against self-incrimination, the right to assistance of counsel in a criminal trial, the right to confront witnesses, the right to compulsory process, the right not to be placed in jeopardy of life or limb more than once upon accusation of a crime, the right not to have illegally obtained evidence introduced at a criminal trial, and the right to a jury of one's peers.

The history of the quarter century following that Madison Lecture need not be told in great detail. Suffice it to say that each of the guarantees listed above has been recognized as a fundamental aspect of ordered liberty. Of course, the above catalogue encompasses only the rights of the criminally accused, those caught, rightly or wrongly, in the maw of the criminal justice system. But it has been well said that there is no better test of a society than how it treats those accused of transgressing against it. Indeed, it is because we recognize that incarceration strips a man of his dignity that we demand strict adherence to fair procedure and proof of guilt beyond a reasonable doubt before taking such a drastic step. These requirements are, as Justice Harlan once said, "bottomed on a fundamental value determination of our society that it is far worse to convict an innocent man than to let a guilty man go free." There is no worse injustice than wrongly to strip a man of his dignity. And our adherence to the constitutional vision of human dignity is so strict that even after convicting a person according to these stringent standards, we demand that his dignity be infringed only to the extent appropriate to the crime and never by means of wanton infliction of pain or deprivation. I interpret the Constitution plainly to embody these fundamental values.

Of course the constitutional vision of human dignity has, in this past quarter century, infused far more than our decisions about the criminal process. Recognition of the principle of "one person, one vote" as a constitutional one redeems the promise of self-governance by affirming the essential dignity of every citizen in the right to equal participation in the democratic process. Recognition of so-called "new property" rights in those receiving government entitlements affirms the essential dignity of the least fortunate among us by demanding that government treat with decency, integrity and consistency those dependent on its benefits for their very survival. After all, a legislative majority initially decides to create governmental entitlements; the Constitution's Due Process Clause merely provides protection for entitlements thought necessary by society as a whole. Such due process rights prohibit government from imposing the devil's bargain of bartering away human dignity in exchange for human sustenance. Likewise, recognition of full equality for women—equal protection of the laws—ensures that gender has no bearing on claims to human dignity.

Recognition of broad and deep rights of expression and of conscience reaffirm the vision of human dignity in many ways. They too redeem the promise of self-governance by facilitating—indeed demanding—robust, uninhibited and wide-open debate on issues of public importance. Such public debate is of course vital to the development and dissemination of political ideas. As importantly, robust public discussion is the crucible in which personal political convictions are forged. In our democracy, such discussion is a political duty; it is the essence of self-government. The constitutional vision of human dignity rejects the possibility of political orthodoxy imposed from above; it respects the right of each individual to form and to express political judgments, however far they may deviate from the mainstream and however unsettling they might be to the powerful or the elite. Recognition of these rights of expression and conscience also frees up the private space for both intellectual and spiritual development free of government dominance, either blatant or subtle. Justice Brandeis put it so well sixty years ago when he wrote: "Those who won our independence believed that the final end of the State was to make men free to develop their faculties; and that in its government the deliberative forces should prevail over the arbitrary. They valued liberty both as an end and as a means."

I do not mean to suggest that we have in the last quarter century achieved a comprehensive definition of the constitutional ideal of human dignity. We are still striving toward that goal, and doubtless it will be an eternal quest. For if the interaction of this Justice and the constitutional text over the years confirms any single proposition, it is that the demands of human dignity will never cease to evolve.

Indeed, I cannot in good conscience refrain from mention of one grave and crucial respect in which we continue, in my judgment, to fall short of the constitutional vision of human dignity. It is in our continued tolerance of State-administered execution as a form of punishment. I make it a practice not to comment on the constitutional issues that come before the Court, but my position on this issue, of course, has been for some time fixed and immutable. I think I can venture some thoughts on this particular subject without transgressing my usual guideline too severely.

As I interpret the Constitution, capital punishment is under all circumstances cruel and unusual punishment prohibited by the Eighth and Fourteenth Amendments. This is a position of which I imagine you are not unaware. Much discussion of the merits of capital punishment has in recent years focused on the potential arbitrariness that attends its administration, and I have no doubt that such arbitrariness is a grave wrong. But for me, the wrong of capital punishment transcends such procedural issues. As I have said in my opinions, I view the Eighth Amendment's prohibition of cruel and unusual punishments as embodying to a unique degree moral principles that substantively restrain the punishments our civilized society may impose on those persons who transgress its laws. Foremost among the moral principles recognized in our cases and inherent in the prohibition is the primary principle that the State, even as it punishes, must treat its citizens in a manner consistent with their intrinsic worth as human beings. A punishment must not be so severe as to be utterly and irreversibly degrading to the very essence of human dignity. Death for whatever crime and under all circumstances is a truly awesome punishment. The calculated killing of a human being by the State involves, by its very nature, an absolute denial of the executed person's humanity. The most vile murder does not, in my view, release the State from constitutional restraints on the destruction of human dignity. Yet an executed person has lost the very right to have rights, now or ever. For me then, the fatal constitutional infirmity of capital punishment is that it treats members of the human race as nonhumans, as objects to be toyed with and discarded. It is, indeed, "cruel and unusual." It is thus inconsistent with the fundamental premise of the Clause that even the most base criminal remains a human being possessed of some potential, at least, for common human dignity.

This is an interpretation to which a majority of my fellow Justices—not to mention, it would seem, a majority of my fellow countrymen—does not subscribe. Perhaps you find my adherence to it, and my recurrent publication of it, simply contrary, tiresome, or quixotic. Or perhaps you see in it a refusal to abide by the judicial principle of *stare decisis,* obedience to precedent. In my judgment, however, the unique interpretive role of the Supreme Court with respect to the Constitution demands some flexibility with respect to the call of *stare decisis.* Because we are the last word on the meaning of the Constitution, our views must be subject to revision over time, or the Constitution falls captive, again, to the anachronistic views of long-gone generations. I mentioned earlier the judge's role in seeking out the community's interpretation of the Constitutional text. Yet, again in my judgment, when a Justice perceives an interpretation of the text to have departed so far from its essential meaning, that Justice is bound, by a larger constitutional duty to the community, to expose the departure and point toward a different path. On this issue, the death penalty, I hope to embody a community striving for human dignity for all, although perhaps not yet arrived.

You have doubtless observed that this description of my personal encounter with the constitutional text has in large portion been a discussion of public developments in constitutional doctrine over the last quarter century. That, as I suggested at the outset, is inevitable because my interpretive career has demanded a public reading of the text. This public encounter with the text, however, has been a profound source of personal inspiration. The vision of human dignity embodied there is deeply moving. It is timeless. It has inspired Americans for two centuries and it will continue to inspire as it continues to evolve. That evolutionary process is inevitable and, indeed, it is the true interpretive genius of the text.

If we are to be as a shining city upon a hill, it will be because of our ceaseless pursuit of the constitutional ideal of human dignity. For the political and legal ideals that form the foundation of much that is best in American institutions—ideals jealously preserved and guarded throughout our history—still form the vital force in creative political thought and activity within the nation today. As we adapt our institutions to the ever-changing conditions of national and international life, those ideals of human dignity—liberty and justice for all individuals—will continue to inspire and guide us because they are entrenched in our Constitution. The Constitution with its Bill of Rights thus has a bright future, as well as a glorious past, for its spirit is inherent in the aspirations of our people.

Justice Thurgood Marshall on the Constitution's Bicentennial: Commemorating the Wrong Document? 1987

1987 marks the 200th anniversary of the United States Constitution. A Commission has been established to coordinate the celebration. The official meetings, essay contests, and festivities have begun.

The planned commemoration will span three years, and I am told 1987 is "dedicated to the memory of the Founders and the document they drafted in Philadelphia." We are to "recall the achievements of our Founders and the knowledge and experience that inspired them, the nature of the government they established, its origins, its character, and its ends, and the rights and privileges of citizenship, as well as its attendant responsibilities."

Like many anniversary celebrations, the plan for 1987 takes particular events and holds them up as the source of all the very best that has followed. Patriotic feelings will surely swell, prompting proud proclamations of the wisdom, foresight, and sense of justice shared by the Framers and reflected in a written document now yellowed with age. This is unfortunate—not the patriotism itself, but the tendency for the celebration to oversimplify, and overlook the many other events that have been instrumental to our achievements as a nation. The focus of this celebration invites a complacent belief that the vision of those who debated and compromised in Philadelphia yielded the "more perfect Union" it is said we now enjoy.

I cannot accept this invitation, for I do not believe that the meaning of the Constitution was forever "fixed" at the Philadelphia Convention. Nor do I find the wisdom, foresight, and sense of justice exhibited by the Framers particularly profound. To the contrary, the government they devised was defective from the start, requiring several amendments, a civil war, and momentous social transformation to attain the system of constitutional government, and its respect for the individual freedoms and human rights, we hold as fundamental today. When contemporary Americans cite "The Constitution," they invoke a concept that is vastly different from what the Framers barely began to construct two centuries ago.

For a sense of the evolving nature of the Constitution we need look no further than the first three words of the document's preamble: "We the People." When the Founding Fathers used this phrase in 1787, they did not have in mind the majority of America's citizens. "We the People" included,

"The Constitution's Bicentennial: Commemorating the Wrong Document?" by Justice Thurgood Marshall. *Vanderbilt Law Review* 40, 1987, pp. 1337–1342. Reprinted by permission.

in the words of the Framers, "the whole Number of free Persons." On a matter so basic as the right to vote, for example, Negro slaves were excluded, although they were counted for representational purposes—at three-fifths each. Women did not gain the right to vote for over a hundred and thirty years.

These omissions were intentional. . . .

What is striking is the role legal principles have played throughout America's history in determining the condition of Negroes. They were enslaved by law, emancipated by law, disenfranchised and segregated by law; and, finally, they have begun to win equality by law. Along the way, new constitutional principles have emerged to meet the challenges of a changing society. The progress has been dramatic, and it will continue.

The men who gathered in Philadelphia in 1787 could not have envisioned these changes. They could not have imagined, nor would they have accepted, that the documented they were drafting would one day be construed by a Supreme Court to which had been appointed a woman and the descendant of an African slave. "We the People" no longer enslave, but the credit does not belong to the Framers. It belongs to those who refused to acquiesce in outdated notions of "liberty," "justice," and "equality," and who [strove] to better them.

And so we must be careful, when focusing on the events which took place in Philadelphia two centuries ago, that we not overlook the momentous events which followed, and thereby lose our proper sense of perspective. Otherwise, the odds are that for many Americans the Bicentennial celebration will be little more than a blind pilgrimage to the shrine of the original document now stored in a vault in the National Archives. If we seek, instead, a sensitive understanding of the Constitution's inherent defects, and its promising evolution through 200 years of history, the celebration of the "Miracle at Philadelphia" will, in my view, be a far more meaningful and humbling experience. We will see that the true miracle was not the birth of the Constitution, but its life, a life nurtured through two turbulent centuries of our own making, and a life embodying much good fortune that was not.

Thus, in this Bicentennial year, we may not all participate in the festivities with flag-waving fervor. Some may more quietly commemorate the suffering, struggle, and sacrifice that has triumphed over much of what was wrong with the original document, and observe the anniversary with hopes not realized and promises not fulfilled. I plan to celebrate the Bicentennial of the Constitution as a living document, including the Bill of Rights and the other amendments protecting individual freedoms and human rights.

✤ E S S A Y S

The two essays that follow differ radically in their views of the significance of original intent. In the first, Raoul Berger, who is associated with the Harvard Law School, defends original intent; many of his arguments were later echoed by former attorney general Edwin Meese. Leonard W. Levy, a historian at the Claremont Graduate School, takes aim at both Berger and Meese in the second essay. Levy finds their arguments wanting as a matter of both accurate history and sound law.

Original Intent as a Curb on Judicial Power

RAOUL BERGER

Current indifference to the "original intention"—shorthand for the meaning attached by the framers to the words they employed in the Constitution and its Amendments—is a relatively recent phenomenon. Those who would adhere to it are scornfully charged with "filio-pietism," "verbal archeology," "antiquarian historicism that would freeze [the] original meaning" of the Constitution. We are told that the Framers intended to leave it "to succeeding generations [meaning judges] . . . to rewrite the 'living' constitution anew," an argument opposed to historical fact. The sole and exclusive vehicle of change the Framers provided was the amendment process; judicial discretion and policymaking were in high disfavor; all "agents and servants of the people" were to be "bound by the chains" of a "fixed Constitution." . . .

Why is the "original intention" so important? The answer was long since given by Madison: if "the sense in which the Constitution was accepted and ratified by the Nation . . . be not the guide in expounding it, there can be no security for a consistent and stable government, more than for a faithful exercise of its powers." A judicial power to revise the Constitution transforms the bulwark of our liberties into a parchment barrier. This it was that caused Jefferson to say, "Our peculiar security is in the possession of a written constitution. Let us not make it a blank paper by construction." Given a system founded on a dread of power, with "limits" to fence it about, those who demand compliance with those limits (pursuant to the counsel of four or five early State constitutions) are not to be charged with invoking the shades of the Framers in order to satisfy "the need for certainty. . . . If we pretend that the framers had a special sort of wisdom, then perhaps we do not have to think too hard about how to solve pressing social problems." The issue rather is whether solution of those "pressing social problems" was confided to the judiciary.

Effectuation of the draftsman's intention is a long-standing rule of interpretation in the construction of all documents—wills, contracts, statutes—and although today such rules are downgraded as "mechanical" aids, they played a vastly more important role for the Founders. Hamilton, it will be recalled, averred: "To avoid arbitrary discretion in the courts, it is indispensable that they should be bound down by *strict rules* and precedents, which serve to define and point out their duty in every particular case that comes before them." That Hamilton was constrained thus to reassure the ratifiers testifies to prevailing distrust of unbounded judicial interpretive discretion. Some fifty years later, Justice Joseph Story, perhaps the greatest

Reprinted by permission of the publishers from *Government by Judiciary: The Transformation of the Fourteenth Amendment* by Raoul Berger, Cambridge, MA: Harvard University Press, pp. 363–372. Copyright © 1977 by the President and Fellows of Harvard College.

scholar who sat on the Supreme Court, emphasized that such rules provided a "fixed standard" for interpretation, without which a "fixed Constitution" would be forever unfixed. The Constitution, in short, was written against a background of interpretive presuppositions that assured the Framers their design would be effectuated.

The rules governing "intention" reach far back in legal history; but for our purposes it suffices that English case-law emphasis on effectuation of the "original intention" was summarized in Bacon's *Abridgment* (1736) and restated in 1756 by Thomas Rutherforth, in a "work well known to the colonists." Rutherforth assimilated the interpretation of statutes to that of contracts and wills and stated that "The end, which interpretation aims at, is to find out what was the intention of the writer, to clear up the meaning of his words." And he concluded that "the intention of the legislator is the natural measure of the extent of the law." The influence of these presuppositions on the Founders is no matter of conjecture. On the heels of the Convention, Justice James Wilson, a leading participant, said: "The first and governing maxim in the interpretation of a statute is to discover the meaning of those who made it." Not long thereafter Jefferson pledged as President to administer the Constitution "according to the safe and honest meaning contemplated by the plain understanding of the people at the time of its adoption—a meaning to be found in the explanations of those who advocated . . . it." That view was echoed by Chief Justice Marshall, himself a participant in the Virginia Ratification Convention: if a word "was so understood . . . when the Constitution was framed . . . [t]he convention must have used it in that sense." It was reaffirmed by Justice Holmes: an amendment should be read in a "sense most obvious to the common understanding at the time of its adoption."

Enchanted by judicial fulfillment of libertarian hopes, academe, on one ground or another, has endeavored to discredit "original intention," to rid us of the "dead hand of the past." But neither has openly been repudiated by the Court. To the contrary, it has been the Court's practice over the years to consult the intention of the Framers; the Court's concern, as Louis Pollak remarked, "for the original intent of the framers of the Constitution remains high." An arresting example is furnished by the exchange between two "activists," Justices Black and Goldberg, aligned on opposing sides. To Black's condemnation of judicial "amendment," Goldberg responded: "Of course our constitutional duty is to construe, not to rewrite or amend the Constitution! . . . Our sworn duty to construe the Constitution requires, however, that we read it to effectuate the intent and the purposes of the Framers." So, too, both Justices Black and Frankfurter, on opposite sides of the fence in *Adamson* v. *California,* invoked the original intention.

To impeach the "original intention," academicians sought to discredit resort to "legislative history" in general on the ground that the records are incomplete, that they are inconclusive because strewn with conflicting claims. Such charges are irrelevant to the records of the 39th Congress, a "complete" verbatim record of the entire debates. Insofar as there were conflicting opinions, the views of racist Democrats who sought to kill both the Civil

Rights Bill and the Fourteenth Amendment carry no weight; those of a handful of radical dissentients for whom neither Bill nor Amendment went far enough are overborne by the will of the great Republican majority—for example, to leave control of suffrage to the States. That will is implicitly stated in the §2 curtailment of representation when a State denies or abridges suffrage—recognition of power to do so; it is unequivocally confirmed by the Report of the Joint Committee on Reconstruction, by those in charge of the Bill and the Amendment, and by many others in the course of the debates. On a centuries-old canon of interpretation, that intention is as good written into the text. When a legislature "has intimated its will, however indirectly," Justice Holmes held, "that will should be recognized and obeyed . . . it is not an adequate discharge of duty for courts to say: 'We see what you are driving at, but you have not said it.' " The intention of the sovereign people, whether expressed in convention or through the amendment process, demands even greater obedience. . . .

If the Court may substitute its own meaning for that of the Framers it may, as Story cautioned, rewrite the Constitution without limit. But, Leonard Levy maintains: "Whatever the framers of the Fourteenth intended, there is no reason to believe that they possessed the best insights or ultimate wisdom *as to the meaning of their words* for subsequent generations. . . . Words do not have fixed meanings. As Justice Holmes once remarked, a word is 'the skin of living thought and may vary greatly in color and content according to the circumstances and time in which it is used.' " Of course, were Holmes *drafting* he would use words in their present meaning, but that is a far cry from the view that he would feel free to substitute his own meaning in a subsisting document for that of bygone draftsmen. As we have seen, he felt bound to give effect to the intention of the legislators, and it will hereafter appear that he held that words must be given the meaning they had at the time they were set down. There is, moreover, a serious flaw in the Levy analysis, which appears more plainly in John Wofford's statement that if "the meaning of a word is its use, and if its use can never be found apart from its context, then we need only add that an inseparable constituent of context is the time at which the use occurs to show that a past meaning cannot bind the present." Now one who reads what another has written or seeks to interpret it does not in common usage really "use" the word. It is the writer who "used" it, and the traditional function of interpretation, as Rutherforth stated above 200 years ago, is to ascertain "what was the intention of the *writer?*" On the Levy-Wofford analysis we are free to read Hamlet's statement that he "can tell a hawk from a handsaw," then meaning a heron, as if he referred to our pointed-tooth cutting tool because the meaning of "handsaw" has changed, reducing Shakespeare to nonsense. Even Humpty-Dumpty did not carry it so far as to insist that when Alice "used" a word *he* could dictate what *she* meant. With Willard Hurst, I would underscore that "if the idea of a document of superior authority"—the "fixed Constitution" to which the Founders were attached—"is to have meaning, terms which have a precise history filled content to those who draft and adopt the document [such as "due process"] or to which they attach a clear meaning [such as "equal protection"] must be held to that precise meaning." To hold otherwise is to convert the "chains of the Constitution" to ropes of sand.

Like the Constitution, the Fourteenth Amendment was written against the Bacon-Rutherforth background, clearly restated in 1860. Even Charles Sumner, archradical of the 39th Congress, was well aware that

> [e]very Constitution embodies the principles of its framers. It is a transcript of their minds. If its meaning in any place is open to doubt, or if words are used which seem to have no fixed signification, we cannot err if we turn to the framers; and their authority increases in proportion to the evidence which they left on the question.

A "transcript of their minds" was left by the framers in the debates of the 39th Congress, and they left abundant evidence that, for example, in employing "equal protection of the laws" they had in mind only a ban on discrimination with respect to a limited category of "enumerated" rights. Disregard of that intention starkly poses the issue whether the Court may "interpret" black to mean white, to convert the framers' intention to leave suffrage to the States into a transfer of such control to the Supreme Court.

The Failure of Original Intent

LEONARD W. LEVY

. . . The term "original intent" (or "original intention") stands for an old idea that the Court should interpret the Constitution according to the understanding of it by its Framers. In most cases original intent should be followed when clearly discernible, and it is always entitled to the utmost respect and consideration as an interpretive guide. The Constitution lacks the eloquence and passion of the Declaration of Independence, although the majestic opening of the Preamble, "We the People," summons forth the still radically democratic idea that the government of the United States exists to serve the people, not the people to serve the government. That is fundamental to the Framers' original intent, as is the related idea that government in the United States cannot tell us what to think or believe about politics, religion, art, science, literature, or anything else; American citizens have the duty as well as the right to keep the government from falling into error, not the other way around. That marvelously wise principle, too, is part of original intent. Lincoln summarized it best when he said that this nation was conceived in liberty and dedicated to the proposition that all people are created equal.

Liberty and equality are the underpinnings of the Constitution, the essential ingredients of the philosophy of natural rights that the Framers passed on to posterity and, alas, no longer has the respect it once mustered. Much

Reprinted with permission of Macmillan Publishing Company from *Original Intent and the Framers' Constitution* by Leonard W. Levy, pp. x–xvi, 388–398. Copyright © 1988 by Macmillan Publishing Company, a division of Macmillan, Inc.

that is part of original intent still commands our loyalties, our admiration, and our affection: government by consent of the governed; majority rule under constitutional restraints that limit majorities; a bill of rights that applies to all branches of government; a federal system; a tripartite system of government with a single executive, a bicameral legislature, and an independent judiciary; an elaborate system of checks and balances that limits the separation of powers; representative government; and elections at fixed intervals. . . .

Original intent as constitutional theory is rarely if ever at issue in real cases decided by the Supreme Court. When the Court employs original intent, it refers to the understanding of the Framers respecting a particular provision of the Constitution that is imprecise. In real cases the meaning of the provisions involved in litigation is not clear. Indeed the Constitution tends to be least clear when most involved in litigation; that is especially true of rights as compared with matters of structure. Some of the most important clauses of the Constitution are vague, ambiguous, or, paradoxically, too specific in meaning. The most important evidence of original intent is the text of the Constitution itself, which must prevail whenever it surely embodies a broader principle than can be found in the minds or purposes of its Framers. For example, they had political and religious expression in mind when they framed the First Amendment, but its language contains no restriction. They probably did not mean to extend the rights protected by the Sixth Amendment to "all" criminal prosecutions, but the text says "all" and deserves obedience. They had black Americans uppermost in mind when they designed the Fourteenth Amendment, but its expansive expression applies to all, not only to all races but to people of all religions, creeds, and national or ethnic backgrounds, regardless of legitimacy, sex, or alienage.

Conversely, if two centuries of constitutional government have resulted in wider understanding than the text itself suggests, that is, if the meaning of the text has become expanded beyond its literal phrasing, the text takes second place. Thus, although the Framers did not include "words" as well as "persons, houses, papers, and effects" in the Fourth Amendment and although eavesdropping was commonplace in the eighteenth century, words seized by wiretapping and electronic eavesdropping come within the amendment's protection against unreasonable search and seizure. Similarly, the right against compulsory self-incrimination protected by the Fifth Amendment seems, literally, to apply only in "criminal cases," but the text applies with equal force to nonjudicial proceedings such as grand jury and legislative investigations, to administrative proceedings, and even to civil cases in which questions are posed that might, if truthfully answered, raise a threat of criminal jeopardy. Notwithstanding some advocates of a jurisprudence of original intent, the Constitution cannot be interpreted literally, if only because it is murky at important points. Were it not, the real cases would not keep arising.

Until recently, original intent had no political coloration. Both liberals and conservatives, especially among judges, have relied on original intent to add respectability to their opinions. But, constitutional historians, among others, do not respect judicial versions of history. Clinton Rossiter, a great constitutional scholar of conservative proclivities, censured politicians and scholars as well as judges when he said that most talk about original intent "is as irrelevant as it is unpersuasive, as stale as it is strained, as rhetorically absurd as it is historically unsound." He added that "men of power who know least about 'the intent of the Framers' are most likely to appeal to it for support of their views." . . .

[In 1985] Edwin Meese III, then attorney general of the United States, castigated the Supreme Court in a sensational speech before the American Bar Association for opinions that he disliked, and he demanded that the Court abandon decisions based on its views of sound public policy. The Court, Meese declared, should give "deference to what the Constitution— its text and intention—may demand." In answer to his question, "What, then, should a constitutional jurisprudence actually be?" Meese asserted, "It should be a Jurisprudence of Original Intention." Such a jurisprudence, he added, when "aimed at the explication of original intention would produce defensible principles of government that would not be tainted by ideological predilection." In 1986 Robert H. Bork, then a judge of the United States Court of Appeals for the District of Columbia, argued that judges who do not construe the Constitution in accordance with the original intent of its Framers "will, in truth, be enforcing their own morality upon the rest of us and calling it the Constitution." The present Chief Justice of the United States, William H. Rehnquist, has professed similar views. Conservatives, political and judicial, have sought to preempt original intent as their exclusive bulwark and as the only proper foundation for constitutional interpretation. They give the impression that original intent analysis would legitimate their own constitutional views on controversial questions, and they ignore the extent to which original intent would undermine their own positions. Their assumption that the Supreme Court's versions of history are accurate seems naive. A state jurist with a good eye for the meretricious remarked that people who take seriously the Supreme Court's "historical scholarship as applied to the Constitution also probably believe in the Tooth Fairy and the Easter Bunny."

To say that the Supreme Court should decide constitutional questions in accordance with the intent of the Framers is comparable to saying that the Court has a Tom Sawyer mentality, especially with respect to its devotion to principle. In *Huckleberry Finn*, Tom and Huck set out to rescue Jim. Tom, always the romantic who remembered the adventure stories he had read, knew that the proper way to rescue a prisoner was by digging him out of his prison with a case-knife. They dug and dug for many hours, until they were dog-tired and had blistered hands, yet they had scarcely made any progress. Tom admitted that they would have to use picks "and *let on* it's case-knives." He declared that Huck, being ignorant, might use a pick without letting on, but that would not do for himself, Tom, because he knew better. "Gimme a case-knife," he ordered. Huck handed him one but Tom threw it down and said, "Gimme a *case-knife*." Huck finally caught on and handed Tom a pick; Tom took it and set to work. Huck marveled, "He was always just that particular. Full of principle."

The Supreme Court, also full of principle, uses Tom Sawyer's "case-knife" when it credits original intent for its decisions. Whatever picks it uses as its grounds of decision, it stays respectful of the Constitutional Convention. James Madison, James Wilson, and Gouverneur Morris might, like Moses, be astounded at interpretations attributed to them as the source. On arriving in heaven, Moses did not understand what God was doing and was told that in the future a man named Rabbi Akiba would explain. Moses asked to see Akiba and was transported to the future. He listened to Akiba's discourse on the law but it mystified him; he could not follow Akiba's arguments. Moses felt comforted, however, when one of Akiba's disciples asked the master how he knew the meaning of the law on a certain subject, and Akiba responded, "It is a law given unto Moses at Sinai." The process of seeking original intent is elusive, if not illusive, because the fundamental text may be ambiguous and vague, or overarches a particular situation. In a sense the text, whether Constitution or Talmud, is always unfinished even as it is perpetual; and subsequent teachers or judges must expound its meaning. Their exposition can be a legitimate extension of the original, because the text fixes not only a system but an ongoing process. E. L. Doctorow, the novelist, examined the Constitution as a sacred text whose judicial readings are equivalent to priestly commentaries, and he concluded: "It is in the nature of a sacred text, speaking from the past to the present and into the future in that scriptural voice that does not explain . . . to shimmer with ambiguity and to become finally enigmatic, as if it were the ultimate voice of Buddhist self-realization." A Constitution of this sort does not allow original intent analysis to be dispositive or even meaningful in real cases that raise quite specific questions. Rossiter concluded his book on the Constitutional Convention by affirming, "The one clear intent of the Framers was that each generation of Americans should pursue its destiny as a community of free men." Even if some intent is discernible in a case before the Supreme Court, it is probably so general that no one disputes it and it cannot serve to settle the question.

"Original intent" is not a well-chosen term but it is commonly used and widely understood to mean what the Constitutional Convention understood or believed about the Constitution. Intent, intention, and intendment may be distinguished but I do not find the distinctions fruitful in a discourse meant for nonlawyers. Intent may refer to motive, to purpose, even to reasons, but I think that the commonplace usage of intent, in the context of the debate about the "original intent" of the Framers, refers to what they meant. Nevertheless, "intent" is unsatisfactory because it implies a single or uniform frame of mind, or purpose, or understanding on the part of the Framers of the Constitution and even of the ratifiers of the Constitution. "Original intentions" would have been a far better term. . . .

The historic mission of judicial review is supposed to be the vindication of individual freedoms. To acknowledge that yet to understand and protect only the most obvious and conventional freedoms cancels two centuries of democratic growth by returning us to the world of the Framers. But even in that lost world of two centuries ago, rights were still in evolution, people understood that new rights might emerge, and the Ninth Amendment put the Framers' thumbs down on the "rights" side of the scales that weigh rights against powers. Those who measure individual rights against the rights of society forget that society has a profound stake in the rights of the individual; we possess rights as individuals not only because they inhere in us and serve to fulfill us as individuals but because we function as a free society and maintain its openness by respecting personal differences. The Framers were deeply concerned about the humanity that the fundamental law should show even to the criminal offender not because they wanted to coddle criminals but because they were tough-minded enough to understand that the enduring interests of society require justice to be done as fairly as possible.

No apostle of original intent jurisprudence advocates it with consistency or in a thoroughgoing manner. Rehnquist and Bork have not disparaged juries of less than twelve or nonunanimous verdicts as departures from original intent. To the Framers a jury in a criminal trial consisted of twelve men who rendered a unanimous verdict. President Reagan's Department of Justice did not engage in a campaign to eliminate use immunity from our statutes, and the original intent jurists have not declared that use immunity statutes fall short of the constitutional provision that no person shall be compelled to be a witness against himself criminally. No originalist has explained how a constitutional provision can be superseded by a mere statute, let alone one that requires people to be witnesses against themselves and be subject to criminal penalties of perjury unavailable to the prosecution in the absence of a grant of immunity, whether use or transactional. Attorney General Meese campaigned against the *Miranda* decision, supposedly because the Framers would not have recognized the requirement of the *Miranda* warnings, but he did not campaign against use immunity, which would have been equally alien to them.

Meese also campaigned against the Boland Amendment, which prohibited the expenditure of funds on behalf of the Contras in Nicaragua, and he offered as his explanation that the amendment inhibited the President's inherent powers in the field of foreign affairs; Meese showed no appreciation of the fact that the Framers believed that Congress controls appropriations and expenditures. Indeed, the Constitution provides that money bills should originate in the House of Representatives. If we returned to original intent, money bills would no longer originate, as they do nowadays, in the White House or its Bureau of the Budget, despite the provision in Article I, section 7. Two sections further the Constitution also says that no money shall be expended except in accordance with appropriations made by law, but the Reagan administration encouraged or tolerated the payment of monies to the Contras—monies that belonged in the Treasury, had not been appropriated, and whose payment defied the Boland Amendment, which the President had signed. Article I, section 9, requires "from time to time" a public accounting of all receipts and expenditures. The Central Intelligence Agency receives and expends monies that are never publicly accounted for.

Originalists in Reagan's Department of Justice and on the federal courts insisted on a return to the pristine meanings of 1789, but never with respect to executive powers. The administration that backed original intent analysis allowed "The Enterprise," a secret government within the government, consisting of National Security Administration officers, to make foreign policy without the knowledge of the President (preserving "plausible deniability" for him), or of the secretary of state, or of the secretary of defense, or of any elected officials. The concept of inherent executive powers was foreign to the Philadelphia Convention and if known would have been vehemently opposed by those who ratified the Constitution. The same administration that supported original intent as the basis of constitutional jurisprudence also contended that the War Powers Resolution of 1973 is unconstitutional because it checks the President's inherent executive powers in the realm of foreign policy and with respect to his command of the armed services. The Framers intended that the President should have discretion to repel attacks and suppress insurrections, but they would have thought it was stretching the letter of the law somewhat to engage in foreign adventures on the basis of unmentioned inherent powers. Rehnquist and Bork, who are so tight with rights that they require them to be specified and familiar before according them recognition, are extravagant in recognizing inherent as well as implied executive powers. The administration that supported original intent made war in Libya, Lebanon, Nicaragua, and Grenada, and sent a powerful navy to a war zone in the Persian Gulf, but cried "unconstitutional" when Congress sought to keep it accountable and asked the President to execute the laws faithfully. The more one looks at a jurisprudence of original intent, the more it seems politically motivated as a disguise for political objectives. The more one scrutinizes it, the more it seems to be a pose for reasoning from unquestioned subjective assumptions to foregone subjective conclusions.

The Constitution of the United States is our national covenant, and the Supreme Court is its special keeper. The Constitution's power of survival derives in part from the fact that it incorporates and symbolizes the political values of a free people. It creates a representative, responsible government empowered to serve the great objectives specified in the Preamble, while at the same time it keeps government bitted and bridled. Through the Bill of Rights and the great Reconstruction amendments, the Constitution requires that the government respect the freedom of its citizens, whom it must treat fairly. Courts supervise the process, and the Supreme Court is the final tribunal. "The great ideals of liberty and equality," wrote Justice Benjamin N. Cardozo, "are preserved against the assaults of opportunism, the expediency of the passing hour, the scorn and derision of those who have no patience with general principles, by enshrining them in constitutions, and consecrating to the task of their protection a body of defenders." Similarly, Justice Hugo L. Black once wrote for the Court, "Under our constitutional system, courts stand against any winds that blow, as havens of refuge for those who might otherwise suffer because they are helpless, weak, outnumbered, or because they are nonconforming victims of prejudice and public excitement."

The Court should have no choice but to err on the side of the constitutional liberty and equality of the individual, whenever doubt exists as to which side requires endorsement. Ours is so secure a system, precisely because it is free and dedicated to principles of justice, that it can afford to prefer the individual over the state. To interpose original intent against an individual's claim defeats the purpose of having systematic and regularized restraints on power; limitations exist for the minority against the majority, as Madison said. Original intent analysis becomes a treacherous pursuit when it turns the Constitution and the Court away from assisting the development of a still freer and more just society. . . .

The Court has the responsibility of helping regenerate and fulfill the noblest aspirations for which this nation stands. It must keep constitutional law constantly rooted in the great ideals of the past yet in a state of evolution in order to realize them. Something should happen to a person who dons the black robe of a Justice of the Supreme Court of the United States. He or she comes under an obligation to strive for as much objectivity as is humanly attainable by putting aside personal opinions and preferences. Yet even the best and most impartial of Justices, those in whom the judicial temperament is most finely cultivated, cannot escape the influences that have tugged at them all their lives and inescapably color their judgment. Personality, the beliefs that make the person, has always made a difference in the Court's constitutional adjudication. There never has been a constitutional case before the Court in which there was no room for personal discretion to express itself.

We may not want judges who start with the answer rather than the problem, but so long as mere mortals sit on the Court and construe its majestic but murky words, we will not likely get any other kind. Not that the Justices knowingly or deliberately read their presuppositions into law. There probably has never been a member of the Court who consciously decided against the Constitution or was unable in his own mind to square his opinions with it. Most judges convince themselves that they respond to the words on parchment, illuminated, of course, by historical and social imperatives. The illusion may be good for their psyches or the public's need to know that the nine who sit on the nation's highest tribunal really become Olympians, untainted by considerations that move lesser beings in political office.

Even those Justices who start with the problem rather than the result cannot transcend themselves or transmogrify the obscure or inexact into impersonal truth. At bottom, constitutional law reflects great public policies enshrined in the form of supreme and fundamental commands. It is truer of constitutional law than of any other branch that "what the courts declare to have always been the law," as [Justice Oliver Wendell] Holmes [Jr.] put it, "is in fact new. It is legislative in its grounds. The very considerations which judges most rarely mention, and always with an apology, are the secret root from which the law draws all the juices of life. I mean, of course, consideration of what is expedient for the community concerned." Result-oriented jurisprudence or, at the least, judicial activism is nearly inevitable—not praiseworthy, or desirable, but inescapable when the Constitution must be construed. Robert H. Bork correctly said that the best way to cope with the problem "is the selection of intellectually honest judges." One dimension of such honesty is capacity to recognize at the propitious moment a need for constitutional evolution, rather than keep the Constitution in a deepfreeze.

Sometimes the Framers have to be ignored. . . .

Holmes said, in one of his Olympian moments, "The present has a right to govern itself, so far as it can. . . . Historical continuity with the past is not a duty, only a necessity." The same man, warning against the "pitfall of antiquarianism," declared that he looked forward to a time when history would not be so important "and instead of ingenious research we shall spend our energy on the study of the ends sought to be attained and the reasons for desiring them." Holmes meant that, although we cannot escape history, because it has shaped us and explains how we have come to be where we are, we are not obliged to be static or be bound by original intent.

Two hundred years of expanding the meaning of democracy and of becoming a heterogeneous nation of nations in which the citizens have the remarkable duty and the right to keep the government from falling into error, must have tremendous constitutional impact. History can only be a guide, not a controlling force. How the Supreme Court uses history, origins, and evolution as well as original intent depends on those who serve on the Court, because in the end, we must face up to the fact stated by Chief Justice Earl Warren on his retirement in 1969. Speaking of the Court he declared, "We serve only the public interest as we see it, guided only by the Constitution and our own consciences." That, not the original intent of the Framers, is our reality.

⊹ F U R T H E R   R E A D I N G

Charles Beard, *The Supreme Court and the Constitution* (1962)

Herman Belz, "The Civil War Amendments to the Constitution: The Relevance of Original Intent," *Constitutional Commentary* 5 (1988): 115–141

Raoul Berger, *Congress v. the Supreme Court* (1969)

Robert Bork, *The Tempting of America* (1990)

Jesse H. Choper, *Judicial Review and the National Political Process* (1980)

Edward S. Corwin, *The Doctrine of Judicial Review* (1914)

Murray Dry, "Federalism and the Constitution: The Founders' Design and Contemporary Constitutional Law," *Constitutional Commentary* 4 (1987): 233—250

John Hart Ely, *Democracy and Distrust: A Theory of Judicial Review* (1980)

The Federalist Society, *The Great Debate: Interpreting Our Constitution* (1986)

Paul Finkelman, "The Constitution and the Intentions of the Framers: The Limits of Historical Analysis," 50 (1989): 349–398

James H. Hutson, "The Creation of the Constitution: The Integrity of the Documentary Record," *Texas Law Review* 65 (1986): 1–39

Charles A. Miller, *The Supreme Court and the Uses of History* (1969)

Richard Neely, *How Courts Govern America* (1981)

H. Jefferson Powell, "The Original Understanding of Original Intent," *Harvard Law Review* 91 (1985): 885–948

Jack N. Rakove, "Mr. Meese, Meet Mr. Madison," *The Atlantic Monthly* (1986): 77–86

Neil L. York, ed., *Toward a More Perfect Union: Six Essays on the Constitution* (1988)

APPENDIX

The Articles of Confederation and Perpetual Union

Between the states of New Hampshire, Massachusetts Bay, Rhode Island and Providence Plantations, Connecticut, New York, New Jersey, Pennsylvania, Delaware, Maryland, Virginia, North Carolina, South Carolina, Georgia.*

Article I

The stile of this confederacy shall be "The United States of America."

Article II

Each State retains its sovereignty, freedom and independence, and every power, jurisdiction, and right, which is not by this confederation expressly delegated to the United States, in Congress assembled.

Article III

The said states hereby severally enter into a firm league of friendship with each other for their common defence, the security of their liberties and their mutual and general welfare; binding themselves to assist each other against all force offered to, or attacks made upon them, or any of them, on account of religion, sovereignty, trade, or any other pretence whatever.

Article IV

The better to secure and perpetuate mutual friendship and intercourse among the people of the different states in this union, the free inhabitants of each of these states, paupers, vagabonds, and fugitives from justice excepted, shall be entitled to all privileges and immunities of free citizens in the several states; and the people of each State shall have free ingress and regress to and from any other State, and shall enjoy therein all the privileges of trade and commerce, subject to the same duties, impositions, and restrictions, as the inhabitants thereof respectively; provided, that such restrictions shall not extend so far as to prevent the removal of property, imported into any State, to any other State of which the owner is an inhabitant; provided also, that no imposition, duties, or restriction, shall be laid by any State on the property of the United States, or either of them.

    If any person guilty of, or charged with treason, felony, or other high misdemeanor in any State, shall flee from justice and be found in any of

---

* This copy of the final draft of the Articles of Confederation is taken from the *Journals*, 9:907–925, November 15, 1777.

the United States, he shall, upon demand of the governor or executive power of the State from which he fled, be delivered up and removed to the State having jurisdiction of his offence.

Full faith and credit shall be given in each of these states to the records, acts, and judicial proceedings of the courts and magistrates of every other State.

Article V

For the more convenient management of the general interests of the United States, delegates shall be annually appointed, in such manner as the legislature of each State shall direct, to meet in Congress, on the 1st Monday in November in every year, with a power reserved to each State to recall its delegates, or any of them, at any time within the year, and to send others in their stead for the remainder of the year.

No State shall be represented in Congress by less than two, nor by more than seven members; and no person shall be capable of being a delegate for more than three years in any term of six years; nor shall any person, being a delegate, be capable of holding any office under the United States, for which he, or any other for his benefit, receives any salary, fees, or emolument of any kind.

Each State shall maintain its own delegates in a meeting of the states, and while they act as members of the committee of the states.

In determining questions in the United States, in Congress assembled, each State shall have one vote.

Freedom of speech and debate in Congress shall not be impeached or questioned in any court or place out of Congress: and the members of Congress shall be protected in their persons from arrests and imprisonments, during the time of their going to and from, and attendance on Congress, *except for treason,* felony, or breach of the peace.

Article VI

No State, without the consent of the United States, in Congress assembled, shall send any embassy to, or receive any embassy from, or enter into any conference, agreement, alliance, or treaty with any king, prince, or state; nor shall any person, holding any office of profit or trust under the United States, or any of them, accept of any present, emolument, office or title, of any kind whatever, from any king, prince, or foreign state; nor shall the United States, in Congress assembled, or any of them, grant any title of nobility.

No two or more states shall enter into any treaty, confederation, or alliance, whatever, between them, without the consent of the United States, in Congress assembled, specifying accurately the purposes for which the same is to be entered into, and how long it shall continue.

No State shall lay any imposts or duties which may interfere with any stipulations in treaties entered into by the United States, in Congress assembled, with any king, prince, or state, in pursuance of any treaties already proposed by Congress to the courts of France and Spain.

No vessels of war shall be kept up in time of peace by any State, except such number only as shall be deemed necessary by the United States, in Congress assembled, for the defence of such State or its trade; nor shall any body of forces be kept up by any State, in time of peace, except such number only as, in the judgment of the United States, in Congress assembled, shall be deemed requisite to garrison the forts necessary for the defence of such State; but every State shall always keep up a well regulated and disciplined militia, sufficiently armed and accoutred, and shall provide, and constantly have ready for use, in public stores, a due number of field pieces and tents, and a proper quantity of arms, ammunition and camp equipage.

No State shall engage in any war without the consent of the United States, in Congress assembled, unless such State be actually invaded by enemies, or shall have received certain advice of a resolution being formed by some nation of Indians to invade such State, and the danger is so imminent as not to admit of a delay till the United States, in Congress assembled, can be consulted; nor shall any State grant commissions to any ships or vessels of war, nor letters of marque or reprisal, except it be after a declaration of war by the United States, in Congress assembled, and then only against the kingdom or state, and the subjects thereof, against which war has been so declared, and under such regulations as shall be established by the United States, in Congress assembled, unless such States be infested by pirates, in which case vessels of war may be fitted out for that occasion, and kept so long as the danger shall continue, or until the United States, in Congress assembled, shall determine otherwise.

Article VII

When land forces are raised by any State for the common defence, all officers of or under the rank of colonel, shall be appointed by the legislature of each State respectively, by whom such forces shall be raised, or in such manner as such State shall direct; and all vacancies shall be filled up by the State which first made the appointment.

Article VIII

All charges of war and all other expences, that shall be incurred for the common defence or general welfare, and allowed by the United States, in Congress assembled, shall be defrayed out of a common treasury, which shall be supplied by the several states, in proportion to the value of all land within each State, granted to or surveyed for any person, as such land and the buildings and improvements thereon shall be estimated according to such mode as the United States, in Congress assembled, shall, from time to time, direct and appoint.

The taxes for paying that proportion shall be laid and levied by the authority and direction of the legislatures of the several states, within the time agreed upon by the United States, in Congress assembled.

Article IX

The United States, in Congress assembled, shall have the sole and exclusive right and power of determining on peace and war, except in the cases mentioned in the 6th article; of sending and receiving ambassadors; entering into treaties and alliances, provided that no treaty of commerce shall be made, whereby the legislative power of the respective states shall be restrained from imposing such imposts and duties on foreigners as their own people are subjected to, or from prohibiting the exportation or importation of any species of goods or commodities whatsoever; of establishing rules for deciding, in all cases, what captures on land or water shall be legal, and in what manner prizes, taken by land or naval forces in the service of the United States, shall be divided or appropriated; of granting letters of marque and reprisal in times of peace; appointing courts for the trial of piracies and felonies committed on the high seas, and establishing courts for receiving and determining, finally, appeals in all cases of captures; provided, that no member of Congress shall be appointed a judge of any of the said courts.

The United States, in Congress assembled, shall also be the last resort on appeal in all disputes and differences now subsisting, or that hereafter may arise between two or more states concerning boundary, jurisdiction or any other cause whatever; which authority shall always be exercised in the manner following: whenever the legislative or executive authority, or lawful agent of any State, in controversy with another, shall present a petition to Congress, stating the matter in question, and praying for a hearing, notice thereof shall be given, by order of Congress, to the legislative or executive authority of the other State in controversy, and a day assigned for the appearance of the parties by their lawful agents, who shall then be directed to appoint, by joint consent, commissioners or judges to constitute a court for hearing and determining the matter in question; but, if they cannot agree, Congress shall name three persons out of each of the United States, and from the list of such persons each party shall alternately strike out one, in the petitioners beginning, until the number shall be reduced to thirteen; and from that number not less than seven, nor more than nine names, as Congress shall direct, shall, in the presence of Congress, be drawn out by lot; and the persons whose names shall be drawn, or any five of them, shall be commissioners or judges to hear and finally determine the controversy, so always as a major part of the judges who shall hear the cause shall agree in the determination; and if either party shall neglect to attend at the day appointed, without shewing reasons which Congress shall judge sufficient, or, being present, shall refuse to strike, the Congress shall proceed to nominate three persons out of each State, and the secretary of Congress shall strike in behalf of such party absent or refusing; and the judgment and sentence of the court to be appointed, in the manner before prescribed, shall be final and conclusive; and if any of the parties shall refuse to submit to the authority of such court, or to appear or defend their claim or cause, the court shall nevertheless proceed to pronounce sentence or judgment, which shall, in like manner, be final and decisive, the judgment or sentence and other proceedings being, in either case, transmitted to Congress, and lodged among the acts of Congress for the security of the parties concerned: provided, that every commissioner, before he sits in judgment, shall take an oath, to be administered by one of the judges of the supreme or superior court of the State where the cause shall be tried, "well and truly to hear and determine the matter in question, according to the best of his judgment, without favour, affection, or hope of reward": provided, also, that no State shall be deprived of territory for the benefit of the United States.

All controversies concerning the private right of soil, claimed under different grants of two or more states, whose jurisdictions, as they may respect such lands and the states which passed such grants, are adjusted, the said grants, or either of them, being at the same time claimed to have originated antecedent to such settlement of jurisdiction, shall, on the petition of either party to the Congress of the United States, be finally determined, as near as may be, in the same manner as is before prescribed for deciding disputes respecting territorial jurisdiction between different states.

The United States, in Congress assembled, shall also have the sole and exclusive right and power of regulating the alloy and value of coin struck by their own authority, or by that of the respective states; fixing the standard of weights and measures throughout the United States; regulating the trade and managing all affairs with the Indians not members of any of the states; provided that the legislative right of any State within its own limits be not infringed or violated; establishing and regulating post offices from one State to another throughout all the United States, and exacting such postage on the papers passing through the same as may be requisite to defray the expences of the said office; appointing all officers of the land forces in the service of the United States, excepting regimental officers; appointing all the officers of the naval forces, and commissioning all officers whatever in the service of the United States; making rules for the government and regulation of the said land and naval forces and directing their operations.

The United States, in Congress assembled, shall have authority to appoint a committee to sit in the recess of Congress, to be denominated "a Committee of the States," and to consist of one delegate from each State, and to appoint such other committees and civil officers as may be necessary for managing the general affairs of the United States, under their direction; to appoint one of their number to preside; provided that no person be allowed to serve in the office of president more than one year in any term of three years; to ascertain the necessary sums of money to be raised for the service of the United States, and to appropriate and apply the same for defraying the public expences; to borrow money or emit bills on the credit of the United States, transmitting, every half year, to the respective states, an account of the sums of money so borrowed or emitted; to build and equip a navy; to agree upon the number of land forces, and to make requisitions from each State for its quota, in proportion to the number of white inhabitants in such State; which requisitions shall be binding; and, thereupon, the legislature of each State shall appoint the regimental officers, raise the men, and cloathe, arm, and equip them in a soldier-like manner, at the expence of the United States; and the officers and men so cloathed, armed, and equipped, shall march to the place appointed and within the time agreed on by the United States, in Congress assembled; but if the United States, in Congress assembled, shall, on consideration of circumstances, judge proper that any State should not raise men, or should raise a smaller number than its quota, and that any other State should raise a greater number of men than the quota thereof, such extra number shall be raised, officered, cloathed, armed, and equipped in the same manner as the quota of such State, unless the legislature of such State shall judge that such extra number cannot be safely spared out of the same, in which case they shall raise, officer, cloathe, arm, and equip as many of such extra number as they judge can be safely spared. And the officers and men so cloathed, armed, and equipped, shall march to the place appointed and within the time agreed on by the United States, in Congress assembled.

The United States, in Congress assembled, shall never engage in a war, nor grant letters of marque and reprisal in time of peace, nor enter into any treaties or alliances, nor coin money, nor regulate the value thereof, nor ascertain the sums and expences necessary for the defence and welfare of the United States, or any of them: nor emit bills, nor borrow money on the credit of the United States, nor appropriate money, nor agree upon the number of vessels of war to be built or purchased, or the number of land or sea forces to be raised, nor appoint a commander in chief of the army or navy, unless nine states assent to the same; nor shall a question on any other point, except for adjourning from day to day, be determined, unless by the votes of a majority of the United States, in Congress assembled.

The Congress of the United States shall have power to adjourn to any time within the year, and to any place within the United States, so that no period of adjournment be for a longer duration than the space of six months, and shall publish the journal of their proceedings monthly, except such parts thereof, relating to treaties, alliances or military operations, as, in their judgment, require secrecy; and the yeas and nays of the delegates of each State on any question shall be entered on the journal, when it is desired by any delegate; and the delegates of a State, or any of them, at his, or their request, shall be furnished with a transcript of the said journal, except such parts as are above excepted, to lay before the legislatures of the several states.

Article X

The committee of the states, or any nine of them, shall be authorized to execute, in the recess of Congress, such of the powers of Congress as the United States, in Congress assembled, by the consent of nine states, shall, from time to time, think expedient to vest them with; provided, that no power be delegated to the said committee for the exercise of which, by the articles of confederation, the voice of nine states, in the Congress of the United States assembled, is requisite.

Article XI

Canada acceding to this confederation, and joining in the measures of the United States, shall be admitted into and entitled to all the advantages of this union; but no other colony shall be admitted into the same, unless such admission be agreed to by nine states.

Article XII

All bills of credit emitted, monies borrowed and debts contracted by, or under the authority of Congress before the assembling of the United States, in pursuance of the present confederation, shall be deemed and considered as a charge against the United States, for payment and satisfaction whereof the said United States and the public faith are hereby solemnly pledged.

Article XIII

Every State shall abide by the determinations of the United States, in Congress assembled, on all questions which, by this confederation, are submitted to them. And the articles of this confederation shall be inviolably observed by every State, and the union shall be perpetual; nor shall any alteration at any time hereafter be made in any of them, unless such alteration be agreed to in a Congress of the United States, and be afterwards confirmed by the legislatures of every State.

These articles shall be proposed to the legislatures of all the United States, to be considered, and if approved of by them, they are advised to authorize their delegates to ratify the same in the Congress of the United States; which being done, the same shall become conclusive.

Constitution of the United States of America

Preamble

We the people of the United States, in order to form a more perfect union, establish justice, insure domestic tranquillity, provide for the common defense, promote the general welfare, and secure the blessings of liberty to ourselves and our posterity, do ordain and establish this Constitution for the United States of America.

Article I

Section 1.   All legislative powers herein granted shall be vested in a Congress of the United States, which shall consist of a Senate and a House of Representatives.

Section 2.   The House of Representatives shall be composed of members chosen every second year by the people of the several States, and the electors in each State shall have the qualifications requisite for electors of the most numerous branch of the State Legislature.

No person shall be a Representative who shall not have attained to the age of twenty-five years, and been seven years a citizen of the United States, and who shall not, when elected, be an inhabitant of that State in which he shall be chosen.

Representatives and direct taxes shall be apportioned among the several States which may be included within this Union, according to their respective numbers, *which shall be determined by adding to the whole number of free persons, including those bound to service for a term of years and excluding Indians not taxed, three-fifths of all other persons.* The actual enumeration shall be made within three years after the first meeting of the Congress of the United States, and within every subsequent term of ten years, in such manner as they shall by law direct. The number of Representatives shall not exceed one for every thirty thousand, but each State shall have at least one Representative; *and until such enumeration shall be made, the State of New Hampshire shall be entitled to choose three, Massachusetts eight, Rhode Island and Providence Plantations one, Connecticut five, New York six, New Jersey four, Pennsylvania eight, Delaware one, Maryland six, Virginia ten, North Carolina five, South Carolina five, and Georgia three.*

When vacancies happen in the representation from any State, the Executive authority thereof shall issue writs of election to fill such vacancies.

The House of Representatives shall choose their Speaker and other officers; and shall have the sole power of impeachment.

Note: Passages that are no longer in effect are printed in italic type.

Section 3. The Senate of the United States shall be composed of two Senators from each State, *chosen by the legislature thereof,* for six years; and each Senator shall have one vote.

Immediately after they shall be assembled in consequence of the first election, they shall be divided as equally as may be into three classes. The seats of the Senators of the first class shall be vacated at the expiration of the second year, of the second class at the expiration of the fourth year, and of the third class at the expiration of the sixth year, so that one-third may be chosen every second year; *and if vacancies happen by resignation or otherwise, during the recess of the legislature of any State, the Executive thereof may make temporary appointments until the next meeting of the legislature, which shall then fill such vacancies.*

No person shall be a Senator who shall not have attained to the age of thirty years, and been nine years a citizen of the United States, and who shall not, when elected, be an inhabitant of that State for which he shall be chosen.

The Vice President of the United States shall be President of the Senate, but shall have no vote, unless they be equally divided.

The Senate shall choose their other officers, and also a President *pro tempore,* in the absence of the Vice President, or when he shall exercise the office of the President of the United States.

The Senate shall have the sole power to try all impeachments. When sitting for that purpose, they shall be on oath or affirmation. When the President of the United States is tried, the Chief Justice shall preside: and no person shall be convicted without the concurrence of two-thirds of the members present.

Judgment in cases of impeachment shall not extend further than to removal from the office, and disqualification to hold and enjoy any office of honor, trust or profit under the United States; but the party convicted shall nevertheless be liable and subject to indictment, trial, judgment and punishment, according to law.

Section 4. The times, places and manner of holding elections for Senators and Representatives shall be prescribed in each State by the legislature thereof; but the Congress may at any time by law make or alter such regulations, except as to the places of choosing Senators.

The Congress shall assemble at least once in every year, and such meeting *shall be on the first Monday in December, unless they shall by law appoint a different day.*

Section 5. Each house shall be the judge of the elections, returns and qualifications of its own members, and a majority of each shall constitute a quorum to do business; but a smaller number may adjourn from day to day, and may be authorized to compel the attendance of absent members, in such manner, and under such penalties, as each house may provide.

Each house may determine the rules of its proceedings, punish its members for disorderly behavior, and with the concurrence of two-thirds, expel a member.

Each house shall keep a journal of its proceedings, and from time to time publish the same, excepting such parts as may in their judgment require secrecy; and the yeas and nays of the members of either house on any question shall, at the desire of one-fifth of those present, be entered on the journal.

Neither house, during the session of Congress, shall, without the consent of the other, adjourn for more than three days, nor to any other place than that in which the two houses shall be sitting.

Section 6. The Senators and Representatives shall receive a compensation for their services, to be ascertained by law and paid out of the treasury of the United States. They shall in all cases except treason, felony and breach of the peace, be privileged from arrest during their attendance at the session of their respective houses, and in going to and returning from the same; and for any speech or debate in either house, they shall not be questioned in any other place.

No Senator or Representative shall, during the time for which he was elected, be appointed to any civil office under the authority of the United States, which shall have been created, or the emoluments whereof shall have been increased, during such time; and no person holding any office under the United States shall be a member of either house during his continuance in office.

Section 7. All bills for raising revenue shall originate in the House of Representatives; but the Senate may propose or concur with amendments as on other bills.

Every bill which shall have passed the House of Representatives and the Senate, shall, before it become a law, be presented to the President of the United States; if he approve he shall sign it, but if not he shall return it with objections to that house in which it originated, who shall enter the objections at large on their journal, and proceed to reconsider it. If after such reconsideration two-thirds of that house shall agree to pass the bill, it shall be sent, together with the objections, to the other house, by which it shall likewise be reconsidered, and, if approved by two-thirds of that house, it shall become a law. But in all such cases the votes of both houses shall be determined by yeas and nays, and the names of the persons voting for and against the bill shall be entered on the journal of each house respectively. If any bill shall not be returned by the President within ten days (Sundays excepted) after it shall have been presented to him, the same shall be a law, in like manner as if he had signed it, unless the Congress by their adjournment prevent its return, in which case it shall not be a law.

Every order, resolution, or vote to which the concurrence of the Senate and House of Representatives may be necessary (except on a question of adjournment) shall be presented to the President of the United States; and before the same shall take effect, shall be approved by him, or being disapproved by him, shall be repassed by two-thirds of the Senate and House of Representatives, according to the rules and limitations prescribed in the case of a bill.

Section 8.   The Congress shall have power

To lay and collect taxes, duties, imposts, and excises, to pay the debts and provide for the common defense and general welfare of the United States; but all duties, imposts and excises shall be uniform throughout the United States;

To borrow money on the credit of the United States;

To regulate commerce with foreign nations, and among the several States, and with the Indian tribes;

To establish an uniform rule of naturalization, and uniform laws on the subject of bankruptcies throughout the United States;

To coin money, regulate the value thereof, and of foreign coin, and fix the standard of weights and measures;

To provide for the punishment of counterfeiting the securities and current coin of the United States;

To establish post offices and post roads;

To promote the progress of science and useful arts by securing for limited times to authors and inventors the exclusive right to their respective writings and discoveries;

To constitute tribunals inferior to the Supreme Court;

To define and punish piracies and felonies committed on the high seas and offenses against the law of nations;

To declare war, grant letters of marque and reprisal, and make rules concerning captures on land and water;

To raise and support armies, but no appropriation of money to that use shall be for a longer term than two years;

To provide and maintain a navy;

To make rules for the government and regulation of the land and naval forces;

To provide for calling forth the militia to execute the laws of the Union, suppress insurrections, and repel invasions;

To provide for organizing, arming, and disciplining the militia, and for governing such part of them as may be employed in the service of the United States, reserving to the States respectively the appointment of the officers, and the authority of training the militia according to the discipline prescribed by Congress;

To exercise exclusive legislation in all cases whatsoever, over such district (not exceeding ten miles square) as may, by cession of particular States, and the acceptance of Congress, become the seat of government of the United States, and to exercise like authority over all places purchased by the consent of the legislature of the State, in which the same shall be, for erection of forts, magazines, arsenals, dock-yards, and other needful buildings;—and

To make all laws which shall be necessary and proper for carrying into execution the foregoing powers, and all other powers vested by this Constitution in the government of the United States, or in any department or officer thereof.

Section 9.   *The migration or importation of such persons as any of the States now existing shall think proper to admit shall not be prohibited by the Congress prior to the year 1808; but a tax or duty may be imposed on such importation, not exceeding $10 for each person.*

No bill of attainder or ex post facto law shall be passed.

No capitation, or other direct, tax shall be laid, unless in proportion to the census or enumeration herein before directed to be taken.

No tax or duty shall be laid on articles exported from any State.

No preference shall be given by any regulation of commerce or revenue to the ports of one State over those of another; nor shall vessels bound to, or from, one State, be obliged to enter, clear, or pay duties in another.

No money shall be drawn from the treasury, but in consequence of appropriations made by law; and a regular statement and account of the receipts and expenditures of all public money shall be published from time to time.

No title of nobility shall be granted by the United States: and no person holding any office of profit or trust under them, shall, without the consent of the Congress, accept of any present, emolument, office, or title, of any kind whatever, from any king, prince, or foreign state.

Section 10.   No State shall enter into any treaty, alliance, or confederation; grant letters of marque and reprisal; coin money; emit bills of credit; make anything but gold and silver coin a tender in payment of debts; pass any bill of attainder, ex post facto law, or law impairing the obligation of contracts, or grant any title of nobility.

No State shall, without the consent of Congress, lay any imposts or duties on imports or exports, except what may be absolutely necessary for executing its inspection laws: and the net produce of all duties and imposts, laid by any State on imports or exports, shall be for the use of the treasury of the United States; and all such laws shall be subject to the revision and control of the Congress.

No State shall, without the consent of Congress, lay any duty of tonnage, keep troops or ships of war in time of peace, enter into any agreement or compact with another State, or with a foreign power, or engage in war, unless actually invaded, or in such imminent danger as will not admit of delay.

Article II

Section 1.   The executive power shall be vested in a President of the United States of America. He shall hold his office during the term of four years, and, together with the Vice President, chosen for the same term, be elected as follows:

Each state shall appoint, in such manner as the legislature thereof may direct, a number of electors, equal to the whole number of Senators and Representatives to which the State may be entitled in the Congress; but no Senator or Representative, or person holding an office of trust or profit under the United States, shall be appointed an elector.

The electors shall meet in their respective States, and vote by ballot for two persons, of whom one at least shall not be an inhabitant of the same State with themselves. And they shall make a list of all the persons voted for, and of the number of votes for each; which list they shall sign and certify, and transmit sealed to the seat of government of the United States, directed to the President of the Senate. The President of the Senate shall, in the presence of the Senate and the House of Representatives, open all the certificates, and the votes shall then be counted. The person having the greatest number of votes shall be the President, if such number be a majority of the whole number of electors appointed; and if there be more than one who have such majority, and have an equal number of votes, then the House of Representatives shall immediately choose by ballot one of them for President; and if no person have a majority, then from the five highest on the list said house shall in like manner choose the President. But in choosing the President the votes shall be taken by States, the representation from each State having one vote; a quorum for this purpose shall consist of a member or members from two-thirds of the States, and a majority of all the States shall be necessary to a choice. In every case, after the choice of the President, the person having the greatest number of votes of the electors shall be the Vice President. But if there should remain two or more who have equal votes, the Senate shall choose from them by ballot the Vice President.

The Congress may determine the time of choosing the electors and the day on which they shall give their votes; which day shall be the same throughout the United States.

No person except a natural-born citizen, *or a citizen of the United States at the time of the adoption of this Constitution,* shall be eligible to the office of President; neither shall any person be eligible to that office who shall not have attained to the age of thirty-five years, and been fourteen years a resident within the United States.

In case of the removal of the President from office or of his death, resignation, or inability to discharge the powers and duties of the said office, the same shall devolve on the Vice President, and the Congress may by law provide for the case of removal, death, resignation, or inability, both of the President and Vice President, declaring what officer shall then act as President, and such officer shall act accordingly, until the disability be removed, or a President shall be elected.

The President shall, at stated times, receive for his services a compensation, which shall neither be increased nor diminished during the period for which he shall have been elected, and he shall not receive within that period any other emolument from the United States, or any of them.

Before he enter on the execution of his office, he shall take the following oath or affirmation:—"I do solemnly swear (or affirm) that I will faithfully execute the office of the President of the United States, and will to the best of my ability preserve, protect and defend the Constitution of the United States."

Section 2.   The President shall be commander in chief of the army and navy of the United States, and of the militia of the several States, when called into the actual service of the United States; he may require the opinion, in writing, of the principal officer in each of the executive departments, upon any subject relating to the duties of their respective offices, and he shall have power to grant reprieves and pardons for offenses against the United States, except in cases of impeachment.

He shall have power, by and with the advice and consent of the Senate, to make treaties, provided two-thirds of the Senators present concur; and he shall nominate, and by and with the advice and consent of the Senate, shall appoint ambassadors, other public ministers and consuls, judges of the Supreme Court, and all other officers of the United States, whose appointments are not herein otherwise provided for, and which shall be established by law: but Congress may by law vest the appointment of such inferior officers, as they think proper, in the President alone, in the courts of law, or in the heads of departments.

The President shall have power to fill up all vacancies that may happen during the recess of the Senate, by granting commissions which shall expire at the end of their next session.

Section 3.   He shall from time to time give to the Congress information of the state of the Union, and recommend to their consideration such measures as he shall judge necessary and expedient; he may, on extraordinary occasions, convene both houses, or either of them, and in case of disagreement between them, with respect to the time of adjournment, he may adjourn them to such time as he shall think proper; he shall receive ambassadors and other public ministers; he shall take care that the laws be faithfully executed, and shall commission all the officers of the United States.

Section 4.   The President, Vice President and all civil officers of the United States shall be removed from office on impeachment for, and on conviction of, treason, bribery, or other high crimes and misdemeanors.

Article III

Section 1.   The judicial power of the United States shall be vested in one Supreme Court, and in such inferior courts as the Congress may from time to time ordain and establish. The judges, both of the Supreme and inferior courts, shall hold their offices during good behavior, and shall, at stated times, receive for their services a compensation which shall not be diminished during their continuance in office.

Section 2.   The judicial power shall extend to all cases, in law and equity, arising under this Constitution, the laws of the United States, and treaties made, or which shall be made, under their authority;—to all cases affecting ambassadors, other public ministers and consuls;—to all cases of admiralty and maritime jurisdiction;—to controversies to which the United States shall be a party;—to controversies between two or more States;—*between a State and citizens of another State;*—between citizens of different States;—between citizens of the same State claiming lands under grants of different States, and between a State, or the citizens thereof, and foreign states, citizens or subjects.

In all cases affecting ambassadors, other public ministers and consuls, and those in which a State shall be party, the Supreme Court shall have original jurisdiction. In all the other cases before mentioned, the Supreme Court shall have appellate jurisdiction, both as to law and fact, with such exceptions, and under such regulations, as the Congress shall make.

The trial of all crimes, except in cases of impeachment, shall be by jury; and such trial shall be held in the State where said crimes shall have been committed; but when not committed within any State, the trial shall be at such place or places as the Congress may by law have directed.

Section 3.   Treason against the United States shall consist only in levying war against them, or in adhering to their enemies, giving them aid and comfort. No person shall be convicted of treason unless on the testimony of two witnesses to the same overt act, or on confession in open court.

The congress shall have power to declare the punishment of treason, but no attainder of treason shall work corruption of blood, or forfeiture except during the life of the person attainted.

Article IV

Section 1.   Full faith and credit shall be given in each State to the public acts, records, and judicial proceedings of every other State. And the Congress may by general laws prescribe the manner in which such acts, records, and proceedings shall be proved, and the effect thereof.

Section 2.   The citizens of each State shall be entitled to all privileges and immunities of citizens in the several States.

A person charged in any State with treason, felony, or other crime, who shall flee from justice, and be found in another State, shall on demand of the executive authority of the State from which he fled, be delivered up, to be removed to the State having jurisdiction of the crime.

No person held to service or labor in one State, under the laws thereof, escaping into another, shall, in consequence of any law or regulation therein, be discharged from such service or labor, but shall be delivered up on claim of the party to whom such service or labor may be due.

Section 3.　New States may be admitted by the Congress into this Union; but no new State shall be formed or erected within the jurisdiction of any other State; nor any State be formed by the junction of two or more States, or parts of States, without the consent of the legislatures of the States concerned as well as of the Congress.

The Congress shall have power to dispose of and make all needful rules and regulations respecting the territory or other property belonging to the United States; and nothing in this Constitution shall be so construed as to prejudice any claims of the United States, or of any particular State.

Section 4.　The United States shall guarantee to every State in this Union a republican form of government, and shall protect each of them against invasion; and on application of the legislature, or of the executive (when the legislature cannot be convened), against domestic violence.

Article V

The Congress, whenever two-thirds of both houses shall deem it necessary, shall propose amendments to this Constitution, or, on the application of the legislatures of two-thirds of the several States, shall call a convention for proposing amendments, which, in either case, shall be valid to all intents and purposes, as part of this Constitution, when ratified by the legislatures of three-fourths of the several States, or by conventions in three-fourths thereof, as the one or the other mode of ratification may be proposed by the Congress; provided *that no amendments which may be made prior to the year one thousand eight hundred and eight shall in any manner affect the first and fourth clauses in the ninth section of the first article;* and that no State, without its consent, shall be deprived of its equal suffrage in the Senate.

Article VI

All debts contracted and engagements entered into, before the adoption of this Constitution, shall be as valid against the United States under this Constitution, as under the Confederation.

This Constitution, and the laws of the United States which shall be made in pursuance thereof; and all treaties made, or which shall be made, under the authority of the United States, shall be the supreme law of the land; and the judges in every State shall be bound thereby, anything in the Constitution or laws of any State to the contrary notwithstanding.

The Senators and Representatives before mentioned, and the members of the several State legislatures, and all executive and judicial officers, both of the United States and of the several States, shall be bound by oath or affirmation to support this Constitution; but no religious test shall ever be required as a qualification to any office or public trust under the United States.

Article VII

The ratification of the conventions of nine States shall be sufficient for the establishment of this Constitution between the States so ratifying the same.

Done in Convention by the unanimous consent of the States present, the seventeenth day of September in the year of our Lord one thousand seven hundred and eighty-seven and of the Independence of the United States of American the twelfth. In witness whereof we have hereunto subscribed our names.

[Signed by]
G° WASHINGTON
Presidt and Deputy from Virginia
[*and thirty-eight others*]

Amendments to the Constitution

Amendment I*

Congress shall make no law respecting an establishment of religion, or prohibiting the free exercise thereof; or abridging the freedom of speech, or of the press; or the right of the people peaceably to assemble, and to petition the government for a redress of grievances.

Amendment II

A well-regulated militia being necessary to the security of a free State, the right of the people to keep and bear arms shall not be infringed.

Amendment III

No soldier shall, in time of peace, be quartered in any house without the consent of the owner, nor in time of war, but in a manner to be prescribed by law.

Amendment IV

The right of the people to be secure in their persons, houses, papers, and effects, against unreasonable searches and seizures, shall not be violated, and no warrants shall issue but upon probable cause, supported by oath or affirmation, and particularly describing the place to be searched, and the persons or things to be seized.

Amendment V

No person shall be held to answer for a capital, or otherwise infamous crime, unless on a presentment or indictment of a grand jury, except in cases arising in the land or naval forces, or in the militia, when in actual service in time

---

* The first ten Amendments (Bill of Rights) were adopted in 1791.

of war or public danger; nor shall any person be subject for the same offense to be twice put in jeopardy of life or limb; nor shall be compelled in any criminal case to be a witness against himself, nor be deprived of life, liberty, or property, without due process of law; nor shall private property be taken for public use without just compensation.

Amendment VI

In all criminal prosecutions, the accused shall enjoy the right to a speedy and public trial, by an impartial jury of the State and district wherein the crime shall have been committed, which district shall have been previously ascertained by law, and to be informed of the nature and cause of the accusation; to be confronted with the witnesses against him; to have compulsory process for obtaining witnesses in his favor, and to have the assistance of counsel for his defense.

Amendment VII

In suits at common law, where the value in controversy shall exceed twenty dollars, the right of trial by jury shall be preserved, and no fact tried by a jury shall be otherwise reexamined in any court of the United States, than according to the rules of the common law.

Amendment VIII

Excessive bail shall not be required, nor excessive fines imposed, nor cruel and unusual punishments inflicted.

Amendment IX

The enumeration in the Constitution, of certain rights, shall not be construed to deny or disparage others retained by the people.

Amendment X

The powers not delegated to the United States by the Constitution, nor prohibited by it to the States, are reserved to the States respectively, or to the people.

Amendment XI
[*Adopted 1798*]

The judicial power of the United States shall not be construed to extend to any suit in law or equity, commenced or prosecuted against one of the United States by citizens of another State, or by citizens or subjects of any foreign state.

Amendment XII
[Adopted 1804]

The electors shall meet in their respective States, and vote by ballot for President and Vice President, one of whom, at least, shall not be an inhabitant of the same State with themselves; they shall name in their ballots the person voted for as President, and in distinct ballots the person voted for as Vice President, and they shall make distinct lists of all persons voted for as President, and of all persons voted for as Vice President, and of the number of votes for each, which lists they shall sign and certify, and transmit sealed to the seat of government of the United States, directed to the President of the Senate;—the President of the Senate shall, in the presence of the Senate and House of Representatives, open all the certificates and the votes shall then be counted;—the person having the greatest number of votes for President shall be the President, if such number be a majority of the whole number of electors appointed; and if no person have such majority, then from the persons having the highest numbers not exceeding three on the list of those voted for as President, the House of Representatives shall choose immediately, by ballot, the President. But in choosing the President, the votes shall be taken by States, the representation from each State having one vote; a quorum for this purpose shall consist of a member or members from two-thirds of the States, and a majority of all the States shall be necessary to a choice. And if the House of Representatives shall not choose a President whenever the right of choice shall devolve upon them, before *the fourth day of March* next following, then the Vice President shall act as President, as in the case of the death or other constitutional disability of the President.

The person having the greatest number of votes as Vice President shall be the Vice President, if such a number be a majority of the whole number of electors appointed; and if no person have a majority, then from the two highest numbers on the list the Senate shall choose the Vice President; a quorum for the purpose shall consist of two-thirds of the whole number of Senators, and a majority of the whole number shall be necessary to a choice. But no person constitutionally ineligible to the office of President shall be eligible to that of Vice President of the United States.

Amendment XIII
[Adopted 1865]

Section 1. Neither slavery nor involuntary servitude, except as a punishment for crime whereof the party shall have been duly convicted, shall exist within the United States, or any place subject to their jurisdiction.

Section 2. Congress shall have power to enforce this article by appropriate legislation.

Amendment XIV
[Adopted 1868]

Section 1.   All persons born or naturalized in the United States, and subject to the jurisdiction thereof, are citizens of the United States and of the State wherein they reside. No State shall make or enforce any law which shall abridge the privileges or immunities of citizens of the United States; nor shall any State deprive any person of life, liberty, or property, without due process of law; nor deny to any person within its jurisdiction the equal protection of the laws.

Section 2.   Representatives shall be apportioned among the several States according to their respective numbers, counting the whole number of persons in each State, excluding Indians not taxed. But when the right to vote at any election for the choice of Electors for President and Vice President of the United States, Representatives in Congress, the executive and judicial officers of a State, or the members of the legislature thereof, is denied to any of the male inhabitants of such State, being twenty-one years of age and citizens of the United States, or in any way abridged, except for participation in rebellion, or other crime, the basis of representation therein shall be reduced in the proportion which the number of such male citizens shall bear to the whole number of male citizens twenty-one years of age in such State.

Section 3.   No person shall be a Senator or Representative in Congress or Elector of President and Vice President, or hold any office, civil or military, under the United States, or under any State, who, having previously taken an oath, as a member of Congress, or as an officer of the United States, or as a member of any State legislature, or as an executive or judicial officer of any State, to support the Constitution of the United States, shall have engaged in insurrection or rebellion against the same, or given aid and comfort to the enemies thereof. Congress may, by a vote of two-thirds of each house, remove such disability.

Section 4.   The validity of the public debt of the United States, authorized by law, including debts incurred for payment of pensions and bounties for services in suppressing insurrection or rebellion, shall not be questioned. But neither the United States nor any State shall assume or pay any debt or obligation incurred in aid of insurrection or rebellion against the United States, or any claim for the loss or emancipation of any slave; but all such debts, obligations, and claims shall be held illegal and void.

Section 5.   The Congress shall have the power to enforce, by appropriate legislation, the provisions of this article.

Amendment XV
[*Adopted 1870*]

Section 1. The right of citizens of the United States to vote shall not be denied or abridged by the United States or by any State on account of race, color, or previous condition of servitude.

Section 2. The Congress shall have power to enforce this article by appropriate legislation.

Amendment XVI
[*Adopted 1913*]

The Congress shall have power to lay and collect taxes on incomes, from whatever source derived, without apportionment among the several States, and without regard to any census or enumeration.

Amendment XVII
[*Adopted 1913*]

Section 1. The Senate of the United States shall be composed of two Senators from each State, elected by the people thereof, for six years; and each Senator shall have one vote. The electors in each State shall have the qualifications requisite for electors of [voters for] the most numerous branch of the State legislatures.

Section 2. When vacancies happen in the representation of any State in the Senate, the executive authority of such State shall issue writs of election to fill such vacancies: Provided, that the Legislature of any State may empower the executive thereof to make temporary appointments until the people fill the vacancies by election as the Legislature may direct.

Section 3. This amendment shall not be so construed as to affect the election or term of any Senator chosen before it becomes valid as part of the Constitution.

Amendment XVIII
[*Adopted 1919; repealed 1933*]

Section 1. *After one year from the ratification of this article the manufacture, sale, or transportation of intoxicating liquors within, the importation thereof into, or the exportation thereof from the United States and all territory subject to the jurisdiction thereof, for beverage purposes, is hereby prohibited.*

Section 2. *The Congress and the several States shall have concurrent power to enforce this article by appropriate legislation.*

Section 3. *This article shall be inoperative unless it shall have been ratified as an amendment to the Constitution by the legislatures of the several States, as provided by the Constitution, within seven years from the date of the submission thereof to the States by the Congress.*

Amendment XIX
[*Adopted 1920*]

Section 1. The right of citizens of the United States to vote shall not be denied or abridged by the United States or by any State on account of sex.

Section 2. The Congress shall have the power to enforce this article by appropriate legislation.

Amendment XX
[*Adopted 1933*]

Section 1. The terms of the President and Vice President shall end at noon on the 20th day of January, and the terms of Senators and Representatives at noon on the 3d day of January, of the years in which such terms would have ended if this article had not been ratified; and the terms of their successors shall then begin.

Section 2. The Congress shall assemble at least once in every year, and such meeting shall begin at noon on the 3d of January, unless they shall by law appoint a different day.

Section 3. If, at the time fixed for the beginning of the term of the President, the President-elect shall have died, the Vice President-elect shall become President. If a President shall not have been chosen before the time fixed for the beginning of his term, or if the President-elect shall have failed to qualify, then the Vice President-elect shall act as President until a President shall have qualified; and the Congress may by law provide for the case wherein neither a President-elect nor a Vice President-elect shall have qualified, declaring who shall then act as President, or the manner in which one who is to act shall be selected, and such persons shall act accordingly until a President or Vice President shall have qualified.

Section 4. The Congress may by law provide for the case of the death of any of the persons from whom the House of Representatives may choose a President whenever the right of choice shall have devolved upon them, and for the case of the death of any of the persons from whom the Senate may choose a Vice President whenever the right of choice shall have devolved upon them.

Section 5. Sections 1 and 2 shall take effect on the 15th day of October following the ratification of this article.

Section 6.   This article shall be inoperative unless it shall have been ratified as an amendment to the Constitution by the Legislatures of three-fourths of the several States within seven years from the date of its submission.

Amendment XXI
[Adopted 1933]

Section 1.   The eighteenth article of amendment to the Constitution of the United States is hereby repealed.

Section 2.   The transportation or importation into any State, Territory, or Possession of the United States for delivery or use therein of intoxicating liquors, in violation of the laws thereof, is hereby prohibited.

Section 3.   This article shall be inoperative unless it shall have been ratified as an amendment to the Constitution by conventions in the several States, as provided in the Constitution, within seven years from the date of submission thereof to the States by the Congress.

Amendment XXII
[Adopted 1951]

Section 1.   No person shall be elected to the office of President more than twice, and no person who has held the office of President, or acted as President, for more than two years of a term to which some other person was elected President shall be elected to the office of President more than once. But this article shall not apply to any person holding the office of President when this article was proposed by the Congress, and shall not prevent any person who may be holding the office of President, or acting as President, during the term within which this article becomes operative from holding the office of President or acting as President during the remainder of such term.

Section 2.   This article shall be inoperative unless it shall have been ratified as an amendment to the Constitution by the legislatures of three-fourths of the several States within seven years from the date of its submission to the States by the Congress.

Amendment XXIII
[Adopted 1961]

Section 1.   The District constituting the seat of Government of the United States shall appoint in such manner as the Congress may direct:

A number of electors of President and Vice President equal to the whole number of Senators and Representatives in Congress to which the District would be entitled if it were a State, but in no event more than the least populous State; they shall be in addition to those appointed by the States, but they shall be considered for the purposes of the election of President and Vice President, to be electors appointed by a State; and they shall meet in the District and perform such duties as provided by the twelfth article of amendment.

Section 2.   The Congress shall have the power to enforce this article by appropriate legislation.

Amendment XXIV
[*Adopted 1964*]

Section 1.   The right of citizens of the United States to vote in any primary or other election for President or Vice President, for electors for President or Vice President, or for Senator or Representative in Congress, shall not be denied or abridged by the United States or any State by reason of failure to pay any poll tax or other tax.

Section 2.   The Congress shall have the power to enforce this article by appropriate legislation

Amendment XXV
[*Adopted 1967*]

Section 1.   In case of the removal of the President from office or of his death or resignation, the Vice President shall become President.

Section 2.   Whenever there is a vacancy in the office of the Vice President, the President shall nominate a Vice President who shall take office upon confirmation by a majority vote of both Houses of Congress.

Section 3.   Whenever the President transmits to the President pro tempore of the Senate and the Speaker of the House of Representatives his written declaration that he is unable to discharge the powers and duties of his office, and until he transmits to them a written declaration to the contrary, such powers and duties shall be discharged by the Vice President as Acting President.

Section 4.   Whenever the Vice President and a majority of either the principal officers of the executive departments or of such other body as Congress may by law provide, transmit to the President pro tempore of the Senate and the Speaker of the House of Representatives their written declaration that the President is unable to discharge the powers and duties of his office, the Vice President shall immediately assume the powers and duties of the office as Acting President.

Thereafter, when the President transmits to the President pro tempore of the Senate and the Speaker of the House of Representatives his written declaration that no inability exists, he shall resume the powers and duties of his office unless the Vice President and a majority of either the principal officers of the executive department[s] or of such other body as Congress may by law provide, transmit within four days to the President pro tempore of the Senate and the Speaker of the House of Representatives their written declaration that the President is unable to discharge the powers and duties of his office. Thereupon Congress shall decide the issue, assembling within forty-eight hours for that purpose if not in session. If the Congress, within twenty-one days after receipt of the latter written declaration, or, if Congress is not in session, within twenty-one days after Congress is required to assemble, determines by two-thirds vote of both Houses that the President is unable to discharge the powers and duties of his office, the Vice President shall continue to discharge the same as Acting President; otherwise, the President shall resume the powers and duties of his office.

Amendment XXVI
[Adopted 1971]

Section 1. The right of citizens of the United States, who are eighteen years of age or older, to vote shall not be denied or abridged by the United States or by any State on account of age.

Section 2. The Congress shall have power to enforce this article by appropriate legislation.

The Constitution of the Confederate States of America

We, the people of the Confederate States, each State acting in its sovereign and independent character, in order to form a permanent federal government, establish justice, insure domestic tranquillity, and secure the blessings of liberty to ourselves and our posterity—invoking the favor and guidance of Almighty God—do ordain and establish this Constitution for the Confederate States of America.

Article I

Section 1. All legislative powers herein delegated shall be vested in a Congress of the Confederate States, which shall consist of a Senate and House of Representatives.

Section 2. (1) The House of Representatives shall be chosen every second year by the people of the several States; and the electors in each State shall be citizens of the Confederate States, and have the qualifications requisite for electors of the most numerous branch of the State Legislature; but no person of foreign birth, not a citizen of the Confederate States, shall be allowed to vote for any officer, civil or political, State or Federal.

(2) No person shall be a Representative who shall not have attained the age of twenty-five years, and be a citizen of the Confederate States, and who shall not, when elected, be an inhabitant of that State in which he shall be chosen.

(3) Representatives and direct taxes shall be apportioned among the several States which may be included within this Confederacy, according to their respective numbers, which shall be determined by adding to the whole number of free persons, including those bound to service for a term of years, and excluding Indians not taxed, three-fifths of all slaves. The actual enumeration shall be made within three years after the first meeting of the Congress of the Confederate States, and within every subsequent term of ten years, in such manner as they shall by law direct. The number of Representatives shall not exceed one for every fifty thousand, but each State shall have at least one Representative; and until such enumeration shall be made, the State of South Carolina shall be entitled to choose six; the State of Georgia ten; the State of Alabama nine; the State of Florida two; the State of Mississippi seven; the State of Louisiana six; and the State of Texas six.

(4) When vacancies happen in the representation of any State, the Executive authority thereof shall issue writs of election to fill such vacancies.

(5) The House of Representatives shall choose their Speaker and other officers; and shall have the sole power of impeacement; except that any judicial or other federal officer resident and acting solely within the limits of any State, may be impeached by a vote of two-thirds of both branches of the Legislature thereof.

Section 3. (1) The Senate of the Confederate States shall be composed of two Senators from each State, chosen for six years by the Legislature thereof, at the regular session next immediately preceding the commencement of the term of service; and each Senator shall have one vote.

(2) Immediately after they shall be assembled, in consequence of the first election, they shall be divided as equally as may be into three classes. The seats of the Senators of the first class shall be vacated at the expiration of the second year; of the second class at the expiration of the fourth year; and of the third class at the expiration of the sixth year; so that one-third may be chosen every second year; and if vacancies happen by resignation or otherwise during the recess of the Legislature of any State, the Executive thereof may make temporary appointments until the next meeting of the Legislature, which shall then fill such vacancies.

(3) No person shall be a Senator, who shall not have attained the age of thirty years, and be a citizen of the Confederate States; and who shall not, when elected, be an inhabitant of the State for which he shall be chosen.

(4) The Vice-President of the Confederate States shall be President of the Senate, but shall have no vote, unless they be equally divided.

(5) The Senate shall choose their other officers, and also a President *pro tempore,* in the absence of the Vice-President, or when he shall exercise the office of President of the Confederate States.

(6) The Senate shall have sole power to try all impeachments, When sitting for that purpose they shall be on oath or affirmation. When the President of the Confederate States is tried, the Chief-Justice shall preside; and no person shall be convicted without the concurrence of two-thirds of the members present.

(7) Judgment in cases of impeachment shall not extend further than removal from office, and disqualification to hold and enjoy any office of honor, trust, or profit, under the Confederate States; but the party convicted shall, nevertheless, be liable to and subject to indictment, trial, judgment, and punishment according to law.

Section 4. (1) The times, places, and manner of holding elections for Senators and Representatives, shall be prescribed in each State by the Legislature thereof, subject to the provisions of this Constitution; but the Congress may, at any time, by law, make or alter such regulations, except as to the times and places of choosing Senators.

(2) The Congress shall assemble at least once in every year; and such meeting shall be on the first Monday in December, unless they shall, by law, appoint a different day.

Section 5. (1) Each House shall be the judge of the elections, returns, and qualifications of its own members, and a majority of each shall constitute a quorum to do business; but a smaller number may adjourn from day to day, and may be authorized to compel the attendance of absent members, in such manner and under such penalties as each House may provide.

(2) Each House may determine the rules of its proceedings, punish its

members for disorderly behavior, and, with the concurrence of two-thirds of the whole number, expel a member.

(3) Each House shall keep a journal of its proceedings, and from time to time publish the same, excepting such part as may in its judgment require secrecy, and the ayes and nays of the members of either House, on any question, shall, at the desire of one-fifth of those present, be entered on the journal.

(4) Neither House, during the session of Congress, shall, without the consent of the other, adjourn for more than three days, nor to any other place than that in which the two Houses shall be sitting.

Section 6. (1) The Senators and Representatives shall receive a compensation for their services, to be ascertained by law, and paid out of the Treasury of the Confederate States. They shall, in all cases except treason and breach of the peace, be privileged from arrest during their attendance at the session of their respective Houses, and in going to and returning from the same; and for any speech or debate in either House, they shall not be questioned in any other place.

(2) No Senator or Representative shall, during the time for which he was elected, be appointed to any civil office under the authority of the Confederate States, which shall have been created, or the emoluments whereof shall have been increased during such time; and no person holding any office under the Confederate States shall be a member of either House during his continuance in office. But Congress may, by law, grant to the principal officer in each of the Executive Departments a seat upon the floor of either house, with the privilege of discussing any measure appertaining to his department.

Section 7. (1) All bills for raising revenue shall originate in the House of Representatives; but the Senate may propose or concur with amendments as on other bills.

(2) Every bill which shall have passed both houses shall, before it becomes a law, be presented to the President of the Confederate States; if he approve he shall sign it; but if not, he shall return it with his objections to that House in which it shall have originated, who shall enter the objections at large on their journal, and proceed to reconsider it. If, after such reconsideration, two-thirds of that House shall agree to pass the bill, it shall be sent, together with the objections, to the other House, by which it shall likewise be reconsidered, and if approved by two-thirds of that House, it shall become a law. But in all such cases, the votes of both Houses shall be determined by yeas and nays, and the names of the persons voting for and against the bill shall be entered on the journal of each House respectively. If any bill shall not be returned by the President within ten days (Sundays excepted) after it shall have been presented to him, the same shall be a law, in like manner as if he had signed it, unless the Congress, by their adjournment, prevent its return; in which case it shall not be a law. The President may approve any appropriation and disapprove any other appro-

priation in the same bill. In such case he shall, in signing the bill, designate the appropriations disapproved; and shall return a copy of such appropriations, with his objections, to the House in which the bill shall have originated; and the same proceedings shall then be had as in case of other bills disapproved by the President.

(3) Every order, resolution, or vote, to which the concurrence of both Houses may be necessary (except on question of adjournment) shall be presented to the President of the Confederate States; and before the same shall take effect shall be approved by him; or being disapproved by him, may be repassed by two-thirds of both Houses, according to the rules and limitations prescribed in case of a bill.

Section 8.   —The Congress shall have power—

(1) To lay and collect taxes, duties, imposts, and excises, for revenue necessary to pay the debts, provide for the common defence, and carry on the Government of the Confederate States; but no bounties shall be granted from the treasury; nor shall any duties or taxes on importations from foreign nations be laid to promote or foster any branch of industry; and all duties, imposts, and excises shall be uniform throughout the Confederate States.

(2) To borrow money on the credit of the Confederate States.

(3) To regulate commerce with foreign nations, and among the several States, and with the Indian tribes; but neither this, nor any other clause contained in the Constitution shall be construed to delegate the power to Congress to appropriate money for any internal improvement intended to facilitate commerce; except for the purpose of furnishing lights, beacons, and buoys, and other aids to navigation upon the coasts, and the improvement of harbors, and the removing of obstructions in river navigation, in all which cases, such duties shall be laid on the navigation facilitated thereby, as may be necessary to pay the costs and expenses thereof.

(4) To establish uniform laws of naturalization, and uniform laws on the subject of bankruptcies throughout the Confederate States, but no law of Congress shall discharge any debt contracted before the passage of the same.

(5) To coin money, regulate the value thereof, and of foreign coin, and fix the standard of weights and measures.

(6) To provide for the punishment of counterfeiting the securities and current coin of the Confederate States.

(7) To establish post-offices and post-routes; but the expenses of the Post-office Department, after the first day of March, in the year of our Lord eighteen hundred and sixty-three, shall be paid out of its own revenues.

(8) To promote the progress of science and useful arts, by securing for limited times to authors and inventors the exclusive right to their respective writings and discoveries.

(9) To constitute tribunals inferior to the Supreme Court.

(10) To define and punish piracies and felonies committed on the high seas, and offences against the law of nations.

(11) To declare war, grant letters of marque and reprisal, and make rules concerning captures on land and water.

(12) To raise and support armies; but no appropriation of money to that use shall be for a longer term than two years.

(13) To provide and maintain a navy.

(14) To make rules for government and regulation of the land and naval forces.

(15) To provide for calling forth the militia to execute the laws of the Confederate States; suppress insurrections, and repel invasions.

(16) To provide for organizing, arming, and disciplining the militia, and for governing such part of them as may be employed in the service of the Confederate States; reserving to the States, respectively, the appointment of the officers, and the authority of training the militia according to the discipline prescribed by Congress.

(17) To exercise exclusive legislation, in all cases whatsoever, over such district (not exceeding ten miles square) as may, by cession of one or more States, and the acceptance of Congress, become the seat of the Government of the Confederate States; and to exercise a like authority over all places purchased by the consent of the Legislature of the State in which the same shall be, for the erection of forts, magazines, arsenals, dock-yards, and other needful buildings, and

(18) To make all laws which shall be necessary and proper for carrying into execution the foregoing powers, and all other powers vested by this Constitution in the Government of the Confederate States, or in any department or officer thereof.

Section 9. (1) The importation of negroes of the African race, from any foreign country, other than the slaveholding States or Territories of the United States of America, is hereby forbidden; and Congress is required to pass such laws as shall effectually prevent the same.

(2) Congress shall also have power to prohibit the introduction of slaves from any State not a member of, or Territory not belonging to, this Confederacy.

(3) The privilege of the writ of *habeas corpus* shall not be suspended, unless when in cases of rebellion or invasion the public safety may require it.

(4) No bill of attainder, or *ex post facto* law, or law denying or impairing the right of property in negro slaves shall be passed.

(5) No capitation or other direct tax shall be laid unless in proportion to the census or enumeration hereinbefore directed to be taken.

(6) No tax or duty shall be laid on articles exported from any State, except by a vote of two-thirds of both Houses.

(7) No preference shall be given by any regulation of commerce or revenue to the ports of one State over those of another.

(8) No money shall be drawn from the treasury but in consequence of appropriations made by laws; and a regular statement and account of the

receipts and expenditures of all public money shall be published from time to time.

(9) Congress shall appropriate no money from the treasury except by a vote of two-thirds of both Houses, taken by yeas and nays, unless it be asked and estimated for by some one of the heads of departments, and submitted to Congress by the President; or for the purpose of paying its own expenses and contingencies; or for the payment of claims against the Confederate States, the justice of which shall have been judicially declared by a tribunal for the investigation of claims against the Government, which it is hereby made the duty of Congress to establish.

(10) All bills appropriating money shall specify in federal currency the exact amount of each appropriation and the purposes for which it is made; and Congress shall grant no extra compensation to any public contractor, officer, agent, or servant, after such contract shall have been made or such service rendered.

(11) No title of nobility shall be granted by the Confederate States; and no person holding any office of profit or trust under them shall, without the consent of the Congress, accept of any present, emoluments, office, or title of any kind whatever, from any king, prince, or foreign state.

(12) Congress shall make no law respecting an establishment of religion, or prohibiting the free exercise thereof; or abridging the freedom of speech or of the press; or the right of the people peaceably to assemble and petition the Government for a redress of grievances.

(13) A well-regulated militia being necessary to the security of a free State, the right of the people to keep and bear arms shall not be infringed.

(14) No soldier shall, in time of peace, be quartered in any house without the consent of the owner; nor in time of war, but in a manner prescribed by law.

(15) The right of the people to be secure in their persons, houses, papers, and against unreasonable searches and seizures, shall not be violated; and no warrant shall issue but upon probable cause, supported by oath or affirmation, and particularly describing the place to be searched, and the person or things to be seized.

(16) No person shall be held to answer for a capital or otherwise infamous crime, unless on a presentment or indictment of a grand jury, except in cases arising in the land or naval forces, or in the militia, when in actual service, in time of war, or public danger; nor shall any person be subject for the same offence to be twice put in jeopardy of life or limb; nor be compelled in any criminal case to be a witness against himself; nor be deprived of life, liberty, or property, without due process of law; nor shall any private property be taken for public use without just compensation.

(17) In all criminal prosecutions the accused shall enjoy the right to a speedy and public trial, by an impartial jury of the State and district wherein the crime shall have been committed, which district shall have been previously ascertained by law, and to be informed of the nature and cause of the accusation; to be confronted with the witnesses against him; to have com-

pulsory process for obtaining witnesses in his favor; and to have the assistance of counsel for his defence.

(18) In suits at common law, where the value in controversy shall exceed twenty dollars, the right of trial by jury shall be preserved; and no fact so tried by a jury shall be otherwise re-examined in any court of the Confederacy, than according to the rules of the common law.

(19) Excessive bail shall not be required, nor excessive fines imposed, nor cruel or unusual punishment inflicted.

(20) Every law, or resolution having the force of law, shall relate to but one subject, and that shall be expressed in the title.

Section 10. (1) No State shall enter into any treaty, alliance, or confederation; grant letters of marque and reprisals; coin money; make any thing but gold and silver coin a tender in payment of debts; pass any bill of attainder, or *ex post facto* law, or law impairing the obligation of contracts; or grant any title of nobility.

(2) No State shall, without the consent of Congress, lay any imposts or duties on imports or exports, except what may be absolutely necessary for executing its inspection laws; and the net produce of all duties and imposts, laid by any State on imports or exports, shall be for the use of the Treasury of the Confederate States; and all such laws shall be subject to the revision and control of Congress.

(3) No state shall, without the consent of Congress, lay any duty of tonnage, except on sea-going vessels, for the improvement of its rivers and harbors navigated by the said vessels; but such duties shall not conflict with any treaties of the Confederate States with foreign nations; and any surplus of revenue, thus derived, shall, after making such improvement, be paid into the common treasury; nor shall any State keep troops or ships of war in time of peace, enter into any agreement or compact with another State, or with a foreign power, or engage in war, unless actually invaded, or in such imminent danger as will not admit of delay. But when any river divides or flows through two or more States, they may enter into compacts with each other to improve the navigation thereof.

Article II

Section 1. (1) The Executive power shall be vested in a President of the Confederate States of America. He and the Vice-President shall hold their offices for the term of six years; but the President shall not be reëligible. The President and Vice-President shall be elected as follows:

(2) Each State shall appoint, in such manner as the Legislature thereof may direct, a number of electors equal to the whole number of Senators and Representatives to which the State may be entitled in Congress; but no Senator or Representative, or person holding an office of trust or profit under the Confederate States, shall be appointed an elector.

(3) The electors shall meet in their respective States and vote by ballot

for President and Vice-President, one of whom, at least, shall not be an inhabitant of the same State with themselves; they shall name in their ballots the person voted for as President, and in distinct ballots the person voted for as Vice-President, and they shall make distinct lists of all persons voted for as President, and of all persons voted for as Vice-President, and of the number of votes for each; which list they shall sign, and certify, and transmit, sealed, to the Government of the Confederate States, directed to the President of the Senate. The President of the Senate shall, in the presence of the Senate and House of Representatives, open all the certificates, and the votes shall then be counted; the person having the greatest number of votes for President shall be the President, if such number be a majority of the whole number of electors appointed; and if no person shall have such a majority, then, from the persons having the highest numbers, not exceeding three, on the list of those voted for as President, the House of Representatives shall choose immediately, by ballot, the President. But, in choosing the President, the votes shall be taken by States, the Representative from each State having one vote; a quorum for this purpose shall consist of a member or members from two-thirds of the States, and a majority of all the States shall be necessary to a choice. And if the House of Representatives shall not choose a President, whenever the right of choice shall devolve upon them, before the fourth day of March next following, then the Vice-President shall act as President, as in case of the death, or other constitutional disability of the President.

(4) The person having the greatest number of votes as Vice-President shall be the Vice-President, if such number be a majority of the whole number of electors appointed; and if no person have a majority, then from the two highest numbers on the list, the Senate shall choose the Vice-President; a quorum for the purpose shall consist of two-thirds of the whole number of Senators, and a majority of the whole number shall be necessary for a choice.

(5) But no person constitutionally ineligible to the office of President shall be eligible to that of Vice-President of the Confederate States.

(6) The Congress may determine the time of choosing the electors, and the day on which they shall give their votes; which day shall be the same throughout the Confederate States.

(7) No person except a natural born citizen of the Confederate States, or a citizen thereof, at the time of the adoption of this Constitution, or a citizen thereof born in the United States prior to the 20th December, 1860, shall be eligible to the office of President; neither shall any person be eligible to that office who shall not have attained the age of thirty-five years, and been fourteen years a resident within the limits of the Confederate States, as they may exist at the time of his election.

(8) In case of the removal of the President from office, or of his death, resignation, or inability to discharge the powers and duties of the said office, the same shall devolve on the Vice-President; and the Congress may, by law, provide for the case of the removal, death, resignation, or inability both of the President and the Vice-President, declaring what officer shall

then act as President, and such officer shall then act accordingly until the disability be removed or a President shall be elected.

(9) The President shall, at stated times, receive for his services a compensation, which shall neither be increased nor diminished during the period for which he shall have been elected; and he shall not receive within that period any other emolument from the Confederate States, or any of them.

(10) Before he enters on the execution of the duties of his office, he shall take the following oath or affirmation:

"I do solemnly swear (or affirm) that I will faithfully execute the office of President of the Confederate States, and will, to the best of my ability, preserve, protect, and defend the Constitution thereof."

Section 2.   (1) The President shall be commander-in-chief of the army and navy of the Confederate States, and of the militia of the several States, when called into the actual service of the Confederate States; he may require the opinion, in writing, of the principal officer in each of the Executive Departments, upon any subject relating to the duties of their respective offices; and he shall have power to grant reprieves and pardons for offences against the Confederate States, except in cases of impeachment.

(2) He shall have power, by and with the advice and consent of the Senate, to make treaties, provided two-thirds of the Senators present concur; and he shall nominate, and, by and with the advice and consent of the Senate, shall appoint ambassadors, other public ministers, and consuls, Judges of the Supreme Court, and all other officers of the Confederate States, whose appointments are not herein otherwise provided for, and which shall be established by law; but the Congress may by law vest the appointment of such inferior officers, as they think proper, in the President alone, in the courts of law, or in the heads of departments.

(3) The principal officer in each of the Executive Departments, and all persons connected with the diplomatic service, may be removed from office at the pleasure of the President. All other civil officers of the Executive Department may be removed at any time by the President, or other appointing power, when their services are unnecessary, or for dishonesty, incapacity, inefficiency, misconduct, or neglect of duty; and when so removed, the removal shall be reported to the Senate, together with the reasons therefor.

(4) The President shall have power to fill all vacancies that may happen during the recess of the Senate, by granting commissions which shall expire at the end of the next session; but no person rejected by the Senate shall be reappointed to the same office during their ensuing recess.

Section 3.   (1) The President shall, from time to time, give to the Congress information of the state of the Confederacy, and recommend to their consideration such measures as he shall judge necessary and expedient; he may, on extraordinary occasions, convene both Houses, or either of them; and, in case of disagreement between them, with respect to the time of adjournment he may adjourn them to such time as he shall think proper; he shall receive ambassadors and other public ministers; he shall take care that the laws be faithfully executed, and shall commission all the officers of the Confederate States.

Section 4. (1) The President and Vice-President, and all civil officers of the Confederate States, shall be removed from office on impeachment for, or conviction of, treason, bribery, or other high crimes and misdemeanors.

Article III

Section 1. (1) The judicial power of the Confederate States shall be vested in one Superior Court, and in such inferior courts as the Congress may from time to time ordain and establish. The judges, both of the Supreme and inferior courts, shall hold their offices during good behavior, and shall, at stated times, receive for their services a compensation, which shall not be diminished during their continuance in office.

Section 2. (1) The judicial power shall extend to all cases arising under the Constitution, the laws of the Confederate States, or treaties made or which shall be made under their authority; to all cases affecting ambassadors, other public ministers, and consuls; to all cases of admiralty or maritime jurisdiction; to controversies to which the Confederate States shall be a party; to controversies between two or more States; between a State and citizens of another State, where the State is plaintiff; between citizens claiming lands under grants of different States, and between a State or the citizens thereof, and foreign States, citizens, or subjects; but no State shall be sued by a citizen or subject of any foreign State.

(2) In all cases affecting ambassadors, other public ministers, and consuls, and those in which a State shall be a party, the Supreme Court shall have original jurisdiction. In all the other cases before mentioned, the Supreme Court shall have appellate jurisdiction, both as to law and fact, with such exceptions, and under such regulations as the Congress shall make.

(3) The trial of all crimes, except in cases of impeachment, shall be by jury, and such trial shall be held in the State where the said crimes shall have been committed; but when not committed within any State, the trial shall be at such place or places as the Congress may by law have directed.

Section 3. (1) Treason against the Confederate States shall consist only in levying war against them, or in adhering to their enemies, giving them aid and comfort. No person shall be convicted of treason unless on the testimony of two witnesses to the same overt act, or on confession in open court.

(2) The Congress shall have power to declare the punishment of treason, but no attainder of treason shall work corruption of blood, or forfeiture, except during the life of the person attainted.

Article IV

Section 1. (1) Full faith and credit shall be given in each State to the public acts, records, and judicial proceedings of every other State. And the Congress may, by general laws, prescribe the manner in which such acts, records, and proceedings shall be proved, and the effect thereof.

Section 2. (1) The citizens of each State shall be entitled to all the privileges and immunities of citizens of the several States, and shall have the right of transit and sojourn in any State of this Confederacy, with their slaves and other property; and the right of property in said slaves shall not be thereby impaired.

(2) A person charged in any State with treason, felony, or other crime against the laws of such State, who shall flee from justice, and be found in another State, shall, on demand of the executive authority of the State from which he fled, be delivered up to be removed to the State having jurisdiction of the crime.

(3) No slave or other person held to service or labor in any State or Territory of the Confederate States, under the laws thereof, escaping or unlawfully carried into another, shall, in consequence of any law or regulation therein, be discharged from such service or labor; but shall be delivered up on claim of the party to whom such slave belongs, or to whom such service or labor may be due.

Section 3. (1) Other States may be admitted into this Confederacy by a vote of two-thirds of the whole House of Representatives, and two-thirds of the Senate, the Senate voting by States; but no new State shall be formed or erected within the jurisdiction of any other State; nor any State be formed by the junction of two or more States, or parts of States, without the consent of the Legislatures of the States concerned as well as of the Congress.

(2) The Congress shall have power to dispose of and make all needful rules and regulations concerning the property of the Confederate States, including the lands thereof.

(3) The Confederate States may acquire new territory; and Congress shall have power to legislate and provide governments for the inhabitants of all territory belonging to the Confederate States, lying without the limits of the several States, and may permit them, at such times, and in such manner as it may by law provide, to form States to be admitted into the Confederacy. In all such territory, the institution of negro slavery, as it now exists in the Confederate States, shall be recognized and protected by Congress and by the territorial government; and the inhabitants of the several Confederate States and Territories shall have the right to take to such territory any slaves lawfully held by them in any of the States or Territories of the Confederate States.

(4) The Confederate States shall guarantee to every State that now is or hereafter may become a member of this Confederacy, a Republican form of Government, and shall protect each of them against invasion; and on

application of the Legislature, (or of the Executive when the Legislature is not in session,) against domestic violence.

Article V

Section 1. (1) Upon the demand of any three States, legally assembled in their several Conventions, the Congress shall summon a Convention of all the States, to take into consideration such amendments to the Constitution as the said States shall concur in suggesting at the time when the said demand is made; and should any of the proposed amendments to the Constitution be agreed on by the said Convention—voting by States—and the same be ratified by the Legislatures of two-thirds of the several States, or by conventions in two-thirds thereof—as the one or the other mode of ratification may be proposed by the general convention—they shall thenceforward form a part of this Constitution. But no State shall, without its consent, be deprived of its equal representation in the Senate.

Article VI

1.—The Government established by this Constitution is the successor of the Provisional Government of the Confederate States of America, and all the laws passed by the latter shall continue in force until the same shall be repealed or modified; and all the officers appointed by the same shall remain in office until their successors are appointed and qualified, or the offices abolished.

2. All debts contracted and engagements entered into before the adoption of this Constitution, shall be as valid against the Confederate States under this Constitution as under the Provisional Government.

3. This Constitution, and the laws of the Confederate States, made in pursuance thereof, and all treaties made, or which shall be made, under the authority of the Confederate States, shall be the supreme law of the land; and the judges in every State shall be bound thereby, any thing in the Constitution or laws of any State to the contrary notwithstanding.

4. The Senators and Representatives before mentioned, and the members of the several State Legislatures, and all executive and judicial offices, both of the Confederate States and of the several States, shall be bound, by oath or affirmation, to support this Constitution; but no religious test shall ever be required as a qualification to any office or public trust under the Confederate States.

5. The enumeration, in the Constitution, of certain rights, shall not be construed to deny or disparage others retained by the people of the several States.

6. The powers not delegated to the Confederate States by the Constitution, nor prohibited by it to the States, are reserved to the States, respectively, or to the people thereof.

Article VII

1.—The ratification of the conventions of five States shall be sufficient for the establishment of this Constitution between the States so ratifying the same.

2. When five States shall have ratified this Constitution in the manner before specified, the Congress, under the provisional Constitution, shall prescribe the time for holding the election of President and Vice-President, and for the meeting of the electoral college, and for counting the votes and inaugurating the President. They shall also prescribe the time for holding the first election of members of Congress under this Constitution, and the time for assembling the same. Until the assembling of such Congress, the Congress under the provisional Constitution shall continue to exercise the legislative powers granted them; not extending beyond the time limited by the Constitution of the Provisional Government.

Adopted unanimously by the Congress of the Confederate States of South Carolina, Georgia, Florida, Alabama, Mississippi, Louisiana, and Texas, sitting in convention at the capitol, in the city of Montgomery, Ala., on the eleventh day of March, in the year eighteen hundred and sixty-one.

Howard Cobb
President of the Congress.

[Signatures]

Supreme Court Nominations, 1789–1990

Name	State	Date of Birth	To Replace	Date of Appointment	Confirmation or Other Action*	Date Resigned	Date of Death	Years of Service
WASHINGTON								
John Jay	N.Y.	12/12/1745		9/24/1789	9/26/1789	6/29/1795	5/17/1829	6
John Rutledge	S.C.	9/1739		9/24/1789	9/26/1789	3/5/1791	7/18/1800	1
William Cushing	Mass.	3/1/1732		9/24/1789	9/26/1789		9/13/1810	21
Robert H. Harrison	Md.	1745		9/24/1789	9/26/1789 (D)		4/20/1790	
James Wilson	Pa.	9/14/1742		9/24/1789	9/26/1789		8/21/1798	9
John Blair	Va.	1732		9/24/1789	9/26/1789	1/27/1796	8/31/1800	6
James Iredell	N.C.	10/5/1751	Harrison	2/8/1790	2/10/1790		10/20/1799	9
Thomas Johnson	Md.	11/4/1732	Rutledge	11/1/1791	11/7/1791	3/4/1793	10/26/1819	1
William Paterson	N.J.	12/24/1745	Johnson	2/27/1793	2/28/1793 (W)			
William Paterson †			Johnson	3/4/1793	3/4/1793		9/9/1806	13
John Rutledge ‡			Jay	7/1/1795	12/15/1795 (R, 10-14)			
William Cushing ‡			Jay	1/26/1796	1/27/1796 (D)			
Samuel Chase	Md.	4/17/1741	Blair	1/26/1796	1/27/1796		6/19/1811	15
Oliver Ellsworth	Conn.	4/29/1745	Jay	3/3/1796	3/4/1796 (21-1)	12/25/1800	11/26/1807	4

Boldface—Chief Justice
Italics—Did not serve
‡ Earlier court service. See above.
† Earlier nomination not confirmed. See above.
D Declined

W Withdrawn
P Postponed
R Rejected
*Where no vote is listed, confirmation was by voice vote or otherwise recorded.

ADAMS

Name	State	Born	Seat of	Nominated	Confirmed		Resigned	Died	No.
Bushrod Washington	Va.	6/5/1762	Wilson	12/19/1798	12/20/1798			11/26/1829	31
Alfred Moore	N.C.	5/21/1755	Iredell	12/6/1799	12/10/1799		1/26/1804	10/15/1810	4
John Jay ‡			Ellsworth	12/18/1800	12/19/1800	(D)			
John Marshall	Va.	9/24/1755	Ellsworth	1/20/1801	1/27/1801			7/6/1835	34
JEFFERSON									
William Johnson	S.C.	12/27/1771	Moore	3/22/1804	3/24/1804			8/4/1834	30
H. Brockholst Livingston	N.Y.	11/25/1757	Paterson	12/13/1806	12/17/1806			3/18/1823	16
Thomas Todd	Ky.	1/23/1765	New seat	2/28/1807	3/3/1807			2/7/1826	19
MADISON									
Levi Lincoln	Mass.	5/15/1749	Cushing	1/2/1811	1/3/1811	(D)		4/14/1820	
Alexander Wolcott	Conn.	9/15/1758	Cushing	2/4/1811	2/13/1811	(R, 9-24)		6/26/1828	
John Quincy Adams	Mass.	7/11/1767	Cushing	2/21/1811	2/22/1811	(D)		2/23/1848	
Joseph Story	Mass.	9/18/1779	Cushing	11/15/1811	11/18/1811			9/10/1845	34
Gabriel Duvall	Md.	12/6/1752	Chase	11/15/1811	11/18/1811		1/14/1835	3/6/1844	23
MONROE									
Smith Thompson	N.Y.	1/17/1768	Livingston	12/8/1823	12/19/1823			12/18/1843	20
J. Q. ADAMS									
Robert Trimble	Ky.	11/17/1776	Todd	4/11/1826	5/9/1826	(27-5)		8/25/1828	2
John J. Crittenden	Ky.	9/10/1787	Trimble	12/17/1828	2/12/1829	(P)		7/26/1863	
JACKSON									
John McLean	Ohio	3/11/1785	Trimble	3/6/1829	3/7/1829			4/4/1861	32
Henry Baldwin	Pa.	1/14/1780	Washington	1/4/1830	1/6/1830	(41-2)		4/21/1844	14
James M. Wayne	Ga.	1790	Johnson	1/7/1835	1/9/1835			7/5/1867	32
Roger H. Taney	Md.	3/17/1777	Duvall	1/15/1835	3/3/1835	(P)			

Name	State	Date of Birth	To Replace	Date of Appointment	Confirmation or Other Action*	Date Resigned	Date of Death	Years of Service
Roger B. Taney †			Marshall	12/28/1835	3/15/1836 (29-15)		10/12/1864	28
Philip P. Barbour	Va.	5/25/1783	Duvall	12/28/1835	3/15/1836 (30-11)		2/25/1841	5
William Smith	Ala.	1762	New seat	3/3/1837	3/8/1837 (23-18) (D)		6/10/1840	
John Catron	Tenn.	1786	New seat	3/3/1837	3/8/1837 (28-15)		5/30/1865	28
VAN BUREN								
John McKinley	Ala.	5/1/1780	New seat	9/18/1837	9/25/1837		7/19/1852	15
Peter V. Daniel	Va.	4/24/1784	Barbour	2/26/1841	3/2/1841 (22-5)		5/31/1860	19
TYLER								
John C. Spencer	N.Y.	1/8/1788	Thompson	1/9/1844	1/31/1844 (R. 21-26)		5/18/1855	
Reuben H. Walworth	N.Y.	10/26/1788	Thompson	3/13/1844	6/17/1844 (W)		11/27/1867	
Edward King	Pa.	1/31/1794	Baldwin	6/5/1844	6/15/1844 (P)			
Edward King †			Baldwin	12/4/1844	2/7/1845 (W)		5/8/1873	
Samuel Nelson	N.Y.	11/10/1792	Thompson	2/4/1845	2/14/1845	11/28/1872	12/13/1873	27
John M. Read	Pa.	2/21/1797	Baldwin	2/7/1845	No action		11/29/1874	
POLK								
George W. Woodward	Pa.	3/26/1809	Baldwin	12/23/1845	1/22/1846 (R. 20-29)		5/10/1875	
Levi Woodbury	N.H.	12/22/1789	Story	12/23/1845	1/3/1846		9/4/1851	5
Robert C. Grier	Pa.	3/5/1794	Baldwin	8/3/1846	8/4/1846	1/31/1870	9/25/1870	23
FILLMORE								
Benjamin R. Curtis	Mass.	11/4/1809	Woodbury	12/11/1851	12/29/1851	9/30/1857	9/15/1874	5
Edward A. Bradford	La.	9/27/1813	McKinley	8/16/1852	No action		11/22/1872	
George E. Badger	N.C.	4/13/1795	McKinley	1/10/1853	2/11/1853 (P)		5/11/1866	
William C. Micou	La.	1806	McKinley	2/24/1853	No action		4/16/1854	

	State	Birth	Seat	Nominated	Confirmed	Vote	Resigned	Died	No.
PIERCE									
John A. Campbell	Ala.	6/24/1811	McKinley	3/22/1853	3/25/1853		4/30/1861	3/12/1889	8
BUCHANAN									
Nathan Clifford	Maine	8/18/1803	Curtis	12/9/1857	1/12/1858	(26-23)		7/25/1881	23
Jeremiah S. Black	Pa.	1/10/1810	Daniel	2/5/1861	2/21/1861	(R, 25-26)		8/19/1883	
LINCOLN									
Noah H. Swayne	Ohio	12/7/1804	McLean	1/21/1862	1/24/1862	(38-1)	1/24/1881	6/8/1884	19
Samuel F. Miller	Iowa	4/5/1816	Daniel	7/16/1862	7/16/1862			10/13/1890	28
David Davis	Ill.	3/9/1815	Campbell	12/1/1862	12/8/1862		3/4/1877	6/26/1886	14
Stephen J. Field	Calif.	11/4/1816	New seat	3/6/1863	3/10/1863		12/1/1897	4/9/1899	34
Salmon P. Chase	Ohio	1/13/1808	Taney	12/6/1864	12/6/1864			5/7/1873	8
JOHNSON									
Henry Stanbery	Ohio	2/20/1803	Catron	4/16/1866	No action			6/26/1881	
GRANT									
Ebenezer R. Hoar	Mass.	2/21/1816	New seat	12/15/1869	2/3/1870	(R, 24-33)		1/31/1895	
Edwin M. Stanton	Pa.	12/19/1814	Grier	12/20/1869	12/20/1869	(46-11)		12/24/1869	
William Strong	Pa.	5/6/1808	Grier	2/7/1870	2/18/1870		12/14/1880	8/19/1895	10
Joseph B. Bradley	N.J.	3/14/1813	New seat	2/7/1870	3/21/1870	(46-9)		1/22/1892	21
Ward Hunt	N.Y.	6/14/1810	Nelson	12/3/1872	12/11/1872		1/27/1882	3/24/1886	9
George H. Williams	Ore.	3/23/1823	Chase	12/1/1873	1/8/1874	(W)		4/4/1910	
Caleb Cushing	Mass.	1/17/1800	Chase	1/9/1874	1/13/1874	(W)		1/2/1879	
Morrison R. Waite	Ohio	11/29/1816	Chase	1/19/1874	1/21/1874	(63-0)		3/23/1888	14
HAYES									
John M. Harlan	Ky.	6/1/1833	Davis	10/17/1877	11/29/1877			10/14/1911	34

Name	State	Date of Birth	To Replace	Date of Appointment	Confirmation or Other Action*	Date Resigned	Date of Death	Years of Service
William B. Woods	Ga.	8/3/1824	Strong	12/15/1880	12/21/1880 (39-8)		5/14/1887	6
Stanley Matthews	Ohio	7/21/1824	Swayne	1/26/1881	No action			
GARFIELD								
Stanley Matthews †			Swayne	3/14/1881	5/12/1881 (24-23)		3/22/1889	7
ARTHUR								
Horace Gray	Mass.	3/24/1828	Clifford	12/19/1881	12/20/1881 (51-5)		9/15/1902	20
Roscoe Conkling	N.Y.	10/30/1829	Hunt	2/24/1882	3/2/1882 (39-12) (D)		4/18/1888	
Samuel Blatchford	N.Y.	3/9/1820	Hunt	3/13/1882	3/27/1882		7/7/1893	11
CLEVELAND								
Lucius Q. C. Lamar	Miss.	9/17/1825	Woods	12/6/1887	1/16/1888 (32-28)		1/23/1893	5
Melville **W. Fuller**	Ill.	2/11/1833	Waite	4/30/1888	7/20/1888 (41-20)		7/4/1910	22
HARRISON								
David J. Brewer	Kan.	6/20/1837	Matthews	12/4/1889	12/18/1889 (53-11)		3/28/1910	20
Henry B. Brown	Mich.	3/2/1836	Miller	12/23/1890	12/29/1890	5/28/1906	9/4/1913	15
George Shiras, Jr.	Pa.	1/26/1832	Bradley	7/19/1892	7/26/1892	2/23/1903	8/2/1924	10
Howell E. Jackson	Tenn.	4/8/1832	Lamar	2/2/1893	2/18/1893		8/8/1895	2
CLEVELAND								
William B. Hornblower	N.Y.	5/13/1851	Blatchford	9/19/1893	1/15/1894 (R, 24-30)		6/16/1914	
Wheeler H. Peckham	N.Y.	1/1/1833	Blatchford	1/22/1894	2/16/1894 (R, 32-41)		9/27/1905	
Edward D. White	La.	11/3/1845	Blatchford	2/19/1894	2/19/1894		5/19/1921	17
Rufus W. Peckham	N.Y.	11/8/1838	Jackson	12/3/1895	12/9/1895		10/24/1909	13

	State	Birth	Predecessor	Nomination	Confirmation		Death	No.
MCKINLEY								
Joseph McKenna	Calif.	8/10/1843	Field	12/16/1897	1/21/1898	1/5/1925	11/21/1926	26
ROOSEVELT								
Oliver W. Holmes	Mass.	3/8/1841	Gray	12/2/1902	12/4/1902	1/12/1932	3/6/1935	29
William R. Day	Ohio	4/17/1849	Shiras	2/19/1903	2/23/1903	11/13/1922	7/9/1923	19
William H. Moody	Mass.	12/23/1853	Brown	12/3/1906	12/12/1906	11/20/1910	7/2/1917	3
TAFT								
Horace H. Lurton	Tenn.	2/26/1844	Peckham	12/13/1909	12/20/1909		7/12/1914	4
Charles E. Hughes	N.Y.	4/11/1862	Brewer	4/25/1910	5/2/1910	6/10/1916	8/27/1948	6
Edward D. White ‡			Fuller	12/12/1910	12/12/1910			10 ‡
Willis Van Devanter	Wyo.	4/17/1859	White	12/12/1910	12/15/1910	6/2/1937	2/8/1941	26
Joseph R. Lamar	Ga.	10/14/1857	Moody	12/12/1910	12/15/1910		1/2/1916	5
Mahlon Pitney	N.J.	2/5/1858	Harlan	2/19/1912	3/13/1912 (50-26)	12/31/1922	12/9/1924	10
WILSON								
James C. McReynolds	Tenn.	2/3/1862	Lurton	8/19/1914	8/29/1914 (44-6)	1/31/1941	8/24/1946	26
Louis D. Brandeis	Mass.	11/13/1856	Lamar	1/28/1916	6/1/1916 (47-22)	2/13/1939	10/5/1941	22
John H. Clarke	Ohio	9/18/1857	Hughes	7/14/1916	7/24/1916	9/18/1922	3/22/1945	6
HARDING								
William H. Taft	Ohio	9/15/1857	White	6/30/1921	6/30/1921	2/3/1930	3/8/1930	8
George Sutherland	Utah	3/25/1862	Clarke	9/5/1922	9/5/1922	1/17/1938	7/18/1942	15
Pierce Butler	Minn.	3/17/1866	Day	11/23/1922	12/21/1922 (61-8)		11/16/1939	17
Edward T. Sanford	Tenn.	7/23/1865	Pitney	1/24/1923	1/29/1923		3/8/1930	7
COOLIDGE								
Harlan F. Stone	N.Y.	10/11/1872	McKenna	1/5/1925	2/5/1925 (71-6)		4/22/1946	16

Name	State	Date of Birth	To Replace	Date of Appointment	Confirmation or Other Action*	Date Resigned	Date of Death	Years of Service
HOOVER								
Charles E. Hughes ‡			Taft	2/3/1930	2/13/1930 (52-26)	7/1/1941		11 ‡
John J. Parker	N.C.	11/20/1885	Sanford	3/21/1930	5/7/1930 (R, 39-41)		3/17/1958	
Owen J. Roberts	Pa.	5/2/1875	Sanford	5/9/1930	5/20/1930	7/31/1945	5/17/1955	15
Benjamin N. Cardozo	N.Y.	5/24/1870	Holmes	2/15/1932	2/24/1932		7/9/1938	6
ROOSEVELT								
Hugo L. Black	Ala.	2/27/1886	Van Devanter	8/12/1937	8/17/1937 (63-16)	9/17/1971	10/25/1971	34
Stanley F. Reed	Ky.	12/31/1884	Sutherland	1/15/1938	1/25/1938	2/25/1957	4/2/1980	19
Felix Frankfurther	Mass.	11/15/1882	Cardozo	1/5/1939	1/17/1939	8/28/1962	2/22/1965	23
William O. Douglas	Conn.	10/16/1898	Brandeis	3/20/1939	4/4/1939 (62-4)	11/12/1975		36
Frank Murphy	Mich.	4/13/1890	Butler	1/4/1940	1/15/1940		7/19/1949	9
Harlan F. Stone ‡			Hughes	6/12/1941	6/27/1941		4/22/1946	5 ‡
James F. Byrnes	S.C.	5/2/1879	McReynolds	6/12/1941	6/12/1941	10/3/1942	4/9/1972	1
Robert H. Jackson	N.Y.	2/13/1892	Stone	6/12/1941	7/7/1941		10/9/1954	13
Wiley B. Rutledge	Iowa	7/20/1894	Byrnes	1/11/1943	2/8/1943		9/10/1949	6
TRUMAN								
Harold H. Burton	Ohio	6/22/1888	Roberts	9/19/1945	9/19/1945	10/13/1958	10/28/1964	13
Fred M. Vinson	Ky.	1/22/1890	Stone	6/6/1946	6/20/1946		9/8/1953	7
Tom C. Clark	Texas	9/23/1899	Murphy	8/2/1949	8/18/1949 (73-8)	6/12/1967	6/13/1977	18
Sherman Minton	Ind.	10/20/1890	Rutledge	9/15/1949	10/4/1949 (48-16)	10/15/1956	4/9/1965	7
EISENHOWER								
Earl Warren	Calif.	3/19/1891	Vinson	9/30/1953	3/1/1954	6/23/1969	6/9/1974	15
John M. Harlan	N.Y.	5/20/1899	Jackson	1/10/1955	3/16/1955 (71-11)	9/23/1971	12/29/1971	16

Name	State	Birth date	Justice replaced	Date nominated	Vote	Date confirmed			
William J. Brennan, Jr.	N.J.	4/25/1906	Minton	1/14/1957		3/19/1957		7/20/1990	5
Charles E. Whittaker	Mo.	2/22/1901	Reed	3/2/1957		3/19/1957	3/31/1962	11/26/1973	22
Potter Stewart	Ohio	1/23/1915	Burton	1/17/1959	(70-17)	5/5/1959	7/3/1981	12/7/1985	
KENNEDY									
Byron R. White	Colo.	6/8/1917	Whittaker	3/30/1962		4/11/1962			3
Arthur J. Goldberg	Ill.	8/8/1908	Frankfurter	8/29/1962		9/25/1962	7/25/1965		
JOHNSON									
Abe Fortas	Tenn.	6/19/1910	Goldberg	7/28/1965		8/11/1965	5/14/1969	4/5/1982	4
Thurgood Marshall	N.Y.	6/2/1908	Clark	6/13/1967	(69-11)	8/30/1967			
Abe Fortas ‡			Warren	6/26/1968	(W)	10/4/1968			
Homer Thornberry	Texas	1/9/1909	Fortas	6/26/1968		No action			
NIXON									
Warren E. Burger	Minn.	9/17/1907	Warren	5/21/1969	(74-3)	6/9/1969	9/26/1986		17
Clement Haynsworth Jr.	S.C.	10/30/1912	Fortas	8/18/1969	(R, 45-55)	11/21/1969			
G. Harrold Carswell	Fla.	12/22/1919	Fortas	1/19/1970	(R, 45-51)	4/8/1970			
Harry A. Blackman	Minn.	11/12/1908	Fortas	4/14/1970	(94-0)	5/12/1970			
Lewis F. Powell, Jr.	Va.	9/19/1907	Black	10/21/1971	(89-1)	12/6/1971	6/26/1987		16
William H. Rehnquist	Ariz.	10/1/1924	Harlan	10/21/1971	(68-26)	12/10/1971			
FORD									
John Paul Stevens	Ill.	4/20/1920	Douglas	11/28/1975		12/17/1975			
REAGAN									
Sandra Day O'Connor	Ariz.	3/26/1930	Stewart	8/19/1981	(99-0)	9/21/1981			
William H. Rehnquist ‡			Burger	6/20/1986	(65-33)	9/17/1986			
Antonin Scalia	Va.	3/11/1936	Rehnquist	6/24/1986	(98-0)	9/17/1986			

Name	State	Date of Birth	To Replace	Date of Appointment	Confirmation or Other Action*	Date Resigned	Date of Death	Years of Service
Robert H. Bork	D.C.	3/1/1927	Powell	7/1/1987	10/23/1987 (R, 42-58)			
Anthony M. Kennedy	Calif.	7/23/1936	Powell	11/30/1987	2/3/1988 (97-0)			
BUSH								
David H. Souter	N.H.	9/17/1939	Brennan	7/23/1990	10/6/1990 (90-9)			

Sources: Leon Friedman and Fred L. Israel, eds., *The Justice of the United States Supreme Court, 1789–1969: Executive Journal of the United States Supreme Court, 1789–1969:* Executive Journal of the U.S. Senate, 1789–1975; Congressional Quarterly *Almanacs,* 1971, 1975, 1981, 1986, and 1987.